Project on the City 1

Harvard Design School

edited by * chuihua judy chung * jeffrey inaba * rem koolhaas * sze tsung leong *

Great Leap Forward

essays by * bernard chang * mihai craciun * rem koolhaas * nancy lin * yuyang liu * kate orff * stephanie smith

with commentary by * qing yun ma *

design by * alice chung *

www.taschen.com

"Persist with Party's Principles,
One Hundred Years Without Change"
Shenzhen, 1996.

商业地位

北栅商业大厦占地20000平方米，为6层现代化建筑。一至二层为全中央空调式商场，内有商铺400多间，并配备饮食、娱乐、金融、电讯和医疗等服务设施。三至六层共有152个住宅单元可供客商使用。三层平台设有大型停车场。汽车可从大厦东面的车道自由上落

"Eminent Commercial Status"
Pearl River Delta, 1996.

现已推出！

Guangdong Villas

新的编章
新的奉献

"Guangdong Villas:
A New Chapter, A New Contribution"
Zhongshan, 1996.

"Chiao Fu Garden, Your Ideal Home"
Dongguan, 1996.

"Dongguan New Town Center District,
Yi Tai Garden Already on Market"
Dongguan, 1996.

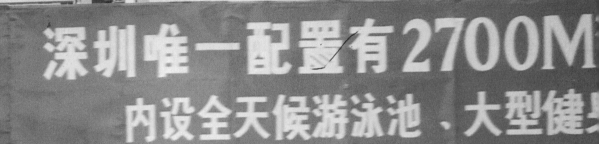

深圳唯一配置有2700M

内设全天候游泳池、大型健身

金寶

位于上

发展商：深圳工程咨询公司

直销电话

Harvard Design School Project on the City

GREAT LEAP FORWARD

Editors
CHUIHUA JUDY CHUNG   JEFFREY INABA
REM KOOLHAAS   SZE TSUNG LEONG

Design
ALICE CHUNG

Essays by
BERNARD CHANG   MIHAI CRACIUN
REM KOOLHAAS   NANCY LIN   YUYANG LIU
KATE ORFF   STEPHANIE SMITH

Commentary
QINGYUN MA

HARVARD DESIGN SCHOOL
2001

Project on the City Director Rem Koolhaas
Project on the City Coordinator Jeffrey Inaba

Great Leap Forward
Editors Chuihua Judy Chung, Jeffrey Inaba, Rem Koolhaas, Sze Tsung Leong
Design Alice Chung
Design Schema Alice Chung with Sze Tsung Leong
Contributing Editor Qingyun Ma
Manuscript Editor Cathy Lang Ho and Lauren Neefe
Associate Editor Michael Kubo
Production Associates Christopher Chew, Megan Feehan, Salomon Frausto

Special thanks to Harvard Design School Peter Rowe, Dean; Patricia Roberts, Associate Dean;
Jorge Silvetti, Chairman, Department of Architecture; K. Michael Hays, Professor of Architecture;
Sterling Deweese, Financial Services; and Graham Foundation for the Advancement of the Arts.

First published 2001 by Taschen GmbH
Hohenzollernring 53, D-50672 Köln
www.taschen.com

ISBN 3-8228-6048-4
Library of Congress Cataloging-in-Publication Data available
A CIP catalogue record for this book is available from the British Library

Printed in Italy
This book is printed on Munken Lynx 115 g/m^2, www.munkenpapers.com

CONTENTS

INTRODUCTION		24	Rem Koolhaas
CHRONOLOGY	*Pearl River Delta*	30	Yuyang Liu
IDEOLOGY	*Shenzhen*	44	Mihai Craciun
ARCHITECTURE	*Shenzhen*	156	Nancy Lin
MONEY	*Dongguan*	264	Stephanie Smith
LANDSCAPE	*Zhuhai*	336	Kate Orff
POLICY	*Guangzhou*	418	Yuyang Liu
INFRASTRUCTURE	*Pearl River Delta*	466	Bernard Chang
GLOSSARY	*Project on the City*	702	

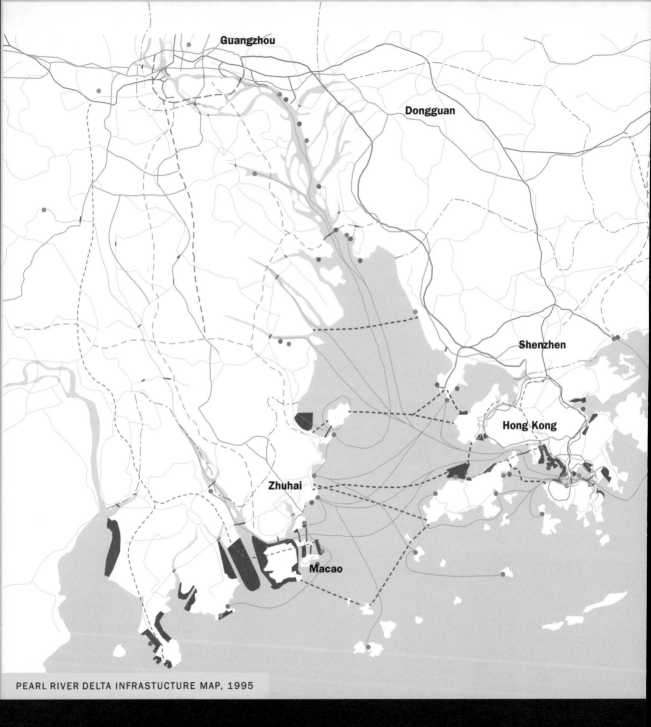

PEARL RIVER DELTA INFRASTUCTURE MAP, 1995

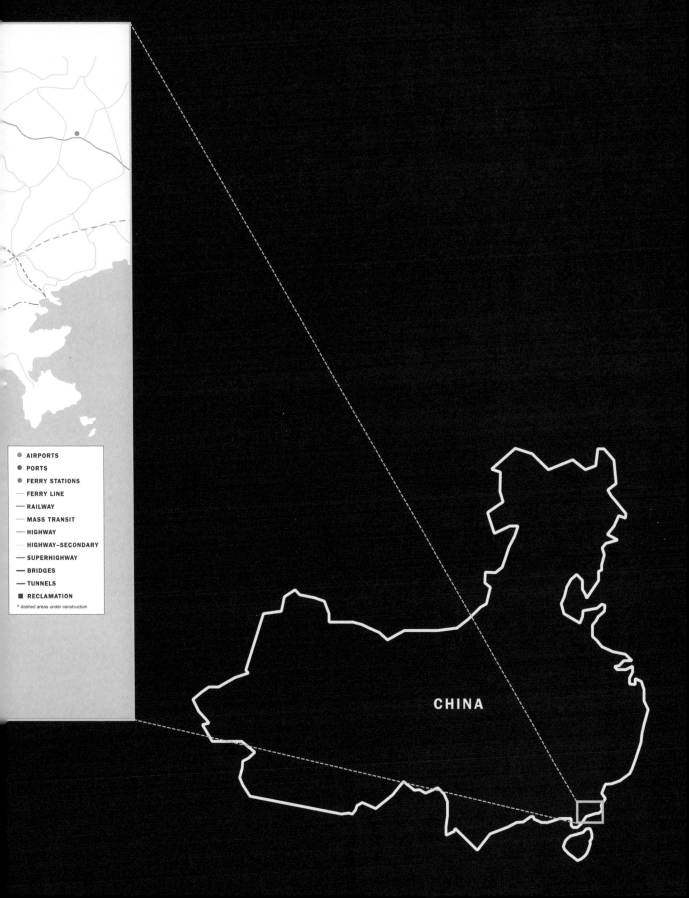

AIRPORTS
PORTS
FERRY STATIONS
FERRY LINE
RAILWAY
MASS TRANSIT
HIGHWAY
HIGHWAY–SECONDARY
SUPERHIGHWAY
BRIDGES
TUNNELS
RECLAMATION
* dashed areas under construction

CHINA

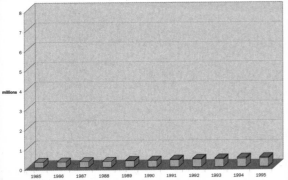

GUANGZHOU

HONG KONG

ZHUHAI

MACAO

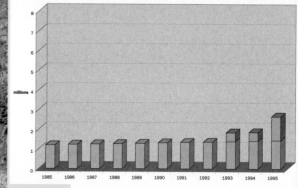

DONGGUAN

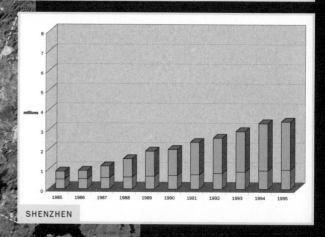

SHENZHEN

POPULATION 1985–1995

 floating population

 registered population

PEARL RIVER DELTA 1985

urbanized area

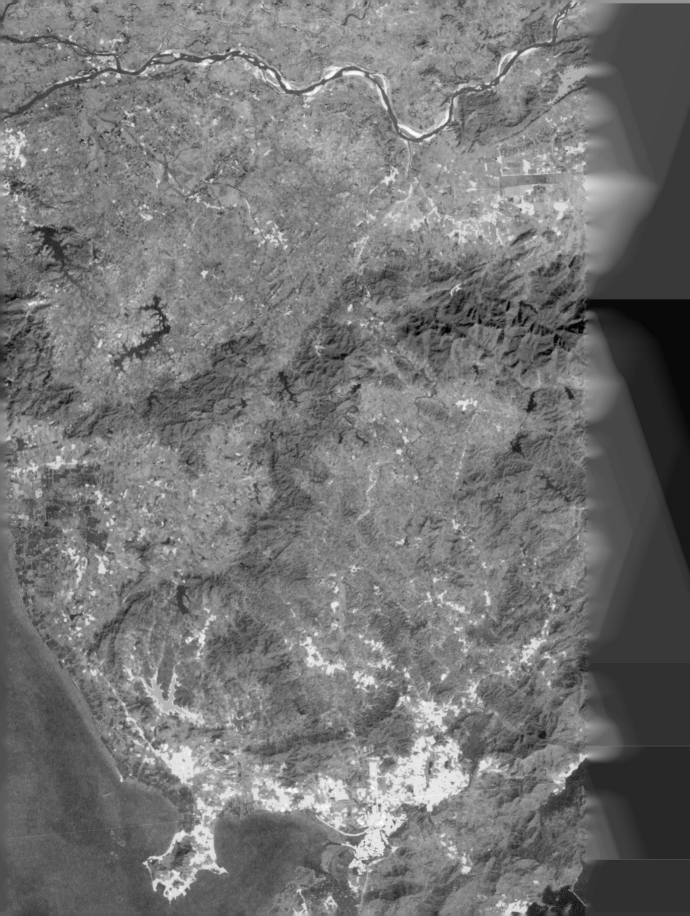

PEARL RIVER DELTA 1995

urbanized area

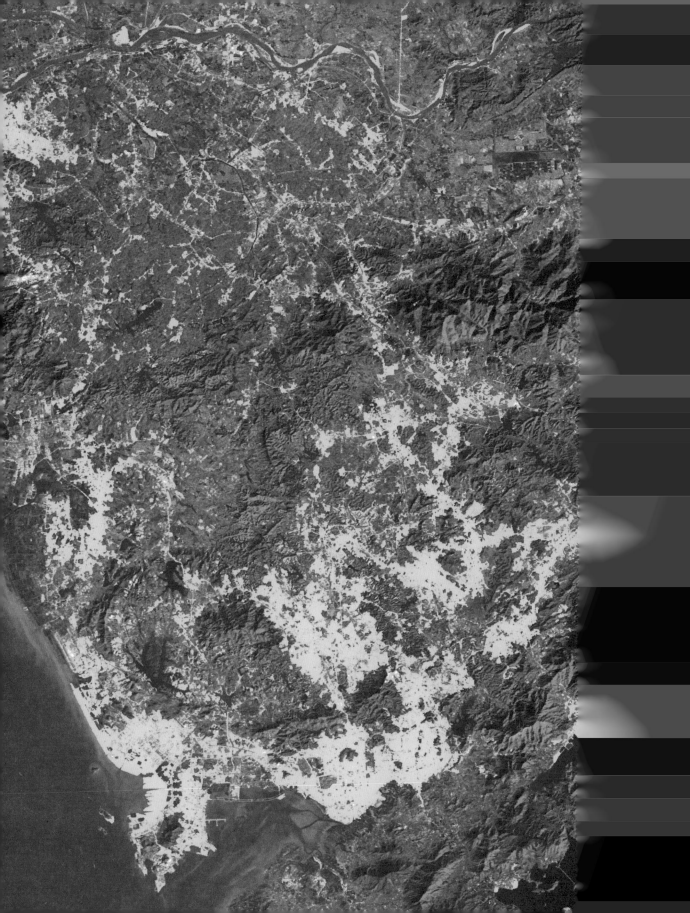

INTRODUCTION

Rem Koolhaas

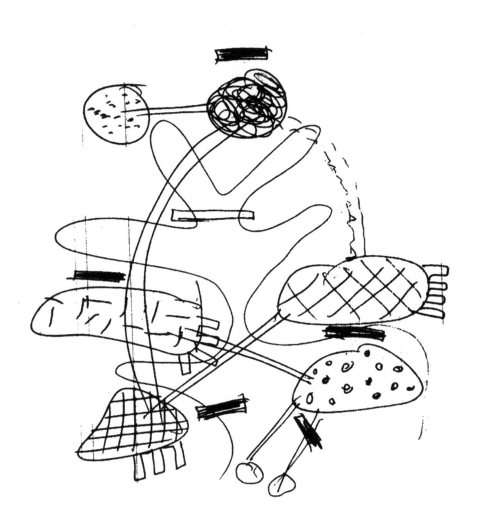

CITY OF EXACERBATED DIFFERENCE©

Maybe Team X and Archigram were, in the sixties, the last real "movements" in urbanism, the last to propose with conviction new ideas and concepts for the organization of urban life. In the long interval since their time, there has been a huge increase in our understanding of the traditional city; there has been the usual ad hoc intelligence and improvisation, and the development of a kind of plastic urbanism, increasingly capable of creating an urban condition free of urbanity. At the same time, Asia has been in the grip of a relentless process of building, on a scale that has probably never been seen before. A maelstrom of modernization is destroying everywhere the existing conditions in Asia and everywhere creating a completely new urban substance. The absence, on the one hand, of plausible, universal doctrines and the presence, on the other, of an unprecedented intensity of production have created a unique, wrenching condition: the urban seems to be least understood at the very moment of its apotheosis.

The result is a theoretical, critical, and operational impasse, which forces both academia and practice into postures of either confidence or indifference. In fact, the entire discipline possesses no adequate terminology to discuss the most pertinent, most crucial phenomena within its domain nor any conceptual framework to describe, interpret, and understand exactly those forces that could redefine and revitalize it. The field is abandoned to "events" considered indescribable or to the creation of a synthetic idyll in memory of the city. There is nothing left between chaos and celebration.

Great Leap Forward is based on fieldwork conducted by thesis students, in the fields of architecture, landscape architecture, and urban design, at the Harvard Design School. The project consists of a series of interrelated studies that together attempt to give an initial overview of the emerging urban condition(s) in China's Pearl River Delta (PRD), a region that, according to reliable predictions, is destined to grow to 34 million inhabitants by the year 2020 and, through sheer size alone, to play a critical role in the twenty-first century.

Research was conducted over the course of 1996, beginning with a group visit in January—a counterclockwise journey that started in Shenzhen Special Economic Zone and ended in Hong Kong. Over the summer, individual investigations focused on specific locations and subjects, but it seemed hopeless for such a small group of people to reconstruct the events in the PRD. Therefore, each student was coupled with one major subject and the urban condition where that subject would be most tangible or pertinent:

Bernard Chang	INFRASTRUCTURE	Pearl River Delta
Mihai Craciun	IDEOLOGY	Shenzhen
Nancy Lin	ARCHITECTURE	Shenzhen
Yuyang Liu	POLITICS	Guangzhou
Kate Orff	LANDSCAPE	Zhuhai
Stephanie Smith	MONEY	Dongguan

Together these studies describe the PRD's urban condition, a new form of urban coexistence that we have called CITY OF EXACERBATED DIFFERENCE©, or COED©. Beyond the particularities of each condition that we found, *Great Leap Forward* introduces a number of "copyrighted" terms, which represent the beginning of a conceptual framework to describe and interpret the contemporary urban condition. The emergence of the PRD with the suddenness of a comet, and the present "cloud of unknowing" that creates a kind of stealth envelope around the PRD's existence and performance, are in themselves proof of the existence of parallel universes that utterly contradict the assumption that globalization equals global knowledge.

CITY OF EXACERBATED DIFFERENCE© (COED©) The traditional city strives for a condition of balance, harmony, and a degree of homogeneity. The CITY OF EXACERBATED DIFFERENCE©, on the contrary, is based on the greatest possible difference between its parts—complementary or competitive. In a climate of permanent strategic panic, what counts in the CITY OF EXACERBATED DIFFERENCE© is not the methodical creation of the ideal, but the opportunistic exploitation of flukes, accidents, and imperfections. Although the model of the CITY OF EXACERBATED DIFFERENCE© appears brutal—to depend on the robustness and primitiveness of its parts—the paradox is that it is, in fact, delicate and sensitive. The slightest modification of any detail requires the readjustment of the whole to reassert the equilibrium of complementary extremes.

CHRONOLOGY

Yuyang Liu

1911 Led by **Dr. Sun Yat-sen** and his collaborators, the **October Revolution** ends five thousand years of imperial rule in China and begins a new paradigm in the country's course of development. Immediately after the abdication of the Qing Dynasty (1644–1911), Yuan Shi-kai, a Qing general-turned-warlord, seizes control of the throne for eighty-three days before being ousted by Sun's republicans. With no clear successor, China disintegrates into social turmoil.

1912 Under the leadership of Sun, the Chinese Revolution Association (Zhongguo Geming Tongmeng Hui), founded in 1905, is reorganized to become the **Nationalist Party (Guomindang)** in Guangdong Province. In the meantime, the new republic undergoes a period of factionalism, wherein regions are primarily controlled by various warlords rather than by the central government. Although the Nationalists receive strong support from wealthy landowners and merchants in the coastal eastern and southeastern cities (which had long been open to Western influences), there is growing opposition from Chinese intellectuals anxious to recover the nation's lost sense of unity and greatness. Many of these intellectuals eventually become Communists.

1921 The **Chinese Communist Party** (CCP) is founded in Shanghai; its members include the young **Mao Zedong**. In 1923 the Nationalists and Communists join forces to defeat the warlords and to reunify the country through the Northern Expedition, sending joint troops from Guangdong to fight in regions as far north as Manchuria. Their collaborative venture successfully clears away smaller factions, setting the stage for opposition between the two parties during the next decade.

1925 Sun, by this time regarded as the founding father of the new China, dies of liver cancer, leaving the fragile nation in a precarious state of unbalance. Now led by the Japanese-trained General Chiang Kai-shek, the Nationalists launch an offensive against the Communists, forcing them to hide in the rural southern province of Jiangxi.

1934 Blockaded by the Nationalists, Chinese Communist forces under Mao Zedong begin the **Long March** from Jiangxi Province to Yan-an in the Shaanxi Province, 6,000 miles to the northwest. The march lasts until October 1935; Mao's forces, led by future Party figures **Zhou Enlai**, **Peng Dehuai**, **Lin Biao**, and **Deng Xiaoping**, are on the move for 268 out of 365 days.

1911

1915

1920

1925

crossing eighteen mountain ranges and six major rivers. Only 8,000 to 9,000 of the original 80,000 men survive the continual rearguard actions against the Nationalist troops. Over the course of the march, the CCP becomes battle-hardened, spreading its message and ideology throughout the countryside.

1935 Mao Zedong becomes chairman of the CCP.

1937 The **Japanese invasion** of China forces both the Nationalists and the CCP to shift their military efforts from fighting each other to defending against Japanese aggression. In September, a CCP manifesto entitled "Together We Confront the National Crisis" announces the CCP's alliance with the Nationalists against Japanese forces; the **united front** between the two lasts through the course of World War II. But the CCP remains focused on increasing its strength against the Nationalists: Mao reminds CCP cadres, "Our fixed policy should be 70 percent expansion, 20 percent dealing with the Guomindang, and 10 percent resisting Japan."[1]

1945 Struggle between the Nationalists and the CCP resumes as Japan is defeated. After the end of World War II, the Nationalist government faces tremendous inflation, corruption, and mounting Communist opposition.

1949 Chiang and the Nationalists are defeated by the Communists and forced to flee to Taiwan. On October 1, Mao Zedong proclaims the founding of the **People's Republic of China** (PRC). From its inception, the PRC is marked by instability. Symptomatic of Mao's oscillation between socialist ideals, personal ego, and an unstable status quo, frequent factional struggles within the party elite result in sudden policy shifts. The liberal faction, favored by Deng Xiaoping, Zhou Enlai, and many intellectuals, emphasizes the role of central planning in implementing pragmatic programs for economic development. The radical faction, favored by Mao, seeks to remove social distinctions—between city and country, worker and peasant—and advocates the relentless push toward a classless, egalitarian, agriculture-based society. Throughout this period, Mao maintains his position and strengthens his power as the paramount leader of the PRC by manipulating the struggles among factions and purging perceived forces of resistance.

1949–56 Mao and his colleagues direct their attention toward the reconstruction of the nation and the economy. The CCP promotes industrial-based development following the Soviet model, seeking cooperation between intellectuals and technocrats from China and the Soviet Union. The CCP recruits more than six million new members, emphasizing the enrollment of industrial workers and educated groups. Land reform is introduced as a progressive process: Collectivization, or the redistribution of land obtained from large landlords to small tenants, is adopted as a first step toward the eventual creation of communes.

1950 In June the government announces the **Agrarian Reform Law**, aimed at abolishing "land ownership of feudal exploitation" and reorganizing the countryside into collectives. The law confiscates land from those identified as landlords (those who own land but live entirely on "usury and the exploitation of others") or rich peasants (those who own and work their own land, but also hire or rent their land to others to increase their income). The land is then redistributed to poorer peasants and hired hands with little or no property. Within two years, just under 120 million acres of land are redistributed to 300 million peasants.[2]

1951–52 Mao launches a series of rectification campaigns to consolidate CCP control over industry and labor. The **Three Anti Campaign** targets corruption, waste, and bureaucracy among party officials, bureaucrats, and factory and business managers, increasing CCP control over labor by uniting workers against corrupt managers. The **Five Anti Campaign** targets remaining Chinese industrialists and businessmen in cities; massive confiscation of private property ends the independent operation of capitalists in China.

1953–57 The Soviet-modeled **First Five-Year Plan**, focusing on heavy industry, is adopted to increase industrial growth by extracting surplus from agriculture. The plan seeks to correct the imbalance between the interior and coastal regions, which occupy less than one-fifth of the land but produce 70 percent of industrial output. Of the 694 major industrial sites initiated during this period, 472 are in the interior provinces.[3] Workers are reorganized into *danwei* (urban communes); industrial production is dramatically increased.

1956 Mao launches the **Hundred Flowers Campaign** to rectify "bureaucratism, sectarianism, and subjectivism" within the CCP through constructive debate.[4] Declaring "Let a hundred flowers blossom; let a hundred schools contend!" intellectuals are encouraged to openly voice their concerns over CCP abuses.[5] By May, the campaign prompts an enthusiastic outpouring of intellectual criticism of CCP practices across China. According to Mao, it will be "a movement of ideological education carried out seriously yet as gently as a breeze or a mild rain"; concerns will be discussed in the form of "comradely heart-to-heart talks."[6]

1957 Mao launches the **Anti-Rightist Campaign** to stifle intellectual criticism of the CCP. Over 300,000 intellectuals are branded rightists, sent to labor camps or jail, "rusticated", or driven to suicide.[7]

1958–62 The **Second Five-Year Plan** organizes the country into 7 economic regions. During this period, the investment ratio between the interior regions and coastal regions is 56–44 percent.[8]

1958 Introducing the principle of "continuing revolution," Mao launches the **Great Leap Forward**, a push to achieve rapid, equal growth in both industrial and agricultural production through the power of mass mobilization.[9] A "spontaneous energizing of the whole nation," the movement, based on decentralizing economic decision-making to increase CCP power in rural areas, centers on a large-scale effort to end private plot farming and to group existing collectives into communes—large, self-sufficient cooperative units subdivided into smaller production brigades.[10] By fall, some 750,000 agricultural cooperatives are re-organized into 23,500 communes, averaging 22,000 people or 5,000 households each.[11] Each commune is planned as a self-supporting community for agriculture, small-scale local industry, and education. The separation of men, women, and children into different living and working units and the sharing of kitchens, mess halls, and nurseries represents a radical departure from the traditional Chinese family structure. Within a year, amazed by a flood of astounding production reports across the country, euphoric CCP leaders praise "the all-round, continuous leap forward in China's agricultural production and the ever-rising consciousness of the 500 million peasants."[12]

1959 The Great Leap Forward is acknowledged as a massive failure. In the fervor of the campaign and the fear of local cadres to report disappointing results, actual production figures have been disastrously over-exaggerated: The announced figure for grain production in 1958, 375 million tons, is later corrected to 250 million.[13] Optimistic attempts to redistribute industry to small-scale, rural enterprises, such as backyard steel furnaces, decimates the overall level of Chinese industrial production. Among the Great Leap Forward's economic consequences are massive shortages of food and raw materials, the deterioration of industry, and the physical exhaustion of the population. As the grain supply drops to catastrophic levels, an estimated 20 million people die of famine.

In the wake of the Great Leap Forward, CCP policies are modified to decentralize control, restore material incentives to workers, and house reunited families. Mao steps down as head of state of the People's Republic (though he remains chairman of the CCP), appointing **Liu Shaoqi**—author of the immensely popular *How To Be a Good Communist*—as his successor.

During a CCP Central Committee meeting in Lushan, Defense Minister **Peng Dehuai**—a devoted supporter of Mao and veteran of the Long March—writes a personal letter to Mao expressing his concern over the negative effects of the Great Leap Forward. Days later, Mao openly accuses Peng of "right opportunism" and "betrayal of the fatherland."[14] The Eighth Plenary Session quickly issues a series of resolutions including a "Directive of the Central Committee of the CCP on Opposing Right Deviationist Thinking," "Safeguarding the Party's General Line and Opposing Right Opportunism," and "Resolutions on the Errors of the Anti-Party Clique Headed by Peng Dehuai."[15] Soon after the Lushan meeting, an Anti-Right Deviationist movement spreads throughout the party.

Lin Biao—a devoted supporter of Mao and veteran of the Long March—replaces Peng as defense minister and head of the **People's Liberation Army (PLA)**.

1955

1960 Lin Biao launches an indoctrination movement within the PLA to strengthen Mao's reputation most significantly by compiling *Quotations from Chairman Mao Zedong*, known more commonly as the "little red book." The book quickly becomes a subject of study throughout the army, elevating Mao to a new level of reverence as the revolutionary leader of modern China

1960–64 Liu Shaoqi implements a centrist recovery program aimed at reintroducing some measure of private plot farming and material incentives, in addition to the production quotas set by the government. Seeing a resurgence of capitalist tendencies and a loss of revolutionary fervor Mao begins a series of rectification efforts to eradicate liberalization within the CCP.[16]

1963 The **Socialist Education Campaign**, a "comprehensive program to reintroduce basic socialis values into Chinese society," attempts to eradicate rural corruption across the country. The party emphasizes the "Four Clean-ups": accounting procedures, granary supplies, propert accumulation, and work-point allocation in communes. Thousands of cadres are relocated to the country to learn from peasant conditions and encourage rural class struggle.[17]

1966–70 The **Third Five-Year Plan** unites economic policy with national defense strategy. The country is geographically divided into a three-tier system of zones: The first tier includes the eastern seaboard and the Sino-Soviet border; the second tier includes the centra provinces; the third tier includes the southwestern provinces. Economic development is focused on the third-tier zones.

Seeking to purge conservative opposition within the CCP according to the principles o Maoism and "continuing revolution," the **Cultural Revolution** emerges as a comprehensive rectification of the cultural realm. In a complete reordering of the power structure, criticism and "struggle sessions" are held throughout the CCP to root out perceived rightist, capital ist, or bourgeois influences. A string of purges travels up the CCP ranks; eventually Deng Xiaoping—a devoted supporter of Mao and veteran of the Long March—and Liu Shaoqi Mao's chosen successor as chairman, are denounced as bureaucrats and "capitalist road ers" and subjected to public humiliation.

The campaign quickly spreads to all levels of society. Calling for a vigorous attack on the "Four Olds"—old customs, old habits, old culture, and old thinking—the radical faction o the Party, led by Mao's wife Jiang Qing, agitates for mass-mobilization. Students are told "Everything that does not fit the socialist system and proletarian dictatorship should be attacked."[18] The Eleventh Central Committee of the CCP announces the formation of the Red Guards, a "shock force" to take the movement directly to the people. Millions o youths, armed with Mao's quotations, rebel with revolutionary fervor against elders, rightis party officials, and eventually, each other.[19] Without central leadership or a clearly defined enemy, the movement grows in scale and intensity, each faction was attacking the previous with increasing violence.

1967 By January, the country is reduced to a state of chaos. Open warfare between students, radical factions, local governments, and the PLA completely destabilizes and undermines all political and social structures. Workers turn against managers, students against teachers, children against parents, neighbors against neighbors. Most universities are closed, and the British Embassy is burned down. Seeking to prevent a complete social collapse, the CCP authorizes the PLA to disband all "counterrevolutionary organizations," initiating a fierce crackdown against radical groups. Hundreds are killed in clashes; reports describe rivers dammed with dead bodies.

In an attempt to restore the struggle along clear lines. the **Campaign to Purify Class Ranks** attempts to classify definitively millions of cadres, officials, and landowners according to their backgrounds and perceived ideological alliances. Hundreds of thousands o cadres and intellectuals are assigned to May Seventh Cadre Schools, which combine inces sant indoctrination and study of Mao's works with hard agricultural labor.[20]

1969 A veteran of the Long March, editor of the "little red book," and Mao's most trusted and deeply loyal supporter for decades, Lin Biao's reputation grows as the People's Liberation Army becomes the primary force responsible for maintaining order in the aftermath of the Cultural Revolution. At the national party congress. Mao declares Lin his chosen successo as chairman of the state.

1970 Mao "remove[s] the post of chairman of the state, vacant since Liu Shaoqi's arrest, from the draft constitution, which [means] . . . that Lin [Biao] [can] not succeed to such a post."[2]

1971 Lin Biao reportedly tries to organize Mao's assassination, fails, and dies in a mysterious plane crash in Mongolia while attempting to flee to the Soviet Union.

1971–75 The **Fourth Five-Year Plan** continues to favor China's interior region. The country is recon figured into ten economic regions, with central and western provinces receiving 57.5 percen of total government investment.[22]

1972 Mao allows Premier Zhou Enlai—a devoted supporter of Mao and veteran of the Long March—to set about the reconstruction of the nation. The following years are marked by ar uneasy balance of power between liberal and radical factions. The moderate Zhou slowl implements economic reconstruction policies and restores many of the experienced and skilled cadres. Stressing economic development over ideological campaigns, Zhou calls fo the modernization of industry, national defense, science, and technology. His efforts are later referred to as the **Four Modernizations**. In order to speed economic growth, Zhou encourages increased contact with the West.

1972 President Nixon—a devout anti-communist—visits China. At the conclusion of the trip, a joint communiqué issued by the United States and China calls for "the normalization of relations between the two countries," pledging an increase in "people-to-people contacts and exchanges º [in] science, technology, culture, sports, and journalism."[23]

1973 The radical left **Gang of Four**, headed by Mao's wife Jiang Qing, shares political power with the party's central right. Under the auspices of Mao, the Gang of Four controls the media and CCP propaganda, launching a joint **Anti-Lin Biao Anti-Confucius Campaign** to both discredit Lin's legacy and attack the humanistic, traditional values represented by Confucius. Lin Biao, according to the Gang, is one of "the Confuciuses of contemporary China."[24] The Gang of Four eventually broadens the campaign to a full attack on the conservative policies of Zhou Enlai's administration.

Deng Xiaoping is rehabilitated as vice-premier—a shift apparently engineered by an ailing Zhou Enlai, who promptly begins grooming Deng as his successor.[25]

1976–80 The **Fifth Five-Year Plan** begins to shift development efforts away from the central and western regions to the eastern provinces. As a result of power shifts within the CCP, concerns over national defense give way to a development model focusing on maximizing economic production, rather than a geographic balance of investment and industry.

Zhou Enlai—a stabilizing force in Chinese politics as premier for over twenty-five years and the man credited with guiding the country through the turmoil of the Cultural Revolution—dies on January 8, 1976. Deng Xiaoping, Zhou's chosen successor and the de facto premier in the last year of Zhou's life, delivers the eulogy at the memorial service on January 15th.

Shortly thereafter, Deng disappears from public view. On February 7, to the shock of CCP radicals and moderates alike, Mao names **Hua Guofeng**—then a sixth-ranking vice-premier and minister of public security—as acting premier of the State Council. The selection, apparently an "ideologically safe" choice until the Gang of Four can assume power, places Hua, no Deng Xiaoping, in position to succeed Mao as chairman. Under the pressure of the Gang of Four, the Central Committee dismisses Deng from all CCP and government posts but allows him to "keep his party membership so as to see how he will behave himself in the future."

Mao Zedong dies on September 9, 1976. In the absence of any constitutional provisions for the transfer of power, Jiang Qing and the Gang of Four conspire to seize power over Hua Guofeng, now firmly in line for succession (Mao's handwritten instruction to Hua before his death, "With you in charge, I am at ease"). The Gang distributes six million rounds o ammunition to militias in Shanghai; Hua and senior party cadres, backed by the minister of defense and military commanders in Canton, Shanghai, and Peking, prepare for a counter-coup. On October 5 the **Gang of Four is arrested** for crimes committed during the Cultural Revolution; on October 24, one million soldiers and civilians celebrate at a victory rally in Tiananmen Square.

Deng is reappointed to the vice-chairmanship, the Politburo, and the Military Affairs Commission. Seeking to strengthen his position by criticizing those responsible for blocking him from succession, Deng launches indirect attacks on both Hua Guofeng's leadership and the entrenched dominance of "Mao Thought."[26]

1978 At the **Third Plenum of the Eleventh Central Committee of the CCP** in December, Deng out-lines his plan for enacting the Four Modernizations. Calling for the decentralization of control "from the leadership to the lower levels," he advocates stronger divisions in the respective roles of the CCP, local governments, and enterprises. According to his plan, the CCP will not interfere in the development of enterprise, and business managers are to be given greater authority over labor management and production operations. "Carrying out the Four Mod-ernizations," Deng proclaims, "requires changes in all methods of management, actions, and thinking which stand in the way of such growth. Socialist modernization is therefore a profound and extensive revolution."[27] Advocating greater openness towards foreign invest-ment and technology, Deng states that "China needs to expand its contacts with foreign countries. º In Guangdong, this means opening its doors to Hong Kong."[28] Before the end of the conference, China announces corporate agreements with Boeing and Coca-Cola.

In a further reversal of Mao's seclusionist economic approach, Deng Xiaoping introduces the **Open Door Policy**, a comprehensive program to modernize the (socialist) Chinese econo-my relative to the (capitalist) global market. The policy calls for increased contacts to foreign trade and investment, the decentralization of economic decision-making to allow greater response to market forces, and gradual legalization of the transaction and transfer of land to promote economic development.

1979 On January 1, China and the United States announce the opening of full diplomatic rela-tions. On January 28, Deng Xiaoping visits the United States, "the beautiful imperialist"; images of Deng greeted by cheering crowds in Washington, D.C., are beamed back to China.

1980 The Open Door Policy is inaugurated in China by the establishment of four **Special Economic Zones** (SEZ) in Guangdong Province: Shenzhen, Zhuhai, Shantou and Xiamen. The zones are designated as territories for accelerated economic development and the controlled importation of foreign technology and capital. The SEZs offer skilled, non-unionized labor, develop transportation networks and offers to build plants to the specifications of foreign investors. The SEZs are strategically located near anticipated sources of foreign capital: the Pearl River Delta, Shenzhen borders Hong Kong and Zhuhai borders Macao; meanwhile Shantou and Xiamen lie across the coast from Taiwan.[29]

1981–85 The **Sixth Five-Year Plan** implements a "two-way adjusted policy," by which a system of compensation is intended to balance differences in regional growth. Development in coastal regions is accelerated through preferential policies, introduction of foreign technology and management, and an influx of foreign capital investment. Interior provinces are compensated through the development of energy and raw materials.[30]

1981 In a final reordering of the power structure, the **Sixth Plenary Session of the Eleventh Central Committee of the CCP** accepts the resignation of Hua Guofeng, already reduced to a figurehead, as CCP chairman. Hua remains on the Committee as the most junior of the six vice-chairmen, "a powerless but nevertheless respectable position."[31]

Now firmly under the control of Deng Xiaoping, the Sixth Plenary Session embarks on the official task of reevaluating Mao's legacy. Both a response to the suffering brought by the Cultural Revolution and a means of ensuring the continuation of control and power in the aftermath of social upheaval and economic stagnation, "de-Maoification" becomes a necessary prelude to future government action.[32] The new government stresses that the criticism concentrates on de-idolizing Mao and pointing out his personal mistakes, not on undermining Mao's fundamental ideological significance. While maintaining tribute to Mao's "indelible" achievements, the Committee declares that his rule was "not free of shortcomings and mistakes."[33] Reports one Hong Kong daily, the CCP's analysis concludes with the assessment that "Chairman Mao was probably 70 percent correct and 30 percent wrong."

1983 The **Anti-Spiritual Pollution Campaign** attacks the contamination of Chinese culture by Western influences and ideas—including the effects of foreign investment brought by the Open Door Policy and the Special Economic Zones. Provincial leaders in Guangdong, formerly critical of radicals during the Cultural Revolution, respond by redirecting momentum to a new target: conservatives resisting the reforms. Conservative hard-liners are criticized for equating competition, individual enterprise, and commodity economics with capitalism for their lack of enthusiasm in studying foreign developments, and for their unwillingness to abandon old methods.[34]

As coastal regions receive more autonomy from CCP controls, inner regions begin to feel the pressure of competitive disadvantage. Inland provinces, demanding Beijing reinstate policy of centralization, map out strategies to sabotage the economic reforms. In response, reformers adopt a new strategy of inter-provincial cooperation to encourage joint ventures and trading between inland and coastal regions. Enterprises from coastal provinces can now reinvest earnings back into inland areas, increasing flow and exchange between the coast and the hinterland; the arrangement intensifies the effect of regional influences on national politics, and conversely, of national (or even international) repercussions on regional politics.

1984 In January, Deng tours Guangdong Province as a gesture of support for the fledgling Special Economic Zones. The visit provides a huge boost to the development of the SEZs: the volume of building construction in Shenzhen nearly doubles over the following year.

The status of Special Economic Zone is extended to fourteen coastal cities and the island of Hainan in Guangdong Province. The Pearl River Delta is named one of three "development triangles" targeted for expanded economic development. They will act as "filters" for science and technology, helping China to "discard the dross and select the essential."[35]

1986–90 The **Seventh Five-Year Plan** seeks to further reduce the imbalance among eastern, central, and western regions. Policies focus on reforming traditional industries through new technologies. In the central and western regions, attempts are made to revive agriculture, transportation, and mining.[36]

1987 Land-use reform is initiated in Guangdong province to deregulate property development within the confines of the socialist property system. Under the reforms, the PRC retains ownership of land, but the right to use land is transferred or leased to developers through negotiation, tendering, or auction. Thus urban land is owned by the state, but leased and controlled by the Planning Bureau; agricultural land is owned by collectives, enabling peasants to join together and sell land-use rights to developers, turning many into millionaires overnight. The government can still expropriate or demand rights to use collectively owned land, but must reasonably compensate peasants, often in the form of IOUs. The government also charges a land-use tax from the user, which is typically applied toward infrastructure projects.

Deng formally retires from all government positions, but remains the paramount leader of the CCP.

1988 The Party approves the **Coastal Development Strategy** (CDS) to increase the export capacity of coastal regions by linking them with the inland. Two-hundred and eighty-four cities and counties in fourteen coastal regions are opened to trade and foreign investment, and regarded as places where raw materials are processed and assembled for export. These coastal areas include Liaodong and Shandong peninsulas in the northeast, the Yangtze River Delta and Shanghai in the central coastal area, and the Pearl River Delta in the south.

1985

1989 The CCP issues the **Law of Transfer of Land-Use Rights** in Shenzhen, furthering the split between ownership and land use. Within the system of collective ownership, the law allocates the land-use rights for one hectare of land to each household, prompting a burst of speculative real-estate development. With proximity to the Special Economic Zones as its prime asset, the value of farmland in the Pearl River Delta immediately skyrockets.

1991–95 The **Eighth Five-Year Plan** ends the two-tiered price system, based on a fixed price for certain products and a floating or fluctuating price for other goods. For the first time, policymakers begin to develop a cross-regional approach between coastal and interior provinces through improved transportation infrastructure. Many of the open coastal cities flourish; with a 27 percent annual growth rate, the Pearl River Delta becomes the "Gold Coast" of China.

1992 Deng Xiaoping's second tour of the Pearl River Delta—a reprise of his much-celebrated visit in 1984—reaffirms the importance and status of the Special Economic Zones in realizing the goals of the Open Door Policy. Already prosperous, the visit sparks a renewed surge in development throughout the region.

1997 Deng Xiaoping dies.

1997–2000 The **Ninth Five-Year Plan**—the first of the post-Deng era—is a benchmark of China's transformation from a planned economy to a "socialist market economy." Seven economic regions are established, crossing existing provincial and city boundaries. While eastern regions are targeted to develop more export-oriented industries, 60 percent of international assistance loans to China are directed toward central and western regional development efforts. Simultaneously, the government encourages the flow of investment funding from the southeast—including the Pearl River Delta—toward the country's midwest in return for a flow of labor supply.[37] While preserving taxes and other privileges of the coastal provinces, the Plan shifts the focus of development to sustained growth in agriculture and the rural economy, greater self-sufficiency in grain production, a higher standard of living for farmers, and faster development in agro-processing industries.[38] The plan outlines the intention of leveling the playing field for all the provinces—inevitably reducing the competitive advantage of regions such as the Pearl River Delta by expanding the benefits of the reform to the rest of China.

1990

1995

1. Immanuel Hsu, *The Rise of Modern China* (New York: Oxford University Press, 2000), 588, 589.

2. Ibid., 652, 653.

3. Lin Wu-lang; Chen Tai-ming; Kuo Ai-ai. *Mainland China Regional Economic and Industrial Development* (Taipei: Executive Yuan Mainland Committee, 1999), 31–42.

4. Jonathan D. Spence. *The Search for Modern China* (New York: Norton & Co., 1999), 540.

5. Hsu, 663.

6. Spence, 540–41.

7. Ibid., 543.

8. Lin et. al., 31–42.

9. Mao's definition of this concept is given in Jerome Ch'en, *Mao Papers: Anthology and Bibliography* (New York: Oxford University Press, 1970); cited in Jonathan D. Spence. *The Search for Modern China*, 547.

10. Spence, 545.

11. James Wong, *Contemporary Chinese Politics* (London: Prentice-Hall International, 1995), 149.

12. Spence, 548.

13. Ibid., 550.

14. Hsu, 693.

15. *History of Chinese Communist Party: A Chronology of Events 1919–1990* (Beijing: Foreign Language Press, 1991), 280–81.

16. Hsu, 695.

17. Spence, 561.

18. Ibid., 575, 577.

19. Hsu, 700.

20. Spence, 580, 582.

21. Spence, 584–85.

22. Lin et. al., 31–42.

23. Spence, 600.

24. Ibid., 603.

25. Hsu, 764.

26. Ibid., 764–76.

27. Spence, 621–22.

28. Ezra Vogel, *One Step Ahead in China: Guangdong Under Reform* (Cambridge: Harvard University Press, 1989), 41.

29. Spence, 636–38.

30. Lin et. al., 31–42.

31. Hsu, 825.

32. Ibid., p. 780.

33. Spence, 623; Hsu, 827.

34. Vogel, 89.

35. Spence, 667.

36. Lin et. al., 31–42.

37. Ibid., 31–42.

38. "World Bank and China," *World Bank Country Brief* (1999): 4.

2000

2005

Contents

RED

47   Urbanism
53   De-urbanism
59   Anti-urbanism

INFRARED©

67
71   The American Dream
79   Planning the Market

SHENZHEN SPECIAL
ECONOMIC ZONE

83   Winning Hands
87   ZONE© I
111   CULTURAL DESERT©
117   SCALE©
123   LINEAR© City

BLOCK©

133
141   CHINESE SUBURBIA©
149   ZONE© II

IDEOLOGY

SHENZHEN

Mihai Craciun

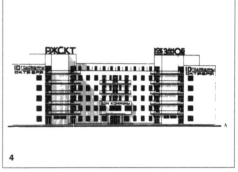

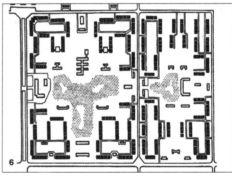

[1] *Soviet propaganda poster; 1924. Industry shapes the socialist city as an inverted twin of the capitalist metropolis.* [2] *Dziga Vertov's* Man with a Movie Camera; *1929. According to S. Frederick Starr, Vertov's films "taught about the Future by documenting the present." See S. Frederick Starr,* Melnikov: Solo Architect in a Mass Society *(Princeton: Princeton University Press, 1978), 5.* [3] *Palace of Labor, designed by the Vesnin brothers; Moscow, 1920. With firm lines, the Soviet Constructivists outline a genuine vision.* [4] *Communal housing, Vesnin brothers; Moscow, 1920. New programs that furthered the goals of the Soviet revolution and established essential differences between the socialist industrial city and its capitalist equivalent earned architecture the role of what S. Frederick Starr calls the "art of the dictatorship of the proletariat."* [5] *A superblock, designed by Meskov and Masselnikov; Moscow, 1926. Any reference to metropolitan density stirs ideological suspicion.* [6] *A micro-district, or* microrayon, *U.S.S.R., 1950. The* microrayon *demonstrated the postwar Soviet formula for ideal urban density, approaching urbanism as science. Socialist cities were able to maintain the illusion of the Future long after the West had declared its crisis. The manipulation of urban quantities would guarantee ideological survival.*

RED

If Utopia is illusion, then ideology is illusion decreed, imposed: it mandates optimism. The fever of great expectations underlies an obsession with the Future and a refusal to accept the present. Indeed, each day's miseries are Utopia's raw matter; the project of constructing social perfection is directed first at the masses. Communists throughout modern history have inherited a Utopian ideology that mandates belief in an ideal history.

In working toward their goals, communists found ideological campaigns to be their tools of choice. As both manifestos and test-tube revolutions, ideological campaigns fulfilled the communist goal of linking theory with practice. Always conceived at a large scale, they also formed the script—the code—of the destiny of cities under communist regimes. As communists embraced the goal to transform society, cities became both the stage of their revolution and the measure of their progress.

Communists' fascination with the Future has translated, during the 20th century, into attempts to merge Utopian visions with the realities of modern industrial cities. The image of the industrial city was adopted as symbol of the *red* "class struggle"; the socialist city was seen as an inverted twin of the capitalist metropolis.[1] The idealism that imbued industrial cities was conveyed in early Soviet manifestos such as *Epoch and Style,* Moisei Ginzburg's Constructivist digest of the machine aesthetic, or Dziga Vertov's cinematographic experiment *Man with a Movie Camera.*

Communist, or *red,* ideology—rooted in the instability of the metropolis—found in the dynamism of industrial cities a catalyst for an elusive search for utopia. Spurred by the enchantment of the communist vision, the idea of the "good" metropolis became the foundation of the cities of socialism. For communists, this impractical idea became both destiny and dogma. In trying to realize it, the communists of the Industrial Age faced a wrenching contradiction: while *red* ideology depended on the critical mass of the proletariat and was therefore committed to industrialization, it also sustained an Oedipal agenda that systematically denounced the metropolitan origins of its Utopian vision.

Early on in the Soviet Union, the architecture and urbanism professions were tainted with negative associations, linked as they were with the creation of the metropolis. They were forced into ideological captivity: after silencing the Constructivist avant-garde in the 1930s, the communist party assumed control over urbanism. To reinforce Karl Marx's assertion that the success of the proletariat's struggle depended on the existence of large industrial cities, urbanism became the statistical expression of communist ideology, a science assigned to organize vast numbers.[2] Urban planning was reduced to devising formulae for repetition, coherence, and prefabrication. The Vesnin brothers' 1920 prototype of a superblock, designed to infuse metropolitan density in half-rural Moscow, resurfaced after World War II as the *microrayon*—the basic unit of the socialist city, guaranteeing predetermined density. Soviet academics drafted a blueprint of the Cold War socialist city, carbon-copied throughout the U.S.S.R., and later adapted in other communist countries.

The standardization of architectural and urban practices ensured that socialist cities would maintain the illusion of Future long after the West had declared its crisis. Shaped by *red* ideology's optimism, socialist cities were characterized by hyperbole: expansion, overstatement, and an "aestheticization" of numbers. Conceived only as a part of totality,

A theater of mandatory optimism, Beijing in the 1950s. Chairman Mao,
a crane, and the ghost of a factory—the "natural" consequences of the
Communist revolution—loom over cheering crowds.

architecture lost the significance of the individual. Each new project was a fragment, secondary to an overwhelming whole. With the absolute opening to the collective, socialist cities, from East Berlin to Beijing, conformed to a ubiquitous blueprint that set forth the freedoms offered by numbers: freedom from tradition, from the individual, from taste.

Urbanism

At a time when Comintern (Communist International, a congress established by Lenin in 1919 to encourage socialist revolution in other countries) polarized revolutionary fervor, the ideological focus of the communist movement was unity. *Red* ideology strove, above all, for a monolithic party and a consistency of its principles. Urbanism was called to represent this closed, unitary system by searching for a canon, rules of composition, and the repetition of an accepted model.

Despite communism's emphasis on unity—or maybe because of it—in China, the *red* era was marked by instability, ideological swerves, and a perpetual testing of loyalties. For Mao Zedong, leader of the Chinese Communist Party (CCP), ideological campaigns were a strategy for maintaining control by instating a climate of incertitude and fear. The beginning of Mao Zedong's ideological campaigns can be traced back to the Long March of 1934–35, which gathered all the future Politburo members into a tightly knit group.[3]❋ Soon after, Mao seized upon mass movement, stressing ideological activism, as an essential political tactic. The Rectification Campaign (1942–44) served to consolidate Mao's role as leader of the Communist party.

A steadfast Communist, convinced of the perfectibility of an idea or system, Mao Zedong assumed control over the destiny of cities by gradually developing his version of Marxism—"with Chinese characteristics." The urbanism of the *red* era illustrates his growing distrust in the metropolitan formula that shaped the Soviet socialist city. Of peasant roots, Mao's revolutionary interests resided in the countryside, not in cities. His *red* campaigns began with an expression of loyalty to Soviet urbanism based on industrialization, but soon moved toward a furious rejection of this paradigm. After abandoning the revolutionary role of cities entirely, Mao attacked the idea of the city itself.

Immediately after the People's Republic of China (PRC) was established in 1949, the Chinese Communist Party focused its ideological agenda on cities. The Three Anti Campaign (1951), directed at factory and business managers, and the Five Anti Campaign (1952), directed at the surviving capitalists and merchants, consolidated the CCP's control over industry. The First Five-Year Plan (1953–57), together with the collectivization of agriculture through land reform campaigns initiated in 1950, began the transformation of the economy, not to mention its urban planning, along the Soviet model. Cities were reorganized around self-sufficient industrial "neighborhoods"—*danwei*, or urban communes—"production units" that governed every area of urban life, from work to leisure. In this way, China's *red*

❋ The **Ideology of Mao Zedong** was influenced by Chinese philosophies that had existed long before the establishment of socialist China and long before the ideologies of Marx and Lenin. In his 1919 speech entitled "The Obligations of Students," Mao enunciated his vision of an ideal society, known as the *Xing Cun,* or New Village, a concept that was profoundly influenced by the Confucian notion of *Da Tong,* or Great Unity. In his notes on Confucius' *Liji* (*Notes on Civility*), Mao commented: "Confucius knows the significance of this perfect, peaceful state of society. It is society above the ones separated by wars and even the ones developing in peace. Confucius calls it *Hu.* The so-called *Da Tong* is what *Hu* means. We are *Hu.*" (*Hu,* which translates to "swan," alludes to an ultimate level of ambition and purity; a swan represents a transcendental spirit in Chinese art and literature.) Another more direct influence on Mao's ideology is the *Book of Great Unity,* written by Kang Youwei, a social reformer and scholar in the late Qing Dynasty. In this book, Kang formulated an ideal society composed of a number of institutions and guided by a set of very clear social principles. For instance, children should be taken care of by a Children's Institution instead of by their families; husbands and wives should separate after a year living together; people should work for all institutions for free, and so on. Mao's later experiment with the People's Commune (*Renmin Gongshe*) was an attempt to physically manifest his utopian ideology and the true model for his slogan "Communism with Chinese Characteristics."
—Qingyun Ma

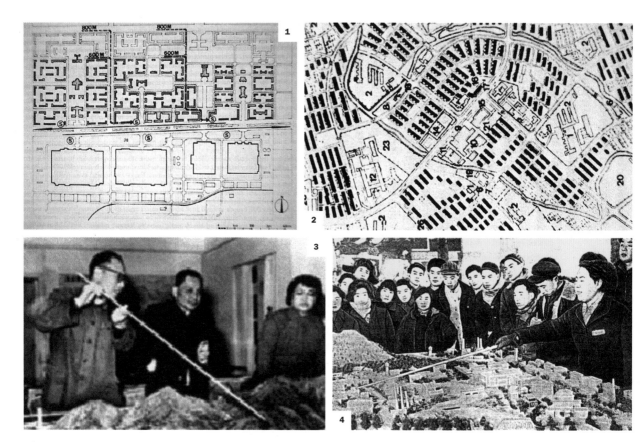

[1] *Plans for a* danwei, *an urban commune, with a mix of residential and industrial buildings; Beijing, 1954.* [2] *A* danwei *in Shanghai, 1956. "China's strategy for urban construction is clearly wedded to her strategy for industrial development and is contingent upon her progress in industrial construction."* [3] *In this photograph from the 1950s, Deng Xiaoping, then a member of the Chinese Politburo, listens to a city planner. A perpetual idealization of shortcomings, planning systematically extracted an imaginary Future from the realities of the present.* [4] *Planning of Beijing, from the Soviet magazine* Arhitektura, *1956. "We'll see a forest of chimneys from here!" Mao Zedong proclaimed from Tiananmen Square.*

urbanism became "wedded to her strategy for industrial development and . . . contingent upon her progress in industrial construction."[4] Writes C. P. Lo in his 1980 essay "Shaping Socialist Chinese Cities":

> The communist ideal of a city . . . should be "centralized, highly standardized and uniform type of social organization." City planning should be integrated with the overall economic planning of the state. . . . Spatially, no part of the city should attract or repel certain classes. In brief, the city's plan should express the classless nature of the society. In order to achieve such an ideal, communist city planning aims at (a) standardization of housing, (b) controlling the size of the city, (c) laying out a city center to give a political-cultural-administrative center image rather than an area of retail concentration, and (d) employment of neighborhood unit concept in planning aimed at dividing the city into self-contained units.[5]

Planning formed the basis of the CCP's ideological and political agendas. It played a key role in submitting cities to the control of *red* ideology and toward the actualization of the ideals of the Comintern. Planning also allowed the inexperienced Party to overcome an ideological impasse when confronted with the instability of the industrial city. A perpetual idealization of shortcomings, a smoothing of misery, planning systematically extracted an imaginary Future from the realities of the present. With planning came the Soviet model of industrialization, which focused on cities. Under its influence, a candid Mao Zedong declared in the early 1950s, looking over Beijing from the grand entrance to the Forbidden City: "We'll see a forest of chimneys from here!"[6] While supporting the communist rhetoric of class struggle, the factories were a clear, immediate way of representing the revolution: the transformation of society from rural to urban, from the archaic countryside to the modern industrial universe of the proletariat. Factories advertised the socialist city as a "double" of the metropolis, a mechanical city wresting the power of industrial dynamism from its original.

"Walking on Two Legs" was one of the slogans of the 1958 Great Leap Forward, described by one writer as "a mighty paroxysm of round-the-clock labor. The face of the country was changed with new roads, factories, cities, dikes, dams, lakes, afforestation, and cultivation, for which 650 million Chinese had been mobilized in nationwide efforts of unparalleled intensity and magnitude."[10]

De-urbanism

Mao assumed leadership trying to overcome the conflict between the theoretical reliance of Marxism on a minority of urban, *red* proletariat and the realities of China's vast, rural population. His frustration over the Soviet model of industrialization grew as he increasingly perceived it to be unfit for the social conditions of China. He soon came to focus his ideological campaigns on the countryside, launching his thesis "Marxism with Chinese Characteristics" as a local, specific reaction against the Comintern's narrow focus on cities. He targeted Chinese cities to be transformed "from centers of consumption to centers of production"; they were to relinquish their existing roles as centers of commerce and trade, to become, instead, heavily industrialized to serve agriculture by manufacturing products that were unavailable in the countryside.[7] This bias toward the countryside and against cities would mark the entire period that Mao was the head of the Party. Again, C. P. Lo writes:

> *The Communist Chinese government therefore tended to regard most cities as "consuming" because the city dwellers have been engaged in commercial activities which are not productive in the socialist sense. The task is therefore to convert them to "producing cities" cities, i.e., cities devoted to industries at large or small scales. This dichotomous division of cities is of course highly idealized, but it points toward the importance of industrialization as a national goal of economic planning and a driving force in city planning.*[8]

After China's falling out with the Soviet Union in 1958, Chairman Mao's attention shifted entirely to the countryside. Having silenced the economists through the Hundred Flowers Campaign (1956) and its aftermath, the Anti-Rightist Campaign (1957), and replaced them with cadres for the purpose of mobilizing the masses, Mao Zedong launched the Great Leap Forward (1958–62).✱

What John King Fairbank called a "paroxysm of round the clock labor," the Great Leap Forward substituted ideological ardor for economic realism, advocating the simultaneous development of agriculture and industry with the slogan "Walking on Two Legs."[9] The "forest of chimneys" emerged in the Chinese countryside: one million "backyard" furnaces were built in an attempt to achieve instant industrialization and the "socialization" of the means of production.

The Great Leap Forward was the first major step toward enacting Mao Zedong's goal of de-urbanization: the industrialization of the countryside and its autonomy from cities. Driven by his belief in the ability of the countryside to transform China, as well as his distrust in the Soviet model, Mao Zedong now rejected the urban while retaining industry solely as a necessary economic factor. Following the Marxist theory of canceling the differences between city and countryside, de-urbanization called for the abolition of cities in favor of "field urbanism," an evenly distributed industry intermingled of agriculture and residential areas. First imagined by the Soviet Constructivist avant-garde in the 1920s, de-urbanization was the red, communist version of Ebenezer Howard's Garden City. It followed the assertion that the red

✱ The impact of the **Great Leap Forward** on China's urbanism must be examined against a larger social-political context. The Great Leap Forward was only one part of a larger national campaign, called the Three Red Flags (*San Mian Hong Qi*); the other two parts were the Principal Line of Socialist Construction ("Construct Socialism Faster, Better, and More Efficiently") and the People's Commune. As the name implies, the "flags" were intended to fly everywhere and direct every aspect of social life in China, both urban and rural. Although the cause for the Great Leap Forward was complex, the competition between the Soviet Union and China should be considered a major factor. In November 1957, sixteen socialist nations and sixty communist parties sent their delegations to Moscow for the 40th anniversary of the Soviet Revolution. Mao, who had never before traveled to a foreign country, led China's delegation. In the closing ceremony, Nikita Khruschev called for an international competition between socialism and capitalism in his famous speech, "Declaration of Peace." He set forth the goal for the Soviet Union to surpass the United States in fifteen years. This ignited Mao's burst of ambition. He responded in his speech: "If the Soviets can surpass the U.S. in fifteen years, there is no reason that China cannot surpass the U.S. in fifteen years. The most important measurement of our goal is the overall output of steel." Mao's unrealistic goal of directing the country towards steel production led China into a frenzied industrial movement nationwide. —QM

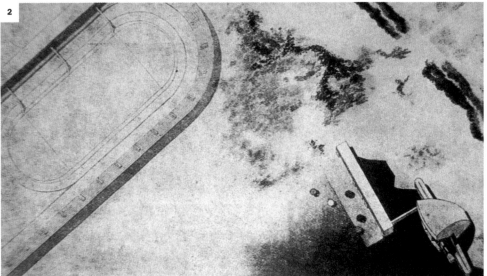

[1] The People's Commune Is Good, *a painting by Rui Guanting, 1958. "Urban Hierarchy in China.... The uncertainty about the extent to which official definitions of urban and rural settlements have been adhered to in enumeration work adds to the difficulties of interpretation. The extension of administrative boundaries of cities since 1958 to include vast areas of agricultural land, and the dilution of employment differentiation further reduce the feasibility of studies based on taxonomy of settlement." T. N. Chiu, "Urbanization Processes and National Development," in* China: Urbanization and National Development, *95.* [2] Project for a "Green City," Moisei Ginsburg and Mikhail Barshch, 1929. *The project, a "wedge [of a] Utopian campaign to abolish cities," was controversial. Observed one historian, "Based on the recently expounded theories of the Russian sociologist M. A. Okhitovich (which were drawn in turn from works by the French economist Charles Gide), the Ginsburg-Barshch plan would have cut a pair of automobile roads through the territory and strung houses along them, with public facilities at appropriate intervals. . . . Ginsburg here emerged as the enemy of all compulsion in society. In the plan as a whole he opposed 'natural' order to geometric order." S. Frederick Starr,* Melnikov: Solo Architect in a Mass Society, *168–76.*

revolutionaries did "not suffer only from the living, but also from the dead"—an insinuation that their agenda was hindered by the very presence of cities built by previous generations.[11] Although impractical, de-urbanization best suited Mao Zedong's goal of drawing the rural worker into the class struggle of the proletariat.

The Great Leap Forward ended with the disastrous famine of 1959. The years following were years of economic recovery during which the stabilizing role of the *danwei* and of the cities became the basis of China's new welfare state. So did the farming of private plots and selling of products in local markets, fostering individual responsibility and a call to material concerns.

The failure of the Great Leap Forward, coupled with the shadow of distrust cast over intellectuals in the aftermath of the Hundred Flowers Campaign, resulted in a deep rift between two opposing intellectual factions within the Chinese Communist Party: the radicals, who "sought to return to fundamental principles," and the liberals, who "sought fundamental change."[12] The "radical" intellectuals, clustered around Mao, fervently supported the idea that commitment to Marxism-Leninism and the power of will alone had the capacity to transform reality. They also shared Mao's belief that the masses, if mobilized, could overcome economic or bureaucratic obstacles and achieve the communist ideals through class struggle. The "liberal" intellectuals, associated mainly with the Party bureaucracy, sought a degree of autonomy for China's intellectual activity that would allow the development of economic, technological, scientific, and administrative skills and would advance China to a stage of development closer to that of Western countries. Mao did not favor this type of development, regarding it as reminiscent of the Soviet model and unfit for the unique condition of China, with its population largely engaged in a rural economy. The will to overcome the conflict between these two factions lay at the core of most of Mao's "rectification" campaigns between the late 1950s and the early 1970s—up until his last days as Chairman of the CCP. It would also extend into the years marked by the leadership of Deng Xiaoping.

This division at the heart of the Party sparked Mao Zedong's renewed thirst for ideological warfare and brought thousands of cadres under attack as revisionist, Soviet-oriented, or "capitalist remnants." The publication of fourteen of Mao Zedong's poems marked the beginning of the Socialist Education Campaign (1963), the first in a new series of campaigns targeting intellectuals. Directed at those engaged in the arts and their perceived Soviet-style revisionism, these campaigns called for the ideological rectification of the cultural realm. Repeatedly, Mao Zedong saw "culture"—the conventions arising from cities and their persistent clinging to values—as a quest for permanence and individualistic concerns that thwarted the goals of the revolution by imposing difference and dissuading unanimity. The Yang Xiangzhen Campaign and the Feng Ding Campaign, directed against Soviet-educated Marxist theoreticians, were centered around an allegorical debate between Taoism and Confucianism.[13] Mao's theoretical argument, that "two unites into one" takes precedence over "one splits in two," disguised an attack on the lingering criticism of the Great Leap Forward and the "liberal" cadres who upheld the idea that socialism could coexist with capitalism (an anticipation of the debates of the 1980s).

Over the course of these campaigns, Mao Zedong introduced the figure of a *red,* revolutionary peasant as the Chinese counterpart to the canonical Marxist urban proletarian. This idealized, self-sacrificing figure—open to manipulation and self-described as a "cog in the machine"—served as basis for the Middle Man Campaign (1963) and the Four Clean-ups

[1] *In July of 1966 Mao Zedong, age 73, swims across the Yangtze River. His athletic feat symbolizes his commitment to communism and marks the beginning of the Cultural Revolution.* [2] *Red Guards, 1966: Rebuilding unanimity by restoring a shattered consensus. "With the notable exception of the Cultural Revolution, Maoists and Party bureaucrats sought to maintain the appearance of consensus."* Merle Goldman, *China's Intellectuals: Advise and Dissent, 7.* [3] *"Rusticated" youth, 1968. "Ten million or so Red Guards, after they got out of hand in 1968, were sent down to the countryside."* John King Fairbank, *China: A New History, 402.*

(1964), advanced as "rectifications" of cinema and literary theory.[14] These campaigns challenged the view that the goal of the peasant—the middle man caught between old and new societies—was to improve his own life and livelihood instead of working toward establishing a new egalitarian society. They were a final warning that Mao Zedong was ready to abandon the cities and focus the revolution entirely on the countryside.

In July of 1966, Mao swam across the Yangtze River; news of his act electrified the masses. The Cultural Revolution (1966–72) thus made its debut as an allegory of the commitment to *red* ideology: Mao Zedong had literally "crossed the river," and for those who shared his commitment, there was no return from the road to a complete revolution. Directed against those who had taken the "capitalist road," the Cultural Revolution stopped the budding market-socialism that appeared after the Great Leap Forward.

The failure of the Great Leap Forward and the rejection of the Soviet model had cast doubt over central planning. Mao Zedong introduced the concept of "local self-reliance," the economic guideline of the Cultural Revolution that avoided both central planning and the free market. This model helped revive the failing socialist economy briefly, by giving farmers increased control over their production. However, it also accentuated ideological polarities. The Cultural Revolution's splinter campaigns—the Three Loyalties Campaign (1968–69), the Campaign to Purify Class Ranks (1969–70), and the later Line Education Campaign (1973–77)—reinforced ideological commitment as a criterion of social legitimization, stressing the demands of class struggle against the evil of following the private road to prosperity. These campaigns reinforced the Cultural Revolution's main imperative: to achieve the spontaneous transition from socialism to communism by eradicating the differences between countryside and city.

As the apogee of Mao Zedong's ideological campaigns, the Cultural Revolution achieved the *de-urbanization* of China. It was carried out under the slogan "Destruction for Construction": millions of people were "rusticated," or sent to the countryside*; city populations stagnated or decreased; city activities were completely arrested, including the closing of universities and the destruction of foreign embassies. With the Third Front Campaign and the Cultural Revolution's twin, Mao Zedong finally achieved "industrialization without urbanization." He banished industries to remote mountain areas, succeeding to remove the urban connotations of factories.

❋ The **dispersion of urban youth to the countryside** was in actuality a strategy to sustain urban growth while avoiding potential social problems caused by overpopulation. Although efforts were made during the First Five-Year Plan to improve urban infrastructures and increase employment, China's economic state was still very bleak by the mid-1960s. From 1966 to 1968, millions of students in cities were graduating from high schools and colleges, without the prospect of jobs. They eventually became "accumulated spare labor," posing a serious problem to the Party and city managers. This volatile situation directly precipitated the Revolutionary Mobile Connection (*Geming Chuanlian*) and Educated Youth Up to Mountains and Down to Villages (*Zhi Shi Qingnian Shang Shan Xia Xiang*), the two primary campaigns of the Cultural Revolution. It should be noted that the Cultural Revolution was only one of a series of efforts to balance the population between the city and countryside. There were two other significant efforts in the early 1950s and the late 1970s. It may not be an exaggeration to state that population balance was the real, though concealed, motive behind the major political campaigns in China's recent history. —QM

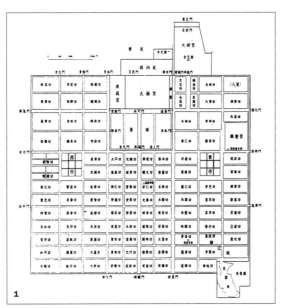

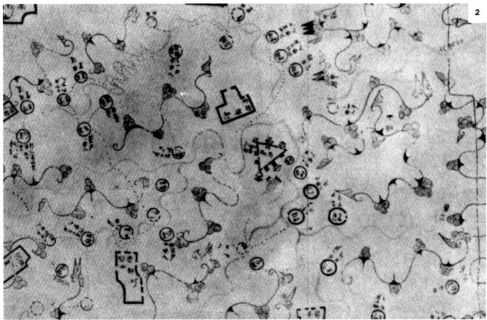

[1] *Gridiron layout of ancient city Chang'an (Xian). The Anti-Confucian Campaign (1973–75) attacked the symbolism of traditional Chinese cities. Repeatedly, Mao Zedong saw "culture," the conventions arising out of cities, with their quest for permanence, as thwarting the goals of the revolution, imposing difference and dissuading unanimity.[2] Eighteenth-century map with* feng-shui *markings. Traditional urban forms and traditional urbanism were branded as counterrevolutionary, imbedded with Confucianism. Their gridiron layout, north-south orientation, axiality, symmetry, and feng-shui readings were denounced as instances of "nature dominating man."*

Anti-urbanism[※]

Despite Mao Zedong's attempts, the Cultural Revolution failed to unify the CCP. The partitioning of *red* ideology over the course of Mao's campaigns, had brought structural changes and specialization. Polarized, the "radical" and "liberal" factions began to launch campaigns against each other.

The post-Cultural Revolution "radical" campaigns were carried out by the Gang of Four, a group led by Mao's wife, Jiang Qing, which remained obstinately devoted to Mao and the red ideological line. The Dictatorship of the Proletariat Campaign and the Water Margin Campaign were directed against the liberal, reform faction of the Chinese Communist Party, led by Zhou Enlai, the premier of China. In turn, the liberals, who were leading the effort to revitalize China's economy, launched the Four Modernizations (1972), which called for the modernization of science, technology, industry, agriculture, and the military in an attempt to open China to the West.

Ideology draws its strength from the constancy of its rancor. The cities remained Mao Zedong's source of discontent, the home of his ideological opponents. Having annihilated the urban effectiveness of the factories with the Third Front Campaign, Mao Zedong tried again to force the victory of *red* ideology by subverting the idea of the city itself.

Mao Zedong's last ideological battle, the Anti-Confucian Campaign (1973–75), attacked the symbolism of traditional Chinese cities.[15] Traditional city forms and traditional urbanism were branded as custodians of counterrevolutionary ideals, imbued as they were with Confucian ideals. Their gridiron layout, north-south orientation, axiality, symmetry, and abidance of *feng-shui* principles were denounced as instances of "nature dominating man." Mao advocated the ancient Chinese Legalist thought over Confucianism, stressing that the Legalist ideal of nonsymmetrical, self-sufficient cities would be closer to the Communist position of linking city and countryside. Writes C. P. Lo in "Shaping Socialist Chinese Cities":

> *All this emphasis on symbolism came under strong attack by Chinese city planners especially during the time of the Anti-Confucius Movement in 1975. The symbolic and geomantic considerations in the siting and layout of the city were thought to imply Nature's domination over man and man's desire to conform to Nature—a deterministic philosophy believed to be advocated by the Confucius school. The Communists tended to reject this and favored the Legalist school of thought headed by Kuan Tze who believed in man's ability to conquer Nature, and upheld a more pragmatic approach in city planning.[16]*

Behind this denunciation of Confucianism and praise of Legalism was an attack on the city-oriented reform faction of the Chinese Communist Party that had been critical of Mao's policies. Mao linked this criticism with the ancient Confucian practice of "good government," according to which any official had the duty to criticize the government when it deviated from established ideals. This criticism, denounced as ideological, could be persecuted based on the same ancient principle that "rectification of [an opponent's] ideas would lead to rectification of policy."[17] Through historical analogy, Mao extended the allegorical debate

※ **Anti-urbanism** was not the essence of China's urbanization strategy during Mao's regime. On a conceptual level, urbanism should be discussed as a part of the Great Unity, Mao's ambition to create an ideal society. Since the Great Unity required the fusion between industry, agriculture, commerce, culture, education, and defense, it engendered an urbanism that did not recognize the difference between the urban and the rural. It was a total urbanism. Its society and environment, Mao proclaimed, was brand-new, with no precedent in the East or West. It was to give birth to novel urban scenarios best characterized in political sayings such as, "Urbanization Without Industrialization," "Urbanization Free of Sub-Urbanization," "Cities Floating On Rural Lands," "Villages Carved In Urban Areas," and so on. Thus, industrialization in early socialist China focused on the realignment of urban and rural areas. If industrialization was one measure of urbanity, it elevated urban intensity throughout the whole landscape. —QM

Local market; Guangzhou, 1978. Mao insisted that the asceticism of rural life was the ethic required to complete the Communist revolution that imposed the equality of rural insufficiency.

between Confucian and Legalist ideals to the fundamental issue of the Cultural Revolution: "whether China should give priority to class struggle and continuing revolution, or to national and social unity and economic and scientific development." [18]

The Anti-Confucian Campaign aimed to eradicate the last vestiges of the "Old Habits" that had persisted after the Cultural Revolution, calling for the rejection of Confucian (urban) values of "idealism, humanism, and traditionalism." [19]✿ Mao insisted that the asceticism of rural life was, for the Chinese masses, the ethic required to complete the Communist revolution. Seeking to achieve the *red*, Communist goals by discarding the role of cities, Mao equivocally imposed the equality of rural insufficiency.

✿ The **Anti-Confucian Campaign** was only a mask for the Anti-Lin (Biao) Campaign, and had little to do with the criticism of traditional urban forms. Lin Biao, after a series of attempts to overthrow Mao, was killed in a plane crash fleeing to the Soviet Union. Feeling betrayed and anguished, Mao launched the Anti-Lin Campaign to eliminate the forces and influences of Lin's allies. But there was a huge dilemma: being Mao's closest colleague and most trusted successor, Lin had played a critical role in the Cultural Revolution and in building Mao's status as a political idol. To criticize Lin meant to doubt Mao's theory and practice. The Anti-Lin Campaign was hence renamed the Anti-Confucian Campaign and was crafted as a tactic to offset the criticism towards Mao himself. The Anti-Confucian Campaign referred to the theoretical debate between Confucianism and Legalism, a legacy of the First Emperor Qin, who was considered a symbol of reform and revolution. Legalists were the Emperor's political aides who had advocated new non-Confucian orders and laws for a centralized government. —QM

In the southern province of Guangdong, factories
are scattered across the countryside, relics of
China's Great Leap Forward.

"The feat most publicized abroad was the campaign begun in July 1958 to produce steel from small 'backyard' iron smelters without special guidance or equipment. Some 30,000 to 50,000 smelting furnaces were reportedly set up by the end of September, and a million in October. 100 million people were engaged in this 'battle for steel.'"

John King Fairbank, *China: A New History* (Cambridge: Belknap Press of

Deng Xiaoping was Time magazine's Man of the Year in 1985. He received the same honor in 1978.

INFRARED©

INFRARED© Driven underground by the forces of global economy, the Chinese Communist Party safeguards its totalitarian ideology by moving into the invisible spectrum of politics. INFRARED© is a covert strategy of compromise and double standard, a preemptory reversal of history that links 19th-century idealism with the realities of the 21st century.

After exhausting its resources for raising hopes or misery, any ideology reaches the limits of its powers of seduction. Ideology draws strength from its stockpile of Utopian vision and its survival depends on the speed at which it burns this reserve. When overwhelmed by the difficulties of putting its doctrines into practice, ideology is forced to bury the promise of the Future under the demands of an urgent, preparatory present. Such modification announces a crisis of vision: the concealment of Utopian beliefs under the sanction of historical realities is an emergency tactic. The underground is, therefore, a *state*—a condition—or perhaps the only public aspect of an ideology seeking to survive.

China at the end of the 1970s witnessed the decline of *red* ideology—a foreshadowing of a society forever cured of the Future. In the wake of Mao's death in 1976, the fear of a reversal to Maoist totalitarianism coupled with the alarming legacy of the Chairman's break with the Soviet Union brought the Communist vision into crisis. The apogee of the CCP's paralysis was summed up by Hua Guofeng, Mao Zedong's unmemorable successor, in the principle of the "Two Whatevers": "Whatever policies Mao has made, we will resolutely safeguard, and whatever instructions Mao has given, we will forever follow."[20] Mired in this impasse, Communist ideology in China seemed ready to surrender to a permanent standstill.

This is where INFRARED©, the concealment of Communist, *red* ideals, assumed its role: to save Utopia at a moment when it was being contested on all sides, when the world kept accumulating proofs of its ravages and miseries. When faced with the sum of errors and horrors committed in the name of its claimed truths, an exhausted ideology is ready to accept compromise. Communist ideology in China retreated underground, tunneling and ramifying according to the opportunistic potentials of its vision. Utopia mutated into *reform*—the sub-visionary but effective tactic of compromise. INFRARED©, *the ideology of reform*, is a campaign to preempt the demise of Utopia, a project to conceal 19th-century ideals within the realities of the 21st century.✱

With the demands of compromise, a necessary re-selection of believers reenacted conditions from the past. "Isolation strengthens ties" seemed to recall the memories of the Yan'an years and of the

✱ The notion of **infrared** is an explicitly Chinese, Deng-era formulation, and should be perceived through the following vantage points:
1. Separation between economic foundation and ideological super-structure: During Mao's era, the integration between the two was heavily stressed. Since Deng, separation of the two has become more common practice, and has become a prerequisite condition for China's "infrared" policy.
2. Deng's unique personality: Deng was characterized by Mao as "Soft Outside, Solid Inside" (*"Li Ying Wai Ruan"*). Owing to his very nature, Deng survived all the political campaigns against him. This was also the reason why Mao, before his death, reappointed Deng as China's new leader. It is this infrared personality of Deng's that ensured the flexibility of China's social experiments since the 1970s.
3. Consolidation of government: Through the 1960s, the oversized bureaucracy and deteriorating commitment of Party members weakened the effectiveness of Party policies. Deng made governmental consolidation one of the first strategies of his political reforms. This streamlining sharpened the Party's strength in its ability to execute new policies. —QM

In 1962, Deng Xiaoping, a veteran of the Long March, offers grassroots wisdom as solution to the economic impasse of the Great Leap Forward: "We must make the illegal legal. To quote an old saying from Sichuan province once uttered by Comrade Liu Bocheng, 'It doesn't matter if the cat is yellow or black as long as it catches the mouse.'" Quoted in Ruan Ming, Deng Xiaoping: Chronicle of an Empire, *5.*

Long March. The Communist party retreated underground, sinking this time into its own shadow, recalling the years of its invisible existence in Guangzhou, in the midst of the Guomindang. A self-imposed exile, its apparent abdication allowed the search for new powers.

❀   ❀   ❀

If architecture is the display of ideology, in retrospect this assumption provokes a heightened expectation of objectivity. Even more, if ideology is taken to be a willed distortion of realities, assisting the interests of the group that underwrites it, then architecture and ideology are placed at opposite poles of reliability. Architecture is evidence that offers for scrutiny realities concealed by words or beliefs; its stability—its *reality*—grinds down the firmness of past convictions. At the scale of cities, the accumulation of even the most banal architectural *facts* may become equated with *true* statements.

As the *red* era approached its end and its epic of factories declined, its critics must have exhaled, relieved. The Communist mythology dried up. After 1976, the Party repudiated the spent icons of the *red* era. Gone were the banners, the uniforms, the little red books, the public "self-criticisms." The heroism of an ideology once conceived as boundless and irrefutable gave way to pragmatism.

The factories were the icons of the *red* era. Industrial architecture became a closed universe where all idiosyncrasies were smoothed over to produce uniformity through repetition. Architecture had been called upon to represent the eternal present of Utopia, the literal construction of the Future. As the vigor of the revolution withered without having accomplished the goal of universal wealth, the factories—once symbols of the *real*, but now remnants of a failed start—were reduced to surreal, ghostly apparitions littering the countryside. Such stark embodiments of the misery of the proletarian universe made Party cadres shiver, but still, they did not abandon their commitment to *red* ideology. Unable to accept failure on such massive scale, the Party decided to survive as its own critic. Having opted for eventually crawling back from the grave, the Party changed its strategy from attack to concession toward the West.

Shorter than Mao . . . Deng Xiaoping knew that he could never achieve the stature of his predecessor. His pragmatism was a necessary threat to Mao Zedong's idealism. Loyal but cast as a rebel, Deng had been made a model of "ideological rectification."

The American Dream

"Modern industry has established the world market, for which the discovery of America paved the way." —*Karl Marx,* The Communist Manifesto *(1848)*

Notorious for criticizing cadres who supported Mao's argument that "ideological and class struggle would increase economic production," Deng Xiaoping had been purged twice during the Cultural Revolution and labeled an "unrepentant capitalist roader."[21] An adept pragmatist, he used catastrophe as tactic, issuing disastrous statistics, threatening reports, and prophecies of an imminent ideological meltdown. His ORACULAR MAGIC© were gathered in 1975 in the "Three Documents," a report on China's science, technology, and industry.[22] Deng Xiaoping tried to force the country to open to the West. He presented a bleak picture of the Chinese economy in the aftermath of the Cultural Revolution and advocated the development of science and technology for all sectors of the economy, including agriculture.

> ORACULAR MAGIC© A seemingly random, essentially unpredictable way of defining "aims," "goals," and "deals" that depends on an amalgamation of Confucian and Communist traditions and practices. Now operative in a new market-based context as the foundation of MARKET REALISM©.

In 1977 Deng Xiaoping was restored to his former post as vice-chairman of the Chinese Communist Party. By the following year, he was attacking the policy of the Two Whatevers and launched a theoretical debate that set out to reinvigorate the Party's ideological strategy. Deng published an article entitled "Practice Is the Only Criterion for Truth,"❋ in which he proposed to reform the Party's ideological strategy along the principle of finding "truth from the facts." He wrote:

> *The current debate about whether practice is the sole criterion for testing truth is also a debate about whether people's minds need to be emancipated. . . . In this sense, the debate about the criterion for testing truth is really a debate about ideological line, about politics, about the future and the destiny of our Party and nation.*[23]

Deng summed up the central INFRARED© guideline: Communists must take advantage of the present and bring their ideological impasse to an end—even if this meant choosing history over Utopia. To ease this difficult task, Deng allowed one satisfaction: that of the inherent conflict. To be a Communist and to embrace the present—this is a tactic of contradiction, a symbol of a new time. Deng Xiaoping challenged his cadres to begin building a paradise not imagined, but visible and tangible. Utopia would, thus, survive paradoxically in a post-Utopian era, driving a subterranean effort that uses history to construct history's own end.

❋ **"Practice Is the Only Criterion for Truth"** (*"Shi Jian Shi Jian Yan Zhen Li De Wei Yi Biao Zhun"*) is the title of an article that changed the path of China's modern history. The political environment at the time, shortly after Mao's death when the Gang of Four was still in power, was dangerously unstable. Although Deng and Hua Guofeng were appointed to be in charge of the CCP's daily life, they were confronted fiercely by the hard-core right-wing factions of the Party. A new political battle seemed inevitable. An early version of the article was first discovered by the editor of the newspaper *Sunshine Daily* (*Guangming Ribao*). It was then forwarded to Hua and then to Deng, who immediately sensed that releasing the article would ignite incredible public sympathy and mass energy that could help them win this political battle. Experts in mass movement, the two leaders personally modified and intensified the original article and had it published in the *Sunshine Daily* on 11 May 1978. Immediately, it incited people's frustrations as well as hopes. This was the battle that ended the CCP's history of battles. —QM

Deng Xiaoping and Chen Yun at the Third Plenary Session of the Eleventh Central Committee in December of 1978. At that session, the Central Committee reaffirmed the Party's Marxist and organizational lines, yet made the strategic policy decision to shift the focus of its work to socialist modernization.

What truth did Deng refer to? Evidently, he didn't refer to the truth that dares to denounce any "truth"—any ideology—as untrue. Committed to actualize the Communist vision, Deng advanced the "truth" of facts—a truth whose meaning is limited to the value of the experiment, to the outcome of trial and error. The INFRARED© principle—"practice is the only criterion of truth"—immediately transformed planning from a pregnant but perpetual deferral of completion into a dynamic, open testing of possibilities, a vigorous array of victories and failures. It asserted that Communists should no longer plan equality but pursue the equality of opportunities suggested by the market—in short, borrow the thinking underlying the American Dream. INFRARED© ideology suggested that, with the help of the market, the validity of Marxist-Leninist and Maoist thought could be found in an economic overhaul. For those seeking to match utopian beliefs with reality, capital *can* be a measure of truth.

In their search for a new science of truth, Communists were now allowed to idealize the United States. Legitimized by their interest not in history but in hastening its end, they could claim the *American Dream* as a model for instigating action and the search for happiness, fated for all. To Communists, the *American Dream* gave history a purpose, or better, revealed history's role to be solely transitional.

❀   ❀   ❀

INFRARED©, then, thwarted the traditional interpretation of ideology as a direct relation between idea and expression. Deng Xiaoping's ideological project was directed not toward the invention of new icons, but rather toward altering the perception of familiar images. Years later, contemplating the results of his ongoing reform, Deng Xiaoping would elatedly describe the new relation between ideology and the cadres' actions in language that echoed capitalist efficacy: "Their slogan is 'time is money, efficiency is livelihood.' In buildings undergoing construction, one floor is finished every day and the entire building is completed within a couple of weeks or so."[24]

The representational space of communism shifted from factories to metropolitan constructions—highrises and freeways—denoting mobility and displacement. As tactical devices, these fleeting presences conceal the persistence of Utopia. The transformation of cities would accompany this ideological shift. Deng's principle of "finding truth from facts" began the campaign of transforming Chinese cities, following the American model. The Party abandoned the Third Front policies and began focusing on new industries—service and trade—in its quest to make all cities ideal cities.

❀   ❀   ❀

Modernization, the key word of this ideological shift and a synonym for opening to the West, became linked and limited to saving Utopia. After 1978, modernization became a necessary, welcome condition supporting the Party's reform agenda; it was no longer perceived, as it was during Mao's reign, as a "birthmark of socialism arising out of capitalism." INFRARED© ideology's roots go back to Zhou Enlai's Four Modernizations campaign. Dubbed "the Elastic Bolshevik" around the time Richard Nixon's visit to China in 1972, Zhou had encouraged the separation between politics and the professions after the failure of the Great Leap Forward campaign. For him, science and technology provided the concept that could enable

*Deng Xiaoping in 1984 reviewing an honor guard on the 35th anniversary of
the founding of the People's Republic of China.*

an ideological shift. Deng Xiaoping, Zhou's close associate, enacted the Four Modernizations in 1978, revising the Party's strategy of government and establishing contact with the West, especially with the United States.

To demonstrate China's willingness to open its economy to Western technology and capital, Deng toured the United States in 1979. At the same time, to satisfy the Party's sudden desire to court the "Beautiful Imperialist," Deng Xiaoping offered communism as a hidden principle, the unseen platform of globalization. Sacrificed, communism was given a second life in a trade-off between ideological orthodoxy and power. The "invisible hand of the market" proved to be an all-inclusive concept that could substitute the *red* theme of class struggle and guarantee the Party's continued political control, even as it established contacts with the West. Deng Xiaoping's words grasp the contradictions that characterize the INFRARED© policy of opening up to the West:

> We will unswervingly follow a policy of opening to the outside world and actively increase
> exchanges with foreign countries on the basis of equality and mutual benefit. At the same time,
> we will keep clear heads, firmly resist corrosion by decadent ideas from abroad and never permit
> the bourgeois way of life to spread to our country.[25]

To Mao Zedong, Deng Xiaoping had been a necessary threat. Theirs had been a roller-coaster relationship. Loyal but cast as rebel, Deng had been made a model of "ideological rectification." Having studied in France, Deng must have disdained Mao Zedong's obsession with China's rural majority. Deng knew, however, that he could never achieve the stature of his predecessor. To him, to be political was to be envious. Determined to write the future of the Chinese Communist Party, he used his role as a mere successor to trade totalitarian power for ideological poignancy. He fortified the INFRARED© ideology by gradually giving up his Politburo posts and, eventually, eliminating the position of Chairman, announcing in 1982: "I myself will withdraw completely and will give up all positions, including the chairmanship of the Central Military Commission."[26]

By 1987, Deng retired from office, but remained the Party's main ideologue, its "invisible" heart. Without of Mao Zedong's luxury of tyranny, Deng Xiaoping opted for the tyranny of goodness. He proposed to the masses the asceticism of happiness, hurling his subjects on the road of relentless pursuit of self-interest and comfort. Ideology was reinvigorated by the trivial; Utopia was commodified, sold lot by lot.

❁   ❁   ❁

If the role of an epoch in decline is to reveal a society the way it is, to unmask it, to rid itself of the arrogance of its ambitions, then Deng Xiaoping realized that the role of "truth" for the INFRARED© ideology would be to maintain the illusion, to prevent awakening. His ideological campaign was based on a paradox: modernization, which inevitably brought China closer to the West, was also a massive effort to prevent the complete break away from the *red* fictions.

"Crossing the river by touching the stones"—a quaint reference to Mao Zedong swimming across the Yangtze River to boost allegiance to communism—is the slogan under which Deng Xiaoping introduced the Four Cardinal Principles in March 1979.[27] Functioning as an ideological break, the Four Cardinal Principles reinforced the basic political line of the Chinese Communist Party, which holds even today. Advising that progress should be slow and steady, these principles require everyone in China to follow "the socialist path, the dic-

Close associates and champions of the Four Modernizations: Zhou "Elastic Bolshevik" Enlai and Deng "Unrepentant Capitalist Roader" Xiaoping. Their combined thinking articulates (and saves) the future of communism through heresy. Opening Communist China to the capitalist West earns them incredulity from both the conservative and liberal within the Party.

tatorship of the proletariat, the leadership of the Party and Marxist-Leninist-Mao Zedong thought." INFRARED© ideology doesn't nullify the fundamental *red* commitments; rather, using the logic of reform, it finds ways to remain loyal to them.

The INFRARED© project, then, is not the abandonment of Communist ideals but the concealment of them. Communists must discern what they valued in the past and in the present, and how many of their efforts were, or are, illusions. Insofar as they are able to break from past fictions—the very fictions that assured their fame—they will be able to make decisive steps toward knowledge, toward *disillusion*, toward unanimous awakening. This fatal advance will project them outside history, because they have thus ceased to be present in history. Those who have awakened, those without illusions, unavoidably weakened, can no longer be the center of events, because they have realized their uselessness. For them, the interference of truth is lethal to action.

The principle of "finding truth from facts" was therefore Deng Xiaoping's test of loyalty for the cadres of the Chinese Communist Party: they would now have to weigh ideological commitment against realities. When Deng Xioaping proposed the *American Dream* of the free market as a new economic paradigm, he transformed the Communist perception of profit.

In 1978 Deng Xiaoping submitted his thesis at the Third Plenum of the Communist Party and encouraged his cadres to complete their Communist preparation: "Get Rich."

ORACULAR MAGIC© *In the 1970s, adept pragmatist Deng Xiaoping used catastrophe as tactic, issuing disastrous statistics, threatening reports, and prophecies of an imminent ideological meltdown.*

Planning the Market

Seeking "truth from facts" advanced a theoretical proposition. The evidence necessary to reassert the adequacy of Marxist-Leninist-Maoist theses could be found in the realities of the metropolis itself. To save the idea of common ownership, the Party would first borrow the *American Dream* and (re)build its ideological ground in the everyday competition among private interests.

In the early 1980s, the Party launched a series of ideological campaigns of the sort that have marked its history. It launched the Open Door Policy and introduced the notion of a *socialist market economy*. Consistent with its principle of inherent conflict, INFRARED© ideology shifted the Marxist-Leninist-Maoist political practice from an openly antagonistic position toward capitalism to one that accepts compromise between a centrally planned economy and the market. The juxtaposition of planned and free market became the new ideological platform of the Chinese Communist Party, marking a shift from Mao's *red* era to the years of reform.

If the randomness of the market is a seemingly objective "law" capable of building cities, then it could also become the guiding light, leading toward a perfected society and a new citizen. Using the market as a substitute for class struggle, the Chinese Communist Party chose to exert its ideological leadership by merging the political with the economic: cadres as managers. When in 1978 Deng Xiaoping encouraged his cadres to "get rich," he was echoing Lenin who, introducing the New Economic Policy in 1921, called upon Communists " to learn from ordinary salesmen." [28] And just as Lenin excused his ideological compromise as "a tactic, not a new direction," so did Deng advance the instrumentalization of the market as the tortuous path to perfected socialism. [29] Deng's "socialism with Chinese characteristics" (which echoed Mao's "Marxism with Chinese characteristics") transformed socialism into the invisible, stabilizing engine of a market economy. INFRARED© ideology legitimized access to commodities while maintaining the Party's exclusive political control.

Furthermore, INFRARED© asserted that, to support its ideological arguments the Party could *plan* the long-term consequences of the *socialist market economy*. Deng Xiaoping's thesis of "socialism with Chinese characteristics" restored the optimism of Communist ideology: a temporary reversal of the economy to capitalism would make it possible, in the future, to achieve a "perfect" socialist state. Deng Xiaoping identified the cause of China's economic stagnation during the *red* era in the non-conformance between its "means of production" and its "social relations"—a fundamental Marxist axiom. According to Deng, since the majority of China's workers were peasants, Mao Zedong's *red* class struggle could not, in fact, be verified. The *socialist market economy's* role would be, thus to accelerate the modernization of the country's "means of production" and create a new majority class—the modern, industrial proletariat. Only then could the Party accomplish the transition from capitalism to socialism—a second, "truer" revolution.

❀   ❀   ❀

The shift in the ideology of the Chinese Communist Party resulted in the reversal of Mao Zedong's anti-urban strategies. While in Mao's time the countryside had been the focus of fervent ideological campaigns, under the reform—echoing the Soviet Constructivists' emphasis on the metropolitan model—cities are at the center of the INFRARED© ideological

Deng Xiaoping purges the ideology that "purged" him: In "One Country, Two Systems," he stated, "In recent years, China has worked hard to overcome 'Left' mistakes and has formulated its policies concerning all fields of endeavor in line with the principle of proceeding from reality and seeking truth from facts. After five and a half years, things are beginning to pick up."

campaign. Entire new cities and the resurgence of the modern metropolis are telling of the transformations undergone by Chinese Communist ideology of the past two decades.

INFRARED© ideology uses the market—and the image of the metropolis—in the service of Marxism. The conflicts and contradictions of the metropolis conceals a belief in the redemption of Utopia. INFRARED© ideology takes over the unmitigated yet clear, structured forces of the Western metropolis and stresses only those aspects that fit its underlying ideas of compromise and concealment. Distorted, the contradictions and seemingly random juxtapositions extrapolated from Western urban models become the icons of the reform.

Advanced by the political elite of the Chinese Communist Party, the ersatz metropolis appears, structured on a syntactical set of blueprints controlling combinations of formulaic architectural types. The frivolity of this metropolitan replica is disguised by instrumental reference to the authority of the market, taken over ideologically as a repository of "knowledge." In fact, for INFRARED© ideology, the market does not function simply as a normative model summoned from without to ratify the correctness of urbanism; rather, it intervenes as a *conceptual* process that makes planning more fluid. *The market, in fact, designates the inner limits of urbanism under the reform*, functioning as a means of re-absorbing and ordering ideological tensions and contradictions. In other words, the market authorizes the interplay of permutations and mutations, endowing the formal urban system with flexibility. A calculated ambiguousness is built into this concept of the (socialist) market, at times focusing on the unity of principles and at other times favoring the diversity of phenomena, capable of authorizing every choice that is made in its name and controlling their outcomes and potentialities.

The techniques of simulating the metropolitan image are a direct consequence of Deng Xiaoping's call to pragmatism. They no longer intervene only at the level of representation, the way factories denoted the *red* class struggle. Insofar as they act on perceptive mechanisms, these techniques must extend their influence to conceptual mechanisms. The shift from *red* (representation) to INFRARED© (perception) blurs the borders between fantasy and reality.

Ultimately, economic reform questions the role of cities in relation to the Party's future. INFRARED© ideology shows that Mao Zedong's anti-urban policies were an entirely mistaken strategy: campaigning against the Four Olds and the cities destroyed communism's own ground. According to Deng Xiaoping and reform cadres, the modernization of cities under a "planned commodity economy" is more effective in securing the future of the Chinese Communist Party and the relevance of its doctrines.

*Deng Xiaoping tours the United States in 1979. Holding the key to the Future,
the United States could now be idealized.*

SHENZHEN SPECIAL ECONOMIC ZONE

Winning Hands

According to legend, an artificial island was built during imperial times at Guangzhou in the Pearl River Delta.[30] Its declared purpose, to shelter foreigners, concealed the less generous but urgent call to keep "barbarians" away from Guangzhou, an ancient walled city and capital of the Guangdong province. Though local resistance against foreigners' presence was strong, it was a matter of decades—and many wars—before the imperial government was forced to concede Guangzhou and a series of other coastal cities as "open ports" that allowed commerce with the outside world. In 1842, as a result of the Opium War, the British acquired the island of Hong Kong, just south of Guangzhou, as a trading post. More than a century earlier, the island of Macao, only a few miles west of Hong Kong, had been ceded in a similar way, to the Portuguese. Due to their proximity to these colonies, Guangdong Chinese experienced, fortuitously, Western customs and built communities. It didn't hurt that no one could remember the settlements that existed on those islands before.

The beginnings of modern China are linked, therefore, to territorial manifestations of an ideological dispute and its modern urban settlements are the result of a bargain. The land concessions in the Pearl River Delta established the idea of a different China—a China of enclaves. There, a new ideology was founded, based on parallel regimes of identities. The ensuing dialectic between an inside (perceived as real and Chinese) and an outside (perceived as virtual, or Western) pervades the history of modern China. The enclaves, where modernization has been defined in terms of coexistence rather than overall transformation, harbor the juxtaposition between tradition and Western influence. Inspired by their fortuitous uprooting, many Chinese from the Pearl River Delta became the founders of *ethnic* communities throughout Southeast Asia and the rest of the world (Chinatowns). Over time, the Pearl River Delta became the paradigm of Chinese modernization and entrepreneurial spirit, an area where Western interference became assimilated as know-how. It was no coincidence that Dr. Sun Yat-sen, the most prominent figure of the 1911 revolution against the imperial government and "father" of the Chinese Republic, was born in the Pearl River Delta. His vision of a modern China drew on Western political and economic models. During the brief period of the Chinese Republic, he was the first to suggest that modernization required the transformation of Chinese cities. Western urbanism and planning were the templates of Dr. Sun Yat-sen's political vision.

The enclaves boast diversity and adaptability. Drawing on Guangzhou's notorious culinary license, anything can be assimilated in the enclaves. Paradigms of exoticism—as much for China as for the West—the enclaves exaggerate the cosmopolitan possibilities of the metropolis. Their extreme contrasts are both programmatic and exemplary. The notorious "walled city" of Hong Kong (the ultimate slum, now demolished) contrasts starkly with the stratospherically priced mansions on Victoria Peak; the welfare paradise of Macao is strikingly set against the gambling economy that fuels it.

This insistence on the extreme and ludicrous urban assemblage is possible because the enclaves are *extraneous* metropolises. Politically powerless, satellites of faraway cities, their difference from their mother-cities is an essential one. Each city, at its origin, is an autonomous, self-governed entity, left to defend itself with its own ideology. The enclave is a

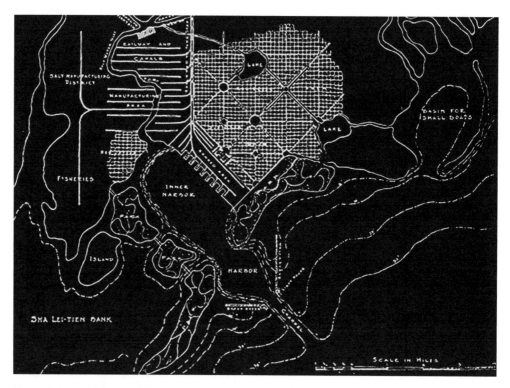

Dr. Sun Yat-sen's 1922 proposal for a new northern harbor, north of Tianjin, appeared in the book International China *(New York: Putnam, 1929). "My idea is to develop this port as large as New York," remarked the "father" of the Chinese Republic. The enclaves of foreigners in the Pearl River Delta established a precedent for China's modern urbanism. Starting with their model, Dr. Sun was the first to suggest that modernization required the transformation of Chinese cities.*

metropolitan *consequence*. It recycles all aspects of its mother-city, save the idea of community, of public and participation. Its essence is transience, the temporary arrangement of interests. A perpetually divided community, the inhabitants of the enclave are the voluntary prisoners of a historical arrangement, whether they are living in slums or gated communities.

As epicenters of modernization, the enclaves make clear that the territory, seen as extraneous to the city or at best as its geographical extension, is subject to the powers residing in cities. The land is silent: it undergoes the fate decided for it by urban interests. The cities decide how the territory will be used, if it will remain agricultural or not. The development of the territory, its industrialization and ecological concerns are all urban arguments.

Ironically, this "triumph" over the territory expands the influence of the cities beyond their control. The enclaves, by now the source of a new urban model sustained by economic robustness, threaten the cities with obsolescence.

❊   ❊   ❊

After 1949, the foreign enclaves of Hong Kong and Macao were ignored in China; they were ideological Pandora's boxes, better left aside. Both places underwent a period of stealth development and slipped into relative ideological insignificance, lone survivors of a colonial past. In the West, they made the headlines only periodically, to mark the exodus of refugees fleeing Mao Zedong's campaigns to fill the sweatshops in Kowloon or Macao.

In August 1980, after decades of neglect, the Pearl River Delta suddenly reacquired relevance as Deng Xiaoping proposed to suspend ideological orthodoxy and pursue the gains of compromise. "Seek Truth from the Facts" articulated the new ideological agenda of the Party—to test Zhou Enlai's Four Modernizations thesis by surrendering openly *red*, Communist commitments and offering part of the economy to the market. Labeled as *reform*, this underground pursuit of utopian ideals opened the possibility for a new way of looking at reality, a new code for the city and its spatial and technical definitions, armed with new instrumental knowledge.

The homeland of an international network of overseas Chinese, the Pearl River Delta could provide the foreign capital needed to fuel *open-door* economic reform while the region's mercantile background could serve as the foundation of a new *socialist market* economy.

As a consequence of Deng Xiaoping's call for economic reform, the Fifth National Congress of the Communist Party decided to apply "flexible" economic measures specifically in Guangdong. Making reference to the "dirty realism" of the Pearl River Delta, officials proposed to use the "winning hands" that the province had at its disposal in the interests of reform.[31]

Following the precedent of establishing Hong Kong and Macao as concessions for trade with foreigners, the Party chose to adopt the enclave model for these new *socialist market* experiments, designating select regions in the Pearl River Delta as Special Economic Zones (SEZ). The first SEZ, established in 1980, was Shenzhen (near the China–Hong Kong border), soon followed by its smaller neighbor, Zhuhai, which stretches along the border with Macao. Modernization was once again confined to enclaves.

文锦广场

'95 1

特区党的生活

TEQU DANG DE SHENG HUO

The Chinese Communist Party periodical for the Shenzhen Special Economic Zone (1995).

ZONE© Imposes limits, but not spatial content. A vague term, ZONE© is preferred by the Chinese Communist Party over "city" because it is conceptually blank. A ZONE© is open to the impurities of ideological manipulation. It purges historical contents from territories where they have been imposed and replaces them with the dynamics of global economy. A ZONE© remains programatically unfulfilled, an urban condition that never achieves focus or intensity. ZONE© is the birthplace of CHINESE SUBURBIA©.

✱ **Zone** is the translation of a Chinese word, *qu*. While zone is only a recent concept in urban planning and architecture, *qu* has been in Chinese literature since the Zhou dynasty (1027–771 B.C.). Examination of this character can offer some critical discussions related to the notion of the SEZs.

Based on the *Ci Yuan* (*Source of Words*), the most reliable reference book on Chinese etymology, *qu* was first used to mean a designated commercial area in a military territory. Its definition has since been extended to these meanings: an act of categorizing or differentiating; a designated area within a limit; a small unit of measurement; and, in literature, diminutiveness and inferiority. Pictographically, the character is composed with an open boundary containing a number of elements, which may or may not resemble each other. Ideographically, it implies a limit that is defined by a single principle or a single purpose that is military, political, or ideological. Therefore, it is simultaneously the most artificial and conceptual physical construct. The fact that the character itself has an open boundary is very suggestive. It is to prevent the sterility caused by isolation. Life within the boundary is neither the default consequence of what is in the boundary, nor the necessary preconception of the boundary. It is guarantor of differences. Through the contemporary history of China, *qu* has had a very dynamic life, appearing as the White Zone (*Bai Qu*), Red Zone (*Hong Qu*), Marginal Zone (*Bian Qu*), and Liberated Zone (*Jie Fang Qu*). —QM

Once the Party approved the establishment of Special Economic Zones,✱ the entire area along the China–Hong Kong border became surrounded with barbed wire. Checkpoints were set up, tightly isolating this chosen swath of land from the surrounding Chinese province—an insurance against capitalist "spiritual pollution."[32]

The Shenzhen Special Economic Zone grew around what had been a sluggish village located at the border with Hong Kong. In the beginning, a crude industrial area was hastily built under the pressure of ideological urgencies. Although imagined as an enclave for experiments with the market, the zone was still modeled to be a socialist city—a cluster of *danwei*, urban communes. Dubbed an "export zone," it was given as an "experimental" investment area to foreign developers, most of them from Hong Kong.

Carved out of the Communist "mainland," the Special Economic Zone offered the promise of a fresh start. At the moment when the Party's confidence in its own ability to rebound from its past failures was at an all-time low, the SEZ became the vessel of a renewed confidence, the project that harnessed the Communist zeal to a new campaign.

Established at the peak of Communist anxiety, the Shenzhen SEZ links utopia and pragmatism. The zone synthesizes the INFRARED© ideal of finding "truth" in reality while, at the same time, presses beyond realities to construct new public symbols.

A propagandistic device, the SEZ sets aggressive goals for urbanism and architecture. The "message" of the zones is emphasized in Deng Xiaoping's prophetic words that advertise the ideology of the reform:

Special Economic Zones are a window to technology, management, knowledge, and foreign policies. Through the zones, we can import technology, acquire knowledge, and learn about management, which is also a form of knowledge. The Special Economic Zones will become a foundation for opening to the outside world. We will not only benefit in economics and personnel training, but also extend the positive impact of our country on the world.[33]

Deng Xiaoping's analogy between "window" and ZONE© establishes a diagrammatic approach to the city that contrasts with Mao Zedong's revealing image of a transformed

A construction billboard in Shenzhen.

Beijing ("a forest of chimneys"). His remarks underline the changes in the Party's perception of the relation between ideology and cities: from "forest" to "window," from the literal to the implied. Loaded with the ideological significance of the Party's underground control, the "window" is an intermediary space that can open or close the possibility of viewing. A figurative space, it frames a metropolitan similitude where the freedom of seeing substitutes for real experience.

ZONE©, a "window" open to previously forbidden realities, nurtures a renewed understanding of Utopia. As a simulated metropolis, the Shenzhen SEZ provided the stage where new freedoms could be released; controlled access to commodities marked the Party's "popular front." The ZONE© opened up a narrow path between reality and representation, it advertised common standards directed at the collective imagery. A new code of the city was addressed to an incipient, virtual "middle-class" with the intention of channeling its desires into a new ideology. If *red* ideology upheld the socialist city as a symbol of the collective and of the Revolution, the *socialist market economy* redefined the collective as mass—a collection of diverse identities, the expression of heterogeneity. In the SEZs, INFRARED© ideology pairs the collective of the *red* ideology with the idiosyncratic, the ephemera of market preferences.

❁   ❁   ❁

The SEZs are the cradles of a culture of contradictions. The consumerism sanctioned by the Party in exchange for modernization and participation to the global economy is in contrast to the Communist regime itself. (It is said that in the Special Economic Zones the mere presence of Party representatives was initially put under question. To camouflage its presence, the Party merged the positions of Party secretary and factory manager; the zone entrepreneur is now a cross-identity-cadre/manager.[34]) In the ZONES©, the syncretism *socialism-capitalism*—an expression of a hybrid ideology—sustains a fragile ecology of juxtapositions. These *pragmatic* constructions (Eastern-Western, global-local, market-planned) maintain an impure, simultaneous allegiance to both Utopia and the realities of consumer desires. The juxtapositions are held in a tenuous balance, susceptible to reselection, rearrangement, and even dispersion once the ideology that binds them shifts. Just as their colonial enclave precedents, the ZONES© are temporary spaces, transient arrangements that depend on the slightest transformations or conversions of ideology.

The SEZs also marked a departure, a turning away from the socialist city—the city of standard production. INFRARED© ideology dismantled all the assumptions of the *red* era: uniformity, typology, and control. The opening of a *socialist market economy* under Deng Xiaoping's call to "find truth from facts" brought socialist planning into crisis. Not only would the chaos of the *socialist market economy* challenge the relative stability of urbanism and architecture, but the programmatic contradictions of the reform would discard the assumed correspondence between ideology and form. The ZONE© is a periphery, a conceptually gray area. This is the territory where the planners of the SEZ would have to imagine a new beginning, new certitudes. Could Utopia be a no-man's-land?

"Seek Truth from the Facts"

Shenzhen Special Economic Zone, view of Luohu area, looking northeast.

"One Step Ahead"
Shenzhen Special Economic Zone, view of Luohu area, north.

"Get Rich Faster"
Shenzhen Special Economic Zone, view of Shekou area, west

"The Four Windows: Technology, Management, Knowledge, and Foreign Policies"

Shenzhen Special Economic Zone, view of Luohu area, north.

"Unswervingly Follow a Policy of
Opening to the Outside World"
The border between Shenzhen Special Economic Zone and Hong Kong.

"One Hundred Years Without Change"
Shenzhen Special Economic Zone, view of Luohu's business center.

"Behind market-oriented cliches, the pale traces of a genuine vision"

Shenzhen Special Economic Zone, office buildings comprise an ideological palimpsest.

"Keep Clear Heads, Firmly Resist Corrosion by Decadent Ideas"

Shenzhen Special Economic Zone, view of an early danwei (cluster of

In the Shenzhen Special Economic Zone, the old town is the ground for an ideological counter-purge.

The scrapping of the old town of the Shenzhen Special Economic Zone. "Destruction for Construction" proves to be the most obstinate legacy of the Cultural Revolution.

CULTURAL DESERT©

CULTURAL DESERT© China's euphemism for the Pearl River
Delta. The fortuitous result of NEGLECT©, geographical circumstance and relentless ideological campaigns. Under Mao Zedong,
the Cultural Revolution tried to force the victory of the red ideals
by imposing a moratorium on the cities and on the market. To the
INFRARED© ideology, the CULTURAL DESERT© is ground for
an equally efficient ideological counter-purge that uses urbanization and the exaltation of the MARKET© to save Utopia. The
ZONE© is the planned equivalent of the CULTURAL DESERT©.

It is said that at the heart of the metropolis there is nothing. In the Special Economic Zones, this *nothingness*—the consequence of breaking away with the past—is the basis of modern- ization and of new freedoms. It is this nothingness that the planners of the SEZs seek today. Only the tabula rasa can enable possibilities otherwise hindered by the traditional obliga- tion of cities and architecture to be stable.

Located far from China's political and cultural centers, Beijing and Shanghai, the Pearl River Delta had been derided during past centuries as a "cultural desert"—a prejudice made clear against the Chinese merchants dealing with the West. Nevertheless, its *nothing- ness* has always proved to be a fertile ground for new ambitions. The *compradores*, the Guangzhou middle-class of the Imperial era, turned their outcast status to profit. Their famed wealth only intensified Pearl River's "blank" condition. It became an incentive for exposure to Western influences and a catalyst for modernization.

In a similar way, INFRARED© ideology exploits all past erasures: those of Pearl River Delta's enclaves and those of Mao Zedong's campaigns. Deng Xiaoping seized the opportu- nities offered by the CULTURAL DESERT© and persuaded his cadres to allow the Pearl River Delta to move "One Step Ahead." The area's notorious disregard of the central gov- ernment's authority could be exploited as *entrepreneurial spirit*, needed to activate the market reform. At the same time, the opportunism that characterizes the CULTURAL DESERT© would enable the cadres to take advantage of the contradictions of the INFRARED© ideology.

However, before the *socialist market* experiment could take place, the CULTURAL DESERT© had to be enhanced, made more efficient. Deng Xiaoping encouraged his cadres to "purge the 'left' mistakes" of the previous decades: the INFRARED© ideology had to avoid the pitfalls of the *red* era campaigns. The cadres chose ZONE© as the planned equivalent of the CULTURAL DESERT©. ZONE© was chosen to be the solution to the entire array of ideo- logical conflicts that had surrounded the cities in the past. ZONE©, a vague term, defines the urbanism of the reform. A ZONE© can be anything: its spatial characteristics are inde- terminate. ZONE© is only a condition of a limit.

The construction of the Shenzhen Special Economic Zone was inaugurated under the slogan "Three Paths and One Leveling."[36] The words sum up the INFRARED© planning strategy: urbanism bracketed between *infrastructure* and *tabula rasa*. The "leveling," a lit- eral "rectification" of the territory, bestowed an ideal, a blank status, on the area. Only in

this way the Shenzhen Special Economic Zone could achieve in practice the theoretical transformations introduced by the shift to an underground ideology. Conceived as a vast, ideological *no man's land*, the ZONE© established a disruptive presence—a sudden enhancement of the CULTURAL DESERT©.

The Shenzhen Special Economic Zone radiates the consequences of the *open-door* economic reform while, at the same time, it obstinately resists any contamination of its enclave of contradicting values.

[1] *Unwanted authenticity in the Shenzhen Special Economic Zone; the old town of Luohu, 1996. As late as the 1990s, the old town of Luohu, the "traditional center" of Shenzhen and a Qing dynasty outpost, is still untouched by the apocalyptic changes that surround it. The town appears archaic, a cumbersome "window" to the past. Its purity draws good intentions to save it, to readapt it. Planners draw its "reform," yet, it cannot be saved. Its "authenticity" is its greatest flaw: the area is "densely and poorly constructed," and "has a low-level infrastructure, ineffective transport facilities and disappointing quality of environment," according to an official 1990 report celebrating Shenzhen's general planning and design. The old town district is in dire need for improvement. It is rearranged. The (red) factories are moved out of town "to increase land use for commercial, residential, and afforestation purposes." Statistics invoked as a tactic to stop the bulldozers only weaken its case: "33.4 hectares and 8,408 residents from 2,311 families." The district's smallness fails to stir the interest of the SEZ's planners. Efforts to save it are futile. The old town becomes a Cantonese enclave in a sea of Mandarin-speaking immigrants to the zone. Without faithful advocates, by the mid-1990s, most traces of old Shenzhen is gone. [2] Commerce in the (razed) old town of the Shenzhen Special Economic Zone. Seen through the lens of* INFRARED© *ideology, the town's only salvageable assets are "its commercial and service industries . . . flourishing, accommodating a large number of business dealers and labor forces."*[35] *The old shops are spared, surgically severed from the houses that contained them and continuing to line the streets. The old town is now a ghostly bazaar—shopping flavored with ethnic connotations. The Special Economic Zone has its own Chinatown.*

3

4

[3]*Shenzhen Special Economic Zone, patches of vulnerable farmland and natural reserves. The gradual advancement of urbanization takes advantage of all previous erasures, such as those that resulted from colonial influence and from Mao Zedong's campaigns.* INFRARED© *ideology didn't have to create a* DESERT©; *it was already there, waiting to be enhanced, made more efficient.* [4] *The Shenzhen Special Economic Zone and the areas under its administration. Theorem: For urbanism, the failure to coherently theorize the effects of modernization is the key to satisfying the vast ambitions of the reform.*

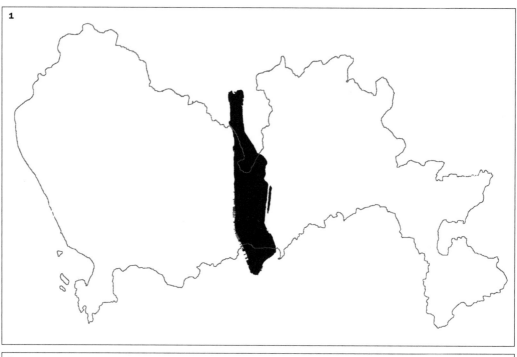

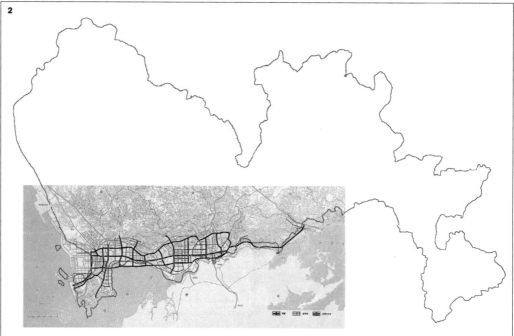

[1] *The area of Manhattan compared to Shenzhen Special Economic Zone.*
[2] *Traffic plan for the Shenzhen Special Economic Zone, designed by Beijing China Academy of Planning; 1985. Distilled down to an essential traffic pattern, the plan underscores the* INFRARED© *redefinition of the city as infrastructure.*

SCALE©

SCALE© dictates a system of static proportions that strives to control variation. The INFRARED© ideology replaces the perfection of a model with impetus. Every new project creates a new set of standards; every reassessment of goals urges a jump of SCALE©. SCALE© used to imply the harmonic. In the ZONE©, SCALE© includes the insufficient and the excessive.

"Urban construction in Shenzhen is large in scale."[37]

At the onset of a massive campaign of urbanization, planning is confronted with the challenge of creating order out of vast, seemingly chaotic numbers. The planners of the *socialist market*, ideologically committed to generating "facts," confront the opposite challenge: how to create maximum substance with minimum means.

The instability of the market provided the inspiration. A new concept of the city emerged as planning assumed *variation* as its objective. According to the planners of the Special Economic Zone, the *socialist market economy* requires, according to Sun Kegang, "Shenzhen's city planning to constantly readjust itself and forecast the development scale in accordance with the changes."[38] This new concept freed the "city" from the obligations imposed at the beginning of the industrial era. The zone was to be independent from the idea of a *standard* that upheld a semblance of essence and imposed a law of constancy—such as the socialist city produced by and for the masses. The Shenzhen SEZ embodied a new state of urbanism where fluctuation of the norm replaced the permanence of law, where the city (if "making" a city was still possible) assumed its place in a continuum by *variation*: precariousness replaced type. The confrontation between market and planning consistently canceled any obvious continuity between today's realities and tomorrow's goals: it humiliated vision. The planners of the SEZ confess to: "guiding urban construction mainly according to short-term targets;" and "repeatedly readjusting the long-term targets." Under the spell of their ideological commitment, these planners see the waning of their competence as evidence of a new science. They make improvisation their method: According to Sun Kegang, "Shenzhen's planning work was constantly perfected in terms of its breadth, depth, level, content and form."[39]

Under the pressure of an ostensibly impossible task—to create an instant metropolis—the planners systematically underestimate actual numbers. The history of Shenzhen Special Economic Zone is dominated by constant acceleration: a race between the seemingly inexhaustible possibilities of the market to mutate and the planners increased ability to reshuffle objectives. As paradigm of the Open Door Policy, the ZONE© is evidence for the planner's interest in finding devices that favor dynamic processes capable to engage the sudden changes in scale imposed by the market. In the ZONE©, the changes of scale combine the particular of each architectural project with the synthesis of a new urban space.

❀   ❀   ❀

INFRARED© ideology committed Utopia to an ambitious, unprecedented plan for capital. The logic of *subjective reaction* seemed to be for the planners the only "method" capable of withstanding the crushing freedom of numbers and the demand to oversee the production

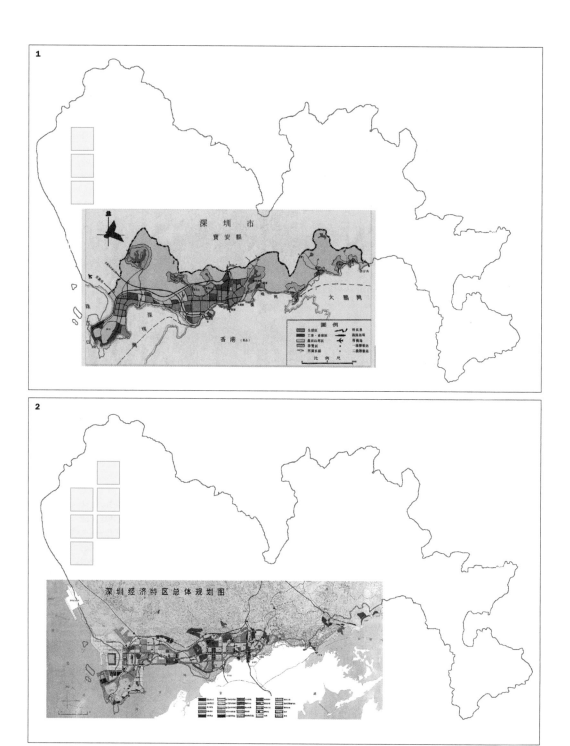

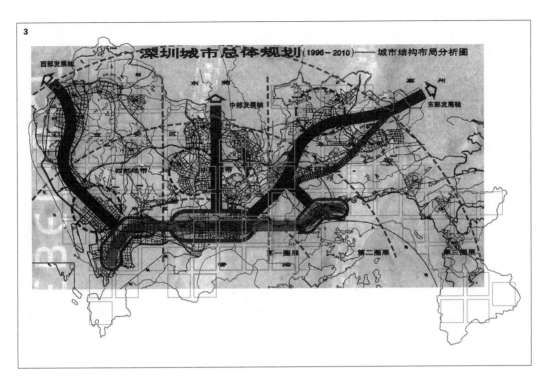

3

深圳城市总体规划(1996−2010)—— 城市结构布局分析图

[1] *The first master plan of the Shenzhen Special Economic Zone, by the Guangzhou Planning Institute; 1982. In two years, the city's population grows from 30,000, to 300,000 and finally, 800,000. The area of the zone is adjusted from 3 square kilometers to 10, then 60. Foundations are poured for 300 skyscrapers. Each blue square represnts 20 square kilometers.* [2] *The second master plan of the Shenzhen Special Economic Zone, by the China Academy of Planning in Beijing; 1985. A "second stage of development" is declared and the size of the SEZ is doubled, to 122 square kilometers. In four years, the SEZ has more than 1 million inhabitants. In 1989, when its population reached 1.5 million, the size of the area was readjusted again, to 150 square kilometers.* [3] *The third master plan of the Shenzhen Special Economic Zone, by the Shenzhen Institute of Urban Planning; 1996. The 1990s were inaugurated with six new areas of development spiraling out of the original Special Economic Zone. The zone is declared a "city" and the adjoining territory is put under its administration. By 1997 the Shenzhen Special Economic Zone had become a metropolitan area of 2,020 square kilometers and 3.79 million people.*

"Floating" population: former peasants and workers from inland provinces, many of them having left their hometown danwei clandestinely, ensure the zone's economic vitality.

of a vast urban expanse. When confronted with the unrepentant objectives of the *socialist market economy*, the traditional method of controlling the *formless* through *design*—a capricious compromise between theory and practice—proved to be just as out-of-date as the industrial city it had served in the past. For the first time in the history of urbanism, the planners of the Special Economic Zone used *chaos* as a measure of their achievements.

In 1980 the Shenzhen SEZ was expanded from 3 to 10 square kilometers; its population instantly grew to 300,000.[40] The development took place in Luohu, the area surrounding the train station along the border with Hong Kong. According to the Party's Science and Technology Modernization imperative, the Shenzhen Special Economic Zone was deemed to be a "learning laboratory of capitalist modes of operating business, hi-tech manufacturing, and construction." This first phase of development aimed at transforming Shenzhen from "a small town into a medium size city." In its infancy the zone developed at an astonishing 12 square kilometers a year. Foundations for more than 300 skyscrapers were poured, forming in less than a decade an "instant" skyline, rivaling that of nearby Hong Kong.

Between 1980 and 1982 Shenzhen's population swelled from 300,000 to 800,000. Under the shock of this first demographic wave, the area of the SEZ was increased from 10 to 60 square kilometers. The Guangzhou Planning Institute drafted the first master plan for Shenzhen between 1982 and 1983. An economy centered on the light industry was transferred from Hong Kong. Consequently, the population continued to grow rapidly, fueled by immigration from northern provinces: the zones promised financial gain. As planners consistently underestimated numbers, the population growth exceeded expectations. The number of migrant workers soon rivaled that of registered residents.

In 1984 the SEZ officially entered its second stage of development. A revised master plan was drafted in Beijing and the area of the Special Economic Zone was doubled to 122 square kilometers. For the first time, the central government publicly acknowledged the presence of the temporary or "floating" population. In four years, the population of the SEZ had exceeded 1 million inhabitants—800,000 permanent residents and 300,000 "floating" workers.

In 1985 as market consequences again exceeded the planners' estimates, "quick changes" became a planning concept. In 1989 the area of the Special Economic Zone was readjusted again, expanded to 150 square kilometers, while the population now approached 1.5 million. In the same year, the zone became the official laboratory for the real-estate market in Communist China. The Law of Transfer of Land-Use Rights was inaugurated in Shenzhen, unleashing speculative real-estate development. As planning targets were systematically voided by market demands, Hong Kong—the Asian metropolis notorious for extracting efficiency from demographic crisis and a paradigm of unrestrained capitalist freewheeling—became the urban model of the reform. Chinese planners declared Hong Kong an "official case study."[41] Through Hong Kong, the planners of the Special Economic Zones could finally reach for other metropolitan paradigms, whether Asian (such as Singapore) or Western (Manhattan).

Overwhelmed by the sudden increase in the volume of construction, the Shenzhen SEZ's local government shunned legislative confirmation of the master plans. "Forecast" became a new planing concept that avoided the embarrassment of official afterthoughts. Master plans became "nonlegal" and for "government-use-only."[42]

The 1990s were inaugurated with six new areas of development, their magnitude underscored by names that helplessly indicate geographic orientations swirling out and around the Special Economic Zone: the Southeast Area, the Northeast Area, the North Area, the West Area, and the Northwest Area.

By 1996, Shenzhen Special Economic Zone had become a metropolitan area of 3.5 million.

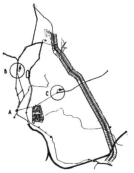
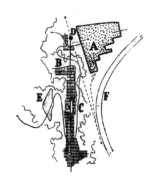

[1] *Since its beginning, the linear city has been associated with socialist ideals. In 1892 the Spanish philanthropist Soria y Mata published* Ciudad Lineal—*a project designed to remedy the problems brought by modernization to Madrid. The* Linear City *was his manifesto for social progress made possible through urbanism.*

[2] *Project for an ideal industrial city, by Tony Garnier; 1914. The linear city is a 19th-century invention, an antidote for the overcrowded Western metropolis.*

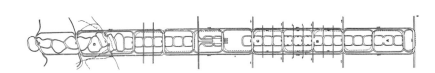

[3] *Project for the new town of Magnitogorsk, Siberia, by Ivan Leonidov; 1929. The Soviet linear city arrived in China in the early 1950s, with the "specialists" who helped Mao set up the People's Republic. By then, the idea already had three decades of theoretical debate and experiments behind it. The Spanish linear city had been reprinted by El Lissitzky in 1930 in his Constructivist manifesto* Russia: Architecture for the World Revolution.

LINEAR© **City**

> LINEAR© The *socialist market economy* defines the present as
> an era of opportunistic juxtapositions and uses the LINEAR© city
> as the blueprint for an ideological puzzle of urban forms and pro-
> grams. The *socialist market economy* exposes, therefore, the
> LINEAR© city as being akin to the PICTURESQUE©; the irra-
> tional is rationalized, planned according to a logic that finds beauty
> in disorder and virtue in the bizarre.

*"In opening industrial and development zones along highways to form "linear cities," the PRD
is following the pattern of linear development."*[43]

Immersed in the contradictions of the reform, the planners of the Special Economic Zone
are now devoted to improvisation and disorder. Having lost their vocation for clarity, they
see in the rationality of modern urbanism an ascetic possibility—a *therapy*. Eager to discard
their anxieties, the planners set out to transcend the contradictions of the *socialist market
economy* and to direct the consequences of economic deregulation toward a structural
process, to transform the zone into a *specific* landscape.

The Shenzhen Special Economic Zone is a border city. Taking maximum advantage of its
location, the zone stretches along the entire boundary between China and Hong Kong. This
controlled, but permeable line—a jigsaw puzzle of rice paddies—is the zone's most important asset and a source of inspiration for its planners. The *linearity* of the Special Economic
Zone establishes the most efficient economic and ideological boundary between both sides:
the ZONE© is both an area of fiscal deregulation and a geographical buffer between the
Communist mainland and Hong Kong.

"Three Paths and One Leveling," the slogan that inaugurated the construction of the
Shenzhen Special Economic Zone, delineates the formula of a minimally yet ambitiously
planned city. Along with the necessary erasure—the preparatory "leveling"—Shenzhen is
shaped as a LINEAR CITY©.✱ Between its first (1982) and second (1984) master plans, the
Shenzhen SEZ was laid out as a linear instrument for organizing the flow of capital.
Although stretching 50 kilometers along the border with Hong Kong, its layout numbers
only three east-west avenues (the "three paths") and twelve north-south cross-connections.
It is precisely this scarcity of connections and the freedom from a preestablished pedestrian
"grid" that forms the basis of all future urban incarnations. Distilled
to an "essential" traffic pattern, the plan of the zone underscores the
INFRARED© redefinition of the city as *infrastructure*. Recognizing
that Hong Kong owes its prosperity to its infrastructures—container
ports, tunnels, bridges, and highways connecting the harbor with the
New Territories (a warehouse-hinterland storing containers and people alike)—the Shenzhen SEZ advertises itself as a colossal infrastructure, a link between the financial incentives of the *socialist market
economy* and the international capital flowing out of Hong Kong.

Under Deng Xiaoping's reform, the active, functional mechanism
of the city has acquired an infrastructural vocation, owing to the

✱ Shenzhen's **linearity** is completely
unintentional. It is the result of the connection of two points: Luohu and Shekou. While the former is a historic, dense
residential settlement directly across
the border of the New Territory, the latter
is a new industrial manufacturing site
across the Hong Kong bay. Their location,
along the same line, offers the most efficient link and maximum exposure to
Hong Kong. —QM

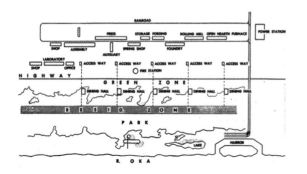

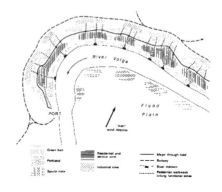

[4] *Project for a linear city by Nikolai Miliutin, taken from his* Sotsgorod *(The socialist city); 1930. For Miliutin, a Soviet bureaucrat, the linear city matched the goals behind the theory of the socialist city. He proposed to organize all socialist settlements as industrial linear cities.*

[5] *Plan for Stalingrad, by Nikolai Miliutin; 1930. The strongest influence on Miliutin seems to have come from industrial processes. Although he never made open references to American industry, his linear industrial city is the ideal Fordist city. In spite of Miliutin's ideological prudence, one of the first assembly lines in the Soviet Union was prefabricated in Detroit, shipped to the U.S.S.R. and assembled under Albert Kahn's—the architect of Ford factories—supervision. This factory, the Stalingrad Tractor Plant, was built together with residential areas as a linear city.*

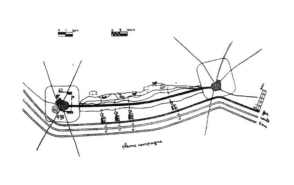

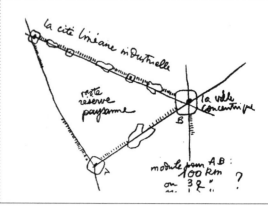

[6] *The planning principles of the linear city became part of the modernist doctrines articulated by CIAM (Congrès Internationaux d'Architecture Moderne). Under the influence of Miliutin's* Sotsgorod, *Le Corbusier's urban planning theory adopts the idea of the linear city, as illustrated by his project for an Industrial Linear City of 1942.*[45]

[7] *The ability of the linear city to transform the relation between urbanism and territory is seized upon by Le Corbusier in his 1945* Trois etablissements humains *(Town-planning of three human establishments). His jubilant remarks seem to anticipate the role imagined by planners for the Shenzhen Special Economic Zone: "The linear industrial city has a consequence of crucial significance, one that has the value of a principle: it creates pure peasant reserves, vast reserves, and yet it establishes the purest imaginable contiguity between land, industry, the peasant, and the worker. A contiguity that signals the possibility of contact: a land that is clean, revivified and whole: an industry that is brilliant, optimistic, radiant with order, intensity and beauty. A reversal of industrial life."*[46]

INFRARED© ideology that informs it. *Infrastructure* merges ideology with spatial organization. Intended as a compromise between planning and the market, the SEZ is not a figure, but a dynamic, flow-organizing device that synthesizes the network of infrastructures—the *infrascape*—that forms interconnected corridors of development.

Since conventional urban geometry such as the Manhattan grid would only hinder the inherent mutability of the *socialist market*, the layout of the Special Economic Zone is purposely crude—to allow experiments to fill in the blanks. Even more, the indeterminacy of the plan is what allows it to become paradigmatic. The Special Economic Zone is programmed to become a model or, better, the first link in a tentacle-like chain of development that will opportunistically crisscross the Delta. City planners announce:

> A megalopolis is usually developed along some major economic development axes. However, these axes are not simply transportation lines. They are major production, transportation and communication corridors. These axes usually consist of the complex transportation networks and their associated production and urban networks.[44]

In spite of its enclave status, the SEZ's role, therefore, is a regional one. As a hub, the task of the Shenzhen Special Economic Zone is to bind the entire Pearl River Delta into a vast, interconnected economic system.

Linearity bestows the "rationality" attributed to its modernist genealogy. In Shenzhen, however, the predictability and repetitiveness of the linear city have given way to the indeterminacy and mutability of the market. The planners had originally chosen the linear model as an ideal prototype of zoning: a simple, seemingly easy to control series of parallel bands of program. "Zoning," accepted as the canonical (CIAM) modernist strategy of arranging the city according to a taxonomy of discrete, yet interrelated functions—residence, industry and institutions—is undermined in the Special Economic Zone by the opportunism of the *socialist market economy*.

In the Special Economic Zone (seen as a planned, ideal city) the "modernism" of the linear layout had been adopted as a symbol of the reform's ideological openness. However, like any Utopian projection, the LINEAR© city remains essentially a *plan*, disconnected from its volumetric extension. Wary about their inability to control the consequences of their own project, the SEZ planners began to cast doubt over the linear city model. The planners now had to save their original idealization of the ZONE© from the brutal effects of the market. Their preemptory caution warned that linearity "may limit the long-term development of the city by demanding large-scale investment in basic infrastructure and destroying the farmland and environment along the transport routes."[47]

In an effort to control the effects of market deregulation, the planners subdivided the linear city into BLOCKS©, imagining each as a self-sufficient world. An article that appeared in a Chinese urban planning journal describes the Shenzhen experiment as "where a modern urban planning started [in China]," observing that it "adopted the mode of multi-centers with eight groups, which had greater flexibility and was suitable for an open city to be constructed by blocks, a brand-new method for the shape of modern cities."[48] Tamed into "greater flexibility," the linear city is now a collector of events, a register of market episodes, each one switched on or off by the flow of available funding.

If the West criticized the linear city for its excess of structure, the planners of the Shenzhen SEZ resent the fact that linearity does not provide *enough* structure. The BLOCKS© give away this obsession with control. Ideological, rather than prompted by the logic of supply and demand, the BLOCKS© concentrate what linearity disperses. Each BLOCK© may be

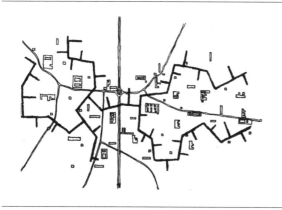

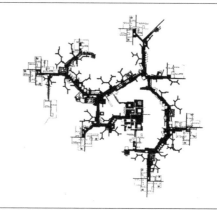

[8] *Alison and Peter Smithson's Golden Lane project; London, 1952. In the early 1950s, the linear city reemerges in the work of Peter and Allison Smithson as a critique of England's postwar suburbs—the new towns founded on Ebenezer Howard's idea of the garden city. For them, the linear city is to be the catalyst of a renewed community. "Association" is the word that accompanies their formulation of a pedestrian elevated city.*

[9] *Two decades later, Georges Candilis and Shad Woods—members of the Team X group that included the Smithsons—put the utopian ideas advanced in the Golden Lane project into practice. The (partially built) project for a new community at Toulouse Le Mirail, commissioned by the socialist mayor of Toulouse, injects "urban identity" into the French suburbia. Like the Smithsons' Golden Lane, the linear suburb by Candilis and Woods separates vehicular and pedestrian traffic.*

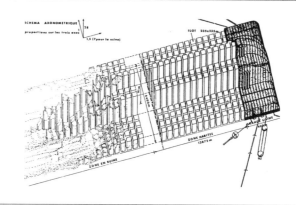

[10] *Kenzo Tange's Tokyo Bay project; 1960. In the West, the 1960s represent the last moment of optimism for the postwar urbanism. The linear city becomes the blueprint of technopolis (as in Kenzo Tange's plan for Tokyo Bay) and for the world city (as prophesied by Doxiadis).*

[11] *Project for prefabricated linear suburbs, by J. Bakema; 1969. In 1969 the Italian group Superstudio resorts to the idea of a linear "city-as-machine" to critique postwar urbanization. Compelled by modernization, the linear city marches "forward like a majestic snake through constantly changing landscapes" and "defecates perfectly equipped, prefabricated suburbs."*

structured around a *theme*, an alias of a market niche: high-tech parks, ethnic towns, theme parks, business center. Allowing for the use of the city "one part at the time," the breakdown of the LINEAR© city, and with it, of zoning, is—to use the words of Shenzhen's planners—the consequence of a "strategic composition of the environment." "The unique environment of Shenzhen [is] a belt-like entity of urban blocks built in light of the SEZ's topography and functions." Furthermore, its "geographical characteristics and urban layout determine the pattern of people's activities—a combination of vertical activities within the belt and horizontal activities within each block."[49]

The substitution of zoning—the firm apportioning of parts—with that of a *system*, an open mechanism capable of absorbing the varied combinations of the market and their corresponding formal manifestations, points to a shift in the vocation of urbanism. In the SEZ, planning proceeds by establishing lines of development, free from any attempt to define the "substance" of the city. The line functions as an "abstract machine": it organizes multiplicity, the discrete events of the *socialist market economy*, in the manner of a computing device.

Competition between various areas of the zone (BLOCKS©) has replaced classical interaction and leads to inner changes of the system. Overall, the tendency of the linear city is to *shrink*: privileged BLOCKS© polarize activity from neighboring ones. As a consequence, with every new version of the ZONE©'s master plan, the planners reduce the number of BLOCKS©. If in Shenzhen's beginning (1984), the zone was composed of eight BLOCKS©, the number decreased to five (1990), and then three (1996).[50]

❀ ❀ ❀

Shenzhen Special Economic Zone, a LINEAR© city, derives coherence from mere sequence. Its simple geometry, idealized by SEZ planners as modernist, does not impose constancy. It only connects and collects the opportunistic events of the *socialist market economy*.

The modernist linear cities organized shortsighted repetitions of a singular social pattern. Linearity became an ideological statement, an awkward evenness of utopian opportunities. A best example, the Soviet linear city related, in an efficient way, discrete groups (the workers) to discrete spatial clusters (workplaces, residences, et cetera). These relationships were organized linearly and sequentially:

work — residence — work — residence . . .

In the Shenzhen Special Economic Zone, the tension between the linear scheme, favoring dispersal, and the BLOCKS©, favoring concentration, leads to the redefinition of LINEAR©. The SEZ is a complex series of discontinuous spatial events: instead of one sequence, several sequences take place simultaneously, at different speeds, on different spatial tracks. The *socialist market economy* has canceled linearity's former ideological significance. In Shenzhen, the line no longer represents a purpose: it simply connects A to B, B to C, D to E. The line is now a *timeline*, a chart of the ZONE©'s program:

residence — factory — residence — factory . . .
farming — market — farming — market . . .
travel — golf — travel —— golf — travel . . .

The planners of the Shenzhen Special Economic Zone have translated INFRARED© ideology into a new urban model that abandons the assumed order of the socialist city. The SEZ is a

Shenzhen's Central Business District. Tamed into "greater flexibility,"
the LINEAR© city is now a collector of events, a register of market episodes
switched on or off by the flow of available funding.

city of montage: different spatial frames are juxtaposed, with references to real or imagined models recreated in the BLOCKS© of the linear city. Only a *cinematic* experience of the ZONE© can reveal the exhilarating effects of its seemingly purposeless heterogeneity. It provokes a new perception of time as arrhythmic, jolting and intertwined, a time of the ephemeral. This perceptual perplexity signals the presence of the artificial and the hybrid.

❀   ❀   ❀

Linearity now admits the *ad hoc*, the casual juxtapositions of urban programs and forms, conforming to the demands of the *socialist market*. When it resurfaces in Shenzhen, linearity is no longer an "essence" (as it was for its modernist predecessors), a guarantee of the Utopian consistency of an urban model. It is not even the backbone of a complex megastructure or urban "machine." Linearity is simply a thread, a vector loosely stitching together an assemblage of disparate market experiments. Its fluidity is a manifesto for the infrastructural vocation of the ZONE©, quietly endorsed by INFRARED© ideology. Subdued, the ideological role of linearity is to be a symbol of the ZONE©: modernism as openness to the instability of the market.

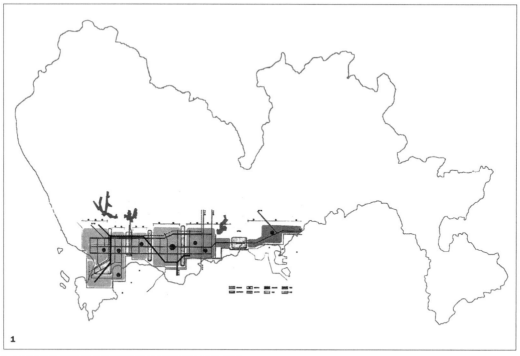

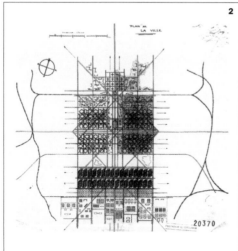

[1] *Shenzhen Special Economic Zone, a* BLOCK© *diagram, by the Beijing China Academy of Planning, 1985. The* BLOCKS© *redefine the linear city, "a belt-like entity of urban blocks built in light of the SEZ's topography and functions." In 1989 the Shenzhen SEZ consisted of five* BLOCKS©*:* **Shekou–Nantou,** *which includes the western port, an industrial area, the Shenzhen University campus, and the Hi-Tech Park currently under construction;* **Shahe,** *encompassing the Overseas Chinese Town, where three theme parks and one twenty-four-hour golf course were developed alongside speculative residential projects;* **Futian,** *including the SEZ's future administrative and business center, the Shenzhen Golf Club, and the earliest amusement park, the Honey Lake resort, interspersed with industrial and residential areas;* **Shangbu–Luohu** *(the site of the Old Town), the earliest and present business and industrial center of Shenzhen, located at the border check-point with Hong Kong; and* **Shatoujiao–Yantian** *district in the east, where a new port is currently under construction. The "three paths" that run east-west are: an industrial road along the SEZ's northern border, a road currently being reclaimed from the bay along the southern border, and Shennan Road, the main thoroughfare. Shennan, in fact, is the only element that connects all five* BLOCKS© *and confers the overall* LINEAR© *configuration.* [2] *The prototype of a zoned linear city, Le Corbusier's La Ville Radieuse (1933).*

BLOCK©

> BLOCK© In the ZONE©, the BLOCK© is an ideal of INFRARED©
> versatility, an ideological *unit*. Its theoretical as well as physical
> extent may be stretched or dwarfed to absorb the unpredictability
> of the market. The BLOCKS© are test grounds where the oppor-
> tunities and failures of the market are played out, "structured"
> and phased in a search for illusory control.

The frivolity of the modernist theoretical assumptions under which the ZONE© was founded—a rational urban formula whereby linearity, consigned to a figurative role, establishes
mechanical rather than essential connections—pushed the Party and its planners into an
ideological overload.

To lift the burden of their unfulfilled, Utopian drive, they turned their attention to the
BLOCKS©. Within the ZONE©, the BLOCK© no longer denotes the conventions of its west-
ern counterpart: a "kernel" of urbanism, scale, neighborhood, public, private, et cetera.
Instead, a *theme*—a "center of commercial activities"—lies at the core of each BLOCK©.
This unstable market-dependent mosaic of economic experiments is the essence of the
ZONE©'s urbanism. In the words of its planners, the Special Economic Zone is "a pluralistic
urban environment of natural and man-made scenic wonders built according to the functions of the block."[51]

An urban enclave supports each theme, complete with residences and factories (*danwei*).
These themes, ambiguously classified as parks (science and technology, agricultural, high-
tech, amusement, and so on), are carefully separated to avoid cross-contamination between
failure and survival: "partial environments will be different from each other."

The autonomy of the BLOCKS©—a consequence of their themed experiments—is well
calculated: a prime example of how, in the ZONE©, the instability of the market is the "eure-
ka" of urbanism. Together, the collection of BLOCKS©—the Special Economic Zone—sets
the stage for every personal and collective drama of market experimentation. The themes of
the BLOCKS© hold surrogate metropolitan freedoms. They are Utopia substitutes.

❀   ❀   ❀

No other BLOCK© translates the original intuitions of INFRARED© ideology (the enclave-
based market experiments) more openly into programmatic realities than the Overseas
Chinese Town. Its planners define the Overseas Chinese Town as "a base for introducing
home overseas capital, advanced technology and talented personnel."[52] Disguised as ethnic
nostalgia, the theme of this BLOCK©—the *socialist market* funded by foreign capital—is
the economic formula of the ZONE© itself.

Set up as an enclave within an enclave (the SEZ), the Overseas Chinese Town is a showcase BLOCK©. When its construction begins, the ideological pressure behind its planning is
the highest in the ZONE©. The Overseas Chinese Town is expected to become the paradigm

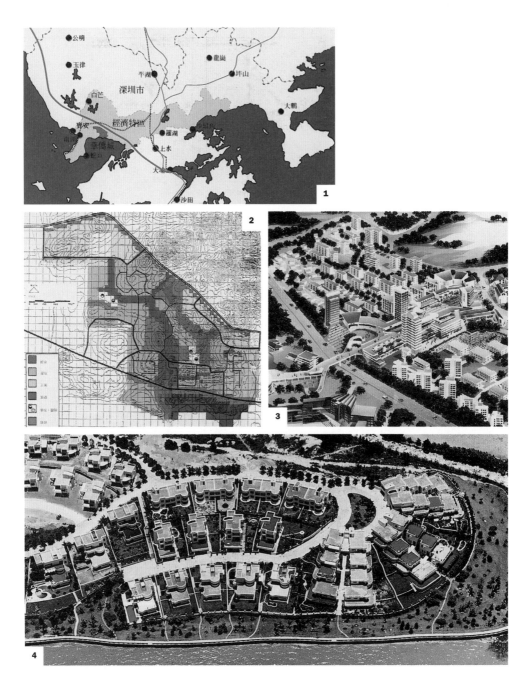

[1] *The Overseas Chinese Town, a district in Shenzhen SEZ, is a showcase* BLOCK©, *established as an enclave within an enclave. Master plan by the Shenzhen Planning Institute and Dadi Corporation, 1985.* [2] *The planned identity of the Overseas Chinese Town is the outcome of a combined expertise in Asian ideals and pragmatism.* [3] *Bird's-eye view of an early version of the Overseas Chinese Town. An Asian Metropolis infused with* INFRARED© *idealism.* [4] *Shenzhen's Oriental Garden is scant achievement compared to the ambitiously planned Overseas Chinese Town.*

of reform, a model of INFRARED© urbanism. A "city exclusively for returned overseas Chinese" ("exclusively" and "returned" not taken literally), it is imagined as a manifesto of the "Asian metropolis," or "an organic combination of natural and artificial environment."[53]. A team of Singapore planners and Hong Kong developers is hired. The result that is expected from their combined expertise in Asian ideals and pragmatism is *identity*: "building and road construction are required to depend on the original terrain and the designs to be of both modern and south China style."[54]

The heightened ambitions that surround the planning of the Overseas Chinese Town are undermined, however, by the urgencies of the market. Just like all the other BLOCKS©, the Overseas Chinese Town must be self-sufficient and, in the beginning, it must follow the pattern of the ZONE©: cheap labor in exchange for foreign capital. Shennan Road—the main east-west avenue or "path" of the ZONE©—slices the Overseas Chinese Town in two. To the north, on the razed land of former Shahe and Huajia villages (with occasional plots of farmland still intact), a series of *danwei* is hastily built: stark factory and dormitory slabs, no different form others in the ZONE© or beyond. To the south, there are scant achievements of the BLOCK©'s ambitious master plan: a "Continental-style" hotel and an Oriental Garden, a cluster of villas overlooking the bay—the Special Economic Zone's initial flirtation with the real-estate market.

It is a disappointing start for the cadre-managers of the Overseas Chinese Town. The gap between their original ambitions of infusing the Asian Metropolis with INFRARED© ideals and the humiliating cash-for-labor formula that by now seems to plague the *socialist market economy* causes them to question their original assumptions. It is a period of transition, self-doubt. The master plan is formally brilliant but conceptually inarticulate. "The special zones will become a foundation for opening to the outside world."

Suddenly, Deng Xiaoping's words seem pregnant with new possibilities, directions hitherto not explored. "Shenzhen is an open city," the ZONE©'s planners echo the refrain. In 1985 the cadre-managers readjust the program of the Overseas Chinese Town and with it, the ZONE© itself, to pursue the tourist industry. The planners are given a new task and, beginning in 1986, three theme parks (quaint reverberation of the definition of a BLOCK©'s core) are built in less than a decade along the Shenzhen bay: Splendid China, the Folk Culture Village, and Window of the World. A fourth is rumored to follow. In 1989, when Splendid China is completed, the cadre-managers define it as "a window of China's history, culture, and tourist resources."[55] Their attention has shifted from the city's master plan (and its painful memories) to the promising (and cash-rewarding) theme parks. Sensing the proclivity of the theme park toward Utopia, the cadre-managers revel in the chronic idealization of its symbols and layout. Unrepentantly and endlessly, the cadre-managers repeat Deng Xiaoping's "window" metaphor: the Utopian enclave is the *theme* of the ZONE©, of the Overseas Chinese Town, of the *theme park*.

Since urbanism consistently falls short of its ideals, it is up to theme parks to inject *meaning* into the CULTURAL DESERT© of the Special Economic Zone. For the planners, the theme park is now the only *program* capable to legitimize urbanism, to add interest to any new urban scenario. The kitsch of the theme parks delivers the *context* eschewed by the savvy dogmatism of the original master plan. The Overseas Chinese Town becomes an INFRARED© Tower of Babel. The theme parks scatter signs of the city even before the "city" was present. Because icons in the theme parks (Eiffel Tower, the Colosseum, the Imperial Palace) supplant "context," everything else (buildings, roads, landscape) became a provisory background.

[1] *Splendid China theme park, Shenzhen Special Economic Zone, 1987. "The crystallization of collective wisdom": a spontaneous insight offered by ideological platitudes outwits the dogmatism of planning. Again, ideologues score against experts.* [2] *Splendid China: The manipulation of perception adds drama to (regained) ideological confidence. At last, ideology can deliver pleasure: "Thirty hectares, . . . eighty scenic spots . . . arranged scientifically according to their real scenic places."*

After the opening of the real estate market in 1989, the presence of the theme parks made the hopelessly dormant idea of the "Asian metropolis," begun years earlier, newly desirable. Land-use value replaced the earlier economic role of factories. Dormitories built just a few years previously are torn down to make room for new speculative developments. The edges of the theme parks are blurred and the *themes* spill across Shennan Road. Overlooking the Window of the World, a European City theme park was developed. Twenty-story-high residential towers, densely packed on the site, carry roof pediments, replicas of replicas in the neighboring theme park. The views of the theme park from these apartment buildings are their most expensive asset.

❀   ❀   ❀

Authenticity eventually becomes a dead-end for the planners of the Overseas Chinese Town. They imagined a perfect "city" distilled from the best urban antecedents to yield the authentic. However, their dry idealism could not support the "dirty" agenda of the *socialist market*, its inherent compromise. The "window," an INFRARED© concept susceptible to ideological transgression—to *borrowing*—allowed the cadre-managers to load the theme parks with theoretical potential.

An underground connection seems to have been established between the ZONE© and the theme parks: urban imposture is suspected to release conditions that exceed the planners' ability to theorize. The ZONE© is authentic only when it recycles and erodes the fetishes that fill the mythology of urbanism.

Bird's-eye view of the Window of the World theme park in the Shenzhen Special Economic Zone. The technology of the bizarre supports a shameless exploitation of ideology, word for word.

Window of the World. Kitsch in the theme parks delivers the "context" that eschews the savvy dogmatism of urbanism.

[1] *Guangdong Villas: with proximity to the Shenzhen Special Economic Zone as its prime asset, the value of farmland skyrocketed after 1989: it came to yield that harvest formerly only allowed in the special economic zone—real estate equity.* [2] *Villages of only a few hundreds became towns of tens of thousands.*

CHINESE SUBURBIA©

> CHINESE SUBURBIA© Urbanization without a doctrine of the city. If in the West, "suburban" is a derogatory term for unwelcome spin-offs of the city, in China, SUBURBIA© is the essence of urbanization. The new Chinese city strives for SUBURBIA©.

The end of cities is written in their beginning. Eager to achieve perfection, the planners of Utopias only hasten their demise. Their efforts reveal how the history of cities is (only) a series of ideological frames, a dialectic between failed visions and renewed beliefs. Endless combinations of the idea of the city—the result of ever faster changes and a search for technological adaptability—have brought the role of cities, as stable, self-governing communities, to the brink. After having lent their urbanity—their *genetic code*—and the potential for change to ever more unrestrained formulas, to sprawl, cities seem prepared to disappear at the very moment when urbanization will have arrived at its apogee. Just as ideology vanishes underground, cities seem ready to write their last chapter.

Deng Xiaoping's reform gave a new meaning to Mao Zedong's arduous efforts to cancel the differences between city and countryside. The cadre-managers of the Shenzhen Special Economic Zone, guided by INFRARED© ideology, proved that urbanization could succeed *without* a doctrine of the city. Streamlined as a simple conduit for capital, infrastructure and speed, the linear urbanization in the Pearl River Delta established a model for the rapid modernization of the countryside. Released from its former *red* obligations to control, urbanization was made entirely dependent on the demands of the *socialist market economy*.

Toward the end of the 1980s, urbanization exceeded the borders of the Special Economic Zones. As the rising cost of labor began to hinder growth, Beijing became wary about the future of the ZONE©. It was forced to step up the development of Shenzhen Special Economic Zone as a regional center, steering its economy toward high-tech industry, finance, and services. Manufacturing was pushed north, beginning the development of the adjoining countryside. Spurred by new opportunities, the "metropolitan" development outside the SEZ grew faster and faster, as adjoining villages, efficient because cheaper, attracted capital. The rippling effects of the ZONE©'s economy accelerated the industrialization of surrounding countryside and created a deregulated hinterland of new, ad hoc *profit zones*.

The central government, concerned about its weak control over the effects of economic deregulation, decided on the next step. In 1989, Beijing issued the Law of Transfer of Land-Use Rights, in a move to increase and protect the scope of the *socialist market economy*. The split between ownership and land-use rights enabled INFRARED© ideology to appropriate the consequences of economic deregulation as evidence supporting the *truths* of the reform. The Law of Transfer of Land-Use Rights expanded the range of the *socialist market economy* through real estate speculation, while allowing the Party to retain control of the Future. By opening up the real-estate market, INFRARED© ideology could extend its influence to the entire Pearl River Delta and begin to export the lessons of the Special Economic Zones (the know-how and how-not-to of modernization) to the Chinese countryside. The Law of Transfer of Land-Use Rights—aimed at regulating a deregulated landscape outside the Special Economic Zones—only triggered a "gold rush," an even more unrestrained develop-

[1] *Longgang Administrative Area of the Shenzhen Special Economic Zone.
Farmers* lent *their land-use rights to Hong Kong developers. In this new
danwei, where golf cart tires and plastic toys are manufactured, factories
flank one side of the main street while dormitories flank the other.* [2] *Migrant
workers housing in Longgang. Temporary workers, migrants from northern
provinces, quickly moved in.* [3] *Suburban villas. The farmers—entrepreneurs
and landlords overnight—moved out, to live in new villas, closer to Shenzhen.*

ment. The law allocated one hectare of land to each household as a source of wealth. With proximity to the Shenzhen Special Economic Zone as its prime asset, the value of farmland skyrocketed after 1989. Suddenly, it came to yield the harvest that had been allowed only in the SEZ: real estate equity. Farmers in the Pearl River Delta became real estate developers. Up to 50 percent of the farmland quickly came on the market. Land not originally listed for development was made more tempting: farmland was bulldozed to make it "desirable." Cleared, the territory advertised its condition of being in reserve. Villages of only a few hundreds suddenly became towns of tens of thousands. The Pearl River Delta's farmers lent their land-use rights to Hong Kong developers; developers built new *danwei*; temporary residents, migrants from northern provinces, moved in. The farmers—now entrepreneurs and overnight landlords—moved out, to live in new villas closer to Shenzhen.

CHINESE SUBURBIA© thrives on urban "genetics": golf courses, entertainment, luxury apartments. These splinters of metropolitan "lifestyles" spread along vectors of development, corridors of capital. The migration of funds is matched by the movement of nomad developers and the floating population—adventurers struggling for opportunity.[56] Both celebrate SUBURBIA©: the developers shun financial control, and the floating population shun their former work-communes. CHINESE SUBURBIA©, a sector of the world economy, emancipates the nomads.

The Law of Transfer of Land-Use Rights thus secured the necessary support for the reform (and for INFRARED© ideology) from the rural majority in the Pearl River Delta. Development—the new call to ideological participation—is now a joint venture between farmers and the local governments committed to attract capital.

The Special Economic Zone is the birthplace of CHINESE SUBURBIA©.✽ In the West, *suburbia* denounces the disassembling of former communities, the segregation of cities along social and economic lines. In China, SUBURBIA© defines the unrelenting development that inundates the countryside. In the words of the planners, the fresh "sub-city-centers . . . are [still] engaging in traditional agricultural activities." Development in the countryside is fed by capital overflowing from the Special Economic Zone: suburbanization is the *dross* of modernization. Caught between a duty to order and the commitment to deregulation, the planners admit that the staggering demographics of the countryside are "a phenomenon" of "population deposition."[57]

CHINESE SUBURBIA© is a hybrid of city and countryside. Nature and agriculture are now part of the urban program as *reserve*—or *reservations*.[58] Their inclusion into the realm of the *urban*, enclaves of rural life, transformed the Special Economic Zone itself. The ZONE© no longer has an outside: one cannot exit this "city" anymore. After the introduction of the Law of Transfer of Land-Use Rights, planners try to reassert theoretical control. They draw a parallel between the suburban development in the Pearl River Delta—in their words, a "gray area"—and "Desakota," "a new spatial arrangement" in the industrialized countryside of South East Asian countries identified by Western researchers as "a place being simultaneously influenced by the urban and rural impacts."[59]

At the beginning of the 1990s, a third phase of planning begins in the Shenzhen Special Economic Zone. In 1992 Deng Xiaoping visits the Special Economic Zones to encourage

✿ The notion of the **Chinese suburbia** should be put in its historical context. After 1954, one of the goals Mao set for the country was to diminish the "Three Great Differences" ("*San Da Cha Bie*")— the difference between the urban and the rural, the industrial worker and farmer, intellectual work and labor work. Instead of a naturalist strategy of creating a transitory middle zone (suburbia?), Mao chose to separate the urban and rural by demographic control and ideological education. The failure to achieve this goal and its subsequent disasters elevated the desire for this zone. —QM

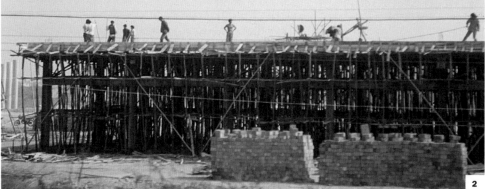

[1] CHINESE SUBURBIA© *thrives on urban "genetics."* [2] *Splinters of metropolitan lifestyles spread along vectors of development—corridors of capital.* [3] CHINESE SUBURBIA©, *a sector of the world economy, emancipates the nomads.*

their sagging development. To weaken the competition between the fast-growing country-side and the lagging SEZs, Beijing elevates villages and towns north of Shenzhen to the status of "cities," but puts them under the administration of the ZONES©.

The Shenzhen Planning Institute, a branch of the Chinese Academy of Planning in Beijing, thus assumes control over the adjoining countryside.✱ The ZONE©'s planners extend their authority over the suburban areas through newly established local offices at county level. Though the planners of the Special Economic Zone are "commissioned" by local governments to guarantee coherence, in practice, this encompassed only roads, crude infrastructures. Planning by this point is the accomplice of unrestrained development. Under the pressure of the market, the only strategy left is *capitulation*: all planning is, by then, retroactive, a record of construction taking place faster than planners can anticipate.

Humbled by this staggering growth, the planners declare a new ambition for suburban development: "Judging from the geographical position, population size, and levels of development, the PRD region, developed along the Hong Kong–Shenzhen–Guangzhou axis, has already possessed most of the formative characteristics of a megalopolis."[60]

The third master plan (1996) accounts for the expanded areas of development, transforming the Shenzhen SEZ from an enclave into a "megalopolis." Dispersal is the new goal, favoring acceleration over accumulation. Baoan and Longgan, the two counties north of the Special Economic Zone that were incorporated within its administrative borders, cover over 1,000 square kilometers—an area as large as Hong Kong and the New Territories together.

The planners begin to assess the consequences of suburbanization:

By the end of 1991, the number of permanent residents in the PRD was 32.8 million. Among them, 27.5 were local residents and 5.3 million were non-local residents. . . . Moving into the 21st century, the number of local residents in the region will grow to above 30 million. When an additional 40 million of non-local residents are included, the urbanization rate of the region will reach a level of about 63 percent. Apart from a few exceptions, the majority of the counties in the PRD will be upgraded to cities.[61]

The modernization of the Pearl River Delta generates ever greater quantities, preparing cadres and planners for the next campaign: after the ZONE©, the region.

✤ **Shenzhen** was planned by remote control, or from afar. The Chinese Academy of Planning in Beijing has been involved in a large variety of issues and decision-making with regards to Shenzhen's development. Every major move in Shenzhen's building and growth was influenced by planning authorities in Beijing, either through official channels or through personal influences. Although not abnormal in China, Shenzhen's planning procedure has had obvious consequences: constant tension between idea and reality, between distant wishes and immediate needs. The remote-control idea once existed as the collective proposition of planning during Mao's era under one ideology, but has been replaced by a mélange of principles and approaches: idealistic, classical, picturesque, poetic, pragmatic, *feng-shui*-istic, thematic, Chinese, Western, Singaporean, and so on. This free mix has been demonstrated by the international nature of recent participants in international and national competitions, whose contributions can be considered another form of remote-control planning. —QM

CHINESE SUBURBIA©, a hybrid
of city and countryside.

[1] *Hong Kong and* [2] *Shenzhen at night: "A center of two fans:" twin city*
Shenzhen-Hong Kong. In a radical swerve of regional politics, Deng Xiaoping
reveals that the Special Economic Zone is not a mere recipient of wealth, but
the guardian of the former colony's future.

ZONE© II

One Country, Two Systems. Ideology draws maps. Borders shift as territories hitherto closed off, inaccessible, suddenly reveal new potentials. As difference is perceived no longer as a threat but as a model, these territories become the extensions of an ideological "mainland." Hong Kong and Macao—the enclaves of the market economy shunned by Mao Zedong—inspired (and funded) Deng's Xiaoping's thesis of finding "truth from facts": with the Party's shift to an INFRARED© ideology, the enclaves became both indispensable models of modernization and the financial reservoirs of the *socialist market economy*. As their return to China approached, the Party initiated a campaign to upgrade their enclave status.

In 1984 Deng Xiaoping begins talks with the British government for the return of Hong Kong to China. He introduces the principle of "One Country, Two Systems," announcing that Hong Kong will remain an enclave of the market economy after the British departure. Ironically, as a basis for these talks, he advances the ZONE© as the concept underlying the Future of the former British colony: Hong Kong will become a Special Administrative Zone. Thus, Deng Xiaoping extends to Hong Kong the very model that Hong Kong lent to the mainland experiments of open-door reform: for the INFRARED© ideology, the ZONE© is a political warranty. Soon, Macao's Future is drafted along the same lines.

Deng Xiaoping's successful negotiation is not without ambiguities. The return of Hong Kong and Macao to China suddenly makes the role of the Special Economic Zones less clear. If the ZONES©' proximity to Hong Kong and Macao were an advantage in the beginning, now it seems to be a weakness. Will the SEZs become *another* hinterland? To restore momentum, Deng Xiaoping reinforces their post-1997 role. In the words of the ZONES©'cadres-managers: "Only when Deng Xiaoping . . . pointed out in 1984 that Shenzhen should play the role as 'four windows' and 'center of two fans' did we come to understand the importance of the Special Economic Zone."[62]

In a radical swerve of regional politics, Deng Xiaoping reveals the special economic zones to be not merely recipients ("windows") but also guardians of the Future *special administrative zones* / ex-foreign enclaves. The *special economic zones* would become ideological and administrative switch boxes ("centers of two fans") between the *global* market economy of the former colonies and China's *socialist* market economy.

After Deng Xiaoping professed that Hong Kong and Shenzhen will become *twin cities* to mutually "compensate" for each other's weaknesses and strengths, the region's planners seize upon his vision:

> *By 1997 and 1999, Hong Kong and Macao will become part of the PRC and will pursue the policy of "one country two systems". By then, the economic and cultural connections between Hong Kong, Macao and the rest of the PRD will become stronger. The flow of human resources, goods, capital and news in the region will also become easier. These favourable factors, together with the intimate personal, historical and geographical relationships in the region, will make Hong Kong and Macao more important as "windows" of the mainland.*[63]

In 1997 Hong Kong's return to China triggers a reversal of roles: the Shenzhen Special Economic Zone is now the model, the "correct" metropolis, a conduit of INFRARED© ideology. Its role is to replicate and to transform the Pearl River Delta into a system of enclaves simultaneously based on coexistence, juxtaposition, and maximum difference. The Hong Kong Special Administrative Zones is now merely one of these *new* enclaves.

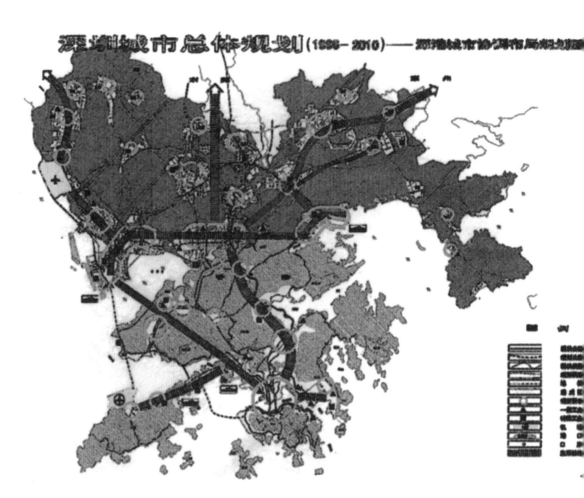

*"A center of two fans:" twin city Shenzhen–Hong Kong. In a radical swerve of
regional politics, Deng Xiaoping reveals that the Special Economic Zone is not
a mere recipient of wealth, but the guardian of the former colony's Future.*

The Party's readiness to maintain the market economy in Hong Kong, and thus effectively to preserve its separation from the socialist mainland, constituted the basis of Deng Xiaoping's negotiation for its return to China. "One Country, Two Systems" is the corollary of INFRARED© that makes the underground role of the Party most explicit: merging capitalism with the socialist realities of China depends entirely on the (unseen) control of Communist ideology.

While the "One Country, Two Systems" principle precipitates the reintegration of China, modernization leads to its cultural and spatial fragmentation. The ZONES© (be they "special economic" or "administrative") are a re-mapping, a remaking of the territory and of its urban organization that conforms to the objectives of INFRARED© ideology. Geographical changes thus follow the Party's ideological shift.

Pioneering for a Second Time. After the collapse of the Communist Eastern Bloc in Europe and the dissolution of the Soviet Union at the end of 1980s, China remained the apparent flag bearer of international communism. Caught in the middle of economic reform, China took over the Soviet Union's leading position not programmatically, but by default. Has it really assumed control of this role or, as a consequence of Deng Xiaoping's ideological reform, has it succumbed to globalization and ceased to be communist at all? Is INFRARED© ideology a form of *resistance*—an ideological "guerilla"—against the overwhelming forces of the global economy—or is it only the first step toward an *awakening* leading to the abandonment of communist ideals?

These vexing questions point to an increased relevance of the Special Economic Zones. Shouldn't the *ideal* of reforming society through urbanism and trying to achieve in practice the communist idea of the "good" metropolis, albeit hopelessly resorting to a *socialist market economy,* confirm the leading role of the Party? The ZONES© maintain the Party's role in shaping cities and preserve the communist ambition of large-scale planning. At the same time, by continuing the Party's (underground) control over the social and economic transformations taking place within their borders, the ZONES© preserve the relevance of communist, Utopian commitments.

"One Hundred Years Without Change," the slogan displayed under Deng Xiaoping's portrait in the heart of the Shenzhen Special Economic Zone, is both prophecy and threat. The message might seem ironic, given the overwhelming, daily changes that surround it. Taken literally, it seems to imply a deal: one hundred years more of unrelenting reform under the Party's leadership. And after that?

In 1997 Deng's death is mourned in the Shenzhen Special Economic Zone. Weeping crowds lay wreaths under his portrait displayed in the center of the Luohu BLOCK©—where it all started. They are grateful: the ZONE©—with its glittering skyscrapers looming over a gigantic construction site where nothing ever seems at rest—has opened, for each and everyone, a "window" to a personal Utopia.

The cadre-managers of the ZONE©—now leaders of the Pearl River Delta—call for a new campaign: to enact Deng Xiaoping's prophecy of the "center of two fans." Introduced with

*"Good Luck!"—a boomtown mascot in the Pearl River Delta. The Special
Economic Zones strive to reconnect Communist ideology and modernization,
a relation previously taken for granted but shattered by the ideological
excess of previous decades. The* ZONE© *is a place where this synthesis can
be engineered. The impure association between Communist ideology and
the market leads to a culture of contradictions. To maintain their tenuous
agreement, differences must be constantly created and exaggerated.*

the slogan "Pioneering for a Second Time," its ambitious goal is to transform Shenzhen Economic Zone's status from a province of international capital into a metropolitan center. The cadres-managers are now investors. The planners of the ZONE© hastily prepare the next master plan: 500 square kilometers are slated for development through 2010, a *new* enclave under the ZONE©'s administration. Deng's words, displayed under his portrait, resonate in their minds. For them, modernization is an ideological commitment—or maybe a curse.

The new campaign begins immediately after the return of Hong Kong to China, spirits heightened by the actualization of Deng's vision of "One Country, Two Systems." The border between Hong Kong and Shenzhen has been maintained, guaranteeing a protective, enclave status to both ZONES©. Their continued separation from the "mainland" allows their unhindered modernization and participation to the global market economy. An INFRARED© paradox emerges: Hong Kong's financial vigor depends now on Shenzhen's ideological and political stability. Hong Kong is *given* to Shenzhen: the deregulated *socialist market economy* absorbs the insufficiencies and inefficiencies of the capitalist market. It is its secret partner.

As an economic crisis sweeps over the Pacific Rim at the end of the 1990s, the world wonders about the robustness of China's economy as it surfs the ups and downs of the market. The Shenzhen Special Economic Zone lurks behind the headlines. Deng Xiaoping's "deal" between INFRARED© ideology and the international capital funding the *socialist market economy* has transformed the Pearl River Delta into a vibrant urban area that adds distortions—or maybe corrections—to the global market flux.

1. Nineteenth-century socialists and communists adopted the red flag as symbol of their ideology.

2. From Karl Marx's *The German Ideology*: "Competition isolates individuals, not only the bourgeois but even more the proletariats, despite that it brings them together. It takes a long time before these individuals can unite, apart from the fact that for this union—if it is not to be merely local—big industry must first produce the necessary means, the big industrial cities and inexpensive, quick communications." See L. H. Simon, editor, *Karl Marx: Selected Writings* (Indianapolis/Cambridge: Hackett Publishing Company, 1994), 142.

3. A detailed history of the communist ideological campaigns in China is gathered in Merle Goldman, *China's Intellectuals: Advise and Dissent* (Cambridge: Harvard University Press, 1981) and John King Fairbank, *China: A New History* (Cambridge: Belknap Press of Harvard University Press, 1992).

4. C. P. Lo, "Shaping Socialist Chinese Cities: A Model of Form and Land Use," in *China: Urbanization and National Development*, C. K. Leung and Norton Ginsburg, editors (Chicago: University of Chicago Press, 1980), 143.

5. Ibid., 132.

6. Jianying Zha, *China Pop* (New York: New Press, 1995), 63.

7. T. N. Chiu, "Urbanization Processes and National Development," in *China: Urbanization and National Development*, 95.

8. C. P. Lo, "Shaping Socialist Chinese Cities: A Model of Form and Land Use," in *China: Urbanization and National Development*, 132.

9. John King Fairbank, *China: A New History*, 365–71.

10. Ibid.

11. Friedrich Engels, quoted in Nikolai Miliutin, *Sotsgorod* (The socialist city), (1930). Engels quoted Karl Marx's *The Eighteenth Brumaire of Louis Bonaparte*: "The tradition of all the dead generations weighs like a nightmare on the brain of the living"; from L.H. Simon, editor, *Karl Marx: Selected Writings*.

12. Merle Goldman, *China's Intellectuals: Advise and Dissent*, 8.

13. Confucianism, Taoism, and Legalists' thought, all have their roots in ancient China, where they developed around 500 B.C. "The Confucian ideal centers on the enlightened and highly cultivated individual who contributes his wisdom for the benefit of the state. The idealized social order reflects the degree of progress individuals have made to this enlightened state of being, with elaborate rules of conduct regarding filial piety and service to one's sovereign. Taoism holds a contrary view that emphasizes the contradiction between the artificial world of civilization and the true world of nature. . . . Taoism's rejection of the evils of civilization is responsible for the fact that, throughout China's history, Taoist teachings have been adopted as the rallying point of revolutionary peasants. The Legalists rejected the Confucian view of the state as family. Instead they regarded the state as a machine and man as a cog in that machine. The Legalists aspired to an omnipotent and omniscient state and viewed man as an instrument to be manipulated to that end." See E. Heikkila and M. Griffin, "Confucian Planning or Planning Confusion?" *Journal of Planning Education and Research* 14, no. 4 (Summer 1995).

14. Merle Goldman, *China's Intellectuals: Advise and Dissent*, 104; these latter campaigns were a prelude to Michelangelo Antonioni's 1972 furious critiques of China's realities.

15. Ibid., 166.

16. C. P. Lo, "Shaping Socialist Chinese Cities: A Model of Form and Land Use," in *China: Urbanization and National Development*, 144.

17. Merle Goldman, *China's Intellectuals: Advise and Dissent,* 4.

18. Ibid., 166.

19. During the Cultural Revolution, Mao encouraged the Red Guards to "destroy the Four Olds": old thinking, old culture, old customs, and old habits; Merle Goldman, *China's Intellectuals: Advise and Dissent,* 166.

20. Ruan Ming, *Deng Xiaoping: Chronicle of an Empire* (Boulder: Westview Press, 1994), 6.

21. Ibid., 219, 222.

22. Ibid., 166.

23. Deng Xiaoping, "Emancipate the Mind, Seek Truth from Facts, and Unite as One in Looking to the Future" (13 December 1978), in Ruan Ming, *Deng Xiaoping: Chronicle of an Empire*, 48.

24. Ibid.

25. Deng Xiaoping's opening speech at the Twelfth National Congress of the Chinese Communist Party (1 September 1982).

26. Ruan Ming, *Deng Xiaoping: Chronicle of an Empire*, 164.

27. Merle Goldman, *China's Intellectuals: Advise and Dissent*, 9.

28. "Communists must learn to trade," Lenin exhorted. See George Fyson, editor, *Lenin's Final Fight: Speeches and Writings, 1922–23* (New York: Pathfinder Press, 1995), 37.

29. Ibid., 48.

30. Known as White Swan Island, it is currently the location of a hotel catering mainly to foreigners.

31. Ruan Ming, *Chronicle of an Empire*, 88.

32. Once the Shenzhen SEZ was established, Chinese officials were wary that the area along the China–Hong Kong would be besieged by "political campaigns against liberalism, against humanism, and against spiritual pollution." From Ruan Ming, *Deng Xiaoping: Chronicle of an Empire*, 133.

33. Ibid., 134.

34. The standard organization of the *danwei* (production unit) has two top officials: the manager/director and the Party secretary. As a means of veiling the presence of the Party in the SEZ, the two positions are given to a single person.

35. Ibid.

36. The China Academy of Planning in Beijing developed the original planning strategy for Shenzhen. The Shenzhen Planning Institute (a local branch of the China Academy of Planning) is currently responsible for supervising all development in the SEZ and the surrounding territories that fall under its administrative power.

37. Sun Huasheng, Ruan Zupei, "Shenzhen's Brand-New Urban Environment: An Organic Combination of Urban Culture, Human Activities and Urban Environment," in *Shenzhen Urban Planning and Design: A Compilation for the First Decade Celebration of Shenzhen Special Economic Zone.*

38. Sun Kegang, "Shenzhen City Planning and Planning Management," in *Shenzhen Urban Planning and Design: A Compilation for the First Decade Celebration of Shenzhen Special Economic Zone.*

39. Ibid.

40. Ibid.

41. "The City Planning Administration is now ready to transfer Hong Kong planning experiences of phasing and layering and carry out new planning reforms accordingly and finally to work out zoning ordinance to be submitted to the Future Shenzhen People's Assembly for promulgation." Zhou Ganshi, "Press Forward To Reach the Contemporary State of Art of Urban Planning," in *Shenzhen Urban Planning and Design: A Compilation for the First Decade Celebration of Shenzhen Special Economic Zone*, 14.

42. Sun Kegang, "Shenzhen City Planning and Planning Management," in *Shenzhen Urban Planning and Design: A Compilation for the First Decade Celebration of Shenzhen Special Economic Zone*.

43. Cheng Tianxiang, Ng Kim Wai, *An Urbanization Strategy for the Pearl River Delta in the 21st Century* (Hong Kong: Center for Hong Kong and Macao Studies of Zhongshan University and Guangzhou and Center of Urban Planning and Environmental Management of the University of Hong Kong, 1995), 6.

44. Zhou Ganshi, "Press Forward To Reach the Contemporary State of Art of Urban Planning," in *Shenzhen Urban Planning and Design: A Compilation for the First Decade Celebration of Shenzhen Special Economic Zone*, 6.

45. Kenneth Frampton, "The Other Le Corbusier: Primitive form and the Linear City 1929–1952," in *Le Corbusier: Architect of the Century* (London: Arts Council of Great Britain, 1987).

46. Ibid., 6.

47. Xheng Tianxiang, Ng Kim Wai, *An Urbanization Strategy for the Pearl River Delta in the 21st Century*.

48. Xu Zhou, "A Review of Urban Planning in China in the 1980s," *China City Planning Review* 11, no.1 (1995).

49. Sun Huasheng, Ruan Zupei, "Shenzhen's Brand-New Urban Environment: An Organic Combination of Urban Culture, Human Activities and Urban Environment," in *Shenzhen Urban Planning and Design: A Compilation for the First Decade Celebration of Shenzhen Special Economic Zone*.

50. Ibid.

51. Ibid., 104.

52. "Shenzhen SEZ Overseas Chinese Town General Planning," in *Shenzhen Urban Planning and Design: A Compilation for the First Decade Celebration of Shenzhen Special Economic Zone*.

53. Sun Huasheng, Ruan Zupei, "Shenzhen's Brand-New Urban Environment: An Organic Combination of Urban Culture, Human Activities and Urban Environment," in *Shenzhen Urban Planning and Design: A Compilation for the First Decade Celebration of Shenzhen Special Economic Zone*.

54. Ibid., 21.

55. *Shenzhen, Splendid China, Miniature Scenic Spot* (San Francisco: Getherease Inc.).

56. "Floating population" is the unofficial name for the growing number of Chinese migrating to new places of opportunity, such as the Shenzhen Special Economic Zone, but who are not registered as official residents. The success of market reform depends significantly on this reservoir of labor.

57. Xheng Tianxiang, Ng Kim Wai, *An Urbanization Strategy for the Pearl River Delta in the 21st Century*, 4.

58. See the "Agricultural Science Park" in Shenzhen. In 1997, the Special Economic Zone Government passed laws to protect the remaining farmland from development.

59. Xheng Tianxiang, Ng Kim Wai, *An Urbanization Strategy for the Pearl River Delta in the 21st Century*, 4.

60. Ibid., 4.

61. Ibid., 2, 9.

62. Shenzhen Mayor Li Hao's speech at the founding of Shenzhen Municipal Urban Planning Committee.

63. Xheng Tianxiang, Ng Kim Wai, "The Return of Sovereignties," *An Urbanization Strategy for the Pearl River Delta in the 21st Century*, 7.

Contents

CHINESE ARCHITECT©   *161*

ARCHITECTURE©   *163*
    165   ARCHITECTURE© = Stocks
    167   ARCHITECTURE© = Commodity
    173   ARCHITECTURE© = Profit
    175   ARCHITECTURE© = Status
    179   FENG SHUI©
    181   SHENZHEN SPEED©
    183   *Chaogeng*
    183   Architectural Recipes
    185   Winning Competition Entries
    191   Historical Manuals
    191   Drawings = Commodity
    193   Construction Improvisation
    193   Foreign Growth

GREAT LEAP FORWARD©   *205*
    209   MORE IS MORE©
    211   More = Vacancy
    217   CURTAIN WAR©
    226   FACTORY/HOTEL/OFFICE/HOUSING/PARKING©

MORE IS LESS   *243*
    245   Poor Construction
    245   Hybrid Buildings
    247   Illegal Structures

FLOATING©   *249*

LESS FOR MORE   *255*
    255   *Min Qi*

ARCHITECTURE

SHENZHEN

Nancy Lin

There is $^{1}/_{10}$ the number of architects in China as in the US . . .

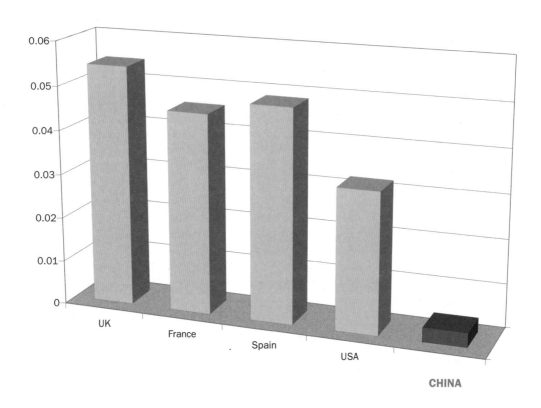

# of architects as a percent of total population

. . . designing 5 times the volume of projects . . .

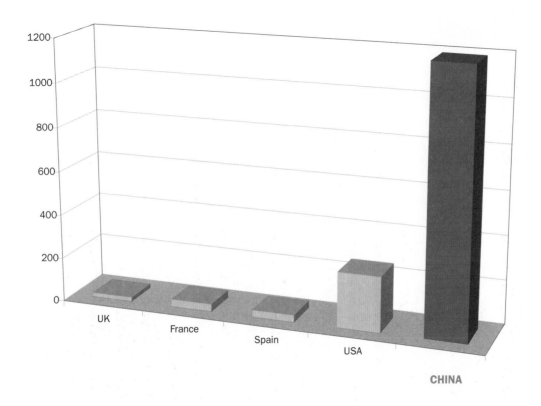

Total construction per architect (millions m²)

. . . earning $1/10$ the design fee.

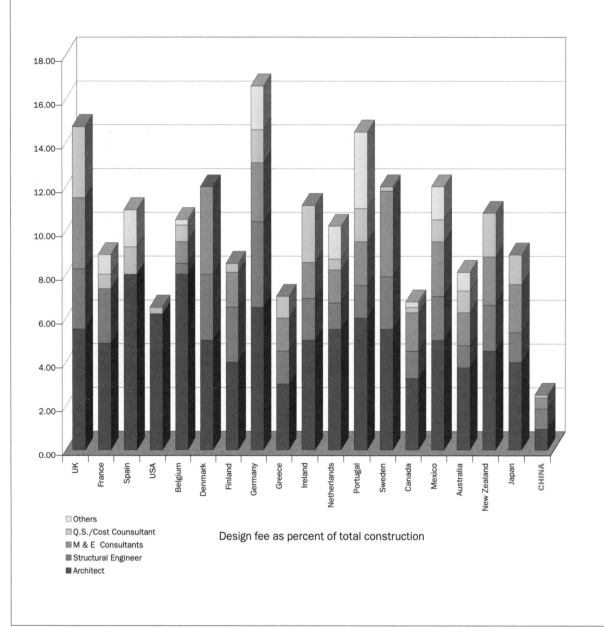

Design fee as percent of total construction

Legend:
- Others
- Q.S./Cost Counsultant
- M & E Consultants
- Structural Engineer
- Architect

Countries (left to right): UK, France, Spain, USA, Belgium, Denmark, Finland, Germany, Greece, Ireland, Netherlands, Portugal, Sweden, Canada, Mexico, Australia, New Zealand, Japan, CHINA

CHINESE ARCHITECT©

CHINESE ARCHITECT© The most important, influential, and powerful architect on earth. The average lifetime construction volume of the CHINESE ARCHITECT© in housing alone is approximately three dozen thirty-story highrise buildings. The CHINESE ARCHITECT© designs the largest volume, in the shortest time, for the lowest fee. There is one-tenth the number of architects in China than in the United States, designing five times the project volume in one-fifth the time, earning one-tenth the design fee. This implies an efficiency of 2,500 times that of an American architect.

The scarcity of Chinese architects, the low fees paid to them, and the massive amount of work each undertakes in a short amount time define the CHINESE ARCHITECT©. The notions of "architect" and the "practice of architecture" known to Western culture have changed.

In 1996 there was only one architect for every 30,400 people in China.[1] In the rural areas, there was one architect for every four million people in 1989.[2] Compare this to the architectural profession in the US (1:3120), France (1:2200), Spain (1:2070), and Great Britain (1:1840).[3]

At the same time, the design fee schedule in China is among the lowest in the architectural profession worldwide. Depending on the region, the total design fee, including fees for architects and all consultants, averages only 1.5 percent to 2.5 percent of the construction costs.[4]

In addition, in 1996 the total construction volume for housing alone in China was 1.19 billion square meters.[5] It is analogous to saying that each Chinese architect is on average responsible for producing 29,240 square meters of housing construction each year, or the equivalent of one thirty-story apartment building. When comparing the total construction volume of residential buildings in square meters, the differences for the U.S., France, Spain, and the United Kingdom, are 5-fold, 36-fold, 38-fold, and 66-fold, respectively.[6]

Architectural design is produced ten times faster in China than in the U.S.[7] In a Dongguan firm with a staff of thirty-five architects, design work per project takes on average ten days to finish, whether a single-family house, a multilevel apartment, or a highrise office building. In 1995 alone, the same office undertook more than 120 new design projects. For a thirty-story residential highrise, it takes one Shenzhen architect seven days to finish the design and complete a set of drawings. Yet, a project of similar scale requires two to three months to design in an American architectural office.[8]

Advertisement for new residential architecture.

ARCHITECTURE©

> ARCHITECTURE© Stocks, commodity, profit, status; otherwise only marginally related to the art and science of building. ARCHITECTURE© is designed in the Pearl River Delta under unprecedented pressures of time, speed, and quantity.

The implementation of the Open Door Policy in 1978 and the establishment of Special Economic Zones (SEZs) in the coastal areas of the Pearl River Delta stimulated an amount of land development and urban construction unprecedented in the history of Chinese architecture.[9] Shenzhen, a former fishing village with a population of 25,000 and a land area of 3 kilometers, was transformed into a base for agricultural and industrial export products in 1979 when the Shenzhen Municipality was established. Covering 2,020 square kilometers, Shenzhen is approximately twice the size of Hong Kong, and located on the eastern side of the Pearl River Delta, directly north of Kowloon. In 1980 the Shenzhen Special Economic Zone, an area of 327.5 square kilometers (40 kilometers from east to west, 7 kilometers from north to south) was established after the Standing Committee of the National Congress passed and published the Regulations on Special Economic Zones in Guangdong Province, marking the official beginning of the Shenzhen SEZ.[10]

Previously, with the establishment of Communist China in 1949, land and property developments had been excluded from economic activity. The government dominated state ownership, and acted as financier, landowner, developer, and investor in all urban land and property developments. Not only did central and local governments control regulations and planning, but also controlled physical urban construction by providing public housing and offices, and factories to enterprises. But, with unprecedented economic reforms in 1978, the economy shifted from strict self-reliance and self-sufficiency to inclusion of the global economy. The new policies encouraged the coexistence of public and private participation.[*] Private and collective developers, therefore, were allowed to register and operate in China, and collective design firms were set up in the 1980s.[11]

Shenzhen's proximity to Hong Kong positioned it as an ideal gateway to mainland China. In 1981, six hundred projects involving foreign participation were set up or were underway, and in the downtown area of Shenzhen alone, forty highrises with a total floor area of 3 million square meters were constructed. Between 1981 and 1983, nearly 2 million cubic meters of rock and earth were removed and 95 hectares were leveled for the creation of the Shekou Industrial Area.[12] In 1983 more than 4,000 professional technical personnel from twenty-nine provinces, municipalities, and autonomous regions throughout country were working on the planning, construction, and management of Shenzhen. In 1984 more than 100,000 staff and workers from the construction ranks of the central departments and other areas were working day and night at various sites in the Shenzhen SEZ.[13] These activities marked the beginning of the first private real estate development in China since the establishment of the Chinese Communist Party in 1949.[14]

The accumulation of ARCHITECTURE© in Shenzhen has created a new kind of city that may serve either as an exceptional model to be followed or a deformation to be ignored. These transformations prove that the classical disciplines of planning, and design are no longer viable. Architecture is not the known and familiar, but has transformed into ARCHITECTURE©, coincident with capital, speed, and quantity.

深市地产股分类指数全景图

1640.60

812.68

■ 在新一轮经济发展中,
房地产业将面临空前的发
展机遇,深市地产板块将
大有作为。

Panoramic view of Shenzhen's Categorized Stock Exchange Index. In this new turn of
economic development in the Pearl River Delta, ARCHITECTURE© and the real estate
industry promises Shenzhen a bright future.

Shekou Improvisation

If it was not for last night's high tide, how
suddenly came
This many illusory buildings, factories?
Ah, past crabs lived place,
Today, everywhere steel's sounds, electric flashes!

—by Xueqiang Liu and Yu Chun[15]

❀ **Reform of Shenzhen Land**
There have been three phases in the process of Shenzhen's
land use reform: (1) Housing Stock Compensation Deal; (2)
Real Estate Development collaborative; and (3) Land Use Fee.
Given the socialist ideology and China's constitution regarding
the ownership of national land, the first phase was truly a revolutionary act, and it was achieved with tremendous political
controversies. The person who was responsible for this
ground-breaking reform was Luo Jinxin, who was the Vice-
Director of Shenzhen's Bureau of National Land, a native Cantonese. As a common practice in China's political life, any new
policy must be supported by the fundamental theories of Marxism and Leninism. Land reform is no exception. Luo started
his thinking by reading into Lenin's writing on the early phase
of socialism in the Soviet Union. He wielded a quote from
Lenin to shield himself from political controversy: "Housing,
factory, et cetera . . . should not be handed to individuals and
associations for free, at least in the early stage of socialism.
Abandoning private ownership of land property does not mean
diminishing the rent value of land. Rent value, through reform,
can be beneficial to the whole society."
    The concept of the Housing Stock Compensation Deal is
simple: the city provides the land, and foreign developers
cover costs of development, design, and construction. They
share the profit. It was recorded that the split between the city
and the developer was 8.5 to 2.5. The first Hong Kong developer who pioneered the joint venture housing development is
Liu Tian Zhu. The first contract was signed in 1980, on New
Year's Day. As result, the city of Shenzhen made millions of
Hong Kong dollars, something city officials never dreamed
about. Although the city earned cash, it did not resolve the
serious housing shortage caused by the drastic increase in
population. As a reaction, the policy of Real Estate Development Collaborative was made. It is different from the first
phase, in that the city, instead of sharing profits, owns a certain percentage of the housing units. During this period, the
city also invested in infrastructure projects to make the land
more desirable for foreign developers, a strategy that has
proved effective. Shortly after the implementation of the second policy, the city became aware of the shortcomings of both
policies. In the first scenario, there was a three-year waiting
period for the cash return because the housing market was
not active enough. Meanwhile, in the second, the housing
units available to the city were insufficient and not at the right
standard for local residents. In addition there was no cash
return to support other ventures of the city.
    It was then that the third policy, Land Use Fee, was
launched. This time, land was no longer for free; it was
leased for a period of fifty years. The benefit of this policy is
obvious: the city gets cash as soon as the contract is signed,
bears no risk of the market, and can use the money to develop other projects that are more meaningful to the city and
less so to developers. The combined result of these three
policies is the complete sell-out of Luo Hu District. It is truly a
result of marriage between SHENZEN SPEED© and Deng
Xiaoping's "Truth by Practice" theory. —Qingyun Ma

ARCHITECTURE© = **Stocks**

ARCHITECTURE© has become a channel for
investment. Building construction has become
such a profit-making tool that a building's primary function is no longer to serve human needs.
The traditional concepts associated with architecture such as aesthetics, comfortable environment, advanced building technology, and human
occupancy have been suppressed to emphasize
quantitative measures like construction volume,
capital investment, construction time, cost, and
profit return.

    In these various states, architecture is no
longer only present in physical form: architecture
is everything, appearing as a topic of daily conversation, as well as an abstraction of numbers,
published like stock quotes in newspapers. Taxi
drivers, ordinary residents, architects and planners all talk about architecture.[16] Stories of new
buildings, construction, and real estate markets
make headlines and frontpages of local newspapers nearly every day. Mutating from traditional
architecture, ARCHITECTURE© has become the
most overwhelming activity of the city.

    Real estate prices are analyzed like trading
stocks and securities, with market fluctuations
described in points, akin to the Dow Jone's
Index. Reported in the *Shenzhen Special Zone
Daily* in May 1996: "Although the prices for real
estate property have dropped, Shenzhen still
remains at the top in the nation at 1,223 points.
Beijing is second at 1,089 points and Shanghai
is third at 922 points." The real estate
"exchange" is the architectural casino where
investors gamble for high returns. The index indicates how many investors have placed their
"bets," or down payments.

Architectural vendors on the streets of Futian; Shenzhen, July 1996.

Real estate billboards have become the most accessible method by which architecture is perceived and consumed, because most buyers do not see what they are purchasing in the pre-sale phase.

ARCHITECTURE© = **Commodity**

Real estate transactions have been changed dramatically by the commodification of architecture. The Shenzhen City Real Estate Property Exchange Center was established in May 1995 to manage the changes in real estate procedures, by providing consultations on purchasing property, financing mortgages, paying taxes, and other policy-related issues associated with real estate. The Exchange Center has completed 1,270 transactions since its establishment.

The Exchange Center also organizes large-scale exhibitions to promote and sell new building projects. During one exhibition, the Third Shenzhen Commodity Housing Promotional Exhibition held in August 1996, about fifty developers and brokers gathered to provide services and information for 120 projects. At every exhibition held at the Exchange Center, property transactions take place at "architectural stalls." At exhibitions held outside of the Exchange Center, architecture vendors are found almost everywhere: streets, atria and lobbies of office buildings, and department stores.

At these stalls, the "one-dragon-method service" is provided, ranging from purchasing to obtaining real estate property certificates which developers offer on-site. In these stalls, models, master plans, unit plans, and elaborated renderings of projects are displayed, videotapes of completed buildings are shown, and shuttle buses for site visits are available. Customers shop from one stall to another comparing prices and special offers like shopping for clothes. The exhibitions make shopping for houses so easy that they have become the most efficient and effective way to sell "commodity buildings." For example, at the 1996 Futian Real Estate Property Promotional Exhibition, over 70 percent of units were sold.[17]

Exhibitions also conduct pre-sales of commodity buildings.[18] Pre-sale is a phenomenon resulting from increased interest in real estate developments. A certain percentage of units are sold prior to the commencement of construction of a project to reduce risks for developers. In an exhibition held in May, 80 percent of all units from Yitian Garden were pre-sold even before the sales permit was obtained. Because the sales went so well in the exhibition, developers sent out notices to pre-sold buyers, already urging for down payments when it was still illegal for the developer to conduct any sale.

Because people do not see what they are buying during the pre-sale phase, advertisements become indispensable. Building plans, elevations, and perspectives rendered in beautiful colors on large billboards on streets and construction sites are the most visible advertisements. The shear amount of billboards present in the city for the frantic developments turn billboards into public art works by which architecture is visualized. In addition, phrases such as "limited offer," "sale ends in seven days," "20 percent off," and "celebrate the Moon Festival, welcome the National Day Special Sales" fill the full-page real estate property advertisements in newspapers as if architecture is a commodity people purchase daily. The importance of real estate advertisements is indicated by the fact that publishers are now compiling not only books on best housing projects, but on best billboards and advertisements as well. Billboards and advertisements have become the most accessible method by which architecture is perceived and consumed.

Architectural stalls selling housing projects at the Promotional Exhibition for Housing in the lobby of the Shenzhen World Trade Center, 1996.

入深圳户口

Models and drawings displayed in architectural stalls at the 1996 Promotional Exhibition for Housing at the Shenzhen World Trade Center. Buyers often make purchases based only on representational models.

Land fees amount to *45–49%* of overall development costs . . .

Cost distribution for highrise (at least 18 floors) housing developments

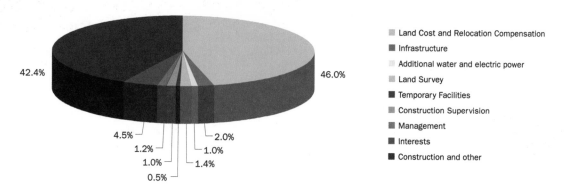

- 46.0%
- 42.4%
- 4.5%
- 1.2%
- 1.0%
- 0.5%
- 2.0%
- 1.0%
- 1.4%

■ Land Cost and Relocation Compensation
■ Infrastructure
■ Additional water and electric power
■ Land Survey
■ Temporary Facilities
■ Construction Supervision
■ Management
■ Interests
■ Construction and other

. . . but are waived for *3 years* to lure overseas Chinese developers.

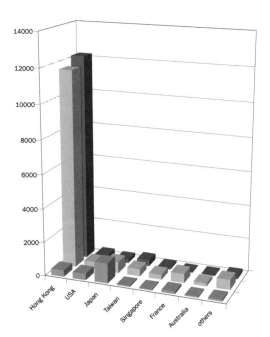

Investment sources

	Hong Kong	USA	Japan	Taiwan
	12190	297	214	356
	11670	457	653	426
	384	376	1195	69

	Singapore	France	Australia	others
■ # of Contracted Projects	97	30	33	188
■ Agreed Value (millions US$)	293	560	173	600
■ Actual Value (millions US$)	59	145	59	108

"If You Have Land, You Will Make Money; If You Have a House, You Can Get Rich," is a motto that drives developers and buyers alike.[19] Following Deng Xiaoping's proclamation, "To Get Rich Is Glorious," profit-seeking has become a legitimate goal for everyone. The profit from real estate development in China was seldom less than 30 percent, a significant return compared to the international profit average of 6 to 8 percent.[20] In Shenzhen, the net profit was reported to be RMB 3.3 billion (about $413 million USD, with an exchange rate of about $1 USD to RMB 8), from a total income of RMB 9.1 billion ($1.1 billion USD) generated from selling commodity housing—a profit rate of 36 percent.[21] Since most companies underestimated their profits to avoid tax payments, the actual profit margin was likely much greater. Developers construct overwhelmingly luxurious commercial and residential buildings for which high profit margins are guaranteed.[22]

Even for low-income and affordable housing projects, the Chinese government guarantees 10 to 15 percent profit as an incentive to developers.[23] Compared to the international average, profits for low-income and affordable housing projects in China are already twice the international standard. How is such a high return possible?

The overpricing of real estate property is the main factor in the high return for developers in China, and makes Shenzhen one of the most unaffordable places worldwide in relation to local per capita income. According to a survey conducted by the World Bank, the international standard of housing affordability (a ratio of average cost of a housing unit to the annual income per household) fluctuates between 3:1 and 6:1. In the U.S., for example, a housing unit is 2.8 times the annual income per household, which is slightly below the international standard.[24] In Shenzhen, however, the ratios are 8:1 and 12:1, with housing prices at 1.36 and 2 times the average international housing price.[25] Likewise in the Luohu and Futian districts, the average prices for residential units in highrises in 1995 were $8,000 USD and $7,500 USD respectively, amounting to a difference of about 15 times the annual income per household.[26]

Another reason for the high profits are the costs developers save on land fees which reduce development costs dramatically by at least 45 to 49 percent.[27] Since most developers in Shenzhen are from Hong Kong, Macao, and Taiwan, land fees are waived for overseas Chinese companies for the first three years to lure development interest.[28] This incentive policy reduces initial land costs, and hence increases profit margins for investments. To take advantage of these low land fees, many mainland Chinese enterprises are set up as Hong Kong subsidiaries, or "cover-up" companies.[29] Disguised as Hong Kong companies, mainland Chinese companies enjoy benefits unavailable to domestic firms, and re-enter China as overseas companies to invest and develop projects.

Construction costs average only 30 percent of the actual sale price, giving developers profits of 58 percent for multilevel and 47 percent for highrise buildings.[30] The average construction costs in Shenzhen is RMB 1,300 ($143 USD) per square meter for multilevel housing, and RMB 2,000–2,500 ($313 USD) per square meter for a residential highrise (more than eighteen floors).[31] The average sale price in 1995 of multilevel units and highrise units is RMB 4,267 and RMB 6,279 per square meter, respectively.[32] Despite these figures, developers in China still claim "the return for developers is already so low that there is no room for price adjustments."[33]

Sale Price for Multilevel and Highrise Commodity Housing in Shenzhen SEZ, 1984–1996

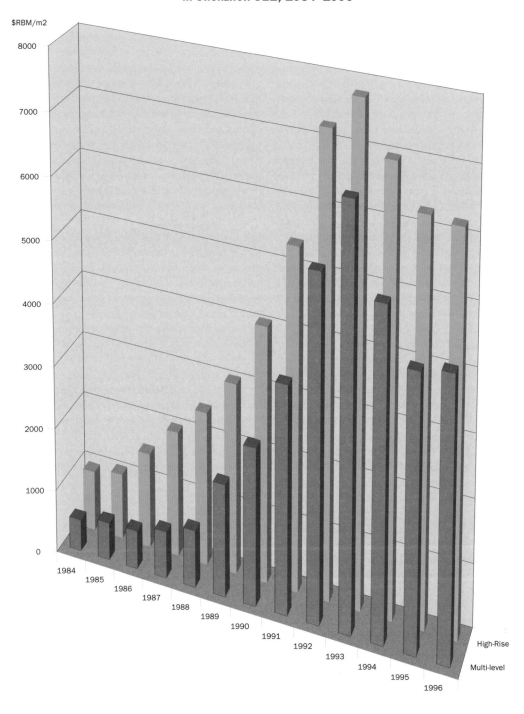

ARCHITECTURE© = **Status**

When the Special Economic Zones were established in 1980, the Chinese government limited access to these areas, establishing new borders which Chinese citizens could only cross by applying for residency. Thus, for many, ARCHITECTURE© is a means to obtaining residency in Shenzhen, a position connoting high social status in China.

In October 1995, the Shenzhen Municipality implemented a housing policy for Longgang and Baoan districts, described by one residential development's sales brochure as the "Buy a house and get registered policy . . . kill two birds with one stone."[34] All in a single step, this policy stimulates the buying of commodity housing, legitimates permanent residency, and provides a sheltering roof. Individuals buying government-approved housing can receive three to four blue registration cards (depending on the size of the unit), which allows permanent residency in Shenzhen for one to three years, fulfilling their "green card dream."[35]

The success of this policy is suggested by the fact that 90 percent of all transactions completed in the 1995 Real Estate Trading Exhibition of Shenzhen were for projects associated with the registration system.[36] Within ten months, the total sale in Longgang and Baoan reached 8,916 units, twice the previous year's total sales in these areas.[37]

GREEN CARD DREAM© Shenzhen's policy of "Buy a House and Get Registered; Fulfill Ones' Green Card Dream" allows the establishment of residency in Shenzhen when purchasing a home. Residency in Shenzhen is a highly desirable achievement, providing home-buyers an immediate elevation in social status. The GREEN CARD DREAM© also provides Shenzhen's FLOATERS© immediate permanent residency. The GREEN CARD DREAM© keeps the buying of housing in Shenzhen at an accelerated pace.

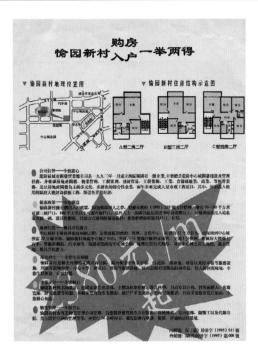

"Buy a house and get registered; kill two birds with one stone; fulfill your Shenzhen dream!" Shenzhen Longgan Central Town, Cheerful Garden New Village.

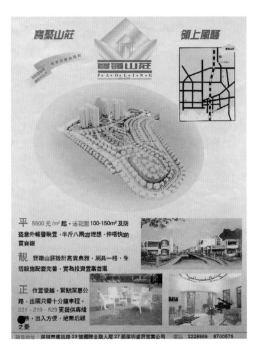

"Detached house for the price of a multilevel apartment; buy a house and get registered!" Treasure-collecting Mountain Villa, 1996.

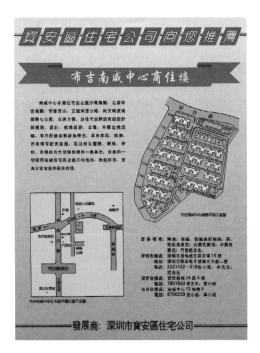

"All ready-constructed buildings; buy a house to get registered!" Buji Nan Wei Center, 1996.

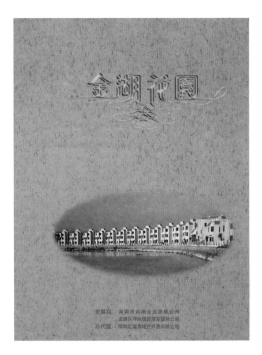

"Ready buildings, direct sale, low prices; get keys once paid in full; instantly process closing and property deed; instantly receive registry!" Golden Lake Garden, 1996.

"Move to Shenzhen, grab your chance: the dream-household registry, the favored location, the unbeatable price, the perfect development!" De Xing Garden, 1996.

"Become a client for free; buy one get one free; special prizes for buyers; open-to-the-public drawings!" Shenzhen Famous Town International Square, 1996.

Wal-Mart, the world's biggest retail store, opened its first Sam's Club and Wal-Mart Superstore in Shenzhen in August 1996. Because of its FENG SHUI©—geographical advantages and great consumption power—Shenzhen was Wal-Mart's first choice for its inaugural location in China.

FENG SHUI©

With ARCHITECTURE© evaluated like stocks and commodities, its profitability must be guaranteed. The traditional practice of *feng shui* has become more than rules for proper orientation, but is now a way to ensure financial success. In its original sense, *feng shui* is geomancy, used to obtain the correct orientation for new sites and buildings, a set of interpretations which share the same roots as Eastern medicine, based upon empirical knowledge about channels through which *qi*, energy, flows within the human body. Traditionally, abiding by *feng shui* protects against catastrophe. In its new interpretation, FENG SHUI© is not used as a set of guidelines, but as justification of geographical advantages to generate commercial success.

Shenzhen has been named, "Feng Shui Treasure Land," to claim its ideal proximity to Hong Kong as the "special zone" for investment within China.[38] To promote investments for the Futian central business district, the development plan was based on the "blossom in the center," a *feng shui* idea which helps physically collect good *qi*. Used in its modern context, FENG SHUI© attracts investors as well. The center of the development was oriented on the north-south axis of the Lotus Mountain located in the north of Shenzhen, whose exact location was found with a compass by the Director of the Planning Bureau. Even when the American company Wal-Mart opened the first Sam's Club and Wal-Mart Supercenter in Luohu, they consulted experts and located near rivers for good FENG SHUI©. Wal-Mart's presence is expected to bring prosperity to the region.

FENG SHUI© Geomancy originally used to determine optimum site and building orientations, FENG SHUI© now is used to fabricate ideal conditions from scratch, functioning as advertisement and becoming a self-fulfilling prophecy that both predicts and insures the inevitable success of commercial development. FENG SHUI© also is used retroactively to correct bad *qi* (energy) accumulated in modern architecture. In pursuit of financial profitability, FENG SHUI© coalesces ARCHITECTURE© and landscape into the PICTURESQUE©, providing the necessary precursor to SCAPE©.

Buildings with more than 18 floors in Shenzhen, 1982–1994

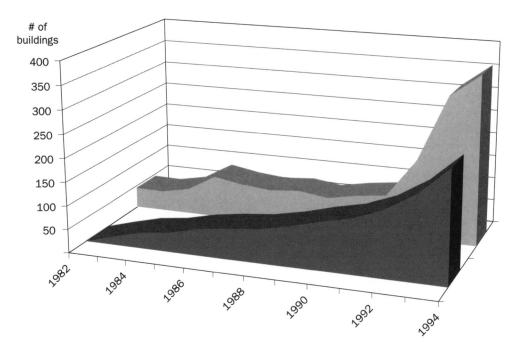

Industrial Output of Shenzhen, 1979–1995

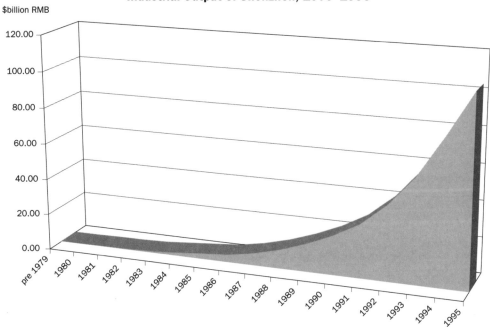

SHENZHEN SPEED©*

> SHENZHEN SPEED© Unit of abrupt growth. Architectural design in China has accelerated to keep pace with SHENZHEN SPEED©. Designers in the Shenzhen Special Economic Zone have set records: 5 designers x 1 night + 2 computers = 300-unit single family housing development; 1 architect x 3 nights = 7-story walk-up apartment; 1 architect x 7 days = 30-story concrete residential highrise.

Shenzhen Speed

Shennan Boulevard: Slender black and white
Gigantic enough to occupy the whole city
It howls to the poet's soul
"quick quick quick, quick quick quick
running cars are like flying bullets."

"Bullets are flying happily"
The Poet's soul says to his ears

His ears say to the pen and paper
"I hear the speedy wind
I hear the dizziness
I feel the wheels of Shenzhen rotating desperately"

—Li Li, "Shenzhen Speed,"
Poet Comes To Shenzhen (1996).

"Speedy design" is practiced with enthusiasm in Shenzhen. A master plan for a project consisting of 300 single-family houses only took a team of five designers to finish in one night. The complete design and drawings for a detached house only required one day. The detailed drawings for the entire project to be used as construction documents took fifteen days to complete. The master plan of a 2,000-student college campus took two people one month to finish. The design and the architectural drawings of a city gymnasium with a seating capacity of 5,000 took three people two months to complete.[39] It becomes normal for architects and designers to finish the complete package of a project's schematic design within eight to ten days or even less. The young architects' abilities to finish the schematic design drawings of a large scale project in just one or two days become issues to be bragged about in conversations. The ways one can finish a set of construction drawings within a very short time are popular stories shared among friends. "Architectural details become an non-issue because there is no time for any detail," said one architect.[40]

The increased industrial activity and rapid population rise not only forced construction of structures to accommodate the population swell and created economic opportunities for real estate development, but also set record speeds for growth in construction. Before 1979, the tallest building in Shenzhen only had five stories. Within three years, the total floor area for buildings completed in Shenzhen increased fifteen-fold, from 0.13 million to 1.95 million square meters. The number of completed buildings taller than eighteen stories increased from 1 to 237 between 1982 and 1994 and the total number including buildings under construction increased from 46 to over 600 between 1982 and 1996. As indicated by the 1,256-fold increase in Shenzhen's industrial output between 1979 and 1995, the sudden influx of capital investment was beyond imagination.[41]

❋ Speed
The shocking speed in Shenzhen is inherent in China's contemporary cultural situation, which can be detected through the traditional obsession with efficiency and the new idea of standardization acquired from the West through the Soviets during the 1950s. For a large country like China, speed makes sense. In the field of construction, speed is a result of straightforward construction technology, freer choices of material, unlimited labor resources, and the undivided responsibility of the contractor. The confidence in construction speed in turn motivated the speed of design, which in turn is facilitated by a profession-based, multidisciplinary education system. Constantly updated CAD programs and monographs of world architects (from which to emulate designs) magnified the speed of design in Shenzhen. —QM

What a *Shenzhen Speed!*
Huxin Garden Restaurant Completed and Opened in 80 Days!

From the *Shenzhen Commercial Daily*, (17 July 1996).

Chaogeng*

"Design fast hands," a phrase describing the rapidity of architectural design in Shenzhen, is often linked to the motto "time is money," indicating that clients are willing to pay more for faster service, especially with the motivation of profit-making.[42] "There is great pressure to complete revenue-generating structures quickly. . . . After a long and often exasperating period of building program approval and lease negotiation, developers want their buildings to go up overnight."[43] Because the demand for rapid design is high, and fees at design institutes are low, architects are given attractive incentives by developers to *chaogeng,* or moonlight for services outside of design institutes.[44] *Chaogeng* has become so popular that almost all architects have doubled up on projects outside of the design institutes.[45] Normally, a lump-sum fee in cash is negotiated between the architect and the developer for *chaogeng* projects. Partial fees are paid in advance and full cash payment is paid when drawings are delivered.[46]

Although a residential highrise is considered a complicated project type that requires special consultants, it has become one of the easiest tasks for *chaogeng* architects. In general, the average time to construct a fifteen-story and thirty-story concrete building was ten months and eighteen months, respectively.[47] The fastest highrise project has been done in just seven days. According to Sun Yimin, an architect and professor with the South China Institute, "There is only so much you can do to the plan of a residential highrise. Since the plan is pretty much the same for all buildings, all of the work really is done on giving the building a 'hat' or some variations in the facade."[48]

According to Tzou Hsiaoshi, one of the first private architects in Shenzhen, the projects undertaken by architects are classified into "face" projects or "stomach" projects. A "face" project, normally done in the design institute, reflects one's ability to design. A "stomach" project, or *chaogeng,* is undertaken merely for mon-

etary purposes, because the income earned from these projects can amount to ten and twenty times the average income an architect earns from a design institute. With "stomach" projects, an architect can be highly paid compared to other occupations in China.[49]

Architectural Recipes

With speed as the main factor in architectural design, an architect assumes the role of a chef who cooks from set recipes. Prepared by architects by composing architectural elements, languages, styles, forms, and standard details, "architectural recipes" are pattern books from which customers may order a building design. Publications of architectural recipes—which fill the design section of bookstores—are collections of projects edited by prominent architects and professors. Designers frequently do not associate their names with these recipes, thus architects who use these recipes often do not know the origins of these projects.

Architectural recipes have become indispensable references to every professional architect and student. Existing projects or previous designs are recycled with minimum alterations. Designs are processed simply by replacing new labels and "hats," a method that has become the most common for architectural design. "We collect a lot of brochures, pattern books, and projects from Taiwan and Hong Kong, so it is very easy to find a project where I have an entire

* **Chaogeng**
Although it gained popularity during the peak years of Shenzhen's growth, *chaogeng* has never been a legal form of practice, therefore never recognized by design institutes. A design institute could be criticized if any of its employees were discovered to be involved in legal disputes related to *chaogeng* practice. This is not to say that professionals in design institutes do not participate in *chaogeng* while officially employed by a design institute. The situation is quite the opposite. The careful ones keep a very low profile while the more aggressive ones would choose to leave the institute and become professional *chaogeng*-ers. A designer could stay with an institute and continue to pay a loyalty fee to attain the privileged status of "inactive employee."

The speed of Shenzhen also urges design institutes to reform their traditional way of practice. Setting up a small studio under a special financial arrangement with the institute is popular. It is legal and protected by the institute. It is called *chenbao.* Although less profitable in comparison to *chaogeng,* it becomes more and more preferred, particularly during an economic slow-down. It should be noted that architects in China still consider themselves, and are considered by others, intellectuals. Therefore they still bear the Confucius legacy of success, which is measured by one's career status and social establishment. In China, professionals are ranked by the government and given benefits in accordance to the ranks. The number of years one has worked in a design institute is a basic factor. Time away under the loyalty fee is not counted. Without these ranks, one is not qualified for benefits such as free or subsidized housing, let alone fame and recognition, which can bring more benefits. This is the main reason in recent years one sees a major back flow of "*chaogeng* army". —QM

Architectural recipe books in the Guangzhou Book Center.

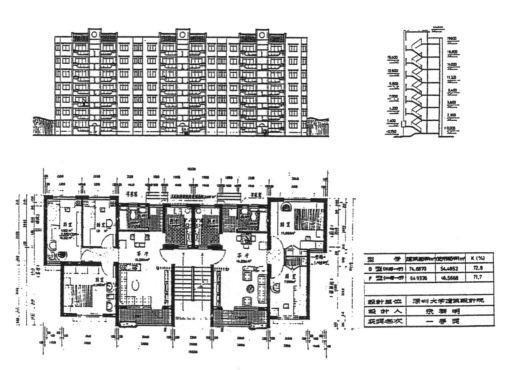

These winning entries in a 1993 housing design competition appeared in *Beijing City's Excellent Residential Design Collection*, published by the Beijing City and Town-planning Committee.

set of construction drawings from which I revise to fit into a new building," says architect Sun Yimin.

Often these architectural recipes contain tips on techniques for more efficient design and faster construction, all to facilitate SHENZHEN SPEED©. One such volume, *Jianzhu Xue Bao* (An architectural resource), a series published by the Jiangsu Design Institute, contains many essays and diagrams elaborating the conclusions made from research in design, planning, construction, land use, housing, et cetera.

In the essay "Residential Space and Reasonable Floor-to-Floor Height," Zhang Mo Shin conducted research to calculate the ideal height for housing in China.[50] He concluded that reducing the present standard floor-to-floor height of 2.8 meters to 2.7 meters was a more economical way to design housing, giving a net floor height of 2.6 meters (8.5 feet), which design institutes considered a reasonable height for standard housing.

In order to increase efficiency in erecting residential superblocks, a group of architects proposed, in an essay entitled "Planning and Design of Superstructural Housing," to separate the processes of design and construction between structural members (i.e., load-bearing walls, floor slabs, roof, and utility cores) and "separable parts" (i.e., partitions, furniture, facilities, and kitchen and bathrom fixtures of kitchen and bathroom).[51] Thus, the structural members would be designed and fabricated first, with the separable parts following closely behind. The essay also offered efficient solutions for housing design and building configurations and gave "multiple variations" based on these proposals.

Another essay, "Further Investigation of Conservation in Land Area Used in Housing" by Jin Zi, proposed the proper land area in building construction for land conservation, taking into account such issues as building height and distances between buildings. He presented light and shadow diagrams to determine the duration of sunlight and shade.[52]

Winning Competition Entries

One source for architectural recipes is competitions. Starting in the early 1980s, annual competitions have been held to find the most efficient plans and sections for slab, lowrise, highrise, and single-family housing. National standards for floor area per unit are used in designs, and plan efficiency is carefully calculated in terms of usable-living floor area per dwelling. Housing design becomes a scientific study of the ultimate floor-to-floor height, the ideal room dimension and proportion, and the best plan configurations for different housing typologies and orientations. In order to control the use of electricity, the government regulated the implementation of central control air conditioning unit by local design institutes. Furthermore, strict regulations on sun exposure and natural ventilation are enforced by government agencies. Chinese architects understand that China's limited resources must serve an immense population, hence the efforts to produce efficient housing.

Since the climate varies dramatically from region to region in China, competitions are held in different areas to ensure thorough studies of suitable housing plans for all of China. The Ministry of Construction recommends that winning entries to be used by developers and design institutes to achieve maximum efficiency in the construction and design of housing. For example, Beijing's Planning and Construction Committee addressed all the design institutes and interest groups in the *1993 Beijing City's Excellent Housing Design Collection:*

"In order to further promote and raise our city's housing design level, we demand each winner to improve and finish their winning entries especially on the elevations and plans. Within the near future, finish the construction drawings so that they will become our city's 1993 typical drawings (series). We will also execute the winning entries in a housing development, and try to finish the construction in one year. Through this execution, good housing will be demonstrated to the entire city and be promoted further."[53]

高层建筑标准层平面形式及其布局举例（图中阴影部分为垂直交通及服务设施面积）

矩形平面
（美）纽约松树街
88号楼

五角形平面
（美）休斯敦
某办公大厦

六角形平面
（美）克利夫兰
某办公大厦

八角形平面
（美）路易斯维尔
杰弗逊大厦

十字形平面
（加拿大）多伦多
玛利亚广场大厦

八字形平面
（俄罗斯）莫斯科
原经互会大厦

三角形平面
（美）匹兹堡
钢铁总公司大楼

Y字形平面
北京，北京西便门
高层住宅）

圆形平面
香港，香港合和
中心

丁字形平面
北京，北京长城
饭店

双矩形交迭平面
上海，上海宾馆

弧三角风车平面
上海，上海虹桥
宾馆

腰鼓形平面
广州，广州白天鹅
宾馆

L形平面
北京，北京西苑
饭店

带中庭平面
（美）亚特兰大
海特摄政旅馆

S形平面
上海，上海华亭
宾馆

弧形平面
（美）洛杉矶
世纪广场旅馆

组合平面
（巴西）巴西利亚
政府办公大厦

Architectural Recipe 1
Examples from the *Pictorial Guide to Speedy Architectural Design*.

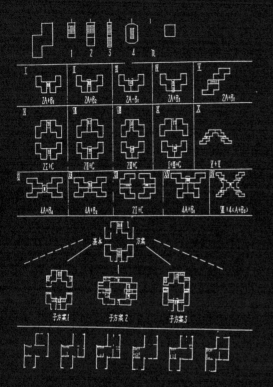

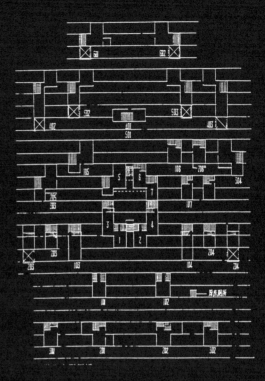

Architectural Recipe 2
The Design Process for Superstructural Housing: In order to increase efficiency in housing design and construction, a group of architects proposed to separate structural members (i.e., load-bearing walls, floor slabs, roof, and utility cores) and "separable parts" (i.e., partitions, furniture, facilities, and fixtures of kitchen and bathroom) in the process of design and construction. From, "Planning and Design of Superstructural Housing," in the series *Jianzhu Xue Bao* (An architectural resource), published by the Jiangsu Design Institute (February 1995).

Architectural Recipe 3
Housing Design: Diagram showing multiple variations on residential units. From "Planning and Design of Superstructural Housing," *An Architectural Resource* (February 1995).

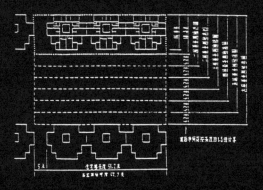

Architectural Recipe 4
Investigations of Land Area Conservation: Dotted lines represent land areas required for one-to-five-story Type B buildings. From "Further Investigation of Conservation in Land Area Used in Housing," *An Architectural Resource* (April 1995).

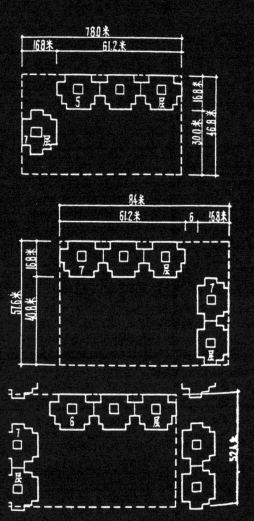

Architectural Recipe 5
Diagrams showing land areas used for a combination of five-to-seven-story buildings. From, "Further Investigation of Conservation in Land Area Used in Housing," *An Architectural Resource* (April 1995).

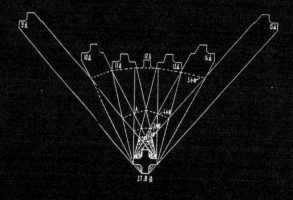

Architectural Recipe 6
Light and Shadow Diagrams: Shaded portions represent areas that do not receive at least two hours of sunlight. From, "Further Investigation of Conservation in Land Area Used in Housing," *An Architectural Resource* (April 1995).

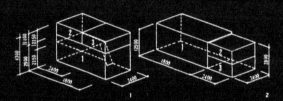

Architectural Recipe 7
Residential Space and Reasonable Floor-to-Floor Height: The Jiangsu Design Institute conducted research to calculate the ideal for housing in China. The institute concluded that reducing the present standard floor-to-floor height of 2.8 meters to 2.7 meters is a more economical way to housing design. The 2.7-meter floor-to-floor height will produce a net floor height of 2.6 meters—a reasonable height for standard housing with or without air conditioners in China. From "Residential Space and Reasonable Floor-to-Floor Height," *An Architectural Resource* (March 1993).

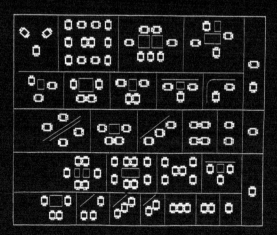

Architectural Recipe 8
Diagram showing variations in the configurations of several buildings. From, "Planning and Design of Superstructural Housing," *An Architectural Resource* (February 1995).

A commodity drawing of the Shenzhen Fang Zhi Building (left) and the imitated building (right). Drawings become commodities; developers will purchase perspective drawings or rendered elevations from an architect before a project is designed. The "image" is all that is needed for a project to be built.

Advocating the use of winning entries from housing competitions has altered the traditional concept of design in China.[54] Each site and program is no longer considered a unique issue. Rather, housing design becomes an application of formulas and architects misinterpret the meaning of building typologies as patterns. The architect's role is reduced to revising and recycling the best and the most efficient designs found in their recipe books.

Variable factors in design have shifted. Architectural design is no longer affected by programs and design is no longer site-specific. An exemplary case is that of the Shenzhen Fang Zhi building. Due to the client's financial difficulties the twenty-story tower was truncated literally from the building without any modification in the original design.[55] Finance determined the building's height and its final design.

Historical Manuals[※]

Historically, engineers, masons, and carpenters were responsible for the production of architecture. According to historian of Chinese architecture Wilma Fairbank, "The Chinese had never considered architecture an art," and regarded architecture the work of artisans or craftsmen.[56] Architectural characteristics were developed by carpenters for centuries, and common practices in architectural principles, methods, design, and construction were initially conveyed orally from master to apprentice, and in later centuries, collected in manuals and guidebooks.[57] Analogous to Vitruvius' *Ten Books on Architecture* and Palladio's *Four Books on Architecture*, these manuals became the primary sources for the production of architecture. Two manuals on architecture from earlier dynasties that have survived are *Ying Zao Fa Shi*, the Sung Dynasty rules for structural carpentry, first published in 1103 and written by the court architect, Li Chieh; and *Ying Zao Ze Li*, the Qing Dynasty builder's manual, published in 1734 by the state's Department of Works, and consisting of seventy chapters dealing with calculations of building materials and rules for timber carpentry.[58] Sustaining common architectural principles over many centuries was a widespread practice, a belief expressed by the phrase, "If the sky does not change, the method does not have to change."[59]

Drawings = Commodity

When the client of Shunde Shujiang Refrigerator Factory Building saw an architectural drawing done by an architect in southern China, he insisted that the style of his own new factory had to be identical to the drawing. The architect thus essential copied the rendering and the factory was built accordingly.[60]

The architect in this case had "made the clothes first before finding a customer and made clothes before taking measurements."[61] Drawings have become commodities; developers will purchase perspective drawings or rendered elevations from architects before a project is designed. An "image" is all that is needed for a project to be built.

※ **Classical Manuals and Architects**
The Song Dynasty *Construction Orders and Types* (*Ying Zao Fa Shi*) and Qing Dynasty *Construction Principles and Examples* (*Ying Zao Ze Li*) are China's only surviving volumes of classical literature on construction. The Chinese Society of Construction discovered and investigated them in the 1930s. Liang Sicheng, a graduate from the University of Pennsylvania, was the leader of the society. It has been a consensus among Chinese scholars, including Liang, that these documents describe systems and methods of quantity survey and material calculation. They were primarily used by the Imperial Government to control construction materials and avoid waste. It is highly unlikely that they were used as resource for the production of architecture. They were equivalent to today's cost estimate manuals and code books.

The most interesting aspect of these two classical books is the coded terms and passwords used to describe various construction situations. Sometimes a phrase is just a name for one piece at a specific location; other times it describes a whole set of things and the way they are put together. For instance, *xuan shan* (suspending mountain) is a construction method of roof; *tou xing* (steel heart) is a piece in a column capital; and *ying bu lou* (eagle does not nest) is a treatment of the top of masonry wall. The reason for their unique appellations is related to the protection of technologies used by a specific group of builders (usually a family). These techniques were, in essence, family secrets.

Liang (with the collaboration of his architect wife, Lin Wei-Yin) did two things to decode these phrases. One is field investigation; the other is graphic interpretation. Their persistent effort is critical yet destructive to the original material, bringing more understanding to them, but ruining their original purpose, allowing anyone to use them as design manuals. —QM

A commodity drawing of the Shunde Shujiang Refrigerator Factory Building (top)
and the original, imitated building (bottom).

Construction Improvisation

SHENZHEN SPEED© has become the norm in Shenzhen that buildings begin construction even before drawings are finished. Contractors simply improvise and build buildings according to their own methods on-site, because construction documents frequently provide insufficient specifications, and architects are not expected to clarify projects during construction. On-site interpretation by contractors becomes more important than construction drawings.[62]

The speed in architectural design and the rapid production of drawings can never be imagined in Western architectural culture simply because of different expectations. Buildings in the U.S. demand architects to create detailed instructions and specifications in the preparation of construction documents as well as during the construction process, with site visits and supervision to ensure proper implementation of design.[63]

Foreign Growth

What most observers do not realize is that ARCHITECTURE© could not have been built with SHENZHEN SPEED© without the participation of foreign architecture firms. Even at the speed at which CHINESE ARCHITECTS© design, they could not fulfill all the demands for new development. With this in mind, the central government allowed foreign professionals to fill unmet needs, but they are only allowed to work in China with caution, with their activity strictly regulated. According to the Ministry of Construction's 1992 Regulations on Establishing Jointly Managed Sino-Foreign Design Projects, foreign architecture firms are required to cooperate with an officially licensed Chinese design institute.[64]

Because foreign firms may not engage in the full range of their architectural services, the production of construction drawings, the design of mechanical systems, quality control, construction management, and labor supervision are all supervised by local design institutes. By law, only the design institutes are qualified to have licenses to practice architecture and obtain permits for building construction. Foreign firms can act as consultants to design institutes or enter competitions held by local developers and planning commissions. In addition, they can become partners in joint ventures by winning bids for planned real estate developments.[65]

Even though the government has set up legitimate channels to produce architects by establishing more than fifty new architectural programs and institutes since 1990, professional training, however, does not happen instantly.[66] Between 1986 and 1990, there was only an increase of 809 to 1,500 graduates from architectural schools.[67] The new species of architect, the CHINESE ARCHITECT©, cannot be produced with sufficient speed through architectural education and training. Compared to the American architectural profession, it will take China 115 years to reach the comparative ratio of architects to population.[68] Not until then will the first Chinese architect be jobless.

Before China has a complete and mature registration system for architects and engineers, the design profession in China will be regulated and, at the same time, deregulated.[69] It will be regulated for quality, but deregulated in terms of culture. "When the Chinese ask us to give them the 'American Model,' do we do what has been asked, and provide them with what we know to be the best, or do we suggest other alternatives that respect the Chinese culture?" said an urban planner at Skidmore, Owings, and Merrill in New York.[70] Many more Western developers, architects, planners, and landscape architects are participating in the creation of the ARCHITECTURE© of China. Will Chinese architecture be completely globalized with this influx of international influences? Or rather, through Chinese inhabitation, adaptation, and conversion, will another type of architecture emerge?

Diwang (King of Land) Building (far left), Shenzhen, set the fastest speed of high-rise construction in the world. The sixty-seven-story, 384-meter-tall concrete office building took only three years to complete. Kumagai, the Japanese contractor and developer of the project, developed a new additive to speed up the curing process for concrete in order to accelerate the process of construction. This new technology enabled the record-breaking speed of 2.5 days per floor in concrete construction.

This cluster of curtain wall buildings is the new financial center that redefines Shenzhen's skyline. The glass panels are in bright purple, green, blue, and brown. Five images of the financial center taken from different angles were used in the Yearbook of Shenzhen and Hong Kong Real Estate 1997 to illustrate Shenzhen. The construction of the financial center is an index to the maturing financial industry of Shenzhen. As described in the yearbook, "Shenzhen's financial industry is mature and stable. The city's regionally concentrated financial center is already being established. In 1995, there are already 1,051 financial organizations and service centers citywide."

The Diwang Building (middle) set off the race for the construction of the array of buildings in the future financial center.

A sculpture was cut in half and attached to
the Haiwang (King of Sea) Building, a symbolic highrise curtain wall building proudly
presented by the architects of Shenzhen
as a gateway to the city in 1994.

The International Technology Building, developed by the Shenzhen North Engineering Development Company, has become one of the landmarks of Futian since its completion in 1996. The "revolving" restaurant on top of the building does not revolve, but continues one of Deng's myths in Shenzhen. In 1992 when Deng visited Shenzhen, the revolving restaurant on the 49th floor of the Shenzhen World Trade Center (the first commercial highrise in Shenzhen) was the first place Deng visited. Deng referred to the revolving restaurant as the "one center" representative of Shenzhen, which has, since then, given rise to the oft-copied formula: "revolving restaurant = modernization = success."

红灯禁止右转

GOLDEN SEAHORS
FURNITURE
MARKET

The degree to which Shenzhen's skyline had changed was not obvious until the multitude of building scaffolds were taken down. When the colorful curtain wall panels were revealed, within days, these buildings became the new symbols of Shenzhen, proclaiming the city's commercial eminence to the world.

Shenzhen: the Future Blueprint is Not a Dream

本月 15 日，深圳市全市总体规划将首次在深圳博物馆展出，并公开征求市民的意见。设计师们说——

深圳： 未来蓝图不是梦

□ 本报记者　戴磊　刘烨萍/文　孙盈海/摄

你家住深圳南头，工作单位却在火车站。但每天可以喷地铁上班。来回只需半小时到 40 分钟；你的孩子可能会在居住地附近读收费普通的寄宿中小学，使你的负担大为减轻；

在福田中心区的城市卡轴线两侧，包括广场，绿地和雕塑小品的宽 80 和 100 米的步行区，让你充分享受自然……

未来不是梦，以上这些情景，将在本月 15 日首次全市总体规划的大型展览中，你会吃惊地发现——那就是你下一世纪的新家园。

规划赶不上变化

在深圳市的城市设计中心——深圳市城市规划设计研究院，设计师们告诉记者：深圳的城市规划是三年就修订一次，但仍然赶不上飞速的扩张速度。

深圳城市为爆炸出来的城市，天一变的成长速度实令当初的蓝图设计者们始料未及。1985 年

From Cash magazine (August 1996).

GREAT LEAP FORWARD©

GREAT LEAP FORWARD© 1. Extravagant hyperdevelopment marked by periods of stagnation. 2. Optimistic production even in the face of immanent disaster or prolonged suffering. 3. An unofficial campaign to modernize China, overseen by a socialist structure leaping toward a market economy that simultaneously achieves staggering success and catastrophic failure. 4. A modern reinterpretation of Mao Zedong's early campaign, the Great Leap Forward.

More than 44,000 acres of cropland in the southern province of Guangdong were handed over to developers in 1992, a move that swiftly replaced terraced rice fields and traditional villages with postmodern villas and office towers.[71] On billboards as large as houses, Zhuhai's mayor announced, "Development is the only way"—a proclamation carried out with a zeal akin to Mao Zedong's enthusiasm for accelerated industrial production during the first Great Leap Forward. Mao's motivating chant, "Quantity, Speed, Quality, Economy" ("*Duo, Kuai, Hao, Sheng*"), could be resurrected as the slogan—with an emphasis on quantity and speed—for this modern phase of unprecedented development.[72]

Since the PRD has been the first experimental ground for China's Open Door Policy, among all cities, Shenzhen is the focus of future development. While adhering to a modern socialist economy, Shenzhen is striving to become an international city in the 21st century. The busy tower cranes operating twenty-four hours a day, 365 days a year, indicates that new buildings are participating in a modernization never seen before in the city. Predictions are that by 2006, the Pearl River Delta will become the "world's most active economic belt."[73] "It is the most ambitious construction campaign in history," according to Tunney Lee of Hong Kong's Center for Planning, Architecture, and Development, commenting on the PRD's development efforts.[74] Observed by *The Guardian*:

"The urban sprawl growing in the PRD will become home to 40 million people, leapfrogging Mexico City and Tokyo-Osaka to become the largest in the world within a decade if it continues at its present rate. A population greater than most of the states of Europe will be packed into an area no larger than Greater London. The new cities in the megalopolis are dense, raw, chaotic, and vast. They have shopping malls and skyscrapers, airports, and business parks. The population doubles and redoubles in a single lifetime and open fields mushroom into a skyline of skyscrapers with urgency."[75]

But at the same time, the effort to modernize has been obstructed by its own enthusiasm. Hyperspeedy design and hyperdevelopment have created uneven growth (both physically and socially), debilitated structures, created homelessness and illegal activities, all to promote this new experimentation with the market economy. What has developed is a condition that engenders growth and decay, decadence and paucity.

Total Building Construction in Shenzhen, 1979–1994

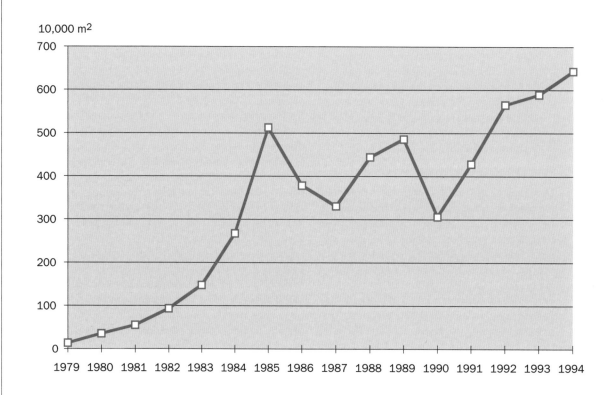

10,000 m²

Building Construction in Floor Area in Shenzhen, 1979–1994

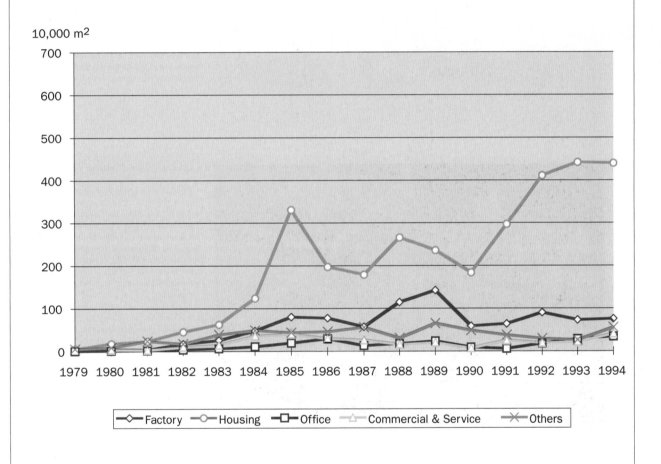

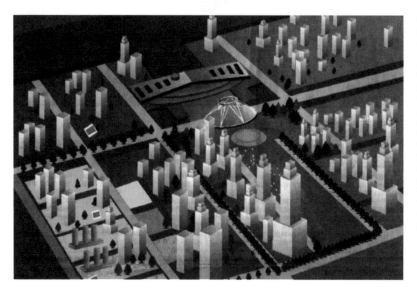

深圳 500 亿再造城市奇迹

福田中心区建设蕴含无限商机，深圳市府已制定多项优惠政策

The China Twin Tower, a 400-meter tall, all-glass curtain-wall building, is the centerpiece of the RMB 50 billion ($6.25 billion USD) project to create a central business district (4.13 square kilometers) in Shenzhen. The district is divided by Shennan Road into two areas: the northern commercial center for trade, finance, and information, and the southern area for institutions, government administration, culture, technology, and exhibitions. The China Twin Tower will be taller than the 384-meter Diwang Building, formerly the tallest building in Shenzhen. There will be more than 100 buildings of 200 meters or more in height, approximately fifty-five stories tall. The center will contain a residential population of 77,000, and a working population of 310,000, including 198,000 people working in the commercial center.

Crystal Island, a multipurpose glass complex: in 1996 five firms were invited to participate in a design competition for "Sunny New City," a new central business district in Shenzhen: John M. Y. Lee of Timchula Architects, Ltd., New York; SCAU, France; B + H, Canada; Huayi Designing Consultants, Hong Kong; and Architecture and Urban Design Consulting Company, Singapore. The winning entry was the Crystal Island scheme by Lee of Timchula Architects, conceived as a multipurpose glass complex consisting of exhibition hall, public recreational area, and restaurants. It is larger than the Winter Garden, the glass atrium of the World Financial Center in New York. From "America's M.Y. Lee's Crystal Island Scheme," *Cash* (20 August 1996).

MORE IS MORE©

MORE IS MORE© The conclusion of an evolution that began with Mies as "less is more"
and passed through Venturi as "less is a
bore," now ends in a paroxysm of the quantitative in the PRD as MORE IS MORE©. Five
hundred square kilometers of urban substance is built every year, of which 6.4 million
square meters is found in Shenzhen alone. In
addition to quantity, redundancy proliferates:
five international airports exist, with two
more nearing completion; in one building
alone, twelve different curtain wall systems
are used (see CURTAIN WAR©), while five
lighting systems are deployed in a single
15-square-meter room; ten revolving restaurants are constructed within four square
blocks; 414 holes of golf are open for play,
and 720 more are under construction.

Imbued with an inherent optimism, all buildings
in the PRD attempt to be the tallest, biggest,
longest, quickest, best, and most comfortable.
Competing for the largest is Star Place in Sun
City which will be the "largest mall ever built
when completed . . . enclos[ing] nearly 6 million
square feet, more than either the Mall of America (4.2 million) or Canada's West Edmonton Mall
(5.2 million), to become PRD's shopping
mecca."[76] Competing in the "longest" category
is: Guangzhou's new train station, with the
longest roof span in Asia, and Zhuhai Airport,
with the world's longest runways. Competing for
the "quickest": Shenzhen city for the world's
fastest record for concrete construction. And for
"most comfortable": Sun City in Huiyang,
designed as a "switched-on utopia where well
trained professionals and executives pursue the
good life."[77] It was also carefully planned to
become China's version of Silicon Valley.

Fifteen new shopping centers were constructed in Shenzhen before the end of 1996, as part
of a plan to develop the city through commerce.

The Shenzhen Municipality proposed to use
"large commercial and wholesale centers as the
structure, large shopping plazas and retail
stores as the support, and supermarkets and
chain stores as a foundation." Within the second
half of 1995, five large-scale department stores
appeared Shenzhen: Friendship Center (24,000
square meters), Wanjia (17,000 square meters),
Dashijie (50,000 square meters), Baihuo Plaza
(40,000 square meters), and Far East (30,000
square meters).

Even the world's largest retailer, wanted to
locate in the land of hyperbole. In August 1996,
Wal-Mart opened its first Sam's Club and Wal-
Mart Superstore in Shenzhen, the first choice
for a location in China because of its geographical advantages and great consumption power.
Wal-Mart plans to open two hundred stores in
China with initial investments concentrated
in Guangdong.[78]

Not only are retailers confident about Shenzhen's commercial industry, but the Shenzhen
Municipality stated that consumption power will
increase along with developing tourism,
increase in population, and reduction in taxes.
The relatively low rents and low costs in Shenzhen's developments, approximately one half
that of Hong Kong, will attract investments from
Hong Kong corporations and other large foreign
companies. "Commercial industry is like an aircraft carrier. It will continue to go forward in the
sea of commerce."[79]

Percent of Unsold Spaces in Shenzhen, 1986–1995

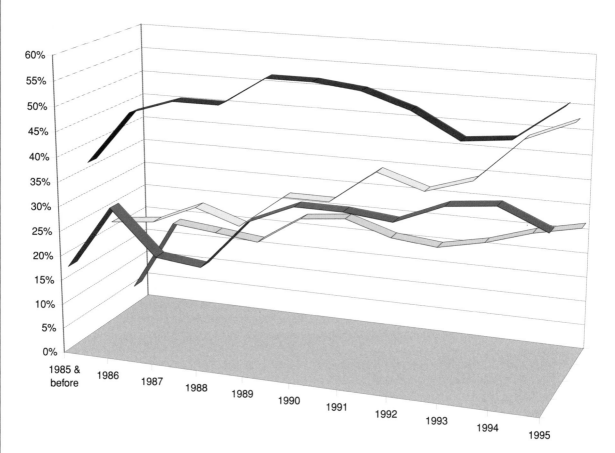

- ■ Factory
- ■ Office Building
- □ Commercial Space
- □ Housing

More = Vacancy

Between 1979 and 1994, the construction volume in Shenzhen increased persistently, with annual averages of 48, 49, 57, and 64 percent for factory, housing, office buildings, and commercial buildings, respectively, and 32 percent for all other buildings.[80] During the same period, the average annual increase of all construction volume in Shenzhen was 41 percent.[81] This expansion reflects a 405-fold increase in the total floor area of all buildings.[82] With a "hurry-up-and-build" attitude, Shenzhen planners pushed for the completion of private developments at unimaginable volumes.

Even though the increase in the total floor area of buildings in Shenzhen was dramatic, the surge did not reflect the real condition of supply and demand.[83] The PRD real estate market actually suffered from high vacancy and low sale rates. General vacancy rates hover near 50 percent, while the vacancy rate for commercial space reached 64 percent in 1994.[84] The percentage of unsold units in commodity housing projects, factories, commercial and office buildings averaged 30, 30, 45, and 50 percent, respectively.[85]

Luohu, the overnight city, built with SHENZHEN SPEED© is turning into an old city with vacant buildings.[86] Nevertheless, Shenzhen's Central Business District (CBD), the most ambitious plan of the decade, is underway and will be realized in 2010.[87] It is said that "Ten years ago, thrive Luohu; ten years later, prosper Futian."[88]

For commercial spaces and office buildings, the vacancy rates were far higher than unsold rates. In 1996 the Shenzhen Development Center and the Luohu Commercial City each had a vacancy rate of over 70 percent.[89] The Shenzhen Development Center is a forty-three-story "comprehensive commercial mansion" consisting of offices, shopping arcade, restaurants, exhibition hall, disco club, and a five-star hotel equipped with tennis courts and swimming pool, and a helipad on the roof.[90] The vacancy rate as of July 1996 was 70 percent.[91]❀

Luohu Commercial City is a six-story building with a floor area of 71,000 square meters. In 1996, 70 percent of the building was vacant. At its opening in August 1995, two hundred stores were initially registered; but now, only sixty stores are operating, and primarily used as display showcases. Thus, the owners of the buildings are now offering special deals: "rent for three years and get one year rent free."[92]

Empty for seven years since its completion and sold to the Zhongsheng Investment Company in 1996, even before occupation, the brand new four-story Shenzhen Tourist Center will be demolished to make way for a multi-use complex. Replacing the tourist center will be the foundation of two new twenty-eight-story towers, which will include space for offices, hotel, shopping arcade, and restaurants. The new towers will supplement the original 20,000-square-meter floor area with an additional 90,000 square meters.[93]

❀ **Unsold Ratio**
The unsold ratio in Shenzhen is not as troubling as the number indicates. Firstly, it is a strange phenomenon made by artificial overlapping of a real estate market and housing production, which has no common ground. In Shenzhen, during late 1980s and early 1990s, the average construction cost was RMB 1,000–1,500 per square meter, which is one-tenth to one-fifteenth the cost of building in the West or Hong Kong. One explanation for the high sales prices is that the majority of the housing stock was financed by Hong Kong developers and intended to sell to Hong Kong residents. In many cases, one-third of the overall sale would already meet the financial goal. On top of this critical offset between the construction cost and sale price, most of the housing projects are put on the market before construction even begins. It is more critical to developers to get immediate cash flow than long-term assurances of sales, for often their only asset is the land-use right and development permit (and not cash). —QM

Shenzhen Development Center is a forty-three-story-high "comprehensive commercial mansion," consists of offices, a shopping arcade, restaurants, an exhibition hall, a disco club, and a five-star hotel, with tennis courts, a swimming pool, and a helipad on the roof. It is "finished with the latest glass curtain wall and it shines like a gigantic crystal sculpture." Its vacancy rate as of July 1996 was 70 percent.

Shenzhen Tourist Center
Upon completion, the Shenzhen Tourist Center has been empty for seven years and was sold to the Zhongsheng Investment Company in 1996, before ever being occupied. The brand new four-story building is slated for demolition, to make way for a multi-use complex. Replacing the center will be the foundation of two new twenty-eight-story towers, which will include space for offices, hotel, shopping arcade, and restaurants. The new towers will supplement the original 20,000-square-meter floor area with an additional 90,000 square meters.

Luohu Commercial City is a six-story building with a floor area of 71,000 square meters. In 1996, 70 percent of the building was vacant. At its opening in August 1995, two hundred stores were initially registered; but now, only sixty stores are operating, and primarily used as display showcases. Thus, the owners of the buildings are now offering special deals, such as "rent for three years and get one year rent free." The building, located in front of the Luohu train station and encircled by heavy vehicular traffic all day, is nearly impossible to access by pedestrian shoppers.

Building Supply in Shenzhen

Factory

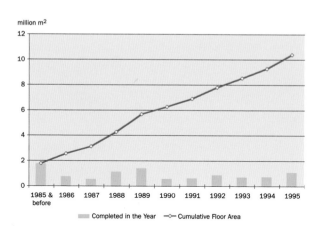

Commercial Space

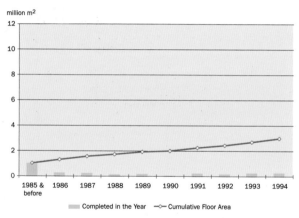

Office Space

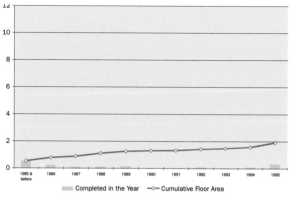

Supply and Demand

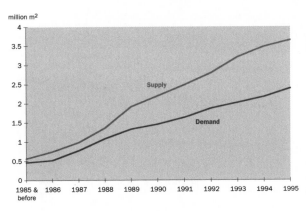

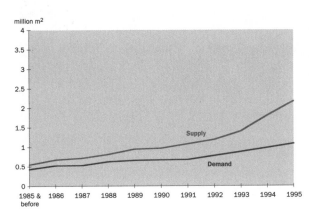

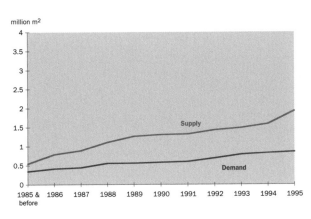

Percent Unsold

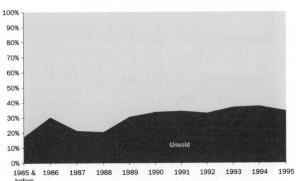

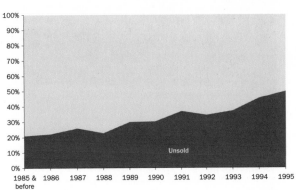

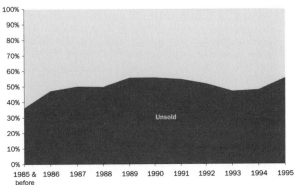

At least five glass-panel curtain wall systems compete in this shopping arcade in
downtown Shenzhen.

CURTAIN WAR©

CURTAIN WAR© A battle between different ARCHITECTURES© to utilize the maximum variety in glass-panel systems on one façade to form a competing whole; includes the use of multiple curtain-wall systems to distinguish separate programs on one façade. The curtain wall in the PRD is no longer associated with simplicity, precision, and tautness, but with a new baroque, assuming a vital role in the PICTURESQUE© order.

Curtain wall, atrium, scenic elevator, and revolving restaurant are four architectural elements which represent modernization in China. Therefore, they become the standard elements seen in all major cities. But, in the PRD, the significance of the curtain wall* has escalated beyond mere element and has come to embody the ideals of the GREAT LEAP FORWARD© and the optimism of MORE IS MORE©. Diversified curtain wall panels emerge from behind bamboo scaffolds on every building, springing like bamboo shoots after a spring rain. Often one building will contain more than one curtain wall panel system, in some cases at least ten, all forced together to compete with each other in order to compose a whole.

Utilizing multiple curtain wall systems, however, often fails to meet standardization criteria, construction efficiency, and massive prefabrication for curtain wall construction. For instance, although creating mechanized airflow is indispensable in an enclosed curtain wall building, many operate without air conditioners or mechanical ventilation systems. To save electricity and overall costs, air conditioners and mechanical ventilation systems are either not designed or not operational. Operable panels for emergency exits are popped open for natural ventilation and for the installation of window air-conditioning units. At one construction site, galvanized angles used to fix the aluminum frames holding the glass panels, had holes burned into them without further re-galvanization.

Glass curtain walls in China entail a new expression, divergent from the Western version. The corporate image expressed by the slick glass surfaces, perfection in construction, alienation from the outside world, and costly maintenance is not present. Rather, the curtain wall is merely used as a symbol for modernization and technological advancement, which satisfies Chinese cities' desires to proclaim their commercial eminence to the world. For example, the Shenzhen Development Center boasted a finish of "the latest glass curtain wall, shinning like a gigantic crystal sculpture."[94]

❋ Curtain Wall
Curtain wall construction is another facilitator of Shenzhen speed. If the structural frame and floors can be built at a speed of 2.5 floors per day, the timber and glass panel system is the only candidate to match. Flexibility is the second advantage provided by curtain wall construction. Glass can be cut into any shape and turned in any direction. With the right sealant, it can even be transformed into curtain roof. Because a sophisticated curtain-wall system can be costly, Shenzhen has localized their manufacture to make it more affordable. Instead of the double-layered, low-E, transparent type, the localized curtain wall is highly reflective and tinted with sharp but environmentally friendly colors such as blue, green, and brown, sometimes purple. All these strategies have reduced the cost dramatically. For the first time, it liberated design creativity with lower cost and higher speed. —QM

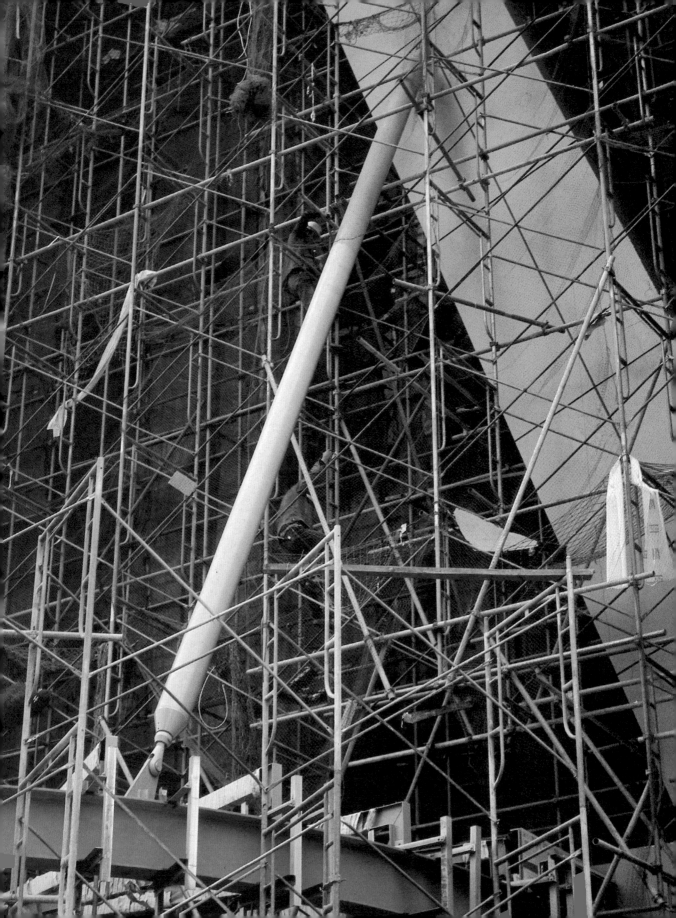

華加日暴增

The labor intensive bamboo scaffolds are used in curtain-wall construction in Shenzhen. Like the curtain walls competing in color and shape, bamboo scaffolds, too, are customized for each building.

The history of function turnovers in the original Huafa Electronics Factory Building can be observed from the different claddings of the façade. The window-tuned panels, popped-open operable panels, aluminum panels, and large fixed-glass windows are different systems forced into a competing whole.

During the construction process, operable
glass panels (intended for emergency exits)
are propped open for natural ventilation.

新闻大厦 招租 电话 22739334

Once the building is completed and in use, its operable glass panels continue to be propped open. The smooth and taut finish of the typical curtain wall facade is compromised for natural ventilation since many buildings operate without air conditioners or mechanical ventilation systems.

The operable glass panels for emergency
exits are propped open to hold air conditioning units, and used as windows with
canopies from which to hang laundry.

FACTORY/HOTEL/OFFICE/HOUSING/PARKING© The status of all floor space in the PRD is generic. Each programmatic function is provisional, and every occupancy is only temporary. A consequence of MORE IS MORE© in which the changing market force buildings to transform rapidly to accommodate multiple uses.

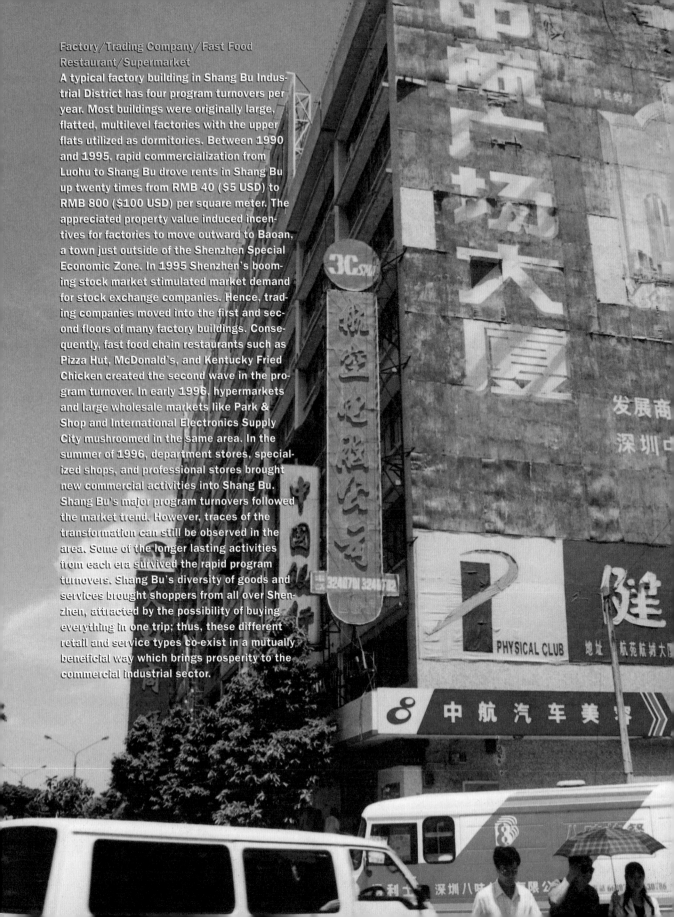

Factory/Trading Company/Fast Food Restaurant/Supermarket

A typical factory building in Shang Bu Industrial District has four program turnovers per year. Most buildings were originally large, flatted, multilevel factories with the upper flats utilized as dormitories. Between 1990 and 1995, rapid commercialization from Luohu to Shang Bu drove rents in Shang Bu up twenty times from RMB 40 ($5 USD) to RMB 800 ($100 USD) per square meter. The appreciated property value induced incentives for factories to move outward to Baoan, a town just outside of the Shenzhen Special Economic Zone. In 1995 Shenzhen's booming stock market stimulated market demand for stock exchange companies. Hence, trading companies moved into the first and second floors of many factory buildings. Consequently, fast food chain restaurants such as Pizza Hut, McDonald's, and Kentucky Fried Chicken created the second wave in the program turnover. In early 1996, hypermarkets and large wholesale markets like Park & Shop and International Electronics Supply City mushroomed in the same area. In the summer of 1996, department stores, specialized shops, and professional stores brought new commercial activities into Shang Bu. Shang Bu's major program turnovers followed the market trend. However, traces of the transformation can still be observed in the area. Some of the longer lasting activities from each era survived the rapid program turnovers. Shang Bu's diversity of goods and services brought shoppers from all over Shenzhen, attracted by the possibility of buying everything in one trip; thus, these different retail and service types co-exist in a mutually beneficial way which brings prosperity to the commercial industrial sector.

Hotel/Office/Retail/Recreation/Restaurant
Hotels[113] in Shenzhen have acquired roles in addition to providing accommodations for travelers. When the Shenzhen Economic Zone was established in 1979 after the implementation of the Open-Door Policy, there were shortages in luxury residences, office buildings, and commercial space for businessmen and travelers. Hotels were among the first to provide these accommodations before sufficient buildings could be built. Since hotels easily provide facilities such as restaurants, conference, business and recreational centers, hotels became the most accessible buildings, providing instantaneous floor space for other programs. The "hotel" becomes a complex with independently operational functions, accessible not only to guests, but also to the public. The function of a hotel frequently becomes a minor part of the multi-operational "hotel."

Stadium/Night Club/Car Dealer/
Car Repair/Driving School

By day, Shenzhen Stadium is an athletic facility, by night it is a nightclub. The Chicago Club and Mexico Club are twenty meters away from each other at the Shenzhen Stadium, each with its own entrance, both located under the staircase of the bleachers. At the entrance to the clubs, the stadium's green field encircled by an orange running track can be seen through a glazed wall. Although the Chicago Club only opened in April 1995 and the Mexico Club followed in six months, their low-profit strategy allowed them to take over the night recreational business quickly, so that by the end of 1995, their names were synonymous with Shenzhen nightlife. The original intent of the Chicago Club was to provide sports fans with a place to watch live games, introducing the phrase "sports bar" to the Chinese vocabulary. These clubs turned an otherwise remote and underutilized stadium into an affordable snack-disco-beer-bar. Ball games are rarely played in the stadium these days, as other activities have entered the facility. Car dealers and repair services have taken over the entire space underneath the bleachers, and a driving school uses the parking lot as a practice course. Although Shenzhen Stadium is now everything besides a sports stadium, it is utilized twenty-four hours a day.

Although beset with legal and management
problems, Yi Jing Garden is the oldest high-
class residential development in Shenzhen,
consisting of detached houses and seven-
story walk-up apartments. Replete with
facilities such as kindergarten, corner gro-
cery stores, playgrounds, parks, hair salons,
and a pharmacy, Yi Jing Garden is a self-
sufficient environment. A master plan of the
development, a sculpture, and a plaque with
inscriptions reading "Excellent Residential
Environment Award" are displayed in front of
its community park. Although intended for
residential use, 80 percent of the single-family houses in Yi Jing have been adopted as
offices and government institutes. The only
hint of their non-residential use is the signs
hanging on their front doors. In some, the
first floor is used as office and second floor
as living quarter. Additions of elaborated
Chinese temple roof, curtain wall wrapping
in the terrace, brightly colored tile cladding,
and high walls at the property line have
mutated most detached houses from their
original form. The only similarity among all
houses is the "steel chicken cage" placed
for protection over every window and door.

Factory/Bowling Center
The "Berlin Bowling Center" is located on the third floor of a factory building. A neon sign covering the entire second floor of a factory has an arrow directing customers to the entrance on the side of the building. The large external staircase leads to the blue entry canopy on the third floor, which is supported by four round columns covered with mirror-like panels. At ten o'clock in the morning, only two customers are in the forty-lane bowling center. The lights are turned off and no natural light can enter the building. A man behind the semicircular snack bar near the bowling lanes takes drink orders. A can of Coke costs RMB 50 ($6.25 USD) All the equipment—lanes and balls—are imports from the United States. With the finished floor and ceiling, the net clearance of the bowling area is less than two meters.

Department Store/Dormitory/Game Room
In a department store, construction was in progress in one of its U-shaped wings. A terrace and additional stairs in the atrium were being added. A neon sign reading "Recreational Town" has been put in front of a gigantic, nearly completed game room. Only one wing of the dormitories on upper floors is being occupied. The connecting corners between the dormitory and other commercial floors have been cut off, so all the linking doors have been turned into solid walls.

Multi-use Booths
At least one hundred booths per floor are
selling electronic parts in the International
Electronics Supply City and fifty shoe stores
are selling shoes of similar styles, colors,
materials, and prices in the Shoe Town. The
shops and booths are all lined up neatly in
columns and rows, allowing easy access for
customers. Most buildings are not finished,
thus leaving the original structure of the
factory building exposed.

Office Building/Entertainment Center/
Game Zone/Food Court
Occupying an entire wing of the third floor of
an office building in Futian, this entertainment floor has games found in a typical American amusement park. Stuffed-animals and
advertisements are hung from the exposed
structure of the unfinished dropped ceiling.

Office Building/Entertainment Center/
Game Zone/Food Court
The other wing on the third floor of the same
office building is a Western-Oriental fast-food
court. The offerings range from fried chicken
to hamburgers to Chinese food. The colorful
neon lights and the arrays of advertisements
decorated the exposed ceiling. Loud music
and the televisions are playing at the same
time. "No photos" signs are attached on the
columns in the middle of the food court.

妇儿医院超负荷 医者患者两无奈

吊瓶挂在树枝上

The Shenzhen Women and Children's Hospital suffers from poor conditions due to a severe shortage of necessary facilities.

【本报讯】住在莲花北村的谢小姐可说是祸不单行，她家的天花板在昨天连续两次坠下水泥板砸块，还差一点把人给砸了。

昨天凌晨3时，住在莲花北村66栋305房的谢小姐正在熟睡，突然被一声巨响震

一声巨响惊睡梦
大块水泥砸在床

醒，只见主人房的天花板上掉下了一块约1平方米大小的水泥板砸块下来。掉下来的水泥板砸块正好落在大床的床尾，差一点就把她给砸了，顿时谢小组吓得脸如土色。

谁知祸不单行，当日早上约9点，谢小姐家的客厅天花

板又掉下一块水泥下来，此时幸好谢小姐外出找管理处的同志，才安然无恙。

记者昨天下午来到谢小姐家，只见她家客厅的中央出现了一个约1.5平方米的缺口，客厅满地都是摔烂的水泥板砸块，主人房亦同样有一个大缺

口，一些水泥块还残留在床边。

市住宅局闻讯后，立即派人到现场勘查，表示尽快为住户维修房屋。据了解，从上月至今，该住宅小区已有4户居民家的天花板发生水泥块坠落。

（锦言）

A woman living in Shenzhen's Lotus Village was awakened by a loud thud at three o'clock in the morning when one square meter of concrete slab fell down in her bedroom. After waking up, she found that another 1.5 square meter piece of concrete ceiling had fallen in her living room. Four similar incidents had already occurred in Lotus Village. Clipping by Yang Jin, "Awakened by a Loud Sound: A Large Concrete Piece Fell in Bed," *Shenzhen Special Zone Daily* (1996).

While high-priced commodity buildings are over-supplied, private developers do not construct enough hospitals, factory dormitories, and affordable housing for which there is an urgent demand. Nor can infrastructural facilities (sewage, power) provide adequate or reliable service. The imbalance between the oversupplied commodity buildings and the undersupplied basic necessities illustrates the phenomenon of obsession with "quantity" or "bigness" which heeds the systems of capital—fueling the demand for quantity—rather than responding to the needs of the population.

Even though the Shenzhen's Women and Children's Hospital opened in 1984, its facilities are below 1970s standards in China. With the total land area of less than 10,000 square meters and the total floor area only 16,000 square meters, space for adequate service is insufficient.[96] The hospital was designed for an urban population of 300,000, but since its opening, outpatient service has increased from 300 patients a day to 1,300 in 1995, with peak activity at 2,300. The number of child-births in the hospital has increased from 500 to 5,000 per year within a decade, with one-fifth of all childbirths in Shenzhen taking place here. Due to insufficient hospital beds, more than 1,000 sick children could not be hospitalized in 1996. Spaces not originally intended for medical use have been re-programmed: the 100 square-meter clinic lobby accommodates an average of 200 children in need intravenous drips daily; and the garden has been converted into an "outdoor hospital" populated by parents holding drip bottles, or even bottles hung on trees.[97]

Even when facilities are constructed, they are built to be larger and taller without care for practical need. The construction of the future city hospital in downtown Shenzhen was halted after 30,000 square meters had already been excavated for the foundation. The original design for the hospital included a seven-story clinic building, a nine-story administrative building, a twenty-five-story ward building, a training center, and a pharmacy. The budget for the project was RMB 380 million ($47.5 million USD). After officials and representatives from the Public Health Bureau and the City Planning Office met on the site, "the design was criticized for being too advanced and too lavish . . . a twenty-five-story ward is too tall; it does not suit the medical needs," said the head of Public Health Bureau. A final decision was made to compress the ward to a twelve-story building, to eliminate the training center and the pharmacy, and to reduce the distance between the clinic and ward. According to the project's engineers, reworking the foundation would waste RMB 1–2 million ($125,000–250,000 USD) for work already completed. Nevertheless, future costs would be reduced by RMB 10 million ($1.25 million USD). "Reduce scale, better structure, without compromising functions; quickly construct a high-standard comprehensive hospital," was the new target according to the *Shenzhen Special Zone Daily*.[98]

No matter how fast urban infrastructure facilities are constructed to keep pace with rapid architecture developments, the increased capacities for power and sewage plants, and telecommunication networks can never satisfy the demand generated by new building construction. According to statistics provided by the Shenzhen Planning Department, sewage treatment plants in Shenzhen can only provide 30 percent of the current demand. Sewage facilities are only sufficient for 50 to 60 percent of new construction. The main reason for this discrepancy is that construction of infrastructural facilities is largely sponsored by the Shenzhen government, while construction of buildings is sponsored by private capital.

At the same time, China is wasting its limited land supply. China has 7 percent of the world's

This construction site appeared to be a duckweed pond at first sight in the torn-down section of Shenzhen's old town. Although the pond suggested the construction had halted for a while, the activities and the temporary labor housing on the site indicated that the construction was in progress.

Among all problematic buildings, the high-risk group was the "five-lack buildings," which were built by farmers in the villages and towns without the five essentials: design, drawings, permits, construction supervision, inspections, and reports. In April 1995, a seven-story housing project collapsed entirely in the Jiangxi Province. In December, an eight-story office building in Sichuan Province collapsed before it was ever occupied. "Five-lack buildings" were responsible for the collapse or dangerous state of one-eighth of the 700 million square meters of rural buildings completed between 1982 and 1983, according to the *Shenzhen Commercial Daily* (18 July 1996).

farmland, which feeds 22 percent of the world's population. Nevertheless, according to government's statistics, there are more than 3,000 large-scale parcels of land put together by developers which have been left vacant and undeveloped.[99] The government claims that improper "land flow" within the real estate market is the inherent problem. Organizations with developing power are unable to claim development sites, landlord institutes and companies needing urgent capital do not sell their "golden sites," moreover, large corporations with sufficient capital do not have access to downtown parcels. Consequently, the market is not effectively stimulated. This urgency in preparing land for development thus decreases the economy of China's limited farmland.

Even when commercial buildings are erected with great speed and abundance, they are not planned for efficient access, so many commercial areas have become neglected. The Luohu Commercial City has been a meager success since its opening because of its poor siting and entry locations. Although the first floor is reserved for public facilities and the second to sixth floors are commercial spaces, there is no direct pedestrian access to the building. Located in front of the train station, with heavy vehicular traffic looping around the building all day, the only safe route to enter the building is through its neighboring immigration building. There is neither surface parking nor a parking garage available. One store owner complained, "Not one person has entered my store in ten days."[100] Although sold as the "National Gateway's First City," it is now an "urban island" isolated in a sea of cars.[101]

Poor Construction

Speedy design and construction have created "more is less" problems, which are impossible to remedy in China. According to a survey conducted on building inspections for problematic buildings in 1995, 40 percent of the problems were associated with design. Poor construction accounted for 30 percent, bad material and other issues accounted for another 30 percent of the problems. Leakage in roofs and ceilings, peelings of walls, unclosable windows and doors, and foundation settlements were the most common problems found in the building inspections. In 1995, during the rainy season in Shenzhen, many buildings constructed with hollow bricks had severe leakage. The extensive complaints received by the government agencies led to doubts of whether hollow bricks were a proper building material. It was only after an investigation conducted in a manufacturing plant that the name of the hollow brick was cleared. The cause of the problem was proven to be poor construction rather than hollow bricks.[102]

According to a survey conducted by the Department of National Construction in Beijing, of the 700 million square meters of rural building completed between 1982 and 1983, one-eighth is deemed to have collapsed or to have been in a dangerous state within the first year simply due to a lack of technical supervision.[103]

Hybrid Buildings

In most Asian cities, five stories is the height limitation for walk-up apartments, a number derived from a calculation of cost efficiency and human physical tolerance. In China, seven stories is the official maximum height for walk-up apartments. But, because of many factors, the number of levels is often raised to unbelievable heights. With the introduction of split-level designs and the utilization of escalators in commercial spaces at ground level, residents enter the building one-half or one-story up or down from the ground entry. These devices add extra levels to walk-up apartments so maximum heights can be extended to eight stories.

In downtown Shenzhen, there is a fifteen-story apartment building without an elevator. It is a hybrid of highrise and walk-up typologies. When first built, it was one of the few highrise buildings in Luohu. Without providing the essential vertical circulation, even though the marriage

A highrise walk-up.

of the two typologies challenge the physical toler-ance of its residents, the building is fully occu-pied. Does this hybrid building represent a new housing type for China?

Illegal Structures

"More is less" is evident as a result of fast developments, where loopholes were not only created in the process of design and construc-tion, but also in management and property transactions. Many apartment complexes are poorly managed, illegal structures, developed through a "collective fund," wherein projects built with funds raised by high-tech enterprises and government agencies for the companies and agencies themselves.[104] To support these high-tech enterprises and governmental agen-cies, the Shenzhen Municipal Government had reduced land fees for these self-developing pro-jects. No property could be sold or transferred as a profit-generating commodity in the market. All economic activities were restricted by the government, the co-owner of the houses of the "collective fund" projects.

Residents of one illegal complex, Yi Feng Gar-den, awoke one morning to discover that "overnight, the houses they purchased no longer belonged to them."[105] Sen Da, its developing company had gone bankrupt. Since the property deed belonged solely to the company and was mortgaged, the apartments were to be auc-tioned. Residents had to buy back their proper-ties from the bank, although they had already purchased their units. Furthermore, the apart-ment building was oversold. Nine units were dou-ble-sold; the residents who arrived first could claim their units. While waiting for a resolution, people who bought units that were occupied could only build and live in temporary structures in the parking lots.

Notwithstanding the skyrocketing prices for real estate in 1992 and 1993, a 50 to 60 per-cent price increase from 1991 tempted many government agencies. At the sight of profits, developing agencies sidestepped the laws and illegally advertised these housing projects as commodity housing. Although individual property ownership certificates cannot be obtained (because the unit price for "collective fund" pro-jects are on average 20 to 35 percent cheaper than commodity housing), many buyers are seduced by the "collective fund" developments. According to an unofficial 1996 estimate, there were at least one million square meters of "col-lective fund" housing in stock. These projects not only disturbed the real estate market, but caused disputes between buyers and develop-ers. Since the contract between the developer and the buyer was illegal, the consumer's rights were not protected by law.

The problems caused by the "collective fund" housing projects created a difficult situation for the Land Bureau and the Planning Department of Shenzhen. The Land Bureau retained, fined, con-fiscated, or dismantled buildings according to the different effects they had on the urban environ-ment of Shenzhen. Also, additional construction of amenities and infrastructure were undertaken by the government to remedy the problems and reduce residents' anxieties.

FLOATING© A migrant condition, held by two-thirds of Shenzhen's population, who do not have jobs, legal status, or homes
in the SEZs, yet are officially registered in their original provinces
of residence. Attracted to the hyperdevelopment of the coastal
cities and the SEZs, FLOATERS© form mobile reservoirs of flexible labor, a necessary ingredient for SHENZHEN SPEED©.

Shenzhen's Population, 1979–1995

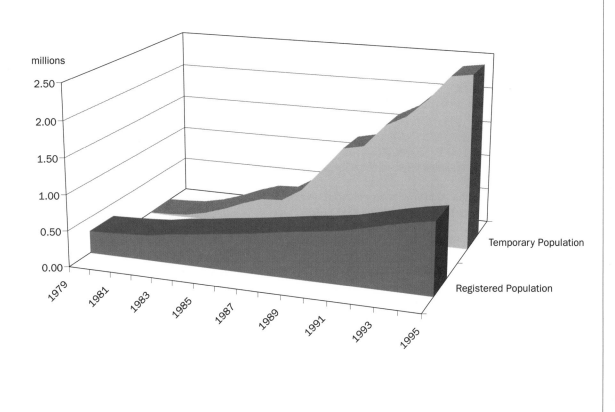

As a condition of "more is less," FLOATING© is a temporary situation that affects two-thirds of Shenzhen's population. Most temporary residents are service industry staff, factory laborers, or construction workers who have come from farming villages and neighboring countries to participate in hyperdevelopment. With these new residents, Shenzhen's population had tripled and re-tripled within sixteen years, from 3.1 to 34.5 million, a 1640-fold increase of the temporary population.[106] According to the Shenzhen Statistics Department, the number of temporary residents between 1979 and 1994 increased from 1,500 to 2,459,600.

Even with these figures, the exact number of the floating population is difficult to determine. The Shenzhen Municipal Government could not keep accurate files on rental units and their occupants, whose majority are *san wu ren kou* or "three-no's-people" (people with no job, no registration, and no home). Often, these residents cannot be filed, because landlords underreport or do not report them at all, to avoid paying an 18 percent tax on collected rent. In 1995, 2,600 rental units out of the estimated 68,913 in Baoan, and 30 out of 16,000 in Nanshang paid their taxes. In an attempt to register the floating population, in 1996 the Shenzhen Municipal Government installed 1,222 Floating Population Management Stations in locations where rental units are concentrated.[107]

Because living costs are too high, more than 900,000 people (one-quarter of Shenzhen's population) live in 250,000 rental units which are frequently overcrowded and poorly managed.[108] Fire codes, safety regulations, and minimum living conditions are often not met. In Baoan, 500 laborers live in an overcrowded 1,000 square-meter factory dormitory that has few exits and one narrow corridor. On January 1, 1996, an uncontrollable fire took fifty-six lives. The tragedy was a direct result of high density, inadequate fire escapes, insufficient fire extinguishers, and flammable construction materials. Only after this incident did poor living conditions and violations in rental regulations draw "official" attention.[109]

Another crucial reason for the inadequacy of residences is the severe shortage in affordable housing and the overabundance of high-priced commodity housing which the majority of the population cannot afford. Of the 62 percent of housing projects constructed in Shenzhen between 1979 and 1994, commodity housing comprised 50 percent. As previously mentioned, housing prices were already twice as much as the high end of the international standard. The majority of the temporary residents, the "immigrants" who work day and night to support the industries in Shenzhen, cannot afford these accommodations. Even professionals with moderate incomes cannot afford to buy homes without bank loans. However, the financial structure in China is so underdeveloped that only a limited number of commodity housing developments are allowed to be purchased with mortgage payments.[110]

Instead, only those who can afford inflated housing prices are being targeted by commodity housing developers. A survey in the 1995 China Market Report suggested that the top 10 percent of the richest people in China own nearly 50 percent of China's private wealth. The wealth accumulated was mostly generated from transactions in the stock market, real estate market, security and bond markets. Since regulations in the financial system are not yet well established, there are many loopholes through which bribery and other illegal practices routinely fall through. "Just by using absolute power and making use of the government's capital, enormous amounts of private wealth are collected and redistributed in a very short time."[111] The majority of the 7.2 billion square meters of housing sold in 1995 was high-end commodity housing.

A FLOATING© Life 1

Behind the Seibu Department Store is the hub for the floating population in downtown Luohu. Everyday in the heat of summer, topless men sleep on the balcony of a group of five- and eight-story walk-up apartments, for it is more comfortable to sleep outdoors than indoors. "There is no fan, no air, no light, and no space in these rooms," said John Huang Liu, a temporary resident who lived in this neighborhood when he first arrived in the Shenzhen SEZ. Because the living spaces are too small, people spend more time on the street than in the buildings.

This area is the only place in downtown Luohu where the floating population can stay without being checked. Anyone can stay for RMB 60 a night without giving a name or any personal information. Many people first lived here when they arrived in the SEZ. To accommodate the growing life in this area, the buildings expanded outward and upward. Not only were additional rooms constructed with corrugated steel sheets on the roofs and balconies, internal staircases were converted into rooms. It is unclear whether the vertical columns supporting the added-on external staircases slightly bent are due to heavy traffic or poor construction.

Liu spent two months in a three-bedroom unit with two families in an eight-story apartment building. His room was three square meters. The two families, each consisting of two parents and two children, occupied the two 6-square-meter rooms. The landlord turned a large part of the living room into his room. The unfinished plywood partition blocked the only windows in the space, leaving the remaining living room extremely dark even on a bright day. All nine residents shared one bathroom, one kitchen, and one truncated living room. The building's staircase and rooftop are strewn with garbage, junk, and water puddles. Web-like antenna and phone lines cross everywhere on the roof. The five-story apartments across the street only sit 0.7 to 2 meters apart from each other on all sides. Through these narrow slits, the windows and front doors rarely receive sunlight. Kitchen exhaust blows from one apartment to another. Corner stores, barbershops, and other supporting facilities have claimed enclaves inside this self-sufficient "walled village."

Of his experience there, Liu related: "Eighty percent of the people living in these five-story apartments are prostitutes or drug addicts. When I was living here, I frequently heard and saw the police busting into the apartments at night. In the beginning, I was very curious and always wanted to check it out. However, the frequency made it so normal that I began to live without noticing anything in the end . . . if you have a camera in your hands, they might think you are turning them in with evidence . . . the conditions do not improve because the buildings are owned by an official."

全统计, 深圳现有外来打工者数百万人, 其中大约有70多万人住在出租屋

在拥挤简陋的出租屋中相互关心、相互提携, 共同创造着属于自己的家

悲亦喜出租屋

A FLOATING© Life 2

The living conditions in Baoan, an industrial town just outside of the SEZ, is no better for the floating population. There is no formal contract between lessee and lessor. Owners of the apartments post ads when there is vacancy. The security deposit is the only tie between the two parties.

The scarcity of space is so extreme that often one bed is shared by at least two people, with about twelve people sharing a room of 20 square meters. For rental units in the Da Yang Tian industrial area of Baoan, each bed is shared by at least two people. A paper screen is the only provision of privacy. A story in the local newspaper *Shenzhen Commercial Daily* described "an eighteen-year old girl [who] sandwiched between two males in her room, went to sleep everyday wearing jeans and a belt tied into knots."

A FLOATING© Life 3

The shops on the street in front of the Chao-Shan village are all family-owned liquor and cigarette wholesalers. Each family lives in one or two floors of the "steel-skin houses" added above the store owned by the family. In one case, the Wong family's seven members and two relatives share two rooms on the second floor of his shop, while two workers live on the third floor in a 1.5 meter by 2.5 meter steel-skin house. Like the Wong family, storeowners on the street began working a decade ago as laborers doing any work available. After saving enough money, each individual built his own house and business.

According to the Wong family patriarch, "Everyone who was here earlier between 1980 and 1988 has made money . . . then, we built our own houses and shops . . . it is very easy since we all had been construction workers at some point in the past." There was no land fee at the time, and everyone just claimed a plot and built along the street with the cheapest material they could find. Although corrugated steel sheets are the cheapest and easiest with which to build, they trap heat in the hot and humid summer and are unstable structures susceptible to fire. Several years ago, a fire burned down more than ten homes and stores on the street. The fire spread quickly, destroying nearly

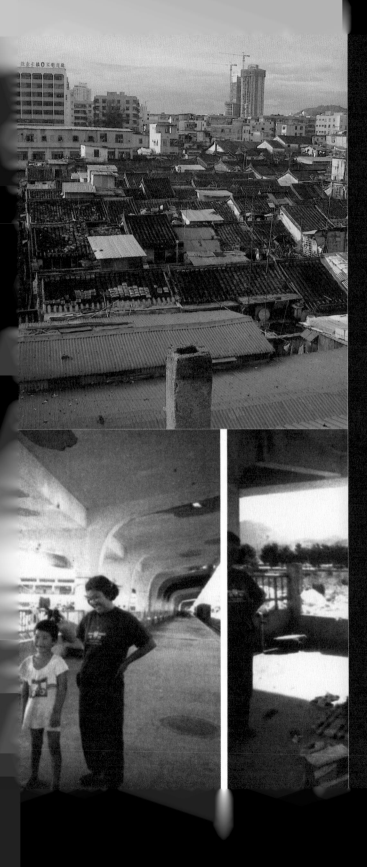

everything. Like other shop owners on the street, the Wongs started from zero again after the fire. But they are millionaires today.

A FLOATING© Life 4
On the east side of Shenzhen, the Chao-Shan village houses the floating population of two Guangdong cities from which it takes its name: Chaozhou and Shantou. Farmers who had lived here previously all moved to highrise apartments after making enough money in early years of Shenzhen's development. The original village people sold the land-use right of their collective land and developed a twelve-story office build-ing across the street from the village.

A FLOATING© Life 5
Many in the floating population do not have cov-ered shelter in Shenzhen. Xiaoyan, a seven-year-old girl, her two brothers, and her parents live on the platform of a cargo train terminal in Shenzhen, their second home. Two or three times every year, when there is no field work in their home province of Anhui, they travel to Shenzhen and other cities by hopping onto cargo trains. "Whenever we get caught, we just hop down and wait for the next train that comes by," Xiaoyan's father said. To make a living in the off-season, Xiaoyan and her family recycle materials found in junk yards, garbage bins, warehouses, and markets. As a third job, Xiaoyan is one of a group of young "pro-fessional beggars" stationed outside Shenzhen's five-star Shangri-la Hotel and train station.

Xiaoyan's mother once went to Hong Kong by hiding beneath a train, in the gap between the spare tires which is just large enough for a human body. Although she was caught by Hong Kong Police at the train station upon arrival, her three-day stay in the prison before being deported was positive. "Hong Kong policemen were nice and courteous. . . . I had three meals everyday and every meal had meat!" she said. Although the train platform is inconvenient as a home, every year Xiaoyan's family returns. "Beijing, Shanghai, Guangzhou— we have tried many places already. Still, Shenzhen has the most to pick from." From "Floating Home," *Focus* (December 1995–January 1996) 64.

市中心医院设计过于超前怎么办？市领导与有关部门负责人现场办公确定——

规模缩小结构优化功能不减
尽快建成高水平综合性医院

【本报讯】（记者滕礼）昨天下午，骄阳如火。李子彬、李德成、王炬、袁汝稳四位领导与市规划局、卫生局等有关部门负责同志在市中心医院现场办公，并将这所医院规划过于超前的住院楼"砍"去一半。

这所我市未来最大型医院尚未完成桩基工程，预计投入3.8亿元，是市政府为民办实事项目。记者看到为桩基而挖的坑像一个巨型大口，面积近3万平方米，正在停工待建。市卫生局同志向市长介绍：按原设计的规划，包括7层高的门诊楼、9层高的一级科室楼和25层高的住院大楼。规划中还有一个制剂室和一个培训中心。设计十分超前，工程十分巨大。

李子彬等沉吟不语。

在此之前，有关这一工程建设规模曾一再引起过争论。渐渐地，一种意见被谨慎地提出来：能否收缩规模，降低造价，减少投资，集中精力尽可能快地建一所高水平的综合性大医院？在未来医院的模型面前，卫生局长周俊安说："现在看，25层住院楼太高了，不符合医学要求。而且要10部电梯，建成后运行费用也相当可观。病房是按每间1—2人设计，也过于超前。我走了国外五、六十间医院，很少见有哪间公立医院如此奢华的。"

李子彬、李德成、王炬和袁汝稳仔细询问：按现在设计，3.8亿元能不能拿下来？一级科室能否并到门诊楼和住院楼去？如果改动，现在的桩基有没有用？重新修改设计要多长时间，浪费将有多少？

卫生局、规划局和负责设计的工程师谈了自己的看法。大家赞同优化结构，降低造价。制剂室和培训中心可以砍去。修改设计、重新打桩从眼前看会浪费一、二百万元，但从长远看起码可节省一个亿。

在详细听了各方面意见后，李子彬说，住院楼压缩到12层，门诊楼保持不变，病房设计容量大些。这样功能不减，结构优化，又能一气呵成。至于门诊楼与住院楼之间距离是否缩小，一级科室楼如何分化，病房与职能部门之间分配比例，这些都需要由专家去定，市长也不能包办。总的原则是用尽可能少的钱办最多的事，办得科学、合理。

他最后问道："能不能保证在1998年底给市民建起一所设备先进、功能齐全的大医院？"在场同志朗声回答："没问题。"

"Contemporary architecture in China is like a person who has been starving for a long time. He doesn't need a gourmet meal; he needs something that will nourish him," writes S. Stiebomg in "Building in China: The Promise, Problems, Perspectives," *Progressive Architecture* (March 1996).

LESS FOR MORE

Restrictive regulations on construction and design began to surface in 1995. By 1996 the *Shenzhen Special Zone Daily* announced, "Psychological and physical states of buyers and sellers are maturing soberly." Not only have local regulations been implemented, provincial policies are established to control further rapid increases. The "Huge and Sudden Profit Era" of the real estate market has ended, declared the *Shenzhen Special Zone Daily*.

To regulate the quality of construction, the government suspended the licenses of fifty construction firms from outside Shenzhen in 1995. Within six months, the construction of two hundred housing units was forced to stop due to poor quality. Shenzhen began regulating its own construction industry according to national standards in July 1996. As a new policy, national standard documents (including two certificates and one report) are required before construction commences. Moreover, design and construction issues which had been previously ignored begin to surface.

To stabilize real estate property prices, which had doubled for commodity housing and office space between 1990 and 1992, the Land Bureau of Shenzhen initiated regulations to control development, supervise transactions in real estate property exchange centers, and limit the supply of land plots.[112] The central government also stopped providing bank loans and reduced financial incentives.

Luxury commodity buildings and projects in Guangdong Province were overdeveloped to the extent that Guangdong's Provincial Government declared "no new land will be approved from August 1996 to the end of 1997 for any new commodity building developments."[113] Land transfers from technological and industrial developments into luxury residential, resort, golf, and recreational developments were restricted. To prevent further imbalances between luxury and affordable housing, "high class" projects were restricted to 18 percent of all developments annually.[114] To absorb some of the oversupplied buildings, the government bought vacant luxury-developments and commodity housing units.[115] Sixty-five percent of all rental units (amounting to 8.5 million square meters) have now established management systems.

All of these new regulations, however, were not implemented to halt development completely but to promote more equal development so that modernization could occur more evenly throughout the Shenzhen SEZ. Finally, the social costs of new developments are being considered. For example, the government effectively "digested" the overbuilt luxury developments and commodity housing by selling or leasing them as affordable or low-income units.[116] An already-built area of 29 billion square meters of will be rebuilt according to higher-quality standards.[117] Rural housing will receive more attention than urban housing, with volumes of 3 billion and 1.2 billion square meters, respectively, expected to be built, while housing construction is kept at annual increase of 15 percent. In 2000, the area of urbanization will increase from 28 percent to 35 percent, with 230 new towns and cities added. Development will continue in Shenzhen according to broader urban planning goals.

Min Qi

When *min qi*, which translates literally to "people's energy," or public enthusiam, is high, impossibilities can be overcome and irremediable conditions overlooked. Although conditions in Shenzhen appear to be dramatic, the city operates with an elegance, different from the scientific version of the West. It operates with an unimaginable optimism and indifference to logic.

I found a stamp store while I was wandering in the podium of Fu-Shing Garden, the twenty-eight-story residential tower where I lived in Futien. I have been collecting stamps for twenty years because stamps are indicators for important activities, people, and culture for each country. The first two sets of stamps that caught my eyes were "Making the City Green" and "Making the Desert Green." They were both printed in early 1990s. "How ridiculous" was my immediate reaction to seeing "Making the Desert Green." Nevertheless, the title is charged with incredible optimism. It implies China's confidence in challenging impossibilities.

The subtitles for "Making the City Green" are: "Constructing a Green Great Wall; Flourishing Forestry Brings Prosperous Living; The Citizen's Obligation in Planting Trees; Making the City Green and Beautifying the City."

When real estate prices were decreasing in 1995, newspapers were filled with statements such as: "the market is in the digestive stage but is under stable development"; "the prices are stable but falling"; "the market is calm, but soberly maturing"; and "seeing hot in cold; prosperity is growing from desolation." [118] These statements show that a zealous optimism drives *min qi* to overlook unfavorable conditions. For example, in response to the housing vacancy of 1.81 million square meters in Shenzhen in 1995, the Deputy Director of Land Bureau of Shenzhen replied:

"If we look at other commodities such as watches, televisions, and bikes, the overstock is much more than real estate property in terms of percentage . . . the overstock is in the environment and the climate. Overstock does not mean un-saleable. Shenzhen has a population of 3.35 million. Sale of 1.65 million and pre-selling 2.0 million square meters in floor area is already great."[119]

Min qi also helps change a present difficulty into a bright prospect for the future. People can see empty buildings as a sign that China thoroughly anticipates a great and prosperous future, when every building will be filled. According to Zheng Lei, a private architect and developer in Shenzhen, "We are building for the future. If there is no demand presently, it is okay. There are so many people in China, there will be demand some day. We like to see building activities because they represent prosperity."[120] Describing the phases of Shenzhen's anticipated evolution, the *Shenzhen Special Zone Daily* projected, "Tomorrow, Shenzhen people will see a beautiful and poetic design. Next year, Shenzhen people will see a sculpture of the new city center. In the future, Shenzhen people will live in an elegant and advanced modern city."[121]

The unbridled optimism created by *min qi* is analogous to the mentality created by the original Great Leap Forward campaigns. Even when economic disaster was forthcoming, a bright future lay ahead. Encouraging the nation to look beyond the present difficulty, Mao said, "Generally speaking, the overall situation is very good; even though problems are not few, the future is bright."[122]

❀ The **design institute** (*sheji yuan*), like the basic social unit *danwei*, is the only legal entity recognized by the Chinese government in the practice of architecture and construction. A design institute is always affiliated with a sector of industry or a level of governmental hierarchy. By this rule, each ministry is supposed to have at least one design institute and every province, every city, town, county would have their own design institutes. For instance, there is the Aviation Design Institute belonging to the Bureau of Civic Aviation; the Railroad Design Institute belonging to the Ministry of Transportation; the Hydropower Design Institute belonging to the Ministry of Hydropower; the Beijing Municipal Design Institute and the Shanghai Civic Design Institute belonging to their respective cities. A design institute is supposed to receive commissions within this context. The idea is that through internalization of financial, material, and labor transactions, maximum efficiency is achieved. This dynamic is reflected in the opposition of two famous Chinese proverbs: "Fat water does not flow out" (*fei shui bu wai liu*) versus "Sheep wool comes from sheep" (*yang mao chu zai yang shen shang*). Reinterpreted for the contemporary socialist dilemma, the proverbs become: "global idealism" (*quan qiu guan nian*) versus "local protectionism" (*di fang bao hu zhu yi*).

Since the economic reform took place during the early 1980s, design institutes have undergone a series of changes. The most obvious among them is the propagation of new design institutes. Trade boundaries and administrative hierarchies are demolished; new design institutes are granted for newly established businesses ranging from entertainment groups to educational institutions. Another critical shift is that job commissions are no longer guaranteed to design institutes by government, which immediately threw the institutes, old and new, out to the street. They are forced to learn the concept of marketing. This alone causes many complexities in the reorganization of design institutes. The traditional large-sized institutes split into many smaller units and many forms. For instance, a design institute would split into a master studio (*da shi gong zuo shi*), a department franchised by courageous young designers/entrepreneurs (*chen bao shi*), and a few designated joint-venture studios (*jin wai he zuo zu*) to name a few. The most significant one, *fen yuan*, is a small branch of an institute. It seems to be a subtle change in form but actually is a complete reinvention in operations, allowing institutes to have branches in many cities—wherever a market exists. This expeditious form of practice contributed largely to the construction of the PRD. The chain of change shifted again in 1994 when the Ministry of City and County Construction and Environmental Protection granted approval for the first group of privately owned design firms. —QM

1. The term "architect" refers to the approximately 40,000 architectural practitioners working in 2,000 registered architecture design institutes and offices in China. The majority of architects in China are not registered or certified by any standardized examinations. The first nationwide registration system, co-sponsored by the China's Ministries of Construction and Ministry of Personnel, was held in November 1995. Therefore, the first group of registered architects emerged in the spring of 1996.

Before the Communists took control of the country in 1949, there were only 200 registered architects in China, mainly in the coastal areas of Shanghai, Tianjin, and Guangzhou. In the early 1960s, the total number of graduates from architectural schools was only about four hundred annually. Since there were no admittances to colleges between 1966 and 1976 (during the Cultural Revolution), no training was available for architects until the annual college entrance examination system was reimplemented in 1977. After 1949 and before 1995, all architectural projects were produced in Soviet-styled design institutes,❀ and the credit of architectural design was given not to an individual designer but to his or her work unit. By law, only the design institutes were qualified to obtain permits for building construction and had license to practice architecture. Still the prevailing model of practice, design institutes employ architects, planners, and engineers in all areas. They are capable of providing full architectural services ranges from schematic design to working drawings. Most are strongly affiliated with universities, drawing design talent from the faculty of prestigious schools of architecture.

Originally, state-owned design institutes served as government design offices. After the advent of real estate development in the 1980s, the state reduced its role in the economy and encouraged private developments. After government subsidies to design institutes were reduced, they reinvented themselves as quasi-private architectural firms and competed in the marketplace.

Rather than register individual designers, the Ministry of Construction grants four classes of registration (A, B, C or D) to design institutes. There are more than 250 Class A design institutes throughout China, with the State Ministry of Construction Institute and six regional institutes being the most important. The large regional institutes often have staffs of more than one thousand and operate branch offices in key cities around the country.

A Class A institute can undertake the design of buildings of any size or type anywhere in the country, whereas those with Class B, C, and D are allowed to work on progressively smaller and less complex buildings in more restricted geographic areas. According to the official statistics of 1994, 97 percent of the two thousand design institutes or architectural firms in China are state-owned, with the remainder classified as collectives.

The Ministry of Construction reviews every design institute annually, assessing the number of its senior architects and engineers and their experience and reputation in order to register any class changes. "Senior architect" is a status and title granted by the Ministry of Construction for an architect who has accumulated many years of experience and has distinguished achievements. Candidates are reviewed by the ministry's "Senior Technical Title Chosen Committee." Senior engineers go through a similar process. "Senior architect" and "senior engineer" are the most prestigious titles and the highest ranks for architects and engineers in China.

The annual registration system was enacted in 1995 to ensure proper standards in design and construction. The goal was also to strive for international recognition in the architectural profession. The government is currently working with the American Institute of Architects to develop a reciprocal-membership system.

Among 9,000 who participated in the first registration examination, 509 passed the complete examination. Architects who graduated between 1971 and 1985 and with nine years of work experience were tested on only four out of nine subjects. Senior architects who graduated before 1970 were registered without taking the examination.

As of June 1997, the total number of registered architects in China was 4,408 (this includes 509 registered architects, 309 specially registered senior architects, and architects registered by passing four subjects). Because part of the registration requires the difficult four-subject examination, many institutes provide false information, or "made experience," for architects in order to increase their registration rates.

Among the 600-architect staff at the Shenzhen General Architectural Design Institute, only one architect had been registered by passing the entire examination. In the city of Shenzhen as a whole, only three architects passed the registration examination. The 1.5 percent registration rate in Shenzhen is very low in comparison to the 5 percent national average. Shenzhen architects claimed to not have enough time to study the published policies and qualification standards. Others claimed that Shenzhen architects were too busy making money, so the incentive to become registered was not high.

Xinhua News Agency (25 October 1995); Grant Sung, "Pacific Rim Country Reports," *Architectural Record* (July 1994): 3; Li Daozhang, "The Teaching of Architecture in China's Institutes of Higher Education," *Chinese Architect* 14, no. 9 (September 1988): 44; Timothy Geisler, "Sprucing Up China's Cities," *China Business Review* (September 1995): 50; Sean Affleck and Helen Goodland, "Changes in China," *Architectural Review* (July 1989): 52; interview with Chang Roumei, architect with the first branch of the Shenzhen General Architectural Design Institute (17 July 1996 and 9 January 1999).
2. Affleck and Goodland, 52.
3. In 1993 there were 26,500 registered architects in France. Architects who complete a five-year education in France are automatically eligible for registration with the Order of Architects and are thereby qualified to undertake a private practice. In Spain, there are 19,000 architects. Once an architect finishes six years of

classes plus a final exam and design project to earn a degree, he or she become automatically licensed to practice. Weld Coxe and Mary Hayden, "Architects And Power: Toward a New Architectural Practice," *Progressive Architecture*, (March 1993): 62–66; American Institute of Architects, *1994 Architecture Factbook* (Washington, D.C.: American Institute of Architects, 1994); Royal Institute of British Architects (London); Timothy Geisler, "Sprucing Up China's Cities," *The China Business Review* (September 1995): 5; and the population census from United Nations, *Monthly Bulletin of Statistics* (November 1998): 1–2.

4. Generally, 50 percent of the design fee is retained by the design institute before it is distributed among the design teams, which function like mini design firms. Thus only 0.75 percent to 1.25 percent of the construction costs are the actual design fees. In Shenzhen, an architectural graduate earns on average a monthly salary of RMB 1,500 (about $2,250 USD annually). Adding bonuses, the number grows to US$4,500–6,250, making it among the highest paid regions in China. An American architect earns 9 to 10 times times what a Chinese architect makes.

Information taken from interviews with Sun Yimin, Guangzhou architect and associate professor of architecture at South China Institute of Technology (July 1996); Sun Huasheng, Chief of Urban Planning and Design Institute of Shenzhen (July 1996); Ma Qingyun, Shenzhen architect and associate dean of the School of Architecture at Shenzhen University (July 1996); Chang Roumei (July 1996); Xu Xiaofeng, architect with the Design Institute of Shenzhen University (February 1999); Sung Xiongyang, Shenzhen architect (February 1999).

5. State Statistical Bureau, *China Statistical Yearbook* (1993): 677.

6. Construction volume statistics are calculated from figures provided in: *China's Statistical Yearbook* (1993, 1997, and 1998); *United Nations' Annual Bulletin of Housing and Building Statistics for Europe and North America*; and United Nations' *Monthly Bulletin of Statistics* (November 1998).

7. See detailed discussion in SHENZHEN SPEED©.

8. From interviews conducted in July 1999, with architects Xu Xiaofeng; Ma Qingyun; Sun Yimin; representatives of Cambridge Seven and Beacon Construction Company; and Yung Yue Sing, architect and developer.

9. According to Zhu Jieming, the old land-use policy in China disabled commercial development of real estate because only state-owned companies could conduct land development. Sensing the strong market pulse, the newly formed Shenzhen Special Economic Zone Land Management Regulation declared the end of the era of free land use in China on 1 January 1982. The Land Management Regulation opened the gate through which private enterprises could legally take up land plots by paying annual land use fees, although the state retained land ownership. Although the Chinese Constitution stated that "no organization or individual may appropriate, buy, sell, or lease land, or unlawfully transfer it in other ways," in September 1987 the Shenzhen Municipality sold the right to use a 5,000-square-meter plot to a local company for a lease term of fifty years. This first step toward land commercialization set a precedent for other transactions to follow. Within three weeks, the Shenzhen Municipality issued an invitation to bid for a plot of 46,355 square meters reserved for commercial housing. In December 1987 a public auction took place for the land use right of a 0.86-hectare housing plot. This sequence of events initiated land commercialization and real estate development in China. Consequently, in January 1988, new legislation passed, the Provisional Ordinances on Land Management of the Shenzhen Special Economic Zone, which allowed rights over leased land to be transferred, assigned,

bequeathed, or mortgaged in the lessee's will within a valid term. In April 1988, an amendment of the 1982 constitution was approved by the National People's Congress that "the right of land use can be transferred in accordance with the law." This introduced market forces into the urban economy as well as into urban land planning and development. The state's omnipotent status in the physical development of China was altered to the extent that it was re-established as a regulator.

Under the new land policy, rents for lands are different according to zone, use, FAR, and lease term. The leasing right for each plot can be obtained through bidding and auction. In order to promote investment and construction, only 50 percent of the land's rental fee is charged during the construction period specified in the contract for new construction. For special projects that are considered "advanced in technology" by the Scientific and Technical Department of Shenzhen, the grace period can be extended to five years. For projects which are "extremely advanced technically," the land fee is waived completely. Also, the land fee is waived for three years for development projects sponsored by investors from Hong Kong, Macao, Taiwan, and overseas Chinese. After the three-year period, 50 percent of the land fee is charged for the next two years. The land fee for enterprise-sponsored projects associated with land reclamation is waived for five to ten years. See *Shenzhen Lu Lu Tong* (Shenzhen: Shenzhen People's Government News Agency, 1993), 88.

10. Shenzhen Special Economic Zone was granted the same political treatment as Guangzhou City after its establishment. See *Shenzhen Lu Lu Tong*, 3–8.

11. In 1995 the Ministry of Construction granted special status to twenty private independent design firms (ten in Shanghai, five in Guangzhou, and five in Shenzhen) to practice in Guangzhou, Shanghai, and Shenzhen on an experimental basis; from an interview with Zheng Lei, executive director of Zonghao Design Architect's Office, one of the first offices granted special status as a private design firm in Shenzhen (18 January 1996).

12. "Society and Environment: Shenzhen Special Economic Zone," Xinhua News Agency (25 May 1981).

13. Z. H. Lu and J. Z. Xu, editors, *Shenzhen* (Hong Kong: Zhongguo Hai Yang Publishing Co., 1985), 49.

14. Non-state property development was initiated in the industrial building development in the early 1980s. The rapid industrial growth prompted many investors to demand premises to rent or to buy in order to begin production immediately in Shenzhen. The industrial buildings and warehouses were mostly self-developments. The owners or the users were also the investors. Hence, non-state capital accounted for 56 percent of the total RMB 1.03 billion ($129 million USD) capital investment in the physical environment of Shenzhen during the first three years of the 1980s, while funding from the central and local governments accounted for 20.4 percent. From *Shenzhen Real Estate Yearbook 1992*.

As a measure of Shenzhen's success, the amount of capital investment it received in 1990 was forty-fold what it had been 1980. The central government was only responsible for 1.4 percent and the local government for 13.1 percent of the total investment. In 1994 non-state investment still amounted to 81 percent of the total capital investment. With non-state capital in the development of Shenzhen, the average annual increment of investment in capital construction reached 44.5 percent throughout the 1980s. As a result, this new commercialized land management system has been adopted by almost every city of China. The Shenzhen experience is being repeated in cities along the coastal regions such as Shanghai, Beijing, Guangzhou, and Xiamen. See Zhu, 194.

15. Liu Xueqiang and Chun Yu, *Shenzhen Fei Hong* (Shenzhen: Hua Cheng Publishing House, 1982). Translated by author.

16. When I traveled in Shenzhen in the summer of 1996, taxi drivers told me stories about different buildings' problems. For example, one related the tale of an unfinished tall building (more than fifty stories high), the would-be-tallest-building of Shenzhen, which had changed owners and designs five times. The construction finally halted after the structure had been completed. Its latest status was it was awaiting a new owner with enough financial power to finish it. Everyone in Shenzhen is interested in seeing construction and talking about architecture because, according to one local resident, "Building construction represents development and prosperity."

17. Jiang Xiu Chuan, "Central District Development Is Nonstop; Futian Real Estate Property Is Full of Strength," *Cash* (7 May 1996).

18. To qualify for pre-sale, certified developers must obtain the following: land-use right, architectural permit, project contract, and an account with a Shenzhen registered bank in order to collect money from pre-sale. They must also have deposited 25 percent of the project budget into the account.

19. Mao Wei, "Gradually Maturing Calmly," *Shenzhen Special Zone Daily* (16 January 1996).

20. Hu Bin, "The Prerequisite for Market Is Demand," *Shenzhen Economic Daily* (1 August 1996).

21. Wang Lei, *Shenzhen Special Zone Daily* (14 October 1996). *Shang pin fang* (commodity building/housing/factory/office) refers to buildings built for sale or for the real estate market. For housing, the term *wei li fang* (low-profit housing) refers to affordable housing built with subsidies from the government. *Fu li fang* (welfare housing) refers to housing built as part of the welfare or benefits for employees.

22. See ARCHITECTURE© for the average profits, 30 percent, for developments and the implication of vacancy rate in buildings.

23. Hu Bin, "The Prerequisite for Market Is Demand," *Shenzhen Economic Daily* (1 August 1996).

24. Wang Lei, *Shenzhen Special Zone Daily* (14 October 1996).

25. Using the high-end international standard of 6:1 (housing cost to income per household) as a reference, the reasonable price for a housing unit is approximately RMB 220,000 ($27,500 USD). In Shenzhen, the 1995 average annual per capita income was RMB 10,534 ($1,317 USD), and the annual income per household was RMB 36,869 ($4,605 USD). Using 70 square meters as the standard floor area per housing unit for China, the unit price in China should be RMB 3,140 ($393 USD) per square meter. However, in 1995 the average price for commodity housing in Shenzhen was already RMB 4,267 ($533 USD) per square meter for multilevel units and RMB 6,279 ($785 USD) per square meter for highrise units.

26. As of July 1996, all the transactions completed for housing units in Luohu district averaged RMB 8,500 ($1,063 USD) per square meter. Wang Lei, *Shenzhen Special Zone Daily* (14 October 1996) and *Yearbook of Shenzhen and Hong Kong Real Estate 1997*, 114, 116.

27. Land fees, including rental fee and tenants' compensation, accounts for 45 to 49 percent of ordinary development costs. *Yearbook of Shenzhen Real Estate 1995* (Beijing: Jian Min Publishing Company, 1995), 73–74.

28. After the three-year grace period, Chinese investors pay rental fees for the land according to market prices. Also, most of the local developers in Shenzhen are collective enterprises jointly owned by government agencies and private investors. These government agencies either have the rights to certain land plots which are available for development or have "channels" from which they can get good deals on rental fees for the use right of lands.

29. Of the agreements signed for all investment projects in Shenzhen between 1979 and 1993, 90.4 percent of all projects were invested in by Hong Kong's companies and 2.6 percent were invested in by Taiwanese companies. *Yearbook of Shenzhen Real Estate 1995*, 73–74.

30. These figures were calculated from figures of costs and sale prices provided in *Yearbook of Shenzhen and Hong Kong Real Estate 1997* (Beijing: Jian Min Publishing Company, 1995), 54. The construction cost accounts for 46 to 50 percent of total development costs. Using the median 48 percent for calculation, the actual total building costs are: RMB 1300/0.48 = RMB 2,748 for multilevels; and RMB 2,250/0.48 = RMB 4,687 per highrises. To calculate percentage gains: percentage profit = (purchase price − cost)/cost; therefore, for multilevels: (RMB 4,267−2,708)/2708 = 57.57 percent; and for highrises: (RMB 6,279−4,267)/4,267 = 47.15 percent.

31. Wang Lei, *Shenzhen Special Zone Daily* (14 October 1996).

32. *Yearbook of Shenzhen and Hong Kong Real Estate 1997*, 114.

33. Wang Jian Bin, "China's Real Estate Property Is Still in Digestive Period," *Cash* (7 May 1996).

34. Baoan and Longgang districts are located in Baoan County. The Shenzhen Municipality consists of the Shenzhen Special Economic Zone (SEZ) and Baoan County. The Shenzhen SEZ consists of Luohu, Futian and Nanshang districts; *Yearbook of Shenzhen Real Estate 1995*, 181.

35. An individual who purchases a commodity housing unit of 70–100 square meters is entitled to three blue registries; one who purchases a unit larger than 100 square meters is entitled to one blue registry. One may be eligible to buy a house and get registered if one is: male and between 18 and 55 years old; female and between 18 and 50 years old; a graduate of junior high school; a spouse or unmarried child of a registered resident, who has observed the country's one child law and has no criminal record. Only property developed by licensed developers and approved by Shenzhen Development and Land Bureau is eligible for the "Buy A House And Get Registered Policy." From "Shenzhen's Major Real Estate Policies," *Yearbook of Shenzhen and Hong Kong Real Estate 1997*, 75–76; Zheng Zhao Xian, "Shenzhen's Commodity Housing Market Is Seeing Prosperity in Cold," *Shenzhen Special Zone Daily*.

36. Ibid.

37. Zhang Pei Fang, "Shenzhen's Real Estate Market Is Warming Up," *Shenzhen Special Zone Daily* (10 March 1996).

38. This term "Feng Shui Treasure Land" appeared in both *Shenzhen Travel Manual 1995*, and in *Shenzhen Special Zone Daily*.

39. Interview with Sun Yimin, project designer for all of the projects mentioned here (19 April 1996).

40. Ibid; and Meng Jian Min, "Architectural Design in the Construction Hot Waves," *Architect* 68 (February 1996): 43.

41. *Yearbook of Shenzhen and Hong Kong Real Estate 1997*, 6, 49.

42. See Meng, 42–43.

43. John Morris Dixon, "Chinese Boom Town," *Progressive Architecture* 75, no. 9 (September 1994): 49.

44. *Chaogeng* or moonlighting, is a job opportunity created for architects in the early 1990s due to the overwhelming growth in the construction industry in China. Though not a part of standard architectural practice, moonlighting became pervasive in places where massive building construction and developments were occurring. Architects, naturally, were motivated to moonlight in order to augment their salaries.

Although there are different ways design fees are paid in the design institute, in general, architects and designers receive minimal compensation for the amount of work they generate, and must pay a loyalty fee that further diminishes their meager salaries. Loyalty fees are annual fees each designer, architect, and engineer is obligated to pay in order to be managed by and remain attached to a design institute. It differs depending on an individual's experience and seniority. After the loyalty fee is paid, overhead expenses such as salaries for administrative staff, costs for stationery, electricity, telephone and a car that is owned by the institute are deducted from the annual revenue generated by each design team. The remaining money is then shared equally among members on the design team.

Here is one example of how fees are distributed in standard design institutes: In the Design Institute of the South China Institute of Technology, with its staff with more than one hundred people specializing in architectural design, landscape design, planning, structural, mechanical, electrical, and various engineering disciplines, each design team functions like a mini firm within the institute. Each design team is led by a head architect who is responsible for getting projects, assembling the right consultants, and negotiating design fees with clients. Designers receive fees based on the projects they bring to the design institute. According to Sun Yimin of the South China Institute, for every project an architect brings to the institute, the affiliate university gets 11 percent of the design fee, the design institute gets 50 percent of the remaining fee, and the architects and engineers split what is left after making contributions to the school and the department. Because there is a regulation on the maximum amount of cash each designer can receive per month, there is a two-year period one has to wait before getting the money from the design institute for projects rendered.

The Shenzhen General Architectural Design Institute was the first architectural institute in Shenzhen, and among the first to be registered as a Class A institute. It operates differently than the South China Institute of Technology. According to Chang Roumei, an architect who has worked in the Shenzhen General Architectural Design Institute's First Branch since 1996, designers are subcontractors of the design institute. The Shenzhen General Architectural Design Institute is not subsidized by the government, like most public institutes. Rather, it is managed by the government.

In 1992 and 1993, when the construction industry was booming, designers earned far more money under this system. However, in 1994, designers did not receive enough projects to generate revenues greater than the loyalty fees and the overhead expenses they were obligated to pay. Thus, designers were working but generating a negative monthly revenue. People needed to borrow money from the institute until a positive revenue was generated.

For example, before 1994 the annual loyalty fee Chang Roumei paid was RMB 110,000 ($13,750 USD). After the recession in 1994, her loyalty fee was adjusted to RMB 100,000 ($12,500 USD) for 1995, and RMB 85,000 ($10,6225 USD) for 1996. On average, Chang makes RMB $1,500 to $3,000 ($188–$375 USD) monthly for rendering architectural services, which translates to a salary of US$2,25 to $4,500 annually.In early 1997, due to financial difficulties, the Shenzhen General Architectural Design Institute was turned into a public design institute managed and subsidized by the Shenzhen government. The "subcontractual" relationship between designers and the institute ended because each design team was unable to get enough projects to support its staff. The design institute is currently being restructured. Interview with Chang Roumei (9 January 1999).

45. Interviews conducted with Sun Yimin (19 April 1996); and Song Xiang Yang and Zhu Xiao Feng, architects with the Institute of Architectural Design at Shenzhen University (July 1996).

46. Because developers negotiate fees directly with the architects, no fee is retained by the design institutes. Under this condition, developers pay less and architects make more.

47. Calculated from data on the 103 buildings completed or under construction listed in the *Yearbook of Shenzhen Real Estate 1994*, 129–32.

48. Interview with Sun Yimin (19 April 1996).

49. Ibid; interviews with Song Xiang Yang and Zhu Xiao Feng (July 1996).

50. Zhang Mo Shin, "Residential Space and Reasonable Floor-to-Floor Height," *Jianzhu Xue Bao* (March 1993).

51. Bao Jia Sheng, "Planning and Design of Superstructural Housing," *Jianzhu Xue Bao* (February 1995).

52. Jin Zi, "Further Investigation of Conservation in Land Area Used in Housing," *Jianzhu Xue Bao* (April 1975).

53. Beijing City and Town Planing Committee, " Regarding the Final Results of the Selection of the 1993 Excellent Housing Design Schemes," *1993 Beijing City's Excellent Residential Design Collection* (Beijing: China Architectural Industrial Publishing House, 1996). Translated by author.

54. The Shenzhen Construction Bureau recommended the best entries from the local 1989 housing competition to developers and interested parties in the construction industry. Because the recommendations were so well received, the Bureau published a collection of housing schemes in 1990, entitled *The Best Housing Design Schemes of Shenzhen*, which included entries from 1989 as well as 1988. The collection was intended to serve as a reference for the construction industry in order to promote better housing quality.

55. Interview with Chang Roumei (17 July 1996).

56. Wilma Fairbank, *Liang and Lin: Partners In Exploring China's Architectural Past* (Philadelphia: University of Pennsylvania Press, 20, 25; and Wilma Fairbank, translated by Liang Congjie, *A Pictorial Guide to Chinese Architecture* (Taipei: OURS, 1991), xiii.

57. Wilma Fairbank, "Achievements, 1928–37," *Liang and Lin: Partners In Exploring China's Architectural Past*, 50.

58. The manuscript copy of *Ying Zao Fa Shi* (Sung Dynasty guidelines for structural carpentry, also seen as *Ying Tsao Fa Shih*) was discovered by architect Liang Sicheng in 1931 in Nanjing's Kiangsu Provincial Library of Sung. Liang was trained at the University of Pennsylvania (1924–28) and became China's first architectural historian. Liang used *Kong Cheng Zao Fa Ze Li* (the Qing Dynasty's builder's manual, also seen as *Kung Cheng Tsao Fa Tse Li*) as a text book. He regarded carpenters as teachers, and Beijing's Qing palaces as resources that could help understand and decode the carpentry terminology used in the *Ying Zao Fa Shi*. Liang and his wife, Lin Wei-Yin, also an architect, initiated the study of China's architectural evolution, and together, searched the Chinese countryside to examine historically significant structures which had survived from previous dynasties into the 20th century. They carefully scrutinized, measured, dated, photographed, and published their research. Due to the World War II, a portion of their research was misplaced and lost for 33 years. In 1984, *A Pictorial Guide to Chinese Architecture* consisting of their research completed between 1931 and 1946, was edited and published by Wilma Fairbank in the United States. See Fairbank, *A Pictorial Guide to Chinese Architecture*, 16, 19, 49–53.

59. Chien Tsu Kuang, "Thoughts on Architects' Registration Examination," *Shin Chien Chu* (February 1996): 52.

60. Song Shao, "Simple Explanation on the Time Features And Cultural Semantics of Guangdong New Architecture," *Guangdong Architecture and Design* (Guangzhou: Guoji Wenhua Publishing Company, 1992).

61. Ibid.

62. Interview with Zhang Lei Zheng (19 January 1996).

63. "An architect spends six months designing a $10 million building for a 4 percent fee and maximum liability. ... A real estate agent sells it in two weeks and receives a 6 percent fee with minimum liability. The lawyer in the deal soaks everyone. Something is wrong!" said Hal Croaddock, a frustrated architect in the United States.

64. See CHINESE ARCHITECT©.

65. Joint ventures between foreign architectural firms and Chinese design institutes take one of two forms: a full-fledged equity joint venture, *hezi qiye*, or a contractual joint venture partnership, *hezuo qiye*, for one or more specific projects. See Timothy Geisler, "Sprucing Up China's Cities," *China Business Review* 22, no. 5 (September 1995): 52.

66. As early as 1895, Tianjin Pei Yang Western Educational Institute (the former Pei Yang University and Tianjin University) had established Civil Engineering Department. In 1923 the first architectural engineering program was founded in Suzhou Industrial Institute. In 1927 National Fourth Chung Shan University, and in 1928 Beijing University and Tung Pei University all established architectural departments. Early architectural programs were small and established in different areas of China. For example, when Liang Sicheng founded the school of architecture for Tung Pei University in Shengang in 1928, the department consisted of two staff members (Liang and his wife Lin) for the first academic year. See Fairbanks, *Liang and Lin*, 42.

The first educational reform of 1952 was an attempt by Communist leaders to destroy the system set up by the Guomindang. "Intercollegiate and departmental adjustments" were made so that specialized departments and schools from each university in a region or province were pooled together to form new institutes following the Russian system. The first educational reform established eight architectural schools between 1952 and 1966, referred to as the "Old Eight Schools." Li Daozhang, "The Teaching of Architecture in China's Institutes of Higher Education," *Chinese Architect* 14, no. 9 (September 1988): 44.) The eight schools are: Beijing's Qinghua University; Nanjing Institute of Technology (renamed Southeast University in 1987); Shanghai's Tongji University; Tianjin University; Guangzhou Huanan (South China) Institute of Technology; Xian Yejing Architectural Institute; Harbin Industrial University; and Chongqing Architectural Engineering Institute.

There are now 54 architectural programs and institutes in China. Further reform to accredit architecture programs began in the 1990s. The Accreditation Committee, consisting of Chinese architects and professors selected by the central government, and professional consultants from the U.S., Australia, and the U.K., was established to evaluate the architectural programs. The goal of the accreditation was to change all architectural programs in China to five-year professional programs. With decision of the state's Academic Degree Committee, students began to receive Bachelor of Architecture and Master of Architecture degrees instead of Bachelor of Science and Master of Science degrees in the eight schools by the end of 1995.

67. Peng I-Kang, "Away from Obsolete, Promote Progresses: A Brief Introduction of Architectural Education of Tianjin University," *Chinese Architect* 14, no. 9 (September 1988): 46–48.

68. In the U.S., there is 1 architect per 3,120 people. If China's population remains at 1,200,000,000, China will need 384,915 architects to obtain the a similar ration of architects to population. Assuming the 60 architectural schools each produce 50 graduates per year (programs in China are small), there will be approximately 3,000 graduates per year. If the graduates are kept at 3,000 per year, it will take 115 years for China to have enough architects. See CHINESE ARCHITECT© for statistics on architects.

69. See CHINESE ARCHITECT©.

70. Interview with an urban planner at Skidmore, Owings, and Merrill in New York (12 December 1996).

71. Thomas Campanella, "Transforming the Good Earth: New Economic Forces Are Changing the Chinese Landscape," *Landscape Architecture* (June 1994): 38.

72. Li Zhisui, *The Private Life of Chairman Mao* (New York: Random House, 1994), 296.

73. "From Hong Kong to Guangzhou: Pearl River Delta Metropolis Will Become The World's Most Active Economic Belt," *Shenzhen Economic Daily* (14 July 1996).

74. See Campanella, 38.

75. "Megalopolis Now," *The Guardian* (24 June 1995).

76. Campanella, 39.

77. See Campanella, 38.

78. Before Wal-Mart's grand opening, there was tension in the retail market of Shenzhen. News headlines, such as "The world's biggest retailer, Wal-Mart Comes Prepared: The Retail Price War Is on the Verge of Breaking Out," indicated the impact of Wal-Mart's presence on Shenzhen. Local retailers pressured the city government to withhold the megastore's commercial permit, causing several months' delay for the grand opening; from "Wal-Mart: A New Force Suddenly Coming to the Force," *Focus* (July, 1996): 46–47. Sam's Club (also owned by Wal-Mart) at Honey Lake and the Wal-Mart Supercenter in Luohu finally opened on August 7 and August 12 in 1996. In three days, the daily sale at Sam's Club already reached RMB 2 million. On its grand opening day, 3,000 people waited outside the 17,000 square-meter Wal-Mart Supercenter before it opened. Together, more than 150,000 people visited Sam's Club and the Wal-Mart Supercenter within the first week of their grand openings; "Wal Mart's $50 million USD Is Selling Craziness," *Cash* (20 August 1996).

79. Guang Jian, "Constructing Prosperous Commercial District," *Shenzhen Economic Daily* (1996).

80. See ARCHITECTURE© for details.

81. The data for the construction volume between 1979 and 1986 is cumulative. Thus, the annual average of 41 percent is based on the increases calculated between 1986 and 1995.

82. *Yearbook of Shenzhen Real Estate 1995*, 92.

83. Ibid.

84. The retail sale in Shenzhen amounted to RMB 30 billion ($3.75 billion USD) in 1995, and has been growing with an annual increase rate of 37 percent between 1991 and 1995. According to the market survey conducted by Wal-Mart, the figure is expected to double in five years, reaching RMB 60 billion ($7.5 billion USD) by the year 2000. "Wal Mart: A New Force Suddenly Coming To The Force," *Focus* (July 1996).

85. The unsold percentages were calculated based on the information provided by the *Yearbook of Shenzhen and Hong Kong Real Estate 1997*, 113, 132, 141, 153.

86. There were 1.6 million square meters of unsold commercial space and office buildings in 1994, and 1.8 million square meters of vacant commodity housing in 1995. It is analogous to saying that 22 forty-story office building (comparable to the size of Shenzhen Development Center, at 70,000 square meters) were vacant, and 25,900 dwellings (or 404 eight-story residential buildings, or 104 twenty-five-story residential highrises) were vacant. In other words, in 1995, there were 181 thirty-story luxury commercial and residential buildings (18,750 square meters per building) vacant in Shenzhen. Although Shenzhen residents cannot afford to buy or

rent these buildings, commodity buildings have been built with an annual increase rate of nearly 60 percent for the last fifteen years.

Even the World Trade Building, the building that represented the glory of Shenzhen, the only building Deng Xiaoping requested to visit on his first trip to the city in 1984, reduced rent by 35 percent and cut building management and maintenance fees in order to keep its vacancy rate at 5 percent or lower. The Hualiang Building not only introduced new amenities sucyh as a swimming pool, cafeteria, convenience stores, but also provides free parking for tenants to keep its vacancy rate at 7 percent. The Baohua Commercial Center, a new building just completed this year, is offering a "one year rent free" program to attract potential lessees.

87. "Strolling Along Shenzhen in 2010," *Shenzhen Economic Daily* (3 September 1996).

88. *Shenzhen Special Zone Daily* (1 July 1996).

89. Zheng Zhao Xian, "Consumer Behavior Changed; Businesses and Real Estates Oversupplied," *Shenzhen Special Zone Daily* (1996).

90. *Guangdong Architecture and Design* (Guangzhou: Guoji Wenhua Publishing Company, 1992).

91. Zheng Zhao Xian, "Consumer Behavior Changed: Businesses and Real Estates Oversupplied," *Shenzhen Special Zone Daily* (1996).

92. Shu Wen, "Luohu Commercial City Rent-Free Special," *Shenzhen Economic Daily* (1996).

93. Luo Hong Yu, "New Building Knocked Down Before Occupation," *Shenzhen Economic Daily* (July 1996).

94. *Guangdong Architecture and Design* (Guangzhou: Guoji Wenhua Publishing Company, 1992).

95. According to 1994 statistics, there are more than 330 middle and high-class hotels in Shenzhen. If motels and lodges are included, the total number is almost 1,000.

96. Zhang Wan Quan, " Drip Bottles Are Hanging on the Trees," *Shenzhen Special Zone Daily* (30 July 1996).

97. Ibid.

98. Li Teng, "Reduce Scale, Better Structure," *Shenzhen Special Zone Daily* (9 August 1996).

99. "Proper Land Flow," *Shenzhen Economic Daily* (11 July 1996).

100. Zheng Zhao Xian, "Consumer Behavior Changed: Businesses and Real Estates Oversupplied," *Shenzhen Special Zone Daily* (1996).

101. Huang Nian, "Why Isn't Luohu Commercial City Flourishing?" *Shenzhen Special Zone Daily* (1996).

102. Kuang Tian Fang, "Leaking in Houses: Blaming Hollow Bricks, Improper Constructions, Un-delayable Inspections," *Shenzhen Commercial Daily*.

103. Sean Affleck and Helen Goodland, "Changes in China," *Architectural Review* (July 1989): 53.

104. Jiang Xiu Chuan and Shi Xu Sheng, "Where Is the Future of 'Collective Fund' Housings in Shenzhen?" *Cash* (8 October 1996).

105. Ibid.

106. *Yearbook of Shenzhen and Hong Kong Real Estate* 1997, 3.

107. Liu Zhi Feng, "Overview of Rental Units' Management," *Shenzhen Commercial Daily* (2 August 2 1996).

108. Shenzhen has a total population of 3.45 million (including floating and registered population).

109. Li Jie, "Remember the Lesson, Ensure Proper Supervision," *Shenzhen Special Zone Daily* (2 January 1996).

110. In Shenzhen, only individuals with the following criteria are eligible for mortgages. The individual must be: a resident of China with an official ID; a foreign investor or overseas Chinese from Hong Kong, Macao, or Taiwan; an individual with stable job and

income, capable of repaying principal and interest; a bank-account holder; 5) able to pay the down-payment.

There are two ways to have mortgages. *Lou yu an jie* is similar to a mortgage in the U.S. One simply pays a down-payment to the developer when buying a house, then secures a loan from the bank with the house as the security. Monthly payments of principal and interest are paid within a fixed term. In general, the repayment period is five or seven years, with the down-payment of 50 percent or 60 percent of property value. The repayment period and interest rate is set by the bank and developer. The developer guarantees his liability for the buildings or developments to be mortgaged. Only 30 percent of all real estate developments have *lou yu an jie*.

Cun yi dai er is when a home buyer deposits 50 percent of the purchase price into a bank to receive a loan for an amount equaling the entire purchase price. The deposit in the bank and the house purchased are used as security. The repayment period of this policy (normally one to three years) and interest rate are agreed upon and set by the individual and the bank. During the repayment period, the buyer receives interest for the deposit. Once all payments are paid in full, the buyer gets the house and the deposit, with interest, back. Wang Jian, "*An Jie* and *Cun Ji Dai Er*: Which One Is Better?" *Cash* (24 May 1996).

111. Yang Hua, "Revealing the True Story of China's Rich and Poor," *World Journal* (20 October 1996).

112. Commodity house price for highrise was RMB 4,050 per square meter in 1990, and RMB 8,259 in 1992. Commodity house price for multilevel was RMB 2,478 per square meter in 1990, and RMB 5,384 in 1992I. Office building price was RMB 3,480 per square meter in 1990, and in RMB 6,800 in 1992.

113. *Shenzhen Economic Daily* (20 August 1996).

114. *Shenzhen Special Zone Daily* (22 July 1996).

115. *Shenzhen Commercial Daily* (30 August 1996).

116. Ibid.

117. "Foreign Real Estate Investors' Great Return," *Da Gong Bao* (16 July 1996).

118. "China's Real Estate Market Is in the Digestive Stage," *Cash* (7 May 1996); *Shenzhen Special Zone Daily* (22 July 1996); Mao Wei, "Soberly Maturing," *Shenzhen Special Zone Daily* (15 January 1996); "Shenzhen's Commodity Housing Market Is Seeing Hot in Cold," *Shenzhen Special Zone Daily* (15 January 1996).

119. *Shenzhen Economic Daily*.

120. Interview with Zhen Lei, a private architect/developer based in Shenzhen (19 January 1996).

121. "The CBD Is Seeking International Consultation," *Shenzhen Special Zone Daily* (26 August 1996).

122. Li Zhisui, *The Private Life of Chairman Mao*, 296.

Contents

CAST OF CHARACTERS   *274*

277   INTRODUCTION: TO GET RICH IS GLORIOUS

287   BROAD WAYS: DEREGULATION, COMPETITION AND URBAN FORM

JUNE 6, 1996. DEAR REM, . . .   *289*

301   THE INDUSTRIAL PARK: PUBLIC/PRIVATE PARTNERSHIP IN A SOCIALIST MARKET ECONOMY

8:30 P.M. JULY 6, 1996   *302*

313   DEVELOPING LUXURY HOUSING

329   EPILOGUE: VIRGIN© CITY

9:00 P.M. AUGUST 19, 1996   *333*

MONEY
DONGGUAN

Stephanie Smith

A lounge area in a Chinese hotel in "Number Two Wife" village. Chinese "mistresses" wait behind the glass for customers.

Dongguan City, July 20, 1996.

Developer culture. Communist party cadres-turned-developers in a hotel lounge. Dongguan is an (in)famous developer's hideout, a "haven for risk-takers."
Dongguan City, July 17, 1996.

A performance in the City Cultural Center.
Dongguan City, June 29, 1996.

Chinese mistresses in a hotel disco. Hotel is a word with many meanings in Dongguan City. . . . "Mr. Fuqi has heard a rumor that a stripper will perform tonight. We watch the singer, and wait for the stripper, and I say, finally, as we sit in the darkness, that I need to know more about mistresses (he points some out), and prostitution (in massage parlors, barber shops, near the bus station, and here, just outside in the hallway. . .)."
Dongguan City, July 6, 1996.

Posters advertising Chinese singers in a hotel lobby.
Dongguan City, July 20, 1996.

Mr. Luo (seated, left), a Chinese real-estate developer and the creator of Beautiful City, with his business partners, in a Beautiful City "single family dwelling," currently used as a meeting room.

Beautiful City, June 3, 1996.

A real-estate developer checking into a hotel. A Chinese joke: if you are a government official in Beijing, you have power; if you are a businessman in Guangzhou, you have money.

Dongguan City, July 8, 1996.

DIARY
Dongguan City 1997
Cast of Characters

Mr. Wu
Dongguan City Planner
Age: 27
Trained as a structural engineer (and said to be very intelligent. Head of Shenzhen University's Design Institute, in Dongguan City, until he was chosen in October 1995 to lead Dongguan's City Planning Office. Currently taking a course in Urban Planning at South China University's Institute of Technology. Moonlights on weekends designing buildings. CCP member. Graduated from Shenzhen University with Half-Town Chan and Bill Wong. Uncle: communist government official
Hometown: Dongguan City

Graduated from Shenzhen University with Mr. Wu and Bill Wong. Father, Uncle: communist government officials
Hometown: Dongguan City

Mr. Fuqi
Assistant Planner, Dongguan City Post and Telecommunication Bureau
Head of Propaganda, Dongguan City Chapter, Communist Youth League
Age: 27
Martial artist. Believer of feng shui fortunes. Translator. Harmonica player. Entrepreneur (restaurant owner). Dongguan City resident permit.
Hometown: North China

Architecture from the University of California, Berkeley. His first building, designed for Dongguan City after returning from the States in 1992, is still the largest and tallest police station in all of China. Father: Chief of Police, Dongguan City
Wife: Architect (Lucy)
Hometown: Dongguan City

Bill Wong
Graphic Designer
Age: 31
Advertising agent and marketer for new developments in Dongguan City. Graduated from Shenzhen University with Half-Town Chan and Mr. Wu. Two years spent in Australia.
Hometown: Dongguan City

Half-Town Chan
Architect
Age:29
Dongguan City's speediest architect (heads an office of thirty-five). Said to have built "at least half the town" of Dongguan. Built the first and only building finished in Dongguan's new city center. Considered the richest architect in Dongguan. Gambler.

Tom Zhang
Architect
Head, Dongguan City Branch, South China University of Technology, Architecture Research and Design Institute
Age:34
Head of Dongguan's most reputable design institute. Beautiful City architect and planner. Hotel designer. Entrepreneur (hotel owner). Trained in Guangzhou, with a Masters of

Mr. Luo
Developer, Beautiful City
Age: 38
Hometown: Dongguan City

January 20–23, 1996
We visit a "city near Guangzhou," where the developers are most powerful, a star city for manufacturing, bowling pins in median strip, empty buildings, run-down hotels, new developments. Without a special driving permit our bus must turn around at city's edge.... I decide to return for a two-day visit.

8:30 a.m. January 25, 1996
I have early morning dim sum with Mr. Ma, our contact at Shenzhen University. He is uneasy about my trip and at the same time wide-eyed, suggesting Dongguan is the place where "prostitutes go bowling" and "billionaires keep their mistresses." He provides me with two "translators" (bodyguards), introduced to me as Peter and Sunny. They give me maps of Dongguan City and development brochures.

They have a small pickup. We drive to their office/loft space in Wu Sha New Technology Park on the outskirts of Shenzhen. They are Mr. Ma's former students and architectural-model builders. We load a coffee table-size model of a housing development into the back of the truck and set off on Gordon Wu's superhighway. Within minutes we exit. We tour a small town just outside the Special Economic Zone boundary—one of the 33 towns that make up larger Dongguan City.

On its outskirts is "Camdor Harbour City," a Taiwanese-funded development of "villas, condominiums, golf and horse-back-riding courses." The brochure advertises a "European level of variety development zone." Camdor Harbour City is one of 20 or 30 golf-course

developments in Guangdong Province. I speak with Nicole, the marketing director. She offers me a round of golf, which I decline, so instead we set out in a golf cart for a tour. Nicole markets villas (HK\$1-3 million; U.S.\$130,000-390,000) and condominiums to factory owners in the area (many of whom are from Taiwan). The golf course is nearly finished and quite beautiful. The villas and condominiums, however, take longer to complete—it is difficult for local labor to build to Taiwanese standards.

There are two options for foreign developers when they propose land use in China outside the Special Economic Zones. Land, which is owned by the local government, is leased for either 20 or 50 years. The 20-year option is cheaper and involves less bribery, but the development is returned to the government at the end of the lease. The 50-year option (which the developers of Camdor Harbour City chose), allows more management freedom and with it more bribery. The rewards, however, are greater. Nicole suggests the central government has no control over local governments—there is "a lot of corruption, every contract is different." She's heard that some of the towns in Dongguan City, usually the larger ones, are known to be "nicer" to developers. Theirs is not, however, and they regret choosing the 50-year option, with its variable and unpredictable conditions.

We continue on to Dongguan City Center (pop. approximately 300,000). Dongguan City sits approximately 20 miles from Gordon Wu's highway. A two-lane

regional road runs through the center of town. Before the construction of Gordon Wu's superhighway, this was the main road from Shenzhen to Guangzhou. Now, it leads only to Dongguan.

Dongguan City Center is very clean. There are few cars, less pollution, more green. Peter points out cars (Mercedes, BMW) with Hong Kong license plates. "Stolen," he says. "Is it dangerous here?" I ask. "There are many rich men in Dongguan," he answers.

We pick up Bill Wong. Bill is a graphic artist/advertising agent/marketer for the new developments going up throughout larger Dongguan City. He attends planning meetings, local-government meetings, etc. We all proceed in the car to lunch. On the way Bill points out one of the larger developments, in a field one or two miles distant. I ask about skyscrapers, and he discusses the city planner's relationship to the central government. "Three different city plans have been submitted, and each time Beijing has requested lower buildings, spreading into the countryside." Bill thinks Dongguan City can't support tall buildings. I ask him why there are so many empty buildings and he says too many people think about one thing—lots of shopping centers, lots of factories and nothing else. He thinks Dongguan City is also kept "backward" by Hong Kong; companies send their old machinery here, for instance, when they open factories.

We have lunch with a factory owner. He arrives at the restaurant late, in a gold BMW. He speaks no English but is able to express his idea that in Dongguan City, "noises are very happy," and there is good opportunity for business. After lunch we take his car and tour the new development Bill pointed out earlier. The factory owner owns a duplex there, still under construction. We have a look. The housing development is fenced and gated. I see at least 10 security guards in this development of maybe 200 duplexes. We tour his house--still unfinished. He is very interested in comparing it to American examples. Is it cheaper? (no), nicer? (...) We tour the rest of the development, East City Center--huge shopping centers, housing, recreational facilities--all, according to Bill, 13% occupied (VIRGIN CITY©). We proceed to the factory....

The factory makes decorative aluminum gates. It's location on a main road is of primary importance to its owner--he

Street in Dongguan City Center

Inoperative revolving restaurants sit atop towers in Dongguan City, 1995. An "outward-looking" building typology perfected in the Special Economic Zones of the Pearl River Delta (PRD), the revolving restaurant proliferated and announced (spatially) Deng's Open Door campaign. During a visit to the PRD, Deng pronounced a revolving restaurant in Shenzhen his favorite building, the very image of his outward-looking economic reforms. While inside, he could view the whole of China. Inoperative copies fill the skylines of the PRD's unsanctioned yet booming development zones.

INTRODUCTION: TO GET RICH IS GLORIOUS

To get rich is glorious.
—Deng Xiaoping, Third Plenum, 1978[1]

Future Wealth

Money cannot be *quantified* in China, a country that has, throughout a history of ambivalent use, flaunted, subverted, and manipulated its worth. China began its deception when the Chinese invented paper money; theirs was the first culture to abstract value.[2] Chinese money was further reduced to invisibility when communism constructed an economy of denial: because imbalanced wealth is a dangerous threat to collective utopia, money has value in the communist state only when hidden or subverted into the hard currency of bribery.

Under Deng Xiaoping's economic reform, China triumphed with its most devastating new abstraction: the value of money (still tainted by corrupt tendencies and often potently visible)[3] resurfaced as "future wealth." Deng's *détournement,*[4] renders this invisible currency not inert and useless (who can spend future wealth?), but ideologically invigorated as a currency of striving. In the socialist market economy, money *will be* used—to "buy" utopia.[5] The socialist market system (another Great Leap Forward) redefines capitalism as a communist strategy; Beijing takes control of the free market to serve the communist agenda.

Deng's system operates as MARKET REALISM©. His ideology—"socialism with Chinese characteristics"—becomes potent as socialist realism reformulated for a new(er) "liberation." Like socialist realism (the Stalinist doctrine that art should depict, in the most realistic way, a final condition of utopia rather than dwell on the imperfections of the present or the sacrifices on the road toward its realization), the socialist market system is a formula for desire simultaneously deferred and consummated. MARKET REALISM© removes the connection

between supply and demand. China's current economic system does not require instant gratification in the form of profit. The Maoist legacy is adapted to the economics of the Open Door reform. "Business for the masses" now creates a speculative furor, another Leap, during which no connection is made between profit and development. Capitalist-style speculation (which defers today's profit for the hope of greater value in the future) and communist-style deferral of reward (that assumes faithful, if blind, sacrifice to the greater whole) merge to form a potent economic hybrid, an accelerated form of capitalism that favors innocence over rationality.

In the MARKET REALIST© system, the moral toil of CORRUPTION© and BANKRUPTCY© replaces the physical toil of the backyard furnace. Socialist realism's physical toil is now an invisible struggle through the complexities of a deal. Global power (and financial identity, modernization, wealth) awaits those who survive, but the destruction that is wrought is still tangible. Money in China finally becomes visible as architecture. Architecture gives form to the crisis and the glory inherent in the (schizophrenic) socialist market economy. Cities in the Pearl River Delta (PRD) are used as tools to encourage further and faster growth. They are spatial indicators of China's modernization, and like tools, they have a singular purpose. Therefore, many are empty: they are abandoned after—or in some cases even before—inhabitation.

This architecture, or "spatial" money—wasted, empty, secretly given away (as bribery), or gambled—is not quantifiable. The exuberance inherent in China's new, freshly solvent, yet irrational system—striving toward utopia (and failing to get there) by making and spending money—renders numerical legibility meaningless. In this system, supply and demand makes no sense. George Bataille's theory of "general economy" (1933) makes what is seemingly incomprehensible suddenly transparent. The general economy replaces the capitalist model of restricted economy (where surplus is automatically reinvested into production) with a model that encompasses both productive and nonproductive spending, or *dépense*.

The Socialist Market Economy

Two years after Mao Zedong's death ends the Cultural Revolution, Deng Xiaoping opens China's doors to the world, an act of self-criticism that announces a (self-imposed) defeat. This sacrifice to modernization—to globalization—is at the same time an unleashing, the pinnacle in a history of "great leaps" that characterize Chinese liberations. A thriving socialist market economy evolves: "socialism with Chinese characteristics." The first five years of reform lift more than 100 million people out of absolute poverty.[6] China's goal: parity with the West by the year 2000.

The socialist market economy, or privatization in an unstable mix of free-market deregulation with communist utopian rhetoric and regulations, operates by relinquishing central control while simultaneously harnessing competitive spirit. China's economic reform enhances the power of communist-party members at county and local levels. These cadres, Deng's new capitalist army, are closest to the money, and Deng's is a race toward the utopia of wealth. The Chinese Communist Party's 57 million members, all potential winners, are given a prime directive: get rich, get rich first, get rich fast.

Privatization

The socialist market economy encourages controlled privatization, a temporary reversion to a "lower" economic form (capitalism) in order to fast-forward modernization.[7] This system, in yin-yang fashion, pairs (communist-style) regulation with deregulation. The first phase of reform attacks China's lumbering collective enterprises by way of starvation; state-owned businesses are weaned from reliance on public funds. But more than just deregulatory release is required to salvage China's industrial sector,

mentions it many times. We park in a lot in front of the narrow, freestanding concrete building. The worker's housing is visible behind. Four stories high, the factory's lower floor is a showroom, small offices for the accounting and marketing departments, and the owner's corner office. His contains a baby grand piano. The project manager of the factory appears, startlingly blue-eyed and blonde-haired, yet Asian in features, voice, and manner. He is, like the factory owner, well under 30 years old.

After our tea he leads me to the stairs. The upper floors are deep, with high ceilings and full windows--lots of natural light. It is quiet. There are about ten workers on each floor, some welding, most assembling parts. The project manager discusses (without prompting) his new investment property (an apartment he owns in one of the new developments) and asks about engineering schools in the States. There is a gentle quality to everything: the light, the delicately welded aluminum gates they are assembling, the men and women.

We leave the factory and proceed to an architect's office, a large, rough loft space, filled with smoke. The 29-year-old architect, Mr. Chan (they call him "Half-Town" Chan because he has built at least half of Dongguan's new construction), heads an office of 35 architects. They've had 120 new projects in the office this year, mostly factories and office buildings in larger Dongguan City. His office spends on average ten days designing a building. Development time in Dongguan City is short, he says, compared to Shenzhen's 2-3 years, but the buildings are just as big. When asked about Beijing's desire for a city plan with lower buildings, he suggests that Beijing has been seduced by its old city, which contains the Emperor's Palace. His influences are Le Corbusier and Mies van der Rohe. Feng shui is used to design every building, he says.

We leave to join 30-year-old Mr. Wu, Dongguan's city planner. He welcomes us into his office (white everything, with a glass wall to view his employees). We pass by what looks to be a kitchen table, at which sits an old Chinese couple--man and woman--smoking, drinking tea, and sketching, working over a city plan. Mr. Wu grew up in Dongguan City, still a village until 10 years ago, now populated by about 3 million people. His family has lived here for over 800 years. Mr. Wu speaks English (this becomes apparent later) but prefers to use a translator during our meeting. I ask to see a current plan and he refuses--it is not finished.... Dongguan City planners don't "plan" anyway, he insists, rather they suggest things-- 30% parks, the location of development, etc. Economics controls the plan, especially building height, he says. Their "suggestions" include expand- ing the city to an "East Center" (which we had visited earlier), "West Center," and "New City Center" (where they plan to relocate the old city center). He mentions that the central government is using Dongguan City as a model for how to change from a "village to a city"--original to modern.

I notice lots of computers, about 15 people working in the office, new furniture. I ask why the city needs a planning office. He says that before, there was bad planning con- trol, not bad planning. With the escalating economic devel- opment they see a need for more control. I ask what falls under the city planner's jurisdiction. We don't plan

freeways, he answers, but they do plan more roads. Dongguan City, he adds, has the first road ever built in China. The first question from the Bei- jing planning office when they see a Dongguan City plan is "what about the traffic?"

I ask again to see plans. He shows me a city plan of a town outside of Zhuhai (Zhongshan City) and says it is their model. This city has more plan- ning control than Dongguan City. He suggests the central government wants more cities like this city. I ask about Dongguan City's relationship to Shenzhen, a Special Economic Zone. He's uncomfortable with the control the government has over people in the zone--cer- tificates to enter, etc. Dong- guan City doesn't want SEZ sta- tus, it is strategically placed between Shenzhen and Guangzhou. I ask (just for the hell of it) if their plans include an air- port. Never, he says, there are too many airports.

I tell him Dongguan City has a dangerous reputation--is felt to be even more dangerous than Shenzhen. He is surprised (and not offended). The town is busy with business, he explains, and he says traffic makes complica-

tions and dangers (this is one of many times he blames too much traffic for all ills; and yet Dongguan City was by far the emptiest, least polluted Asian city I visited).

Mr. Wu begins to make a series of phone calls, and at the same time engage in a con- versation with Bill Wong, my two translators, and the archi- tect Mr. Chan, who has appeared and joined our meeting. They are all friends. It soon becomes apparent that Mr. Wu has arran- ged a hotel for me, has spoken to his wife, who has offered to take me shopping, and they ask me now if I'd like to join all ten of them for dinner.

The Dongguan City flower, in January blooming in profu- sion, had the unmistakable scent of cheap perfume. I watched dancing girls in a cav- ernous, southwestern Chinese- food restaurant on the out- skirts of town. Three midgets appeared to sing Frank Sinatra and then moved into the crowd to tell jokes. Mr. Chan dis- cussed his use of feng shui. "It acts like nature." Mr. Wu told of his upcoming trip to Europe--to Holland and France-- to see cities. We each con- fessed our ages--all well under

long victimized and now close to death after four decades of communism. The central gov- ernment in Beijing—ideologically ambivalent when faced with the realities of privatization but at the same time in need of model success stories to reinforce the value of reform—has approved new sources of investment capital (in a small number of fail-proof test cases). Stocks and bonds from a few ailing companies are sold to privileged Chinese investors.[8]

In this way the forces of privatization are unleashed. Rural companies, encouraged by the newly relaxed policies of low-level, local cadres,

immediately begin to mimic this prostitution, selling themselves in an unregulated, loose manner. Larger enterprises in cities soon follow. The central government reluctantly offers de facto approval, but not before China's savings rate drops from 35 percent at the beginning of reform (twice as high as the rate of any other communist country) to 12 percent as funds are transferred to newly private enterprises.[9]

Becoming Entrepreneurial

Seven years into reform, despite the influx of wealth, one quarter of all state enterprises are losing money. The central government subsidizes them 48 billion RMB (U.S.$7 billion) a year, or 20 percent of the state's annual income. China, fearing bankruptcy itself, finally adopts the Trial Enterprise Bankruptcy Law. Its purpose is not to make enterprises bankrupt, assures *Workers' Daily*, but rather to "increase their vitality." Instead of a business fatality, BANKRUPTCY© in China becomes a newly communist strategy to initiate and accelerate a cycle of death and rebirth. "Bankruptcy Improves Businesses" assures the Chinese Communist Party. The new law will "eliminate backward companies through competition and help enterprises transform pressure into a driving force."[10]

This freedom in failure at last provides the potential for TABULA RASA©, a condition necessary to enact the most radical reform: starting over. With the risk of failure (BANKRUPTCY©) in place, the Chinese government is now functionally entrepreneurial—flexible, market-driven, and looking to gamble (a pre-liberation disposition toward risk resurfaces). Entrepreneurs have always operated most effectively in a condition of TABULA RASA©: a condition of crisis.[11] China is released now to do business. Cadres from the local to the central levels now do business in the name of modernization (yet the CCP still denies membership to entrepreneurs, who are considered exploiters). The TABULA RASA© of BANKRUPTCY© has prepared China for rapid development.

Guangdong Province

Guangdong Province in southern China provides the first testing ground for the experiments of Deng's Open Door economic reform. Long sullied by continued interaction with foreigners through Hong Kong, the Pearl River Delta is abandoned early by the communists as a "cultural desert." For Deng, however, it becomes the perfect area for experimentation. In his vision, geographical proximity to (wealthy) Hong Kong is no longer suspect.[12] Guangdong, now described as "one step ahead",[13] is granted

"special development measures." A radical, anti-communist relaxation of land-use and land-ownership laws couples with ongoing privatization of industry to fast-forward Deng's reform policies.

Guangdong is complicit in reform Deng's economic reform. When Deng's policies are announced, the province simultaneously announces its position of wholesale sacrifice: it will build an "outward-looking economy."[14] In the PRD, the heart of Guangdong Province, new private and foreign-affiliated companies

A map of the Pearl River Delta in a brochure advertising Tai On City, 1996. This map makes the agenda clear: China is building an "outward-looking" economy using foreign funds.

quickly replace state-owned enterprises. Hong Kong factories infiltrate the region. Existing village enterprises in rural areas thrive, released to operate tiny manufacturing and service industries. They absorb surplus labor as Guangdong moves from an agricultural- to

35. Bill Wong boasted of the 20 national swimming champions from Dongguan City since 1960 (we'd passed by the public swimming pool on our way to dinner). They all love Keanu Reeves in Speed.

I dream now about neon softened by polluted air.

Excerpt, Term One Thesis Presentation, May 14, 1996

I am from the West in the United States. I am sympathetic to a Wild West mentality and at home in a new and quickly developing landscape. I am looking for a developer in the Pearl River Delta who is a hero....

3:00 p.m. June 2, 1996

We emerge up high from the green freeway corridor of the Outer Territory of Hong Kong, and I look down to a flat delta plain with Shenzhen (like Oz) in the distance. The border, a thin soupy river, as if acknowledging its upcoming irrelevance, is slowly evaporating in the heat.

We stop here, off the bus, and move out of Hong Kong through a warehouse of corridors and across the river into another low, deep building, and at the end of it and outside in a parking lot is China. It is 3:00 p.m., and on the bus again everyone promptly goes back to sleep. In another twenty minutes we have passed through much of the western half of Shenzhen and again past a border. We flash our passports at the guard through the windows and drive on to the superhighway.

Later at the Dongguan Hotel—a communist-party enclave where I stayed as Mr. Wu's guest in January—Bill Wong meets me, and with my bags loaded onto the back of his scooter, we go to his office. His employees are hard at work on a brochure for an agricultural showroom built by Half-Town Chan. It is the first and only building finished in Dongguan's New City Center. Mr. Wu arrives within minutes. Half-Town Chan is gambling in Macau, Mr. Wu tells me, and therefore cannot join us. We learn later that he has won HK$15,000 (U.S.$2,000). We go to a seafood restaurant. Valets play pool under tents in the parking lot. We sit in a private eating room, with a waitress in attendance and a bathroom and a TV. On most of one wall are fish tanks. Mr. Wu picks seven for us, unlucky, and I choose another, oysters, for eight. The first to arrive is a raw salmon over ice, Japanese-style, then crabs and the hot garlicky oysters—and in the Chinese way, active and collective, we eat and talk of their student days at Shenzhen University. "We no longer want fast change," announces Mr. Wu. Mr. Wu's family book lists the Wu males back 3,000 years. Mr. Wu and Cynthia, his wife, want more babies (they want, of course, a boy). "How many can you have in America?"

I ask Mr. Wu to tell me about Mr. Zhang, the architect he'd mentioned in a letter he wrote to me in May. Mr. Zhang has a lot of work in Dongguan City, Mr. Wu tells me, and he speaks in English. He's also "private," and everyone around the table smiles. If I worked for Mr. Wu (as I'd requested), he would have to ask Beijing. We have finished dinner and I ask, "Where can I stay? A cheap hotel?" and Mr. Wu says, "Don't worry, Mr. Zhang owns a hotel," and I will stay there.

11:30 p.m.

We go to the J.T. Hotel and meet Mr. Zhang. His firm is on the second floor, and we collect in the conference room to drink boiled and steaming water and talk. I tell first of our research at Harvard, and of my previous trip to Dongguan City in January. He slowly begins to show me some of his projects, beginning with his own undergraduate thesis, an industrial city, designed and now built in Shenzhen. It is now midnight and he must return to his work. He offers me an empty office next to his, used only rarely by South China University of Technology professors who visit from Guangzhou to review the Design Institute's work. He asks if I'd like to meet him the next morning to spend time on site with a client.

Mr. Wu has arranged a small room for me on the fifth floor. A hand-off ensues as Bill Wong and Mr. Wu leave me at the door of my room. I realize that Mr. Zhang is responsible for me now.

I get a phone call later that night—Bill Wong—who he tells me "you are very lucky." And I think he means in the American sense—lucky to have him to help me, etc. and I say yes, you and everyone have been so kind, I don't know how to thank you, etc., but he says no, Mr. Wu says you have good feng shui.

10:00 a.m. June 3, 1996

I am in my office to meet Mr. Zhang. I wait until 10:45 and

then we leave. Mr. Zhang, two project architects, two bundles of folded construction drawings, each tied with a red ribbon. We have a driver, and the car has loud horns and police sirens--Mr. Zhang is always late.... We drive 45 minutes to east Dongguan City. On the way, we talk about designing all those factories (Mr. Zhang has done some)-- each must include dormitories and canteens (and I think now of the hotel where I am staying).

Mr. Zhang describes the programs of the various recreational facilities he will build for the client we will visit--two hotels, a massage parlor, an ice-skating rink and bowling alley, a theater, a disco. And when I am showing my (my what? envy? desire?) he must see it, even from the back seat and says, "Why don't you try some floor plans?" Yes, that would be wonderful.

The client, Mr. Luo--a developer--is building the biggest VIRGIN CITY© in Dongguan. Mr. Luo has a compound in Chang Ping, near the Li Cheng (Beautiful City) site and just off a commercial street, where Japanese bonsai trees on stands surround a circular courtyard. We pass through the gate, the security guard opens the car door for me. We enter one of the dark doorways: concrete interiors with fans, many levels, tropical-like sets from Casablanca. In Mr. Luo's office--dark wood, two massive turtle shells on the wall opposite his desk--beautiful Chinese secretaries (like Japanese geishas) wear long traditional uniforms of layered shiny cotton--I never see fabric of that quality here--and I will see more of them, that same uniform, throughout the day in surprising places. They mark the developer's territory.

Mr. Luo is something like a mix of Star Trek's Mr. Spock (Leonard Nimoy) and Roy Orbison--but of course he's Chinese--and very polite (but more bemused than impressed by me), and very cool with diamond ring on middle finder and jade bracelet--spheres on silk thread--and this last proves how far from the American real-estate developer's aura of sleaziness he is. Nothing about him is about selling anything or convincing anyone (a higher form of politician here)--more like an emperor (he doesn't have to get elected).

He drives a jeep around himself (no driver, which is very rare). His main office is in Hong Kong (with 300 employees there and at various site offices--he's got projects in Fujian and Shanghai), but he, like Mr. Wu, Mr. Chan, and Mr. Zhang, grew up in Dongguan City and prefers to be here now, near Beautiful City, which is,

industrial-based economy, a policy of *litu bu lixiang*, ("not engaged in agriculture, but not leaving the village"). The central government's financial contribution to Guangdong's development immediately and steadily declines. Guangdong's contributions to the national budget increase and are soon the largest of any province in China.

The socialist market strategy finds fertile soil in southern China, and this successful pairing of an abandoned Chinese province and an untested economic system create China's most successful model of privatization through deregulation. Guangdong has become modernized in less than ten years.[15]

The Special Economic Zone

China's communist sacrifice to modernization has the inevitable utopian rationale: the anticipation of foreign economic and *intellectual*

investment, with which China will build a global empire. Deng's internal deregulations are coupled, in yin-yang fashion, with a highly visible act—a global press release—of socialist planning control. The centerpiece of Deng's reform strategy, and the flashy force behind Guangdong's success, is the Shenzhen Special Economic Zone, set up to receive controlled dosages of foreign wealth in the form of hard currency and advanced technology. And, most importantly, the incorporation of Hong Kong itself, when in July 1997 Britain releases the island to the mainland.

The spatial equivalent of Deng's Open Door policy is the coastal SEZs (there are four) reprogramming of tiny fishing villages near Hong Kong and Taiwan as capitalist enclaves, future metropolises that offer foreign investors preferential treatment. The Shenzhen SEZ (the most successful, built across the border from Hong Kong) soon teems—a Chinese gold rush—with thousands of entrepreneurial cadres (specialists), capitalist-style private businessmen (local and overseas Chinese), and their mistresses.

Beijing micromanages all aspects of Shenzhen SEZ's creation and operation. Mandarin is spoken in the SEZ, not Cantonese. Beijing erects a border to protect Shenzhen from the deregulated free-for-all that is Guangdong Province. This border also protects the rest of China from the negative influence of capitalism. The zone is also restricted; only those with special SEZ status can enter.

Shenzhen SEZ is Deng's earliest and most fragile success (he is called "designer-general" by the southern Chinese). It grows from a village to a city of three million people in ten years yet, without the necessary infrastructure to support a population of its size. In that same period, it cannot attract any more advanced a technology than instructions for manufacturing Kader Industry's Cabbage Patch Doll.[16]

When designated, an SEZ is privileged forever as an enclave for capitalist experiments and damned forever as the final indicator of a successful ascension to global financial viability, watched by both Beijing and the rest of the world.

it seems, at a critical stage in its development.

On the wall of his office behind me is Beautiful City (1:1,000 scale), one of the many iterations I will see today. It is clearly a vision, his vision (and I'm told later that the site plan was "designed" by this finger-pointing developer. "I think the shrine to my family should go here ... and a tower there."). Mr. Zhang, the architect, has inherited the Beautiful City project half-built and is now, after some minor changes to the master plan (originally designed by a planning/architecture firm from the north and now considered too conservative, too Soviet, the wrong lifestyle for the Pearl River Delta), working on various entertainment and recreational facilities. Today he presents to Mr. Luo and two other men on Luo's team new designs for a hotel, one of two in Beautiful City. Buried deep into the site, it announces the entrance to the tourist and entertainment facilities. I watch him go through the schematics—11x17 pages of photocopied sketch drawings. Then he chooses a few blueprints from the stack of folded-and-

tied to present specific features (he tells me later that unlike most developers he works for, Mr. Luo respects him, listens to his ideas as one professional to another). They spend over an hour as I sit devising my interview questions—Mr. Luo has offered to speak with me formally, and Mr. Zhang has suggested I prepare a list of questions—and then it is time to leave for lunch.

As we are driving, following Mr. Luo's jeep, it sinks in slowly (like everything here—always unfolding into conditions unforeseen, unpredictable)—we are having lunch at Beautiful City—on site with Mr. Luo and his top design and construction men (probably ten around the table). We enter the VIRGIN CITY© (empty, of course) and up the main drive.

*"Single-family dwellings"
in Beautiful City*

On our left is a row of tightly packed two-story housing, and I realize they have turned one of these single-family dwellings into a restaurant—a private club, really—for Mr. Luo and guests.

But before lunch, a quick tour of Beautiful City's tourist area (those that don't

*"I think the shrine to my
family should go here..."*

own units here will pay to enter)—narrow dirt roads winding around hills—beautiful, especially Mr. Luo's shrine to his family cut into a mountainside, something like a miniature Great Wall that sits just in front of the (future) ice-skating rink/bowling alley. Only he and his family can go near it (Mr. Luo's son actually lives at Beautiful City now). Many historic shrines and temples have been finished, including a Buddha figure maybe

Deng's competitive spirit has created an imbalance of wealth: between overheated coastal areas and the tragically underfed hinterland, between communist controlled Beijing and the freewheeling Guangdong Province. His deregulatory reforms are a series of faulty modernizations; the fragile success of the privatization of state industry leads to the failure of inflationary pressure, which leads to economic resuscitation through BANKRUPTCY©, and then again to the failure to attract foreign technology, and so on.

After fifteen years of frenzied modification and mimicry, the national growth rate of fixed-asset investment is at its highest in 1993— 58.6 percent—but within a year it drops to 27.8 percent and then dips again to 20 percent.

"A Shanghai taxi driver—in his mid-20s—says his generation is more optimistic than ever about the future. 'Young people like myself know what our goals are,' he says, as he sips a cola at a Kentucky Fried Chicken outlet on a lunch break, 'We want to save money. Someday we'll be able to buy a car, a house and—why not, maybe its possible—a little airplane.'"[18]

30 feet high. Everywhere there are billboards depicting future buildings, imagined development (Mr. Zhang says Mr. Luo has hired illustrators, not architects, for these visions, and the signs have no relationship to the real design).

We have lunch upstairs in the master bedroom, now filled with a huge circular table, and many men are here and we crowd around, and I'm seated next to the developer, with Mr. Zhang translating at my left. We are served by women in the long uniforms. Iced salmon--with wasabi--(the second time in 24 hours) and other more sinister delicacies. Mr. Luo asks me to prove my proficiency and I snatch a peanut with chopsticks--no mishaps. They discuss the origins of Beautiful City, although very little is translated for me--Mr. Zhang is doing business.

Lunch is nearly over. The fruit begins to arrive, but Mr. Luo waves it away. We walk next door, followed by long uniforms tiptoeing with our fruit, where another single-family dwelling has been turned into a sitting room. Each afternoon, they spend their two-hour break here. We eat the fruit--and for much of it they must show me how to peel, what to spit out-- and I interview Mr. Luo.

He bought the land, 1,500 Chinese acres, in mid-1992 and for one year prepared the site and planned the development, choosing as master planner/ architect a firm from north China who'd done projects in Shenzhen. Construction began in 1994. The first phase of the project is complete (and the original planners have been replaced by Mr. Zhang)-- 250,000 square meters have been constructed, 2,600 units. 1,600 of those units have been sold (only 6 of them to local Chinese), leaving 1,000 vacant units.

300 million RMB (U.S.$36 million) was invested, and 600 million RMB (U.S.$72 million) was returned to investors--they doubled their money. It will take another 8 years to com- plete the project (that is, if the economy picks up) and when completed will have cost 6 billion RMB (U.S.$723 million). I ask if he received any special treatment (tax incentives, etc.) from Dongguan City's local government, and he gets a little sly, and now even more bemused. "Absolutely none..."

As construction began, Mr. Luo started selling the units in Hong Kong. A successful promotion ... The site sits next to the railroad that connects Kowloon to Beijing and is a normal commute at one hour and 20 minutes from Hong Kong. I ask about Gordon Wu's superhighway (at least an hour's drive west from the Beautiful City site), and he is confident that the new infrastructure is only useful for transport of goods, for industry. The train is, and has always been, the most viable mode of transportation in China, he assures me (selling a little, now).

Mr. Luo's buyers/investors are from Hong Kong, Macau, and overseas, so he has developed

SPILLOVER©

The socialist market system, China's Open Door sacrifice to modernization, is a high-risk gamble. Ideologically successful but economically unproved, the socialist market is a revolutionary economy that has caused early and stunning success, and also the hidden failures of wrenching inner struggle.

Fantastic growth, when concentrated in a clearly demarcated economic system (the freewheeling capitalism of the island of Hong Kong), the schizophrenic socialist market in the Shenzhen ZONE©), eventually SPILLS© over into ideologically unprotected VIRGIN© territory. In China, this excess (most visible as export processing factories and luxury housing developments) taints a socialist hinterland with the temptations of unadulterated capitalism. Extra factories, luxury housing developments, and foreign funds (often in the form of bribes) infiltrate the PRD's underdeveloped cities as overflow from the few ill-prepared areas designated to receive them.

It's a balancing act, embodied by two cities in the delta, a yin-yang pairing of purity and contamination. Shenzhen SEZ acts as a filter—purifying capitalism for distribution as foreign currency into Mainland China— and Dongguan City, on Shenzhen's northern border, acts in a secret space of freedom— processing and profiting from the dirty SPILLOVER© Shenzhen cannot contain. Shenzhen's border is weak; Dongguan's is powerfully strong.

If Shenzhen is China's ego, Dongguan is China's id.

a strategy that provides incentives (through entertainment and tourism amenities) to encourage them to come visit more often, maybe even live there.... (Mr. Luo acknowledges that Beautiful City is empty most of the time, and it clearly pains him.) His entertainment and recreation facilities will also attract tourists for short-term hotel stays, as will the 1.6-kilometer-long shopping strip along the main road near the train station. Mr. Luo travels often and all over the world. "To find ideas?" I ask. "Yes, mainly from America." But the shopping strip is a copy of one he'd visited in the Middle East.

We end the interview by taking pictures and then eat more of the special fruits. He serves me, as he's done with the raw salmon at lunch, and is patient as together we peel litchi nuts.

We go once more (Mr. Luo now drives us in his jeep) around the development--a closer look. And end up at the sales office, a cavernous shed done up like a banquet hall--tables and chairs, and where the stage would be there is a stage-size model of Beautiful City. Behind are murals of previous iterations like stage sets--this is entertainment!

I'm given brochures and we leave, go back to Mr. Luo's compound, so Mr. Zhang can get paid, in an extremely long and fitful process--signatures, forms, waiting. Mr. Zhang disappears, leaving me alone with the developer. I drink tea and the developer works, writing at his desk. Nearly an hour goes by (earlier I'd watched Mr. Zhang's driver make a

transaction involving a big pile of notes that he brought in off the street and threw onto the dashboard--American kids can't throw around credit cards with the same effect; here it is closer to the movies, gangsterish). A Chinese geisha appears with a gift for me, a set of pens-- heavy silver ballpoint and fountain pens, and a golden keychain. Owners receive these when they purchase a unit. Mr. Zhang returns and then a secretary appears with a thin tissue paper for Mr. Zhang-- some form of money? It is our signal to go.

On our drive home Mr. Zhang asks, "If you could design a

Models and renderings in the Beautiful City sales office

thesis project, what would you do?" "I would design a city." "How big." "As big as Mr. Luo's." He then suggests that I work on the Beautiful City master plan (Phase Two, which won't begin any time soon). He needs fresh ideas--he can't devote the time to it because they are working on construction drawings for the buildings. He will give me all the original plans and the changes that he's made. "Let's see what you can do with it all," he says...

7:00 p.m. June 4, 1996
Dinner tonight with Mr. Zhang and Mr. Wu ... the same fish restaurant as two nights ago with pool tables under tents. It is the current favorite of Dongguan City's wealthy. Mr. Wu brings me gifts, and I listen to him speak, telling stories in Chinese. I now love the language and I'm listening like it's music and then, all of a sudden, Mr. Zhang will say in English, "Mr. Wu thinks we should go to the top of the tallest building in Dongguan to look at the city" or "Mr. Wu is talking about wandering through cities alone" or, as I watched Mr. Wu tell a particularly long and graphic story-- lots of chop! then long pauses, as everybody watched--a ghost story, really, and then Mr. Zhang says, "Mr. Wu was just answering your earlier question about the empty factories." (ghost city)

Mr. Wu's "ghost" story I finally extract from Mr. Zhang, albeit paraphrased, and it goes like this: Villagers built factories to entice Hong Kong industry (a form of industrial speculation).

Broad ways. Endless vehicle streams. A large number of high buildings. A great many businessmen and tourists. A prosperous scene of the new city, a future metropolis with rural scenery. This is Dong Guan.[19]

Buying Utopia

In the first ten years of China's economic reform, industrial growth in Dongguan, a PRD city between Guangzhou and Shenzhen SEZ, grew at more than 40 percent per year. "If you can make one dollar in Hong Kong you can make two dollars in Dongguan,"[20] boasts a Dongguan official. Theirs is the fastest industrial-growth rate in the world.

Getting rich is glorious in Dongguan. Freshly solvent farmers host feasts in hotels (i.e., bordellos) for Hong Kong factory owners and their bodyguards (after all, "doing business can be bloody"[21]). Migrant workers roam the streets,[22] available to spatialize all utopic visions, constructing export processing factories (and the plastic trees and athletic shoes that pour out of them) and the single-family housing required for the managers who run them. Ensconced in luxury condominiums, playing Mah-Jongg, Wife Number Two, Number Three, and even Number Four greet the tired businessman, who has arrived late in his Mercedes from Hong Kong. The ultimate BUSINESS VACATION©, Dongguan is an (in)famous developer's hideout, the developer rules as secretly and atavistically as any pre-liberation emperor.

Haven for Risk Takers

Dongguan is a Chinese Las Vegas. ZONED© from Beijing's sanctioned hedonism, the city operates like the interior of a themed hotel in Las Vegas, kept perpetually night (no windows

China may threaten your health, writes **Louise Lucas**

and
/ be
here

the
kid-
less-
and
Kit
call
),000
were
ong-

10se
him
Ms
Mr
1der
ison
his
1 in
). In
. no

Danger spots and how to reduce the risks

200 miles
320 km

CHINA

GUANGDONG

Dongguan

Guangzhou   Shenzhen

Shunde

Zhuhai   Hong Kong

Macao

SOUTH
CHINA SEA

The cities of China's Guangdong province are unlikely soon to shed their frontier-town mentality, *writes Louise Lucas.* In the meantime, Mr Stephen Vickers, security consultant and former head of Hong Kong's criminal intelligence bureau, advises foreign businessmen to take the following precautions.

☐ Bring in the professionals should anything go wrong. Hong Kong police can send an Interpol message to China requesting assistance; co-operation between the two is "by and large pretty good".

☐ Before doing a deal with a partner, run a full due diligence check; ensure the activities you plan to pursue are legitimate.

☐ When travelling to China on business, take a colleague and leave at home a full list of names and addresses of people you plan to see.

☐ Have a list of 20 questions to which only you and close relatives know the answers (the name of a favourite novel, the place you spent your honeymoon). This allows investigators to establish whether or not a person is alive once he has been kidnapped and is being held.

☐ Prefer to employ westerners in business dealings. Says Mr Vickers: "Westerners should bear in mind if there is an ugly dispute and you are putting an ethnic Chinese up front he is probably at more risk than a Caucasian. That's not racist, it's just how it is."

Advice from the West about doing business in the Pearl River Delta. 1995.

from which to view the morning sun). As in Las Vegas, twenty-four-hour neon signage keeps people gambling in Dongguan. Speculation is the game that has addicted a newly middle class. Dongguan City, haven for risk takers, where the return on investment—20 to 30 percent—is higher than it is anywhere in China, is as secretive as the developers and corrupt cadres who together control it in an unlikely, but effective, public/private partnership. With danger as the intimidation tactic—only the bravest will exit the superhighway to Dongguan City, where kidnappings and luxury-car theft terrorize the innocent—mystery insures continued desirability and continued profit (milking a return from 50 percent-vacancy rates and a wasted, post-industrialized landscape).

Early promiscuities and (glorious) sacrifices were required to get here. They are visible in Dongguan City. Dongguan's real estate is empty. Dongguan is building emptiness— VIRGIN© cities—not yet taken. Innocent, fresh (but quickly deteriorating) VIRGIN© cities, built with the dirty SPILLOVER© of CORRUPTION© and FAUSTIAN© money from Shenzhen SEZ.

STEALTH© Tactics

Under reform, growth is accelerated by activating competition. Deng's open door dictate, "get rich, get rich fast, get rich first," takes spatial form in the PRD. Shenzhen SEZ competes on the international stage, designed to receive the First World's wealth of high technology. Dongguan is abandoned to the "dark side" of globalization (Nestlé factories, export processing). Turning DISADVANTAGE© into an asset, Dongguan manipulates its geographical gift. The city falls always in the shadow of Shenzhen's shining highrise towers, and it uses this invisibility as strength. As Shenzhen's towers rise, Dongguan—sometimes stealing, sometimes LEARNING© (an enthusiastic innocence)—acts in Deng's secret space of deregulation, with all the STEALTH© of one rejected, ignored. Harnessing the power of looser land-use guidelines

and the free flow of funds gained from bribery, Beijing and Dongguan devise business and occupational tactics simultaneously to quicken spatial growth and insure continued invisibility. In the process, a decentralized network of villages and roads is created, a revolutionary urban form that provides a model for China's spatial and economic evolution.

Growing Rich

Dongguan, lying in the middle south of Guangdong province between Guangzhou-Hong Kong economic corridor, connecting Shenzhen and Huizhou on the southeast, watching Guangzhou from the opposite of the river on the northeast, facing Ling Ding River on the south, is a main passage for many regions of South China and the Pacific coastal countries and regions. Within the bounds many mountains are located in the southeast and in the northwest lie deposited plains with rivers forming a water net and a giant spread of fertile fields. It belongs to a subtropical climate here, sunshine ample, rainfall much, trees and grasses exuberant and climate warm like spring all year around.[23]

Dongguan is Attractive

As early as 1975, Hong Kong uses Dongguan, and much of the rest of Guangdong Province, as industrial hinterland.[24] Squeezed by a labor and land shortage, fearing loss of international competitiveness, Hong Kong manufacturers abandon their high-rent island and move to the mainland.

Dongguan County (as it was called then) is filled with the remains—both human and manufactured—of Mao's 1950s policy the Great Leap Forward, which extended the city into the countryside and created an agricultural, undeveloped string of market villages. Hong Kong needs only basic infrastructure (cities can get in the way of industrial and manufacturing processes): paved roads, reliable electricity. Land is cheap, and labor is very cheap (the bribes necessary to realize construction and factory operation are

This was successful for a few years. Hong Kongers would come up and rent the factories, and the villagers would then share the profits. But Hong Kong eventually decided to build their own factories here, and then moved their operations into them (taking even better advantage of Dongguan's cheap land and labor). Hence the abandoned factories, left behind when they moved. Whole villages of empty factories.

Dongguan City's government wants to move away from the export processing that made the city rich, and like everywhere else in the world, move into high-tech industry. Their slogan: a "second industrial revolution." Mr. Zhang says that they continue to encourage entrepreneurship, but now suggest growing companies. The secret here is to be secret—if the government finds out a business is successful, they start investigating and soon are taxing them more. When a newspaper article was written about Mr. Zhang's architectural work in Dongguan City, his parents were appalled.... Why was that necessary? Mr. Zhang's father is chief of police. Mr. Zhang's first building in Dongguan City was the police station (the largest one in all of China). I ask, "How else do you get clients?" "I have friends like Mr. Wu," he says.

11:00 p.m.
I take a dark drive with Mr. Zhang to Guangzhou. His driver is something like his business adviser and they are engrossed now in a rehash of our dinner with Mr. Wu. We are soon in a traffic jam on the superhighway—a truck has spilled glass,

all three lanes are full. Thanks to Gordon Wu, the superhighway is overlit—a steel pole shining fluorescent orange every 5 meters. Quickly people emerge from the cars, trucks, and buses into this daylight and start a poker game crouched together in one lane, or stretch and sleep on the pavement or the roofs of trucks, or climb the embankment and crouch, talking. We walk ahead past many cars to see the glass pile, and then walk back. We will wait here for two hours. We recline in the back of the car, and Mr. Zhang tells me he has a 30-acre piece of land in Dongguan City, and he tells me his vision.

He will build a gated compound on his land, which sits four meters above the road. His development will be like a castle on a hill. In the middle, a lake will provide fish and birds. Surrounding the water are 30 single-family dwellings, each designed differently, with entertainment and gathering facilities throughout (he assumes buyers will be moving to his castle from somewhere else—Taiwan and Hong Kong, presumably—and they need lots of public space in which to meet one another). The residents would share in the upkeep. Mr. Zhang tells about the early days of communism, when a New China brought everyone together to work for free on projects, like the canal running through Dongguan City Center, which his mother helped build. And to convince people to buy houses in his development, to convince them that his idea is a sound one, he will build his own house first in an exciting, econom-

ic, seductive way. This will prove how nice it will be, and then others will follow. He would like my help with this project. Mr. Zhang will spend the summer suggesting different ways for us to use this land—a collaboration.

June 6, 1996
Dear Rem,
Mr. Wu, Dongguan City Planner, moonlights on the weekend designing buildings. He brings me gifts now, every time we see each other. I will make a list of all of them one day before I leave. He will be a case study for me (if I can say that about someone I feel close to, if I can do that to someone I feel close to...). He is a communist-party member, although we have not talked about this. His age (28) is important. He is part of the new New China, youth put in power because only they are capable of the energy (the naïveté) it takes to grow this fast. Mr. Wu has suggested (not to me) that he and I are connected at a deeper level, maybe in a past life. His last gift, presented to me with Mrs. Wu translating, was a teapot, with Chinese figures imprinted on the outside meaning luck and happiness (feng shui) from what he called the Chinese heart bible. (And yes, I will deal with Mr. Wu's CORRUPTION©, détourned and otherwise—with images of Shenzhen's dead minister of construction all the while in my head...). He is now in North America for 10 days—Vancouver, San Francisco, New York, Hawaii—having canceled last spring's trip to Europe. "America is better," he says.

For the Chinese I am a kind of apparition. I've not yet

From the 1995 Dongguan Yearbook Rich and Civilized Dongguan: *"The Modern Comprehensive Public Infrastructure. Broad roads. Perfect anti-collision wall. Green belts and drainage ditch. Modern bus-stops. Striking signs. When night comes, the luxurious street-lamps on the roadsides, as the bright pearls in the vault of heaven, light the whole city as if it were daytime."*[26]

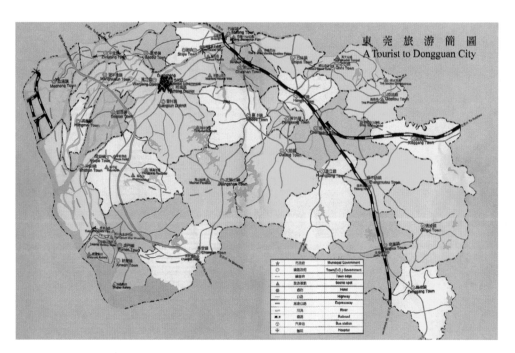

A tourist map of Dongguan City's thirty-three towns, 1994. From the Chinese strategist Sun Tzu's The Art of War: *"Hiding order beneath the cloak of disorder is simply a question of subdivision; concealing courage under a show of timidity presupposes a fund of latent energy; masking strength with weakness is to be effected by tactical dispositions."*[27]

reduced through connections: 650,000 Hong Kong residents have ancestral homes and family in Dongguan). Hong Kong's textile, food-processing, footwear, and electronics-assembly enterprises flood Dongguan County and many other small towns in the delta. Dongguan begins to grow rich.

In 1980, Shenzhen SEZ, designed by Deng to control and profit from exactly this infiltration, filters Hong Kong's invasion of the PRD into one contained area. The SEZ is created to couple with Hong Kong in a partnership that will introduce global business practices and new technologies into China. Dongguan, newly addicted to industrial growth, is lost in the fanfare.

Watching China's "opening" from the other side of a new border, Dongguan sees skyscraper foundations poured at SHENZHEN SPEED©, it see investors—seduced by tax incentives, simple entry/exit procedures, and access to the labor market—fund a shiny model city. Dongguan sees Shenzhen as China's future.

As Shenzhen's towers rise, Dongguan acts in Deng's secret space of deregulation. Dongguan mimics Shenzhen's successes and its mistakes. The city LEARNS©.

Since the reform and opening toward the outside, the people of Dong Guan have caught the favourable time to exert all kinds of advantages, make a start to accumulate funds by processing imported raw materials, carry out building the infrastructures of the city on a large scale, take the road of industrialization and mass production, so the framework of a big modern city has been formed.[25]

Roads

Dongguan insures success with one subtle, realizable, infrastructural tactic: while the delta's SEZs (Zhuhai and Shenzhen) construct flashy superhighways and international airports (today sitting vast and empty), Dongguan builds roads. With the income earned from land leasing, the only incentive Beijing allows Dongguan, the city pours a web of pavement,

connecting Dongguan's villages (full of tiny factories) to distributors in all directions.

Then, as the SEZs beg for high-tech business and tourism (foreign currency) from America and Japan, Dongguan approaches Hong Kong (poaching now from Shenzhen) with an offer of cheap land and labor, a secret complicity (like insider information) that allows in-the-know businessmen to avoid Shenzhen's rising costs (manufacturers don't want to pay for skyscrapers). Dongguan offers (unsanctioned) SEZ-style tax incentives and relaxed land-use laws to cement the deal with Hong Kong.[28]

In 1982 Dongguan's tactics are discovered by Beijing; the city is caught stealing from the SEZ (i.e., Dongguan's success at attracting Hong Kong investors threatens Shenzhen). As punishment, Beijing designates Dongguan County a model of how to grow from an historic village into a city and bestows upon Dongguan legal powers of persuasion. Dongguan County is renamed Dongguan City, And then Beijing returns its attention to Shenzhen. With city status, the privileges Dongguan has for so long simply taken—the tax incentives and loose land-use policies, the freedom of local-level decision making—are now bestowed. Beijing's act makes visible Dongguan's secret intention, and Dongguan will now be watched. Dongguan is left with no choice but to plan and construct the model city that is Beijing's desire.

Thirty-three Towns

Dongguan's city planners (who are government officials) abandon Dongguan's STEALTHY© mission. Using Beijing's suggestion—"from a village to a city"—they devise a plan.

Dongguan City is rezoned into thirty-three towns (Dongguan's city center comprises four of the thirty-three). Dongguan planners adapt a Garden City model, with satellite towns surrounding an historic core, to Dongguan's existing condition. Villages outside the core are zoned as satellites, but each village is also made singular and given an asset to promote seen a Western face, a non-Chinese. But in a sense that's not true. In beauty shops and department stores they show pictures of blonde women. So when I go running, or make any movement out of my hotel room, it is a spectacle for them, and for me a kind of pure loneliness. Exactly what I imagine being famous is like, but darker (yes, I imagine fame can be dark, too, but a child cried, cowering against his mother, when I smiled at him yesterday)--absolutely no anonymity.

We watch TV in the canteen. I notice that not only do they re-create their pre-liberation history as tourism (Splendid China), but they now have an obsession with historic soap operas, on TV in the canteen afternoon and night (which I can't help but contrast with the faded Cultural Revolution music videos played in between the soap opera segments. These videos are, for me, especially potent--dancing workers and agricultural landscapes, reels of Mao; and so faded, like old postcards. I ask if they were really made during the Cultural Revolution, but they weren't, they're new). After lunch we take a nap. They are living on the insides and the backsides of this hotel and retire there, in bunks (half the hotel was never finished, so these rooms have dirt floors, and some literally with mounds of dirt in the middle of the room). I go to my room and sleep.

I've been trying to find the New City Center. A large plot of land at the edge of Dongguan City Center was designated as the New City Center by the local government. The master plan for the area includes gov-ernment buildings, exposition centers, retail, housing. Nothing on the site is currently occupied, save for an Agricultural Exposition Center, designed by Half-Town Chan, which is finished and operating, and a tall post office to house all post and telecommunications operations, which will be occupied next month. Other buildings are under construction, although the project is on hold--empty, abandoned for lack of funds, the sudden refusal of the city government to move their operations to the new site, and a resistance to the project by the community (it is too far from work and all the buildings are empty, they say). Plans to salvage the project inexplicably include adding more land to the site footprint.

Also included in the New City Center master plan is an area designated to integrate the existing (old) city center with the new, in order to de-densify the urban core. Held as separate from the rest of the plan, it is the first project Mr. Wu has undertaken in his role (since October) as Dongguan City Planner. He has a six-year deadline to solve the problems of this integration. To add to the complication, a new New City Center is being designed to replace the first. It seems the former Dongguan mayor (infamous--jailed now for CORRUPTION©) sited the original close to his hometown, and the new mayor prefers a site closer to his own village, further west).

I work in the office in the afternoons. I'm studying the various iterations of Beautiful City. The first plan was rejected as "too Soviet." They had hired northern Chinese designers who couldn't provide enough exuberance. Mr. Zhang (my boss) was hired to make a new plan, although much of Phase One of the original design has been built. I'm not yet getting paid, not officially working on it (but unofficially I am, of course, preparing it for use in my thesis). Mr. Zhang is very busy--he has ten buildings in the office now--and is often in Guangzhou, where the institute is head-quartered. Sometimes I read Jameson (I brought along Post-modernism); often I write. I usually wander around the city before dinner.

I spent half an hour in the post office to mail your last letter, just trying to figure it all out--some primitive machines for pasting together an envelope--no licking here. Yesterday I spent hours cashing travelers' checks at the bank. ... In fact, I have much to tell about "money" now that I'm here--many frustrations (it shouldn't surprise us that money will be my only rub, my only friction.... Has it always been so for me? or until you made it so by choosing me. I no longer remember, ... but I'm probably assured now, for good or bad, of getting rich). Life without credit: money is so very tangible here. The men carry purses to hold their cash. The buildings, the developments, are just bigger purses--there is nothing else to do with the extra money (Bataille...).

I've been reading Conrad's Heart of Darkness--I feel like the storyteller awaiting rivets at the edge of the jungle.

based on infrastructure or topography (a "rail-sides colony" in the only place in Dongguan where two railroad lines meet, a "mountain colony" with Hong Kong's hilly profile, or a "seaside colony" connected to the waterways of the delta).

Not a few years ago, several comprehensive industrial and commercial cities and towns were set up, such as Chang An, etc. For overall arrangement, the area is divided as: railsides colony centered in Chang Ping focusing on storing, producing, trading and transporting; mountain colony centered in Tong Xia focusing on of R & D and real estate developments, seaside colony centered in Hu Men.[29]

Dongguan immediately reconceptualizes its new decentralized plan as European, (a patchwork, a loosely woven fabric connected with threading highways, inspired by the European continent). Each of the thirty-three towns, controlled by a town leader (a local communist official), is asked to declare its intention to become an international city, creating the accelerated growth that would accompany that vision. Each is asked to provide a five-year plan for the realization of the vision.

The provincial government appoints a mayor (a figurehead) to control the whole of Dongguan City; and together with Dongguan's city planner (who has the power only to *suggest* action), the mayor will regulate the realization of the city's vision. [30] Deng's reforms, a combination of deregulation and competition, are now embodied in urban form. Dongguan is organized into a decentralized, low-visibility network that harnesses competition to create power. Innocently, maybe even naively, Dongguan has created a perfect model for China's evolution.

Shifting Centers
Dongguan is not a tiny fishing village, as Shenzhen and Zhuhai, at the beginning of reform. Dongguan's historic center has thrived for more than 800 years and is roughly 100,000

people strong when Deng opens China's doors. The thirty-three-town model now designates the historic center as four districts, each with a village leader and an autonomous government. A tangle of Chineseness, the city center is now shared by the four town leaders—none of whom want it.

Infrastructurally DISADVANTAGED© compared to others of the thirty-three towns (it is separated from the superhighway, the delta, the rail lines), the old city also prohibits the construction of new buildings and roads. There is no TABULA RASA© here. Each town leader wants a newly constructed center, and each wants his district to be the center. The nature of the town leaders' competition to become international cities, therefore, is necessarily creative, and so successful that it provides a model for many similarly DISADVANTAGED© villages.

A new city center will be constructed, it is decided. The mayor will determine which district will receive it. Locations are proposed, plans are drawn, and locations are shifted (based on bribery—each town leader attempting to receive the bribe). False starts litter the landscape. Dongguan's mayor finally positions the city center to direct growth toward his own village. Halfway to completion, the mayor of Dongguan City is sacrificed (hanged) by the Chinese Communist Party for CORRUPTION©. The new city center immediately shifts again, to the southwest (leaving behind two occupied buildings), where the new mayor's hometown is located. During the five years that these shifts occur, the four district leaders quit waiting (why wait?), and each builds a new city center of his own.

Miniaturizing Shenzhen
Dongguan also realizes it must compete overtly with the Shenzhen SEZ. The city constructs a village to take advantage of its greatest asset: proximity to Shenzhen. Chang An, a miniature sweep of planned, linear city, is realized as a replica of the SEZ, a mirror (warped to reduce scale) facing the border. A model

茶山
Chashan

擁有美好的明天
possess beautiful futare

一個現代化城鎮已經呼之欲出，一座又一座的花園別墅、高層禹住大廈，一個又一個具有規模的大型綜合開發區正動工興建，明日的茶山更是繁花似錦、璀璨奪目。

一個現代化的城鎮已經呼之欲出　　A modern city is rising

38

"An Embryonic Modernized City," 1995. A developer's brochure from one of Dongguan City's thirty-three towns. (In Rich and Civilized Dongguan, Dongguan Yearbook, 1995).

industrial village, Chang An announces Dongguan's challenge to Shenzhen: a showdown between gold-rush towns. Chang An, situated on the national highway where Shenzhen meets Dongguan, is positioned to receive the SEZ's SPILLOVER© and soon teems with development-zone proliferation.

Dongguan, with these visible acts, is complicit in the STEALTH©-proof planning-control mechanisms of the state (still in place despite Deng's deregulations). Beijing notices Dongguan's rising fixed-asset investment rate and makes a second visit in 1985. Praising Chang An as a model city (it is a thriving but still tiny village of 31,000, with 120,000 FLOATING© workers), Beijing encourages Dongguan to quicken its growth. With new incentives (freshly won from Beijing) immediately transferred, wholesale and without reservation, directly from Dongguan's city government to Dongguan's socialist-market cadres, each town is asked to LEARN©. They will mimic Chang An's successful evolution "from a village to a city" (each

cadre will be a city within a city). The whole of Dongguan is now doomed to repeat Chang An's success, in keeping with the speed at which China can merge with the global economy.

Dongguan's thirty-three competing villages, using the same incentives as Shenzhen SEZ (each with a speculating communist cadre as its town leader), together realize the fastest growth rate in the world for more than ten years.[31] As a model city, Dongguan is designated by Beijing as an economic experiment. But unlike the SEZ, Dongguan will be a condition the outside world won't see. Dongguan's experiment is designed to create an economic system for China, not a system for the global economy.

It will be months until he can repair his boat. Chinese time ... I'm dying to start designing one of Mr. Zhang's ten buildings. Two days ago Mr. Zhang suggested I could do one or two (?!) while I'm here. We'd been playing badminton and driving home. He showed me one of his buildings (the police station). He talked about the ease of building here, the relaxed rules, the need. I know he is serious about giving me one, he has more than enough work. And soon it will be that I'm forced to design a building in two weeks. I think that is what is supposed to happen here, at a fundamental level. And funny, me impatient--all the things that we suspected about the condition here are true, and more. ... FAUSTIAN MONEY©, FAUSTIAN© everything.

I hear music just now as I write and out the office win-

dow watch a funeral procession-- pipes and drums, followed by white-robed and hooded mourners. The casket comes last-- beautiful carved red

The "Translators Institute" in Dongguan City Center

wood in the shape of a flower's stem and bud, carried on bamboo poles. They rise over the bridge in front of me and head out of town, stopping at a generic factory truck-- canvas-backed. The casket is loaded in back as they file into an old white school bus--headed for the cemetery. No flowers, but a sign board

with a photo of the dead and white tissue streamers. Here what should be black is white. I live in the negative (or is it positive?) image...

2:00 p.m. June 8, 1996
Bill Wong had introduced me to a high-school friend, Thomas Tong, who runs a Translators Institute in Dongguan City Center. They would like me to teach. I go with Bill Wong on the scooter to the Science Museum, a hollow building with a globe out front, atrium inside. It forms one of two civic squares in downtown. After we drink, tea I'm asked to teach two classes on crime in America--a trial run. I will follow a chapter in their schoolbook. It outlines safety issues for Boston, and I ask if I must necessarily agree with these safety tips. They suggest I speak from experience....

5:30 p.m. June 18, 1996
I sit in Mr. Zhang's office and we talk about Beautiful City. He inherited a developer's plan of a Soviet-style development, half-constructed. His first corrective step was to regularize the street pattern (many streets did not meet). He then redesigned Phase Two, repositioning two of the podium towers, adding a symmetrical megablock and more parking. Some lowrise retail strips in this section had been constructed--small streets with markets--and Mr. Zhang designed a tent structure to enclose them. Chinese don't like to shop outside of a podium, he insists. Moving back into Phase One, he added wandering paths and landscape between the concrete towers, before tackling the real task at hand: the design and construction of five recreational buildings, placed in the master plan around a lake on the site.

As we talk, I remind him I'm writing about money. He says (again), let's go into business together. The single-family house--the next big thing here, he says. This is the way architects can take advantage of the Chinese market. We must make enough money to do the really interesting architecture projects, he tells me (and I can't help but think how interesting his current projects are....). We will buy prefabricated houses and sell them in Dongguan City, setting up models and a showroom on his vacant piece of land. I ask if the current market supports these kinds of home sales, and he produces a brochure from a development outside of Guangzhou. Look, these houses are selling for

U.S.$150,000-$200,000. And I say, Are they selling? Yes, yes, and he shows me the low vacancy rates. If we can construct them as prefabricated houses that we ship from the States, our profit will be huge. I agree. He asks me to go back to my hometown and arrange a joint venture. And we could represent any number of other building-materials companies here on his land, he says.... (I can't imagine anything more FAUSTIAN© for me than the single-family house--maybe worse than designing and building these huge developments on farmland (or maybe not).

8:00 p.m. June 18, 1996
He's given me a building! ... on the lake at Beautiful City

The site for a building beside the lake ...

80 meters long
20 meters wide
3-4 stories high
open program (recreational)
atrium

June 21, 1996
Dear Rem,
I have been asked to do two things this summer while working for Mr. Zhang's architecture firm in Dongguan City: finesse the master plan for Beautiful City, and more urgently, help design one of the recreational buildings--a clubhouse at the Beautiful City site--5,000 square meters, a

long and thin footprint roughly 80 meters by 20 meters, 3-4 stories high, to begin construction this fall or winter (or maybe spring, in this slowing economy ...). I've decided the open program will most likely include guest rooms, a restaurant, boating facilities (it is on a lake), table tennis, an art gallery (!?), and anything else we suggest that the developer, Mr. Luo, approves of. I will be assisted on the project by Mr. Liu, a graduate student at the Design Institute (in Guangzhou) that Mr. Zhang's firm is associated with. Mr. Zhang has just left for one month to visit family in America. On his return to Dongguan City, Mr. Zhang will present design drawings to Mr. Luo, with the construction-drawing stage set to begin as I leave in mid-August.

Many conditions make this project (for good or for bad) less hurried--a 4-week design-- than others in the office and in other architecture offices I've visited (i.e., Half-Town Chan's): two other larger recreational buildings for this same site, a hotel and a theater, will be constructed first, the clubhouse is effectively third in line. And Mr. Zhang's buildings take longer; he is attempting to introduce American standards and practices here. Without much success. His employees often leave, dissatisfied, after only a few months, because Mr. Zhang asks them to change the design many times and work on details. Also, very few developers are willing to participate in this experiment. In the project I will work on, the developer is in fact salvaging his empty city

(250,000 square meters planned, designed, and built in two and one-half years) by hiring Mr. Zhang to design lifestyle, and is therefore willing to spend a little extra money and time. For instance, the hotel's construction drawings are finished now, eight months after the project was begun. Mr. Zhang usually spends about six months getting to this stage, most architects here average 4–6 months, and Half-Town Chan-- known here to be the richest architect, the one who's sacrificed the most to money, "I design my buildings in 10 days. ..."--probably spends 2–4 months (at the most) before construction begins. All the above includes construction drawings and assumes building designs are not being recycled, but designed fresh.

The topic of gossip around the office is always how Mr. Zhang is negotiating with the many developers/clients who hurry him, insist on certain building materials because of special relationships with suppliers, (for awhile the blue-tinted-glass factory was everybody's best friend), refuse his details. So, I've found our speedy-architecture model to remain, for the most part, intact.

Two conditions--related to development and MARKET REALISM©--are also present here. At the micro-project by project-level, failure (the empty VIRGIN CITY©) is beginning to evolve into a renewal. In some cases, the developer is attempting to salvage the development (if it is valuable enough, and if he has not gone bankrupt ...) by adding entertainment/ recreation/tourism. Less valu-

able, smaller-scale projects are simply abandoned or undergo a radical change in program, either due to BANKRUPTCY© and subsequent renewal under a new owner or to a developer's short attention span. Here they play at entrepreneurship. At the macro (MARKET REALISM©) level, the intensity of development in the delta has been slowing after peaking in 1993, but at the same time, there is a renewed speculative fervor (of a slightly different nature) generated by the approaching 1997 handover (Hong Kong returning to Chinese rule).

There are 80 architecture firms in Dongguan City, some collaboratives, others nearly private, all loosely connected to design institutes. Mr. Zhang now has ten projects in the office and does not yet have to look for work--clients come to him. In four years he's completed roughly 40–50 projects (and that's nothing compared to Half-Town Chan's hundreds), but the nature of the projects is changing. Instead of factories, podium/towers in developments, and big government buildings (Mr. Zhang's first building in Dongguan City after his return from the States in 1992 is still the largest and tallest police station in all of China--his father is chief of police ...), the work now seems more about "image." "Redesign the facade of a half-completed strip mall that has just been given a new program--ice-skating rink turned to bowling alley," he's told. (This is the other project I was offered this summer and will probably work on after the clubhouse). This change of program mid-project is common here, devel-

opers continuously evolve their strategies. Mr. Zhang himself owns a half-completed building and has asked me to help start various companies to fill it up (he also owns a huge plot of land and wants us to do something very FAUSTIAN©--single-family dwellings--there, too). Mr. Zhang has suggested that many of the incomplete, empty buildings are the result of strategies evolved out of existence. Now, they simply design infill, usually recreation/ tourist attraction, always a complex mix of programs, or an open program, like the clubhouse I will design for the desolate Beautiful City--what I've called above a kind of salvaging operation that attempts to enhance the Western space planned and built here over the last 5–8 years.

7:00 p.m. June 23, 1996
I am to be presented at a lecture at the Science Museum. They insist I sit on the panel up front. I am introduced in Chinese, most likely as a visiting scholar from Harvard, here to study growth in Dongguan City. They promote the course I will teach to advanced English speakers (they were pleased with my treatment of crime in America and would like me to stay on.... I've decided to call my course "American Culture"). I am, of course, silent during the presentations, but when they call for questions, the first is directed to me: "What do you think of Dongguan's city planning?" I tell them that being in Dongguan City excites me, that it is beautiful in many ways but is also continuing to grow very quickly and is therefore diffi-

cult to manage. I say that I am confident, however, that the Dongguan City Planner (my friend Mr. Wu) is working now at solving Dongguan City's current problems. (I am often asked why I've come here. It is easiest to answer, I've come here to study money. This is clearly understood. Dongguan has a reputation. Any other answer--beauty, architecture, culture, inspiration--is met with bewilderment, even distrust....). Tonight they seem only to hear me say "Dongguan is beautiful," and later I find out this has discredited me: I am now highly suspect.

6:00 p.m. June 25, 1996
Tony Lee, director of the Translator's Institute, where I teach, invites me to another wedding. Many of those involved in the institute are there, and I always enjoy them for their bravery with English. Tony Lee has been devising ways we might do business together--tonight's idea is a collection of famous contemporary Western quotes, compiled by me, translated by him; and when he senses my reaction, this evolves into an architecture dictionary of terms and styles. I am seated next to someone new, Mr. Fuqi. Later we watch the bride's parents perform Tai Chi, and when I suggest I'd like to learn, Mr. Fuqi offers to teach me. His major in college was English, and his accent is purely American (causing immediate, and deceptive, familiarity). We talk about computers. I need a printer that can read a Macintosh disk. His might. We decide to leave the wedding together to go find out. We go to my hotel.

7:30 a.m. June 26, 1996
Mr. Fuqi calls, and 10 minutes later we are crossing the street with his older brother. We are having dim sum at

Mr. Fuqi

Honesty OK, the restaurant next to my hotel. We eat rice porridge with congealed pig's blood ("You mean, in America they just throw the blood away?"). I say, What are Americans thought to be like? He says, Casual, romantic (like Hollywood), creative.

We go off alone on his motor scooter in search of a Tai Chi sword for me (we cannot begin the lessons without it). Department stores are closed, a sports store is out of stock. We go to the Mountain Temple Park anyway, instead of Tai Chi, Mr. Fuqi wants to visit the fortune tellers.

We are led by old women to the alley of fortune tellers, and Mr. Fuqi chooses a youngish, straggly bearded one--this will be a feng shui fortune telling. We sit in heat, strong incense but lightness--staring out at a green slope with rows of statues. Women wander through them, giving gifts to deities-- bigger mountain, lush, behind them. The fortune teller speaks at length to Mr. Fuqi, explaining--what?--maybe the procedure, the cost, and then Mr. Fuqi takes his place on the

bench. They speak in Mandarin for over an hour--much palm and face reading, pointing at me sometimes, and I understand two words--feng shui. The fortune teller writes what he says down with a fountain pen, with much underlining, and then, when Mr. Fuqi is satisfied, he asks him to tell my fortune. He asks for my birthday--March 9, 1967--and time of birth, which I (bravely) make up, 11:20 p.m. He briefly reads both palms and my face, and makes notes, then asks me to stand up and walk across he room to the door and then come back.

A Feng Shui Fortune
My palm shows 2 lifelines; I am now in my second life-- which is full of luck and success--my first being tragic and difficult;

my palm shows a triangle in the middle that means I will be an owner/director of a company;

my success line is very straight--I have had and will have much success;

I will make my money overseas;

I have no reason to worry about money, I will be rich;

I have a habit of worrying about small things that I shouldn't worry about;

I should marry at the age of 30-31;

my first child will be a son-- very smart--and then I will have more sons;

my husband may not be an official but will have money;

I shouldn't gamble, for me it is not the way to make money (which does not mean,

I make sure to confirm, that
I shouldn't take risks);

there will be much luck and
success for me, especially in
the next few years;

my ancestors are very lucky
(their tombs are also in a
very good place).

I pay him 100 yuan, and as we
get up to leave Mr. Fuqi translated the fortune teller's
parting words to me, "congratulations." I ask Mr. Fuqi, Why?
Congratulations for what? and
he says simply that I have good
fortune. I insist on knowing if
Mr. Fuqi has told the fortune
teller who I am (although it
is almost enough simply to be
caucasian/American/foreign).
Mr. Fuqi promises he kept me
a secret....

Later at lunch he begins the
inevitable scheming--how we can
make money together (especially
after hearing what that fortune
teller had to say ...). I must
go to meet his uncle, a developer ("they call him a billion-
aire"), when I'm in Hong Kong.
I can convince him to develop
projects in Dongguan City
because I have expertise and
know a good development climate
when I see one (I'm fascinated,
actually, to hear this billion-
aire's reasons for not investing here, since I'm sure he's
considered it). Mr. Fuqi will
use his connections here in
Dongguan City to facilitate the
project (he is assistant planner at the Dongguan City Post
and Telecommunication Bureau--
a government office). I ask him
about the development pace in
Dongguan City, and he predicts
(somewhat enigmatically) "a
very fast train will sometimes
run out of track." ...

He takes me back to the
hotel (my hotel's name means
"gathering in heaven," he tells
me--why haven't I thought to
ask before?). When will we see
each other next? I ask. I say I
want to go to the Cultural Cen-

*"Cultural Center" in
"Times Square"*

ter (with men outside in yellow
Buddhist-monk costumes), near
his office in what he calls
"Times Square," and he is very
uninterested in this--can't you
go alone? you want to go to a
disco? not really knowing what
I want.... He says, I'm not
sure I will have time.... I'm
somehow despondent.

6:30 p.m. June 27, 1996
A call and Mr. Fuqi asks, do
you have your sword? (He has
insisted I go off alone to the
department store as a way to
begin learning Chinese. "Look
the word for sword up in your
dictionary and say it to them."
... I have gone there and managed, after drawing a picture
and speaking some English, to
purchase a tin, colorful,
adjustable sword.)

I must not be seen with you,
he says, we must go somewhere
secret. During the Cultural
Revolution, they would think
you were a spy, he has told me.
But I, it turns out, am not the
sole reason for his paranoia.
No young people practice the
martial arts anymore. Chairman
Mao's sports programs have

turned China into a country of
weight lifters, tennis players
and gymnasts (especially in
Dongguan City, where the
national weight-lifting cham-
pion lives). Mr. Fuqi is all
of these things but was also
taught martial arts as a child;
he is graceful, and his parents
thought he might one day be an
actor or dancer.

We go after dinner on the
scooter out to where the river
meets the canal, looking for
flat ground. I want to be next
to the water, but a thick grass
grows right up to the edge,
and so we cross the canal over
a very thin concrete bridge,
into a litchi grove, and then
a rice field, then up around a
hilly cemetery--urns of ashes
surrounded by concrete curving
walls, hundreds up and down
the hillside. We are both in
awe (but don't point he says,
you cannot point at the
graves). This is why Dongguan
City is so prosperous, this
burial ground has good feng
shui, he tells me. Down again
into the back side of town and
to places we've both never
seen, and then past a vast
development, all pink, and
neo-Roman. This place I've
been looking for.... East
City Center--so empty. It is a
place I'd been last January,
13% occupied....

We are lost--they are adding infrastructure--and after
detours and torn up roads
finally emerge near the sports
stadiums. We stop in a back
parking lot, nondescript (if I
can say that about China ...).

I learn Tai Chi--a Tai Chi
body works like a spinning
sphere, deflecting all aggression. Act like a cat, he tells
me. My Tai Chi teacher, he

says, said: "I will not teach someone I do not understand. ... One must pass a series of moral tests before beginning the martial arts, so that one will always use them for good purpose...." And has he already tested me, I ask?

It is so dark now, so we sit in the parking lot to talk (his English is mysteriously good--he's traveled to America, AT&T paid for his trip, they want Dongguan City's Post and Telecommunication Bureau's business ...). He calls Dongguan the "development city." He asks me what I think will happen when China gets rich--will we change? We discuss this for some time. I tell him I'm writing a thesis, a book about money and Dongguan City, and what has happened to me here (and he immediately senses that it is not only formal research but also personal, and says, 'Mr. Fuqi' will be a chapter, right?). He talks about his work--he's on a team that decides where and when to build post and telecommunication offices. In the beginning (just after the economic reforms), theme buildings (Las Vegas as the model) were inevitably proposed by architects--one wanted to put a 2,000-square-meter lobby on a 6,000-square-meter site, he says derisively. Mr. Fuqi told him no, a waste of land and money. Now they have developed a Post and Telecommunication aesthetic (a James Bond/Soviet spy elegance, glossy wood paneling ...).

We drive off, past a children's amusement park, where all the rides are inflated plastic structures. "I want to see a building that you've built in Dongguan City some day ..." he tells me. We drive around for gas, out past the Capital Hotel--Dongguan's buildings more singular at night, one masterpiece after another in the moon. We end up at Dongguan Hotel's Coffee S hop for a banana split and talk of China's political history, the brilliance of Chairman Mao, Deng's health, doing business in China, going to America, famous buildings Harvard alumni have designed. He wants to see drawings of my building (he doesn't know much about design, only planning, he says), but first we go to his office in search of litchi his colleagues have brought in from the country, and not finding any, we sit at the computer. He has a Beijing opera CD-ROM that explains the origins of all the costumes. As we hear the opening music, he says "I can play that on my harmonica."

It is late now, midnight, too late to see my drawings, and he drives me to my hotel-- Gathering Place in Heaven-- singing aloud the words to a John Denver song--"Country roads, take me home...." (imagine with the full moon, and we are driving parallel to the canal, past the dark buildings, trees reflected in water, litchi sellers with candles to illuminate their fruit, empty streets--it is so late....), and he leaves me. He has woken up and become somehow coherent at the same moment I swing off the scooter. When will I see you again? I say.

11:00 a.m. June 28, 1996
Mr. Fuqi calls and asks to see me in my office. He's spoken to his uncle in Hong Kong. I am to go and see him (I am traveling to Hong Kong during the next weekend to renew my visa), to have an interview. Mr. Fuqi would like me to work for him (in Mr. Fuqi's vision, I will open an agency in Dongguan City and work from there for the developer). I must bring the brochures from the Beautiful City development, he tells me (See, Dongguan is a good place for investment....).

Then he sees--for the first time--the building sketches and plans on my desk and pours over them. I imagine he must be disappointed (he is inscrutable). I know he is used to seeing images (of Las Vegas hotels, 1990s Soviet architecture), and my drawings don't really look like anything. I feel inadequate, badly educated for this Chinese condition (I thought we Harvard graduates were supposed to be so exportable...).

2:30 p.m. July 4, 1996
I go back to East City Center alone. I approach a guard at the front. What do I say? I smile. Can I come inside? I point. I lock my bicycle to his

East City Centre development

guard station and begin to walk up the ramp. It is a vast mall podium unfinished, resting above a parking garage and playground, with towers rising above. A central arcade has a glass roof. I am on top of the

THE INDUSTRIAL PARK: PUBLIC/PRIVATE PARTNERSHIP
IN A SOCIALIST MARKET ECONOMY

"I have two souls inside me." —Faust [32]

A Feudal Battlefield

When new incentives are given to Dongguan's socialist market cadres—the thirty-three town leaders—the SEZ's potent powers of seduction are, in effect, given to villages of 10,000 farmers.

Free now to control land,[33] Dongguan's town leaders play on a feudal battlefield of warring villages. In their factionalized minicombats, to defeat the enemy is to offer the loosest regulation, the lowest taxes, and the quickest factory construction. Dongguan's internal struggles and any destruction they wreak are kept secret from Beijing.[34] And anyway, cities are rising! (if only to five or six stories), and statistics show the success of soaring growth rates.

Soon, however, legally bestowed deregulations are not enough. Competition is fierce, and town leaders are predatory and LEARNING©. Encouraged by Beijing's entrepreneurial leanings (bankruptcy has just been tentatively declared legal), the cleverest village leaders—"one step ahead"—evolve from land managers to land speculators ("I have two souls inside me").

Foreign Funds

By 1988, Beijing has fully released Dongguan, raising its status to "Prefecture Equivalent City." Any control Guangdong Province has is given over to Dongguan's town leaders. Dongguan's villages can legally offer low-cost land leases, special tax incentives, preferential access to local markets, and utility subsidies. In Chinese terms, prefecture status presupposes a foreign focus (a view outward, beyond even Hong Kong), and a complicity in Guangdong Province's agenda of wholesale sacrifice.

Hard at work creating an outward-looking economy,[35] Guangdong supports Dongguan's prefecture designation. Local banks are encouraged to loan money for investment and to manage foreign exchange. Village leaders can approve foreign-owned enterprises, obtain foreign loans, regulate foreign personnel entry, and offer flexibility in providing preferential measures to attract foreign investment.

Beijing descends again to designate Dongguan City the "National Symbol for Export Processing." Dongguan is now dependent upon export processing; yet the success of the operation depends on foreigners who could be lured to other areas of the delta where there is cheaper land and labor, and a lower cost of living. Dongguan, like Shenzhen before it, is pricing itself out of the market. Development-zone proliferation infiltrates the delta, and Guangdong Province is blanketed with official and unofficial development zones, all competing with Dongguan. A huge population in the delta now depends on a continually growing economy.

The Open Door Policy correctly prophesizes foreign money as the crucial symbol of modernization. To gain control of global capital, a notoriously slippery and dirty seduction, China forces foreign money into a wrenching process of purification. Foreign funds, formerly tainted with the threat of capitalist contamination, are newly anonymous when filtered through a SEZ. Clean foreign money can now circulate through Shenzhen SEZ into China.

Directing foreign currency through the SEZ, however, denies it freedom to roam. An imbalance is inevitable (a conceptual market, full of ideological punch but without a rigorous supply-demand base, is not corrective). No longer able to protect, to cleanse, Shenzhen releases its excess (which is not yet clean) as SPILLOVER©. A new kind of industrialization moves outside Shenzhen's border into unprotected and hidden areas. Foreign funds (often podium, and I can see through to the inside, the vast core.

How to describe the emptiness, the density of construction, the lack of green or landscape, the refined program--pure shopping, residential and nursery schools. Pink, postmodern, and each block of towers is subtly different and pushed together-- why would this be? a breakdown at the level of detailing, as if many architects (young, collective, FLOATING©) were asked to work successively, building up this city in pink for mistresses. Can't quite explain how extraordinarily silent it was, and massive, and very much hermeneutic/ whole--wholeness?. It feels trapped in a kind of aspic, an uncorrupted surface stillness, preserved as proof of the viability of Western (and Hong Kong) planning. Somehow the building feels like the future (i.e., apocalyptic ...), and one imagines the future occupation (RECLAMATION©).

It is profoundly silent here and empty until I see two women with their children rising up the escalator from the unfinished shopping podium. They carry shopping bags and are dressed seductively in pant suits and Chanel gold belts-- for one instant seeming so natural, as if there really were stores here. There is, actually, a store here, opened on the first floor of one of the residential towers. I go inside, where a family sits waiting--two sisters, one with baby breast-feeding, and husband asleep on the counter. A Chinese market, plucked from Dongguan City's inner core.

I want to come back at night-- the real test of a VIRGIN CITY© condition--how many lights are on? I imagine Southern California seen from above, lit by the underwater lights of a thousand swimming pools, and know that here the podium would glow the same way through the cheap blue glass.... It feels like Western space--I am still and quiet for the first time since coming to China.

8:30 p.m. July 6, 1996
Mr. Fuqi is about to buy a restaurant. He and three others will go into business together. His (schizophrenic) dual role is as silent partner (because he is working for the government and cannot, therefore, be an entrepreneur) and promoter/ manager. He takes me to see it in an area just behind my hotel--my backyard, yet I have never been here. All neon, nightclubs, and outdoor restaurants, light at night and Hong Kong-ish. His restaurant is next to a massage parlor (with a glass facade etched with naked female figures in Art Deco style) and just beyond are the empty developments that start at the first ring road around Dongguan City Center. It is very much at the edge of the light (and this is the one thing that worries him, makes him hesitate). He will renovate the space and add new signage, he tells me (Will you help? he asks....).

I ask him to take me to East City Center, night now. Empty, (something this big can be so dark and quiet, how?) but he says it won't sell because it is too crowded (he means the buildings are too close together, especially compared to New

World Garden, the development of townhouses next door ...). Stars and moonlight, no other light, no other life.

11:30 p.m. July 6, 1996
We drive back on the ring road toward the inner city, and he asks if I'd like to go to a hotel. I say yes ("hotel" is a word with many meanings in Dongguan City; tonight Mr. Fuqi refers to a mixed-program nightclub...). He pulls off at one of the buildings that line

OK Hotel

the ring road. The facade is like an aluminum factory shooting sparks, all done with Christmas-tree lights. We enter, and flanking the inner door are two rows of women in pink pantsuits. They welcome us as we pass through and on up two grand stairs to the third floor. It is very much a Las Vegas, but of the fifties as much as the late eighties. We are seated in a very small curving couch near the stage. A woman brings us tea and an elaborate tray of fruit carved like birds. It is not normal to order drinks, although they are on the menu (I see Mr. Fuqi frown as I contemplate it, and so I don't).

We have come to this particular hotel (there are hundreds in Dongguan City Center) because Mr. Fuqi has heard a rumor that a stripper will in the form of bribes) infiltrate the PRD's underdeveloped cities as overflow.

Fantastic growth, no longer in controllable dosages, spreads into the rest of the delta. Shenzhen has grown rich as a filter. Glass towers have risen as surrounding areas have handled the dirtier tasks of globalization. Dongguan City—acting in a secret space of freedom, processing and profiting from the SPILLOVER© Shenzhen cannot contain. Fearing Beijing's wrath (the wrong set of statistics can be deadly), Dongguan is again forced to relinquish its secret mission. Through attention-hungry town leaders, it succumbs to temptation and adopts the most visible of tactics: the high-tech foreign investment mantra.

Just imagine, friends, how the interprises of foreign trade, "external processing & assembly," Sino-foreign joint venture, co-op venture and foreign monopoly, like a flock of robust steeds carrying the city's "external economy" will be galloping straight towards tomorrow, a more exciting tomorrow! —Dongguan's Achievements in Reform, *Dongguan Yearbook, 1996.*[36]

Winnerway

One of Dongguan's four competing districts, with access to roads and labor as its only advantage, builds as a city center a vast industrial park—Winnerway—designed to attract foreign investment in the form of a joint venture with overseas technology corporations. Winnerway is fail-safe, a partnership of East and West supported by Beijing.

Its town leader—a public/private partnership given human form—is an embodiment of the socialist-market ideal. As an official, he controls land use and the dissemination of land lease funds to farmers. As a developer, he attracts foreign partnerships and builds a huge corporation. On both sides he is CORRUPT© (first, when he doesn't transfer land-use fees to farmers—so common now that the farmers have begun to protest at the provincial level; and second, when he takes bribes (gifts) from foreign partners—as is normal when working in the private sector in China).[37]

Winnerway is an extraordinarily successful industrial village, which makes a feudal Rolls Royce-driving lord of the socialist-market landlord. Winnerway is Dongguan's first company to be traded on Shenzhen's (B) stock exchange. Winnerway's town leader is considered now to be the richest man in Dongguan.[38]

A FAUSTIAN© Contract

With controlled privatization, socialist-market cadres (constructing the future) engage in a FAUSTIAN© contract by introducing into China

perform tonight. We watch the singer and wait for the stripper, and I say, finally, as we sit in the darkness, that I need to know more about mistresses (he points some out) and prostitution (in massage parlors, barber shops, near the bus station, and here, just outside in the hallway ...). He seems to already know that this will be important (Dongguan has a reputation), and I have very little explaining to do. He simply agrees to help me understand (and he seems boyishly titillated by the prospect). Each new singer focuses our attention—yes,

I think she is about to take that off—but to our disappointment the stripper never materializes. We leave, and as we drive to my hotel, he says, You are seeing things that no American ever sees....

9:00 p.m. July 7, 1996
I am groggy—a phantom hangover (the one I should have had)—and I don't leave the hotel until evening, when I take a walk back to Mr. Fuqi's restaurant. I realize along the way that the whole area has been planned—and can feel the Soviet housing blocks under the new signage. It is a

development now full, taken (RECLAMATION©).

Later Mr. Fuqi arrives at my hotel, and we talk in my room and watch To Catch a Thief on TV, and I tell him I've gone back to the area near his restaurant. You know, he says, they call it the "Number-Two Wife Village." ... (I'd gone at dinnertime and watched girls in pajamas and high heels on the street serving food from a card table—the bordello's canteen). Is it the only one in Dongguan City? No, but it is known, even in Hong Kong. It is the most famous one—typical, he calls it.

Midnight July 7, 1996

Mr. Fuqi and I go to a hotel just across the street--I've seen it from my office window lit up at night. This one is more of a disco, more Western.

Mr. Fuqi's restaurant

And the floor shows are better-- all Saturday Night Fever: two Chinese men in bright-yellow suits, with sheer nylon T-shirts underneath; four small women in taffeta puffed mini-skirts and black motorcycle boots; then other girls appear on stage in bikinis--only one brave enough to take her bra off just before they all rush off the stage. Later I watch various self-mutilations by musclemen--bricks swinging from nipple clamps, a pseudo-martial arts knife show. No blood as he presses the blade into his chest and is then struck by a bench swung at him like a baseball bat by another male dancer. Still no blood.

Slowly (why so slow?) I understand where I am--a bordello. I've uncovered the place where billionaires keep their mistresses. They can bring their own, or spend the evening with one of the crowd hovering in every corner of the room-- 100 yuan (U.S.$12). They are not prostitutes, says Mr. Fuqi, no sex allowed.

I watch Mr. Fuqi's growing interest in a corner table full of older men--why aren't they arranging mistresses for themselves? And then it becomes clear as a woman and a small boy appear. It appears to be the mistress and child of one of them, but it is the wife, Mr. Fuqi tells me. The men are putting on a show for her. See, they seem to say, nothing happens when we go out together, we just talk business, maybe play a game of Mah-Jongg.

Mr. Fuqi says these girls are all from somewhere else, the north (and I realize suddenly, as Mr. Fuqi talks, that for those in the south, the north is a kind of utopia-- clean water, white-skinned women). He offers a theory he has concocted. He says the city in the north where these beautiful women (white skin, tall) come from was the city of two strong dynasties, but as they lost their power, the wives and concubines and mistresses of the emperors and court were forced to marry the common people, thus producing beautiful daughters. In Dong-guan City (in the south) it is

the possibility of damnation. A FAUSTIAN© contract is signed when Beijing—at the local level—turns over, goes to the other side (the private, the entrepreneurial). The joint venture introduces the devil of globalism into China. Foreign funds (and foreigners' bribes) are FAUSTIAN MONEY©. FAUSTIAN MONEY© money pays for speculation in this MARKET REALIST© condition.

The socialist-market cadre is inherently FAUSTIAN©: the devil of the private sector within the soul of a communist cadre. The freedom to be two in one is a schizophrenia that makes Dongguan crazy. Everything that follows is the tale of Dongguan's destruction. What did the city trade for complicity in the private sector? What was the deal? A trade of utopia for dystopia. (Faust's is a story of lost innocence.) The city, the landscape, and the buildings show the deal that was made with the devil.

Officials from the local to central levels do business in the name of modernization. Winner-way is widely copied (each town leader expects the same rewards from his position), and it is a mimicry that destroys. The showy high-tech factory is employed as a model in a system that works at the scale of export processing (a low-skill manufacturing base), and the balance is upset—as if a spaceship had fallen from the sky with technology from another planet.

Dongguan, reeling from the injection of uncontrolled and unplanned for foreign capital, is, unlike Shenzhen SEZ, without Beijing's protection. Dongguan is rejected, no longer viable as a manufacturing mecca (rising costs, over-industrialization). The city's inevitable release (into failure) is a release that makes starkly visible the ruptured socialist-market system. Dongguan is a landscape of abandoned and bankrupt factories and industrial parks. A landscape of lost utility.

difficult to be healthy--the water is bad, and the girls' skin is not lovely.

10:00 p.m. July 9, 1996
Mr. Fuqi says we could go to a place that spins, up high, to look at the city. There are actual revolving restaurants here....

We go up the Oriental Hotel 15 stories and then stepping through the door we are inside it, spinning past Dongguan City once an hour. The space is thin: room for two tables, and the floors are hard wood. And Dongguan is panorama. What do they spend their electricity on? I see the Christmas lights of many hotels, but very few other buildings are lit. I see a metallic public sculpture almost directly below us--the center of the inner city. The streets glow. We eat sandwiches (it is a Western menu). I drink a beer. We design his restaurant in candlelight, his facade and new signage (he draws the plans carefully and correctly). He says, "Architects are like psychoanalysts--they reveal the people they serve."

I suggest a pseudonym, so when I quote him in my book he won't be implicated (he's been watching me write nearly everything he says down). We spend some time deciding what it will be. He suggests Rooster (in English), his birth year. I say no, it sounds too silly, like a cartoon, but what are the rooster's characteristics? Crowing as the sun rises, an alarm clock, a wake-up song ... "I will wake up China," he says, and I say, "No, you will wake up America."

The moon somehow follows our revolutions, always in our view, and he talks about leav-ing his northern hometown. Losing your hometown means part of you is dying, he says. We agree. He says when he goes back he can't accustom himself to it--he needs more stimula-tion now. We agree. Later I ask what kind of significance the moon has in China--the gold full moon hangs above East City Center--and he tells me that when you look at a full moon you become homesick....

when the moonlight shines
through the window
I take it for frost
when I look up
the moon
I begin to miss my hometown
--Li Bai, Tang Dynasty[56]

Dongguan--a darker night here, especially from above (and a different kind of day that stays light late, infusing the streets at man-height like a carnival, or a Las Vegas 24-hour cycle). Dongguan--city of secrets (with danger being the biggest secret of all--does it even exist, or is it just a rumor?). The neon sign won't work on me (I don't read Chi-nese), so no words hide the architecture, but I must be shown everything else.

10:00 a.m. July 12, 1996
Bill Wong has asked me to look at a friend's development--Sun-shine Hillside Villas--in Chang Ping (one of the 33 towns and the site of Mr. Luo's Beautiful City). Bill Wong and Mr. Li, the developer, pick me up and with us are two men "from Bei-jing." We drive east out of the city. Bill Wong has news of Mr. Wu's trip to America. "Very nice," Mr. Wu has said, "but when I returned I loved Dong-guan even more."

Bill Wong measures time by how many of the 33 towns we pass through (Chang Ping is three towns away....), each about 10 kilometers apart. I ask about new unfinished developments, visible at every turn. He tells me of the new government directive--develop-ers who can't finish projects (for lack of money) must plant trees, they must landscape the half-finished, deteriorat-ing property.

We arrive at the litchi mon-uments and wide streets of Chang Ping. As we approach the site I ask what I will see. Mr. Li's project is 1.4 million square meters of development in two phases. The first is 740,000 square meters: a com-mercial podium, a hotel (3 floors), and a tourist area with a lake. Phase two is 300,000 square meters of vil-las, six apartment towers (both 5-6 and 12-16 floors). Each villa is on a 600-square-meter plot, with a 100-square-meter building footprint (2 stories high). The rest of the land is landscaped. In the future, Mr. Li would add a school and a hospital.

We drive off the village road, we are here (?), onto dirt and a piece of stunning raw land. Tents and shacks, and two workers welcome us. We spread the plans out and I feel like I'm on an African safari, plotting a hunt. I try to fig-ure out first what's going on, and second, what they expect me to do.... They explain the project and we drink tea, lots of flies (no real-estate office here). The site plan is tacked to the wall. It is compact, circular, and they won't tear out mountains (a new strategy), but will build villas on the

A decaying industrial park, Dongguan City, June 1996. "We are absolutely sure that with the grand base of industry, the perfect investment circumstance, the completed modern services system as well as all kind of talents with rich experiences and the concern and support from all the people, Chang An will show its brilliance once more. May Chang An be known by the world, may it step to the world! We'd like to extend our heartfelt welcome to all the friends and economic organizations from abroad or home. Let's work side by side for another wonderful future." —Gao Beilun, manager of Chang An town, in To Rouse and Exploit Splendid Future.

Failed (BANKRUPT©³⁹) speculative industrial parks litter Dongguan. Foreign investors, rejecting Dongguan's homemade high technology, have learned to construct their own factories to take advantage of cheap land and labor. After a town's failure, the leader often moves to another to start the same process again (experienced now), leaving the villagers behind. Or he goes to America—the Dongguan get-rich-quick scheme one last gamble before leaving. The villagers that are left behind, the victims of the socialist-market cadre's greed, pay off their former town leader's loans to the Construction Bank of China.

Dongguan is now both failed—abandoned city centers, obsolete industrial parks—and rich with the successes of its industrialization. Full of factory managers (in town three days a week), rich farmers, corrupt cadres, and Hong Kong businessmen, a growing middle class is rising in Dongguan with Deng's reforms.

slopes, utilizing the landscape as amenity.

The project began with a search for planners with experience, working with this type of land (a similar climate, topology). Mr. Li traveled to a southwestern province near Vietnam with lots of sun and hills and hired a planner. This first plan exploded all of the mountains and designed everything flat (Mr. Li laughs, he thinks that these planners fell victim to wanting what they can't have—they live in the mountains, they want to live on flat land....). He talks about other developments in Chang Ping, especially about Mr. Luo's Beautiful City, which they've been following closely. It is too flat. Mr. Li says that this is Mr. Luo's development strategy, his vision: you can have a villa and a view either together or separate (and it is separate in Beautiful City—with the mountains and lake hidden off to the side, the rest on flat ground), and we want the villa and the view together.

Next, they tried a Guangzhou firm, whose plan was also flat and—even worse—too dense. Finally, Mr. Li found the "best planning firm in China," in the form of government planners working out of Shenzhen.

I ask them how they will phase it—what of the Phase One plan will get built first? are any buildings designed?

They've phased Sunshine Hillside Villas this way:

1. build a wall around the site (in the mountainous areas a porous wall, and on the flat areas more of a security wall)
2. roads

3. green on edges of roads/ underground prep
4. a strip of samples—medium towers and villas on either side of one street, tourist hotel closer to the commercial-strip edge.
To complete the above (especially #4), they need U.S. $8 million.

Mr. Li's site

They have so much land (they won't answer when I ask how much it costs, but it was cheap, they say), but not enough money, so they will start with the two rows of short apartment towers and a grouping of villas, and sell those to finance amenities and further villas. Their strategy has been to spend their money

on site preparation, so already the plumbing work is done. The site is cleared (and Bill Wong has made a brochure of this prepared land—dirt). They would like to avoid the failure that has befallen previous developers who've left buildings standing unfinished but sold (i.e., selling to Hong Kongers by making promises with a deceiving photograph).

Feng shui has been used; they will place a large villa for the developer at the top of the center mountain—the feng shui master forecasts this spot will help him keep control of the land.

4:30 p.m. July 12, 1996
I get a phone call from an industrial designer, John, who'd been to the institute's lecture and seen me introduced. He asks some questions about factory design in America. He, too, speaks English extraordinarily well (they speak almost too well; I'd sometimes rather interpret the Chinese/English of Mr. Wu or Half-Town Chan). After about two minutes, I've told him all I know about American factory design and ask him about Chinese factories.

He works in Winnerway, what he calls the biggest industrial district in Dongguan City. His office is at a high tech-factory complex on the site. I ask

Winnerway's real estate office

Sacrifice

The Chinese Communist Party attempts to control the socialist market economy through sacrifice. It is the operation that cleans and purifies through destruction. Shenzhen is pure, Dongguan is destroyed. Both are equally sacrificed: Shenzhen to embody the new communist ideal of modernization, Dongguan to the deregulatory frenzy of globalization.

By the mid-1980s in China, verdicts had been reversed on the five black categories: capitalists, landlords, rich peasants, counter-revolutionaries, and bad elements. All were newly called "advanced elements of the working class." This advancement pushed forward communist risk takers (socialist-market cadres) into the untested socialist-market system as pioneers; the advancement used them to chart the efficacy and the boundaries of the socialist market economy. Sacrificed by Beijing to the unquantifiable effects of money, these cadres are now tainted and useless. Money in China is in service to the state, as are the cadres that gamble with it (buildings are a gamble in a country addicted to risk, in a country where there's no other game in town). Like a sacrificial ceremony, a balance of transgression (corruption, now *détourned* into CORRUPTION©) and punishment is necessary for the smooth operations of the socialist market economy.

The socialist-market cadre regulates land use but also speculates as a developer. To reduce the effects of this schism, a *détournement* of bankruptcy (into BANKRUPTCY©, no longer failure) and corruption (into CORRUPTION©, no longer suspect) redefines the most fatal and feared tenets of the capitalist canon.[40] *Détournement* is a form of TABULA RASA©, though TABULA RASA© is never complete; there is always the potential (and often actual) reappearance of original meaning. To preserve the ability of the private sector to create wealth in relative secrecy, a few CORRUPT© cadres are taken down (hanged) as an example to the rest of the world of the purifying (TABULA RASA©) process of communism (just as Shenzhen SEZ was offered as a sacrifice to modernization).

about factory housing, and he says the residential area where he lives has been integrated into the old village fabric. He offers to show me.

I meet John at the Silverland Hotel. He is very excited to show me his factory, but first I've asked for maps and brochures so we go to Winnerway's real-estate office. It is huge, with a huge scale model under glass pushed back in the corner. I go closer; there is some of everything. The site spans Dongguan's big river, and they've taken an island in the middle for rows and rows of single-family houses. The existing urban fabric in this model has been removed (relocated?), but I know in "real life" they've kept some of it, inserting Winnerway in between.

We cross the river to a dusty field (with the ubiquitous billboard of "development to come" ...) and tour the new factory, a high-tech science-fiction movie, spacesuits, whispering. An ugly building.

We walk back to the Silverland Hotel through the development; existing fabric out of control on the inside, planned by Winnerway on the edges. The Cultural Revolution did not destroy the south so completely--so here there are still village temples to worship ancestors and money gods. John is a Methodist and tells me stories of the democracy movement--he was at Tiananmen Square. He came to Shenzhen in search of money but could find no job--there are no factories there. He ended up working in a hotel. (John will eventually leave Dongguan, too--in December, 1996, he will defect to America....)

We arrive at the house of the landlord: he is a rich man, a developer, a village representative, a government official, an owner of a Rolls

The landlord's house

Royce, a BMW, a sprawling villa; he is a sports sponsor, a city builder. He controls

DEATH MARCH: Former Shenzhen official Wang Jianye, who steadfastly maintained his innocence, on his way to his execution last week for taking $1.2 million in bribes

"Death March: Former Shenzhen Construction Minister Wang Jianye, who steadfastly maintained his innocence, on his way to execution for taking $1.2 million in bribes." —Time Magazine, January 1996.

"It is always the purpose of sacrifice to give destruction its due, to save the rest from a mortal danger of contagion." —Georges Bataille, The Accursed Share .

Capitalist activity within the socialist market economy carries with it the potential of death (the unquantifiable risk of operating under the *détourned* rules of CORRUPTION©), and therefore the potential of consecration as one sacrificed. Sacrifice makes the socialist-market cadre recognizable and glory-ous: the cadre is saving the rest from the danger of capitalism. Infused (recognizable) with the aura of the sacred (sanctioned by Beijing as one step ahead), the (quasi) private-sector cadre is worshipped and mimicked by would-be speculators: farmers and factory owners suffering from boredom in a slowing, over-industrialized economy and looking to spend money.

Dongguan's release is exactly halfway between the exuberance and optimism of striving towards the utopia of wealth and the dystopia of sacrifice and failure. Dongguan is balanced (in China's perpetual state of yin-yang). Industrial failure allows Dongguan's release into the post-communist freedom of luxury. Flush with funds after years of growth, the city's pressure extends. It begins to spend. It builds into the overbuilt, wasted landscape scores of luxury developments.

land, has built industrial facilities that he, representing the village, rents out to mostly foreign companies, like TDK, where John works. He also speculates in housing developments (at least 50% of which Mr. Yang insists are lived in by mistresses--factory managers from Hong Kong spend the week here in Dongguan).

8:00 a.m. July 15, 1996
I meet John at McDonalds. We will go to Zhung Mu Tou--the most developed, he says, of the 33 towns. "Everyone made money there," he says. (And it is, he says, free of factories, too--what do they do there?). I've invited Mr. Fuqi to come. They are opposites. Mr. Fuqi, with his ties to the communist government, a coveted Dongguan City resident permit (which means he's not a FLOATER©), a member of the new entrepreneurial Chinese middle class, gifted with languages, visited America, and John, living illegally in Dongguan, technically trained, gifted with languages, hungry for information, lost, a freedom fighter. They immediately, and for the whole day, bicker. John keeps calling Mr. Fuqi a rich man. He's envious and speaks through Mao, and Mr. Fuqi denies it, but is proud, too. Mr. Fuqi wants to talk with me about signage (still designing his new restaurant) and he ignores John, and we compare the strips and strips of neon and plastic out the bus window while John tells me stories in my other ear about corrupt village leaders. It is my first time on a Chinese bus.

John has described Zhung Mu Tou as sitting in between two mountains. It is a town that

looks like a city--all 33 towns aspire to look like this--and is smaller than I imagined, mostly under construction, and empty. We stop in the first development office I see. Tai On City. This developer's vision is to build a minicity of shopping, recreational rooms, an athletic club, all in a vast podium, with residential towers above (the brochure pictures show Roman baths). I interview the real-estate broker. They missed the last wave, he says, in 1992-93 (Deng's PRD visit), but expect another after the 1997 handover. This development is slated to be complete by then. Much of Zhung Mu Tou's construction was begun in 1992-93. And when finished they sold well. Developments here are 70-80% sold, but not occupied. The city is occupied on weekends, he says.

We are on foot and walk far out of town to finally end up at a sprawling development--rows and rows of villas and condominium towers. I want to

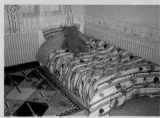

A condominium in Zhung Mu Tou

go into a tower and we arrange this with the real-estate broker. In the lobby of the building (a dark shell) sit a family handing out brochures and giving tours. We tour a condominium interior. I've never seen Mr. Fuqi more excited. For me, they are smallish apartments, nice enough when white, but our model was decorated in Western style: purple paint, teddy bears.

We catch a tour bus back into town, and I realize that

Hong Kongers on a site-seeing tour

it is filled with Hong Kongers on a site-seeing tour, looking to buy flats (Zhung Mu Tou-style tourism).... The whole town is devoted to selling real estate. I ask John what in Zhung Mu Tou is desirable as a tourist destination (they are marketing the lack of factories, environmental qualities, physical similarity to Hong Kong). It seemed to me a dusty second place to Dongguan City Center (although again this comment makes me highly suspect), and I confuse John with my questions. Recreation for him is karaoke bars, entertainment centers, space--which Zhung Mu Tou will eventually have in abundance--not the history and density of Dongguan City. I keep pushing them to answer my uestion--why would people come here for the weekend? The whole downtown is only real-estate offices.

Home again on the bus, with Mr. Fuqi sleeping like a heated baby against me and John brooding in the seat behind.

11:30 p.m. July 18, 1996
I go with Mr. Fuqi to China City, the biggest and most expensive hotel in Dongguan City. Mr. Fuqi points out the sign in front of the hotel, advertising rooms by the hour-- 50 yuan per person. It is the first time I've seen this and I quiz Mr. Fuqi--he is so casual--it is for men and their mistresses--no big deal, but I tease him because I know he is "acting cool." He tells me once in a hotel he saw some Russian mistresses, blonde--maybe they think I am his Russian mistress? I ask him about secrecy and he explains it is the Chinese way--don't show what you have, who you are, don't be distinctive, let others find out about you.... He tells me it took him a long time to learn this, it was not instinctive for him.

He tells me the next morning that he will be sequestered for the weekend in a local hotel for a League conference (Communist Youth League).... I have suspected he was a member but haven't asked--it is the one taboo subject.

Midnight July 19, 1996
He finally calls from the hotel, sitting alone in a spacious room on the outskirts of Dongguan City Center. He has slept all afternoon (we'd been out until 2:30 a.m. the night before) during the lectures on goal setting and leading a meaningful life, and is now wide awake. He was bored: when the lecturer said the first sentence, Mr. Fuqi knew the second. He tells me he is responsible for dissemination of propaganda. Officially? I ask.... What is your title?! Head of Propaganda, Chinese Communist Youth League, Dongguan City Chapter.

I have a barrage of questions.... We talk late into the night. What does he do?-- it seems he gets told of the policy changes from the central

A developer in a hotel lobby

government and is asked to tell everyone--promotion ... What is communism? I ask. "A black chicken or white chicken, it doesn't matter, as long as it lays a golden egg." (He's quoting Deng.) He has used this with me many times before to explain the socialist market economy. What about outside of the economic condition, what about the political or social conditions?--harder for him to answer. He's heard a rumor, not from the central government, but from a workmate, that the next reform will be towards democracy ... he is very excited by this, but at the same time without aphorism-- they must one day give him a way to explain a "communist democracy." ...

11:30 a.m. July 20, 1996
I have dim sum with Mr. and Mrs. Wu, Bill Wong, and Half-Town Chan. We recreate January's table of friends, and our conversation is again mostly about feng shui and gambling (Mr. Wu's tale of betting and losing $1,000 in Las Vegas is the highlight). Vancouver and San Francisco are Mr. Wu's two favorite cities (he'd also gone to New York, D.C., Hawaii, Los Angeles). America is so empty, he says. Copying America doesn't work here, he has realized. Mr. Wu wants to show me his apartment.

Mr. Wu wants to live in New World Garden, but he explains the nature of his own wealth. Young people like Mr. Wu will help change China, make it good in the next 20 years, he tells me. We may not make money like businessmen, but we still have wealth because the government takes care of us--travel, apartment, car.

We arrive at one of the generic developments on the other side of the ring road, about three miles from the center of town, and climb six flights up into a building that I assumed from the outside was abandoned. The interior is Chinese fullness, and Loos-like with level changes and a bed raised on a platform. His baby has fallen asleep in my arms. Turtles keep the ghosts away, both when alive and dead, he says, when I ask about the shells hanging on the wall. And Mrs. Wu has disappeared and returns with a cold and heavy turtle shell, which she sets on the coffee table. It starts to move. They have a pet. How will I write about Mr. Wu, standing in front of me now in his jeans and white sweatshirt?

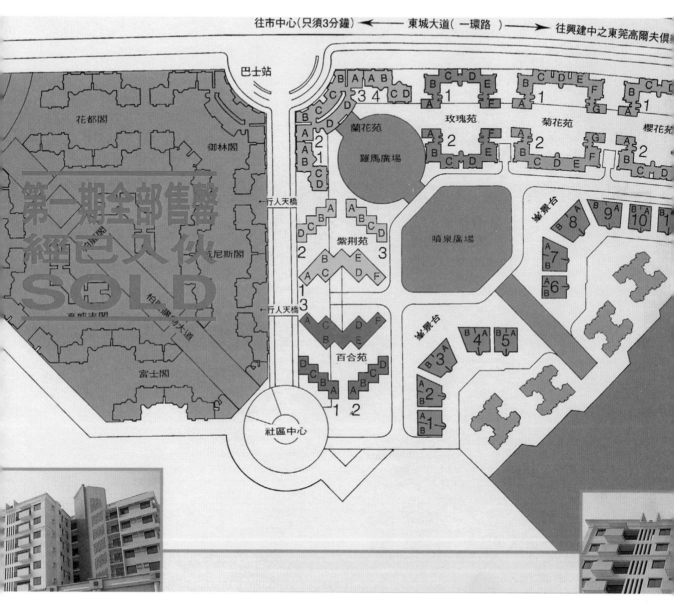

"He must waste the excess, but he remains eager to acquire even when he
does the opposite, and so he makes waste itself an object of acquisition."
—Georges Bataille, The Accursed Share.

DEVELOPING LUXURY HOUSING

"AFTER FOUR YEARS OF DEVELOPMENT, THIS EXTRAORDINARY LAND NOW GLOWS. Unrelenting spirits have sculpted this wide piece of land into a self-sufficient economic zone, a splendid place for residence & leisure alike" —*"Camdor Harbour City Today & Her Future,"* Camdor Harbour City brochure, 1995.

"Dirt has mana, spiritual power. It horrifies yet attracts us. Because we repress it, we fear it, and thence its power. It spoils the pattern and yet is the material for a new pattern. It has potential. Some sacred rituals will celebrate dirt, perhaps to express the unity of opposites, or to atone for culturally imposed separation. Such rites internalize our ambiguities and make available the dangerous powers of the unclean. Those who cross the boundary of purity, who abandon themselves to filth or dreams or frenzy, acquire a special strength." —*Kevin Lynch,* Wasting Away.[41]

Speculative Fever

Dongguan is, after ten years with the fastest growth rate in the world, a microcosm of China's failing economy. China's problems (inflation, a bankrupt industrial sector, and finally, the Tiananmen Square incident) threaten further reform. When foreign funds are finally pulled out of the PRD by wary investors—the most fail-safe of China's booming regions—Deng travels south to encourage further and faster growth. He will salvage his Open Door Policy.[42]

Deng's tour is an announcement to the world (more sacrifice): *The Pearl River Delta is a landscape in crisis!* There opportunity is in crisis, as every developer knows. Overseas Chinese speculators quickly descend to take advantage. Taiwan and Southeast Asian Chinese boost their investment in a greedy speculative fever disguised as renewed nationalism.

Overseas investors—well-schooled in Western-style capitalism—assess the PRD's market risk as high. Deng's excessive deregulation; a communist party teeming with corrupt cadres; no clear difference between the public and private sectors; China's nonexistent legal system;[43] and various temporary regulations, which lack the full force of law, all contribute to the high-risk condition in the delta. Speculators, therefore, concentrate on investment in projects with short payback periods and higher near-term profit potential. Six months after Deng's visit, a 242-percent increase in foreign investment surges into the delta, 31 percent of which goes into various speculative real estate–development projects.[44]

When overseas developers infiltrate Dongguan to do business, [45] they are received by a population grown rich from land leasing, export processing, and CORRUPTION©. [46] Dongguan—relaxed under deregulation, intimately connected to Hong Kong's capital through insider information, and the most over-industrialized of the delta's cities—is fully prepared to receive the overseas wealth. The thirty-three towns' leaders, given a second chance to grow rich, release huge plots of land for the construction of luxury developments.

The first vast, Western-inspired developments go up—pink postmodern towers and red-roofed single-family housing developments, built by Hong Kong architects—and are quickly successful, sold to Dongguan's newly wealthy. But overseas developers pull out, distracted by newer and safer possibilities in the newly released Shanghai area, leaving Dongguan's homegrown (indigenous) speculators to continue on MARKET REALISM© ideology. Rational speculation turns irrational. Deng, on tour, has just encouraged another boom (continue the economic revolution!), and it is no longer enough simply to buy real estate. In China's climate of modernization through growth, each must do its part to make money and to build

Dongguan cloaks itself in a rumor of danger. The security force at Camdor Harbour City, a golf resort and gated housing development in Dongguan City, 1994.

cities. Development is the ideal job in the privatizing socialist market economy.

Developer Culture

The socialist market cadre is now functionally entrepreneurial—flexible and market-driven within the communist system. Flush with funds (bribery is the gift that eases millions of square meters of construction into existence in China each year), fearing sacrifice (the occasional example preserves the system), and allowed to fail under new BANKRUPTCY© laws, a pre-liberation disposition toward risk resurfaces.

The speculating thirty-three-town leaders spawn a flock, a congregation of followers. Developers in China are not required to have a license; anyone with a down payment can get a loan from a bank and start a development without knowing anything about business or construction. Soon a private sector of powerful farmers-turned-developers evolves in Dongguan (they are responsible for modernization).

The followers, however, are private and therefore not at sacrificial risk (bribery is only bribery in China if it is taken by an official). As the controlled system of crime and punishment turns into an imbalance of developer power, private-sector developers are worshipped as politicians, even oracles. The transfer of the sacred aura to those without the potential of death changes the nature of the festival in Dongguan.

Mimicking their overseas peers (an irresistible model: in town three days a week, driving a Mercedes, installing mistresses), the private-sector developers develop not only buildings, but also a culture. Forty-five years of communist restriction of luxury, the overt use of money, and spending cause Dongguan's secret space to be used first for spending into pre-liberation activity; the developers' spending is a release of communist inhibition. Living like emperors, they are the secret society of the new reform. Developers shape Dongguan, mold it into their playground as the ultimate BUSINESS VACATION©. Now this is tourism!

Dongguan creates a reputation. It cloaks itself in the rumor of danger as its final, definitive STEALTH© tactic. [47] Dongguan depends on secrecy to stay viable as a haven for risk takers; Developer power (and therefore making money) depends on secrecy (to discover and capitalize on underutilized—actually or ideologically—markets). Dongguan's secret location; its infrastructural inaccessibility; its closed borders, through which money can pass but from which nothing comes; and its mystery all make it easy to construct a story of danger (to preserve further autonomy).

July 22, 1996

Rem,

I have found the mistresses and I know where they live (especially in a five-square-block development just behind my hotel, called Number-Two Wife Village). I understand Dongguan City's planning vision (it is CITY OF EXACERBATED DIFFERENCE© in microcosm--33 towns, with Dongguan City Center-- where I am living--as the biggest, each understood as a city within a city, actively distinctive and competitive, connected by superhighways. They consider it a European model), and I see it building up around me. I have seen the night here--I eat dinner at midnight with a Chinese man and candlelight in a revolving restaurant. I have found extraordinarily successful industrial villages that have made feudal Rolls Royce-driving emperors of their communist-party-member landlords, and I've also seen the destruction of a town of failed speculative factories (yes, the ghost city). I learn to cook

A failed village

Chinese food with Mr. Wu (Dongguan City Planner), his wife, and their family. I know that it is all empty here (some estimate Dongguan City's real estate, i.e., all buildings, is 50% occupied) and I know

that it is more than anywhere. I smoke in hotels (hotel here is just another name for bordello) and watch dancing girls and martial-arts magicians, and design my building.

8:30 p.m. August 2, 1996

I arrange a dinner with my students at Mr. Fuqi's restaurant. I ask them about Mah-Jongg.... "They gamble in your hotel, right?" No, I say, the nightclub there has closed down, abandoned on the third floor (not understanding). "No," they say, "you live in that privately owned hotel. The owner has connections to government officials?" Yes ... Mr. Zhang, his father is chief of police. "I know the hotel," they say, "it is the most secure place to gamble, in the private rooms. That's why you see so many police cars out front, they are all gambling" ... Ahh ... the J. T. Hotel ... "Gathering Place in Heaven." And I say to Mr. Fuqi--why didn't you tell me? and he says there are many more secrets, I can't tell them to you all at once, but you will know them all eventually. Many things that aren't supposed to happen anywhere happen here, he says. I thought my hotel so pallid, so pseudo-Californian, interesting only because of worker inhabitation of the unfinished backside, and now a layer of Chineseness exposed--the secret program ...

Clemen, sitting at my right, works for East City's Architecture and Construction Control Board. He tells me about his plan to move to Shenzhen in order to escape the people in Dongguan City. He is from Sichuan and feels foreign in

Dongguan, but in Shenzhen everyone is foreign and he will feel more at home. He has a T-shirt that says "crazy" on it in English, and he asks me what it means--does crazy mean "frontier"?, he asks.

7:00 p.m. August 5, 1996

Echo, 28 years old and one of my students, asks me out to dinner. He's worked as an architect in Dongguan for the last four years. He works with 20 other architects in a collective. The government pays their bills, provides housing and a minimal salary, and all commissions they keep for themselves.

Architects from all over China came to Dongguan to build after hearing Deng encourage accelerated growth. From 1992-94 Echo designed 20 buildings. It was competitive. "We worked only for money--if we didn't say yes to the developer's demands, someone else would." "Developers would bring photos from America, usually government offices or hotels in Las Vegas, especially the pyramid.... I would try, anyway, to show them photographs of other kinds of buildings" (and he tells of bringing out the Kahn book--can I design something like this? and the developer would answer, no--red bricks are for poor people). "We would draw the elevation from their picture, and at the same time design the foundation so they could start construction." Buildings take 2-4 weeks to design through construction drawings. "Just give me the foundation plan, I have to get started," the developers would say.

Echo seems stripped bare by the loss of control over his

YAN HE ROAD COMMERCIAL AND RESIDENTIAL SECTION

Is another important section developed by our company after Winnerway Garden. It covers more than 56,000 square meters and has eighteen multi-storyed buildings. Above the first two stories are low-price apartments, favoured by citizens of Dongguan. There are almost 400 stores which occupy more than twenty thousand square meters. This section is beside Highway 107 on the south, near Dongguan Canal and the south branch of Dong Jiang River on the west, and close to the urban districts of Dongguan City and Guan Tai Road on the east. The traffic in this section is convenient, and the facilities such as warehouse are perfect, so it meets the need of the products import and export in large scale. With the permission of the city government, we have established Dongguan Winnerway Subsidiary Foodstuff Market of Dongguan City here, which is the center of Dongguan and the neighbour hood for gathering and distributing subsidiary foodstuff and commodities.

窗前景緻優悠寫意 華山蒼翠 波光霞影....

如斯美景盡在馬鞍山"新港城"

長安鎮鳥瞰一覽
A view of Chang'an Town

城建篇
Construction

不是城市勝似城市

長安市政建設,以"高起點規劃、高標準建設、高效能管理"為要求,規劃、建設、管理同步進行。

1990年,長安鎮拳鎮政府用超電規劃的發展戰略,制定了《長安鎮1991—2010年總體規劃》,在城鎮建設中,突出抓好道路建設,新建成了150公里長的主幹道路,把送貿業全線,同時高標準建設好配套排水、供電、通訊、公共服務設施、綠道緣化等配套設施;興建了兩座11萬千伏變電站,建成了日供水量6.8萬立方米的自來水廠;加快啓動移動電話、無綫電話、圖文傳真等通訊業務,程控電話裝機容量達14000門,平均每戶擁有一部多電話,被廣東省評爲東莞市第一個"電話鎮"。

為了完善城鎮的功能,長安鎮參照中等城市的規模建設了中心小學、中學、幼兒園、文化中心、體育中心、公園、影劇院、醫院、省資運汽車總站、綜合市場、中心市塔、三星級酒店、旅游度假村、夜光燈高爾夫球場等一大批文化娛樂設施,爲當地群衆、投資商人提供了優良的工作和生活環境。

城鎮秩序井然,實透過强化的管理,長安鎮不斷强化環衛、綠化、環保、交通、市場、城監、治安等方面的管理,使城鎮管理達到平不斷上新檔次。1994年,分別獲得"全國造林綠化百佳鎮"、廣東省城鎮規劃建設管理"南向杯"連續榮獲"南向杯"獎,以及東莞市"文明鎮"稱號。

長安如錦——長安一街道
Chang'an Yihuan Road——Treees shade the streets

A Town Better Than a City

The construction program of Chang'an is carried out with top-level design, high-standard construction and efficient administration.

In 1990, the local government draws up "A General Construction Plan of Chang'an Town from 1991 to 2010" by forerunning developing strategy. We dedicate ourselves to the construction of transportation network. A 150-kilometer-long leading road runs through the town. High-standard construction of public service facilities of drainage, electricity-supply, communication and of afforesting environment has been completed. There are two 110,000V power transmission and transformer stations and one waterworks plant whose daily water-supply capacity reaches 68,000 cubic metre. The wireless telephones, pagers and Fax have been in use. There are 14,000 sets of controled telephones. Each household owns more than one telephone on an average. Chang'an has been honoured with the title of the first "Telephone Town" in Dongguan City.

In order to perfect the town's basic facilities, Chang'an, following the construction of medium-sized city, has set up quite a few facilities of culture and entertainment, such as central primary school and middle schools, kindergartens, cultural centre, sports center, parks, the-

WU SHA NEW TECHNOLOGY PARK
烏沙新科技工業區

The Best Location in Southern China For Setting Up Your Factory

WU SHA, CHANG AN, DONG GUAN

東南中國投資設廠的首選靚地……

"O divine art of subtlety and secrecy! Through you we learn to be invisible, through you inaudible, and hence we can hold the enemy's fate in our hands." —*Sun Tzu,* The Art of War.

Squander

Dongguan embodies the socialist market economy at its most ambivalent. It has at once the entrepreneurial strength of a gentrifying communist cadre and the fragility of one addicted to risk. Infected with a speculative fever, Dongguan twists incoherent in its sickbed, a wasteland of emptiness, danger, and destruction. Having sacrificed itself as China's National Symbol for Export Processing (i.e., as Hong Kong's hinterland), it now rejects industry. With the profits from empty developments, Dongguan's developers keep building, now all excess (for themselves, their architects and their mistresses: a collective dramatization of Bataille's *dépense*).

The speculating congregation, led by a powerful secret society of developer-politicians, soon litters Dongguan with architectural copies—all pink towers and single-family housing (they say oversimplification is the sign of a powerful private sector). Dongguan's developers are risk takers. Like the socialist-market cadres they copy, they are gamblers (speculation is the only legal form in China), playing with FAUSTIAN© money chips: foreign currency from joint ventures and bribes (unfiltered by Shenzhen), and the earnings from a destroyed industrial landscape. They are playing in the market, and they replace financial analysis with optimism.

Dongguan's developers operate via salvage operations. Working within a competitive and overdeveloped market, they construct an architecture of modification and adjustment. Dongguan's developers work quickly. Born of SPEED© and LEARNING© (an automatic operation, no time to plan), spatial experiments are tested and abandoned (PHOTOSHOP© cut-and-paste operations that merely illustrate various potentials).[48] This architecture is never static, but rather in a constant state of renewal based on market predictions, boredom, or lack of money (BANKRUPTCY©).

Gambling is an addiction. High stakes, fast returns, spectacular failure. Soon, despite salvage operations, developments are failing (they aren't running numbers. . . . The future wealth of 1.2 billion people is still imminent, and Hong Kongers, early buyers, have now quit investing. There are too many unfinished projects). Using bank loans to buy land and pour foundations, the developers LEARN© and begin selling property before developments are completed. Hong Kong businessmen seduced by the potential of cheap housing invest anyway. Exuberant marketing efforts insure continued sales (Dongguan is practiced in the art of competition).[49] Developments stand empty (they cannot yet be occupied) but sold. Speculation continues.

Finally the central government in Beijing cracks down. It directs its admonishments to Shenzhen. To stabilize overheated property markets and to cool investment fever, Beijing asks the Guangdong authorities to implement credit restrictions, designed to slow investment in luxury housing. In order to limit construction, Beijing sets quotas for the amount of land available for development. It stabilizes land-use prices, and it initiates a property rights–registration system to prevent the transfer of agricultural land to commercial purposes. Guangdong follows the measures according to a sixteen-point austerity plan, which includes calling in loans being diverted to speculative schemes and controlling real-estate speculation in the development zones.

Dongguan, outside the SEZ, copies the incentives but never the restrictions. Local governments in Dongguan continue to promote new real-estate investment; revenues from the sale of land-use rights are still Dongguan's single largest source of development funds. Dongguan is not only out of central control, it is out of local control (China is not ruled by laws; it is ruled by men).

Socialist-market cadres are hard at work on the new frontier of the socialist market economy; and when they can milk profits from the destroyed landscape and variable conditions of doing business there (bribery, connections),

陽光工業區　新\概\念\高\科\技\工\業\城

攜手并進　共展宏圖

陽光房地產開發公司
地址：東莞市萬江區金泰金宇 2 號樓　　郵編：511717
電話：(0769)2282250　2282253　傳真：(0769)2272986

Developer's brochure depicting potential development in Dongguan, 1995.
The foundation is poured, and the properties are sold to Hong Kong investors,
who assume the project will one day be completed.

Two examples of speculative development, in Zhung Mu Tou and in Chang An, 1996. Speculating, developers litter Dongguan with pink towers and single-family housing.

own work and now dreams of teaching architectural history in Shanghai. He tells me the history of his family during the Cultural Revolution: they were "rich," with a house of their own, which was taken from them and never returned.... (It is still very raw, his story.)

He says, "My favorite film is Paris, Texas."

And at the end of dinner he says, "There is a Buddhist saying: if you are on a boat with someone, it means that you have already known them, in another lifetime, for 10 years; and if you are married to someone, it means that you have already known them for 1,000. We are sitting here now together, which means we've probably known each other, in another lifetime, for at least five years; and since we've spent two hours together, in less than 1,000 years we will marry one another."

11:30 a.m. August 12, 1996
I go to East City Center's golf course clubhouse (a shed across the street from the city). I will meet the construction manager on the project, David. When he walks in, I smile because he is a Californian surfer, a dropout type. He has abandoned America for Thailand, with a Thai wife, and speaks two Asian languages fluently, and now they have a child.

He lives in East City Center. We go to see his apartment. Driving up the podium ramp he says, You won't believe it, but

this whole development is built for second wives (I know, and I smile). His apartment is undistinguished/nice (he has a new stereo blasting hard-core surfer

East City Center

punk and L.A. rap music). I ask him to tell me about living here. Phase One (the concrete phase) is 30% sold (10-15% occupied at any one time). The whole place, including the villas out back (but not New World Garden) is owned by a very wealthy Thai man (but like everything, it is a 50% joint partnership with the government, and he points to the government office on site as we walk in). I ask if it's central or local, and he says the government's 50% is usually split between—30/20 or 40/10.

Phase Two of East City Center, David feels, will be

better (LEARNING©), there will be landscaping here—not all concrete, and a public sculpture—a cascading waterfall that he is helping to design. He describes the exact way it will spill from between two residential towers.

I ask him about Dongguan. David has heard from government officials here that Dongguan City is considered the second test bed, to replace Shenzhen, which in their opinion has failed (it grew too fast without infrastructure, no one can do business there because it is too closely watched, the atmosphere is too American). They will be more careful with Dongguan because they don't want to fail, he says. We agree on how invisible Shenzhen is here, no one acknowledges its existence—who needs Shenzhen with all the direct ties to Hong Kong and overseas?

We go out past the reservoir to the golf course.... huge, incredible land shaping, with later phases building villas into the mountains. He's a landscape architect. I ask about environmental issues. "I know I will go to hell," he says. "This golf course used to be rice fields—how will they feed themselves?" (The continuous FAUSTIAN© sentiment from those overseas who work here).

7:30 a.m. August 15, 1996
The Unbearable Lightness of Chang An. Mr. Fuqi arrives to pick me up at the hotel and we

they become sacred doing the dirty work at the edge. Developer power continues in a Wild West frenzy. After the market bottoms out, they use themselves as clients, filling their empty condominiums with two, three, four mistresses. Dongguan goes from *National Symbol of Export Processing* to *Development City* in less than five years.[50] In Dongguan, the developer replaces the communist official as role model; but like a politician, the developer has kept hidden from his followers the risk, the CORRUPTION©, and the emptiness.

Empty and abandoned buildings in Dongguan City, 1996. Space where a "truly indigenous culture" will emerge.

EPILOGUE: VIRGIN© CITIES

On account of sufficient attention paid to the cultural development at a time of extensive assimilation of material developments, Shenzhen has successfully averted the unsavory aspects of incursions of foreign culture...however, it is only a beginning, a truly indigenous culture is yet to emerge and surely it will if the present policy can be further implemented. —Shenzhen Urban Planning and Design: A Compilation for the First Decade Celebration of Shenzhen Special Economic Zone *(Shenzhen, China: Shenzhen Urban Planning Institute, 1990).*

Spatial Output

Dongguan is building emptiness: VIRGIN CITIES© not yet taken; innocent, fresh (but quickly deteriorating) VIRGIN CITIES©, built with the dirty SPILLOVER© of CORRUPTION© and FAUSTIAN MONEY© from Shenzhen. Deng's future wealth offers ideological justification. As under any communist system, reform requires a strategy of statistics; and the socialist market economy judges success not in terms of industrial output (the number of pounds of iron ore melted in a backyard furnace per week was China's previous measure of success) but in terms of spatial output (rising cities).

Village cadres during the Great Leap Forward padded industrial output figures to please Mao, causing the death of millions from starvation. Today's socialist-market cadres also manipulate by counting the raw space of spatial envelope (whether a building is finished and occupied is irrelevant). Dongguan's concrete shells are used to pad output levels. Instead of causing death, however, the strategy represents China's rebirth. Dongguan is spending on waste, but the spending is not necessarily wasteful: an empty building can be profitable. Newly developed but unoccupied cities represent a spatial new frontier for re-inhabitation.

RECLAMATION©

(or Surviving Globalization)[51]

Dongguan reaches its limit then goes beyond it into excess. It builds emptiness. Yet the optimism and ideological striving toward Deng's utopia of wealth continue (overbuilding is a sign of energy, of confidence), redirected toward what may be a condition of ideological and economic liberation. It would be liberation from industrialization, or even from a regulated market economy of checks and balances. Dongguan's developers use a landscape of crisis (a TABULA RASA©) as grounds for an economic and cultural renewal, visible in Dongguan's architecture.

RECLAMATION© is a liberated-market operation. It depends and thrives on a cycle of failure and rebirth. RECLAMATION© is an indigenous takeover of failed, empty space by the populace of the largest nation on Earth. The VIRGIN CITY©, standing nearly empty—not yet taken—is TABULA RASA© for re-inhabitation. RECLAMATION© is spatial; it is an act of material addition and adjustment. RECLAMATION© is also programmatic; it is the flexible occupation and reoccupation of space. Western (American and Soviet) typologies are turning Chinese in Dongguan. An indigenous culture has (re)emerged and is visible in Dongguan.

RECLAMATION© fills. . . . RECLAMATION© cares not at all about aesthetic, only about potential. An empty building, any empty luxury development, any empty Soviet housing block, is a condition of waiting (and of wanting). Any typology in Dongguan can be RECLAIMED©. The built landscape offers a full range of design aesthetics to choose from. The history of the modern movement, in fact, can be seen in Dongguan—from the international style, through soviet constructivist– and communist-style projects, to late modernism (the curtain-walled tower) and into a postmodern (or classically inspired) aesthetic. All is

RECLAIMED© equally and in similar ways. A project's aesthetic, origin, or style is not important: only its emptiness, its potential.

Corbusian Radiant Cities, relentlessly copied by Chinese urban designers, are drawn and modeled pure; but they are built and occupied Chinese-style (becoming quickly impure, yet more real, when taken by this indigenous population). Pink, postmodern luxury-housing and shopping-mall developments, empty but for the scattered mistresses of developers and factory owners, are slowly taken over by local shopkeepers, who sell vegetables in the empty podiums. RECLAMATION© takes empty Western space and makes it Chinese.

And if emptiness is good, then the unfinished is better. Dongguan's buildings are shells. Building standards are extremely low. Buildings are constructed of poured-in-place concrete with brick infill and are often—because there has been overdevelopment—left unfinished (without cladding, insulation, windows, etc.). They are also abandoned and unoccupied (post-industrialization). This is a condition of exposed materiality (there are no white walls—there is no purity—anywhere). Theirs is not substandard; it is a new standard for user-driven design strategies.[52]

RECLAMATION© takes advantage of the Chinese liberation of use and utility. As RECLAMATION© overtakes Western typology, it also overtakes program. In Dongguan, any predesigned program will be changed, will be adapted. Program is simply pretext: a hotel is inhabited like an office, or it is turned into an office. Floor space is indeterminate. Even Soviet-inspired projects are adapted by developers, who add a southern Chinese exuberance in the form of entertainment (bowling alleys, skating rinks, dance halls).

The spatial action of RECLAMATION© is to make density by adding physical layers, and complex and malleable programs. Any RECLAIMED© condition originated near a dense area. Density in China spreads.[53]

RECLAMATION© is a celebration of density. Long considered by Western architects to be a problem (attempts to de-densify the urban core abound), density is in China a necessity. Chinese culture draws from collective inhabi-

go for breakfast at McDonalds. It is raining hard and we get on a bus to Chang An--grey and sooted interior, tinted windows, us to the very back, soaking. We arrive at the gate of Dr. Sun Yat-sen's ancestor's village (a huge monument ... they do Zhongshan City, Sun Yat-sen's birthplace, one better here....). Sunday-afternoon laziness and we eat a slow lunch under green fishtanks next to a table full of businessmen and mistresses. They interested in me, me interested in them. Mr. Fuqi tries to convince the better waitresses to move to Dongguan City Center to work for him.

In Chang An there are only factories. But the planning is nice, more West than the West.

Mr. Fuqi asks me then, simply--because this is the reason, after all, that we'd come here-- if I'd like a massage....

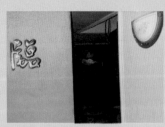

A "hotel" in Chang An

So we go to a hotel and up three flights to a waiting area--and it's only for men, so we subvert the usual policies (he has connections here). I'm given a guest room in the hotel for a shower and another for a steam bath, and then the girl will meet me in another room and so on, and so I do this and she does.

We lounge on the recliners afterwards, with tea and watermelon, and pay the bill. Stepping back outside to blue sky now, and everything seems quite different. We wait for a bus to Dongguan City Center near the new post office (Mr. Fuqi planned it....) in a wide open space with a soaring circular walkway rising above the roadway--warm wind and green landscape and white buildings--my favorite time in late afternoon, crisp now, windy and no more dead heat. Look at those clouds, yes, and he says beautiful clouds, like your name ... (my Chinese name is Shi Li Yun--Beautiful Cloud). I say, Have you ever read the book The Unbearable Lightness of Being? (I realize I'm addicted to his answers to questions like this). "No." ... and I try to

"Someone once said with certainty that there might be a cultural desert behind the economic oasis. The practice by people in Dongguan has refuted the seemingly eternal law." (The Flowers of Civilization Blossom Everywhere, *Dongguan Yearbook, 1994).* [54]

tation. The Chinese create density as a desired condition of collectivity. After RECLAMA-TION©, a single building will be occupied by a whole village.

One Step Ahead

Dongguan is a pioneer of the socialist-market system. The socialist-market cadres, developers, architects, and planners who made it now act as communist China's first (quasi) private sector. Their role as political, social, and cultural groundbreakers takes them and Dongguan "one step ahead" into the schizophrenic morass that is the socialist market economy. Their activity on this frontier has an unintended result. While industrial parks are abandoned to destruction, and Western-style luxury-housing developments are sold unfinished and empty, money and its liberating effects have created in Dongguan a new economic and cultural environment. It is an environment that could potentially liberate China from the TABULA RASA© that is globalization.

Dongguan's liberated condition is an argument for leaving space open to indigenous takeover. It is proof that certain architectural conditions (empty, open, blank, unfinished) have potential as grounds for RECLAMA-TION© anywhere.

"...the voluntary effacement of the architecture..."[55]

1. With this pronouncement, Deng unleashed China into capitalism.
2. Upon his return to Italy, Marco Polo tries to explain Chinese financial institutions in terms of "alchemy and flight" "The great Kaan causes sheets to be spent for money. The great lord has the alchemy perfectly." Henry Yule, ed., *Book of Ser Marco Polo, Volume 1* (Hong Kong: South Asia Books, 1993).
3. Money has become *physical* as blocks of cash—men carry purses to hold it all. China, where money is a prop, is the celluloid gangster's dream. In China's underdeveloped economy, no credit cards or electronic exchanges exist to dilute the symbol.
4. "*Détournement* proposes a violent excision of elements from their original contexts, and consequent destabilization and re-contextualization through rupture and realignment." Asger Jorn, *Detourned Painting* (Brookfield, Vermont: Ashgate, 1984).
5. "Think of it as Faustian money (Spengler), namely that which is not minted, but thought of as an efficient center coming up out of a life which elevates the thought to the significance of a fact. Think-

ing in money generates money—that is the secret of the world—economy." Marc Shell, *Money, Language, and Thought: Literary and Philosophic Economies from the Medieval to the Modern Era*, (Berkeley: University of California Press, 1982).
6. Deng Xiaoping's *private* wealth, hidden but estimated to be approximately U.S.$4 billion, makes him one of the richest men in the world and is an illustration of China's *imbalanced* wealth despite a communist agenda.
7. "When he traveled westward into Texas he had occasion to experiment the truth of the remark, that in traveling towards the frontier, the decreasing scale of civilization and improvement exhibits an accurate illustration of *inverted history*." (Henry Nash Smith, "The Garden and the Desert," in *Virgin Land: The American West as Symbol and Myth* (Cambridge, Mass: Harvard University Press, 1978), 174–84.
8. "In the gloomy bank lobby, under a chandelier shaped like a giant octopus whose outstretched tentacles held white glass globes, we lined up with ten or fifteen other people before a single wooden desk. There, two sullen-looking women sat before piles of fatigued ten yuan notes banded into one-hundred-bill packets. Since China's largest denomination note was at the time ten yuan and since personal checks were almost unheard of, all large purchases had to be paid for with these ungainly bricks of cash. In this sense, even with its new security exchanges, China was still much closer to a frontier economy than to one furnished with the sophisticated financial institutions of the industrialized world, conducting instant transactions by computer. As we waited two women counted off blocks of currency like clerks at a horse-track betting window, stuffed them into a simple wooden drawer and then issued wallet-size bond certificates to investors. The only sound in the room was the clicking of abacuses and the grinding of several Lilliputian-size air conditioners, which strained hopelessly away against the humid air." Orville Schell, *Discos and Democracy: China in the Throes of Reform*, (New York: Doubleday, 1989), 50–51.
9. Since privatization, many companies still obtain either "state-owned" or "collective" designations by various means in order to avoid the political stigma attached to being a private enterprise in a socialist economy.
10. Gu Ming, director of the state council's Economic Legislation Research Center, quoted in *New China News Agency* (August 1986).
11. It is said that the Chinese meaning of the word crisis includes a sense of danger, and of opportunity.
12. Then chairman of the New York Stock Exchange, John J. Phelan Jr., visits to advise Beijing in 1991. A Chinese publication describes it as a chance for China to share the experiences of an elder brother. Phelan notes that China has an "insatiable need for capital." (*Peoples' Daily*).
13. Ezra Vogel, *One Step Ahead in China: Guangdong Under Reform*, (Cambridge, Mass.: Harvard University Press, 1989).
14. Y. M. Yeung and David K.Y. Chu, eds., *Guangdong: Survey of a Province Undergoing Rapid Change*, (Hong Kong: The Chinese University Press, 1994).
15. "Destruction—and technological backwardness—has left the field open." Georges Bataille, trans. Robert Hurley, *The Accursed Share, Volume 1: Consumption*, (New York: Zone Books, 1991).
16. Deng Xioapeng's most costly failure may have been a growing middle class that no longer understands or believes in "socialism with Chinese characteristics." Deng's rhetoric proves empty—a vacuum at the top—and offers no protection from the Western lifestyle. Unwanted elements (McDonald's, freedom fighters, TV, crime) emerge triumphant in Deng's carefully preserved socialist empire.

17. An attempt to make light of those who too slavishly worship the West. (*Peoples' Daily*, February 1987).

18. "Making Money," *Asia Inc.*, December 1995.

19. *Rich and Civilized Dongguan*, Dongguan Yearbook (Dongguan, China: Dongguan Tourist Association, 1995).

20. "In his quest to lure foreign business, Liu has adopted a disarmingly pragmatic view of how to run the economy of this enclave of prosperity in communist China. Without batting an eye, he says his favorite economist is Milton Friedman, the American guru of free markets and minimal government intervention." Reuters, (September 1987).

21. "Recent brutal kidnappings of businessmen traveling in China's booming southern provinces have struck fear into the hearts of executives—and spawned a new business opportunity in Hong Kong. The business is executive protection—in other words, bodyguards. Foreign businessmen worried for their lives are increasingly flanking themselves with bodyguards, paying anything from $100 an hour and up for guards to accompany them while carrying cash, visiting factories or doing business in China. At least two bodyguard companies have sprung up in Hong Kong in the past year to protect visitors to China as crime gallops along with the economy in the mainland's coastal provinces. Beefy freelance bodyguards are a growing breed, ready to contract out for quick executive protection missions to the mainland." Reuters, (August, 1995).

22. Of Dongguan's 3 million people, 1.7 million are "floating," living without the permits that would allow them legal residency in Dongguan. Such permits are necessary in China when moving from city to city. (Vogel, *One Step Ahead in China*).

23. *Rich and Civilized Dongguan*.

24. From 1979 to 1992, Hong Kong manufacturers moved 80 percent of their labor and land-intensive production to Guangdong, investing more than U.S.$17 billion.

25. *Rich and Civilized Dongguan*.

26. Ibid.

27. Sun Tzu, Samuel B. Griffith, ed., *The Art of War*, (London: Oxford University Press, 1988).

28. "Investment into Shenzhen has noticeably declined, from 31% to 23%, as more investors turn their sights inland. Wages outside the SEZ's are 30–40% less, and rising land and labor costs in the SEZ's push low-cost export processing, and other unsophisticated,

explain the title, the words, and don't know why I am bringing it up--feeling disconnected from the ground, closer to heaven, floating--and I can explain the lightness but not the unbearableness, and I say simply that sometimes disconnection can be unbearable.

9:00 p.m. August 19, 1996
One last dinner with Mr. Wu, Mr. Zhang and Lucy, Bill Wong and his girlfriend, and Mr. Fuqi (tonight he's also my spy--when Mr. Wu and Mr. Zhang get together, they talk in Cantonese and tell stories).

I have lunch with Mr. Fuqi at Old Friend Restaurant the next day, a business lunch where I ask him for interpretation and clarification of the dinner the night before. I tell him his role is as my adviser, à la Kissinger ... (he loves this). He tells me Mr. Wu is getting sued by local construction offices because he has too much control over the industry here (this is new control, a crackdown on the industry by the provincial government).

Mr. Wu decides which design institute, engineer, and construction company will go to bid and get the job on government projects. The bidding process is always rigged, so that of the five firms that want the contract, all of them are owned by one person. Mr. Wu is nervous, he says the more power you have, the more you risk getting taken down--sacrificed--for CORRUPTION©. Everyone is CORRUPT©, one just shouldn't get caught, and Mr. Zhang adds, "no risk, no reward." ... Mr. Wu is this week attending a conference, with all government officials, on how to spot and combat CORRUPTION©--they go over case studies, mainly. There has been much discussion of the former mayor; his sons were all in the construction business and were all, like their father, deeply CORRUPT©.

3:30 p.m. August 20, 1996
Bill Wong calls to ask if I'll spend the afternoon looking again at the Sunshine Hillside Villas project, this time in Mr. Li's Dongguan City Center office. Bill Wong and Mr. Li pick me up, and we drive to the building Mr. Li's firm owns. The model is in the lobby (the hills removed as if by habit ...), and then we start a discussion about it in his office.

First we go over the blueprint of the plan and the accompanying booklet--a city planning code given to developers by the Beijing City. This code booklet outlines guidelines for development for these minicities, (i.e., dictates how many schools, how much green space). Mr. Li then asks me how to solve various problems with the plan:

  -how to keep owners from adding to the houses (RECLAMATION©), building high walls, etc., all of which will ruin the view and plan (... I suggest they write rules and regulations the owners must follow)
  -what to do at the edges--for Mr. Li the most desirable areas are closest to the center (... add a running/walking/bike path--they love this idea--and it is nearly 10km around the edge of the site)
  -how to separate the expensive areas--single-family villas--from the cheaper towers--should we build a wall? (... a row of trees)
  -what program for the recreation area in the middle of the single-family villas (... athletic clubhouse)

-should all the villas look the same or be different in groups (... each villa should be different, not different in groups), they tell a story of a housing project in Beijing where the developers copied Windows on the World—there is a Japanese-house section and a Spanish-house section, the favorite, and most laughable (to them) was the outer space section, living in space ships ...

We discuss funding the project—I might be a bridge?—America to Dongguan City, me as a kind of investment guide.

We go out to dinner with the developer, Mr. Li's boss, who has appeared tonight from Beijing. He is a high government official, in construction in Beijing. Sunshine Hillside Villas is one of his side projects. I have driven with him in the big Mercedes to the Royal Regency Hotel for dinner. His joke: if you are a government official in Beijing, you have power; if you are a businessman in Guangzhou, you have money. He is happy to have both.

He explains Dongguan City's development mentality—it's simply about control. Beijing is in control. The south, and especially Dongguan City, is out of control—here the developer is allowed to fill in the space left by the government. He suggests I come back and do urban-design consulting. Everyone needs Western eyes, Western strategies, he says.

6:30 a.m. August 24, 1996
Mr. Fuqi and I go to dim sum on the last morning I am in Dong-guan. He calls me an "architecture missionary" (he has American friends who are Christian missionaries in Shanghai). I am at the Old Friends Restaurant for the last time—he has decided to sell it.... I ask to take a set of chopsticks away with me, so I will be able to eat once I'm back in America.

"You can only become attached to a painting if it resembles you." (Situationist appropriation from *Marie Claire*, 1963)

A Russian exotic dancer

labor intensive industries, north into Dongguan. Labor costs five times as much in Hong Kong as in Shenzhen, ten times as much as Dongguan, land in Dongguan costs 2–3% of what it does in Hong Kong, production costs have increased 20 times in Shenzhen since it was established." (Reuters).

29. *Rich and Civilized Dongguan.*

30. "Developers and architects from the West have also been put off by the Chinese planning system—a nightmare labyrinth of strangely-constituted committees. On one occasion, we were discussing possible changes to a hotel complex with local dignitaries when one man suddenly stood up to denounce the proposal. 'He turned out to be the man who drove me to the meeting,' says John Levy. 'I couldn't believe he could just walk in and have the same clout as the mayor. It's almost impossible to get decisions taken in China.'" *Building Design*, (March 4, 1989).

31. Dongguan covers an area of 2,465 square kilometers and has an official population of 1.36 million people at the end of 1992.

32. Johann Wolfgang Von Goethe, trans. Walter Kaufmann, *Goethe's Faust*, (London: Oxford University Press, 1963).

33. The town leader is now the most powerful political figure in Dongguan City. With control of land use in his village, he determines which farmers get rich. He offers town land for a percentage of a factory or development's profit, or for a flat fee. He is responsible for distributing to his fellow villagers the funds gained from this investment (who then don't have to be farmers anymore and can start companies or buy real estate with their money). No city or province-level planners, or other officials can control the decision of the town leader.

34. Continued marketing efforts allow Dongguan's private sector to prosper; Hong Kong's support allows 60% of Dongguan's population to give up farming. But manufacturing, and the services that sup-port it, has proved to be less labor intensive. 'Streamlining' puts people out of work—failure of the highest order in a still-communist system. This condition is aggravated by a continuing influx of 'floating' population. Also, once Dongguan's preferential policies have been exploited to their fullest Hong Kong's factories hop—one factory to another—in a mad pursuit of tax incentives, resulting in neglected and abandoned industrial sites.

35. "'The Chinese often bring out designs for the project prepared by their own local design institute, which always show the tallest building in the city, usually with a revolving restaurant on top' says Levy. 'Unfortunately, the Chinese are not particularly concerned with the economics of a project and they have to be persuaded to accept your more rational design which can be built within the parameters of the brief given by the foreign partner.'" (*Building Design*).

36. *Dongguan's Achievements in Reform*, Dongguan Yearbook, (Dongguan, China: Dongguan Tourist Association, 1996).

37. "Consider all creations simultaneously as reinvestments, revalorizations of the act of humanity. The object, reality, or presence takes on value only as an agent of becoming. But it is impossible to establish a future without a past. The future is made through relinquishing or sacrificing the past. He who possesses the past of a phenomenon also possesses the source of its becoming. . . . *Détournement* is a game born out of the capacity for devalorization." (*Detourned Painting*).

38. China redefines CORRUPTION© as currency. As bribery, CORRUPTION© lessens the foreign investor's risk as it cements complicity in the communist bureaucracy. For communist officials, CORRUPTION© nonetheless harbors the risk of death; punishment is less common in China's freewheeling socialist market economy but all the more effective therefore as surprise.

39. The new bankruptcy law will "eliminate backward companies through competition. . . . It helps enterprises transform pressure into a driving force." (*Peoples' Daily*, 1987).

40. "The future is made through relinquishing or sacrificing the past." (*Detourned Painting*) CORRUPTION© in the PRD has been *détourned*, a Situationist devalorization. As play, it here emerges as a capitalist gangster's game from the Wild West mentality of the PRD. It is said that Chairman Mao enjoyed walking through "fields of night soil" (shit)—his poetic term for CORRUPTION©. (Dr. Li Zhisui, trans. Professor Tai Hung-chao, *The Private Life of Chairman Mao*, (New York: Random House, 1994).

41. Kevin Lynch, *Wasting Away* (San Francisco: Sierra Club, 1990).

42. "China rules by personal gesture. A spectacular example took place four years ago when Deng Xiaoping, the paramount leader, visited the booming southern province of Guangdong, giving symbolic blessing to untrammeled development. The result of this imperial tour, his last great public performance, was electrifying. Within the party, it routed the conservative camp. Within the economy, enterprise and speculation let rip. Thanks to a surge in building and property speculation, the economy grew by over 12% in 1992–93, faster than anywhere in the world. Mr. Deng, having made his point, then retired for life. Today, even Mr. Deng's most fervent supporters in the leadership rue the inflationary mess and the provincial rebellions that this southern tour left behind." (Dominic Ziegler, "Ready to Face the World," *The Economist*, March 8, 1997).

43. An absence of codified laws governing property rights, taxation, customs, accounting standards, and arbitration procedures.

44. The delta's property market is a highly lucrative one for overseas developers. Although foreign companies are not allowed to own more than 50 percent of a property in China, they take all the profits from a development for the first ten years after completion (rates of return hover around 30 percent in Dongguan, the highest in China) and 50 percent of the profits for the following ten years. (Then the building belongs to China.)

45. Hong Kong speculated in luxury housing long before Deng's tour encouraged accelerated investment. Like Dongguan, Hong Kong made a FAUSTIAN© bargain: when the city's companies shifted labor-intensive operations to the low-cost delta, it—unlike South Korea, Taiwan, or Singapore—failed to climb the 'value-added' ladder. Rather than improve productivity, Hong Kong started to speculate in real estate. High returns were inevitable; Hong Kong is an island, and it has the highest rents in the world. Expanding into the delta to buy up cheap land for housing, especially with the 1997 takeover less than a decade away, made business sense. The balance of supply and demand was upset only after Deng's tour.

46. The PRD's growth rate during this period was 12 percent; Dongguan's was 40 percent.

47. "A spate of recent gruesome abductions involving guns and murder in southern China has put the spotlight yet again on the dangers of business travel there. Hong Kong industrialist Sham Ka-yan, 40, was kidnapped and killed in the southern city of Dongguan even though a ransom of more than $100,000 was paid. His female business partner was murdered after delivering the ransom. Her dismembered body was found dumped in a plastic bag. A real estate contractor and his female companion were abducted from a nearby Shunde karaoke bar. The woman was killed after kidnappers and police staged blazing gun battles. The mass-circulation *Oriental Daily* newspaper in Hong Kong said recently it has heard of more than 70 kidnappings of Hong Kong and Taiwan businessmen in China so far this year." ("Dangerous Business," *South China Morning Post*, 15 January 1996).

48. In China, LEARNING© is a mode of permanent experimentation that has eliminated the notion of failure, which is now declared a LEARNING© experience. China recycles received (often discredited) Western and Soviet development ideas, and adapts them in order to gain access to the new.

49. Deng's utopic MARKET REALIST© vision becomes visible in the developer brochures and 33-town yearbooks of Dongguan. They are filled with MARKET REALIST© imagery—socialist-realist art evolved for use in Deng's socialist market economy. The representation of utopia is imagined as modernization through development. The only difference is that Dongguan's developers and planners realize Deng's two-dimensional utopian reality using PHOTOSHOP©.

50. Deng's privatization is meant to make industrial companies more competitive through the sale of stocks and bonds, but Dongguan privatizes by investing directly into buildings (the buildings have no company attached to them; they are pure speculation). Dongguan's is an endless cycle: those getting rich from speculation and construction (the construction industry is booming, drawing a FLOATING© population from deep in China's hinterland) invest their earnings back into speculation and construction.

51. "Perhaps the successful revolution is no longer successful in the way Tocqueville understood it, as a spontaneous movement of the public mind, a form of spontaneous, concrete ordering of mores to modern values. It is not so much in the operation of institutions as in the freeing of technologies and images that the glorious form of American reality is to be found: in the immoral dynamic of images, in the orgy of goods and services, an orgy of power and useless energy (yet who can say where useful energy ends?), in which the spirit of advertising is more to the fore than Tocqueville's public spirit. But these are, after all, the marks of its liberation, and the very obscenity of this society is the sign of its liberation. A liberation of all effects, some of them perfectly excessive and abject. But this is precisely the point: the high point of liberation, its logical outcome, is to be found in the spectacular orgy, speed, the instantaneity of change, generalized eccentricity. Politics frees itself in the spectacle." Jean Baudrillard, "Utopia Achieved," in *America*, trans. Chris Turner, (London: Verso, 1996), 88–93.

52. "I consider that the problem of quantity can be resolved without lowering the standards by taking the open form as a basis. The half-century of reducing architecture to one decision has made it—and by the same token also the tenants—barren of potential energy of self-determination. The open form, unlike the closed form, does not exclude the energy of the tenant's initiative, but on the contrary treats it as a basic, organic and inseparable component element." In *Team 10 Primer*, ed. Alison Smithson, (Cambridge, MA: The MIT Press, 1968).

53. RECLAMATION© is aided in Dongguan by a restless and growing FLOATING© population, living temporarily and adaptively. (Dongguan's population is 1.3 million permanent and 1.7 million FLOATING© residents.)

54. *The Flowers of Civilization Blossom Everywhere*, Dongguan Yearbook, (Dongguan, China: Dongguan Tourist Association, 1994).

55. Alison and Peter Smithson, in "The Work of ATBAT-Afrique, Collective Housing in Morocco," *Architectural Design* (January 1955).

56. Li Pai, *Li Pai: 200 Selected Poems*, trans. Rewi Alley, (Hong Kong: Joint Publishing Co., 1980).

Contents

INTRODUCTION	*347*	
THE COUNTRYSIDE	*349*	Mao: Rustication
ACQUIRES CITY STATUS	*349*	Deng: Conversion
ZHUHAI TOURIST CITY	*353*	LINGNAN©
SYSTEMATIC	*363*	
DISADVANTAGE©	*364*	Zhuhai Garden City
	368	Fortuities
HAS BECOMING©	*383*	THINNING©
	386	Preparation
	389	FENG SHUI©
	390	PICTURESQUE©
	393	SCAPE©
	396	UTOPIA OF GOLF©

LANDSCAPE
ZHUHAI

Kate Orff

"Without destruction, there is no construction . . ."
Chairman Mao Zedong, 16 May 1966.

RECENTLY EXPLODED AIRPORT SITE

Future site of the Zhuhai Aerotropolis.
Western District, Zhuhai, 1996.

INTRODUCTION

In Zhuhai's remote Western District, 12,000 tons of dynamite systematically explode a nearby mountain range. The series of detonated blasts, said to be heard from as far away as Macau, eventually clear a 100-kilometer road from Zhuhai's Eastern District to its brand-new airport. Alongside the highway, tracts of mangrove forest are in-filled with truckloads of rubble, creating an expanse of flat developable land in all directions.

If tabula rasa was modern architecture's original sin, it has become the battle cry of (post)modern China. During the Cultural Revolution, Mao Zedong's dictum "without destruction, there can be no construction,"[1] professed that new conditions can not arise without destroying the old. Today in the Pearl River Delta (PRD), in keeping with Mao's political catchword, developer-comrades faithfully destruct mountains and bulldoze fish farms in the hopes of constructing a "window to the world" in the Special Economic Zones, in their goal to build a new paradise of "Socialism with Chinese Characteristics." Under Deng Xiaoping's reign, *Wu Tong Yi Ping* ("five pathways and one leveling") guides the struggle to modernize: the pathways are roads, electricity, telecommunications, gas, and sewage; and the leveling is that of large tracts of developable land.[2] This freshly razed blank territory, like the most beautiful paper, awaits the brush strokes of a newly modernized Chinese society.

In Mao's China, modern life did not mean urban life, nor did industrialization lead to densification of city cores. While in the West, industrialization was producing mass concentrations of populations in cities, in China the origin of industrialization was the countryside. Through a series of ideological campaigns and land reforms, city dwellers were actively dispersed into rural communes for "rustication," after which the peasantry was liberated by the Household Responsibility System to leave the land and pursue varied occupations and enterprises. As a result of these reforms, rather than islands of cities surrounded by wilderness, an evenness of city and landscape developed in China from the outset: smokestacks in the middle of rice fields, and factories next to fish farms and housing.

Since the PRD was declared an Open Experimental Zone (OEZ), ferris wheels have gradually appeared between these smokestacks, and peasant vacation villages have emerged where peasants once toiled. While Central Park provided a respite from the urban squalor and density of Manhattan, a 1.24-square-kilometer golf course sits in the middle of Shenzhen as just another fragment of a continuum of golf courses, theme parks, factories, and highrises. In China, nature was never a respite from modern civilization; it was the birthplace of modern civilization. In the new context of the market economy, China's socialist culture is melding into a distinctly Chinese suburban culture.

SCAPE© describes this posturban condition of green texture and evenly dispersed concentrations: a ground of fish farms, parking lots, agrarian fields, and rows of palm trees sporadically gives way to solitary factories, office towers, and multiunit housing. It is an urban typology that is 50 percent landscape and 50 percent architecture, blurring all distinctions between city and country, artifice and nature. SCAPE© is the blueprint of the urbanization pattern of the PRD.[3] Landscape is eclipsing architecture to form the basis of a new *elastic* urbanity,[4] in which solitary highrises spring up from rice paddies, business deals are struck at 3:00 a.m. on all-night golf courses, and earth from exploded mountains forms a thin picturesque coating of roller coasters, highway interchanges, and alligator parks.

MUNICIPALITY

RURAL XIANS

SUBURBAN
DISTRICTS

OLD CITY

 Continuous built-up area, central city, inner city

 District administered towns

 Xian-administered towns

· Commune seat/market towns

THE COUNTRYSIDE ACQUIRES CITY STATUS

The history of SCAPE© can be told through the story of the PRD. Deng's southern tour of the Special Economic Zones (SEZ) in 1992 accelerated the development of the region, and brought new clarity, urgency, and heavy machinery to the construction of a modern Chinese socialist paradise.

In the village of Zhuhai, a newly anointed SEZ on the Western banks of the Pearl River Delta, paradise has found its ultimate expression in the golf resort. If the taut steel-and-glass corporate skyscraper is the symbol par excellence of modern architecture, then the golf bungalow—a hybrid of landscape and architecture—has become the icon of a new brand of THIN© urbanism. It reflects both the history of socialist land policy and the dream of market prosperity.

Marxist-Leninist thought described modernity in terms of contradictions, such as the divides between town and country, between industry and agriculture, and between mental and manual labor. In Chinese urban-planning policy, the eradication of these contradictions was realized spatially through the promotion of autonomous units of production evenly spread across the territory, in a permanent revolution of development. As SEZ agricultural and land-use policies allowed development through market forces, these evenly dispersed units became outposts of urbanism, transforming the countryside into a thin crust of walk-up highrises and vacant golf resorts surrounded by sugarcane fields and theme parks.

Mao: Rustication
Urban policy under Mao Zedong attempted to revolutionize differences between rural and urban settings, and between peasants and city dwellers. In 1950, immediately after Mao came into power, the Chinese Communist Party (CCP) instituted the Agrarian Reform Law, which abolished "the land ownership system of feudal exploitation" and redistributed land to the peasantry.[5]

In 1958, The Great Leap Forward campaign aimed to achieve an unprecedented rate of growth and instantaneous modernization of the country-side. It called for a sudden and dramatic expansion of China's industrial output through the mass participation of peasants in the setting up of furnaces in their own backyards. By the fall of that year, approximately 600,000 backyard furnaces had sprung up across the Chinese countryside, programmatically transforming the hinterlands from areas agricultural production into archipelagos of small industry.[6] By 1962, Zhou Enlai announced an urban policy that aimed to reduce the urban population by 30 million in three years, by dispersing industries and the labor force.

In 1968, the "rustication program" was promulgated under Mao: its aim was to stem migration to cities and eliminate class distinction[7] by forcibly sending educated urban youth to the countryside for several years or permanent settlement. Former city dwellers and rural farmers were gathered together into dispersed communes and encouraged to industrialize, which gradually melded city and countryside populations.

Deng: Conversion
If Mao dispersed industrial production and city dwellers into the countryside to be "rusticated," Deng Xiaoping (in order to prevent the countryside from descending back on the city) enacted policies that instantaneously "converted" the countryside to city status and then restricted population mobility. As part of Deng's agricultural reforms, the commune system was replaced by the "Responsibility System." Deng declared "pao-kan tao-hu" ("full responsibility to the household") allowing peasants to choose their own livelihood, and farmers to grow crops of their own choosing. Individual households acquired control over the production process. Communes were converted to "village and township enterprises."

By imposing the Responsibility System, Deng reprogrammed the entire countryside diversifying the activities of millions of peasants. The policy enabled farmers to grow different types of crops, and even to leave their crops altogether and delve into factory work or to create small enterprises: in

"In order to build a strong and prosperous China, we must take the road of integrating the city and countryside—the road of modernization with Chinese characteristics."
—Zhuhai Mayor Liang, *Survey*, 1995.

short, to pursue urban occupations. Furthermore, the policy provided incentive for workers to pool their land for conversion to more profitable collective activities, such as the formation of factories.

By 1984, 98 percent of farming-based households had been converted to the Responsibility System.[8] Having thus converted the countryside to city status, Deng enacted the Household Registration System, a policy preventing the dispersed urban population from emigrating back to large cities. The farming population was "allowed to leave the land, not the countryside."[9]

After the institution in 1980 of Deng Xiaoping's Open Door Policy, the CCP gradually legalized the transaction and transfer of land, enabling land-use and land-development practices to respond to market forces. Guangdong Province initiated land-use reform in 1987, establishing a socialist real-estate market. Under this real estate system, land is not sold; rather, the right to use land is transferred or leased to developers through negotiation, tendering, or auction. Urban land is owned by the state, and leased and controlled by the Municipal Planning Bureau, while agricultural land is owned by the collective. This means that peasants (with connections to the bureau could potentially join together and sell land-use rights (usually a 40- to 70-year lease, depending on the program) to developers, making millionaires out of peasants overnight.[10]

In the wake of SEZ policy, theme parks began to replace peasant fish farms at a steady rate. In 1991, 300 hectares of land were transferred in the PRD alone.[11] From 1980 to 1993, the cultivated area decreased from 967,000 hectares to 713,000 hectares. As farmers become farmer-businessmen, less land is used for non-export produce and rice cultivation. Land remains fallow, waiting to become property.[12]

Urbanization policy set at the 1980 National Conference on City Planning dictated "control the scale of the large cities, reasonable development of medium scale cities, active promotion of small cities." The conferees' conclusion was twofold: 1. phase out the differences between rural and urban living, and 2. improve the spatial distribution of productive forces.[13] To achieve this goal, Chinese Ministry of Construction officials report-edly planned to build 500 new towns with limited populations which would be strategically placed to control the growth of larger cities.[14]

The cumulative effect of these demographic and land-use reforms has been that urbanization in China is a phenomenon that is being generated in the countryside, rather than in the city. Eventually the physical, legal, and even administrative differences between city and countryside would disappear and become one entity. For example, on March 5, 1979, Zhuhai County was promoted to municipal status. "City" limits were further expanded the year after Zhuhai was declared a Special Economic Zone. In just five years, the city area grew to twenty-four times its original size, from 5 square kilometers in 1979 to a city of 121 square kilometers by 1984.[15] Meanwhile, a state policy converted all of the predominantly rural Guangdong Province into a series of contiguous urban districts. Across China this policy instantaneously increased the area known as "city" by millions of square kilometers: one-fourth of more than 2,000 counties assumed city status. These new administrative zones were immediately planned all the way out to their edges. By the end of 1986, 98 percent of these chartered cities and 85 percent of country towns had been equipped with a comprehensive plan.[16]

To streamline the development process, the separate Land and Building departments were united during 1980-era reforms to create one administrative unit. Permit application times were halved, as developers were required to procure only one certificate from the Planning Bureau's newly combined Building and Land Administration Department.

These urban and demographic policies gave rise to China's most instrumental future subject, one suited for the state's socialist-market economy: the farmer-businessman. Differences between the workers and the peasants were gradually reduced and eliminated, while rural urbanization and mobility restriction created a new breed of countrified urbanite. Sent to the country to learn agrarian virtues and confined to its domain through entrepreneurial incentives, China's modern farmer-businessman inhabits a low-density urban sphere, earning money in countryside industry and relaxing in business-vacation villages.

"National Sanitation City"

"One of the Top Ten Cities on Ideological and Cultural Advancement"

"The 50 Chinese Strongest Cities with Compound Power"

"City of Tourism"

"Advanced City of Environment Protection"

"Advanced City of Urban Planning"

"National Hygienic City"

"Excellent City on Conscription Work for 13 Years Running"

"Advanced City on Family Planning"

"Garden-like City"

ZHUHAI TOURIST CITY

Long regarded as the most remote backwater within the CULTURAL DESERT© of the PRD, Zhuhai, a small fishing village on the delta's western banks, has overcome what Mayor Liang once described as a "state of poverty and blankness" to create a vast phantom-landscape empire, a THIN© city of flower beds, palm-tree edges and empty lots.[17] Since 1980, more than 56 square kilometers of coastline, collective farms, and vegetable plots have been systematically transformed into business-vacation pleasure grounds, where fresh surplus income from the market economy can be enjoyed. Through hard work and the "sheer wisdom and courage of the Zhuhai people," Zhuhai is building a "modern garden-like seaside city" and has miraculously converted systematic disadvantages into happy fortuities of circumstance in an urban Immaculate Conception, in a newly built up area of 56.2 square kilometers since 1980. Its geographic isolation, pleasant natural setting and state of underdevelopment are being refashioned into an idyllic landscape city. Communist sensibilities of collectivity, hard work, and planning have joined forces with the market ideals of speculation and a practiced real-estate pitch to produce a blossoming garden for investment.

The instant urbanization of Zhuhai was achieved by dispersing program elements, such as business vacation hotels, golf courses, factories, clinics, and bungalows, throughout the countryside and then linking these outposts of

CULTURAL DESERT© Chinese euphemism for the Pearl River Delta. The result of NEGLECT©, geographical circumstance, and relentless ideological campaigns, the CULTURAL DESERT© is the only ground where the most radical new ideas can thrive.

inhabitation with infrastructure to create a thin crust of tourist culture connected by a network of palm tree-lined highways.

LING-NAN©

LING-NAN© "South of the Nan-ling mountain range" refers to the geographical barrier between ancient Chinese civilization in the north and the CULTURAL DESERT© of southern China. The word LING-NAN© is claimed by both sides; inevitably synonymous with "tasteless and unrefined"—culturally bankrupt—to those in the north, it means "natural, reasonable, practical, and flexible" to those in the Pearl River Delta. LING-NAN© encompasses the pragmatic and the unworthy: LING-NAN© Garden, LING-NAN© Architecture.

"Since China is a vast country with marked geographical and cultural differences between her northern and southern regions, the styles of landscape gardening vary considerably. Gardens in the north, for instance, tend towards staidness, dignity, and grandeur; those south of the Yangtze River are more delicate, refined, elegant, and flexible, while in southern China they are characterized by ebullience and piquancy."[18]

"As gardens, per se, they [the gardens of Canton] are a little on the vulgar side."[19]

LING-NAN© culture is the apotheosis of landscape, tourism, and entrepreneurship. It derives its name from the Nan-ling mountain range, which physically separates the southernmost part of China (Guangdong and Guangxi provinces), from the country's central and main cultural region. This geographic feature, along with the province's history of contact with the West through ports like Guangzhou,[20] gave Guangdong the reputation of having a "high degree of self-

sufficiency and a tendency towards separatism." The area south of the Nan-ling Mountains is considered to be a CULTURAL DESERT© due to its geographic isolation. Guangdong is viewed by northerners as an uncivilized frontier, to which disgraced officials were exiled as punishment. Although Ling-Nan literally means "gardens to the south of the five ridges," it is colloquially synonymous with the absence of culture and taste. If in the north Ling-Nan signifies cultural bankruptcy, in the south it means natural, reasonable, practical, and flexible.

During the Cultural Revolution, whatever culture had been tenuously established in southern China was largely scraped away. Its blank fallow fields were prepared to host an entirely different way of life and to invent a new culture. Severed from Beijing by the Nan-ling mountain range and therefore forced by SEZ policy to invent a modern city out of a fishing village, Zhuhai has created a LING-NAN© empire. Zhuhai farmers are urged to "be a cultural citizen, build a cultural trend, construct a cultural city!"[21]

Classical Ling-Nan gardens were considered "cruder, and more spartan" (Keswick) than their highbrow counterparts in Suzhou, which were famous for simulating the unfolding experience of Chinese scroll painting and for their spatial and material complexity. The PRD's contemporary LING-NAN© gardens[22] are highly creative and highly dispersed, tactically programmed to lure tourists and provide at least temporary urbanization. All-night golf courses, a peasant vacation village, a Formula One race track, and an array of theme parks like Pearl Land, Alligator Show,[23] the all-you-can-sit-and-eat Tomato Park at Baiteng Lake, Yuan Ming Yuan, and Garden of 1,000 Nations are sprinkled throughout Zhuhai's farthest reaches, luring tourists and Japanese businessmen golfers.

Zhuhai invented a culture of tourism in the hopes of luring potential cultural citizens.[24] Baiteng Peasant Lake Vacation Village, for example, an oasis of abandoned bungalows in the Western District of Zhuhai, was an early joint venture of investors from Hong Kong, Macau Taiwan,

and China. With the infusion of capital from forty investors, the remote fishing-outpost setting was transformed into a real-estate pitch, a "modernized tourist-holiday zone" according to the travel brochure. Following is a description from a Zhuhai tourist brochure: "This picturesque Peasant Vacation Village, 20 km^2 in area with over 40 hotels, nearly 4000 beds, has become one of the 4 key tourist places in Guangdong." "The climate is fine and the air is fresh. The wonderful sights are good combination of natural and artistic, Chinese and Western elements."[25] It has the largest crocodile park (more than 300 crocodiles), the largest butterfly park, a tomato park, scenic boat rides, conference centers, amusement rides, gymnasiums, shopping centers, and restaurants, promising a tempting array of activities for the temporary inhabitant.

> "There is a farmer vacation village near Zhuhai, which is called 'Baiteng Lake.' It is a three-star level international hotel created by a farmer-entrepreneur. . . . We have different kinds of rooms—900 sets of different kinds of rooms. . . . All have a balcony overlooking the water, and the water outside the room is so clear, so transparent and soft, that you can see the swimming fish and stones through the crystal-clear water. On the banks of the lake there are hanging willows, which touch the water gracefully while the green bamboo waves in the wind. . . . The hundred flowers blossom in competition[26]. . . . Standing on the balcony you could just stretch out your arm and fish there, . . . while listening to the frogs singing a song and the insects and worms murmuring. . . . There is a fishing club, a seafood restaurant, a market, an artificial playground, swings, a beach, and different parks: a fruit park, an actual orchard, where you can eat all you want in the park (but you cannot bring the fruits out). . . . There is a flower park and a sort of Tomato Park (i.e., cheap-plant park), which poor people can enjoy. . . . If you go into the Tomato Park, as soon as you enter, you can sit and dig them out yourself!"[27]

Forced by SEZ politics to modernize, Zhuhai evolved from a fishing outpost to a tourist garden city through hard work, inspiration, and a marketing idea.[28] Implementing the long-term tourism development plan worked out in consultation with experts, a series of tourism projects with Chinese characteristics and national features were built, including a park of the four Chinese Buddhist mountains in miniature and a grand re-creation of Yuan Ming Yuan. Yuan Ming Yuan, a scaled re-creation of the Chinese imperial gardens, offers history remade in the form of a desirable brochure image.[29] Since local people were unfamiliar with this type of construction, many of the structures were prefabricated in Beijing.

Innovatively themed landscape substance is appearing throughout Zhuhai. The Pearl Land theme park blankets 6 million square meters with roller coasters, bumper car, and Ferris wheel, and sits adjacent to a freshly smoothed 2-million-square-meter golf course. Yuan Ming Yuan (phase I) is 60,000 square meters, with an 80,000-square-meter lake, covering former communist factories in the Eastern District. It lures the tourist and business vacationer with an abundance of pleasurable activities, including 6,000 square meters of restaurants, hotels, and shopping (with cultural items for sale). Phase II of the Yuan Ming Yuan theme park is called the Gardens of 1,000 Nations. Along a path visitors discover miniaturized gardens of world civilizations unfolding before them—Japanese, French, Egyptian, Islamic. . . . Zhuhai has also built a lush and award-winning park (designed by the Garden Academy division of the municipal government) at the site where the new bridge aimed at Hong Kong touches down in Zhuhai's eastern district, welcoming commuters and tourists into the municipality with a colorful flowerbed.

In the spirit of communist organization, Mayor Liang Guangda instituted the Tourism Regiment, a branch of the municipal government greatly responsible for Zhuhai's renaissance. "During the past decade, we have cultivated a regiment of tourism-business managers, or tourist business-men. We have formulated an efficient system of tourist-business management. We have many ways to train and cultivate these tourist-business managers."[30] Trained at a special tourism academy, this army of managers directs tourists to any of the newly constructed attractions.

In 1994, Zhuhai was home to twenty-two travel agencies, 211 local tourist guides, 815 cooks and dessert chefs, 355 professional tourist drivers, and 12,584 tourist managers. Mayor Liang assured potential investors of the city's commitment to tourism by saying, "we make utmost efforts in investing and exploiting, so to keep tourism of Zhuhai ahead of our domestic counterparts."[31]

As of 1986, there were eighteen official tourist sites in Zhuhai, including Shijingshan Tourist Center, Zhuhai Hotel, and Jiuzhou City. Although the occupancy rate of Zhuhai's seven leading hotels was at that time only 42 percent, the construction of Zhuhai Tourist City continued at a steady pace.[32] More vacation villages were constructed and enhanced, with diversions such as golf, tennis, karaoke, saunas, and boat paddling. Traditional Chinese characters have been adapted in order to describe these new tourism typologies—for example; "hotel" has evolved into a range of other LING-NAN© inspired signs, suggestive of inventive (and sometimes lurid) activities. One sign says, "Liquor Shop: The Place for Guest Residents."

ZHUHAI TOURIST CITY

珠海度假村酒店
ZHUHAI HOLIDAY RESORT HOTEL

珠海旅游城

初设

Hercules at the Baiteng Peasant Lake
Vacation Village.

Western District, Zhuhai, 1996.

The PICTURESQUE© is an aesthetic based on harmonizing disparate elements. In the Pearl River Delta, every view from every point is now inescapably picturesque.

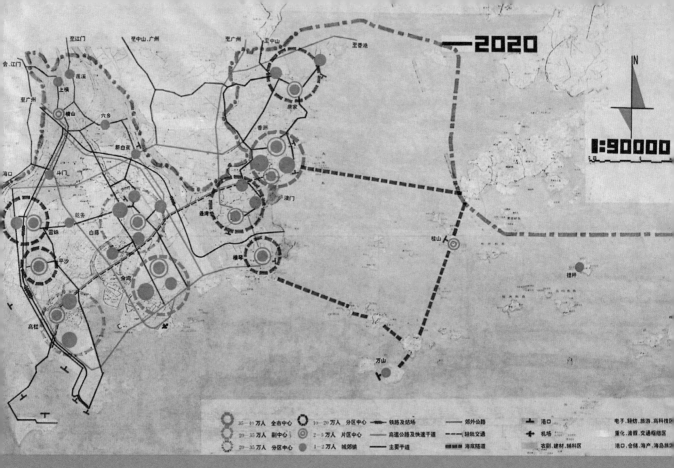

Zhuhai's plan to overtake Hong Kong in 2020. (1995)

Zhuhai has . . .

the lowest population density: 500 people per square kilometer.

the most green are per capita: 41.6 percent of the city.

the best climate: 72.3° Fahrenheit/22.4°Celsius.

the most islands: 146.

China's first Formula One racecourse: 4.3 kilometers long, high speed of 300 kilometers/hour, designed according to international standards.

the longest airport runway: 4,200 meters, capable of handling 12 million passengers per year.

China's only airshow.

China's broadest and least-congested roads: six to eight lanes Zhuhai Grand Road is 60 meters wide.

the deepest port harbor: 290 meters, newly constructed that can handle the heaviest cargo (10 to 20 million tons).

the longest oversea bridge (proposal): Ling Ding Yang Oceanstride Bridge (64 kilometers; six lanes, and the most heavily invested building project in the PRD.

the first full-scope nuclear power plant simulator.

the only building in China modeled on the ancient Yuan Ming Palace.

SYSTEMATIC DISADVANTAGE©

SYSTEMATIC DISADVANTAGE© A condition
in which successive forms of NEGLECT©—
natural, political, economic, cultural—create
an explosive mixture of resentment and recklessness that can be harnessed for sudden
spurts of drastic change.

In August 1980, at the Third Plenum of the Eleventh Central Committee of the CCP, Zhuhai was declared an SEZ. Zhuhai was selected for its commercial potential, due to its proximity to Macau.[33] As an experimental ground for Deng Xiaoping's Open Door Policy, it would become China's "window on the world." CCP officials also tapped Shenzhen for SEZ status for its proximity to Hong Kong. In addition to the inferiority complex caused by neglect, Zhuhai faced the further disadvantage of competing with a more established delta neighbor

Shenzhen's adjacency to Hong Kong enabled easy access to spillover investment, culture, and cachet. Having already converted these assets into substantial urban mass, Shenzhen had a seemingly insurmountable advantage over its remote rival. Far too sparsely populated to generate a critical mass of urban density and isolated from Asia's financial epicenter, Hong Kong, Zhuhai appeared destined to remain provincial and underdeveloped. It lacked both the speedy success of Shenzhen and the established political and cultural clout of Guangzhou.[34]

Tempted by the benefits of a potential Hong Kong–Macau overland connection, Zhuhai initiated the construction of the Ling Ding Yang Oceanstride Bridge: a proposed 63-kilometer elevated roadway, spanning the delta's mouth and connecting Zhuhai with Hong Kong. In its eagerness to connect to the city of riches, Zhuhai officials began construction before securing permission to land the bridge on the delta's

eastern shores. Failing to find a willing recipient, Zhuhai was forced to halt the massive project midstream. Concrete pilings of the aborted bridge stand as a monument to bold LING-NAN© ambition and risk.

Catching wind of the infrastructural fiasco, China's central government severely reprimanded Zhuhai for its administrative and financial recklessness. The wild abandonment with which Zhuhai sought to overcome its disadvantages led to deeper disadvantages. Zhuhai's overextended investments in the Ling Ding bridge, combined with investments in an equally ambitious airport project, were rumored to have left the city bankrupt, leaving it little room for investment in future grand projects.[35]

Zhuhai transformed its disadvantages into strategic advantages, exacerbating its radical difference from Hong Kong. Because of the slowness of its development, Zhuhai was able to learn from the failures of SHENZHEN SPEED©. Zhuhai capitalized on the mistakes of Hong Kong/Shenzhen urbanism. In place of density, Zhuhai proposed openness as part of a mandate to impose green space and diffuse the concentration of buildings.

The Zhuhai Catch-Up Plan 2010 has been broken down into three five-year increments.[36] The First Five-Year Plan centered on infrastructure. It is the 'preparatory' stage, the goal being to first increase infrastructure links and to build industrial structures to connect Zhuhai to the entire Pearl River Delta. The second five-year plan aims to connect Zhuhai with all of China: "Zhuhai will be even more strengthened through a three-dimensional transportation network of high-ways, rail-ways, air-ways and water-ways."[37] The Third Five-Year Plan transforming the economy from farming into industrial development. The Fourth Five-Year Plan is dedicated to new technology. "Our target is to build up within three five year plans a highly modernized Hi-Tech

Industries Developing Zone at world-wide level."
After 2000, Zhuhai hopes to formulate a system
of high and new technology called the "third
industry": this means that commercial stores,
international trade, finance, travel, culture, sports,
and medicine will be the focus, and film, broadcasting, conference centers, etc. will be developed. Subsequent five-year plans decreed by
the central government include the construction
of the Jingzhu Superhighway which will connect
Beijing and Zhuhai, and the GSZ Superhighway
which will run between Heilong Jiang and
Shanya Hainan Island. It is hoped that the highway will be routed through Zhuhai.

Zhuhai's SYSTEMATIC DISADVANTAGE©
was intensified when the central government
eliminated many SEZ privileges and "put on the
brakes" in 1995. The entire Special Economic
Zone policy was questioned during a governmental session in Beijing. Grumbling officials from
China's interior areas complained about widen-
ing regional disparities, sparking the debate that
led to the stripping of Zhuhai's SEZ status.
"Zhuhai, in conjunction with Shenzhen, Shantou,
Xiamen and Hainan, has been feeling the pinch
from the scrapping of preferential policies that
have lured domestic and foreign capital and
expertise. "The SEZs have been hit hard by
uncertainties over their future role in China's
growth plans, as the country wants to create a
level playing ground for business."[38] Foreign
manufacturers initially moved their factories to
Zhuhai to take advantage of cheap land and
labor, but are reacting to the SEZ policy shift by
moving to cheaper inland areas, which now boast
many of the privileges accorded to the no longer
"special" Zhuhai. In response, the city cut indus-
trial-zone land prices by 50 percent and commer-
cially zoned land by 20 percent, in order to slow
migration of investment inland.

Zhuhai Garden City

Zhuhai's state of underdevelopment and pleasant climate were seized by enterprising urban
planners as the setting of a garden city unrivaled
in scope or grandeur.[39] "Garden City" offers a
centralized idea, a unifying, apolitical, and
upbeat slogan that is sufficiently vague to allow
the most ambitious proposals to appear virtu-
ous. Garden City fuses Chinese and Western
concepts, landscape and architecture, countryside and city, control and freedom. Utopian and
Chinese in its vision, Garden City is embraced as
a form of urbanization with Chinese characteristics, or urbanization without density.

Zhuhai planners have embraced Singapore
as a model for their utopia. This mirrors Deng's
own fascination with the garden state. Deng
declared, "We must not only promote economic
development, but also improve social order and
the social mood. Only thus can we say we are
building socialism with distinctive Chinese characteristics. Singapore's social order is good.
Their management is very strict. We must learn
from their experience and strive to do it even
better."[40] Zhuhai urban planners even employed
Singaporean consultants: "On the development
of Zhuhai itself, it was no secret that the city
had been using Singapore as a model for its
town planning, housing program, legal system,
and port management. When we prepared our
urban Master Plan many years ago, we asked
ourselves which international city Zhuhai should
be modeled after. All of us were unanimous that
it should be Singapore," said a Zhuhai official.
He added that "touches such as growing flowers
in balconies of apartments to brighten the look
of the city and planting shrubs along hill slopes
to prevent erosion were all learnt from Singapore." Zhuhai Vice Mayor Zeng Defeng sums up
the intentions nicely: "If you come to Zhuhai and
find it looks like a garden city, you can guess
where we got the idea from."[41]

The Planning Department believes that Zhuhai
will improve on Singapore's design, stating
that "we can go beyond it."[42] As a propaganda

regime, "Zhuhai Garden City" has been so successful that it exists at every level of Zhuhai society. Billboards and advertisements overflow with garden references. Once the site of steel production in backyard furnaces, the economic landscape is today characterized by gardenesque goodness. Enterprises such as the Biowonder Healthy Products Factory in Gongbei Zhuhai advertise Bioenergy Healthy Underpants and the Bioenergy Recovery Mattress. In contrast to industrialized and busy Shenzhen, which hosted the 1993 International Machinery and Industrial Supplies Fair, and the International Waste Regeneration Technology and Equipment Exhibition, Zhuhai continues to host such spirit-enriching events as the International Beauty and Health Care Products Exhibition. One participating factory from Zhuhai is the Long Live Electrical Appliance Group (also in Gongbei), whose advertisement reads like a Garden Special Economic Zone poem, mixing modernism's hygienic mania with commodity zeal:

> To disinfect bacteria and make body
>   more healthy
> To purify air and comfort lung with
>   clean air
> To moisture skin and make it more white
> To be good gift for relatives and friends.

Zhuhai planners were convinced of their Garden City vision and knew the law was on their side. One planner exhorted, "It is a law to make this a beautiful city." When asked about the origins of Garden City, another planner's response was: "The main responsibility is claimed by the city government and planning office." There are laws pertaining to building height (forty stories), building color, building density, floor-area ratio, and building shape, in addition to view lines of the coast, percent of green area (35 percent of the total area of the city), and laws against smoking in public.

After viewing Zhuhai from atop a revolving restaurant in 1984, Deng himself was inspired to inscribe a scroll proclaiming, *"Zhuhai jingji tequ hao"* ("the Zhuhai SEZ is good"). His declaration was a spectacular gesture of support for Zhuhai's project of tourism cum Garden City. It was a green light for Zhuhai's green-thumb planners to plant their city of landscape in search of prosperity.[43] Deng was apparently so taken by Zhuhai's pleasant landscape that he chose to take a 1995 health hiatus on the delta's western shores, rather than in Shenzhen as was originally planned. The BBC reported that "originally he intended to go to Shenzhen, but later, considering that the environment there was not as quiet as in Zhuhai, he went to Zhuhai instead."[44]

"The green area of the city covers 39.58 percent and the per capita public green area is 20.07 square meters. As the whole city is evergreen for all the four seasons and flowers are blooming in every month, the scenery is pleasing to both one's eye and mind and brings people the enjoyment of beauty."
—*Zhuhai Today*, 1995

"Zhuhai aims to be the most vigorous and attractive region in South China."
—Zhuhai Mayor Liang, *Survey*, 1995.

Garden/City
Socialist/Market
Chinese/Western

Fortuities

Zhuhai Planning Regiment transformed their village into a vast Garden City by turning its geographical and cultural disadvantages into strategic advantages. Confronted with the daunting task of imagining a city from nothing, Zhuhai adapted its geographical isolation, underdevelopment, lack of culture, good weather, and other fortuities as tactical advantages. Guided by Singaporean investors and consultants, they declared themselves a Garden City, one that would sit in counterpoint to the crowded slums of Hong Kong and the Eastern Shore. The goal, as explained by an official of the Planning Office, is "to catch up to Hong Kong and keep a contrast."[45] When Zhuhai planners set out to assess their humble city in 1980, they inventoried its unique qualities, which looked something like this:

1: Lots of Land
2: Geographically Remote
3: Pleasant Climate
4: No Culture
5: Bold Mayor
6: Talented Planning Regiment
7: Garden Academy
8: Islands

Fortuity 1: Lots of Land

Zhuhai is not particularly rich in natural resources. What Zhuhai *does* have is flat, developable land. Zhuhai's vast territory precludes any threat of urban density. Although this fact once contributed to its denigrated provincial status, today its abundant land area has suddenly become an asset: land for development is cheap and plentiful. Hong Kong and Macau are both mountainous islands with precious little flat area and land mass. Zhuhai has lots of land and hundreds of mountains available for explosion.

Fortuity 2: Geographically Remote

Zhuhai is from the wrong side of the delta. Far from the Hong Kong–Shenzhen–Guangzhou corridor, the geographic position of Zhuhai has caused its city planners great anxiety. However, officials have realized its remoteness also protects Zhuhai from Hong Kong's urban spillover. Geographic distance could serve as a natural barrier from contamination by the eastern delta cities and lifestyle. Zhuhai could become a safe haven from the ills of density: urbanity based on pleasantness and relief.

"Peasants Riot in China: Security officers in southern China fired tear gas to disperse 500 peasants who rioted for six hours over the confiscation of land. Hong Kong press reports said the violence flared Saturday in the Special Economic Zone of Zhuhai when the peasants gathered outside a government office to protest inadequate compensation over the sale of their land for commercial development. An undetermined number of people were injured in the disturbance." —*The Dayton Daily News*, (2 January 1995).

"In an attempt to speed up industrialization and to attract high-technology industries, Liang last year announced that land prices for industrial sites would be slashed by 50 percent and for commercial property by 20 percent."
—Yojana Sharma, "China Economy: On the Runway, Zhuhai Waits and Waits for Takeoff," *Interpress Service*, (26 January 1996).

"Unified expropriation of land and strict control have been practiced." —Zhuhai Mayor Liang, *Survey*, 1995.

恆昌企業

公司地址：廣東省鶴山市新風路35號　電話

准，由
用」稱
業（集
是集房
聯營、
企業成
承
如既往
開放方
經濟而

公司法定代表人、總經理：易昌

Fortuity 3: Pleasant Climate

Zhuhai does not embrace 20th-century urbanity (vertical growth, high density, 24/7 work ethic); rather it is a culture based on pleasantness, greenery, and dispersal that has inspired a range of urban programs like the downtown beach, Recreational City, Together Happy Garden, and Magic Pigeon Island. Blessed with perennially sunny weather, Zhuhai evolved with leisure at its core. In Zhuhai, pleasant climate is the hallmark of a new type of city, a city unharmed by advancement. Its attractiveness is its counter-evolutionary urbanism: it has avoided the densification of more "evolved" cities, and proposed beaches and parks rather than skyscrapers.

"Dear friends, Zhuhai is a city with mild climate, fresh air, clean environment and picturesque scenery. Its colorful programs for cultural recreation, comfortable accommodation, and delicious food, especially the finest service will surely make your travel pleasant. Zhuhai, the Tourist City, is expecting your coming."
—"A Brief Introduction to Zhuhai," in *Zhuhai Tourist City*, a brochure of the Zhuhai Municipal Tourist Bureau, 1996.

"We grasp every link necessary for the ideological and cultural advancement and make painstaking efforts on the recreational and cultural advancement." —Zhuhai Mayor Liang, *Survey*, 1995.

Fortuity 4: No Culture

Through its distance from northern high culture and society, Zhuhai has been liberated from the shackles of traditional culture. Zhuhai has become free to invent a new society, a pure, open culture of tourism.

Fortuity 5: Bold Mayor

"Zhuhai has 'delusions of grandeur.'
—Gordon Wu, Hong Kong millionaire and
developer of the GSZ Superhighway, interview,
January 1996.

"Mr. Liang moved the mountain to make way
for an international class airport—another surprise. Beijing had approved construction of a
local airfield but was stunned to find Mr. Liang
building what is today China's biggest (500
million dollar) airport."[46]

Mayor Liang, Chief Urban Planner and expert
socialist-businessman, was able to marshal
speculative fervor surrounding the SEZs to
create a "Modern Ling-Nan Seaside City" out
of a fishing village. Liang spearheaded most
of Zhuhai's capital construction projects,
including the international airport, port,
numerous bridges, and thousands of kilometers of six-lane highway, in anticipation of the
coming paradise. It is crucial for the mayor to
propagandize Zhuhai to ensure faith in his
vision, but his enthusiasm for growth and success has run the risk of appearing to stray
from both communist principles and market
sense. A friend at Zhongshan University
explained: "The people in Zhuhai have good
faith in Liang Guangda. But other people think
he is too crazy. He has raised the appeal "See
Zhuhai beyond Zhuhai, See Zhuhai beyond
21st Century!" But people think Mr. Liang has
done more than this. He has built the infrastructure for the second generation. We know
Capital Construction should go before economy development. But there is a limit. Beyond
this it can only push back the economy.
Zhuhai has gone ahead of time too much."

A native of Guangdong, Liang Guangda (b.
1935) presided as mayor of the municipality
of Zhuhai from 1984 to 1995 and has held
the title of Secretary of the Communist Party
of Zhuhai since 1987. Liang joined the CCP in
1958, then became deputy to the 13th
National Congress and to the 7th National
People's Congress. Liang's ability to keep in
favor politically, as well as his bragging and
bravado, is infamous in the region.

One example of Mayor Liang's vision is his pet project, the Yuan Ming Yuan theme park. Yuan Ming Yuan proves what can happen when a mayor mobilizes the right political and aesthetic support.[47] The local government donated land for the project, and Liang funded the project out of the city's coffers: phase I cost 6 million RMB, phase II cost 1 million RMB. Trusted officials were put in place to insure its realization. The director of the Zhuhai Tourist Bureau (a government position) co-directs the construction, while the Planning Office appointed the construction manager who escorted me around the site. The mayor himself chose the site because it has good *feng shui*. Liang, along with a *feng shui* master from Wubei, decided that in order to counteract the disadvantage of one "weak" hill, a miniature Great Wall of China was to be built there, in order to make a strong "left dragon." A pagoda was placed on the "right tiger" hill. The mayor intended this pagoda to become Zhuhai's new icon, replacing the Fisher Girl statue at Lover's Lane.

"A world-wide scaled, comprehensive, modernized with new hi-tech industrial groups and new arts, garden like, coastal Science City shall be set up. We must work hard to make the dream come true!" —Zhuhai Mayor Liang, *Survey*, 1995.

"The whole urban planning process and the development of the city should be considered for the long term—for many, many years later..." —Liao Keqin, Chief Engineer of the Zhuhai City Planning Bureau.[48]

Fortuity 6: Talented Planning Regiment

Zhuhai has converted its sleepy communist bureaucracy into a vital development mechanism. The Zhuhai Planning Regiment executes the mayor's vision with strict control. It started with a physical, cultural, and economic tabula rasa—a clean slate upon which to test planning ideas—and high authority to compel adherence to those ideas. They have envisioned a Flowerbed Empire soon to catch up with Hong Kong through long-term planning and legally enforceable bubble diagrams of pleasantness and prosperity.

The planners of Zhuhai are so forward thinking that they have prepared their city for the long term. From the outset, Zhuhai proceeded by focusing on the distant future. As Mayor Liang puts it, "Zhuhai conducts its city planning and infrastructure well in advance."[49] According to municipal government spokesman Cai Xinhua, Zhuhai was originally designed to accommodate three million people, but the present population is barely one million. Moreover, only 600,000 are permanent residents; the remaining 400,000 are floating migrant workers.[50] It is anticipated that the residential population may increase to 2.5 million by the year 2010 and to 3 million by 2050. This means that even if construction stopped tomorrow, by the year 2010 Zhuhai will still only be 83 percent occupied, and according to the brightest projections, will come to full flower (100 percent occupancy) in the year 2050. Zhuhai planners have taken into account the needs of 2 million people who have not yet materialized. The city is ripe for inhabitation: eight lanes open for traffic in anticipation of the impending demographic and economic boom.

The master plan of Zhuhai is an administrative flow chart consisting of materials, money, pollution, wealth, and landscape. Its territory is accordingly divided into five districts; each assigned a different function. For example, the Central District, which faces Hong Kong, is to be a residential garden paradise, while the Western District is designated to be an industrial zone. It is a law that heavy industry be located there. The residential garden and the industrial zone are separated by an extensive forested landfill project of more than 50

square kilometers. The Zhuhai Regiment imagines this piece of land will serve as a pollution filter and visual screen between east and west, and buffer the flower bed residential district (east) from the heavy industrial district (west).

The Central District: the center of culture and economy.
The Northern District: a rich mixture of tourism and science.
The Western District: the necessary evil of heavy industry, isolated from the other districts.
The Southern District: dedicated to high technology.
The Eastern District: with many islands, a promising base of tourism.

"On the basis of natural topography, that is hill, river, and sea, the city is divided into three districts: the Central District (the Special Zone), the Western District (include Sanzao, Pinsha, Zhuhai-port etc., the Eastern District (Wanshan Archipelago). Every district is composed by several cluster zones, which are different in scale and function. Linked by a rapid transportation system, the districts and cluster zones make up a whole one." —from development brochure, *City Planning and Construction of Zhuhai*, 1994.

"Planners vs. citizens: the relation is getting better." —Mayor Liang Guangda, *Survey*, 1995.

"In order to produce a tidy, clean, and beautiful urban landscape, something will be controlled well in accordance with the urban plan, that as building line, building height, building density, floor-area ratio, building color, building shape and etc. In the same time, the hills, the bank of the river, the seashore, the green ground, the sculptures and etc. should be taken advantage of and become important parts of the urban landscape." —Mayor Liang Guangda, *Survey*, 1995.

珠海市
THE MAP OF ZHU

珠海市風貌規劃
視線通廊圖
珠海市規劃局

VIEWLINES RESTRICTIONS

珠海市風貌規劃
風貌構架圖
珠海市規劃局
同濟大學城市規劃系

PLANNED GREENERY

Fortuity 7: Garden Academy

Zhuhai planners understand that landscape is the most strategic (and cheapest) tool to realize their new city. To this end it has encouraged the energetic Zhuhai Garden Academy to plant away. The Zhuhai Garden Academy, a division of the Agricultural Department of the Municipal Government, which comprises four women, is the symbolic and pragmatic leader in this campaign. It alone has designed, built, and maintained many square kilometers of green. In 1994, for example, the academy completed impressive twenty-eight projects: ten garden constructions, ten greening layouts, and six planning proposals. In total, the academy designed 215,000 square meters, with a total operating budget of 9.2 million RMB. It planted 25,760 trees, 7,000 square meters of afforestation, and 530,000 flower units, and constructed 850 meters of green fence, and placed numerous public art sculptures.

Three of the Garden Academy's 1994 projects won design awards: the Zhuhai Bridge green edges planting, the Gateway Waterfront Park Design, and the Checkpoint Park Design. Most impressive is Lover's Lane, a 50-kilometer seaside road. It is the academy's most celebrated project. Lover's Lane has given Zhuhai a signature landscape for its coastline urbanism. Zhuhai is very proud of it, even though it practically bankrupted the government With the completion of Lover's Lane, Zhuhai is transformed into a Chinese garden on a massive scale, with meandering pathways (highways) linked by carefully planned viewpoints (pagodas) and places of rest and shelter along the way. The Garden Academy is an integral part of the government's plan to develop the entire territory as a garden paradise.

"In order to protect the natural mountain scenery and seacoast, it is stipulated that no one is allowed to set up any building along the sea or the river and that the high level of the hillside buildings cannot exceed the contour line of 25 meters so that one can see the sea by the hill and the mountain by the seashore, and really enjoy the beautiful natural scenery. As a series of measures have been taken for environmental protection during the city con-

struction, the environmental quality of the city proper has been keeping on a fine level. There is no pollution in the city proper, and the quality of air and water is up to the national standard, therefore there is a saying that Zhuhai's air can be canned for export."[51]

Fortuity 8: Islands

"Embellished with 146 islands, Zhuhai is known as the "City of Islands." Surrounded by 6,000 square kilometers of sea it is easy to see why tourism has developed so naturally."
—Brochure, *Zhuhai Window*, 1996.

Zhuhai's territory includes 146 islands. In the past this has been a nuisance, since they are difficult to govern and profit from. Now Zhuhai has turned this problem around. These 146 islands serve as a license for infinite landscape programmatic experimentation. In addition, the islands present a welcome opportunity for exciting infrastructural projects to connect them. The mayor and Planning Regiment now believe these islands, (whose total area is 240 square kilometers!) have great tourism potential. Each island has been assigned its own theme.

Island One Magic Pigeon Island

Qi'ao is a tourist island born from magic pigeon mythology. Its history will become its theme. In 1836, the British landed on the island and tried to conquer it but were defeated by the Qixi people. The British had to pay 300,000 silver dollars as compensation, which was used to fund the construction of a white granite path, dotted with seventeen shrines (a precursor to Zhuhai's own thin urbanism?). The path and shrines are a proposed scenic themed attraction. It is hoped that the island will become a destination for visiting cruise liners.

Island Two Prostitution Island

Wai Ling Dao is the closest Chinese island to Hong Kong. The remote island contains several luxury condominiums, and at least one holiday home, rumored to be exclusively for Zhuhai officials. The island consists primarily of outdoor pool halls and "hairdressing" salons. A majority of the island's 5,000 residents are troops from the People's Liberation Army. A significant percentage of the "hairdressers" are from Hong Kong and Zhuhai.[52]

Island Three A Paradise for Women
Economic Evening News reported that Zhuhai plans to build a "paradise especially for women."

Island Four Monkey Zoo
One of Zhuhai's islands has remained relatively untouched and is rumored to be the home of a species of endangered monkey. The plan for Monkey Island is to protect the species and then attract people as part of an eco-safari tour.

Island Five Central Island
In 1994, a team from Zhongshan University, including planners and transportation specialists, came to Central Island on a research expedition. The team's task was to assess the condition of the island as a potential import/export/entry-port island that will host cultural, economic, and administrative programs. Central Island was to be linked with Cow's Head Island to the north and Metaphysical Island to the south, creating one big island linked by tunnels.

Island Eight People's Liberation Army Outpost
A neighboring satellite of island Wai Ling Dao, the island of many hairdressers.

Island Nine Happy Recreation Island
East Ocean Island is targeted for major tourist and recreational functions. It has a nice beach with yellow sand.

Island Ten Russian Hill Villas Enclave
Security conscious Russian Hill Villa Company has developed this island into a guarded community. It has a bar, a swimming pool, a karaoke club, and a sports facility, and is host to many local officials and government cadres.

Island Eleven The Island Macau Wants
This island, called Henguin is about 350 meters from Macau. It is Zhuhai's second biggest island, with an area of 47.6 square kilometers. It was determined by Guangdong Province to be one of four major development areas and declared an Open Economic Zone (OEZ). Currently there are several projects under construction, including the Henguin Bridge (which connects to the main urban district), a highway circling the island (a "Lover's Lane South"), and a large-scale reclamation effort. The Macau government made a proposal to the Zhuhai Mayor's office to take over and occupy Henguin because they want more space to develop. They want to make it an industrial base, so that they can be more self-sufficient. Zhuhai does not find this proposal to be very interesting. However, Zhuhai prefers to develop it as part of the tourism programming in its Eastern District.

Island Twelve Wailingding Island of the Strange Stones
"A town on the island under the administration of Zhuhai East District, is located to the south of Hong Kong. It is 27.5 kilometers from Macau and Zhuhai to the west, 35 sea miles from Shenzhen to the north. Many high-speed boats and yachts arrive here for its strange stones, blue seawater, and fresh air. The main peak is 312 meters high, which can reach by a hole from the halfway up the mountain. Lingding Bay, Ta Bay and Dadong Bay are ideal places for fishing, swimming and surfing because of the fine and smooth sands and clean seawater. Ye Xuanping, Vice-chairman of the Chinese People's Political Consultative Conference praised it as 'a good place for tourism and holiday.'
—from tourist brochure, *Zhuhai Window*, 1996.

Island Thirteen Isozaki Island
Arata Isozaki was commissioned to design a brand new island from scratch. However, the new mayor has scrapped the Japanese architect's plan for the island because it lacks Chineseness. "It is too much of Hawaii!" the mayor was rumored to say.

ISLAND 1

ISLAND 2

ISLAND 4

ISLAND 9

ISLAND 11

ISLAND 13

"HAS BECOMING"©

Having converted its disadvantages into fortuities, Zhuhai anticipates its future in a highly elastic state of becoming: Zhuhai HAS BECOMING© city. At the core of Zhuhai's present/future plan is landscape, and Zhuhai illustrates that landscape is a key component of urbanization. Its development strategies, tactics of occupation, and tourist culture together create a new model of city making—a "landscape" civilization. Zhuhai has used landscape to manage spatially the pressures, fluctuations, and demands of its emerging market economy.

> "HAS BECOMING"© Future perfect tense invented in the Pearl River Delta that combines the immediacy of achievement with eternal deferment. Terminal striving: "Zhuhai city, with beautiful scenery and good environment, HAS BECOMING a famous scenic spot for tourism and a garden for investment, it is the result of Zhuhai people's wisdom and courage."[53] Essential to an understanding of the Asian condition: there is now, no now there, only later.

Landscape is a consummately cheap form of preparation for settlement, with a boundless capacity to tolerate underdevelopment. Zhuhai is blossoming, though it is nearly empty in all directions. It offers urbanization without density, roads without traffic, billboards without buildings, and land without use. Throughout its 1,630 square kilometers of domain, Zhuhai has laid more than 700 kilometers of palm tree-lined highway, POTEMKIN CORRIDORS© of green for the prospective investor and tourist's eye. It presents the image of THIN© idyll: palm trees and flower parterres along massive distances of road, which are flanked by leveled sites that are waiting to receive future development.

THINNING©

> THINNING© The coating of the largest available territory with the minimum concentration of substance necessary to generate an urban condition.

"The planned density of urban population is kept to 8,000 people per square kilometer. Different groupings are connected with roads, separated by hills and rivers, greens or fields. Zhuhai has formed its own construction style due to its wonderful natural condition and buildings. An urban afforestation system has been completed. 46 percent of the urban area is covered with green plants. Green area per person has reached 22 square meters."[54]

THINNING© is based on the revelation that landscape is the best means to capture large amounts of territory and convert it into speculative development. An urbanization strategy based on based on the organized reduction of density, urban conditions are created with the minimum amount of whatever material is available: plants, debris, trucks, swimming pools. Zhuhai has dispersed its population and built matter into the farthest reaches of the territory, edging its massive infrastructural projects with single rows of palm trees and shrubbery. As Zhuhai's urbanization strategy, THINNING© means that the market, building construction, and landscape construction combine, through planning and administrative policies, in order to produce a crust of green urbanity with maximum coverage, creating a stage set for development. Zhuhai mandates 30 percent green area for all new construction, limits building density, and even actively disperses its residents. "We should be active in pursuing thinner population, higher output value and better economic results. We are bound to be pacesetters."[55]

Zhuhai's innovative urban form was achieved by its "grapevine and bunches" planning ideology. The method, rooted in a landscape metaphor, identifies existing conditions of scenic hills, swamps, viewlines, and *feng shui*. Then, decisions regarding building, or more importantly,

> POTEMKIN CORRIDOR© Just as the Russians, under Potemkin, built villages bigger and healthier than the actual ones for inspection by the czar, so during the Great Leap Forward the entire trajectory of Mao's travels through the country was transformed into linear zones of engineered perfection, where all the ambitions of the revolution were realized as if by magic. Today, the BUBBLES© of the CITY OF EXACERBATED DIFFERENCE© are connected by development corridors that play a similar role as prefigurations of THINNING©.

not building, geomancy, and areas needing explosion and rearrangement are made. The goal is to spread out the urban substance into "bunches of grapes" in the most developable of dispersed sites. Then these distant points are connected with infrastructure, or "grapevines."

Zhuhai planners feel they have developed a unique conceptual framework—one unlike those of the north. Rather than projecting an ideal grid onto the topography, grapevine and bunches are purposefully noncompositional: they are a flexible and opportunistic network, whose form is the result of facilitating the most efficient means of territorial dispersal. In 1995 alone, Zhuhai constructed 132.9 kilometers of highway. At least 717 kilo-meters of that have been built throughout the territory.[56] The most spectacular and wide road, plagued by an occasional water buffalo wandering on the median strip, runs from downtown, past the new airport to the new shipping port.

Zhuhai's urban crust is colonized through innovative tourist programming. Would-be factory sites are now places for all-night swimming pools. Business vacation hotels, golf courses, and vacation bungalows are located in the territory's farthest reaches. The BUSINESS VACATION© village has emerged as an important new development typology. Strategically placed in a distant rural sector, it creates a trace of urbanization, with a minimum population. Rather than requiring permanent settlement, the BUSINESS VACATION© village enables the countryside to be urbanized with a skeleton of staff and occasional visitors. Businessman-vacationers are lured to the countryside for golf holidays, lending these outposts the appearance of inhabitation. Temporary and mobile, the BUSINESS VACATION© village is an optimal method for colonizing a vast territory, in shifts. Each subsequent wave of businessman-vacationers—even spread out over interims of

> BUSINESS VACATION© The way for a few to inhabit the largest possible territory in shifts. In the Pearl River Delta, the reduction of program (STREAMLINING©) coincides with the reduction of city (THINNING©).

vacancy—permits an outpost to exist and survive, because it provides a new supply of foreign income. Zhuhai commands its territory through a temporary hotel population. City and countryside, businessman and farmer, agriculture and industry are merging to create a unique brand of landscape-tourism in Zhuhai and a new way of inhabiting the city (in shifts!).

Preparation

In the quest to construct their urban vision, Zhuhai's leaders discovered that a good deal of preparation is needed. Preparation takes hard work, and striving in politics, geography, and spirituality.

The construction of paradise in Zhuhai has required many large mountains to be exploded. Geography, topography, and culture are scraped away to create desired gross developable land area: space for its own sake. Mountains are removed and used as fill (the marshy inner delta requires 8–10 meters of fill to make a buildable surface) and as sand for concrete. There is no fanfare, save the 24-hour blasts of dynamite. The method is simple:

1. explode the mountain
2. scrape the site of the former mountain flat
3. cart the rubble to the marshy site or to the waterfront to be used as fill
4. erect two billboards: one at the exploded site, one at the filled site, in effect doubling the real estate to be sold

Entire mountain ranges, seen as unfortunate, are simply removed. Rubble from the exploded mountain is then used as fill to create flat developable land along the inner delta or to increase the land area of Hong Kong and Macau. Mountains are exploded, marshlands filled, flattened, and then rented off in auctions to Hong Kong or foreign investors.

These tremendous explosions are accomplished in part because the majority of the Chinese Army Corps of Engineers migrated to Shenzhen precisely when Deng declared the Open Door Policy. In 1980, "some twenty thousand officers and soldiers moved to the SEZ, forming the core of Shenzhen's civil engineering staff."[57]

Government officials have exacerbated the situation in the rush to compete for investment. In order to develop faster than their rivals, land bureaus throughout the PRD strove to clear more and more land and outdo their rivaling municipalities at auction. This process created a permanent state of preparation, or predevelopment, in which voided sites would sit vacant with the aim of enticing speculator imagination. Leveled mountains were ready to become variously a parking lot, rollercoaster ride, a bus station, or a crocodile park, depending upon market demand. In the socialist real-estate market, all surfaces are deemed equally developable: every construction site is pardoned in advance.

Landfill from exploded mountains is sold to the highest bidder. Small islands like Hong Kong and Macau are the most willing buyers, attempting to expand their landmass and connect their islands with landfill from Zhuhai. Sometimes landfill is withheld in order to stall competing projects: "Zhuhai officials delayed the Macau airport project by over six months by refusing to supply sand which was necessary to construct the runway. Macau finally broke the impasse by appealing directly to Beijing, which overruled local Zhuhai officials and resumed landfill shipments."[58] It is estimated that during the development boom in Macau, the cost of Chinese land had gone up by five times.

Competition among Guangdong's counties to attract development has accelerated the rate and timing of explosions. Foreign investors must first approach a city or county development company with a proposed amount of investment and land area required for construction. As local development companies become more competitive with one another, they try to lure foreign business by offering faster (and therefore cheaper) construction times. If the ground has already been declared suitable for construction (i.e., flattened) then the entire process is expedited, and up-front costs are lowered. As a result, sites are often exploded and cleared by the official land development bureau before there is an actual buyer. Preemptive eruptions such as these, however, have led to eager anticipation of the province's future, resulting in numerous false starts where flattened land has been left deprived of the developers fine brush strokes of inspiration. "The [1995] slump in the property market has highlighted problems of property development projects aborted before completion or not started at all. Yuan Geeing, director-general of

Guangdong Province Lands Department, said that this was a problem local government should tackle and that financial support should be given to the aborted projects. '[O]ur main task is to ensure that the leased land is not left idle,' he said." Yuan continued to state that "about 36,000 hectares of idle land that had been leased . . . had been taken back by the authorities."[59] In 1995, it was estimated that 30–40 percent of all flattened sites in Guangdong Province were abandoned before ever being occupied and sit today as blank paper, suitable for beautiful inscriptions and master plans.

These large tracts of TABULA RASA© confirm the resilient and flexible nature of the Chinese method of preparation. THIN© urbanism can accommodate abandonment by either leaving land in waiting or returning it to agrarian use, depending upon economic trends.[60] Land can either be left undeveloped, to serve as an enticement to future geomancers, or converted to agricultural fields, to advance the Zhuhai's urban vision of low density and landscape urbanity.

FENG SHUI© **You Can Make Your Paradise**

FENG SHUI© Geomancy originally used to determine optimum site and building orientations, FENG SHUI© is now used to fabricate ideal conditions from scratch. It functions as advertisement and becomes a self-fulfilling prophecy that both predicts and insures the inevitable success of commercial development. FENG SHUI© is also used retroactively to correct bad *qi* accumulated in modern architecture. In pursuit of financial profitability, FENG SHUI© coalesces ARCHITECTURE© and landscape into the PICTURESQUE©, providing the necessary precursor to SCAPE©.

If exploding mountains are the topographical enabler of development in the PRD, then FENG SHUI© is the spiritual facilitator. In ancient *feng shui* practice, it was typical to "dig a lake and build a hill" to create varied topography, and to enhance the movement and richness of the "vital breath" of *qi* that circulates. In the Pearl River Delta, FENG SHUI© dictates that paradise can be constructed using 10 thousand tons of loaded explosives to level a mountain, in order to place a profitable and highly auspicious cluster of bungalows. The rich Chinese landscape tradition implies that *feng shui* is everywhere: each mountain and body of water is spiritually infused with motion, meaning, and dynamism. This life force called qi, translated as "cosmic currents" is said to be at the origin of the world and always circulating. *Qi* can be enhanced and concentrated by adding variety and richness to a scene—by reconfiguring the landscape and its views (mountains, mirrors, doorways, or even potted plants) to maximize tension among elements.[61]

A principle tenant of *feng shui* is that "you can make your paradise!" If positive *qi* is not deemed present, it is ruthlessly constructed. Since *qi* is everywhere in the Chinese landscape, the operative conviction is that its dynamic power just needs to be flushed out by a mindful geomancer. As a result, huge tonnages of land are rearranged daily to maximize positive qi, as determined by the intuitive theme-park developer or practiced geomancer-consultant. *Feng shui* has played an important role in facilitating development in the name of disposing good energy.[62] In the PRD, *feng shui* experts are also called upon to reverse bad fortune: one might move an elevator 3 feet to the left or shift the entryway to the southern face, in order to transform a development flop into a successful property deal. *Feng shui* also functions as developer scapegoat: when highrise units don't sell, it's blamed on bad *feng shui*.

As with Chinese landscape painting, *feng shui* entails the careful placement of buildings so that they are in harmony with each other and nature.[63] *Feng shui* provides guidelines on how ideally to locate a building within an environment, so that natural and architectural elements enhance each other. The aim is to apply the cosmological theory of *yin* and *yang* spatially, in order to create harmonious balance between nature and building. *Feng shui*, like the picturesque is a condition that can be designed and not just found. "Traditionally, the Chinese have altered their landscape when it was not perfect according to the ideal *feng shui* model. They have also brought the ideal model to their design when they needed to create a man-made landscape."[64]

Good *feng shui* means good golfing. It has become a driving force and marketing strategy behind golf course design and construction. The Beijing Golf Club is reported to have excellent qi. Built directly in the sacred valley of the Ming Tombs, its clubhouse sits barely a two iron-shot away from the ancient archaeological find. Originally built for thirteen emperors of the Ming dynasty, the tombs' location was reportedly directed by *feng shui* masters and today provides pleasing scenery and positive *qi* for the golfing tourist.

Feng shui is also practiced to bring bad fortune. For example, during the Qing dynasty, when land had to be conceded to enemy powers, the government would deliberately select poor sites with bad qi. In consultation with *feng shui* masters, Guangzhou's Shamian Island, for instance, was conceded to foreign victors. According to *feng shui* criteria, this mud land was in a "worst" position. In fact, the foreign housing built on Shamian was overrun by termites. "It was a clear triumph of *feng shui*."[65] Another concession that proved somewhat less auspicious was Hong Kong Island itself, now in a constant state of corrective *feng shui* backpedaling.[66] It was originally disdained by the Chinese as being devoid of *qi* and called the "barren rock." In contrast, the Pearl River Delta has an abundance of positive qi—and particularly good money *feng shui*.

While the Nan-ling mountain range limited the PRD's exposure to culture, it also brought the region good qi. The alpine barrier is the classic *yin* (male), or "dragon" mountain, which interacts with the delta's water, or *yang* (female). Moreover, in its role as south-facing island, Hong Kong strengthens this beneficial *qi* of the Pearl River Delta. The water is said to be "round and money is balanced and flowing in." *Feng shui* masters say "water is an important element in making money."[67] *Feng shui* can enhance the

prospects of any building, predict success and fortune for entire regions, or improve the playability of a golf tee.

PICTURESQUE©

PICTURESQUE© Revenge of the anti-idealistic. A mode of making and perceiving space, invented by Chinese gardeners in the sixteenth century, which insists on the juxtapositions and relationships between objects, rather than their singular presence. "We may look upon pictures as a set of experiments in the different ways in which trees, buildings, water, and etc. may be disposed, grouped, and accompanied in the most beautiful and striking manner, in every style, from the most simple and rural to the grandest and ornamental: many of those objects, that are scarcely marked as they lie over the face of nature, when brought together in the compass of a small space of canvas, are forcibly impressed on the eye, which by that means learns how to separate, to select and combine . . ." —Uvedale Price, *An Essay on the Picturesque*, 1794.

If *feng shui* is the spiritual light of PRD urbanization (literally, a handbook for constructing ideal conditions and increasing real-estate values), then the PICTURESQUE© is the aesthetic mode for its implementation. The picturesque sensibility of juxtaposed landscape and built objects originates from Chinese painting and poetry.[68] The celebration of variety and opposition is expressed through the *yin yang* relationship of architecture and nature. This aesthetic of organized contrast adopted by eighteenth-century Europeans comes back full circle to the PRD in the form of the golf course, the ultimate expression of picturesqueness.

Chinese gardens celebrate varied elements within the bounds of the garden space, generating a microcosm of the universe, a paradise designed for the scale of the strolling visitor.

Good qi, a balance and energy from which the viewer derives pleasure, can be created through the arrangement of a garden's elements. By framing the scene with features that provide texture and variety, the picturesque prepares the viewer for the garden's inhabitation—a perfect tool for the developer selling property.

When architecture and nature are arranged according to *feng shui* principles, each terminally qualifies each other in a perfect arrangement of accommodation and heightened qi. An aesthetic based on harmonizing disparate elements, the PICTURESQUE© facilitates the overall development of southern China by visually preparing the viewer to receive any and all chaotic fragments of construction by integrating them into a pleasing and inhabitable vision. This has become crucial to understanding the PRD phenomenon, for it transforms the most extreme juxtapositions of contrasting elements into pleasant, coherent, inhabitable scenery that delights the mind's eye and titillates the geomancer's compass.

To the viewer versed in picturesque aesthetics, the construction of a highrise tower in a rice field, the addition of a reflecting pool in front of an office building, or the insertion of a Donald Duck sculpture on a median strip, can be apprehended with delight and awe rather than contempt and bewilderment. An aesthetic of visual consumption, the PICTURESQUE© becomes the aesthetic framework in which rampant development can take place and transform every last fragment of wilderness into an inhabitable scene.[69] In the PRD, every view from every point is now inescapably PICTURESQUE©: equal parts highrise, golf course, billboard, tree, sky, and distant (exploded) mountain.

SCAPE©

SCAPE© An (exploded) mountain, a highrise, and rice field in every direction—nothing between excessive height and the lowness of a continuous agricultural/light-industrial crust, between the skyscraper and the scraped. SCAPE©, neither city nor landscape, is the new posturban condition, the arena for a terminal confrontation between architecture and landscape, the apotheosis of the PICTURESQUE©.

Imagine palm trees and concrete block, rice paddy and highrise, exploded mountains and theme parks, next to fish farms and an eight-lane expressway. The urbanization of southern China, which assumed no distinction between city and countryside, resulted in a condition completely new to students of Western urban planning. This urbanization pattern demands we drop the terms "city" and "nature" which have outlived their usefulness, and forces the formation of an entirely new term, SCAPE©. Proved in the Chinese countryside to be a superior carrier of urban growth, SCAPE© hosts varied programs and forms, and is supremely capable of both cheaply fostering growth and lying in wait of future speculation. Landscape's bargain price and pleasing effect allow for a deferral of densification and a reinvention of what used to be reserved for architecture and the public domain. Nature and architecture together now define the scope of the urban realm.

SCAPE© is topography of previously implausible juxtapositions. It is a fertile socioeconomic terrain that simultaneously accommodates and forces a mixture of contrasting programs, political ideologies and ambitions. SCAPE© is the setting in which a farmer a businessman, a geomancer a developer consultant, and shopping malls the sites of highway overpasses. Inspired by socialist dreams to eradicate contradictions of modern life, SCAPE© has flourished in China's socialist-market economy, melding dream and reality, lone highrise and vegetable plot, architecture and nature. SCAPE© marks the global triumph of landscape as the essential substance of urbanization.

Emblematic of this settlement in the market-driven SEZs is the golf course resort, a hybrid of nature and architecture. Hard work and recreation, socialism and tourism have given rise to a new vision of paradise, a UTOPIA OF GOLF©. A quintessentially LING-NAN© invention, the UTOPIA OF GOLF© is an alternative model of urbanism to that of Hong Kong. Learning from their dominant and prosperous neighbor, the cities of the Pearl River Delta have produced an urbanism of open green space and promises of golf and leisure that aspire to dispersal rather than density, thinness rather than depth, mildness rather than edge. What the PRD has learned is that rapid growth may have come at a cost and that pleasant greenery is the speculative antidote to Hong Kong's density.

Revolution

The Cultural Revolution eradicated history and culture, preparing the nation to receive golf courses, theme parks, and alligator shows: a new picturesque setting for a generation without memory. Although golf was once banned in China as a symbol of Western decadence, today courses in China are being constructed at a rate that suggests a revolution of golf. "Earlier this year, the government scrapped seven unauthorized golf course projects in Guangdong Province alone . . . which occupied a total of 706.7 hectares. Guangdong developers looking to benefit from a golf craze had applied to construct 51 golf courses across the booming Pearl River Delta."[70] Analysts predict that by 2010 the PRD will be blanketed by 500 courses.[71]

Golf is now the delta's medium of urbanism, with Jack Nicklaus its Chief Urban Planner. Billboards that once hosted Maoist imagery today are papered with depictions of a Market Realist paradise: highrise developments situated within an urbanism of manicured greens. In place of CCP ideology, banner slogans read "Ready to Tee Off!" An eighteen-hole Guangzhou Luhu Golf & Country Club is located in the middle of City between the railway station and the airport of Guangzhou, while in Zhuhai, the golf course is fast becoming the organizational unit of the city itself.

An integral part of all previously autonomous urban forms, the golf course is becoming the primary focal point of housing projects and highways. A smooth, pleasant, artificial, picturesque surface, golf is the carrier of previously contrary programs: commercial centers, offices, agrarian fields, fish farms, and vacation villas. Just as urbanization has emerged from the Chinese countryside, the golf course is advancing as the triumphant typology of urban space.

UTOPIA OF GOLF©

> UTOPIA OF GOLF© The golf course as the main carrier of urban activity. The first installment of the UTOPIA OF GOLF© takes form in the Shenzhen Special Economic Zone, where three eighteen-hole golf courses and four theme parks radiate from the center.

"Golf Villa is standing by mountains and sea, and is located between golf course of 2 million square meters, and the Pearl Entertainment Park at Taingjia Town"
—Zhuhai Developer's Advertisement, 1996

The golf course is an essentially utopian landscape: it replicates an idealized vision of Arcadian scenery. It manifests a picturesque brand of paradise that is pleasingly apprehended as a whole from a distance yet has varied topography and scenery, to surprise and delight the golfer moving around the course.[72] Like ancient Chinese scroll paintings and the Chinese stroll gardens in Suzhou, the best golf courses are expressed as a succession of unexpected, delightful, and varied views.[73] If the English garden was once dismissed as a rote imitation of the Chinese style, then today FENG SHUI© transforms the layout of the Western golf course back into something quintessentially Chinese.[74] A hybrid of East and West, suburb and community, ancient and modern, casual living and corporate culture, the golf course is the iconic and consummate symbol of globalism, the contemporary *jardin anglo-chinois*.[75]

The golf course is key to the PRD's socialist-realist urbanism. Like the art movement before it, socialist-realist urbanism not only portrays an idealized society, but is also an instrument of transformation of the urban experience itself: rote propaganda for a specific type of smooth, pleasant, controlled, leisure-based inhabitation of the city.[76] By an albeit more pleasant form of control, the urban dweller is subjected to a new ideology, the ideology of golf: he is domesticated, softened, cheered, and coerced into a harmonious relationship with his surroundings, enveloped in a continuous fairway of picturesque tourism.

In the UTOPIA OF GOLF©, golf courses and theme parks become indistinguishable. Shenzhen's Splendid China, for example, sits next to the Shenzhen Golf Club. Like the golf course, the theme park employs the picturesque to create harmony among disparate elements, and creates an instantly consumable landscape experience. At Splendid China, which occupies the Central Business District (CBD) of Shenzhen, much like Central Park in New York,[77] "monuments-to-miniature-scale" are sprinkled among rolling green hillocks and interconnected by a winding path. (Golf carts are supplied for the elderly and foot-weary visitors.) Splendid China perfects the technique of the picturesque stroll, where the garden is expressed as a series of views that unfold to the eye as one moves through space, compressing tourist activity into the space of an afternoon.

Globalization: The JNSD

A golf course delivers instant globalization. The presence of a Jack Nicklaus Signature Design (JNSD) course, is a symbol of ultimate consecration into the global sphere. The golf course implements a universal rule-bound aesthetic, yet it also domesticates the site so that it is consumable, familiar, and unique to its locale: it is the ultimate global development typology. In China, there are four JNSDs under construction. Mission Hills in Shenzhen is a 9 million-square-meter JNSD. In the resort's brochure it is written: "Mission Hills China boasts two 18 hole championship golf courses designed by the legendary Jack Nicklaus. Over the last twenty years, Jack Nicklaus has designed golf courses on five continents, in nearly every terrain and condition possible. Each is a tribute to his commitment to preserving the natural setting of every course he designs, and Mission Hills China is a shining example of this philosophy. Original land contours, lakes, trees, and other natural features are integrated into its unique design."

Roller coaster

Central business district →

Golf garden housing

Shenzhen Golf Club

Jack Nicklaus[78] has probably designed more square meters of landscape than any living landscape architect and earns the highest fees. He went from being the world's greatest golfer to the world's greatest (or at least, most important) urban planner. Jack Nicklaus has brought golf course design to a new plateau, where it rivals all other types of landscape design for cultural and aesthetic prestige as a precise and profitable art. Arnold Palmer[79] and Gary Player[80] also both head full-time design and planning firms, with projects constructed in the PRD.

JNSD is a coveted landscape brand, part of a total package that includes a full line of associated golf programming, consumer and marketing services, such as a pro shop with exclusively licensed items, training facilities, a clubhouse, and most importantly of all, personal appearances by the Golden Bear to lure businessmen to the golf retreat.

Nicklaus has built at least 125 golf courses and has twenty-eight courses currently under construction, half of which are in Asia. There are approximately forty-five JNSD courses already built in Southeast Asia.[81] In the Pearl River Delta, he added eighteen holes to Arnold Palmer's layout at Zhong Shan and also designed the thirty-six-hole Mission Hills Resort in Shenzhen. A record fifteen Jack Nicklaus-designed golf courses have been ranked among the top one hundred greatest golf courses in the United States by *Golf Digest*, and three courses among the top one hundred in the world are JNSD courses. Nicklaus was recently elected to the American Society of Golf Course Architects.[82]

Nicklaus is an expert leveler. A proponent of PRD-style site preparation, the Golden Bear has been known to explode a mountain or two. "It's not unusual for us to have to move mountains. . . . At times we have had to lop off as much as 200 feet off the tops of mountains on either side of the valley."[83]

Nicklaus has worked with pioneer urban planner Desmond Muirhead,[84] on several projects. Muirhead is credited with merging the golf course and residential housing in the 1960s, and is often credited with inventing the golf course community. Muirhead's developments at Mission Hills in Palm Springs, California, and Boca West, in Boca Raton, Florida, are prototypes of golf course real estate. He has written: "I have always maintained that there are two methods of promoting a new residential community and putting it on the map. One is by a shopping center, the other by a golf course. It is almost impossible to build a shopping center before the community is nearly finished, but at any time it is possible to build a golf course."[85] By the end of the 1980s, more than half of the new golf courses opened in the United States were real estate or resort-related courses.[86]

With the invention of the JNSD, the UTOPIA OF GOLF© is complete: it is the ultimate topography of the global economy, an artificial terrain of visual, programmatic, and economic predictability. The Golf Course represents a construction and replication of an aesthetic ideal, of an image of nature that is local and global, branded, marketed, and replicated around the world, and both natural and artificial, inside and out. Twenty-one courses are now open for play in the PRD, and forty are under construction or in the planning phase.[87] The sheer quantity of holes has sparked panic in developers, who are mired in intense competition to attract patrons. Competition inspires creativity: golf courses have begun to distinguish themselves by offering a range of different services and qualities to attract clientele. Programmatic innovations that appear in the PRD include Golf Academy, Golf Simulator, Indoor Hotel Golf, All-Nite Golf, and Female Caddies.

1. Golf Academy "Located in Shenzhen, this is one of the closest courses to Hong Kong. The Gary Player-designed 27 hole Championship course offers night golfing and a full training facility at the Gary Player Golf Academy. What makes the Sand River course unique is the full training facility at the academy. Following the philosophies of Player, everything from nutrition to equipment to a player's mental approach to

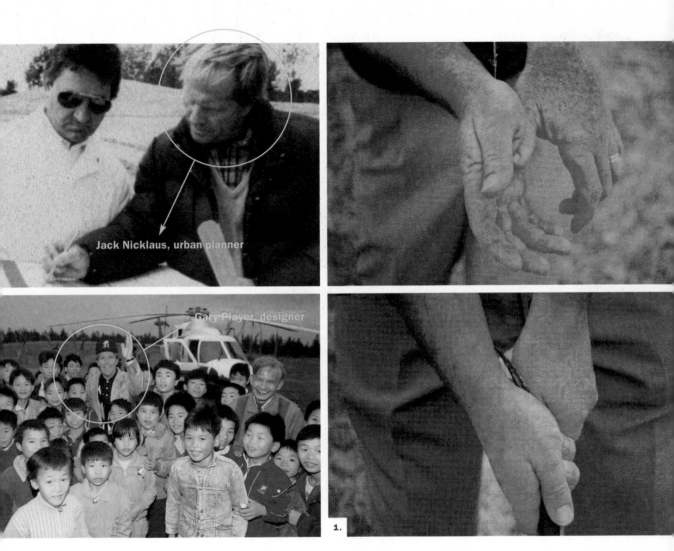

Jack Nicklaus, urban planner

Gary Player, designer

1.

2. 4.

3. 5.

the game will be analyzed to help a golfer improve at any level."[88] Player's bold urban design features seven tennis courts, three swimming pools, eighty-four private villas, forty guestrooms, and six restaurants and coffee shops.

2. Golf Simulator "The simulator provides the opportunity to play golf without having to worry about daylight or weather conditions. Capturing optimum realism in a confined space is achieved through the use of a high-quality video, a computer for tracking the flight of the ball and updating information, an overhead video camera for stroke analysis and optional sound effects."[89]

3. Indoor Golf "'One of the most comprehensive and technologically advanced indoor golf training centers in the world has been established in Hong Kong. Our indoor facility marks the collaboration between an experienced golf instruction organization, Japanese technology, and local Hong Kong capital and management to create a state of the art golf learning center.'"[90] Many hotels now offer golf in the lobby.

4. All-Nite Golf Between Shenzhen and Shekou, near the proposed new civic center, there are two golf courses that are open twenty-four hours. One is called Noble Merchant Outdoor Sports Club, "an ideal place for Noble Merchants." In the brochure, it is written: "Possessed with the flood-lit international par 72 golf course, the Shenzhen Noble Merchant Golf Club is well developed by the Shenzhen Golden Era Investment and Development Corporation and the Shenzhen Golf Service Co. With the natural views of Sand River and its convenient location, it is an excellent place for social functions and leisure resort. The Grandiose Club House is equipped with extensive facilities."

5. Female Caddies "Our golf courses are amongst the most beautiful in the world . . . as, indeed are the local caddies! These colorful and courteous Oriental creatures will pamper you by carrying and cleaning your clubs and holding a parasol to shade you from the sun."[91]

The UTOPIA OF GOLF© describes the completely programmed, consumable, privatized cultural condition of the contemporary moment, wherein urban activities—work, shopping, and recreation—are layering endlessly over each other and all differences between nature and artifice are becoming increasingly blurred. The word UTOPIA© anticipates the ultimate achievement of a Chinese Communist/Western paradise: a smooth terrain where city and countryside, high and low, business and leisure, production and recreation are merging into an altogether new condition.

Throughout the formerly agricultural communist countryside, theme parks and golf villas proliferate, while the PRD eagerly anticipates the decline of its neighboring kingpins. Space and pleasantness abound, while Hong Kong becomes an overcrowded slum of bad *feng shui* and Macau self-implodes into a sentimental European village.

Meanwhile, a thin green crust of golf courses coats the delta's terrain. Another layer is added: bungalows, factories, farmer's housing, clubhouses, skyscrapers, and vacation villages. Soon the golf course will become one with all of urbanity.

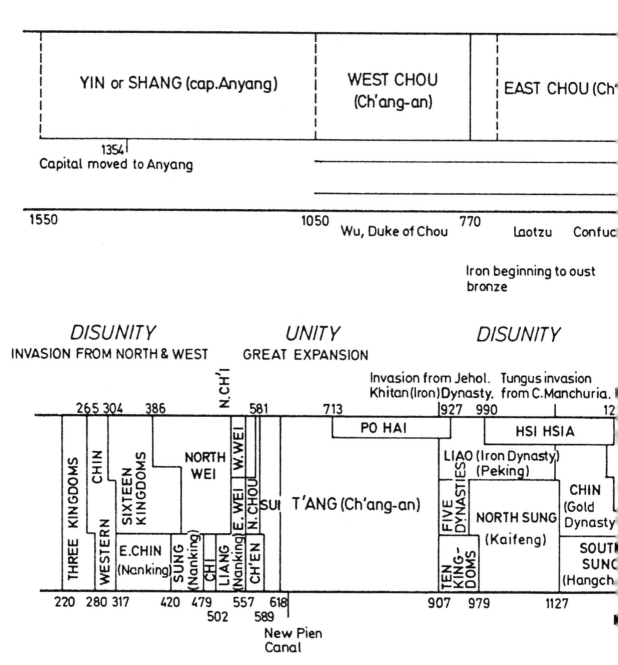

Unity/Disunity : Timechart
(fromT.R. Treagear, China: A C
Wiley & Sons, 1980)

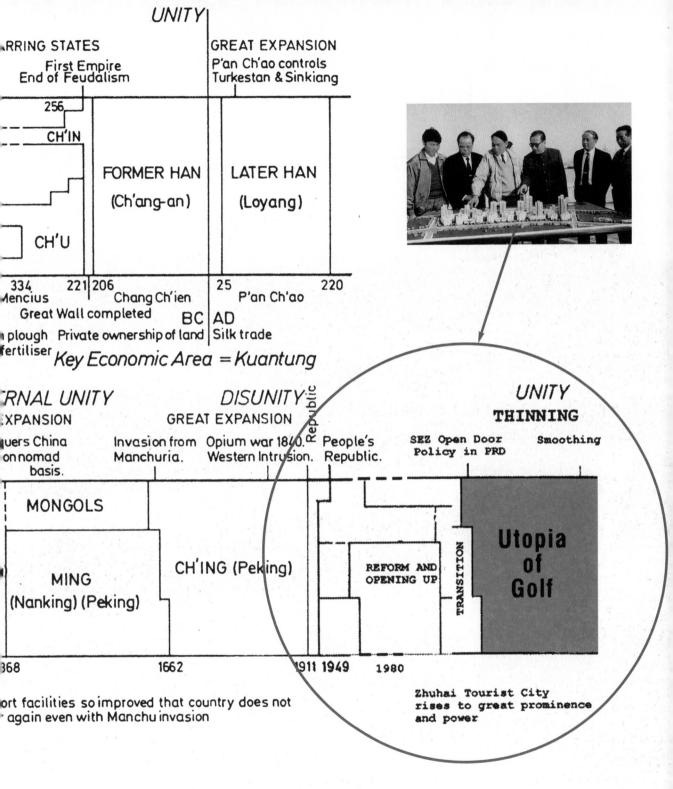

UNITY

RRING STATES

GREAT EXPANSION

First Empire
End of Feudalism

P'an Ch'ao controls
Turkestan & Sinkiang

256

CH'IN

FORMER HAN

(Ch'ang-an)

LATER HAN

(Loyang)

CH'U

| 334 | 221 | 206 | | 25 | | 220 |

Mencius

Great Wall completed

BC | AD

plough   Private ownership of land | Silk trade

fertiliser   *Key Economic Area = Kuantung*

Chang Ch'ien

P'an Ch'ao

RNAL UNITY

DISUNITY

Republic

UNITY

EXPANSION

GREAT EXPANSION

THINNING

quers China
on nomad
basis.

Invasion from
Manchuria.

Opium war 1840.
Western Intrusion.

People's
Republic.

SEZ Open Door
Policy in PRD

Smoothing

MONGOLS

CH'ING (Peking)

REFORM AND
OPENING UP

TRANSITION

Utopia
of
Golf

MING

(Nanking) (Peking)

| 368 | 1662 | 1911 | 1949 | 1980 |

ort facilities so improved that country does not
again even with Manchu invasion

Zhuhai Tourist City
rises to great prominence
and power

phical Survey, New York:

Golf is blanketing the entire earth's surface, with the number of courses growing exponentially. Today there are at least 35,000 golf courses worldwide, approximately 6,000 of which are in Asia.

BT Asian Golf Review, (Singapore Press Holdings, 1996).

Nearly 1,700 golf courses currently
operate in Japan, and 1,330 more are in
the planning and construction phase.
South China Morning Post, 13 April 1996.

Thailand has over 200 golf courses and
will have over 250 by the year 2000.
"Golf in the Kingdom of Thailand," Asia Golf, 24 November 1995.

The Da Yang Golf and Country Resort.

The international standard course with
thirty-six holes.

All-Nite Golf. A business meeting takes place at 3:00 a.m. on all-night golf course in Shenzhen.

1. Circular of the CCPCC, (16 May 1966).

2. Ezra Vogel, *One Step Ahead in China: Guangdong Under Reform*, (Cambridge, MA: Harvard University Press, 1989), 137.

3. The PRD requires a new definition of landscape—one that supersedes the decorative, ecological, redemptive, and ameliorative descriptions it has served in the past. In the PRD, landscape is the material of the urban: a cheap, flexible medium that readily absorbs all forms of construction into a thinly distributed development terrain.

4. "Firstly, Zhuhai is laid out in such an elastic way that large buildings are well dispersed and small ones are concentrated so as to maintain the ecological balance and protect the environment. Secondly, a reasonable building density and height limit is set in the city. And to match the geographical features and natural scenery of the city, low and medium-height buildings are preferred with only a small number of high buildings. Each lot of construction land must be accompanied by at least 35 percent of its area for greenbelt. In addition, adequate attention has been given to the protection of hill and sea views in the course of construction." Zhuhai: A Model City for Comprehensive Improvement of the Urban Environment," *Zhuhai Window*, Zhuhai, 1996.

5. By December 1952, 120 million acres of land had been redistributed to 300 million peasants. The CCP instituted People's Communes in the countryside at least partly to abate the migration to cities. By November 1958, there were 26,000 commune centers. Immanuel Hsu, *The Rise of Modern China*, (London: Oxford University Press, 1995), 653, 656.

6. Ibid., 655.

7. The CCP instituted People's Communes in the countryside at least partly to abate migration to cities. By November 1958, there were 26,000 commune centers. Ibid., 656.

8. Ibid., 844.

9. These land-use policies and demographic changes meant that Chinese urbanization emanated from the countryside rather than from the city. Rather than expanding from already established urban centers, Chinese urbanism converts all parts of its unbuilt sovereignty into a potential city.

10. The government can expropriate or demand rights to use the collectively owned land but must "reasonably" compensate peasants, which often means in the form of IOUs. The government also charges land-use tax to the land user, which is typically used to build infrastructure projects.

11. Si Jinning, et al. *Investment Guide of Real Estate in the Pearl River Delta*, (Guangzhou: Guangdong People's Publishing House, 1993), 11.

12. The PRD is a significant agricultural resource within the whole of China because it has a subtropical climate. It is possible to harvest rice in both the fall and the spring, and therefore increase production onefold. This is called "double cropping." Because it has a subtropical climate, the PRD is especially suited for growing cash crops, rather than staples, such as grains. Important crops are sugar, fruits, and seafood. The PRD has also achieved some degree of national recognition for pioneering the self-sustaining mulberry tree–fish pond system. In 1992, after Deng's southern tour of the PRD region, a wave of agricultural-market reforms was introduced. Agriculture for export became a goal, grain production and distribution were deregulated, and crop diversification was encouraged. The end of 1992 saw the complete transition from the planned production-and-supply system to the free market distribution of agricultural goods. The transformation of the PRD from rice paddies and fish farms into highrises and golf courses was then set into motion. In 1997 due to concerns about the loss of arable land, farmers were prohibited from leasing their plots for nonagricultural uses.

13. Victor F.S. Sit, *Urbanization in the P.R. China*, 1983.

14. Kathy Chen, "Chinese Are Going to Town as Growth of Cities Takes Off," *The Wall Street Journal*, (4 January 1996), A1, A12.

15. *China-Window*, "Profile: Zhuhai Special Economic Zone."

16. Zhao Shiqi, (Beijing: Ministry of Urban & Rural Construction, 1986).

17. Here Mayor Liang recalls the saying, "Firstly poor, secondly blank." Mao Zedong once said that China was characterized by poverty and blankness. . . . Blank paper is . . . 'well suited for writing the newest and most beautiful words and for drawing the newest and most beautiful pictures.' *A Glossary of Communist Terms and Phrases*, (U.S. Joint Publications Research Service, 1969).

18. Yang Hongxun, *The Classical Gardens of China*, (New York: Van Nostrand Reinhold, 1982).

19. Maggie Keswick, *The Chinese Garden: History, Art and Architecture*, (New York: Rizzoli, 1978), 202.

20. During a period of conflict and disunity in the eleventh century, southern China fulfilled the role of escape hatch: people fled south over the Nan-ling mountains to escape the battles, strife, and famine of the north. Since Zhuhai is the southernmost part of mainland China, it became the mythical and literal last resort. The myth is that thousands of migrants committed suicide en masse by walking into the sea. At the turn of the eighteenth and the beginning of the nineteenth centuries, Guangzhou was the only port of entry into mainland China. The serious mistrust of its association and communication with barbaric foreigners, and its geographic vulnerability to penetration and attack from the south left it somewhat outcast from the sphere of influence of the central government.

21. Zhuhai Section, in *Guangdong Yearbook*, (Guangzhou, 1995)

22. If one imagines that ancient Chinese scroll paintings inspired the famous stroll gardens of Suzhou and that eighteenth-century English picturesque landscapes were inspired by the classical paintings of Claude Lorrain then one can understand LING-NAN© gardens to be sparked by socialist realist paintings.

23. "In 'Adventure of Crocodile Island,' the largest crocodile park in China, one can enjoy not only the fierce looks of more than 300 crocodiles, but also the thrilling scenes when animal keepers train crocodiles, and crocodiles spring on the food." *Zhuhai Window*, 1996.

24. Today, Zhuhai ranks seventh among the twenty-two key touring cities in China. The ultimate consumption of space, the rise of tourism as a way to inhabit cities is a result of the combined effect of the market, and the increase in surplus income, leisure time, and mobility. (The more you move, the more you see, and the more you consume.) Tourism is thought to have originated around the same time as the picturesque in eighteenth-century Europe. On the "grand tour," English gentlemen traveled abroad to Italy and Asia in order to find and appreciate scenery. Captured and brought back to England, this scenery often appeared anew in the context of the landscape garden.

25. *Zhuhai Window*, 1996.

26. This is a reference to Mao's Hundred Flowers Campaign, of 1956: "Let hundred flowers blossom, let hundred schools contend!" Mao declared freedom to express opposing ideological and cultural viewpoints just long enough to ferret out his critics.

27. Description of Baiteng Peasant Lake Vacation Village in the *Zhuhai Yearbook*, 1995.

28. Zhuhai's first attempts at establishing a city were uninspired. Because it is geographically adjacent to Macau, the PRD's gaming mecca, Zhuhai sought to skim profits from its neighbor by introducing gambling. However, the effort was dropped as a vehicle for development. Government officials deemed it morally depraved after the municipality lost money and operational control.

29. LING-NAN© culture seemingly enables the people of the PRD to reproduce artifacts without the fear of lost aura. Shenzhen is in the

process of completing its own Yuan Ming Yuan.

30. *Zhuhai Yearbook*, 1995.

31. Mayor Liang Guangda, *Survey*, 1995.

32. "Zhuhai has more than 300 tourist hotels with a reception ability of 7 million persons per year." *Zhuhai Window*, 1996.

33. Before 1980, Zhuhai's adjacency to Macau was the source of disdain and resentment Beijing. Zhuhai had served buffer between corrupt and foreign Macau and the mainland. After its rebirth as a SEZ, Zhuhai's proximity to Macau became an advantage: the city could then leach money, tourist, and commercial expertise from the neighboring colony. Today, Zhuhai threatens to devour the former Portuguese colony and has planned construction on a bridge to connect itself to Macau, much to the surprise and dismay of Macau officials.

34. Zhuhai's goal has been not only to catch up with Hong Kong and Guangzhou, but also to surpass them and become the next Fifth Little Dragon of Asia. In an essay in the *Zhuhai Yearbook* 1995 titled "The Preliminary Thought and Strategic Maneuvers for Zhuhai: How Zhuhai Can Catch Up with the Social and Economic Development of the Four Little Dragons in Asia," it becomes evident that Zhuhai has big goals for the future.

35. Zhuhai as of 1996 was in debt to neighboring city Zhongshan, whose residents, as creditors, can freely enter and exit the once-sacred and fenced-off Zhuhai SEZ border. After Zhuhai was declared a SEZ, it erected a running fence along the border it shares with Zhongshan. The fence stretches as far as the eye can see and consists at times of iron spikes, at times of barbed wire. A taxi driver pointed out that Zhuhai was on the other side of the fence. When asked how he likes Zhuhai, he said that it was OK but that he preferred Zhongshan. He said that he could come and go freely, since the former mayor of Zhongshan City lent Zhuhai money last year to help get Zhuhai out of the bankruptcy caused by the bridge and airport developments. Zhongshan (non-SEZ) residents, as creditors, can cross the border by merely flashing a residency card. The people of Zhongshan are very proud of their territory and have a sense of culture and history. Zhongshan officials have done very well and have been promoted up through the ranks into the central government and into the provincial government of Guangdong, because they are, unlike their neighbors, "sincere."

36. A campaign for Guangdong Province to catch up to the Four Little Dragons of Asia was developed by the central government and implemented through a series of five-year plans. Of the Four Little Dragons, Taiwan and Korea were considered the most important models. It was observed that the size of the land and the population of these two places are more similar to Guangdong than those of the other two dragons, Singapore and Hong Kong. According to this analysis, it was officially estimated that Little Dragon status would be possible in exactly twenty years (or four five-year plans), improvements in worker production rates having been projected based on calculations of a Japanese research institute's findings. There was an elaborate statistical analysis that took into account population increases and other factors, and supported the twenty-year prediction, which suggests proposed incremental goals of improvement. Generally, the Chinese see numbers and statistics as important indicators of the process and state of modernization.

37. Mayor Liang Guangda, *Survey*, 1995.

38. Christine Chan, "Zhuhai's Attractions Fade for Foreigners; the Special Economic Zones Face an Uncertain Future As Beijing Moves to Create a Level Playing Field for All Regions," *South China Morning Post*, (11 January 1996).

39. The Western concept of the Garden City was developed by Ebenezer Howard around 1900 as an idea about how the living conditions of industrial cities in England could be ameliorated. Howard's Garden City combined the healthful and recreational functions of the countryside with the economic functions of the city. He proposed to disperse the central urban area radially into six independent entities, each with a population of 32,000, and diagrammed the total reorganization of settlement patterns. The idea of landscape and urban elements coexisting within the city as a picturesque scene caught hold of the imagination of Europe and America, and was constructed in some form or another around the peripheries of most industrialized provinces. Lewis Mumford observed that Howard's *Garden Cities of Tomorrow* was "unique among utopian books in that its utopia [had] been partly realized."

40. Deng Xiaoping, quoted on 2 April 1992, city of recording: British Broadcasting Corporation, copyright 1992.

41. Sunny Goh, "Zhuhai Considers Getting Singapore to Help Operate International Airport," *The Straits Times*, (8 May 1993).

42. Interview, Planning Office, January 1996.

43. According to "the spirit of the talk given by comrade Deng," the Guangdong Provincial Committee and the Provincial Government were challenged to catch up to Asia's Four Little Dragons in twenty years' time. Thus his 1984 summons set off widespread financial and real-estate speculation in the PRD.

44. "Deng Xiaoping Reportedly Spends Winter in Zhuhai," British Broadcasting Company, (28 February 1996).

45. Interview, July 1996.

46. Craig S. Smith, *The Wall Street Journal*, (29 December 1995).

47. Imperial collapse by landscaping: an historical overview.

Sui dynasty, A.D. Days after Emperor Sui Yang-ti ascended the throne he began to build a second capital to the east to supplement his father's old capital. In a show of defiance he enclosed a landscape park 75 miles in circumference. It included a lake 6 miles long, in which three islands, called the Isles of Immortals, were built and "lavishly endowed with pavilions," in imitation of Han Wu-ti's. Waterways connected the lake with scattered pools and streams, which symbolized the five lakes and the four seas of the ordered universe. Its shore meandered through "a landscape with a thousand prospects and variegated beauty unequaled in the world of men." By imperial decree, exotic and unusual plants, including fully grown trees, were uprooted from nearby estates and transported to the park via specially designed carts to elevate its luxuriousness to a point of unbearable magnificence. It is estimated that one-half of those who worked on the park died during its construction. Soon after a rebellion broke out over his landscape indulgences.

Tang dynasty, A.D. 618–712. The first leader of the Tang dynasty, fearful for his well-being, "took an immediate and firm line on landscaping." He even led his officers and relations on a cautionary expedition to the wrecked palaces of his predecessor. "I do not want you to dig ponds! Nor to make gardens! Nor to build pleasure parks at the expense of farmers! I forbid you to indulge yourselves!" The ground was broken for a Palace of Great Brilliance shortly thereafter.

Tang dynasty, A.D. 712–56. The second leader of the Tang dynasty, took the throne when he was twenty-eight years old. The first fifteen years of his rule were characterized by an "elegant balance of patronage and luxury." He then fell completely and uncontrollably in love with an imperial concubine named Yang Kuei-fei, one of the most famous beauties in Chinese history. The infatuation led him to spend his days and fortunes building extravagant palaces and gardens for his special lady and her sisters. At one site, "a microscopic island mountain of lapis lazuli, around which the girls of his seraglio sculled boats of sandalwood and lacquer."

North Song dynasty, A.D. 960–1126. Emperor Hui-tsung loved stones. Under his rule, the Song dynasty conclusively lost the whole of northern China to the Jurchen barbarians in 1126, when a rebellion was sparked by his landscape operations. It was a clear-cut case of imperial collapse by landscaping.

At the dynasty capital, the refined emperor literally constructed a gigantic mountainous landscape: a colossal pile of stones and rubble of 'ten thousand layered peaks' with ranges, cliffs, deep gullies, escarpments, and chasms. The finest rocks of all were displayed along the imperial carriage road, at the western entrance of the garden. One of these, 50 feet high, stood in the center of the road, with a little kiosk of rocks tied together to guard it. Many stones were anthropomorphic, many named and inlaid with gold characters. "From the highest point in the whole composition the Emperor beheld what seemed to be a microcosm of the universe." The emperor felt that his "artificial cordillera" offered a greater range of experiences than any real mountain in China.

This massively ambitious construction of a mountain range also came about in order to create good feng shui. (Keswick, 56.) Barges carrying rocks blocked canal for weeks, and corruption was rampant at every level. These garden elements were transported from the darkest corners of the territory all the way back to the capital in so-called flower-and-rock caravans. All along the way, houses were torn down, irrigation ditches leveled, and bridges built to facilitate transportation of the rocks and flowers, adding to the suffering of the common people. (Yang, 59.) Imagine a caravan, brimming with precious pieces of a garden, tramping over the countryside, leaving a flattened path of destruction that leads directly to the garden gates.

Assembled from various sources: Congzhou Chen, On Chinese Gardens, (Shanghai: Tongji University Press, 1984); Maggie Keswick, The Chinese Garden: History, Art and Architecture, (New York: Rizzoli, 1978); Yang Hongxun, The Classical Gardens of China, (New York: Van Nostrand Reinhold, 1982); R. Stewart Johnson, Scholar Gardens of China: A Study and Analysis of the Spatial Design of the Chinese Private Garden, (Cambridge: Cambridge University Press, 1991); Ping Xu, Feng Shui as a Model for Landscape Analysis, Harvard University Graduate School of Design Thesis, 1990.

48. Quoted in Elaine Chan, "Property: Asian Focus Zhuhai," South China Morning Post, (8 March 1995).

49. Mayor Liang Guangda, Survey, 1995.

50. Yoji Sharma, "China Economy: On the Runway, Zhuhai Waits and Waits for Take Off," Interpress Service, (26 January 1996).

51. Urban Construction with Characteristics, Zhuhai brochure, 1996.

52. Diane Brady, "Life in Hong Kong," Wall Street Journal, (July 1996).

53. From 'Rising,' a history and summary of Zhuhai's achievements at its 15 year SEZ anniversary, 1995.

54. Mayor Liang Guangda, Survey, 1995.

55. Mayor Liang Guangda, Survey, 1995.

56. Mayor Liang Guangda, Survey, 1995.

57. "The entire Corps was demobilized in 1983. Nearly all of the former Army Corps of Engineers personnel remained in Shenzhen as civilians, however, and became key employees in many of the sizable construction companies, which were more than a hundred in number operating in Shenzhen at the time." Vogel, One Step Ahead in China, 138.

58. Xinhua News Agency, (4 June 1995).

59. In order to reclaim profits lost as a result of abandoned property, Guangdong Province plans to reclaim 90,000 deserted hectares by the year 2000. South China Morning Post, (26 September 1995).

60. Literally translated, feng shui is "wind and water," while the Chinese word for landscape is shan shui, which means "mountains and water." Therefore, the physical landscape is always spiritually infused with meaning.

61. Feng shui master consultants are charged with divining, selecting, or designing sites based upon their potential to accumulate qi.

Fees for feng shui advice vary. In 1982, Choi Pak-lai, one of Hong Kong's most famous feng shui experts, commanded roughly sixty cents a square foot for consultations.

62. In Chinese culture, the aesthetic principle of complementary forms, such as male and female, yin and yang, high and low, rough and smooth, rock and water, evoke mystic harmonies. Feng shui offers a method to construct the ideal landscape—a handbook for creating paradise on earth—based on balancing principles. Traditional Chinese landscape painting similarly strives to capture a balance of architectural elements, humans, and nature, shan (hills) and shui (water), high and low, and open and closed spaces, within the frame of the painting.

63. Ping Xu, Feng Shui As a Model for Landscape Analysis, Harvard University Graduate School of Design Thesis, 1990.

64. Ernest J. Eitel, Feng Shui, (Heian: Heian International Publishing Co., 1873).

65. Hong Kong was conceded to the British in 1842 and initially proved difficult to settle.

66. The success of Atlantic City in America has been interpreted by feng shui masters: "The presence of ocean water on the Atlantic City shore presents a lot of opportunity to make money," but because the water is less than pristinely clear, "the chance of intrigue still exists." Also, "the presence of water in homes, offices, businesses, and restaurants draws in money. Some lucky companies with views of rivers can hang mirrors to reflect water's money-giving qi into their businesses. Water should always be clean and fish should be healthy." Sarah Rossbach, Feng Shui: The Chinese Art of Placement, (E.P. Dutton, 1995).

67. A visual theory about how landscapes can be constructed and appreciated, the picturesque insists on the juxtapositions and relationships between objects, rather than their singular presences. Elements such as rocks, water, trees, and shrubbery are assembled to create a scene, which is characterized by "variety and intricacy." The aesthetic at the root of the English picturesque was imported from China to England via William Chambers as early as 1772, with A Dissertation on Oriental Gardening, written after Chambers visited Guangzhou. The picturesque flourished in the nineteenth century and is now reemerging as a key aesthetic tool after suffering years of derision by the modernist movement for being chaotic and impure. "We are to forgo, or to relegate to a minor place, pleasures arising out of picturesqueness or of what is merely pretty or willful, and to confine ourselves to the sterner delights which severe and pure forms can give us." Frederick Etchells, Introduction to Urbanisme, by Le Corbusier, (1929). However, in the PRD, the PICTURESQUE© has been embraced because it provides a much more flexible and accommodating, and cheaper aesthetic system than the elite, abstract, and totalitarian tenets of modernism.

68. Just as a temple placed amongst the agricultural crops at Castle Howard in Yorkshire transformed its agricultural fields into a picturesque countryside view, the placement of bungalows and Ferris wheels in the outer reaches of the Pearl River Delta has transformed its land into an inviting landscape, suitable for a centerfold in a developer's portfolio. With SEZ policy, investor capital reached the hands of a newly created class of enthusiastic farmer-businessmen, each with an eye on building a communist paradise long deferred. The expansion of bourgeois political and economic liberties has historically run parallel to the expansion of picturesqueness. The free undulating forms and flexible plans that characterize bourgeois gardens in early eighteenth-century England were a deliberate counterpoint to the authoritarian, rational geometries imposed in the formally organized royal estates, such as Versailles, of late seventeenth-century France.

69. *Deutsche-Press Agenteur*, (20 January 1996).

70. Al Campbell, "China Gets into the Swing of Things," *South China Morning Post*, (26 February 1996).

71. "The perfection of their gardens consists in the number, beauty, and diversity of these scenes. The Chinese gardeners, like the European painters, collect from nature the most pleasing objects, which they endeavor to combine in such a manner, as not only to appear to the best advantage separately, but likewise to unite in forming an elegant and striking whole." William Chambers, *Designs of Chinese Buildings, Furniture, Dresses, Machines, and Utensils*, (1757).

72. After all other logic has been subordinated, the visual provides the dominant system of organization in the contemporary city. Objects co-exist and are understood (or not) in terms of their visual relationships.

73. The cross-fertilization of Chinese and Western conceptions of the landscape began as early as 1772, when William Chambers wrote *A Dissertation on Oriental Gardening*, after visiting Guangzhou. Chambers was instrumental in formulating the picturesque theory of landscape, which is analogous to *feng shui* in that both insist on the careful placement of buildings in nature, each terminally qualifying the other in a utopian consistency of architecture and landscape. Chambers wrote: "European artists must not hope to rival Oriental splendor; yet let them look up to the sun, and copy as much lustre as they can, circumstances will frequently obstruct them in their course, and they may often be prevented from soaring high: but their attention should constantly be fixed on great objects; and their productions always demonstrate, that they knew the road to perfection, had they been enabled to proceed on the journey."

74. The English landscape garden—and consequently the golf course—is rooted in the gardens of China. *Le jardin anglo-chinois* is an eighteenth-century term, invented by the French, which disparagingly lumped together the Chinese and English landscape tastes, even to the point of dismissing the English garden as a rote imitation of the Chinese picturesque. The Frenchman Le Rouge wrote: "Tout le monde sait que les Jardins Anglais ne sont qu'une imitation de ceux de la Chine." *Détails des Nouveaux Jardins à la Mode, Paris, 1776–87*.

75. If urban form reflects the influence of factors such as economics, geography, and ideology, it also influences and shapes behavior. *Feng shui* assumes that the character of the landscape plays a formative role in the virtue and fortune of the people who live in it: for example, hills with unstable land at their bases are "considered to be ill omens, which produce women of low morals." Ping Xu, *Feng Shui*, 1990, 43.

76. In Central Park, Frederick Law Olmsted compressed the experience of nature for city dwellers by manipulating section, view, and movement along the transverse roads-and-path system. His goal was to construct a space to which tense and haggard city dwellers could go for an afternoon and be rejuvenated, or to condense the experience of nature into something which could be seamlessly appreciated during the span of an afternoon stroll.

77. The origins of the golf course can be traced to the landscape design of Capability Brown, landscape improver (1716–83). Brown constructed and replicated picturesque landscapes across the English countryside to the point that nature and artifice became completely blurred. He constructed 211 landscape gardens in England during his lifetime, and several in France, Ireland, and Germany. His creations involved the massive movement of land and the construction of hills, forests, and winding lakes. Brown wrote no manifesto; he left no treatise, no poetry, and few drawings, and was denigrated by his contemporaries as being vulgar and dull.

Today, echoes of Brown's vision are evident in the proliferation of the landscape typology of the golf course. As is the practice in golf-course design, Brown added thick belts of woodland to hide unsuitable views and enclose the park, smattered clumps of trees in the middle ground, and built curving lakes. Brown systematically destroyed formal, axial, and linear elements, and existing gardens, and eliminated distracting and unsightly ornament in favor of smooth lines, and a natural appearance.

Brown was not content with the "theater set" scale of his contemporary designer William Kent and began to work at an altogether greater scale—at the scale of all that a human eye can consume in an instant from a distance. Capability Brown shifted the ideology and methods of landscape design from the heightening of all the senses at a garden scale to the broad pleasure of the eye and the ideal image of broad sweeps of landscape and countryside.

78. Arnold Palmer, in 1996 alone, had seven projects in some phase of the design process in Japan, and seven more in the rest of Asia, including Malaysia, Indonesia, China, and the Philippines. Palmer constructed the first golf course in China in 1985, at the Chungshan Hot Spring Resort, just north of the Zhuhai municipality.

79. Gary Player designed twenty-seven holes (nine were lit for all-night golf), a driving range, and a signature golf academy at the Sand River Golf Club in Shenzhen. He is also the designer of the fifty-four-hole Zhaoqing Resort and Golf Club, the largest golf enterprise in China in terms of sheer surface area. Josephine Ma, *South China Morning Post*, (13 April 1996).

80. David Cohen, "Thailand, Lost in the Rough," *The Guardian*, (24 September 1994).

81. Jack Nicklaus was voted 1994 Golf Course Architect of the Year by *Golf World* magazine. In 1974, at the age of 34, Nicklaus opened his own design firm Golden Bear International Inc. in North Palm Beach. Nicklaus had previously worked for several years, starting in 1968, under Pete Dye. Dye, a former insurance salesman, has had a profound impact on the American landscape and went on to design and build some of the world's top courses. He is credited with introducing the American Style of golf-course design. The American Style is characterized by irrigated and precisely clipped turf, and long smooth fairways of more than yards.

82. Gary Rosemarin, vice president of Golden Bear Inc., quoted by the Global Anti Golf Movement.

83. Muirhead writes poetically about the merging of landscape and architecture, of golf and everyday life: "Golf Course communities should not be cold or rigid enterprises but filled with the passions of life and giving. Their design should stir men's blood. We who design these communities must be more than engineers. We must call on emotions and know-how, and we must insist on generating a fundamental human warmth as well as technical correctness." Desmond Muirhead, "Looking Back and Looking Ahead," *Golf Course Real Estate*, 1994, 160.

84. Quote from Desmond Muirhead, Golf Course Architect web site, http://www.golfdesigner.com, 1997.

85. Muirhead & Rando, 1994, 166.

86. "The Provincial Government of Guangdong Province has worked out a set of rules banning golf links from running real estate businesses. The rules stipulate that golf links and related structures should not be diverted for other uses. In addition, the rules say that the total construction area of a golf link should not exceed 20,000 square meters." *Xinhua News Agency*, (24 September 1995).

87. Al Campbell, "China Gets into the Swing of Things."

88. Al Campbell, "Big Drive to Simulate Real Thing," *South China Morning Post*, (9 November 1995).

89. Aravind Vidyadharan, "Golfing Workshop Gets HK into the Swing of Things," *South China Morning Post*, (18 May 1993).

90. Cohen, "Thailand."

Contents

POLICY	431	STRATEGY©
SOVEREIGNTY	435	CONCESSION©
	440	AMBIGUITY©
	443	BORDER©
DIPLOMACY	445	Theme Park Diplomacy
DEVELOPMENT	449	NEGLECT©
	453	NEGLECT REVERSAL©
	456	STREAMLINING©
	457	INCORPORATION©
	459	COORDINATION©
PROJECTION	463	PEARL CITY©

POLITICS GUANGZHOU

Yuyang Liu

President Nixon toasting Premier Zhou Enlai at a banquet in the Great Hall of the People, the assembly building for the National People's Congress.

Beijing, China. 21 February 1972.

A toast between Christopher Patten, the last
British governor of Hong Kong, and Zhou Nan,
former director of the Xinhua News Agency,
Hong Kong Branch, at Zhou's retirement banquet.
Despite the seeming friendliness, the agency
(regarded as the de facto Chinese consulate to
Hong Kong) criticized Patten's reforms of British
policy on China after the Tiananmen incident.
The agency considered this policy shift to be a
violation of the Sino-British Joint Declaration.
Hong Kong, China. 1996.

Premier Deng Xiaoping and President
Jimmy Carter, with their wives, Cho Lin and
Roslyn, wave from a balcony overlooking
the South Lawn of the White House during
the welcoming ceremony for Deng.
Washington, D.C., 29 January 1979

President Jimmy Carter, former president Richard Nixon, and Premier Deng Xiaoping speak at a state dinner in honor of Deng's visit to the United States following the reestablishment of full diplomatic relations between the United States and China.

Washington, D.C., 29 January 1979.

American golf legend Jack Nicklaus meets the president of Guanlan Lake Golf Club and other Chinese officials.

Guangzhou Province, China. January 1960. Chinese Communist leaders gather for a military conference. From right to left: Deng Xiaoping, Mao Zedong, Peng Zhen, Luo Ruiqing, Zhou Enlai, He Long, Lin Biao, and Nie Rongzhen. All but Peng were veterans of the Long March from Jiangxi Province to Shaanxi Province in 1934. Deng, Peng, Luo, He, and Nie were purged from the Party during the Cultural Revolution of the late 1960s. Lin died in an alleged coup attempt against Mao in 1971.

POLICY

STRATEGY©

> STRATEGY© Policy of systematic, abrupt reversal, by which the Chinese Communist Party operates internally to negotiate with external forces. STRATEGY© has defined a perpetual swaying pattern of social and economic development in the Pearl River Delta.

❋ It should be noted that when Deng Xiaoping took over as Premier, policies became characterized by a style of testing and adjusting (known as the experimental "river crossing" style), rather than political reversal, which justifiably characterized the period prior to Deng's leadership at the larger political level. If there is any pattern than can still be characterized by reversal, it is the alternation between central strategy and local methodology. —Qingyun Ma

By characterizing as a constant stream of reversals the political context that led to the explosive development of the Pearl River Delta region, STRATEGY© explains the incredible conditions in the Pearl River Delta taking place today.❋ Contrary to conventional wisdom, the rapid growth and mutation of urban substance in the region was not the result of a smooth evolution of policies or efforts, but of a sudden thrust of momentum for change in Chinese politics. The political struggles of Mao Zedong's era created a tabula rasa condition that left little resistance to new economic policies. The rise of Deng Xiaoping, who single-handedly marshaled into existence the various economic zones and new policies to stimulate the economy, must be understood as a critical moment in China's economic development.

The use of STRATEGY© takes its precedence from the concept of "democratic centralism," which was promoted by the CCP after the 1950s as a way of maintaining political control. In this stage of the political dialectic, "democracy" becomes an adjective that qualifies the self-contained system of "centralism," which in this new interpretation can be attained without sacrificing the foundations of democracy under CCP leadership. The evolution of this concept created the next stage of dialectic, whereby socialism was coupled with a market economy. The resulting socialist market economy ("socialism with Chinese characteristics") has been drastically transforming development in China, especially in the PRD. This post-Mao Zedong brand of communism is a construction of socialism retrofitted to the market economy; it is an integration of the "universal principle of Marxism-Leninism" with the practice of the "Chinese Second Revolution—economic construction, reform, and opening to the outside world."[1]

Prior to 1949, the coastal regions of China had a broad history of industrialization and commerce, receptiveness to investment, and connections to the overseas Chinese population. Beginning in 1949, Mao Zedong's Inland Strategy attempted to equalize wealth and reduce the risk of exposure to foreign attack posed by reliance on coastal cities. In order to gain support from the peasantry and pursue a more equitable distribution of development, Mao reallocated resources from the coastal cities to build up the poorer provinces of the inner region. He argued that the spiritual center of the Communist revolution was not in coastal areas but in inner China. From 1949 until the mid-1970s, economic and political investment was introspective, occurring only in the interior provinces as policies deliberately redistributed industrial plants and skilled workers to scattered inland provinces and provided them with a larger share of the fiscal subsidies and capital investment from the central government.[2]

When Deng Xiaoping took control of the CCP in 1978, the economic development of China was his main priority. In the early 1980s, despite opposition from conservative party leaders that were trying to preserve Mao's ideology, Deng introduced the Open Door Policy, which resulted in significant economic growth. China's GNP grew at an average of 9 to 10 percent a year, and living standards doubled or tripled for most of the population. Gradually, China moved toward a much more decentralized and liberal economy. By 1993, approximately 65 percent of the economy was no longer subject to centralized state planning. Today, approximately 50 percent of the output of the industrial sector of the Chinese economy comes from private enterprises and joint Chinese-foreign ventures. On the local level, the GDP of the southern province of Guangdong alone skyrocketed from U.S.$2.3 billion in 1978 to U.S.$28.7 billion in 1992, a percentage increase of China's overall national GDP from 1.5 percent to 5.2 percent over a fifteen-year span.[3]

❋ Between 1988 and 1989, another political struggle among central government officials emerged on the surface of social life: between the camp of Zhao Ziyang and Hu Yaobang, and that of Li Peng and Yang Shangkun. (Deng Xiaoping supported Li and Yang.) To a large degree, this struggle played a critical role in the students' demonstration in Tiananmen Square. It is interesting to note that both camps were proponents of reform, but one (Zhao and Hu) favored radical political reform to ensure a complete economic reform while the other (Li and Yang) believed that economic reforms would only be successful if the existing political system were sustained. Their debate may be considered the last radical political dynamic in recent history, which has caused and led many party officials to step down, including Party secretary Zhao Ziyang himself. —QM

While China's economic policy has been changing rapidly since 1978, its political adjustment has evolved at quite a different pace. The legitimacy of the CCP has gradually weakened and criticism of the government has increased, witnessed by the 1989 Tiananmen Square massacre,❋ yet the majority of China's population has shown no signs of significant opposition. Such a lack of political resistance has been attributed both to the economic success achieved by Mao's regime and to the memory of chaos during the Cultural Revolution. People wanted national stability.

Deng continued to give top priority to the maintenance of political stability, through the introduction of the Four Basic Principles— socialist road, people's dictatorship, party leadership, and Marxist-Leninist-Maoist thought—and the continuation of one-party rule. In the 1980s, he stated that China would move from a 'socialist planned economy' to a socialist market economy. Deng condemned the negative aspects of capitalism but encouraged learning from "developing capitalist countries, advanced science, technology, and applicable expertise and economic management."[4] He also made changes in the leadership in 1992 that would mark an ideological shift in the future. These changes have strengthened the position of reformers, weakened the position of conservatives, and substantially increased the possibility of a continuation of reform policies by future leaders.

In December 1978, two years after Mao's death, Deng launched a new development strategy. Reversing what Mao had initiated, Deng adopted the coastal strategy, which allowed coastal areas to move ahead more rapidly, experiment with new systems, and become "engines of growth" for the rest of China. Centralized control over investment and allocation of resources was substantially modified to accommodate the Open Door Policy. Under the new policy, areas easily accessed by foreigners and with "good economic foundations"—factories, skilled labor, and port facilities—were given high priority in order to attract foreign investors.

The Open Door Policy was never a clearly articulated set of rules. Rather, it was an ideological shift regarding China's relationship with the West. This shift represented a new official agenda, within which various mechanisms of economic and urban development would evolve into specific strategies or guidelines for development. At the same time, there were still major concerns about the potential for foreign capitalist contamination or even imperialist invasion as the result of any opening to Western influences. The selection of the first coastal location to open to foreigners thus became highly strategic; the place had to be as nonthreatening—or as dispensable—to Beijing as possible, yet it also had to have the potential to succeed in order to prove that the reforms could work. Ultimately, it was decided to designate the first of the Special Economic Zones in the Pearl River Delta.[5]

Guangdong Province

The greater latitude for economic development granted by Beijing since 1980 has been used masterfully by local officials such as Ren Zhongyi, the first CCP secretary of Guangdong Province. Guangdong exploited its advantages by determining and fully utilizing Beijing's limit of tolerance. As Ren announced, "If something is not explicitly prohibited, move ahead; if something is allowed, use it to the hilt."[6] The province was also administered under a special policy that allowed it more leeway than other localities.

Although the Cantonese people have been regarded—and therefore dismissed—by northerners as cunning, opportunistic, and materialistic, Guangdong suddenly represented a special opportunity for Beijing to resolve a number of critical issues, especially sovereignty and finance. In 1979, three years before Margaret Thatcher visited China, Beijing had claimed sovereignty over Hong Kong and Macau, where it did not yet exercise de facto rule. Beijing needed to gain the confidence of the people of these territories, and modernization in the region, especially in the PRD, represented the best opportunity to do just that. Beijing at this time was also acutely aware of its financial constraints, exacerbated by the huge budget deficits that had resulted from unsuccessful investment plans. Guangdong, with almost 80 percent of overseas Chinese originating from the region, had enormous potential to attract overseas investments. Furthermore, many Beijing reformers who had served in Guangdong were convinced that Guangdong cadres were more daring and receptive to trying new strategies. Success in the region, it was felt, would help persuade the conservatives elsewhere to experiment. Beijing was therefore quick to redirect its regional emphasis and change its attitude toward the South.

Up to this point, Beijing still had enough power in the provinces. The CCP had been reconstituted after the Cultural Revolution as party members continued to follow the leadership of the Party Central Committee, yet the highest party officials in Guangdong still had to be appointed and removed directly by Beijing. By 1978, compared to two decades before, the relationship between top officials and locals had changed. In 1952, when Beijing sent Tao Zhu and the Southbound Work Team to take over the leadership of Guangdong, they were accompanied by thousands of outside officials who dominated many parts of the government. This first wave of political invasion would be displaced later by a second wave of newcomers during the Cultural Revolution.[7] When Xi Zhongxun was sent to Guangdong as the first party secretary and governor in 1978, he brought only one personal secretary. Xi and the other officials sent by Beijing were subsequently absorbed into an established provincial structure and, unlike the previous generation of politicians, created no power struggle between the locals and outsiders.[8] This political smoothness allowed attention to remain directed at addressing economic issues and developing new reform strategies in the PRD.

By 1988, the excessive growth created by the Open Door Policy contributed to an over-heated economy and an inflation rate of more than 30 percent. The government decided to implement the Austerity Program and Retrenchment Policy, which aimed to tighten credit for capital construction, crack down on corruption in local governments, recentralize trade and foreign investment, reduce spending by the Party and the government, and revive ideological indoctrination.[9] The Austerity drive, coupled with the aftershock of the Tiananmen Square massacre in 1989 (which stopped most foreign loans), caused the economy to slow down to a temporary recession.

At this time, another round of political struggle emerged between the camp of Zhao Ziyang and Hu Yaobang and the camp of Li Peng and Yang Shangkun, both of which were key proponents of reform directly under Deng. The former camp argued for political reform as an essential part of a complete economic reform, while the latter camp believed that economic reform could be successful only if the current political status quo was maintained. The sympathy of Zhao (who was then party secretary) and Hu toward the student demonstrators in Tiananmen eventually caused them to step down. A subsequent easing of Austerity measures was announced in July 1990 to revive the economy.

SOVEREIGNTY

CONCESSION©

> CONCESSION© Policy of yielding as tactic. Reformulation of the traditional notion of concession: the forceful insertion of a foreign entity into sovereign Chinese territories or the forced yielding of territory as admittance of defeat. Deftly reinterpreted by the Chinese Communist Party to control the importation of Westernness, it allows most of China to remain untainted. The Special Economic Zones, as land sacrificed for free-market experimentation, are examples of CONCESSIONS©.

"When you open the door some flies will get in."
"You can't grow fish in clear water."
—Deng Xiaoping, defending the Open Door Policy, 1980

In the nineteenth century, the PRD became the site of the first Chinese war concessions when Hong Kong and Macau were ceded to the imperialist powers of Britain and Portugal. Deng Xiaoping's Open Door Policy of 1980 repeated the act of relinquishing territory in the same region, this time as a show of strength: The Special Economic Zones (SEZs) were set aside for the purpose of economic experimentation. This reverse scenario enabled China to absorb the lost territories when they were returned to China in 1997 and 1999, respectively.

For 150 years, the loss of political sovereignty has been a source of pain and humiliation for China. Territorial concessions—have repeatedly been made to preserve peace and to pay for defeat in wars with Western nations and Japan, while colonization and domination by these nations, coupled with ceaseless internal conflict, have plagued China's efforts to modernize.

When China reopened its doors in 1842 under foreign pressure for more trade, the result was a fundamental restructuring of its sociopolitical and spatial order. The nineteenth-century geopolitical phenomenon of territorial concession to Western nations by China took place in a number of coastal Chinese cities and regions, including Guangzhou, Shanghai, and the Shandong Peninsula, all as a result of China's defeat in wars against these nations. The defeat of China in the Sino-British Opium War,—fought in Guangzhou between 1839–42, resulted in the territorial concession of Hong Kong—to the British for 150 years. The consequent colonization of China by the British, French, Germans, Americans, Russians, and Japanese, each of which brought its respective customs and rules, profoundly altered the social and cultural landscape of these territories and the regions that came into contact with them.

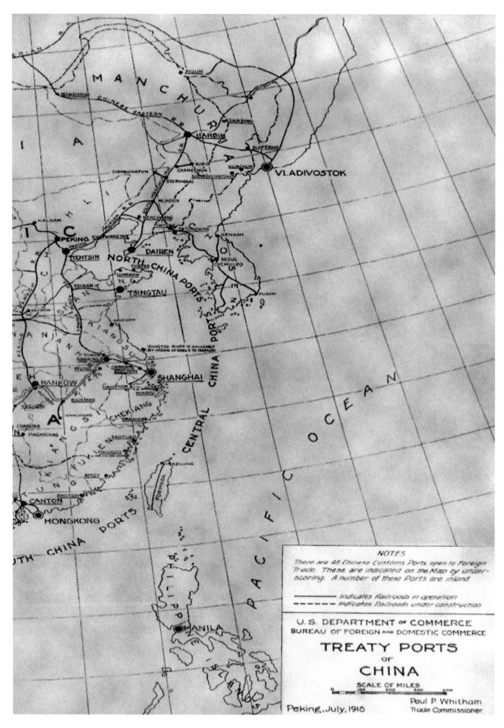

*Map of the old "treaty ports" in China, 1840–1912. China was forced to grant
to Western nations access to coastal cities and regions.*

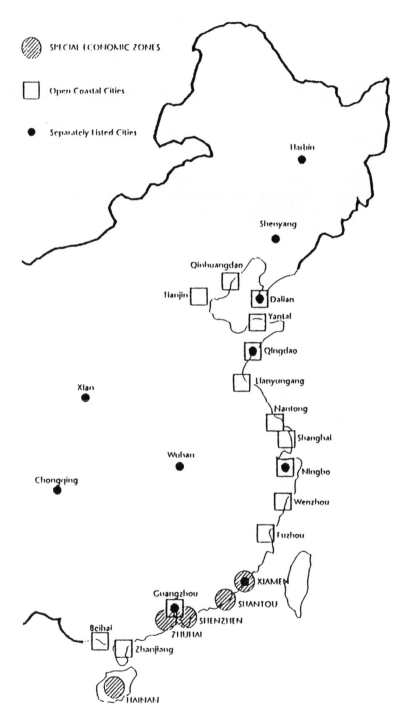

Harbin

Shenyang

Qinhuangdao

Tianjin

Dalian

Yantai

Qingdao

Xian

Lianyungang

Nantong

Shanghai

Wuhan

Ningbo

Chongqing

Wenzhou

Fuzhou

Guangzhou

XIAMEN

SHANTOU

Beihai

SHENZHEN

ZHUHAI

Zhanjiang

HAINAN

Map of the Special Economic Zones (SEZs) and open coastal cities since 1980.

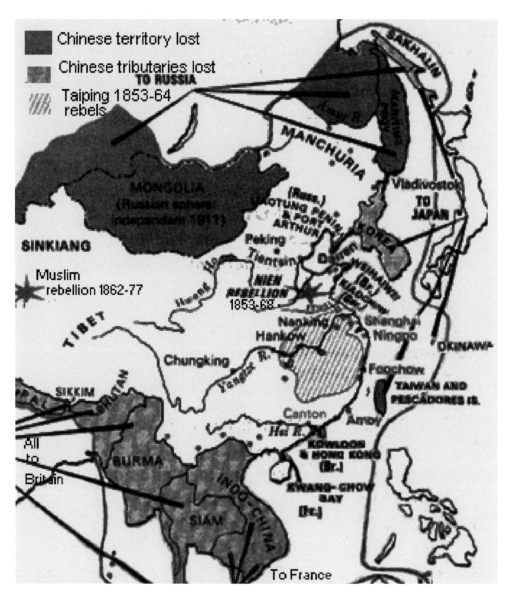

Map of China's territorial loss to imperialist powers, 1840–93. Britain, France, Russia, and Japan took over the Qing Dynasty's tributary sphere, a source of national humiliation and obstacles to modernization in China.

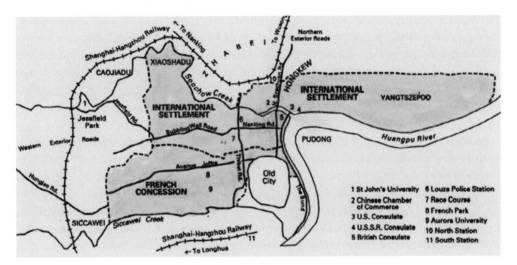

Map of the international settlement of Shanghai, with the Huangpu River
on the right, 1855.

Legend on map:
1 St John's University
2 Chinese Chamber of Commerce
3 U.S. Consulate
4 U.S.S.R. Consulate
5 British Consulate
6 Louza Police Station
7 Race Course
8 French Park
9 Aurora University
10 North Station
11 South Station

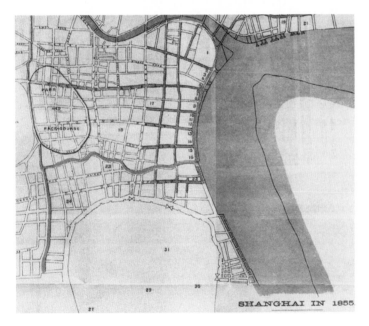

SHANGHAI IN 1855

Map of Shanghai, 1855.

As social entities, these territories became catalysts for ideological progress and political change but at the same time represented an unprecedented national disgrace for the Chinese people. As spatial entities, these coastal concessions restructured the morphological conditions of the cities and regions under the colonizing countries' control and simultaneously affected their economic conditions.

A century later, as the last two colonies—Hong Kong and Macau—were on their way to being returned to the motherland, China made territorial concessions once again. This time, the CONCESSION© was voluntary, made with grand ambitions and specific intentions to any nation or corporation that might be interested. These CONCESSIONS© first manifested in the form of Special Economic Zones and subsequently as Open Coastal Cities, Separately Listed Cities, Economic Development, and so on.

The Special Economic Zones were set up with both economic and political intentions. Economically, they were grounds for experimental policies to be tested and implemented without threatening or "contaminating" the rest of the country. Politically, the new zones were to act as sponges for the soon-to-be absorbed old colonies: Shenzhen for Hong Kong, Zhuhai for Macau. The hope was that the success and openness of the SEZs would give confidence to the new citizens of China just across the SEZ borders.

Despite these ambitions, at certain moments these new CONCESSIONS© represented painful reminders of the old treaty posts:

❊ This policy sounds too shocking to be true. I wonder if the exclusion was the practice of the hotels alone. There have never been any official policies forbidding Chinese to visit hotels that cater to foreigners. —QM

In 1920, in Shanghai, a sign outside of a park in the British territory reads: "Chinese and dogs not allowed."
In 1990, in Shenzhen, a new policy forbids locals from congregating in front of hotels that cater to foreigners.❊

In fact, the Special Economic Zones share many characteristics with the old colonies. Both were created to serve a particularly elite group of people that brings in foreign capital, expertise, and other social or cultural conventions. Both drew on the immense, disadvantaged pool of cheap labor from the hinterland to fuel the growth of the exclusive territories. Both enjoy preferential treatment, with policies and tax incentives to accelerate development. Both, without reservation or hesitation, exacerbate the differences between the protected territory and surrounding regions.

In an effort to appeal to Marxist-Leninist hard-liners and to minimize criticism, supporters of the SEZs described how Lenin's New Economic Policy of the 1920s was important for the Soviet Union at that certain stage of development when power remained firmly in the hands of the government. These reformers argued that political power over these regions would still be in the hands of the authorities and not in the hands of the capitalists: the new system would not be capitalism; it would be "state capitalism."

While the old concessions were symbols of disgrace, the new, voluntary CONCESSIONS©—imbued with a status as prototypes of China's future—have become sources of national and ethnic pride. In a biospatial evolution of the territory, the idea of CONCESSION© has imitated, absorbed, engulfed, swallowed, triumphed over, and transformed its old self.

FDI in Guangdong by Country (US$ millions)

	1990	1992
Hong Kong	985.01	3,038.79
Macau	33.58	123.48
Taiwan	70.32	128.57
Japan	132.23	16.26
Singapore	13.17	17.70
Germany	1.18	2.15
France	19.18	N/A
Netherlands	3.37	0.20
UK	7.01	14.53
USA	136.44	70.24
Australia	8.35	13.21

Utilization of Foreign Captial in the PRD Open Economic Zone and SEZs

	1990	1992
PRD	804	1,891
SEZs	657	1,122

Source: Statistical Yearbook of Guangdong 1993.

Cumulative FDI in China by Region, Year-end 1992 (US$ millions)

	Total	Per Capita	Per 100km²
COASTAL	27,455.99	54.35	25.01
Guangdong	12,051.49	184.70	66.95
Fujian	2,944.64	75.25	24.54
Jiangsu	2,222.45	32.16	22.22
Beijing	2,041.41	185.25	121.51
Shanghai	1,938.55	144.13	323.09
Shandong	1,824.82	21.19	12.17
Liaoning	1,556.41	38.76	10.38
Hainan	944.70	137.71	27.79
Tianjin	610.24	66.33	55.48
Zhejiang	566.12	9.70	5.66
Guangxi	448.38	10.24	1.95
Hebei	306.78	4.89	1.61
INLAND	2,838.51	4.30	0.35
Shaanxi	459.11	13.48	2.42
Hubei	378.85	6.79	2.10
Sichuan	355.60	3.23	0.64
Heilongjiang	290.57	8.05	0.63
Hunan	248.30	3.96	1.18
Henan	245.28	2.77	1.53
Jilin	180.66	7.14	1.00
Jiangxi	169.79	5.45	1.06
Anhui	156.94	3.70	1.21
Guizhou	89.08	2.65	0.52
Shanxi	82.94	2.78	0.55
Yunnan	67.53	1.76	0.18
Xinjiang	54.12	3.42	0.03
Inner Mongolia	42.75	1.94	0.04
Gansu	11.97	0.52	0.03
Qinghai	3.53	0.77	N/A
Ningxia	1.46	0.30	0.02
Tibet	0.03	0.01	N/A
TOTAL	30,294.50	25.99	3.33

Source: China Statistical Yearbook.

The amount of Foreign Direct Investment (FDI) in China since 1990.

Between 1978 and 1995, China received a total of U.S.$128 billion in Foreign Direct Investment (FDI). According to the World Bank, 40 percent of all FDI in developing countries goes to China; China is, in fact, the largest recipient of FDI among developing countries. A recommendation from the World Bank suggests that "these 'better-than-national-treatment' concessions are estimated to have an opportunity cost (in forgone tax revenue) of 1.2 percent of China's GDP."[10] However, the pattern of distribution of FDI in China is highly geographically distorted, with more than 90 percent of the money going to the coastal cities. Investment is also highly disproportional toward the real estate and tourism-related sectors.[11] As China begins to phase out some of the tax preferences given to foreign investors in the SEZs while granting various inland cities the same "open" status that the SEZs receive, the government is beginning to reevaluate the issue of balance between inland cities and coastal cities.[12]

AMBIGUITY©

> AMBIGUITY© Policy of indeterminacy, or half-hearted embrace, to exploit possibilities for political or economic gain. AMBIGUITY© allows tensions and contradictions to coexist in matters of state sovereignty and territory. AMBIGUITY© used by the Chinese Communist Party in one circumstance becomes leverage in another.

With the particular ability to turn weakness into advantage, China has reemerged in the last two decades as a master of international affairs: the Special Economic Zones were created to attract foreign investment, AMBIGUITY© is used as a strategy to negotiate with the British over Hong Kong and with the Americans, Japanese, and other Asian nations over South China Sea offshore oil drilling—all in the name of sovereignty. The issue of sovereignty has become China's favorite playing card in the game of international politics. In fact, sovereignty in China has taken on forms beyond its initial territorial aspect and begun to have other implications and other possibilities; the new manifestation of the idea of sovereignty has found its reincarnated existence in the PRD.

With roots in traditional Chinese military strategy, the advantage of maintaining ambiguity is to confuse the enemy, by "either launching an attack or retreating for defense."[13] In contemporary sovereignty disputes, China maintains AMBIGUITY© by *not* resolving issues immediately, even if intentions or resolutions are clear from the start.

This strategy of AMBIGUITY© has been used extensively and successfully by China in all territorial disputes. Since 1949, for example, China has not successfully taken back Taiwan, which is regarded by China as a renegade province. Even though there have been major and minor skirmishes, both militarily and politically, since the 1950s, Mao had on many occasions expressed his intent to use Taiwan. Neither controlled by China nor legitimately independent, Taiwan was seen by Mao as a bargaining chip against superpowers like the U.S. and Japan. By continuing to use propaganda and rhetoric to suggest the possibility of military action but without actually attacking Taiwan, Chinese politicians take the upper hand in geopolitical leverage.

Another territorial dispute occurred with Vietnam, regarding the Nansha Islands and oil-drilling rights on the South China Sea, and was left in tension because China employed AMBIGUITY©. Since the two countries have resorted to military intervention in previous disputes, the escalation of tension was seen by international political analysts as one of four major "potential threats" in the Asia-Pacific region. According to the *China Daily News*:

> *Shen Guofang, spokesman for China's Ministry of Foreign Affairs, commented on Vietnam's building of fishing docks on the islands as a serious offense to the Chinese sovereignty. "Vietnam has committed an illegal act," he said.*
>
> *Vietnam has been a tough opponent in international negotiation. While China wants to temporarily suspend the dispute on sovereignty issues, and jointly develop this area, Vietnam*

insists on solving the dispute through international laws. Yet, it seems unlikely the question can be solved easily through negotiation, according to analysts, because the ownership right of the oil is unclear. Meanwhile, both parties will talk and drill at the same time. Both countries have signed contracts with American and Japanese oil companies. Both have also sent out military vessels for protection.

There are as many as ninety islands and lagoons in the region. China, Taiwan, Vietnam, Malaysia, Indonesia, and the Philippines have all made claims for sovereignty of these islands.

China gained by keeping the oil-drilling issue in suspense. On the one hand, China continued to drill oil in the area without the risk of losing its rights; on the other, China maintained a powerful bargaining chip for dealing in this region with other nations, especially the U.S., whose interest in oil gives China the great leverage it hopes to retain. Leaving the issue of territorial AMBIGUITY© tangled has also given China leverage for negotiation on other issues.

In both examples, the notion of territory, boundary, or space gets transformed and politicized. It becomes an apparatus or mechanism beyond its spatial manifestation while its very ambiguity gives possibility to other gains and opportunities. How, then, is this geopolitics manifested in the microcosm of the PRD? Both Shenzhen and Zhuhai have been desperately attempting to "integrate" with Hong Kong, and one may speculate that, by integration, a territory of AMBIGUITY© will form.

BORDER©

> BORDER© Boundaries in the Pearl River Delta that are drawn
> and redrawn, and opened or closed according to changing policies
> of inclusion or exclusion of the desired or undesired population.

When the Shenzhen SEZ was first established, an eighty-kilometer fence was erected along the boundary of the Special Economic Zone to control the influx of population from other parts of the PRD as well as from the hinterland. Suddenly, the land was foreign: people needed special documents to enter. The business of border control between the SEZ and the rest of the PRD became so intense that a second border was proposed. It was never realized, however, because the direction of border crossing may be reversed in the future.

Anticipating the problem of border crossing, the Guangdong Border Patrol Armed Police recently activated more than 1,000 members of its force to stage an anti–border crossing exercise on water. This exercise, which took place on the water of Dapong Bay between Shenzhen and Hong Kong, aimed to deter any large-scale "gate rushing" or forceful border crossing between the mainland and Hong Kong from happening just prior to and after 1997.

The fully armed police force steered some twenty speedboats and gun boats into a "combat formation" and intercepted about fifty small fishing boats full of "illegal immigrants." The Guangdong police considered the incident a "premeditated and organized action" in which more than several hundred people were seduced and deceived into conducting an illegal act. If such illegal entry into Hong Kong is not stopped, the police argued, there will be inconceivable consequences to the prosperity and stability of Hong Kong society.[14] Here is a depiction from the actual scene, as recorded by the *Eastern Daily News*:

> *During the exercise, the police found the "targets" on the radar and dispatched the Border Patrol Armed Police squadron, the status of which is equivalent to that of the People's Liberation Army's regiment, for interception. The patrol boats formed a fan-shaped formation to approach the fishing boats. Once the fishing boats were surrounded, the police then made the announcement in four different dialects: Mandarin, Hakkanese, Chaochaonese, and Cantonese.*
>
> *When several of the fishing boats tried to break through the barricade, the police fired "non-fatal weapons" such as smoke gun, tear gas and high-pressure "water dragon" toward the boats. After an hour of struggle and hide and seek between the police and the fishing boats, the exercise officially ended with the fishing boats surrendering as they were forced into a small, shallow water bay.[15]*

Now that the territory has been returned to Chinese sovereignty, Hong Kong fears that the large influx of population from the mainland will jeopardize existing living standards. A quota of 15,000 people per year is currently allowed from China into Hong Kong. A new proposal from China has suggested that the quota be raised to 45,000 people per year.

Although characterized by similar economic and demographic concerns as other "border-crossing prone" areas of the world, the politics of border crossing in the PRD has a twist. Unlike the typical condition, in which the "host nation" actively seeks to reduce the influx of population while the "export nation" passively allows the outflow to persist, in the PRD the situation is reversed: here, the "export nation" (China) actively initiates efforts to stop the outflow, both in the case of the PRD-Shenzhen border and the Shenzhen-Hong Kong border. As a political gesture to reassure the future stability and confidence of the respective host regions (Shenzhen and Hong Kong), the policy of border-crossing control can also work the other way, against a potential reverse flow of population from Hong Kong into China. After 1997, the Hong Kong—Shenzhen border no longer demarcated two countries, but merely two zones of the same geographic region.

In this sense, there is an extraordinary degree of confidence and optimism on the part of PRD officials, for they may be the most forward-looking and visionary of all planners. However, the border between Zhuhai and Zhongshan seems to take on an even newer manifestation of border politics: since Zhongshan City lent Zhuhai six million RMB (almost U.S.$1 million), Zhongshan citizens, as creditors, can now cross into Zhuhai without restriction.

DIPLOMACY

Theme Park Diplomacy

A theme park can provide more than just entertainment and family fun. In the case of Splendid China, a theme park is fully capable of participating in national politics and international relations.

In February 1992, Shenzhen's new theme park, Splendid China—which displays eighty of China's most scenic sites—came to the attention of the international media, when Deng Xiaoping swapped his red-flag limousine for a golf cart and toured around the park. The visit signaled the beginning of a new push for economic reforms in the region. Deng was giving his symbolic blessing to the untrammeled development of the PRD, and the results of the "imperial tour"—Deng's last major public appearance before his death in 1997—were "electrifying" to the eyes of international observers. Economically, enterprise and property speculation surged to achieve a growth rate of more than 12 percent in 1992–93, the highest in the world. Politically, the visit completely de-powered and undermined the communist hard-liners, who had been critical of the "capitalistic" erosion of the region.

On December 6, 1995, Deng's successor Jiang Zemin escorted Cuban president Fidel Castro through downtown Shenzhen, to showcase China's economic miracle. Castro saw two of Shenzhen's most successful joint ventures, the China Bicycle Corporation and the electronics group Konka. He then toured the Splendid China theme park and visited the Shekou Industrial Zone.

Shenzhen newspapers ran a brief biography of Castro's revolutionary background on their front pages. The Chinese media said Castro hoped to experience "new things" during his trip to China and had therefore decided to visit Shenzhen. According to the newspaper *Ming Pao*, Castro told Shenzhen Party Secretary Li Youwei that he was "stunned" by what he saw:

> *"We are extremely interested in Shenzhen's experiences and it is extremely useful for Cuba,"* *he said. "I've never seen such large-scale enterprises and such high-quality products. Both* *workers and cadres here are excellent," Castro wrote in the visitors' book at the bicycle factory. During the afternoon visit to the Splendid China, hundreds of police kept tourists away as* *Castro climbed aboard a miniature electric train to be whisked around the park, where he* *also planted a tree.*[16]

Castro's trip to Shenzhen had a dual significance. It showed, first of all, that as the other previously socialist countries in the world were beginning to concentrate on economic development, Cuba was also under strong pressure to implement a policy of reform and openness. Secondly, according to routine practice in China, a foreign dignitary is received by top leaders in Beijing, then accompanied by lower-ranking officials for the rest of the itinerary. During Castro's visit to Shenzhen, however, Jiang himself accompanied the Cuban leader for two days, demonstrating not only the importance of the visit, but also the government's recognition of Shenzhen's special status.

Shenzhen, 1995. Fidel Castro toasts Jiang Zemin during his tour of China, during which he visited the Splendid China theme park, in Shenzhen.

In fact, even though Jiang formally came to Shenzhen in the name of accompanying Castro, he arrived half a day early in order to hear briefings from Shenzhen officials on their future development strategy. During the trip, Jiang also met a number of Hong Kong politicians to discuss the city's process of transition back to Chinese sovereignty in 1997. In a sense, Jiang was paying more attention to Shenzhen than to Sino-Cuban relations. Just as Splendid China served more than just to entertain, Shenzhen accomplished infinitely more than its original, experimental purpose. Today, the city itself is a sort of theme park, and the theme park has become merely an apparatus of diplomacy, a show of sovereignty.

In the same year, almost 10,000 miles away from Shenzhen, in a land much closer to Castro's Cuba, another theme park also became the subject of controversy. Two miles from Disney World, in Orlando, Florida, lies the body double of Shenzhen's theme park: the Florida Splendid China. With a focus on a replica of Tibet's Potala Palace and China's treatment of Tibet, the park drew fire for presenting a distorted view of Chinese-Tibetan relations. According to Reuters:

> The International Campaign for Tibet, based in Washington D.C., is mounting a campaign against the park and its "insidious political messages," and says it has 60 people collecting signatures asking the state to rule that the park should not be used for school field trips.
>
> It also points out that the honorary committee for the opening ceremony on December 18 contained a number of people more known for their political dealings with China rather than their interest in Chinese culture, including former U.S. president Richard Nixon and former secretary of state Alexander Haig. The Splendid China park, south of Orlando near Disney World, opened nearly two years ago.
>
> China invaded Tibet in 1950, and the Dalai Lama, Tibet's spiritual leader,
> later went into exile with tens of thousands of followers. In the Maoist Cultural Revolution of 1966–76, fanatics destroyed all but a handful of Tibet's 2,000 monasteries. One of the park's exhibits is a model of Tibet's Lhasa Potala Palace, surrounded by statues of Tibetans in colourful robes.
>
> "Our park has nothing to do with politics," said Splendid China spokeswoman Ellen Siu.
>
> But John Ackerly, spokesman for the International Campaign for Tibet, said: "The park is here because the Chinese government wants to improve its image in the West. That's political."[17]

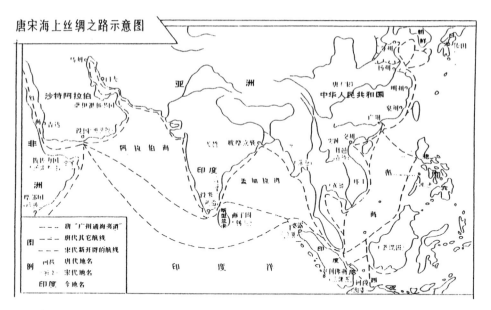

Map of trade routes during the Tang and Song dynasties. Between the sixth and twelfth centuries, when Guangzhou was the largest port in China, traders used the Silk Road by land and the Perfume Route by sea. Trade routes during the Tang and Song dynasties, 6th to 12th centuries.

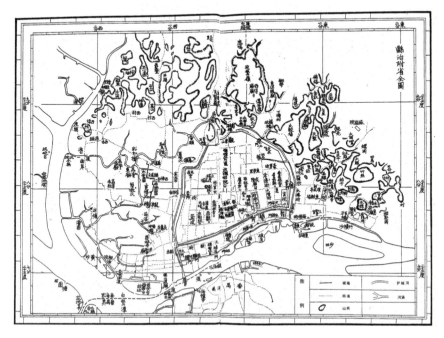

Map of Guangzhou during the Qing dynasty. During the nineteenth century, Guangzhou was the only port that remained open to foreign trade under the closed-door Sea Prohibition policy.

DEVELOPMENT

NEGLECT©

> NEGLECT© Policy of the Chinese Communist Party to chronically disadvantage the Guangzhou region of the Pearl River Delta; it is a policy that has suspended development in the region since 1949.

Perhaps the one city in the delta region that is most threatened by the recent competitive development of other PRD cities is Guangzhou, nicknamed the "tired old man" of the region. While Guangzhou City is responsible for all the other municipalities in Guangdong Province, which includes the entire Pearl River Delta, the provincial capital does not have jurisdiction over the two Special Economic Zones, Shenzhen and Zhuhai. The SEZs receive their authority directly from the central government in Beijing, and therefore are equal in status to Guangzhou.

Constantly outmaneuvered by such smaller, nimbler, and independent-minded municipalities as Shenzhen, Dongguan, and Zhuhai, Guangzhou has suffered for its large population, housing shortage, old industrial plants, and lack of urban infrastructure. The city has also lagged behind other counties because of its bureaucratic slowness, its responsibility as a provincial capital, and the multiple layers of bureaucracy above the level of enterprise: top officials, commissions, bureaus, public corporations, and administrative offices. "Compared to the counties of the Pearl River Delta," observed one of Guanzhou's leading economic officials, "Guangzhou is like a tired old man."

Formerly known as the regional capital of Canton, Guangzhou is situated at the northern end of the Pearl River Delta, facing the South China Sea. A city with more than 2,800 years of recorded history, it has been the most important—and for a long time, the only—port linking China to the outside world. As early as the first century A.D., the city became active as a commercial hub for the Silk Road on the Sea, also known as the Perfume Route. For the next several hundred years, trading activities extended to Southeast Asia, India, East Africa, and cities along the Red Sea coast.

Guangzhou maintained its status as the largest port in China until the Song Dynasty (A.D. 907–1279), when it was surpassed by the Port of Qunzhou in Fujian Province. During the Ming (1368–1644) and early Qing (1644–1911) Dynasties, when China was under the Sea Prohibition—a closed-door policy that outlawed traveling abroad by sea and making contact with Western nations—Guangzhou was the only Chinese port that remained open to foreign trade.

The political history of Guangzhou from the mid–ninteteenth century to the mid–twentieth century essentially highlights that of modern China. In 1839, the Sino-British

广州市城市总体规划图

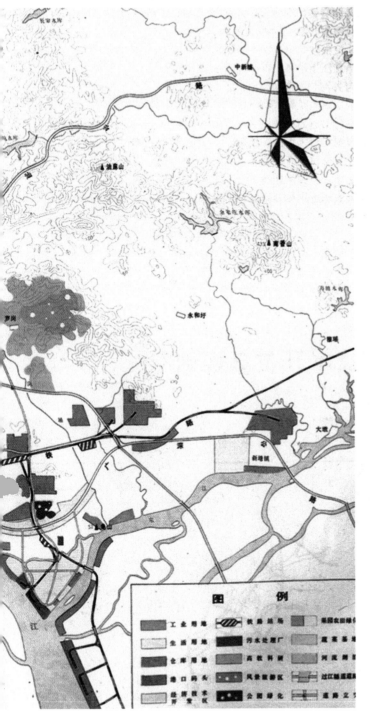

Map of Guangzhou in the present day.

Opium War broke out in Guangzhou; as a result, Hong Kong was given to the British for 150 years. Guangzhou was the site of China's first Republic government, established in 1911 by Dr. Sun Yat-Sen. In fact, three of modern China's most powerful political leaders—Sun, General Chiang Kai-Shek of the Nationalist Party, and Chairman Mao Zedong—resided in the city during the 1920s. In 1927, the Chinese-Soviet government was set up in Guangzhou, though it lasted only three years before being forced out by the Nationalists.

The 8th year during the reign of Emperor Yi of the Zhou Dynasty (887 B.C.), five immortals mounting five rams descended from heavenly clouds to give the blessing that the people of the city would forever be free of famine. "The City of Five Rams" became a legendary name for Guangzhou. —Yang Wansho[18]

As a result of Mao's Inland Strategy, developments in communication, transportation, commerce, and housing in the Pearl River Delta were almost nonexistent between 1949 and 1979. From 1950 until the early 1980s, the number of telephone lines in Guangzhou remained fixed at 29,000; not a single new bridge was constructed during this period. The only housing developments during this period were built either for workers in the new factories or for government bureaucrats around the city government buildings. Guangzhou's

The Guanzhou Economic and Technology Development Zone.

commercial activities suffered severely as the policy favored industrial rather than commercial development. In 1957, there were 3.8 retail stores per 100 people in Guangzhou. By 1978, the number had dropped to 0.3 per 100.[19]

"The sky is high, the emperor is far away…"—ancient Chinese proverb
"Let Guangdong walk one step ahead."—Deng Xiaoping

NEGLECT REVERSAL©

NEGLECT REVERSAL© Method of reversing NEGLECT© for self-advantage by seeking more NEGLECT© or autonomy. Used by the Guangdong province since 1979 to achieve unprecedented economic growth.

❋ The autonomy requested by the provincial government of Guangdong is not necessarily related to the development or economic autonomy of the SEZs. Because the SEZs are not under the jurisdiction of the city of Guangzhou, they are not part of Guangdong and hence are not associated with Guangdong's effort to gain autonomy. —QM

The local government of Guangdong decided to reverse the disadvantage caused by NEGLECT© by requesting more autonomy❋ from the central government and responding independently to its needs. In 1980, Xi Zhongxun, First Party Secretary of Guangdong Province, went so far as to suggest the American federal-state system as a possible model of political hierarchy with Beijing. This daring proposal aroused discomfort among conservative hard-liners and was subsequently dismissed as being inconsistent with the communist tradition.

Since the PRD is far from the capital—geographically and otherwise—leaders in Beijing felt that experimentation could be initiated there without political disruptions threatening the status quo. Furthermore, the region made only minor contributions to China's heavy industry and national income, so the overall risk to the national economy was relatively small. In other words, there was not much to lose.

As the PRD began to exercise more independence in responding to its administrative, agricultural, industrial, transport, commercial, educational, cultural, technical and public-health needs, a new condition, NEGLECT REVERSAL©, has developed in the region over the past fifteen years. The neglecter and the neglected have exchanged positions.

In 1980, as part of the new Special Policy, Beijing agreed to Guangdong's request to pay a fixed lump sum of RMB1 billion (U.S.$125 million) per year to the central government in exchange for retaining the additional provincial revenues for more flexible ways of spending.[20] When Beijing tried to get Guangdong to increase its payment in 1982, Guangdong refused. Eventually, a compromise was reached, whereby the province would "lend money" to Beijing, knowing it would not be repaid. In 1986, Beijing negotiated another such loan with Guangdong. In turn, Guangdong decided to collect taxes from its municipalities.

In 1979, as a way to attract more overseas investors, Guangdong officials began to return properties to families with overseas connections (an estimated one-third of its residents) for private development. Convention centers, hotels, and office buildings were among

Demographic statistics in China.

	CHINA 1997	GUANGDONG	PRD	GUANGZHOU
LAND AREA (KM²)	96,000,000	157,000	42,600	7,434
POPULATION (TOTAL)	125.7 billion	63.64 million	20.8 million	6.84 million
URBAN POPULATION (%)	32.0%	36.8%	40.3%	59.8%

Sources: J. Cheng and S. Macpherson, Development in Southern China *(1995), 115; Guangzhou Tourism Bureau, 1995; The World Bank, "China at a Glance," 1999, 1;* Statistical Yearbook of Guangdong 1993 *(Guangdong: State Statistical Bureau, 1993); Zhou Yi-xin, "Trends of Urbanization in China in the 1980s," and Xu Xue-qiang, "Urbanization of Pearl River Delta: Review and Forecast,"* Chinese Cities and Regional Development, *Yang Ru-wan, ed. (Hong Kong: Chinese University of Hong Kong Asia Pacific Institute, 1993), 123–28 and 369–84.*

A chart of the various classifications of Chinese cities, as defined by the Ministry of Construction, shows that Guangzhou was leader in development.

By population	**Small city**	Non-agriculture population < 200,000
	Medium city	Non-agriculture population > 200,000 but < 500,000
	Large city	Non-agriculture population > 500,000
	Extra-large city	Non-agriculture population > 1,000,000
By hierarchy	**Direct-supervised city**	Reports directly to the State Department of the Central Government; enjoys same status as provincial and autonomous regions.
	Province-supervised city	Reports to the provincial government; has same status as regional government and may supervise one or more counties.
	County-level city	Reports to the regional government; many previous counties and townships were "upgraded" to cities as their population and industrial output grew.
	Planned-itemized city	Administratively under the supervision of the provincial government, P-I cities receive directives from the Central Government on issues pertaining to economic planning and development. The cities' economic performances are itemized and evaluated seperately from the rest of the provinces.
By economy	**Gross > 20 million RMB**	Then a township over pop. 60,000 may declare status of city.
	Gross > 30 million RMB	Then a county over pop. 100,000 may declare status of city.
	Gross > 40 million RMB	Then a county over pop. 500,000 may declare status of city.
	Gross > 1.0 billion RMB	Then a city over pop. 250,000 (non-agriculture) may lead one or more counties.
	Gross > 1.5 bilion RMB	Then a city may apply to be classified as a planned-itemized city.

Sources: Zhu Tiehqin, China Urban Handbook *(Beijing: Economic Science Press, 1987), 47; Diao Tiending,* China's Regional Bureaucratic Overview *(Beijing: Legal Press, 1989), 209–18; Xie Qingkue,* The Contemporary Government of the People's Republic of China *(Shengyang, China: Liaoning People's Press, 1996), 316.*

the most popular development projects. Guangzhou became the first major city in China to have hotels designated for foreigners accept local citizens without special permission.

As part of the effort to solve the subsequent problem of tens of thousands of young people arriving in Guangzhou from the countryside, permits were issued to allow the operation of small eateries and other commercial establishments. Meanwhile, the population in Guangzhou increased from 3.2 million in 1982 to more than 6 million in 1990.[21] Much of this increase can be attributed to the FLOATING© population, the thousands of temporary immigrants from other interior provinces flooding daily into the Guangzhou train station; the number of floaters increased from about 200,000 in 1979 to more than 1.2 million in 1990.

Between 1975 and 1990, spending on urban reconstruction in Guangzhou increased more than tenfold. One public housing project had a higher budget in 1990 than it did during the entire Cultural Revolution. Light industry production, requiring smaller capital investments, doubled between 1978 and 1985.[22]

All of these momentous changes can be attributed to the Special Policy of 1980, which opened a series of new possibilities for Guangdong:

1. Freedom to manage foreign trade: Guangdong branches of national companies were allowed to split off, to retain more foreign currency, and to set up their own promotional organizations and prices in Hong Kong and Macau.
2. Fiscal independence: Beginning in 1980, instead of sending a percentage of revenue as tax to the central government, Guangdong was permitted to pass on a fixed sum, which would remain the same for the next five years.
3. Financial independence: Guangdong banks were allowed to make their own investment decisions. When the province needed to use foreign currency, it notified the central government rather than asking for permission.

The region also gained more authority in determining the distribution and supply of materials and resources, in setting wages above the national guidelines, in allowing the market to determine certain prices, and in establishing an experimental export district, which would subsequently become the Special Economic Zone.[23] This set of new policies represented a reversal of the strategy from Mao's era, which focused on the interior of the country and isolated the coastal regions.

STREAMLINING©

STREAMLINING© Deregulation or simplification of political bureaucracy to enable the accelerated development of a socialist market economy.

As Deng Xiaoping was pushing forward economic reforms at full speed in the PRD and the rest of China, he also criticized the cadre system for its bureaucracy, life tenure, and abuse of power. Deng scolded: "All kinds of phenomena associated with privileges, ... lead to dissatisfaction among the masses." Then, in October 1987, CCP General Secretary Zhao Ziyang presented a new approach: "Advance along the road of socialism with Chinese characteristics." Declaring that "without political reforms, economic reforms cannot ultimately achieve success," Ziyang proposed a series of structural reforms including separating the CCP from the government, establishing a system of consultation with the populace, and conducting elections that would reflect "the will of the voters."[24]

In 1988, Beijing launched two organizational-reform campaigns at the central party and government levels to simplify structure and allocate management authority to local party and government agencies. Zhao's successor, Jiang Zemin, also argued for organizational reforms through a strategy of simplification, decentralization, and change of functions. Then, in 1989, Beijing changed its target from reforms at the central level to reforms at the local (county) level. As a result of Deng's 1992 visit to the PRD region and push for speedy reforms, a number of significant evolutions and mutations within the political structures of local municipalities occurred. At the same time, provincial leaders recognized that the government had too many layers and divisions. Efforts were made by many of the municipalities in the PRD to simplify bureaucracy in order to encourage greater efficiency, more equity, and higher productivity. In the reform process, an attempt was made to reduce the size of government units, primarily by retiring more people and not replacing all who retired.

STREAMLINING© was thus declared as a deliberate strategy for enabling the acceleration of development throughout China. Within the Guangdong provincial party and government structure, the number of leadership posts of departments, committees, offices, and bureaus was reduced from 494 to 232; the number of personnel dropped from 10,422 to 5,500; the number of agencies and units was cut from 84 to 49. In Shenzhen, the number of bureaucratic reductions was equally impressive. Administrative departments were reduced from 37 to 17, and the number of governmental personnel underwent an incredible 61 percent reduction, from 2,237 to 867. A campaign in 1986 further reduced the structure of the Shenzhen government from three layers to just two, greatly expediting the administrative process.[25]

INCORPORATION©

INCORPORATION© Using capitalist tactics as a method of protection from STREAMLINING©.

STREAMLINING© efforts met various roadblocks and countermeasures to survival from the cadres. Over the years, many provincial units continued to expand. The ceiling of 140,000 cadres for the entire Guangdong province was exceeded by 23 percent in 1984. Because the size of each unit determines its bureaucratic status (as a bureau, division, or section), which in turn determines political privileges, wage scales, and other fringe benefits for its cadres, each unit finds inherent advantage in staying as large as possible. In many cases, cadres simply switched from one unit to another, maintaining the total number of people working. "Temporary units," set up to deal with new problems, tended to become semipermanent. By the late 1980s, there were more than seventy "temporary units" at the provincial level, and they somehow proved more persistent than the old units they had replaced.

The most significant method for cadres to avoid the pressure to simplify administrative organs was to INCORPORATE© and set up "corporations," which the government encouraged as a means of separating administrative management from economic management. However, distinguishing in terms of functions between the administrative units and the independent corporations was often difficult. Some bureaus simply used two different names, reporting themselves to the upper level as "corporations" while using the name "bureau" in dealing with subordinate units. In other cases, the parent administrative unit continued to control the funding and personnel management of the corporation.[26]

"When you have a policy, we have a countermeasure"
—local riddle mocking all efforts at centralized policy making

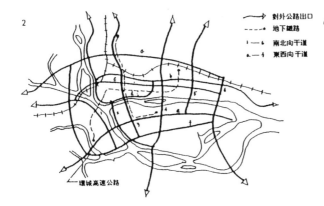

2

Guangzhou's transportation pattern.

對外公路出口
地下鐵路
南北向干道
東西向干道

環城高速公路

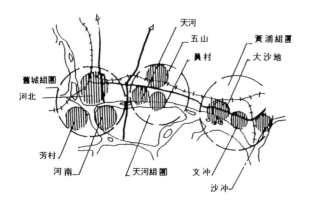

天河
五山
黃浦組團
員村
大沙地

舊城組團
河北

芳村
河南
天河組團
文冲
沙冲

Guangzhou's current development plan.

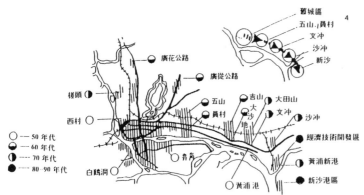

舊城區
五山 員村
文冲
沙冲
新沙

4

Guangzhou's development pattern from 1950–90.

廣花公路
廣從公路
樓頭
西村
五山
員村
吉山 大田山
大沙地
文冲
沙冲
琶洲技術開發區
黃浦新港
黃浦港
新沙港區
番禺
白鵝洞

50 年代
60 年代
70 年代
80–90 年代

COORDINATION©

COORDINATION© Retroactive task, by politicians and planners, of creating coherence in urban development in order to regain lost power in an exploding socialist market economy. An attempt, as in the Pearl River Delta, to mediate various parts of an outwardly unified, but inwardly competitive, whole.

For centuries, Guangzhou had been the center of Cantonese culture, cuisine, and politics. This remained true even after the communists took over, because national policy both favored and demanded that every political center be located in the largest urban center of each locale, thus ensuring centralized control of power and development. Today, various domains within the PRD are experiencing an endlessly polarizing loop of centralization and decentralization. As local municipalities demand more autonomy, wanting to break away from centralized control, the counterstrategy employed by Guangzhou to regain its lost power is COORDINATION©.

Various municipalities in the PRD have been developing independently and competing at all costs for an economic edge. COORDINATION© has become increasingly popular among politicians, planners, and researchers at the regional and provincial levels. After two decades of full-speed growth, runaway development finally caught the attention of PRD planners, who subsequently began to introduce a series of studies and strategies on COORDINATION©. These efforts have resulted in the establishment of such new COORDINATION© agencies as the PRD Economic Planning Committee and publications such as *Planning for the Urban Agglomeration of the Pearl River Delta Economic Region: Coordination and Sustainable Development*.

Other problems, such as protests from Hong Kong citizens who had purchased Guangdong properties, have also resulted in the establishment of a coordinating committee, which includes construction, commerce, and land administration officials from Panyu, Nanhai, Huizhou, Foshan, Zhongshan, and Dongguan. The newspapers chronicle Guangzhou's efforts at COORDINATION©. The following report appears in the *South China Morning Post*:

> Complaints from Hong Kong buyers targeted developers who did not finish projects on time, poor construction and discrepancies between advertised and completed units. Provincial Vice-Governor Tang Bingquan yesterday reassured disgruntled buyers that officials would work for a solution to the problem. "We have the ability to settle the problem. Hong Kong people should remain calm," he said.
>
> Guangdong province announced a ban on new property projects for twelve months. This freeze applies to all residential and commercial projects. Provincial planning commission deputy director Zhen Guorui said the freeze was intended to reduce the stockpile of empty flats in the province, a result of over-building. He said the Government intended to buy some of the stock to sell to Guangdong people at subsidized prices to ease a housing shortage.

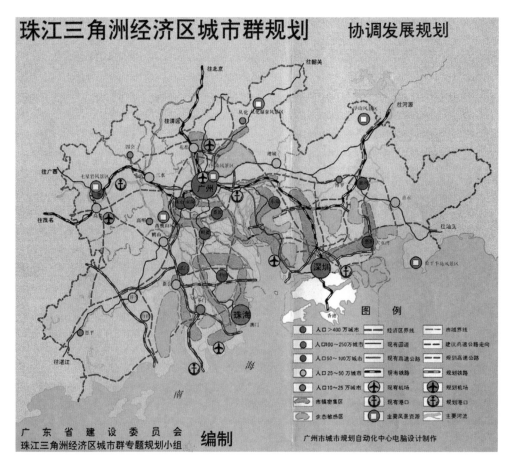

珠江三角洲经济区城市群规划　协调发展规划

广 东 省 建 设 委 员 会
珠江三角洲经济区城市群专题规划小组　编制

广州市城市规划自动化中心电脑设计制作

图 例

Pearl River Delta Coordination Development Plan.

> How much would be spent and how many flats would be bought by the authorities would
> vary from city to city, depending on city governments involved. "It depends on each city's
> earnings," Zheng said. There was no overall figure on how much the provincial Government
> estimated it needed to spend to purchase the empty flats. Guangzhou Vice-Mayor Chen Kaizhi
> said the city would introduce further new measures in the second half of this month to boost
> sales. But he would not say what the new measures were.[27]

Beginning in the late 1980s, after more than four decades of political turmoil and little economic progress and NEGLECT©, centralization gave way to a more decentralized approach
to development as the provincial government of Guangdong became less restricted in making decisions and policies. Today, through COORDINATION© efforts, the provincial government is resuming a centralized strategy against local governments, which in turn may limit
the local governments' chances to tackle problems within their individual counties. As strat-

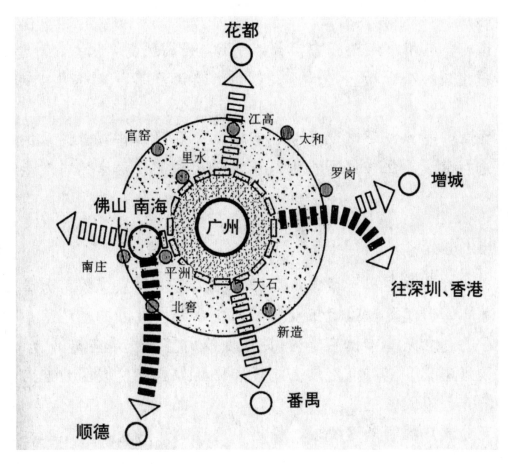

Pearl River Delta Development Diagram.

egy and counterstrategy become routine conceptual operations, the political center may not have the power to resume control of its various parts. Without explicit power, COORDINATION© can only be reduced to the status of euphemism, a term used by those confronted with the increasing autonomy of all the parts that the center can no longer influence.

Meanwhile, as local bureaucratic systems in the PRD have become less and less layered over the last decade, the idea of COORDINATION© may unexpectedly undermine the efficiency achieved through bureaucratic STREAMLINING©. As new agencies are formed to COORDINATE© the development projects of various municipalities, the system becomes once again excessive and convoluted; the actual process of development may end up slowing down as a result. As a prominent international banker put it during a dinner conversation in Hong Kong: "From a layman's point of view, isn't comprehensive planning sometimes too stifling for a city?"

Pearl City promotional advertisement.

PROJECTION

PEARL CITY©

PEARL CITY© A fiction, a fairy tale, the PARADISE© of the PRD.
Lured by the optimism of PEARL CITY©, the PRD region unwittingly
generated its double, the CITY OF EXACERBATED DIFFERENCE©.

Imagine the year 2006. Pearl City is one of the largest, richest urban areas in the world. Including its suburbs, it spans more than 160 kilometers from north to south. Pearl City has a population of more than forty million. The GDP is U.S.$800 billion a year. The average income per capita is about U.S.$20,000 (U.S.$40,000 in Hong Kong and U.S.$10,000 in the fringe of Zhongshan). In terms of purchasing power, even the less affluent rank among the richest 10 percent of Asians.

Pearl City comprises two special administrative regions (Hong Kong and Macau) and two self-governing districts (Shenzhen and Zhongshan). At whatever level, planning is highly coordinated. As a result, Pearl City's infrastructure is the envy of the world. Mass transit systems and networks of highways, bridges, and tunnels enable residents to travel from Stanley Market (on the southern tip of Hong Kong island) to Guangzhou's city center in less than ninety minutes. Road and rail systems connect Pearl City to manufacturing hinterlands as far away as Chengdu and Wuhan. State-of-the-art airports—including Asia's three longest runways, at Chek Lap Kok—transport the world's population within six hours' flying time.

We see few traditional factories or farms in the Pearl City of 2006. The leading industries are trade, investment, transport, communications, tourism, finance, insurance, marketing, design, education, health care, legal services, arts, and entertainment. Manufacturing activities work with cutting-edge technology. Regional and international head offices abound and control operations throughout China, Southeast Asia, Europe, and North America. The companies and the financial industry of Pearl City are world leaders.

The population is 95 percent Chinese (many educated overseas) and is conversant in Cantonese, English, and Mandarin. The remaining two million residents are Japanese, Korean, Southeast Asian, American, British, Australian, Indian, and of other nationalities. Many are architects, economists, chefs, merchants, financiers, engineers, entrepreneurs, and China's best and brightest scientists. Pearl City is the movie capital of the world. Its films are seen by one billion people in the Asia-Pacific region alone, before their release in North America and Europe.

Does this sound too good to be true?

Not everyone is optimistic. Some economists see a danger of the Pearl River Delta stagnating, of the pearl losing its luster and becoming a "Gray City." To achieve this Pearl City, we will need an unprecedented degree of coordination and joint planning among the central, provincial, city, and county governments. Think about the current administrative structure, which does little to promote coordination. These communities are so near, yet so far apart. We must learn to work together—learn to share a vision, turn it into a strategy, and then implement it. Only that way, can we build a Pearl City.

—Adapted from "Pearl City, Here We Come," by David Li Kwok-Po,
in *South China Morning Post* (HK), 6 July 1996.[28]

PEARL CITY© might sound like a fictitious utopia, but the notion of the Pearl River Delta becoming one huge urban conglomerate is anything but a fiction. With a total population of twenty million, the PRD is one of the four most urbanized regions in China. It is also among the most crowded places in the world, having a population density of 500 people per square kilometer.

The urban population of the PRD increased more than 300 percent in about fifteen years, jumping from 3.1 million in 1978 to 9.2 million in 1994 and representing more than one-third of the total urban population (24.3 million in 1993) of China. Meanwhile, between 1980 and 1990, 60 percent of the rural population of the PRD switched from farming to other ventures. Population isn't the only thing that has grown. So has the actual number of cities and townships. Reforms pressured the loosening of criteria for the establishment of a township, and a new policy in 1984 allowed settlements with more than 2,000 people to declare the status of township. Shortly after, the number of new cities and townships in the PRD mushroomed from 33 in 1978 to 458 in 1994.[29]

The sudden burst of population growth and the corresponding number of municipalities has created a fierce battle within the Pearl River Delta for opportunities, resources, and other competitive advantages. Could what emerges out of this seemingly chaotic condition be the prosperous PEARL CITY©?

> *"Forget the border and the crowds at Louhu. In 10 years' time the area stretching from Hong Kong to Guangzhou might well be the most dynamic piece of land in the world."*
> —*South China Morning Post.*[30]

1. James Wong, *Contemporary Chinese Politics* (London: Prentice-Hall International, 1995), 279.

2. Elizabeth Perry and Christine Wong, "The Politics of Industrial Reform," *The Political Economy of Reform in Post-Mao China*, vol. 2 of *Harvard Contemporary China Series* (Cambridge, MA: Harvard University Press, 1985), 210.

3. The figures are derived from the following two sources: Joseph Cheng and Stewart MacPherson, eds., *Development in Southern China* (Hong Kong: Longman Hong Kong, 1995), 301; and *Statistical Yearbook of Guangdong 1993* (Guangzhou: State Statistical Bureau, 1993), 77.

4. Wong, 59.

5. Ibid., 211.

6. Ezra Vogel, *One Step Ahead in China: Guangdong Under Reform* (Cambridge, MA: Harvard University Press, 1989), 81.

7. Ezra Vogel, *Canton under Communism: Programs and Politics in a Provincial Capital, 1949–1968* (Cambridge, MA: Harvard University Press, 1969).

8. Vogel, *One Step Ahead: Guangdong Under Reform*, 87.

9. Lowell Dittmer, "China in 1988: The Continued Dilemma of Socialist Reform," *Asian Survey* 24, no. 1 (January 1989), 24–25.

10. Ibid., 17.

11. Harry Broadman and Xiaolun Sun, "The Distribution of Foreign Direct Investment in China," *The World Economy* (March 1997), 1.

12. Ibid., 17.

13. Sun-Zi, *The Art of War,* trans. Me-Chun Sawyer and Ralph Sawyer (Boulder: Westview Press, 1994).

14. *Eastern Daily News* (HK), (9 August 1996).

15. Ibid.

16. *Ming Pao* (7 December 1995).

17. Reuters World Service (6 November 1995).

18. Yang Wansho, ed., *Guangzhou She Hua* (The Oral History of Guangzhou) (Guangzhou, China: Guangdong People's Press, 1986), 4.

19. Vogel, *One Step Ahead in China: Guangdong Under Reform*, 196.

20. Ibid., 89–90.

21. Lau Kwok-yu, "Issues in Housing Policy in Guangzhou," in *Development in Southern China*, eds. Cheng and MacPherson, (Hong Kong: Longman Asia Ltd., 1995), 115.

22. Vogel, *One Step Ahead in China: Guangdong Under Reform*, 201.

23. Ibid., 85–86.

24. Joseph YS Cheng, "Organizational Reforms in Local Government in Guangdong," in *Development in Southern China*, eds. Cheng and MacPherson, (Hong Kong: Longman Asia Ltd., 1995), 43–44.

25. Ibid., 45.

26. Hong Yung Lee, "China's New Bureaucracy?," in *State & Society in China: The Consequences of Reform*, ed. Arthur Rosenbaum, (Boulder: Westview Press, 1992), 62.

27. *South China Morning Post* (HK), (6 August 1996).

28. The author of this speculative essay, David Li, is a member of the Hong Kong Legislative Council and CEO of the Bank of East Asia.

29. Guangdong Development Committee, *The Planning for Urban Agglomeration of PRD Economic Region—Coordination and Sustainable Development*, (Beijing: China Architecture Industry Press, 1996), 9.

30. *South China Morning Post* (6 July 1996). Louhu is a district between Hong Kong and Shenzhen, where the Customs Building is located.

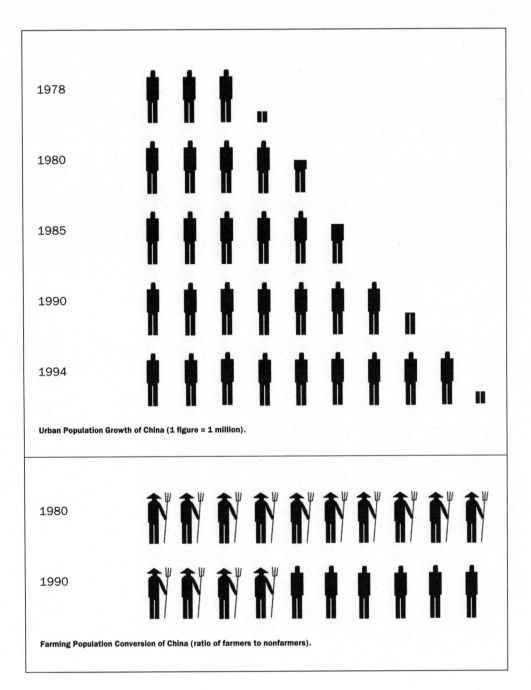

Urban Population Growth of China (1 figure = 1 million).

Farming Population Conversion of China (ratio of farmers to nonfarmers).

Contents

HIGHWAYS	*468*
LAND/WATER TRANSPORT	*510*
BRIDGES	*552*
TUNNELS	*584*
PORTS	*596*
AIRPORTS	*624*
RECLAMATION	*678*

INFRASTRUCTURE
PEARL RIVER DELTA

Bernard Chang

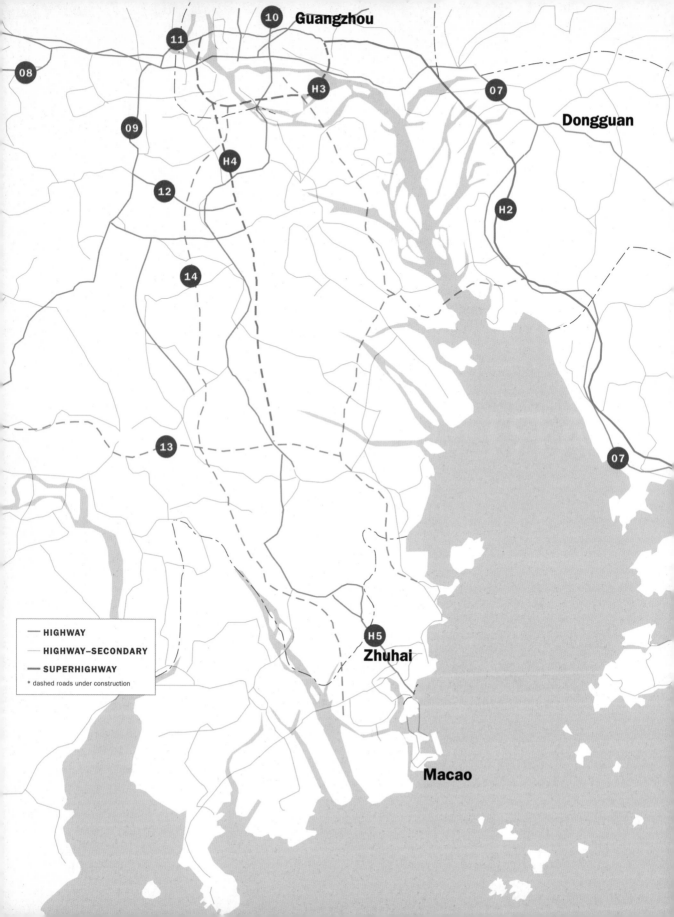

07

16

15

henzhen

H1

H6

g Kong

HIGHWAYS

PEARL RIVER DELTA 471

SHENZHEN–HONG KONG HIGHWAY CONNECTIONS **H1** 473

GUANGZHOU–SHENZHEN–ZHUHAI (GSZ) SUPERHIGHWAY, PHASE I **H2** 479

GUANGZHOU ESW RING ROAD **H3** 489

GUANGZHOU–SHENZHEN–ZHUHAI (GSZ) SUPERHIGHWAY, PHASE II **H4** 495

ZHUHAI **H5** 499

HONG KONG **H6** 503

The Pearl River Delta has built 350 kilometers of state highway since 1996. The highways are mostly connected on the east side of the delta, leaving the west side underdeveloped by comparison. There are currently ten highway projects, which will total 1,500 kilometers in length at completion, under construction. In a period of five years, Guangdong province will have built the largest highway network in China.* The privately funded Guangzhou–Shenzhen–Zhuhai (GSZ) Superhighway phase I, which connects cities on the east side of the delta, channeled 50,000 vehicles per day in 1996; and 1.3 million square meters of retail space are available underneath the elevated section of the highway.

The GSZ Superhighway phase II, which will extend from Guangzhou to Zhuhai, will improve the accessiblity of the cities on the west side. The construction of the Guangzhou ESW Ring Road, was interrupted because construction costs have increased 66 percent. Meanwhile, there are currently three highway connections between Shenzhen and Hong Kong; three more will be added in the near future. Hong Kong's latest highway development concentrates on the New Territories, where an increase in border traffic is anticipated. *China Daily Supplement of Business Week, (16 June 1996).

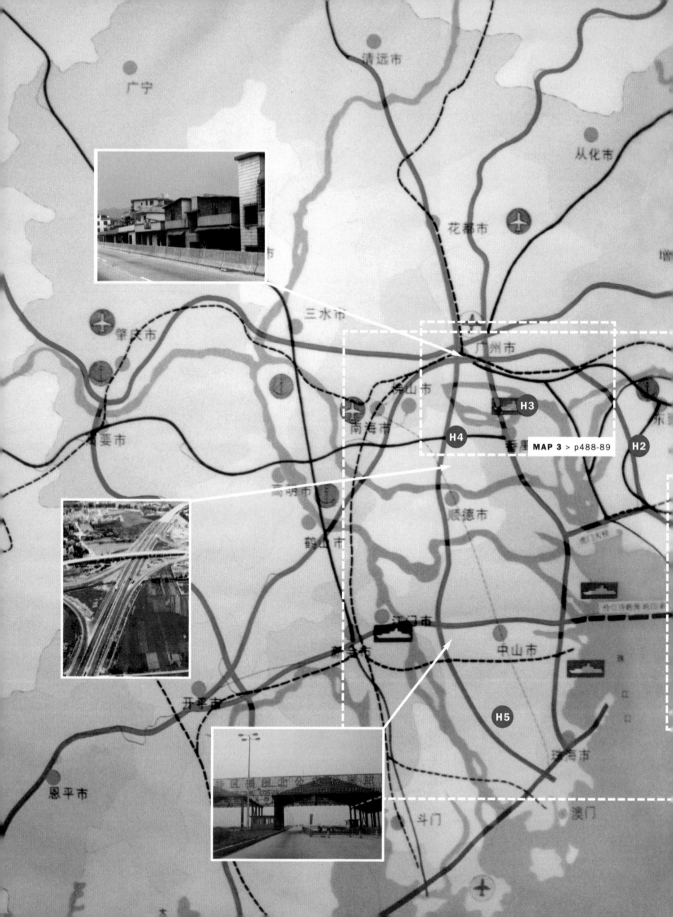

广宁

清远市

从化市

花都市

三水市

肇庆市

广州市

佛山市

H3

南海市

H4

MAP 3 > p488-89

H2

高要市

高明市

顺德市

虎门大桥

鹤山市

江门市

中山市

新会市

H5

开平市

珠海市

恩平市

斗门

澳门

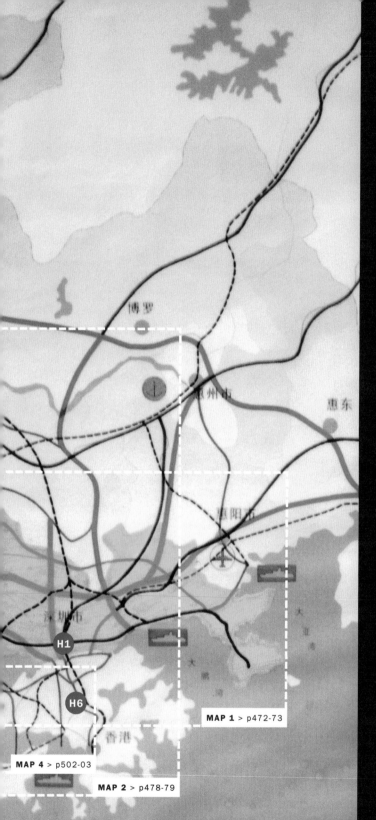

MAP 1 > p472-73

MAP 4 > p502-03

MAP 2 > p478-79

highways > PEARL RIVER DELTA

In July 1996, Guangdong province signed contracts to build 25 highway projects. As listed in the Ninth Five-Year Plan (1996–2000), the projects are worth U.S.$7 billion. Ten highways, totaling 1,500 kilometers and receiving a U.S.$5 billion investment, were scheduled to be built in the PRD within that period. The director of the Guangdong Highway Corporation claims that a 15 to 20 percent return rate for highway projects in Guangdong attracts investors from the United States, France, Malaysia, Hong Kong, South Korea, and the World Bank.

By the end of 1996, more than U.S.$3.5 billion in foreign investment had been contracted for highway construction. The following are the highways that were already in operation in the delta as of December 1996: **H2** GSZ Superhighway, phase I, connecting Shenzhen with Guangzhou; **07** Route 107, linking Shenzhen, Dongguan, Guangzhou, and cities west of Guangzhou, such as Sanshui; **08** Route 105, connecting Guangzhou, Shunde, Zhongshan, Zhuhai, and Macau; **09** Route 325, linking Foshan, Heshan, and other western Guangdong cities; **10** Guangzhou–Huadu Highway, connecting Guangzhou's new airport with the city center; **11** Guangzhou–Foshan Highway, connecting Guangzhou with Foshan Airport; **12** Shunde Highway

The following are the highway projects still under construction: **H4** GSZ Superhighway, phase II, which will connect Guangzhou and Zhuhai; **H3** Guangzhou ESW Ring Road; **13** Guangzhou–Zhuhai East Highway, running along the west bank of the delta, which will link Guangzhou, Panyu, Dongguan Boca Tigris (or Humen) Bridge, Zhongshan and Zhuhai. From Zhongshan, the highway will go west and link Jiangmen with other western cities in Guangdong; **14** Guangzhou–Zhuhai West Highway, running west along Xijiang (the West River), to the GSZ Superhighway, phase II, which will connect Guangzhou with Zhuhai Hengqin Island; **15** Shenzhen–Huizhou Highway, which will connect the Shenzhen Yantian Port with Huizhou, in Huizhou County; **16** Shenzhen–Huizhou Highway, which will link Shenzhen, Longgang, Huiyang, and Huidong, all in Huizhou County, and continue to Shantou County.

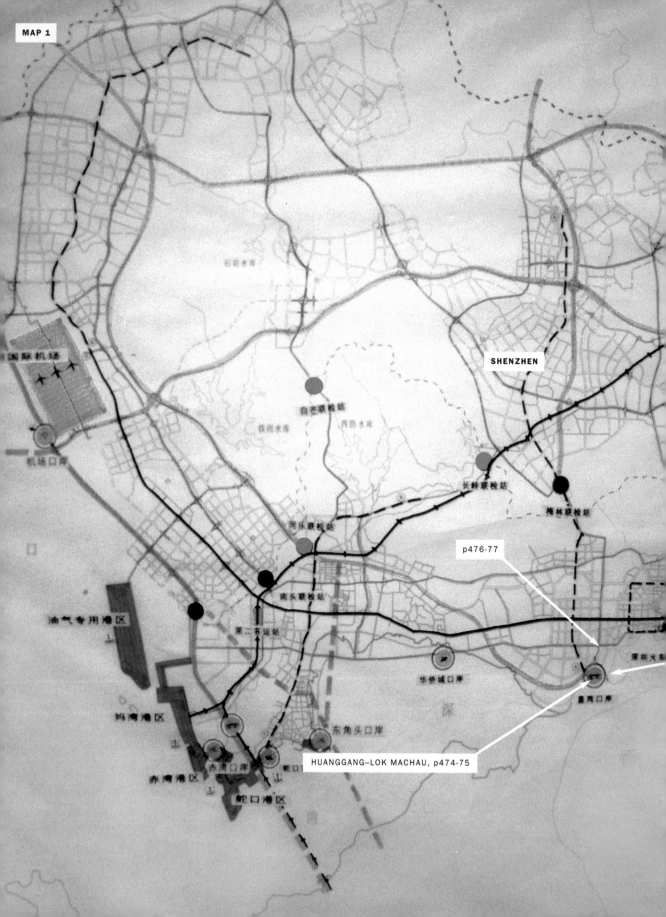

MAP 1

国际机场

机场口岸

石岩水库

白芒联检站

铁岗水库

西丽水库

SHENZHEN

长岭联检站

梅林联检站

同乐联检站

南头联检站

第二客运站

p476-77

油气专用港区

华侨城口岸

皇岗口岸

深圳火车

妈湾港区

东角头口岸

赤湾港区

赤湾口岸

蛇口港区

HUANGGANG–LOK MACHAU, p474-75

深

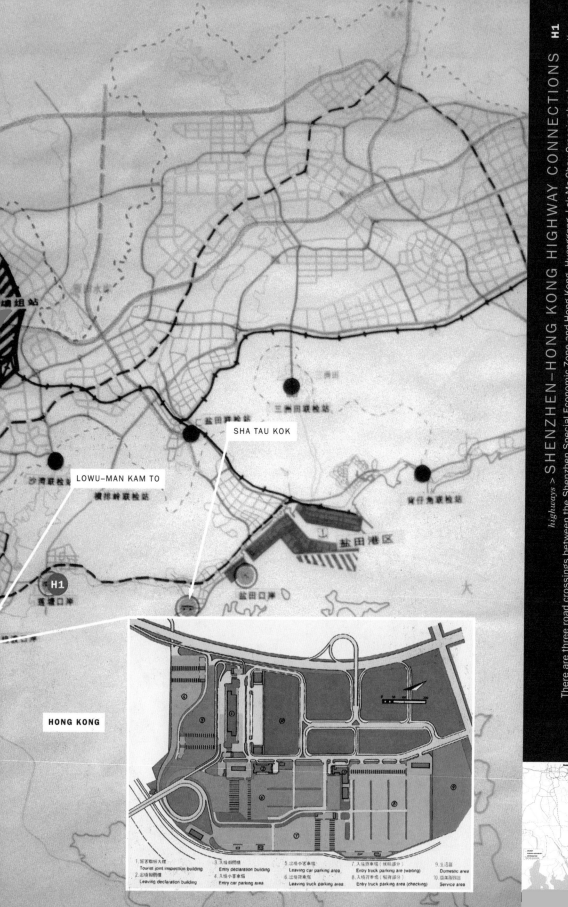

There are three road crossings between the Shenzhen Special Economic Zone and Hong Kong. Huanggang–Lok Ma Chau Crossing has been operating 24 hours a day since November 1994. It had a flow of 12,400 vehicles per day, totaling 4.5 million vehicles in 1995. The GSZ Superhighway, phase I links Shenzhen Huanggang with Shekou Port, Shenzhen International Airport, Dongguan Boca Tigris Bridge, and Guangzhou. Hong Kong–Lok Ma Chau connects with the New Territories Circular Road via Route 2; it continues to Chek Lap Kok International Airport, West Kowloon, and Hong Kong Island via Route 3.

SHA TAU KOK

LOWU–MAN KAM TO

H1

HONG KONG

1. 旅客联检大楼
   Tourist joint inspection building
2. 出境申报楼
   Leaving declaration building
3. 入境申报楼
   Entry declaration building
4. 出境小客车场
   Entry car parking area
5. 出境小客车场
   Leaving car parking area
6. 出境货车场
   Leaving truck parking area
7. 入境货车场（预检部分）
   Entry truck parking are (waiting)
8. 入境货车场（验查部分）
   Entry truck parking area (checking)
9. 生活区
   Domestic area
10. 综合服务区
    Service area

HUANGGANG–LOK MACHAU

Lowu–Man Kam To Crossing operates from 7 a.m. to 10 p.m. It had a flow of 9,100 vehicles per day and a total of 3.3 million vehicles in 1995. Shenzhen–Lowu connects the Futian District, Shekou Port, Shenzhen International Airport, and Dongguan City via Shennan Road, which turns into state highway Route 107. Hong Kong–Man Kam To links the New Territories Circular Road. Sha Tau Kok Crossing opens at 7 a.m. and closes at 6 p.m. It had a flow of 1,780 vehicles per day, totaling 0.65 million vehicles in 1995. Shenzhen–Sha Tau Kok runs adjacent to Yantian Port,

Altogether these three crossings handled 23,280 vehicles per day, for a total of 8.5 million vehicles in 1995. Commercial vehicles accounted for 95 percent of the traffic, and 31 companies operated tourist coach services across the border. The proposed connections between the Shenzhen Special Economic Zone and the future Hong Kong Special Administrative Region are Shekou–Pak Nai, a fixed crossing (see Shenzhen Western Corridor Proposal I), Dong Kok Tau–Sheung Pak Nai, a fixed crossing (see Shenzhen Western Corridor Proposal II), and Liantang Road Crossing, located in a border city between Lowu, and Sha Tau Kok.

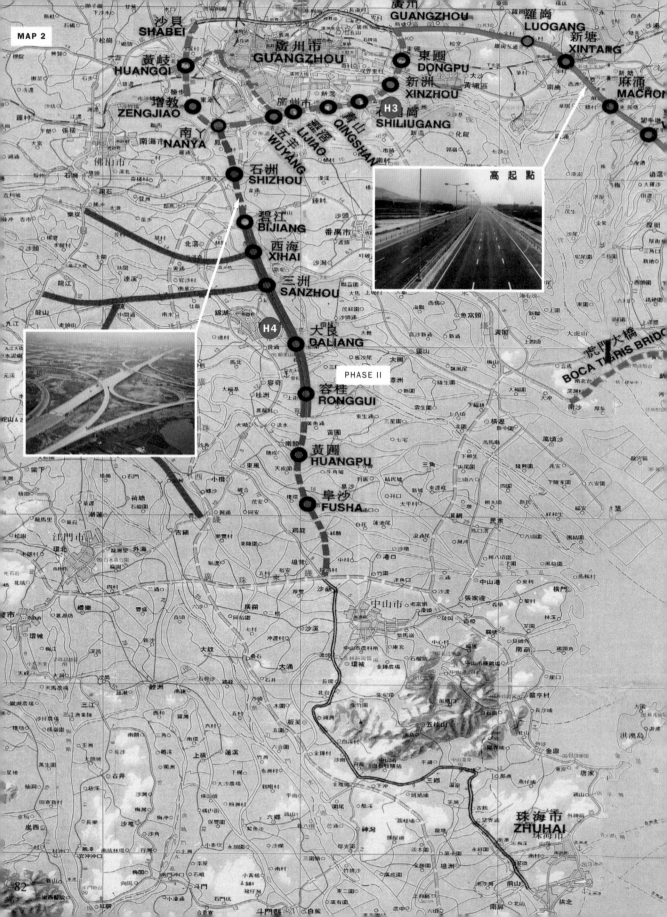

MAP 2

沙貝
SHABEI

黃岐
HUANGQI

廣州市
GUANGZHOU

廣州
GUANGZHOU

羅崗
LUOGANG

新塘
XINTANG

東圃
DONGPU

新洲
XINZHOU

麻涌
MACHON

增教
ZENGJIAO

廣州市
GUANGZHOU

南丫
NANYA

五羊
WUYANG

瀝滘
LIJIAO

青山
QINGSHAN

石榴崗
H3
SHILIUGANG

石洲
SHIZHOU

高起點

碧江
BIJIANG

西海
XIHAI

三洲
SANZHOU

H4

大良
DALIANG

PHASE II

虎門大橋
BOCA TIGRS BRIDGE

容桂
RONGGUI

南朗
黃圃
HUANGPU

阜沙
FUSHA

江門市

中山市

珠海市
ZHUHAI

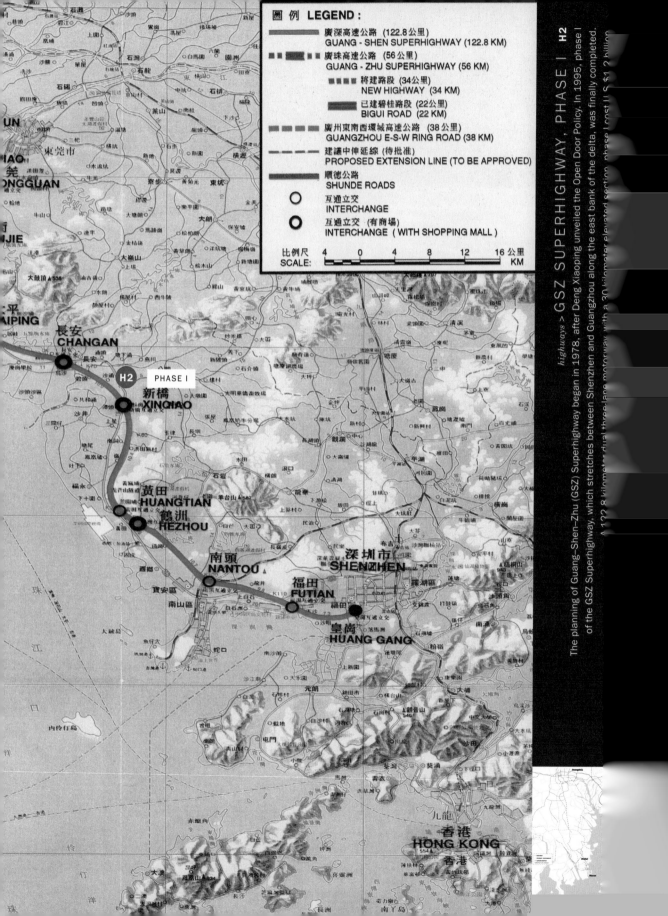

圖例 LEGEND :

廣深高速公路 (122.8公里)
GUANG - SHEN SUPERHIGHWAY (122.8 KM)

廣珠高速公路 (56公里)
GUANG - ZHU SUPERHIGHWAY (56 KM)

將建路段 (34公里)
NEW HIGHWAY (34 KM)

已建碧桂路段 (22公里)
BIGUI ROAD (22 KM)

廣州東南西環城高速公路 (38公里)
GUANGZHOU E-S-W RING ROAD (38 KM)

建議中伸延線 (待批准)
PROPOSED EXTENSION LINE (TO BE APPROVED)

順德公路
SHUNDE ROADS

互通立交
INTERCHANGE

互通立交 (有商場)
INTERCHANGE (WITH SHOPPING MALL)

比例尺
SCALE: 4   0   4   8   12   16 公里
KM

H2   PHASE I

The planning of Guang–Shen–Zhu (GSZ) Superhighway began in 1978, after Deng Xiaoping unveiled the Open Door Policy. In 1995, phase I of the GSZ Superhighway, which stretches between Shenzhen and Guangzhou along the east bank of the delta, was finally completed.

Phase I of the GSZ Superhighway has 16 interchanges, ten of which provide a total of 1,600,000 square meters of property development and 68,000 square meters of commercial development. Nine interchanges have been enlarged to accommodate public transportation;

EXIT 出
Bus
巴士站

Local
S/H
Car

Superhighway Carpark
高速公路停车场

Local Carpark
地方停车场

N

To Guangzhou
往廣州

Local Carpark
地方停车场

Superhighway Carpark
高速公路停车场

To Shenzhen
往深圳

ENTRY 入

Bus
巴士站

EXIT 出

☐ Superhighway
　高速公路
☐ Local Road
　地方路
▨ Toll Plaza
　收费站
▨ Bus Station Building
　巴士站大樓
▨ Petrol Station
　加油站
▨ Shopping Mall
　商場
☐ Shops
　店舖
▨ Development Area (142,522M²)
　發展用地
▨ Superhighway Carpark (41,465M²)
　高速公路停車場
▨ Local Carpark (38,891M²)
　地方路停車場

DONGGUAN INTERCHANGE
PHASE I G-S-Z SUPERHIGHWAY
東莞互通立交
第一期廣深珠高速公路

0　50　100　150　200 M
米

Note: The Northbound Entry is not located within the Interchange.
註：北行入口不在互通立交路網內。

The elevated sections between the Xinqiao and Changan interchanges, and the Dongguan, Daojiao, Wangniudun, Macrong,

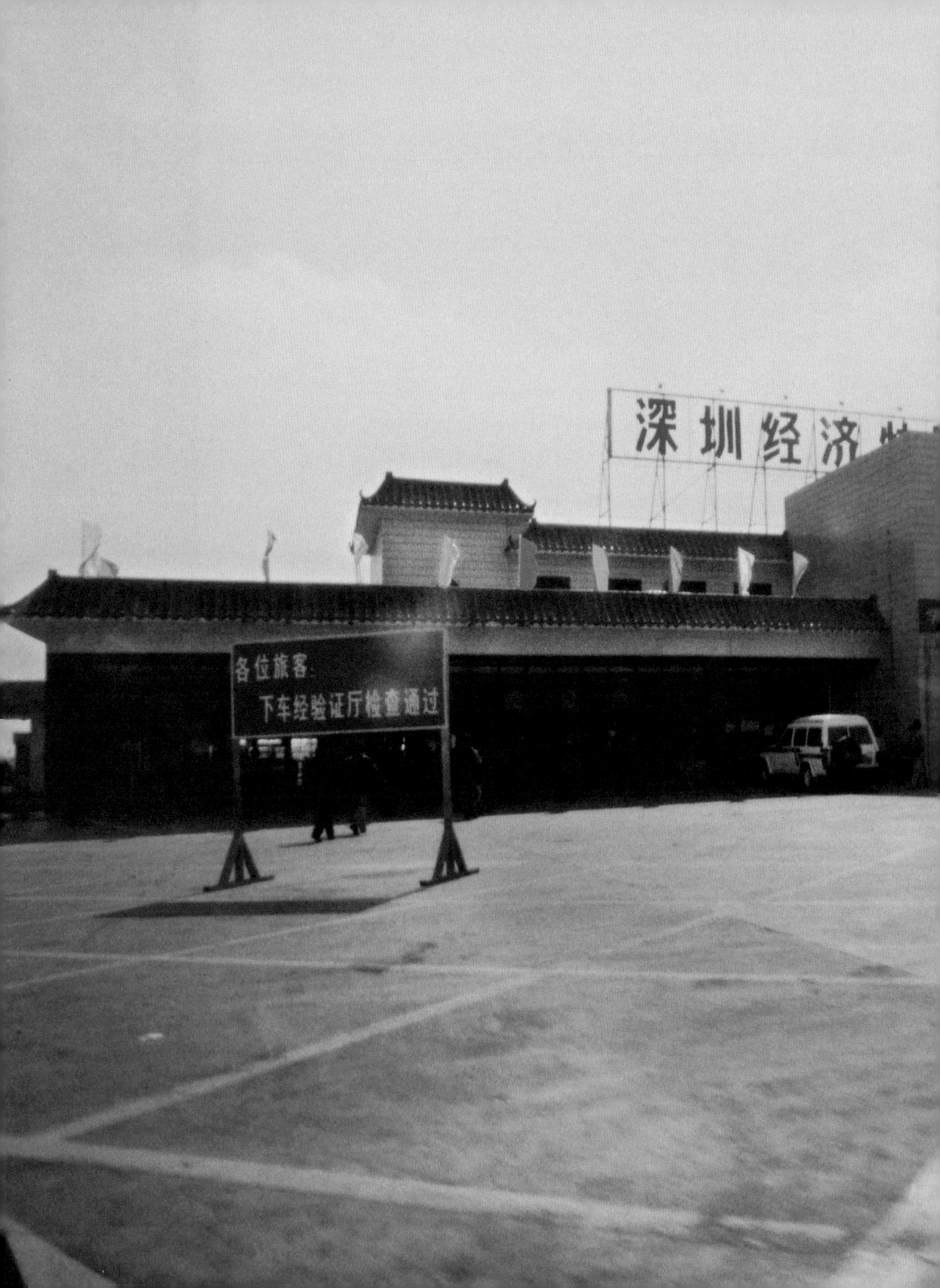
深圳经济
各位旅客:
下车经验证厅检查通过

highways > GSZ SUPERHIGHWAY, PHASE I 04

The GSZ Superhighway project is funded by Hopewell Holdings, of Hong Kong, and created by the company's chairman, Gordon Wu. Hopewell Holdings is entitled to keep 42.4 percent of the tolls collected during the first ten years of operation and 32.8 percent of the tolls collected during the following 20 years. After that, the company will turn over ownership of the highway to the Guangdong provincial government.

ENTERING GUANGZHOU

XINTANG

麻涌
MACHONG

望牛墩
WANGNIUDU

H2

道滘
DAOJIA

東
DOI

高 起 點

Phase I of the superhighway handled 50,000 vehicles per day as of 1996, and the ride between Shenzhen and Guangzhou

Phase I of the superhighway handled

MAP 3

佛

松岗镇

大沥镇

佛山市

山

石湾镇

澜石镇

乐从镇

里水镇

石井镇

新市镇

沙贝
SHABEI

黄岐镇
黄岐
HUANGQI

盐步镇

荔湾区

ZHONGSHAN ROAD VIII

海珠区

GONGYE ROAD

东漖镇

增教
ZENGJIAO

平洲镇

凤鸣镇

南丫
NANYA

五羊
WUYANG

沥滘
LIJIA

石洲
SHIZHOU

陈村镇

碧江
BIJIANG

北滘镇

佛山机场

画例 LEGEND :

廣州東南西環城高速公路 (38公里)
GUANGZHOU E-S-W RING ROAD (38 KM)

建議中伸延線 (待批准)
PROPOSED EXTENSION LINE (TO BE APPROVED)

○ 互通立交
INTERCHANGE

◎ 互通立交 (有商場)
INTERCHANGE (WITH SHOPPING MALL)

● 主要巴士站
MAIN BUS TERMINAL

比例尺
SCALE：

1 0 1 2 3 4 5 公里
KM

highways > GUANGZHOU ESW RING ROAD **H3**

It was planned that Guangzhou ESW Ring Road be a 38 kilometer dual four-lane expressway that would circulate the east, south, and west sides of Gaungzhou. Ring Road would connect with phase I of the GSZ Superhighway at the Guangzhou interchange, with phase II at the Nanya interchange. Piling work for the eastern section of the road was started in mid-1995, and with state highway Route 107 on the north side of the city. Piling work for the eastern section of the road was started in mid-1995, but the project stalled later that year because Hopewell Holdings and the Guangzhou authorities had a disagreement over the costs of the project,

PROPOSED INTERCHANGE WITH MALL

In July 1996, Cheung Kong Infrastructure, of Hong Kong, was invited to join the project, and the cooperation agreement was revised. With a joint investment of U.S.$243 million from Hopewell Holdings and Cheung Kong Infrastructure and a U.S.$12 million investment from the Guangzhou Freeway, the construction of the east-south section of Ring Road resumed. Three other companies agreed in principle to build the remaining part, a 20-kilometer west-south section, which cost U.S.$256 million. Ring Road has 9 interchanges; two of them will be elevated. All of the interchanges provide land parcels for property developments, which are under negotiation between Hopewell Holdings and the Guangzhou government. A 15 kilometer elevated dual 2-lane expressway will be added to connect the Huanqi and Wuyang interchanges.

廣州市
GUANGZHOU

廣州市
青山
QINGSHAN

蘿崗
LIJIAO

五羊
WUYANG

石洲
SHIZHOU

H4

碧江
BIJIANG

西海
XIHAI

三洲
SANZHOU

大良
DALIANG

容桂
RONGGUI

黃圃
HUANGPU

阜沙
FUSHA

LEAVING GUANGZHOU

highways > **GSZ SUPERHIGHWAY, PHASE II** **H4**

Phase II of the GSZ Superhighway, connecting Guangzhou with Zhongshan, was approved by the Guangdong provincial government in mid-1995. The 58-kilometer dual three-lane motorway starts from the Nanpu interchange on Ring Road and runs south to Nanhai. Nine interchanges

Phase II of the highway merges with the already built 22 kilometer Bigui section of the Shunde Highway and continues to the southern district of Zhongshan, where the superhighway joins the upgraded state highway Route 105, which extends as far as the Zhuhai SEZ and the border of Macau. Land acquisitions for the Nanhai and Shunde sections have been completed.

PHASE II G-S-Z SUPERHIGHWAY
POSED INTERCHANGE LAYOUT ON GRADE
第二期廣深珠高速公路
地面互通立交
(UNDER NEGOTIATION & DESIGN)
（在商議階段及設計中）

0   50   100   150   200 M
米

☐	Superhighway 高速公路
☐	Local Road 地方路
☐	Toll Plaza 收費站
☐	Bus Station Building 巴士站人樓
☒	Shopping Mall 商場
☐	Development Area (127,000f 發用地
☐	Superhighway Carpark (13,0 高速公路停車場
☐	Local Carpark (14,000M²) 地方路停車場

ENTERING ZHUHAI

There are two proposed highways for penetration of the Zhuhai SEZ. One carries traffic to the central business district of Zhuhai and Macau's border. The other starts from Shishou and goes through Zhuhai

HIGHWAY TO COME

Within Zhuhai, a proposed grid of highways would connect the CBD and the west side of Zhuhai. Zhuhai Arterial Roads East and West, which consist of the Zhuhai Bridge and three other bridges, are in operation. Macau has 42 kilometers of highway, which wrap around the islands that have three bridges connecting them.

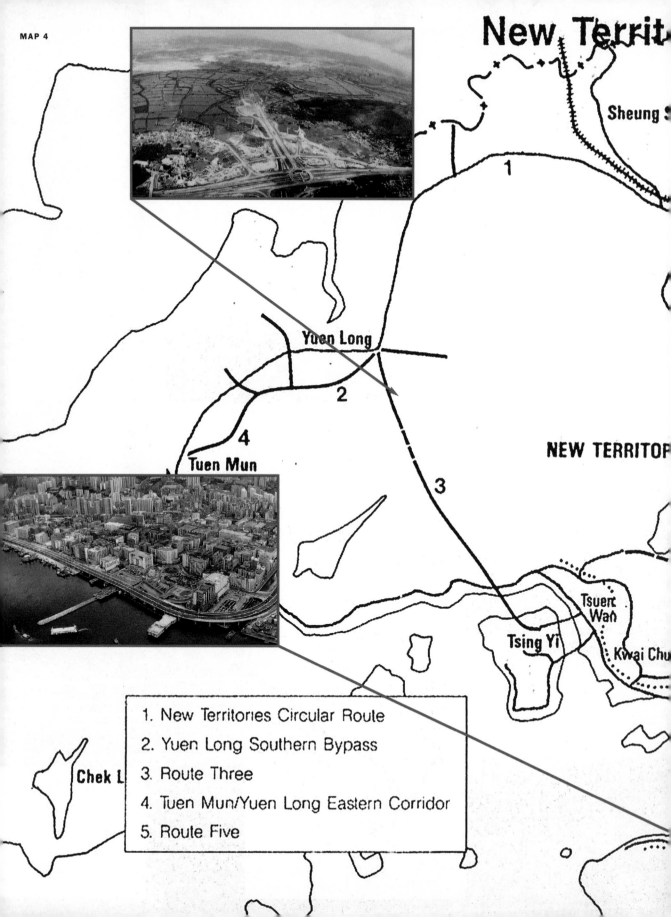

MAP 4

New Territ

Sheung

Yuen Long

Tuen Mun

NEW TERRITOR

Tsuen Wan

Tsing Yi

Kwai Chu

Chek L

1. New Territories Circular Route

2. Yuen Long Southern Bypass

3. Route Three

4. Tuen Mun/Yuen Long Eastern Corridor

5. Route Five

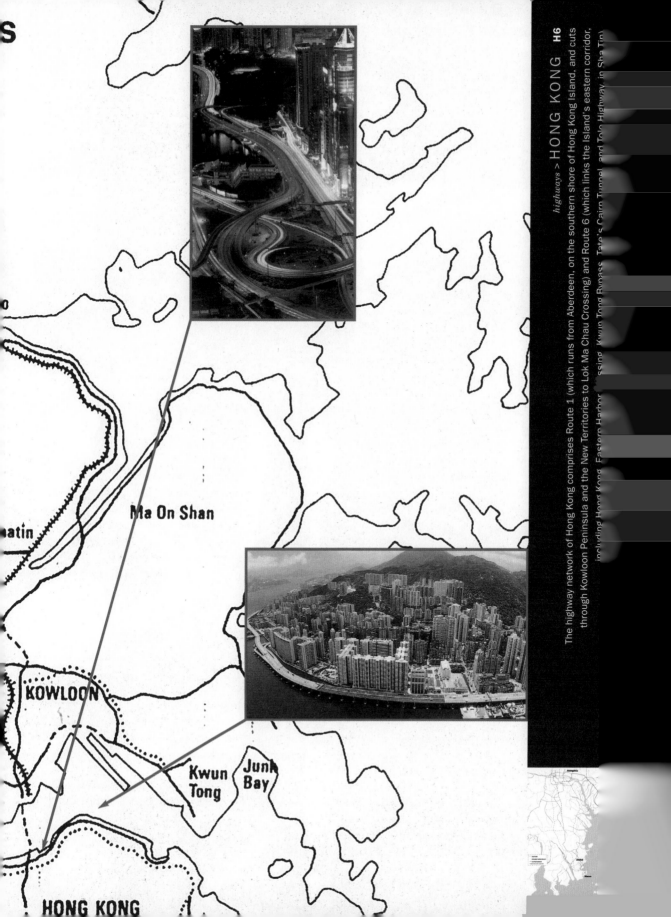

The highway network of Hong Kong comprises Route 1 (which runs from Aberdeen, on the southern shore of Hong Kong Island, and cuts through Kowloon Peninsula and the New Territories to Lok Ma Chau Crossing) and Route 6 (which links the Island's eastern corridor, including Hood Kong Eastern Harbour crossing, Kwun Tong Bypass, Tate's Cairn Tunnel, and Tolo Highway in Sha Tin).

Ma On Shan

atin

KOWLOON

Kwun Tong

Junk Bay

HONG KONG

Route 7 runs westward from the Cross Harbor Tunnel, along the northern shore of Hong Kong Island, via Gloucester Road, Harcourt Road, and Connaught Road, to Hill Road at Kennedy Town. Route 8 runs along the northern shore of the island, from the Cross Harbor Tunnel, through the Island Eastern Corridor, to Shau Kei Wan and Chai Wan in the east. Route 81 links Chai Wan, through Tai Tam and Repulse Bay,

The southern section of Route 3 connects the Chek Lap Kok airport with Tsing Yi Island, through the North Lantau Expressway, Kap Shui Mun Bridge, Ma Wan Viaduct, and Tsing Ma Bridge. It merges with the West Kowloon Expressway, continues to Kwai Chung, and reaches Hong Kong Central District via Western Harbor Crossing. The southern section was completed in mid-1997. The Country Park section of Route 3 links Tsing Yi Island to Au Tau, in Yuen Long, via Ting Kau Bridge and Tai Lam Tunnel, and joins the New Territories Circular Road. Route 2 runs from the Kowloon Bay Reclamation, through the airport tunnel, via the East and West Kowloon Corridors, Tsuen Wan Road, Tuen Mun Road, and Yuen Long Southern Bypass, to the junction of Castle Peak Road and Lok Ma Chau Border Link Road. Route 4 runs along the foothills that separate Kowloon from the New Territories, connects Lai Chi Kok with Kwun Tong, and extends to Tseung Kwan O via the Tseung Kwan O Tunnel.

AIRPORT RAILWAY

MA WAN

TSING YI

RPORT AT
LAP KOK

THE BROTHERS

AIRPORT RAILWAY

WEST KOWLOON EXP

TUNG CHUNG
DEVELOPMENT
PHASE I

LANTAU FIXED
CROSSING

ROUTE 3

KOWLOON

WEST KOWLOON
RECLAMATION

WESTERN HARBOUR
CROSSING

NORTH LANTAU
EXPRESSWAY

CENTRAL &
RECLA
PHA

PENG CHAU

AU ISLAND

CHAU KUNG TO

HONG KONG ISL

HEI LING CHAU

CHEUNG CHAU

LAMMA ISLAND

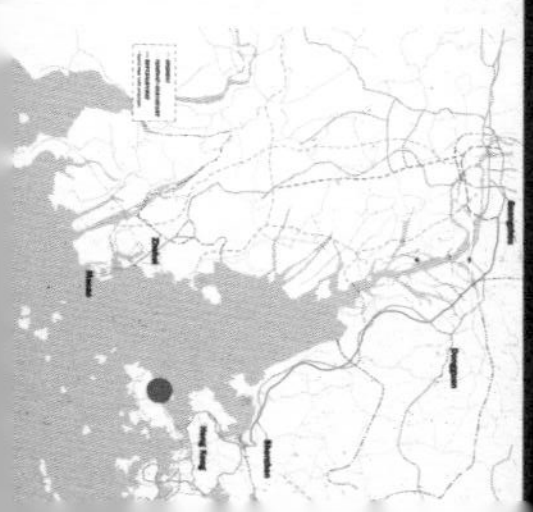

Route 5, a section of the New Territories Circular Road, connects Sha Tin with Tsuen Wan through the Shing Mun Tunnel. The Metroplan of Hong Kong is a comprehensive land use-transportation plan for combined areas of Tsuen Wan, Kwai Chung, Kowloon, New Kowloon, and Hong Kong Island. It provides an overall strategy until the year 2011 for an improved urban environment, the redevelopment of dilapidated districts, the enhancement of Hong Kong's role as an international finance, business, tourism, and trading center. The plan will balance the distribution of employment and provide a multichoice efficient transportation system.

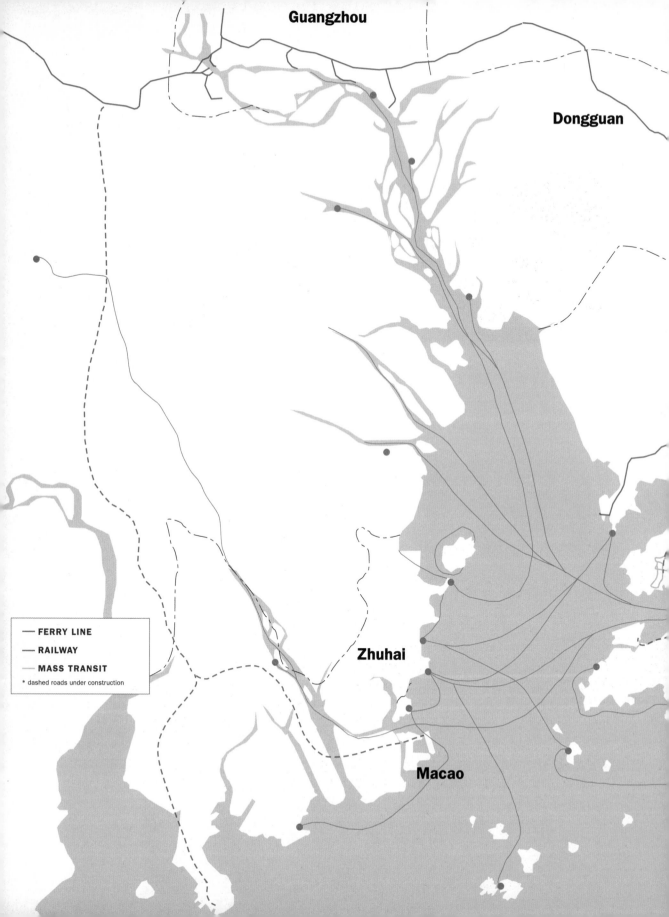

Guangzhou

Dongguan

Zhuhai

Macao

FERRY LINE
RAILWAY
MASS TRANSIT
* dashed roads under construction

henzhen

Kong

LAND/WATER

BICYCLE **L1** 513
AUTOMOBILE **L2** 515
BUS **L3** 521
FERRY **L4** 523
RAILWAY **L5** 529
MASS TRANSIT SYSTEM **L6** 545

Water and land transportation in the Pearl River Delta channeled 4.9 billion passengers at a rate of 155 passengers per second in 1995. The ferry, though an ancient mode of transportation, is still the most efficient way to cross the delta in one hour. In 1994, Shenzhen, Guangzhou, Zhuhai, Macau, and Hong Kong had a total of 1.55 million vehicles and 7,400 kilometers of road. Railways connect cities on the east side of the delta with Beijing and Guangzhou, but there is no railway on the west side to link Zhuhai with the rest of China. Therefore, Zhuhai aims to complete the Guangzhou-Zhuhai Railway by the end of 2003.

The Guangzhou Metro is still under construction. It has been interrupted several times for lack of interest in the project. The investors are more keen on the commercial development along the metro than on the metro itself. In 1995, the Hong Kong Mass Transit Railway handled 2.5 million passengers per day, which is 25 percent of its 6.3 million population.

In 1996, Guangzhou had three million bicycles, which represented 33 percent of the traffic within the city. The implementation of the Guangzhou Metro system and improvements on public transportation networks will cause that percentage to drop to 13 percent by 2010.

Vehicle density of Shenzhen, in the PRD, in 1994: 258,038 vehicles, including 69,710 motorcycles. The city had 944 kilometers of road, which means there were 273 vehicles per kilometer of road.

Guangzhou has 667,323 vehicles, including 448,281 motorcycles. About 4,039 kilometers of road means there are 165 vehicles per kilometer of road. Private transportation between Guangzhou and Hong Kong in 1995 handled 123,000 passengers, 3.1 percent of the traffic between the two cities. Zhuhai has 97,703 vehicles, including 28,800 motorcycles. It has about 584 kilometers of road, which means there are 167 vehicles per kilometer of road. Macau has 68,000 vehicles and about 130 kilometers of road, which means there are 523 vehicles per kilometer of road.

Hong Kong has 458,785 licensed vehicles, including 22,333 motorcycles. There are about 1,717 kilometers of road, which means there are 267 vehicles per kilometer of road. According to the Hong Kong 2011 Development Strategy, nitrogen dioxide levels in Tuen Mun will increase 70 percent between 2001 and 2011, due to the border traffic between Shenzhen and Hong Kong. The figure will go up further

In 1995, express bus services between Guangzhou and Hong Kong carried 700,000 passengers, 21 percent of the traffic from all modes of transportation combined. A bus ride to Guangzhou via the superhighway takes 3 hours; and there are

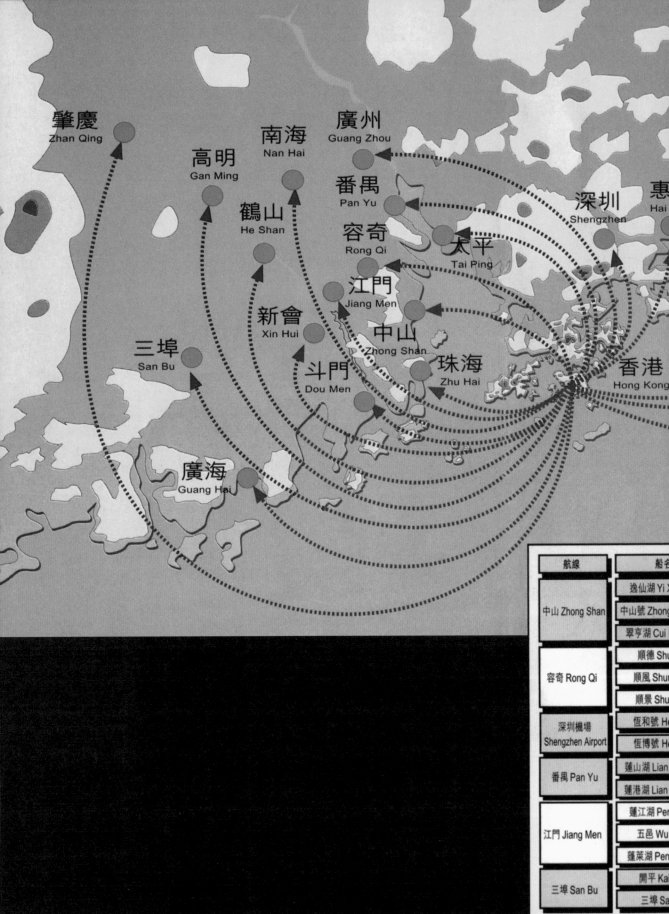

肇慶
Zhan Qing

高明
Gan Ming

南海
Nan Hai

廣州
Guang Zhou

深圳
Shengzhen

惠
Hai

鶴山
He Shan

番禺
Pan Yu

容奇
Rong Qi

太平
Tai Ping

三埠
San Bu

新會
Xin Hui

江門
Jiang Men

中山
Zhong Shan

珠海
Zhu Hai

香港
Hong Kong

斗門
Dou Men

廣海
Guang Hai

航線	船名
中山 Zhong Shan	逸仙湖 Yi X
	中山號 Zhong
	翠亨湖 Cui
容奇 Rong Qi	順德 Shu
	順風 Shun
	順景 Shu
深圳機場 Shengzhen Airport	恆和號 He
	恆博號 He
番禺 Pan Yu	蓮山湖 Lian
	蓮港湖 Lian
江門 Jiang Men	蓮江湖 Pen
	五邑 Wu
	蓬萊湖 Pen
三埠 San Bu	開平 Kai
	三埠 Sa

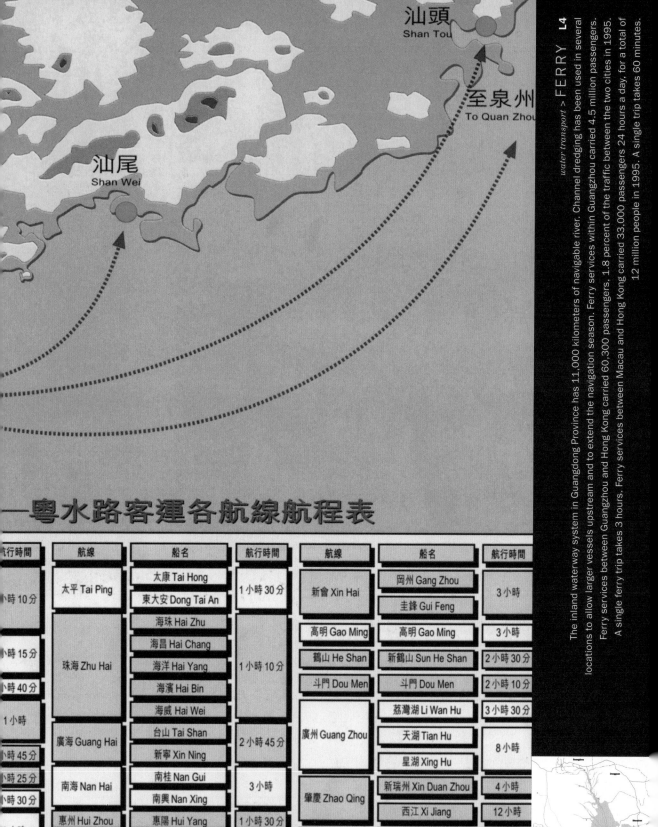

汕頭 Shan Tou

汕尾 Shan Wei

至泉州 To Quan Zhou

water transport > F E R R Y **L4**

The inland waterway system in Guangdong Province has 11,000 kilometers of navigable river. Channel dredging has been used in several locations to allow larger vessels upstream and to extend the navigation season. Ferry services within Guangzhou carried 4.5 million passengers. Ferry services between Guangzhou and Hong Kong carried 60,300 passengers, 1.8 percent of the traffic between the two cities in 1995. A single ferry trip takes 3 hours. Ferry services between Macau and Hong Kong carried 33,000 passengers 24 hours a day, for a total of 12 million people in 1995. A single trip takes 60 minutes.

粵水路客運各航線航程表

航行時間	航線	船名	航行時間		航線	船名	航行時間
時 10 分	太平 Tai Ping	太康 Tai Hong	1 小時 30 分		新會 Xin Hai	岡州 Gang Zhou	3 小時
		東大安 Dong Tai An				圭鋒 Gui Feng	
時 15 分	珠海 Zhu Hai	海珠 Hai Zhu	1 小時 10 分		高明 Gao Ming	高明 Gao Ming	3 小時
		海昌 Hai Chang			鶴山 He Shan	新鶴山 Sun He Shan	2 小時 30 分
時 40 分		海洋 Hai Yang			斗門 Dou Men	斗門 Dou Men	2 小時 10 分
1 小時		海濱 Hai Bin			廣州 Guang Zhou	荔灣湖 Li Wan Hu	3 小時 30 分
	廣海 Guang Hai	海威 Hai Wei	2 小時 45 分			天湖 Tian Hu	8 小時
時 45 分		台山 Tai Shan				星湖 Xing Hu	
		新寧 Xin Ning			肇慶 Zhao Qing	新瑞州 Xin Duan Zhou	4 小時
時 25 分	南海 Nan Hai	南桂 Nan Gui	3 小時			西江 Xi Jiang	12 小時
時 30 分		南興 Nan Xing				潼湖 Tong Hu	14 小時
3 小時	惠州 Hui Zhou	惠陽 Hui Yang	1 小時 30 分		汕頭 Shan Tou	金湖 Jin Shan	
	泉州 Quan Zhou	金湖 Jin Hu	23 小時			南湖 Nan Hu	
時 25 分		南湖 Nan Hu					
	汕尾 Shan Wei	東湖 Dong Hu	8 小時				

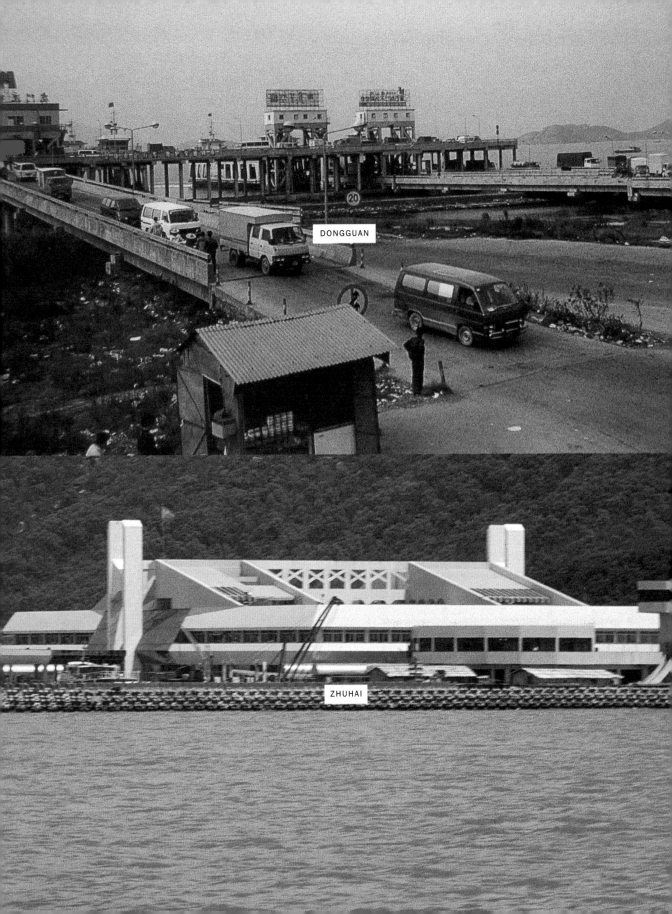

DONGGUAN

ZHUHAI

GUANGZHOU

MACAO

Ferry services within Hong Kong provide linkages from within the Victoria Harbor to the outlying islands and the northwestern New Territories.
The Hongkong & Yaumati Ferry Company Limited owns and operates 80 vessels on 24 ferry routes, which carried 95,000 passengers and 1,200
vehicles daily, for a total of 35 million people and 430,000 vehicles, in 1995. The Star Ferry Company Limited operates 12 vessels on three routes,
which carried 94,670 passengers daily for a total of 34 million people, in 1995. The new terminals are inspired by the form of an ocean liner

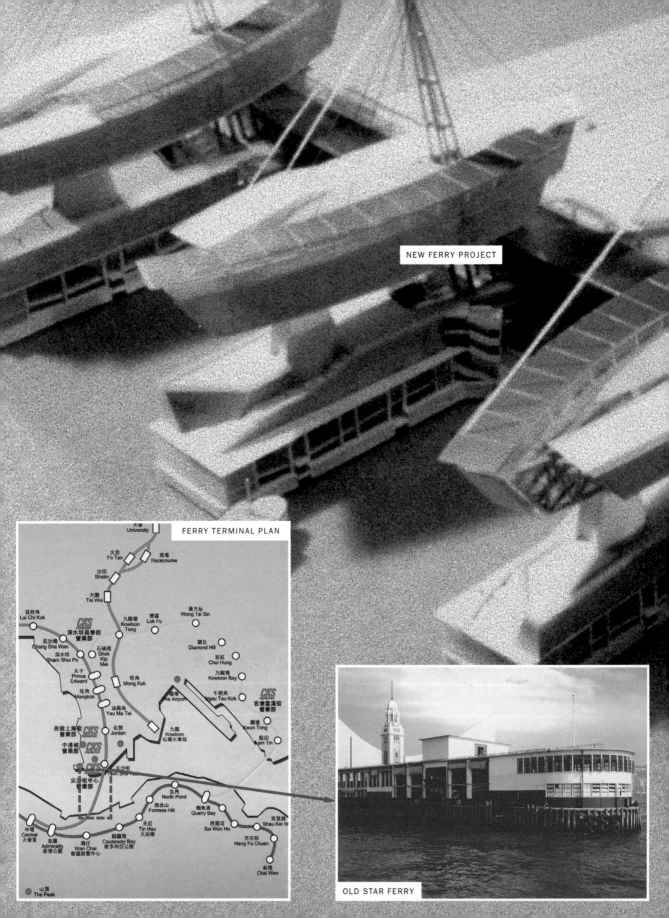

NEW FERRY PROJECT

FERRY TERMINAL PLAN

OLD STAR FERRY

Ferry services among Shenzhen, Dongguan, Guangzhou, Zhuhai, Macau, and Hong Kong carried 7 million passengers in 1995. A total of 28 routes are offered by ten companies. Panyu Nansha terminal, in Dongguan, provides the fastest ferry link in the delta. A new 42 meter twin-hulled catamaran, the Nansha-28, has a cruising speed of 45 nautical miles per hour; it also has a night-vision navigation system, which can extend the present six trips per day to 12 trips per day. It takes 50 minutes to traverse the 38-nautical-mile route from Nansha to Hong Kong, a speed that beats a road trip via the GSZ Superhighway and Dongguan Boca Tigris Bridge. Nansha City received more than 250,000 visitors from Hong Kong in 1995.

SHENZHEN HONG KONG CUSTOMS

The Guangzhou-Shenzhen-Zhuhai (GSZ) Railway, connecting the Hong Kong Kowloon-Canton (Guangzhou) Railway (KCR), begins in Shenzhen-Lowu station and ends at Guangzhou Central station. The GSZ Railway Company operates 26 train services per day between the two cities; a single trip takes 3 hours.

SHENZEN LOWU STATION

GUANGZHOU THIS WAY →

BEIJING

SHENZHEN

BEIJING-SHENZHEN-KOWLOON RAILWAY OPENING

DF₁₁0002

The Beijing-Shenzhen-Kowloon Railway, a 2,356-kilometer railway that links the Beijing West Railway station to the Shenzhen-Lowu station, was completed in November 1995. It started operating in August 1996. The railway, which cost U.S.$4.8 billion, is China's third north-south rail trunk line. It winds through nine municipalities to reach Dongguan Changping, where it starts running parallel to the existing GSZ Railway to Lowu station.

GUANGZHOU THIS WAY →

華強音响
HUAQIANG

GUANGZHOU CENTRAL STATION →

The Shenzhen Shekou-Yantian Railway is a 35-kilometer system that connects Shekou Port, on the west side of Shenzhen, with Yantian Port, in the east. The railway, which crosses the GSZ Railway and the Beijing-Shenzhen-Kowloon Railway, provides freight services only; it started operating in 1995. The Guangzhou government has proposed two elevated railways, at a length totaling 50 kilometers, which will connect the Guangzhou Tianhe Railway station with the Guangzhou Economic and Technology Development Zone, and the northern part of the city with the new Huadu International Airport.

SHENZHEN

BEIJING

GUANGZHOU

2 RAILWAYS RUN PARALLEL THROUGH DONGGUAN

The Hong Kong KCR started operating in 1910, and it was doubled, tracked, and electrified in the early 1980s. The Kowloon-Canton Railway Corporation (KCRC) has been operating the entire system since 1982. It is a 34-kilometer system that has 13 stations and provides train services between Hung Hom, in Kowloon, and Sheung Shui, in the New Territories. Each train has 12 compartments; the system has a total of 351 compartments. The KCR handled 632,700 passengers per day, for a total of 230 million people, in 1995. The railway also provides freight services to the interior of China.

land transport > RAILWAY

The KCRC and GSZ Railway companies provide express train services between the Hong Kong Hung Hom Terminal and Guangzhou Centra
and carried 2.1 million passengers (62 percent of the flow) between the two cities in 1995. There are four round-trip services
A single trip takes 1 hour 55 minutes. Five round-trips were available by the end of 1996 and 12 round trips by 2000. Also by the end

FUTURE ZHUHAI RAILROAD STATION

The Guangzhou-Zhuhai Railway, a 177-kilometer system, will reach the Zhuhai Western District and Gaolan Port via Foshan and Jiangmen counties. Site preparation began in September 1996 and construction followed. Zhuhai aimed to complete the project in three years. At U.S.$500 million, it cost more than other inland railways because of geographic conditions and time constraints. The Zhuhai municipal government was responsible for funding 70 percent of the project, Jiangmen county contributed 10 percent, and the cities along the railway line share 20 percent of the cost.

Tin Shui Wai

Long Ping

Kam Tin

Yuen Long

Existing LRT

Tuen Mun North

West

Tuen Mun Central

Tsue

hek Lap Kok

Airport Railway

Pos
Ter

W
Pass

LANT

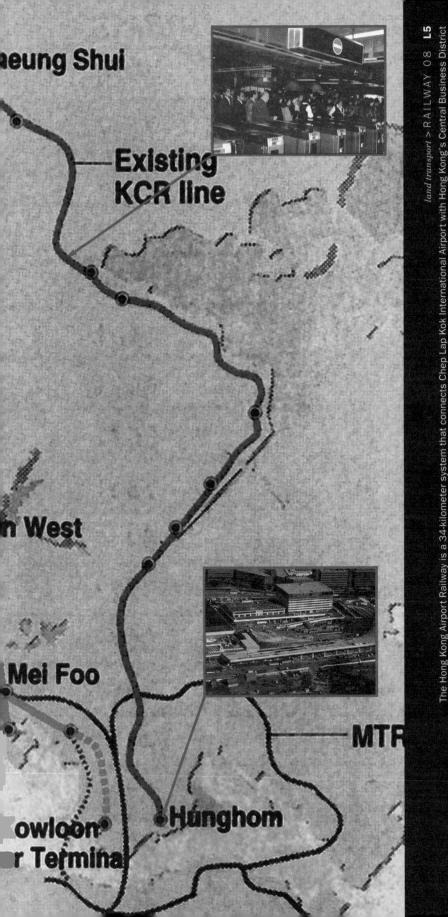

aeung Shui

Existing
KCR line

n West

Mei Foo

MTR

owloon
r Termina

Hunghom

The Hong Kong Airport Railway is a 34-kilometer system that connects Chep Lap Kok International Airport with Hong Kong's Central Business District (CBD). The railway has an Airport Express Line (AEL), which enables passengers to travel from the CBD to the airport in 23 minutes; the Lantau Line (LAL) stops at nine stations. Both lines have a maximum operating speed of 135 kilometers per hour. The AEL operates six-compartment trains and trains with as many as ten compartments; each car carries 64 seated passengers at an 8-minute frequency, or 4.5 minutes if necessary. The LAL is a more conventional mass transit operation and connects to the Tsuen Wan Line of the Mass Transit Railway. At a cost of U.S.$4.4 billion, the system has been operating since 1998, just before the Chek Lap Kok airport opened.

The Mass Transit Railway Corporation finances, develops, and manages the entire project. Stations at Tung Chung. Tsing Yi. Tai Kok Tsui. Kowloon. and Hong Kong contain property developments; a total of 62 hectares of land will provide 1,893,000 square meters of residential development and 937,000 square meters of commercial development.

The Hong Kong Western Corridor Railway (WCR) proposal was published in *Railway Development Strategy* in 1994, after years of numerous studies. The Kowloon-Canton Railway Corporation (KCRC) is responsible for the technical studies for the WCR project. The WCR is a 51.3-kilometer system that runs from West Kowloon to Tuen Mun, with ten stations. The technical studies, which cost U.S.$144 million, were completed in October 1997. The site of the project involves 400 hectares of land, 130 hectares of which are privately owned; the Hong Kong government needs to spend U.S.$640 million to acquire the private land.

The Shenzhen government proposed a mass transit system to replace the multiline light transit proposal that was approved by the State Council in 1992. The new mass transit proposal suggests a 39.5-kilometer system that will run along Route 107, and connect Lowu with Shenzhen International Airport, through Futian District, the Splendid China theme park, Overseas Chinese Village, Nanshan, and Xixiang. The light rail proposals cover the existing CBD and Lowu, and connects Huanggang Crossing with Guanlan Inspection Point, via the future Shenzhen CBD, Futian. It also connects Shekou Port with Changlingpi Inspection Point via Nanshan, Yantian Port with Lowu via Liantang, and Shatoutao Crossing and Lowu with Longgang via Buji Inspection Point.

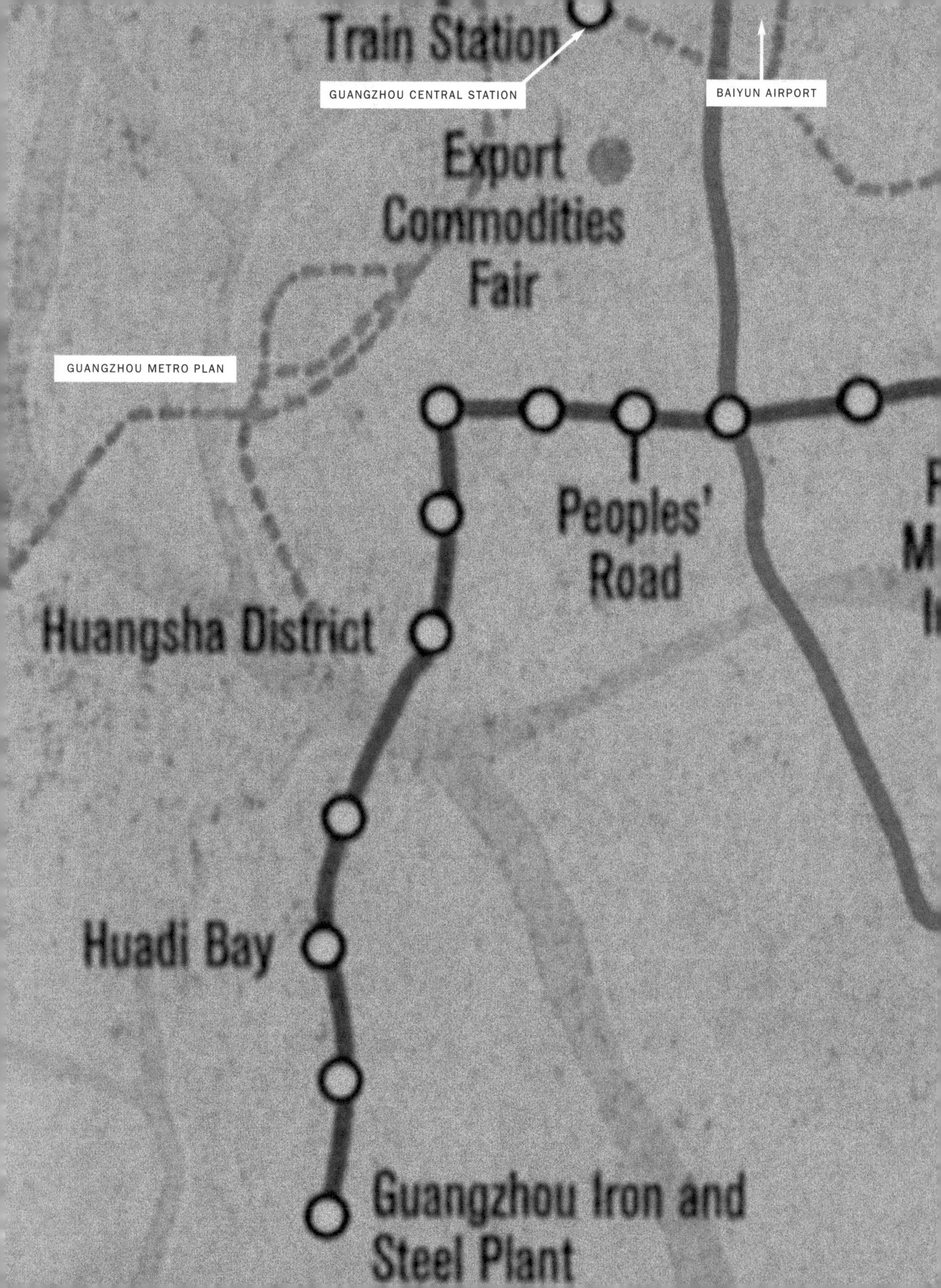
Train Station
GUANGZHOU CENTRAL STATION
BAIYUN AIRPORT
Export Commodities Fair
GUANGZHOU METRO PLAN
Peoples' Road
Huangsha District
Huadi Bay
Guangzhou Iron and Steel Plant

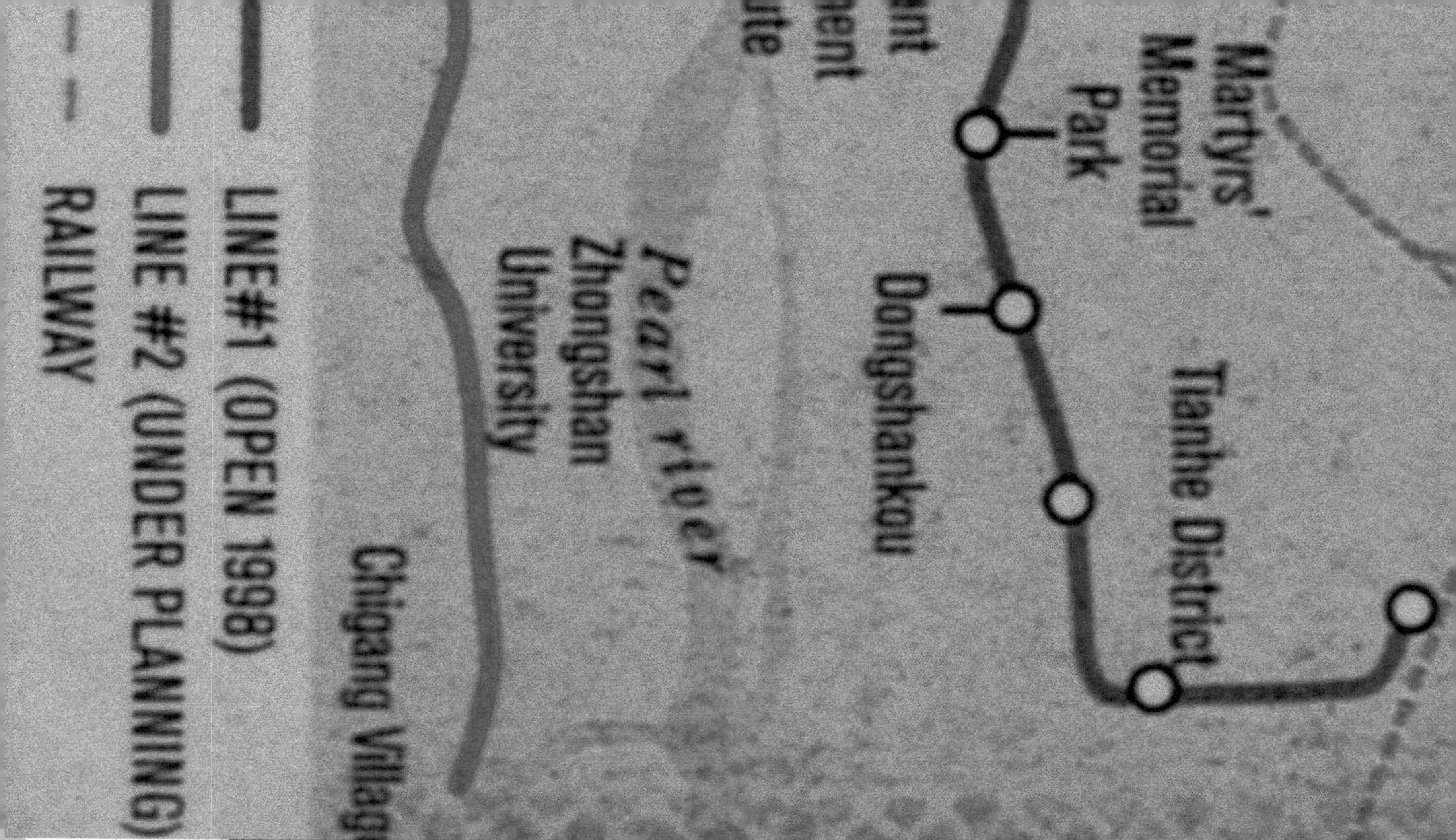

Martyrs'
Memorial
Park

Tianhe District

Dongshankou

ent
ent
ute

Pearl river
Zhongshan
University

Chigang Villag

LINE#1 (OPEN 1998)

LINE #2 (UNDER PLANNING)

RAILWAY

Guangzhou Metro, phase I, an east-west line, is an 18.5-kilometer mass transit system that handles 13.6 million passengers annually with a speed of two minutes per train. The line absorbs 15 percent of the traffic within the city and cost U.S.$1.8 billion. Two kilometers of the rail is above ground, the remaining 16.5 kilometers underground; it operates with 16 stations. There are 24 land parcels, a total of 105,820 square meters of property development, along the metro line and on top of the stations; the development of this property financed the metro construction. Phase II proposes a 26 kilometer system with 22 stations; phase III will be a 13 kilometer subway with nine stations.

HONG KONG METRO STATION

The Hong Kong Mass Transit Railway (MTR), a 43-kilometer three-line system, which comprises 38 stations, handled 2.5 million passengers per day, for a total of 816 million people, in 1995. The system started operating in 1978. The Tsuen Line and Kwun Tong Line, which circulate the Kowloon Peninsula, connect with the Hong Kong Line and run along the north side of the island, through Admiralty and Quarry Bay stations. The system is owned and operated by the Mass Transit Railway Corporation. The Hong Kong Light Rail Transit (LRT), a 32-kilometer system, operates eight routes, with 57 stops in the northwestern New Territories, including Tuen Mun, Yuen Long, and Tin Shui Wai. The rail started operating in 1988. It is owned and operated by the Kowloon-Canton Railway Corporation. The phase III extension was completed in March 1995. A fleet of one hundred cars, running with single or double compartments at 40-60 kilometers per hour, carried 377,000 passengers a day, for a total of 134 million people, in 1995.

land transport > MASS TRANSIT SYSTEM 04 LE

The Hong Kong Electric Tramway, a 13-kilometer double-track system, has been operating on the island, from Kennedy Town to Shau Kei Wan and Happy Valley, since 1904. It has 163 trams and six overlapping lines. The system is owned and operated by Hongkong Tramways Ltd. The trams carried 12,720 passengers a day, for a total of 4.6 million people, in 1995. Hong Kong Funicular Rail, a 1.4-kilometer tramway, has been running from Central to The Peak since 1888; it is operated by the Peak Tramways Company Limited. The system was modernized in 1989. The line carried 11,000 passengers per day, for a total of 4 million people, in 1995

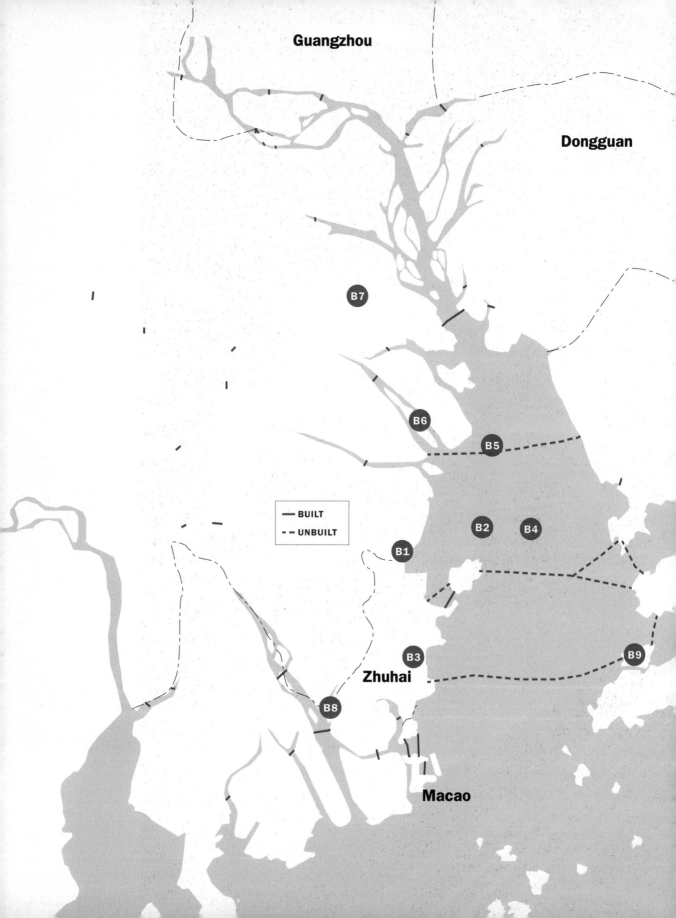

Guangzhou

Dongguan

B7

B6

B5

B2   B4

B1

BUILT
UNBUILT

B3

Zhuhai

B9

B8

Macao

Shenzhen

Kong

BRIDGES

ZHUHAI LINGDING OCEAN BRIDGE PROPOSAL I **B1** 555

ZHUHAI LINGDING OCEAN BRIDGE PROPOSAL II **B2** 559

ZHUHAI LINGDING OCEAN BRIDGE PROPOSAL III **B3** 561

SHENZHEN WESTERN CORRIDOR PROPOSAL I **B4** 563

GOLDEN GATE BRIDGE AT SPLENDID CHINA THEME PARK **B5** 565

SHENZHEN WESTERN CORRIDOR PROPOSAL II **B6** 567

DONGGUAN BOCA TIGRIS (HUMEN) BRIDGE **B7** 569

MACAO TAIPA BRIDGE I AND II **B8** 573

HONG KONG LANTAU FIXED CROSSING **B9** 579

The Pearl River Delta has a total of 1,260 bridges. Most of them are inner-city and river bridges. The most ambitious proposals for new bridges plan for the crossing of the Pearl River Estuary and link Zhuhai, Shenzhen, and Hong Kong. Zhuhai has three such proposals. The construction of the 40-kilometer Lingding Ocean Bridge has started from Zhuahi, but the location of its termination was yet to be determined; it would end either in Shenzhen or Hong Kong. Shenzhen has proposed a 30-kilometer bridge to cross the delta and link its airport to the west bank. Shenzhen has also proposed a 5-kilometer bridge that will link the Western Corridor with Hong Kong. The Dongguan Boca Tigris Bridge was completed in 1997 and was the first bridge to cross the estuary. Macau Taipa Bridge II connects Macau's airport with the mainland of Macau. The 2.2-kilometer Hong Kong Lantau Fixed Crossing will be the world's longest suspension bridge to carry both rail and road traffic.

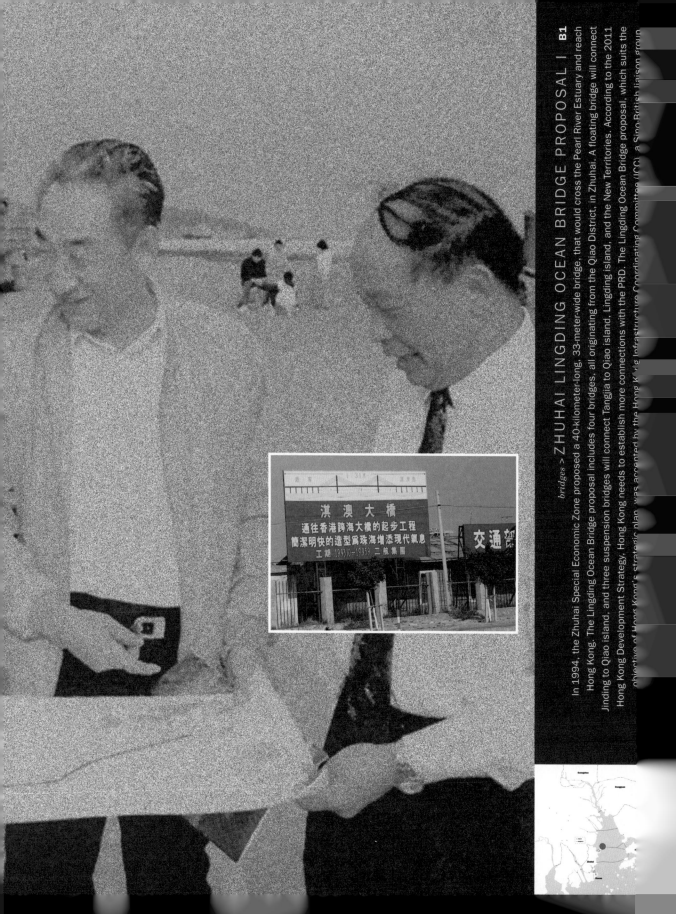

In 1994, the Zhuhai Special Economic Zone proposed a 40-kilometer-long, 33-meter-wide bridge, that would cross the Pearl River Estuary and reach Hong Kong. The Lingding Ocean Bridge proposal includes four bridges, all originating from the Qiao District, in Zhuhai. A floating bridge will connect Jinding to Qiao island, and three suspension bridges will connect Tangjia to Qiao island, Lingding island, and the New Territories. According to the 2011 Hong Kong Development Strategy, Hong Kong needs to establish more connections with the PRD. The Lingding Ocean Bridge proposal, which suits the objective of Hong Kong's strategic plan was accepted by the Hong Kong Infrastructure Coordinating Committee (ICC), a Sino-British liaison group.

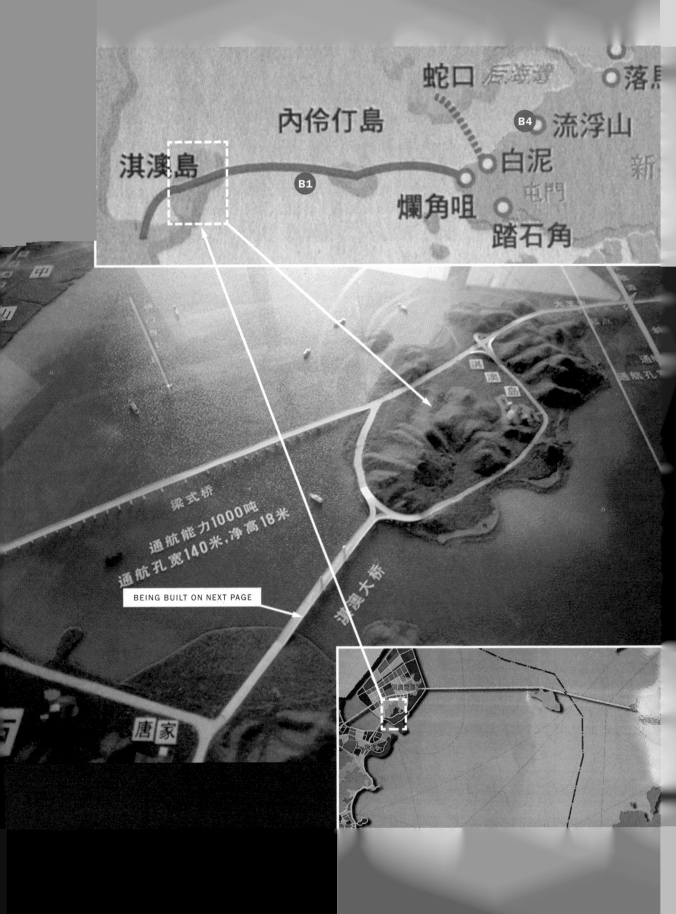

蛇口　后海灣　落馬

內伶仃島

B4　流浮山

淇澳島　　　　　白泥

B1　　新

爛角咀　屯門

踏石角

梁式桥

通航能力1000吨
通航孔宽140米,净高18米

淇澳大桥

BEING BUILT ON NEXT PAGE

唐家

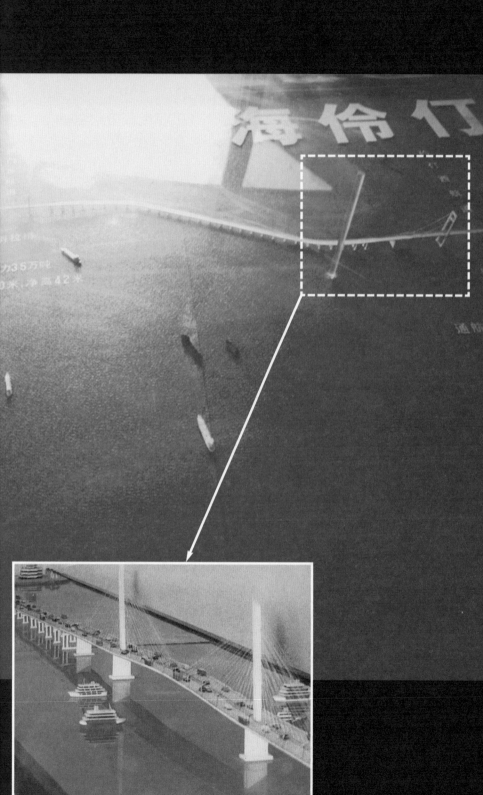

In August 1996, the Hong Kong ICC finally decided that Lan Kok Tsui, in Tuen Mun, would be the landing point for the Lingding Ocean Bridge, in Hong Kong. The committee prepared feasibility studies, and traffic and environmental-impact reports for the project. Submission to the central government followed. In order to improve Zhuhai's accessibility, Zhuhai considers a direct linkage to Hong Kong essential. The Lingding Ocean Bridge will also provide regional linkage between Guangxi and Hong Kong, since the Zhuhai road network had extended to the west side. Water pipes that run alongside the bridge will deliver water to Hong Kong from Xijiang (the West River). The bridge proposal has been partially realized on the Zhuhai side. The Lingding Ocean Bridge will cost approximately U.S.$1.3 billion. The Hong Kong government will pay for the studies of the transport links. Zhuhai will be responsible for the bridge construction. The Zhuhai government has approached the Hong Kong government for financial assistance, but was rejected. Zhuhai also proposed a "land for bridge" deal, as well as a build-operate-transfer method, to attract foreign investors.

557 *Pearl River Delta* | INFRASTRUCTURE

UNDER CONSTRUCTION

The Lingding Ocean Bridge has the option to connect Zhuhai with the Shenzhen Special Economic Zone. Proposal II suggests that the last portion of the Lingding Ocean Bridge, which would start from Lingding Island, would merge with the proposed Western Corridor bridge. at Shekou in Shenzhen, cross Deep Bay, and land in the New Territories. Shenzhen remains skeptical about the two proposals. A bridge across the estuary would disturb the delta current, and the water channel along the east bank of the delta would be affected. Shenzhen officials were also concerned that the Western Corridor bridge would not be able to handle the additional traffic from the Zhuhai side.

QIAO ISLAND

bridges > ZHUHAI LINGDING OCEAN BRIDGE PROPOSAL III **B3**

The third proposal for the Lingding Ocean Bridge places the starting point in Zhuhai Jiuzhou and links to Chek Lap Kok International Airport in Lantau, Hong Kong. The study for the third proposal was initiated by the Macau government. since Jiuzhou is close to the Macau border. When Macau was returned to China in 1999, coordination between Zhuhai and Macau on the bridge proposal began to generate more leverage. Construction of the 1.7-kilometer Qiao Bridge, connecting Tangjia and Qiao island, started in 1994. Some foundation work has been completed: a section of pillars have been planted and some lower sections of the bridge have been shipped to the site to be connected. The Zhuhai Planning Bureau prepared a master plan for Qiao island. "Magical pigeon" is the theme of its future tourist and high-tech industrial community.

西乡

前湾电厂

丹湾港

丹湾电厂

赤湾港

SHENZEN

蛇口水厂

蛇口港

B4

In May 1995, the Shenzhen Special Economic Zone proposed a 5-kilometer, Western Corridor bridge, which would cross the Deep Bay and reach to Hong Kong. The corridor would link Shenzhen Shekou to Tuen Mun, of Hong Kong. Carrying road and rail traffic, the corridor was to be the fourth crossing between the two cities. The Western Corridor proposal, which suited the objectives of the 2011 Hong Kong Development Strategy, would ease traffic congestion on the three existing crossings, which handled 22,000 automobiles a day in 1995. In August 1996, the Hong Kong ICC decided that Pak Nai, in Tuen Mun, would be the landing point for the Western Corridor bridge. The corridor and the proposed Zhuhai Lingding Ocean Bridge would merge with the Hong Kong New Territories Circular Road, and the railway from Shenzhen might join the proposed Western Corridor Railway of Hong Kong. The Western Corridor project will strengthen the transportation network along the east bank of the delta and connect the Shenzhen airport, Shekou Port, and Chiwan Port with Tuen Mun, Kwai Chung Port, and Chep Lap Kok International Airport in Hong Kong. The Western Corridor will cost about U.S.$500 million. The Shenzhen government is seeking investors. The Western Corridor also has the option to connect Shenzhen Nanshan with Hong Kong Tuen Mun: it can be the second crossing and can channel more traffic along the east bank of the delta.

世界之窗

B5

INFRASTRUCTURE

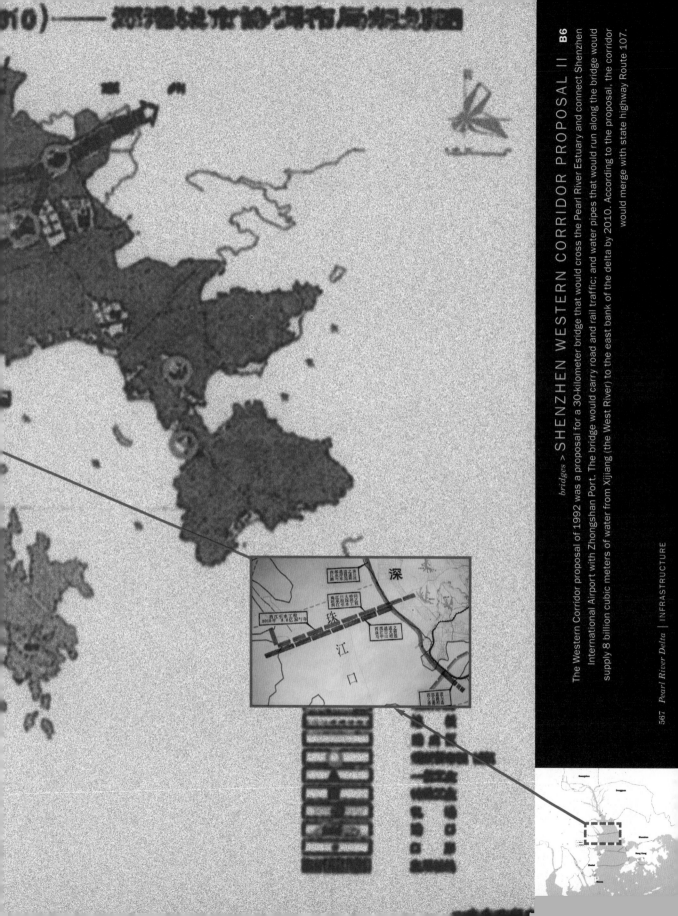

The Western Corridor proposal of 1992 was a proposal for a 30-kilometer bridge that would cross the Pearl River Estuary and connect Shenzhen International Airport with Zhongshan Port. The bridge would carry road and rail traffic; and water pipes that would run along the bridge would supply 8 billion cubic meters of water from Xijiang (the West River) to the east bank of the delta by 2010. According to the proposal, the corridor would merge with state highway Route 107.

深

珠

江

口

The Dongguan Boca Tigris Bridge comprises a 4.58-kilometer-long, 31.5-meter-wide bridge and approach roads, for a total length of 16 kilometers. It will carry six lanes of road traffic, for a daily capacity of 55,000 vehicles. The bridge links phase I of the GSZ Superhighway at Dongguan Taiping Interchange, on the east bank of the delta, with Panyu Nansha, on the west bank.

BEFORE 1994

UNDER CONSTRUCTION 1995

UNDER CONSTRUCTION 1996

BEFORE 1994

AFTER 1996

bridges > DONGGUAN BOCA TIGRIS (HUMEN) BRIDGE 02 **B7**

The entire Dongguan Boca Tigris Bridge project cost U.S.$342 million. Hopewell Holdings. of Hong Kong. took a 30 percent stake in the 30-year build-operate-transfer concession: Guangdong Provincial Highway Construction took 40 percent; and the Panyu City Bridge Administration. the Dongguan City Highway Bridge Development Company, and the Guangdong Transport Investment Company each hold 10 percent of the project. Construction began in 1992. The main suspension, 888 meters in length, was completed in July 1996. Boca Tigris Bridge opened in June 1997 and is the first fixed crossing in the Pearl River Estuary.

571 *Pearl River Delta* | INFRASTRUCTURE

Macau Taipa Bridge II was part of the Macau development strategy. Construction began in 1990, and the bridge opened in February 1994. It cost U.S. $77 million. The 3.9-kilometer-long, 19.3-meter-wide bridge, with a total of 1.1 kilometers of bridge approach at both ends, carries four lanes of road traffic. It links Macau's international airport, Ka-Ho Port, and the Macau Central Business District (CBD).

TAIPA

MACAO →

TAIPA

MACAO →

The Macau Taipa Bridge II crossing, over the navigation channel, has a main span of 70 meters and a vertical clearance of 30 meters. The viaducts and bridges are precast double reinforced concrete slabs, supported by precast piled foundations.

Kap Shui Mun Bridge, Ma Wan Viaduct, and Tsing Ma Bridge belong to the Lantau Fixed Crossing, which connects Lantau Island with Kowloon Peninsula via Tsing Yi Island. The Kap Shui Mun Bridge is a 820-meter cable-stayed crossing that spans Ma Wan Island and Lantau Island. Ma Wan Viaduct, 500 meters in length, connects the Kap Shui Mun Bridge with Tsing Ma Bridge, which spans the Ma Wan Channel to reach Tsing Yi Island.

THE FUTURE VISION

Lantau Fixed Crossing cost U.S.$516 million. Construction began in 1992, and was completed in April 1997. The entire crossing has a dual three-lane road on the upper deck; the enclosed lower deck contains two rail tracks and two single lanes for use in severe weather conditions. The 2.2-kilometer Tsing Ma Bridge is the world's longest suspension bridge to carry both rail and road traffic. There are two reinforced concrete towers, 206 meters in height, holding up a total of 160,000 kilometers of cable—enough to circle the Earth four times.

bridges > HONG KONG LANTAU FIXED CROSSING 03 **B9**

There are three bridge proposals in the 2011 Hong Kong Development Strategy. One proposes a connection from Tuen Mun Circular Route to Lantau Port. Container Terminals 10 and 11. A second proposes a bridge that will start from Lantau Port, cross the Green Bay, and reach Green Island, which became part of Hong Kong Island through reclamation. The bridge of the third proposal extends the Tuen Mun Port Highway to join the North Lantau Expressway on Lantau Island.

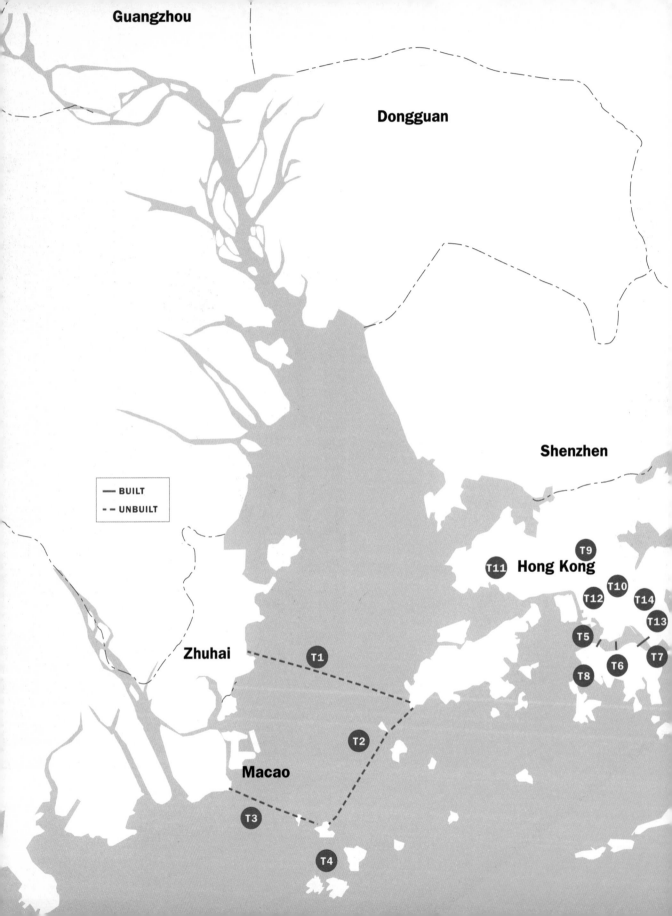

TUNNELS

ZHUHAI EASTERN ISLANDS TUNNELS PROPOSAL   **T1, T2, T3, T4**

HONG KONG   **T5, T6, T7, T8, T9, T10, T11, T12, T13, T14**

587

589

According to a Zhuhai planner, tunnels are less desirable than bridges because they are not visible. However, Zhuhai has prepared the Strategic Program Plan for the Eastern Islands District, to link a group of islands with Lantau Island, of Hong Kong. The plan also assigns a single industry to each island, in order to form a heavy industrial zone. Hong Kong tunnels handled 0.5 million vehicles per day, for a total of 180 million vehicles, in 1995. Air pollution in tunnels affects at least one million passengers for a duration of 2 to 15 minutes per day, depending on how heavily the tunnel is used.

香
洲

港澳小型船
泊引航锚地

禁止抛锚地

油轮过驳锚地

油轮过驳锚地

T1

牛头岛

大
濠
洲

中心洲

桂山

澳门

青
洲
水
道

青洲引航锚地
头洲引航锚地

头引航锚地

引航检疫
及装卸基地

油轮过
驳锚地

T2

禁止抛锚地

小蜘洲

外轮

横琴岛

水
道
西
大

水
道

T3

黄茅岛

万

口澳东
道水

竹洲岛

T4

小万山

白沥岛
列

大万山
岛

外轮锚地

外轮锚地

港

蜘洲

外伶仃

三门列岛

温洲岛

直湾岛

担

一 列

杆

二洲岛

大

担

尾 水 道

佳

蓬

列

岛

北尖岛

庙湾岛

tunnels > ZHUHAI EASTERN ISLANDS TUNNELS PROPOSAL T1, T2, T3, T4

In the Strategic Program Plan, the Zhuhai government proposed a series of tunnels to establish linkage between Zhuhai and Hong Kong, and to develop the Zhuhai Eastern Islands District. **T1** will cross the Pearl River Estuary from Zhuhai Jiuzhou Port to the southern tip of Hong Kong Lantau Island, where the Chep Lap Kok airport and Container Terminals 10 and 11 are located. **T2** will cross the Dayu Haixia Channel and connect the southern Lantau Island with Dong'ao Island via Niutou Island, which will provide storage and good redistribution services. The natural conditions of Dong'ao Island will be preserved. **T3** will cross the Pearl River Estuary and link Dong'ao Island to Hengqin Island via Huangmao Island, Hengqin Island, 20 kilometers south of the Zhuhai SEZ, will become an Open Economic Zone. Huangmao Island will provide storage and good redistribution. **T4** will connect Baili with the Xiaowanshan Islands, which will be occupied by heavy industry.

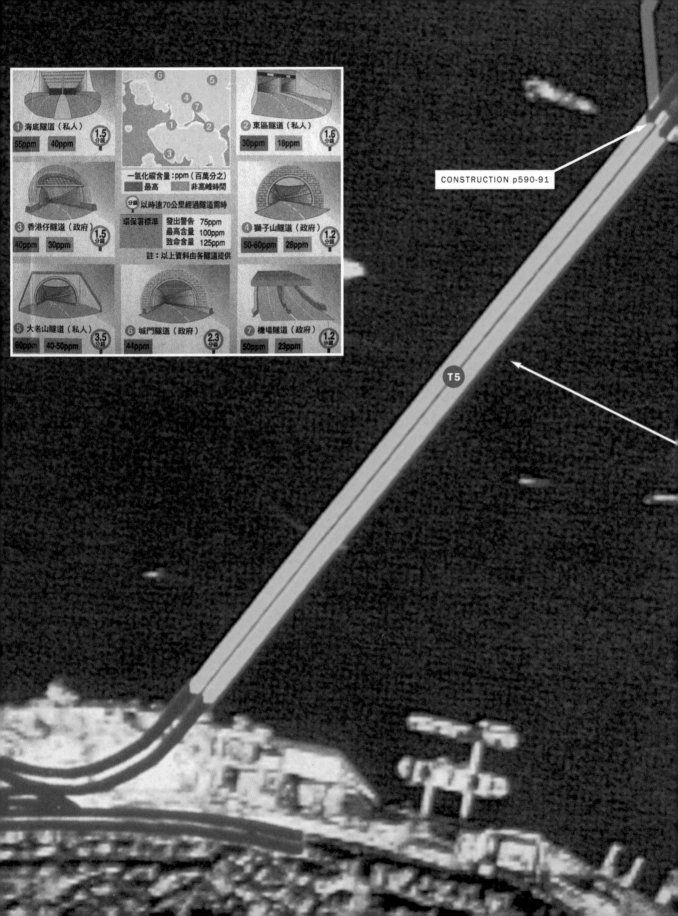

CONSTRUCTION p590-91

T5

一氧化碳含量：ppm（百萬分之）
■ 最高　　□ 非高峰時間

分鐘 以時速70公里經過隧道需時

環保署標準　發出警告　75ppm
　　　　　　最高含量　100ppm
　　　　　　致命含量　125ppm

註：以上資料由各隧道提供

① 海底隧道（私人）
55ppm　40ppm　1.5分鐘

② 東區隧道（私人）
30ppm　18ppm　1.6分鐘

③ 香港仔隧道（政府）
40ppm　30ppm　1.5分鐘

④ 獅子山隧道（政府）
50-60ppm　28ppm　1.2分鐘

⑤ 大老山隧道（私人）
60ppm　40-50ppm　3.5分鐘

⑥ 城門隧道（政府）
44ppm　2.3分鐘

⑦ 機場隧道（政府）
50ppm　23ppm　1.2分鐘

The Western Harbor Crossing, one of the Airport Core Program projects, was opened in March 1997. It is a 1.36 kilometer dual three-lane tunnel, put together by 12 immersed tube sections.

A joint venture between two Japanese firms, Nishimatsu Construction Company and Kumagai Gumi, the construction of **T5** is being managed by the Western Harbor Tunnel Company, which will operate the tunnel for 30 years. The tunnel will cost US $1.6 billion.

tunnels > HONG KONG 03 **T6, T7, T8**

The Cross Harbor (**T6**), opened in 1972, was the first harbor crossing. It connects Hong Kong Causeway Bay with Hung Hom, in Kowloon. The 1.8-kilometer four-lane road-tunnel handled 124,000 vehicles a day, for a total of 45.3 million vehicles, in 1995; it achieved 155 percent of the maximum capacity. The Eastern Harbor Crossing (**T7**), opened in 1989, was the second cross-harbor road-tunnel. It links Hong Kong Quarry Bay and Cha Kwo Ling, in Kowloon. The 2-kilometer 6-lane tunnel handled 86,000 vehicles per day, for a total of 31.4 million vehicles, in 1995; it achieved 75 percent of the tunnel capacity. Aberdeen Tunnel (**T8**) opened in 1982; it circulates between Wong Chuk Hang and Happy Valley. The tunnel handled 58,000 vehicles daily, for a total of 21 million vehicles, in 1995.

593 *Pearl River Delta* | INFRASTRUCTURE

T9

Kwai Chung
葵涌

Kowloon Reserv
九龍水塘

Mei Foo Sun Chuen
美孚新邨

Tai Wai
大圍

T12

T10

Lion Rock Tunnel
獅子山隧道

Route 16
十六號幹線公路

tunnels > H O N G   K O N G   0 4   **T9, T10, T11, T12, T13, T14**

The Shing Mun Tunnel (**T9**) opened in 1990: it links Sha Tin to Tsuen Wan, in the New Territories. It is a 2.6-kilometer dual 2-lane trunk road-tunnel, which handled 52,000 vehicles per day, for a total of 19 million vehicles, in 1995. The Lion Rock Tunnel (**T10**), which connects Kowloon and Sha Tin, in the New Territories, opened in 1967 as a single-tube dual one-lane tunnel. A second tube was added in 1978. The 1.1-kilometer road-tunnel handled 87,000 vehicles per day, for a total of 31.8 million vehicles, in 1995. Tai Lam Tunnel (**T11**), running through the Tai Lam Country Park, connects the New Territories Circular Road with Tuen Mun Road. The 3.8-kilometer six-lane road-tunnel took Bouygues' Dragages et Travaux Publics (HK) Ltd. 38 months to complete: construction started in mid-1996. Route 16 Tunnel (**T12**), 2.2 kilometers in length, serves a section of the 8-kilometer dual 2-lane highway that links Sha Tin with the West Kowloon reclamation. The Tseung Kwan O Tunnel (**T13**) opened in 1990: it links Kowloon with the Tseung Kwan O new town. It handled 36,000 vehicles daily, for a total of 13.2 million vehicles, in 1995. The Tate's Cairn Tunnel (**T14**) opened in 1991; it circulates the northeastern New Territories and Kowloon. The tunnel handled 77,000 vehicles per day, for a total of 28.1 million vehicles, in 1995.

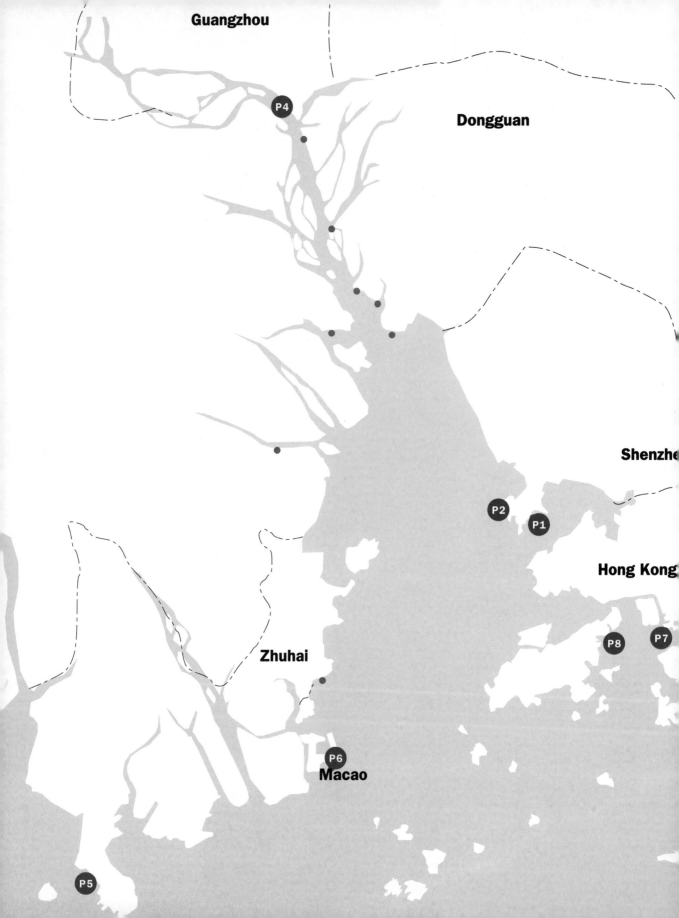

PORTS

SHENZHEN SHEKOU PORT **P1** 599
SHENZHEN CHIWAN PORT **P2** 601
SHENZHEN YANTIAN PORT **P3** 603
GUANGZHOU HUANGPU PORT **P4** 609
ZHUHAI GAOLAN PORT **P5** 611
MACAO KA-HO PORT **P6** 615
HONG KONG KWAI CHUNG TERMINALS **P7** 617
HONG KONG LANTAU PORT **P8** 623

Ports in the Pearl River Delta handled a total of 13.5 million TEUs (20-foot container units) and 250 million tons of cargo, at a rate of 1 TEU every 2 seconds (or 8 tons per second), in 1995. Guangzhou Huangpu Port handled 0.2 million TEUs and 72 million tons of cargo; it ranked as the third busiest port in China that year. According to the 1996 Hong Kong Annual Report, Hong Kong ports handled 12.5 million TEUs and 156 million tons of cargo; they ranked as the second busiest in the world. Ports in other cities of the delta are underutilized. They are handling just 2 to 10 percent of their capacity but plan to be doubled in size every 3 to 5 years.

P3

Shekou Port, one of four international deep-water ports in China, is located on the tip of the Nantou Peninsula, 0.5 nautical miles from Fanshi Water Channel, 45 nautical miles from Guangzhou Huangpu Port, and 20 nautical miles from Macau, Zhuhai, and Hong Kong Victoria Harbor. A dual 2-lane highway connects the terminal with state highway Route 107 and the GSZ Superhighway. A 35-kilometer railway provides linkage between Shekou Port and Yantian Port, in eastern Shenzhen. During 1995, the Shekou Port terminal handled 10 million tons of cargo and 97,000 TEUs, 9.7 percent of its 1 million-TEU annual capacity. The terminal's container-unit capacity will reach 3 million TEUs through additional land procurement and berth construction.

Chiwan Port is located at the tip of the Nantou Peninsula, west of Shekou Port. Terminal construction began in 1983; and it started operating in 1989, with eight berths for cargo handling, seven berths for docking, and a 1.7-kilometer coastline. In 1995, Chiwan Port handled 7 million tons of cargo and 65,400 TEUs, 2 percent of its 3.1 million-TEU annual capacity. The expansion of the port calls for 13 berths of 50,000, 35,000, 25,000, 20,000, 15,000, and 10,000 tons and a 520,000-square-meter dike dock on both sides of the harbor breakwater. As of 2000, Chiwan Port's capacity increased to 8.1 million TEUS.

TO ZHUHAI

TO HONG KONG →

Yantian Port, also one of the four international deep-water ports in China, is located in the northwest of Dapeng Bay, in Shenzhen, is located in the northwest of Dapeng Bay, in Shenzhen, 53 nautical miles from Hong Kong Victoria Harbor, 75 nautical miles from Zhuhai, and 121 nautical miles from Huangpu Port, in Guangzhou. The highways that will link Yantian Port to the GSZ Superhighway and Huizhou are under construction. Yantian Port and Shekou Port are connected by a railway, which was completed in 1995.

The construction of the Yantian Port terminal began in 1987. The facilities are owned by Yantian International Container Terminals Ltd. (YICT), a joint venture of Hutchison Whampoa and Shenzhen Dongpeng Industries. The terminal started operating in mid-1994. In 1995, it handled 0.8 million tons of cargo and 105,700 TEUs, 9 percent of its 1.2 million-TEU annual capacity. The port has three berths of 1,000, 3,000, and 10,000 tons; a 1.4-kilometer quay length on 6 kilometers of coastline; six quay cranes; and 18 rubber-tired gantry cranes. The implementation of phase II of Yantian Port will cost U.S.$17 million began at the end of 1996. The reclamation work has been completed

Phase II of Yantian Port was completed in 1999. The new facilities include three berths of 50,000 tons, which occupy an area of 520,000 square meters; a 950-meter quay length on an extended 10 kilometers of coastline; 11 guay cranes; 17 rubber-tired gantry cranes; and 24,000 square meters of storage space. Ultimately, the port's capacity will reach 80 million tons of cargo annually, and the city of Yantian will accommodate a total population of 100,000 people.

ports > **GUANGZHOU HUANGPU PORT** **P4**

Huangpu Port is located on the east bank of the inner Pearl River, 17 kilometers from the Guangzhou CBD and 50 nautical miles from Hong Kong Victoria Harbor. It is owned by the Guangzhou Municipal Government. Xijiang (the West River) and the Pearl River channels are being deepened. 35,000 dwt vessels can access the port. In 1994, it handled 72 million tons of cargo and 220,000 TEUs. 9 percent of its 24 million-TEU annual capacity. It has 101 berths of 20,000 tons each and a 14-kilometer quay length.

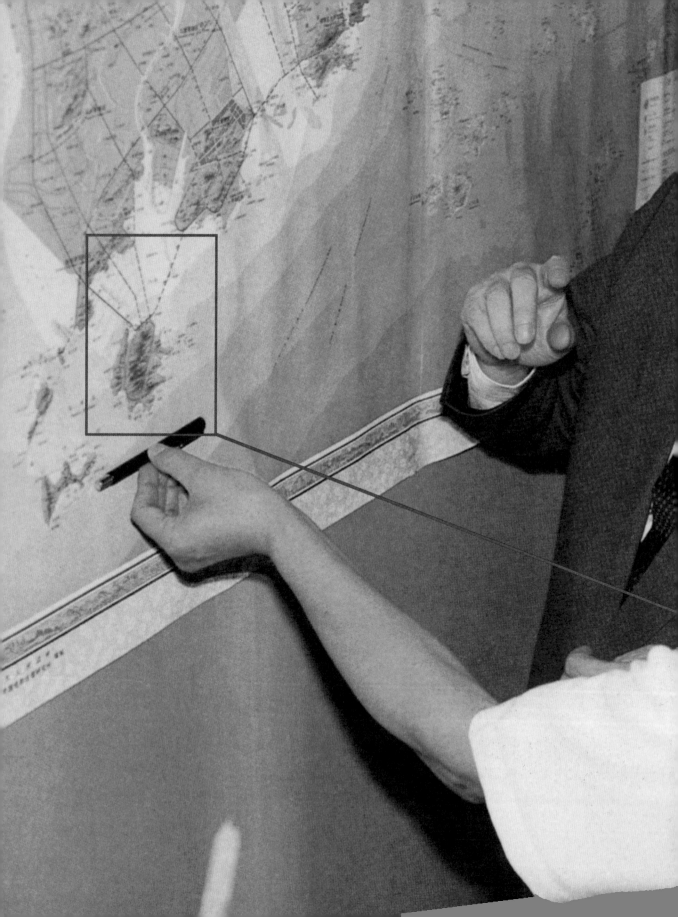

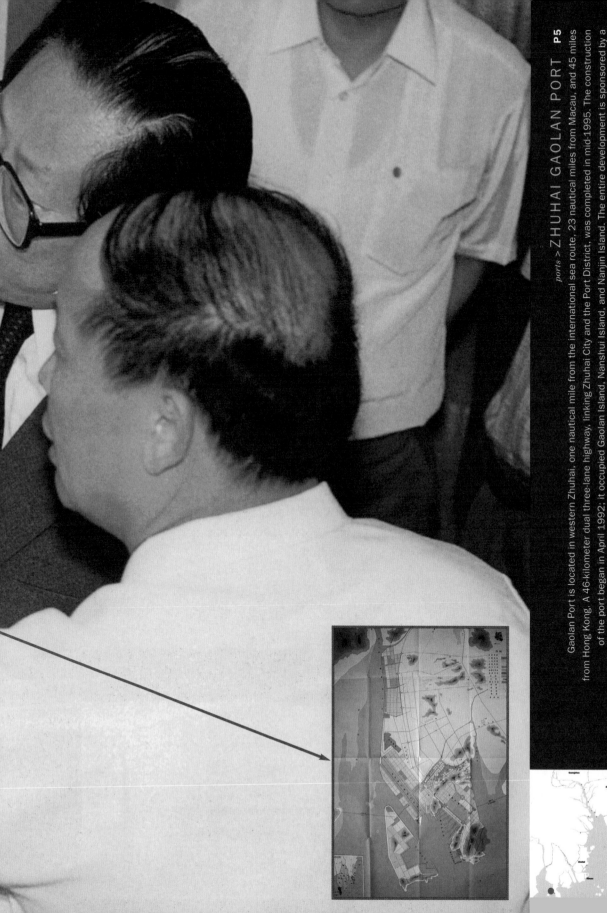

Gaolan Port is located in western Zhuhai, one nautical mile from the international sea route, 23 nautical miles from Macau, and 45 miles from Hong Kong. A 46-kilometer dual three-lane highway, linking Zhuhai City and the Port District, was completed in mid-1995. The construction of the port began in April 1992; it occupied Gaolan Island, Nanshui Island, and Nanjin Island. The entire development is sponsored by a joint venture of Zhuhai Port Authority and Hong Kong Hutchison Whampoa. Phase I of Gaolan Port started operating in December 1994 with the following features: two berths of 20,000 tons each; a quay length of 410 meters, occupying an area of 205,000 square meters; two warehouses, with areas of 10,464 square meters; and an office building of 5,000 square meters.

In 1995, Gaolan Port handled 50,000 tons of general cargo, 5 percent of its 1 million-ton annual capacity. The port's U.S.$400 million cargo terminal will be realized in phase II and will have an annual capacity of 30 million tons. The port has 15 berths of 20,000 tons each, a passenger terminal that handles 40 million visitors annually, and a bulk-goods terminal. The development of Gaolan Port also includes an outer port zone at Nanjin Island, which will handle coal, petroleum, and minerals, up to 100 million tons annually, by means of the following facilities: a 150,000-ton berth for coal handling, a 250,000-ton berth for mineral handling, a dock for 2,000- to 5,000-deadweight-ton ships, and a 78,000-square-meter coal warehouse.

Ka-Ho Port is located on the northeast corner of Coloane Island, two nautical miles from Zhuhai Jiuzhou Port; 20 nautical miles from Shenzhen Shekou Port, 46 nautical miles from Guangzhou Haungpu Port, and 30 nautical miles from Hong Kong Victoria Harbor. Construction of the Ka-Ho Port began in 1988. The terminal is owned by Macauport; Sociedade de Adminstração de Portos (SARL) is responsible for its construction and operation. Phase I of the port development covers 9.6 hectares, 4.5 hectares of which are occupied by the container terminal, which has an annual capacity of 80,000 TEUs. It has one berth, which occupies an area of 7,000 square meters, with a 136-meter quay length, a 1,200-square-meter container freight station, and 5,000 square meters of parking. Phase II will involve an additional 29 hectares of reclaimed land, and the terminal expansion will increase its annual capacity to 400,000 TEUs. A 5.1-hectare oil terminal will also be implemented.

Hong Kong
Harbour
Plan
(1995)

LEGEND

Navigation light
Navigation light buoy
Mooring buoy
Lighted mooring buoy
Mass Transit Railway Station
Local storm signal station
Reclamation works in progress
/Proposed reclamation
Traffic separation schemes

TSUEN WAN

KWAI CHUNG

TSING YI

KOWLOON

HONG KONG INTERNATIONAL AIRPORT
(Kai Tak)

LANTAU ISLAND

HONG KONG ISLAND

Kwai Chung Container Terminals 1–8 are located in the northeast Kowloon Peninsula, east of Tsing Yi Island, in between Ma Wan Channel and Victoria Harbor; 11 kilometers from Hong Kong CBD; 18 nautical miles from Shenzhen Shekou Port; and 45 nautical miles from Zhuhai Gaolan Port. The port's first three single-berth container terminals started to operate in 1972. Four more terminals, comprising seven berths, were constructed along the west Kowloon shoreline in the 1980s. Container Terminal 8 (CT8) is located on the northwest corner of Stonecutters Island. Its construction began in 1991, and it started operating in 1995. CT8 cost U.S.$334 million. It has four berths, which occupy 58.5 hectares of land, and an annual capacity of 1.6 million TEUs.

CONTAINER TERMINALS 1-8

Kwai Chung Container Terminal 9 (CT9) was approved by the Sino-British Joint Liaison Group in August 1996, after a four-year negotiation. Located in southeast Tsing Yi Island, the terminal will have six berths, occupying 70 hectares of land, and an annual capacity of 2.5 million TEUs. Construction began in early 1997 and was completed in 1999. Hong Kong International Terminal (HIT) will build two berths, each 320 meters long, and one barge berth, 60 meters in length. Modern Terminal Ltd (MTL) will build four berths, at a total length of 1,210 meters

CONTAINER TERMINALS 10-11

The terminal development involves a reclamation of 127 hectares of land at the Rambler Channel, 26 hectares of which are designated as a back-up area. A 520-meter waterfront is planned for other uses. Rambler Channel will be deepened from 12.5 meters to 15 meters, to improve its accessibility. Hong Kong ports handled 12.5 million TEUs in 1995. 8.25 million of which went through Kwai Chung terminals. There was a 13 percent annual increase of container throughput from 1988 to 1996. In the first five months of 1996, the Port Development Board (PDB) figures showed that Kwai Chung terminals handled 3.2 million TEUs, which represents a 1.5 percent rise from the throughput handled during the same period of 1995– the smallest amount of growth since the late 1980s.

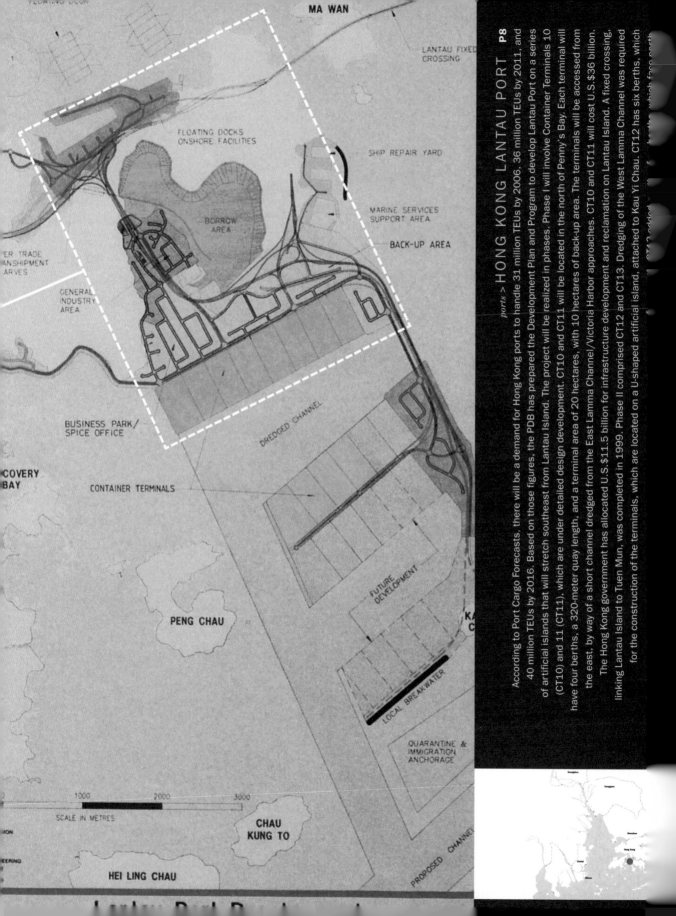

MA WAN

LANTAU FIXED CROSSING

SHIP REPAIR YARD

FLOATING DOCKS
ONSHORE FACILITIES

MARINE SERVICES
SUPPORT AREA

BACK-UP AREA

BORROW
AREA

ER TRADE
ANSHIPMENT
ARVES

GENERAL
INDUSTRY
AREA

BUSINESS PARK /
SPICE OFFICE

DREDGED CHANNEL

COVERY
BAY

CONTAINER TERMINALS

FUTURE
DEVELOPMENT

PENG CHAU

KA
C

LOCAL BREAKWATER

QUARANTINE &
IMMIGRATION
ANCHORAGE

1000   2000   3000

SCALE IN METRES

CHAU
KUNG TO

HEI LING CHAU

PROPOSED CHANNEL

ports > HONG KONG LANTAU PORT P8

According to Port Cargo Forecasts, there will be a demand for Hong Kong ports to handle 31 million TEUs by 2006, 36 million TEUs by 2011, and 40 million TEUs by 2016. Based on those figures, the PDB has prepared the Development Plan and Program to develop Lantau Port on a series of artificial islands that will stretch southeast from Lantau Island. The project will be realized in phases. Phase I will involve Container Terminals 10 (CT10) and 11 (CT11), which are under detailed design development. CT10 and CT11 will be located in the north of Penny's Bay. Each terminal will have four berths, a 320-meter quay length, and a terminal area of 20 hectares, with 10 hectares of back-up area. The terminals will be accessed from the east, by way of a short channel dredged from the East Lamma Channel/Victoria Harbor approaches. CT10 and CT11 will cost U.S. $36 billion. The Hong Kong government has allocated U.S. $11.5 billion for infrastructure development and reclamation on Lantau Island. A fixed crossing, linking Lantau Island to Tuen Mun, was completed in 1999. Phase II comprised CT12 and CT13. Dredging of the West Lamma Channel was required for the construction of the terminals, which are located on a U-shaped artificial island, attached to Kau Yi Chau. CT12 has six berths, which

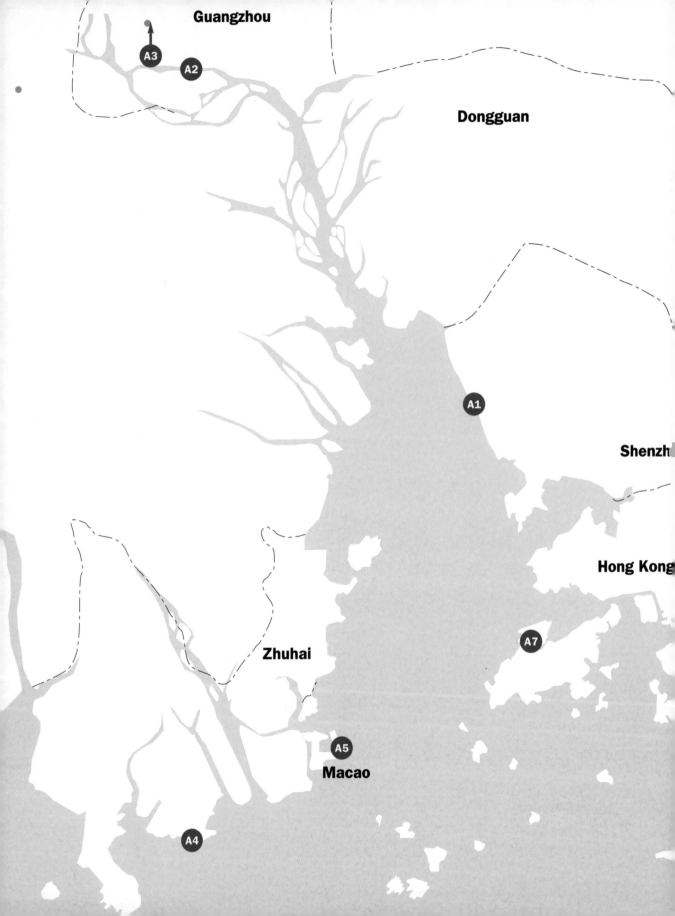

AIRPORTS

SHENZHEN INTERNATIONAL AIRPORT **A1** 627

GUANGZHOU BAIYUN INTERNATIONAL AIRPORT **A2** 633

GUANGZHOU HUADU INTERNATIONAL AIRPORT PROPOSAL **A3** 643

ZHUHAI AIRPORT **A4** 645

MACAO INTERNATIONAL AIRPORT **A5** 659

HONG KONG KAI TAK INTERNATIONAL AIRPORT **A6** 667

HONG KONG CHEP LAP KOK INTERNATIONAL AIRPORT **A7** 673

The Pearl River Delta has five airports in operation: they handled a total of 45 million passengers and 1.8 million tons of cargo in 1995. Shenzhen International Airport is currently China's sixth busiest; it has 6 aircraft movements per hour. Guangzhou Baiyun International Airport is the third busiest in China; it has 15 aircraft movements per hour: Zhuhai Airport has the longest runway in China; but the 4,000-meter runway does not affect the traffic of the airport, because it only serves domestic routes and it is in an isolated location. The Zhuhai Airport has less than 8 aircraft movements per day. Macau International Airport is the only international airport on the west side of the delta; it has 2 aircraft movements per hour. Hong Kong Kai Tak International Airport has 30 aircraft movements per hour: Chep Lap Kok International Airport, which replaced Kai Tak in 1998, handles 35 million passengers a year.

FUTURE EXPANSION

VIEW FROM CONTROL TOWER

The construction of Shenzhen International Airport began in December 1988. The airport started operating in 1991. It is located in Huangtian, on the east bank of the delta, 32 kilometers from the Shenzhen Central Business District (CBD). It is accessed by the GSZ Superhighway and state highway Route 107. The Shenzhen airport is currently China's sixth busiest airport, with 4.1 million passengers in 1995. It provides service to 33 Chinese cities and to Singapore. It has a 3200-meter-long, 45-meter-wide runway; a 3200-meter-long, 23-meter-wide taxiway; a 38,050-square-meter terminal, on three levels; eight boarding bridges for domestic and international flights; and an oil depot, with six 5000 cubic-meter oil tanks.

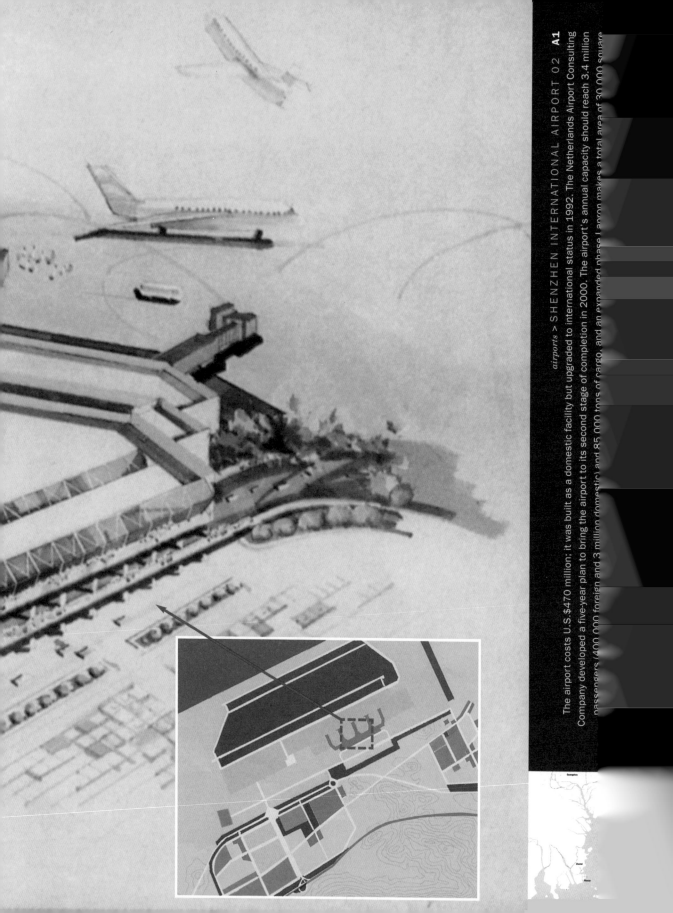

The airport costs U.S.$470 million; it was built as a domestic facility but upgraded to international status in 1992. The Netherlands Airport Consulting Company developed a five-year plan to bring the airport to its second stage of completion in 2000. The airport's annual capacity should reach 3.4 million passengers (400,000 foreign and 3 million domestic) and 85,000 tons of cargo, and an expanded phase I apron makes a total area of 30,000 square

EPARTURE

Final completion of the Shenzhen airport is scheduled for 2025, and the plan calls for a 3,900-meter-long, 80-meter-wide second runway, parallel to the first one; an expansion of the first runway to 3,900 meters in length and 80 meters in width; an expansion of the phase II apron to accommodate 172 large and medium-size aircraft, and 43 cargo planes; a 300,000-square-meter international terminal (including the phase I terminal); a 360,000-square-meter domestic terminal; and a 400,000-square-meter cargo terminal.

airports > GUANGZHOU BAIYUN INTERNATIONAL AIRPORT **A2**

The Guangzhou Baiyun International Airport is located in Baiyun District, 6 kilometers from the Guangzhou CBD. The airport handled 12.5 million passengers and 140,000 tons of cargo in 1995; the number of passengers was expected to reach 18 million by 2000. The airport provides 69 air routes to link Guangzhou with other Chinese cities, and 21 of those routes have an occupancy rate of 90 percent.

DOMESTIC TERMINAL INTERIOR

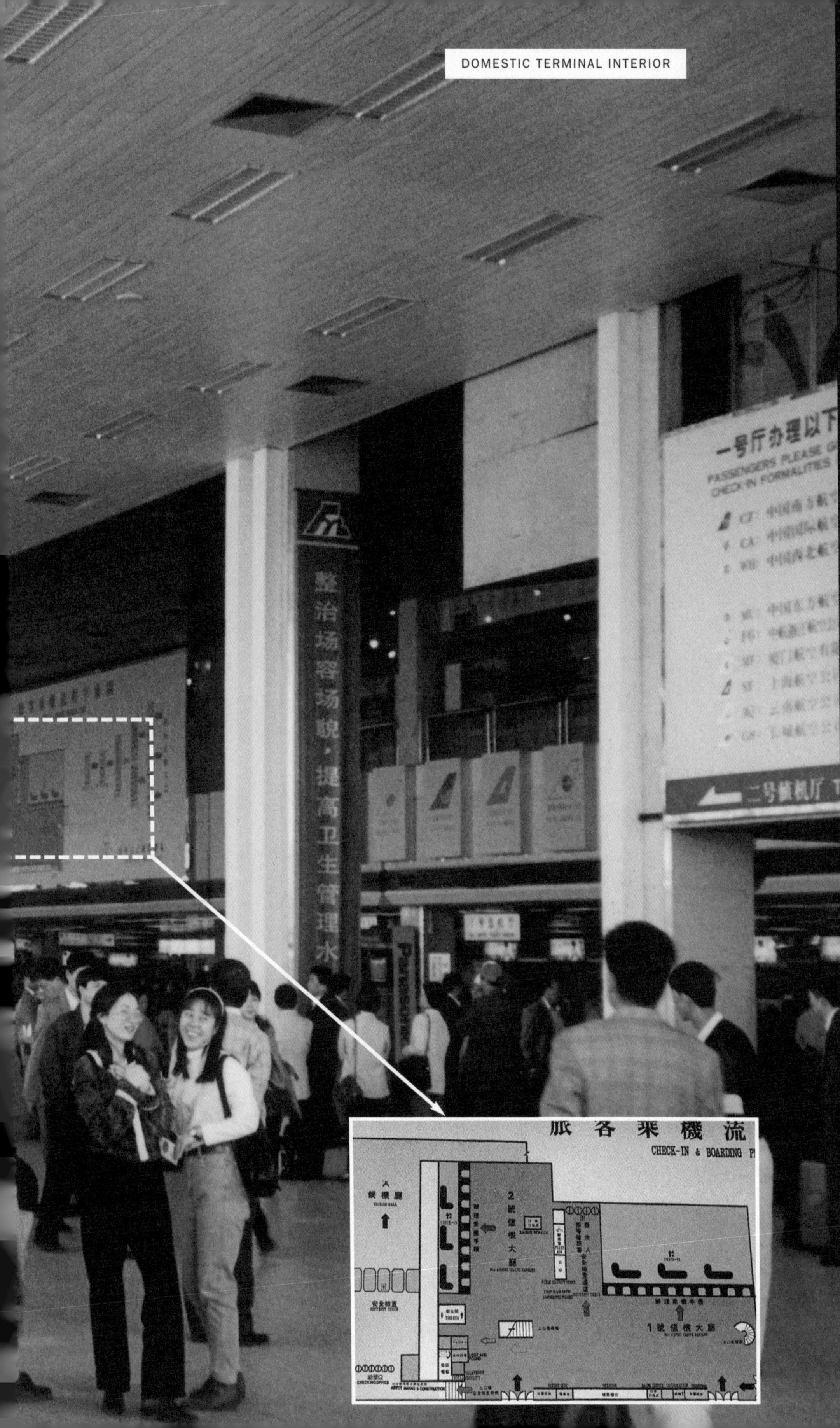

airports > GUANGZHOU BAIYUN INTERNATIONAL AIRPORT 03　**A2**

By July 1995, the Baiyun airport had 13 international routes, of which three maintained an occupancy rate of 68 percent. In 1991, an international passenger terminal was added, and the domestic passenger terminal was upgraded to its present condition. The Baiyun airport has a 70,000-square-meter domestic passenger terminal, with 20 gates, and a 27,000-square-meter international passenger terminal, with three levels.

637　*Pearl River Delta* │ INFRASTRUCTURE

airports > GUANGZHOU HUADU INTERNATIONAL AIRPORT PROPOSAL A3

The proposal for Guangzhou Huadu International Airport was submitted to the State Council for approval in April 1996. The airport is scheduled for completion in 2003. Huadu International Airport will be located in Huadu City, 30 kilometers north of the Guangzhou CBD; it will replace the present airport. A 30-kilometer expressway will connect the airport to Guangzhou. A light-rail transit system will provide linkage within the airport development.

The airport project is funded by a joint venture of Hong Kong-based Yuexiu Enterprises (Holding) Ltd., Guangzhou Development Corporation, and Guangzhou International Trust and Investment. Yuexiu Enterprises will take a 40 percent share, and the other two firms will take 30 percent each. The construction is administered by a holding company under the Civil Aviation Administration of China (CAAC). American, British, Japanese, Australian, Dutch, and Swiss companies have expressed interest in construction and management contracts.

The initial proposal calls for a single-runway airport, which will have an annual capacity of 12.5 million passengers. Current traffic figures show that the single-runway design will not be sufficient. The municipal government prefers a 2-runway design, which will have a capacity of 27 million passengers, 740,000 tons of cargo, and 160,000 aircraft movements annually by 2005. The cost, however, will increase to U.S.$1.5 billion.

Eight thousand residents are being relocated in preparation for the construction of the Huadu airport, which will occupy 15 square kilometers of land. The airport will have 4,000- and 3,700-meter-long, 60-meter-wide runways; two taxiways; a parking apron for 72 aircraft; a 260,120-square-meter passenger terminal; a 30,657-square-meter cargo terminal; a 160,000-space parking lot; and a 23,225-square-meter hotel, with 800 bedrooms. The final phase of the project will add two more runways, which will increase the annual capacity of the airport to 85 million passengers.

The construction of Zhuhai Airport began in December 1992; it started operating on May 30, 1995, after a three-month delay. It is located on Sanzao Island, in the Western District of Zhuhai. A runway, built and destroyed by the Japanese during World War II, remained. Since 1988, that runway has been repaired and used as a military airfield. In 1992, the central government approved the conversion of the airfield to a domestic civilian airport, called the "white elephant." The central government, however, would not finance the project, so Zhuhai was responsible for the funding.

The Zhuhai airport is linked to the city of Zhuhai by an eight-lane highway. Bus service between Macau International Airport and Zhuhai Airport is available; the trip takes approximately one hour. A ferry terminal, 0.5 kilometer from the airport, will provide ferry service to Macau, Hong Kong, and other cities in the delta.

The cost of the Zhuhai airport was U.S.\$470 million. It was built to accommodate the International Civil Aviation standard class flight 4-E. The airport features a 4,000-meter-long, 60-meter-wide runway, the longest in China; a 91,600-square-meter terminal, on two levels: eight international and nine domestic boarding bridges; a 2,160-square-meter cargo terminal; and a 277,000-square-meter parking lot, in front of the terminal building.

Zhuhai Airport operates 30 domestic air routes. In the first four months of 1996, it handled about 250,000 passengers, 2 percent of its 12 million passenger annual capacity. It also dealt with 3,500 tons of cargo, less than one percent of its 600,000-ton annual capacity. The Zhuhai Airport Group Corporation upgraded the airport to international status in 1997. A flight-approach center was built in 1997, to ensure flight-path safety in south China.

中國國際航空航天博覽會
China International Aviation and Aerospace Exhibition.

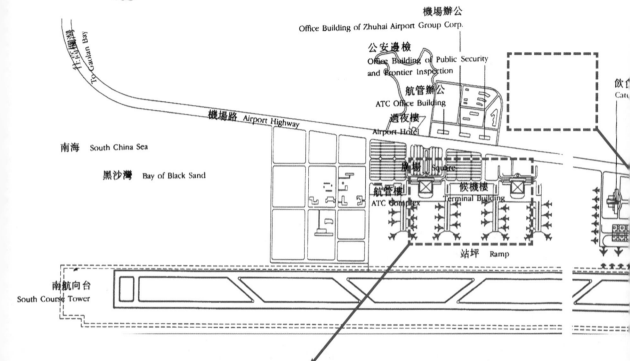

機場辦公
Office Building of Zhuhai Airport Group Corp.

公安邊檢
Office Building of Public Security
and Frontier Inspection

航管辦公
ATC Office Building

遏夜樓
Airport Hotel

飲食
Cate

To Gaolan Bay

機場路 Airport Highway

南海 South China Sea

黑沙灣 Bay of Black Sand

廣場 Square

航管樓
ATC Complex

候機樓
Terminal Building

站坪 Ramp

南航向台
South Course Tower

BUILT

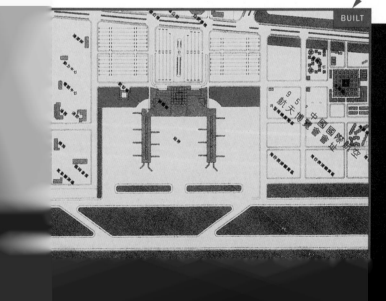

95 中國國際航天博覽會期址

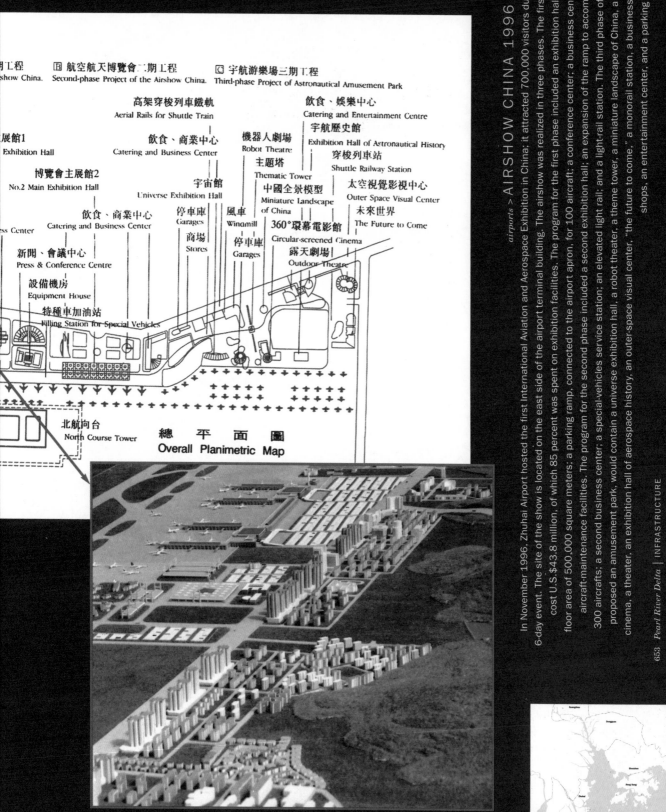

第一期工程 | 图 航空航天博覽會二期工程 | ⓒ 宇航游樂場三期工程
...show China. | Second-phase Project of the Airshow China. | Third-phase Project of Astronautical Amusement Park

高架穿梭列車鐵軌
Aerial Rails for Shuttle Train

飲食、娛樂中心
Catering and Entertainment Centre

飲食、商業中心
Catering and Business Center

宇航歷史館
Exhibition Hall of Astronautical History

展館1
Exhibition Hall

機器人劇場
Robot Theatre

宇宙館
Universe Exhibition Hall

穿梭列車站
Shuttle Railway Station

博覽會主展館2
No.2 Main Exhibition Hall

主題塔
Thematic Tower

太空視覺影視中心
Outer Space Visual Center

飲食、商業中心
Catering and Business Center

停車庫
Garages

中國全景模型
Miniature Landscape
of China

未來世界
The Future to Come

新聞、會議中心
Press & Conference Centre

商場
Stores

風車
Windmill

360°環幕電影館
Circular-screened Cinema

設備機房
Equipment House

停車庫
Garages

露天劇場
Outdoor Theatre

特種車加油站
Filling Station for Special Vehicles

北航向台
North Course Tower

總 平 面 圖
Overall Planimetric Map

In November 1996, Zhuhai Airport hosted the first International Aviation and Aerospace Exhibition in China; it attracted 700,000 visitors during the 6-day event. The site of the show is located on the east side of the airport terminal building. The airshow was realized in three phases. The first cost U.S.$43.8 million, of which 85 percent was spent on exhibition facilities. The program for the first phase included an exhibition hall floor area of 500,000 square meters; a parking ramp, connected to the airport apron, for 100 aircraft; a conference center; a business center; aircraft-maintenance facilities. The program for the second phase included a second exhibition hall; an elevated light rail; and a light-rail station. The third phase of the show 300 aircrafts; a second business center; a special-vehicles service station; an elevated light rail; a robot theater, a theme tower, a miniature landscape of China, a proposed an amusement park, would contain a universe exhibition hall, a robot theater, a theme tower, a miniature landscape of China, a business cinema, a theater, an exhibition hall of aerospace history, an outer-space visual center, "the future to come," a monorail station, a business shops, an entertainment center, and a parking

BUILT

MODEL OF THE FUTURE CITY

airports > ZHUHAI AEROTROPOLIS A4.2

Zhuhai Airport Group Corporation proposed an airport city called Aerotropolis. It is located in Cao Tang Wan, 0.5 kilometer north of Zhuhai Airport. The development, which is similar to the Singapore Airport City, began in 1994. According to the director of the corporation, Zhuhai Airport needs a "modern multifunctional coastal garden aerotropolis" to combine passenger and cargo transportation with commerce, finance, exhibitions, the high-tech industry, information services, aircraft maintenance, tourism, shopping, sports, entertainment, and storage.

SITE OF THE FUTURE CITY

Aerotropolis finances the airport construction by leasing land parcels. The city covers a total area of 25 square kilometers and has a planned population of 100,000 to 120,000. Phase I involved an area of 12 square kilometers and attracted investment from Taiwan, Thailand, and the United States. The master plan is composed of commercial districts, exhibition and conference districts, residential districts, mixed-use developments, sports stadiums, shopping malls, parks, theme parks, hotels, a hospital, a school, a ferry terminal, and a light tower.

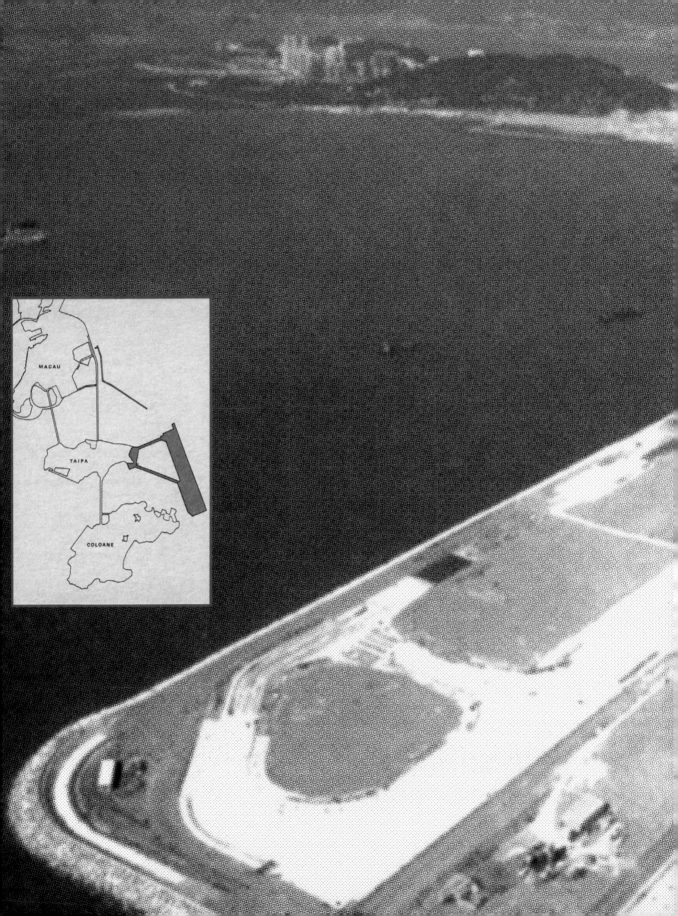

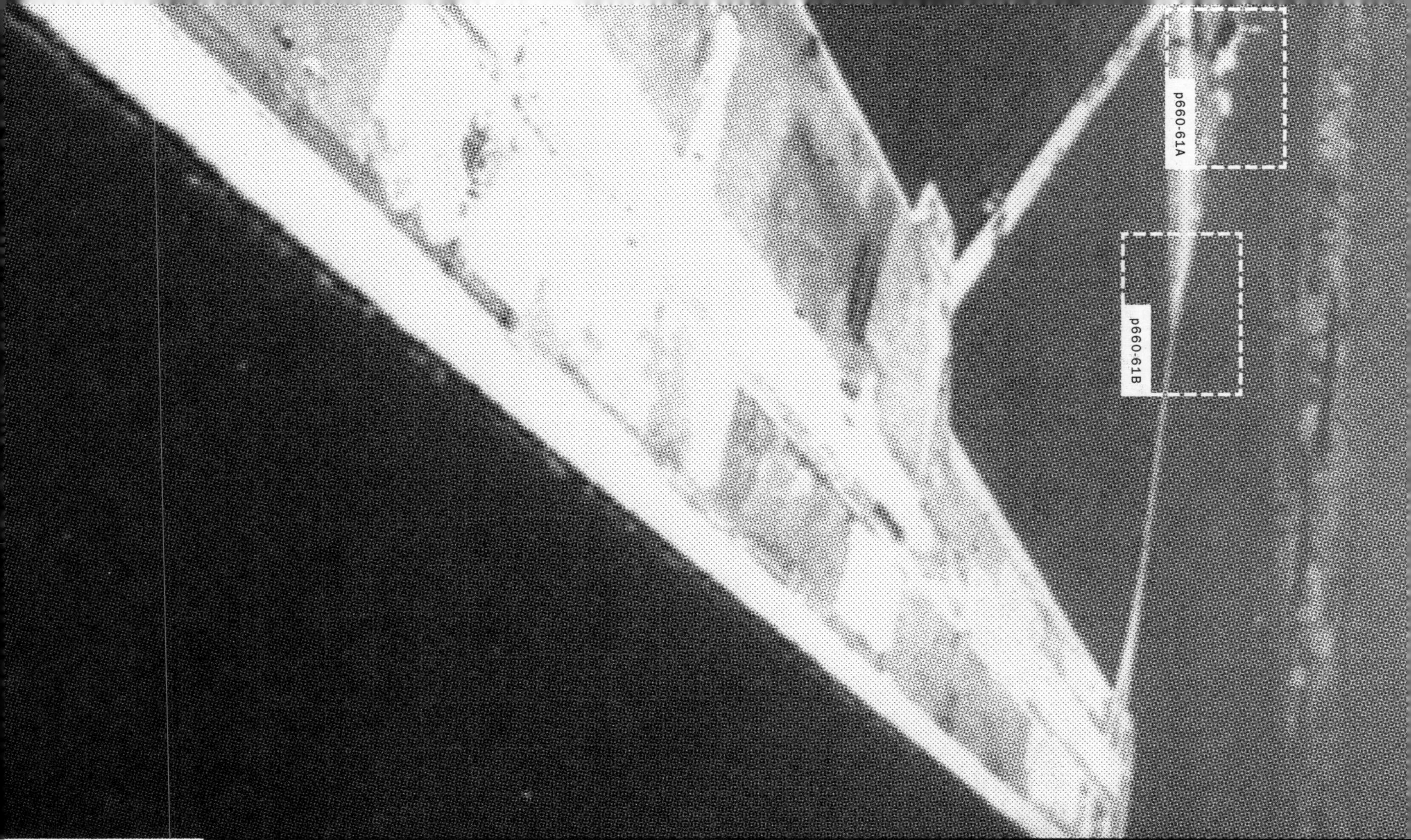
p660-61A
p660-61B

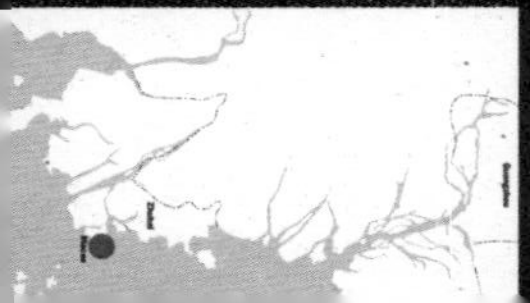

airports > MACAU INTERNATIONAL AIRPORT **A5**

Macau International Airport started to operate in early December 1995. It is located on 115 hectares of reclaimed land off Taipa Island, 15 minutes by road from the Zhuhai Special Economic Zone and 60 minutes by jetfoil from Hong Kong. A railway will connect the airport with Zhuhai, Guangzhou, and other parts of south China. The airport provides linkages between the west bank of the delta and Taiwan, Korea,

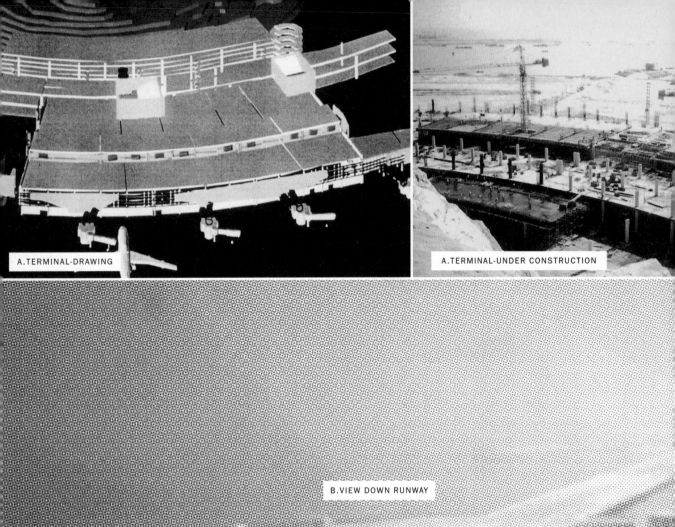

A. TERMINAL-DRAWING

A. TERMINAL-UNDER CONSTRUCTION

B. VIEW DOWN RUNWAY

A.TERMINAL-NEAR COMPLETION

The city of Macau has signed air-service agreements with the United States, and a few European and Latin American countries to open cargo and passenger flights. Those agreements were discussed at the Sino-Portuguese Joint Liaison Group meetings. because they needed the approval of both the Chinese and Portuguese governments. Phase I of the airport cost U.S.$1.1 billion. It meets the standards of the International Civil Aviation Organization and operates under a CAT II permit.

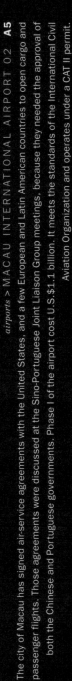

TERMINAL INTERIOR

In the first four months of 1996, the Macau airport handled a total of 246,501 passengers, 16 percent of its 4.5-million-passenger annual capacity. In the first seven months, it totaled 1,963 tons of cargo, less than 2 percent of its 123,000-ton annual capacity. Phase I had the following features: a 3,350-meter runway; two taxiways; a 45,800-square-meter passenger terminal, on three levels; a flow of 2,000 passengers per hour on a one-way flight; four telescopic boarding bridges; a parking apron for 16 parking positions (six large and ten medium-size aircraft); a 16,000-square-meter cargo terminal; a 12,000-square-meter hanger; and operation on a 24-hour cycle.

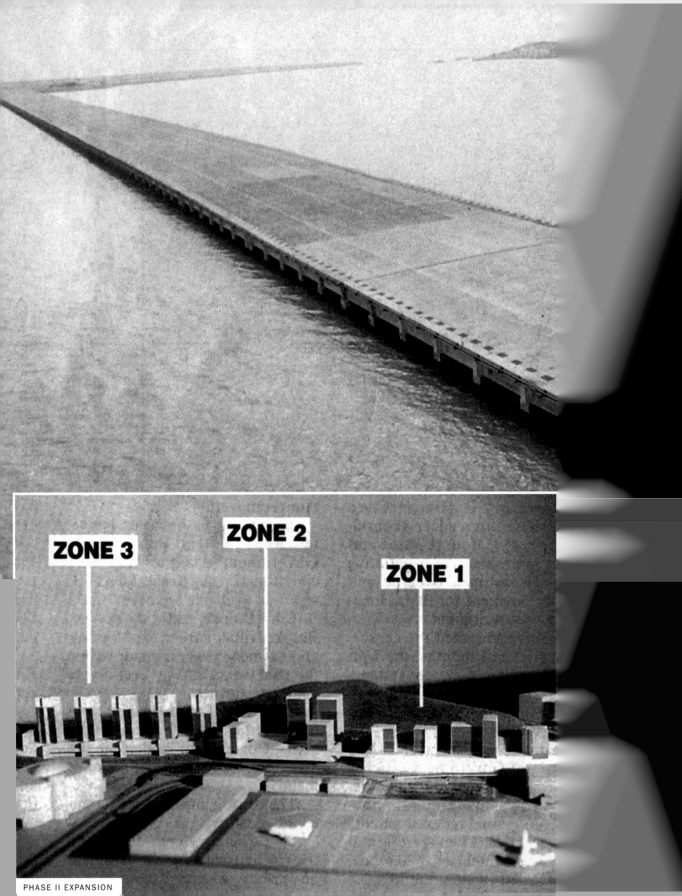

ZONE 3

ZONE 2

ZONE 1

PHASE II EXPANSION

Phase II of the Macau airport involved terminal expansion. Fifty hectares of reclaimed land were added to accommodate other facilities. The annual passenger capacity has reached 6 million. The airport will able to handle 252,000 tons of cargo by 2005 and 297,000 tons by 2009.

p668-69

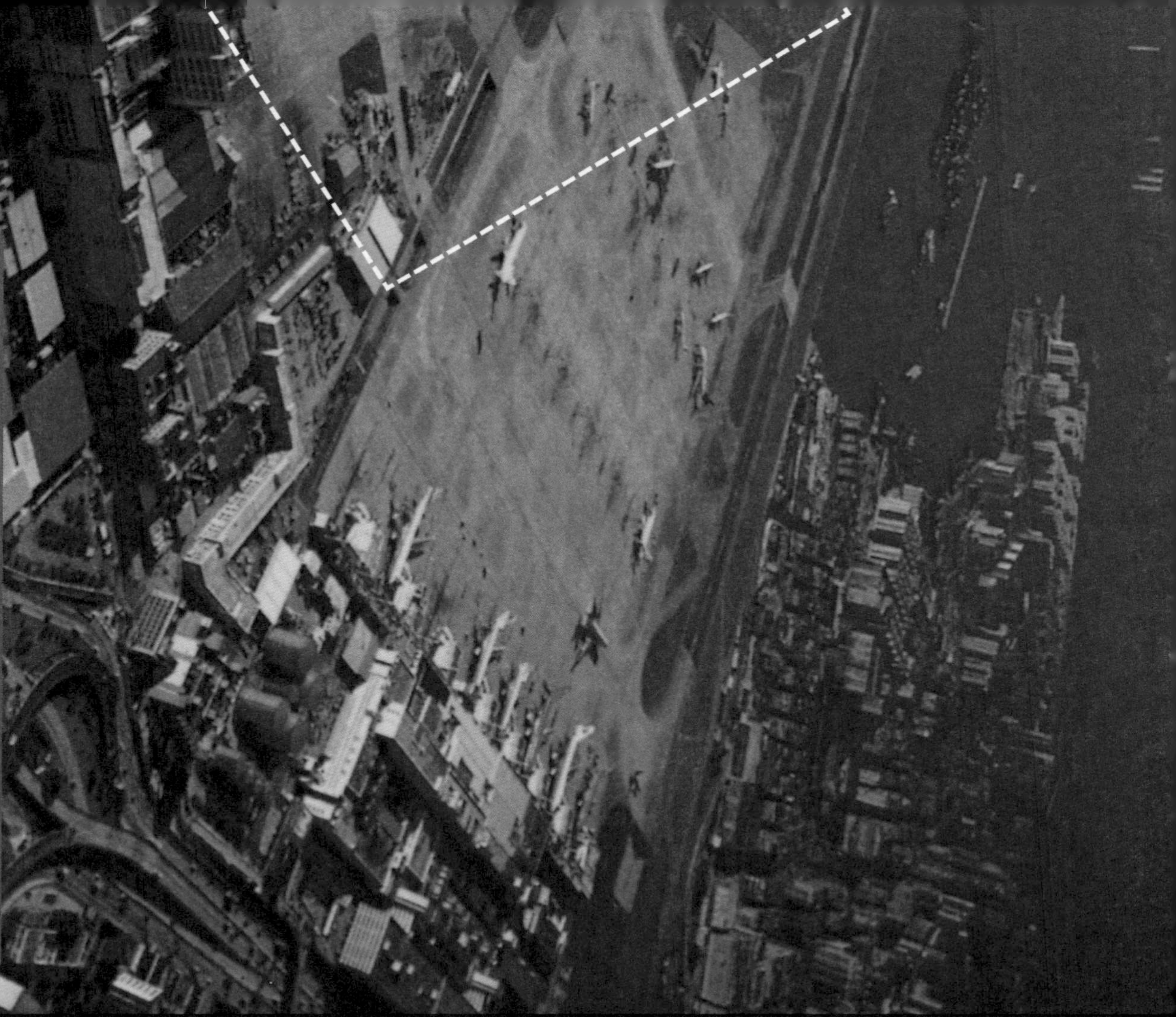

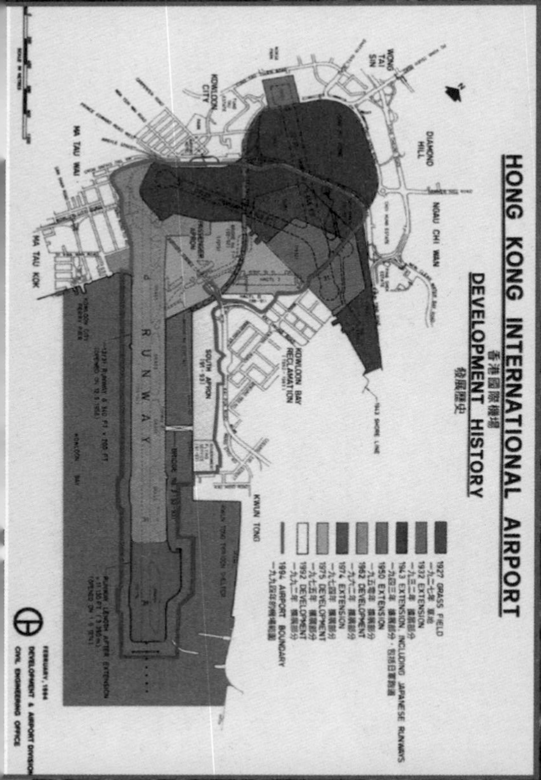

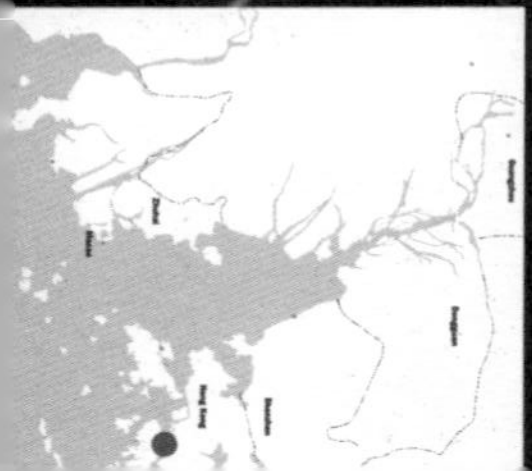

airports > HONG KONG KAI TAK INTERNATIONAL AIRPORT **A6**

Kai Tak International Airport was located in Kowloon Bay, within Victoria Harbor. It began as a Royal Air Force grass airfield in 1927 and has been developed through various stages. To meet international standards, a 2,540-meter runway was constructed in 1958 and extended by 850 meters in 1972. The reclamation of Kowloon Bay in 1975 and 1992 extended the parking apron. In early 1998, the airport was shut down and replaced by a new airport at Chek Lap Kok. The cost of the airport evolved over a long period of development. It had a 3,390-meter runway; a 3,600-meter taxiway; a 4,500-square-meter passenger terminal, on two levels; a 5,100-square-meter cargo terminal; 98 hectares of parking apron for 60 aircrafts; and a multilevel parking garage.

HONG KONG INTERNATIONAL AIRPORT
香港國際機場
DEVELOPMENT HISTORY
發展歷史

1927 GRASS FIELD 一九二七年 草地	
1932 EXTENSION 一九三二年 擴展部分	
1943 EXTENSION, INCLUDING JAPANESE RUNWAYS 一九四三年 擴展部分,包括日軍跑道	
1950 EXTENSION 一九五零年 擴展部分	
1962 DEVELOPMENT 一九六二年 擴展部分	
1974 EXTENSION 一九七四年 擴展部分	
1975 DEVELOPMENT 一九七五年 擴展部分	
1992 DEVELOPMENT 一九九二年 擴展部分	
1994 AIRPORT BOUNDARY 一九九四年的機場範圍	

DIAMOND HILL
NGAU CHI WAN
WONG TAI SIN
1943 SHORE LINE
KOWLOON BAY RECLAMATION
KWUN TONG
KWUN TONG TYPHOON SHELTER
KOWLOON CITY
PASSENGER APRON
SOUTH APRON
BRIDGE
R U N W A Y
Ideal Runway 6 340 FT x 700 FT
(OPENED IN 12.9.1958)
RUNWAY LENGTH AFTER EXTENSION
+ H (30 FT. (3,390 m.)
(OPENED IN 1.9.1974)
MA TAU WAI
KOWLOON POINT PEAKS AREA
KOWLOON BAY
MA TAU KOK

SCALE IN METRES
FEBRUARY, 1994
DEVELOPMENT & AIRPORT DIVISION
CIVIL ENGINEERING OFFICE

In 1994, Kai Tak International ranked second in terms of international cargo and fourth in international passenger traffic. In 1995, the airport had already reached its maximum capacity of 27.4 million passengers; 1.45 million tons of cargo; and 150,118 aircraft movements per day, with an

PLAN FOR FUTURE EXPANSION

In 1996, the Hong Kong government released detailed plans for the redevelopment of southern Kowloon, following the closure of the Kai Tak airport. A total area of 940 hectares was to provide housing for 285,000 people. Some business associations and commuter aviation sectors were in favor of keeping Kai Tak as a city airport; it would have linked at least 20 medium-size cities in Southern China. The Hong Kong Tourist Association, however, wished to organize the "2001: Hong Kong Toward a New Millennium" expo at Kai Tak. The event would have lasted for two years and involve various phases; 20 million visitors were expected. In 2000, the site was developed for recreational and commercial use, including a golf-driving range.

The planning of the Chep Lap Kok International Airport began in 1990. Site preparation started in 1992 and covered a 31-month period of reclamation and excavation. In that time, 938 hectares of land were created and a 1,248-hectare airport platform was formed. Runway and terminal construction began in 1995. Chep Lap Kok Airport opened in 1998 and replaced Kai Tak International.

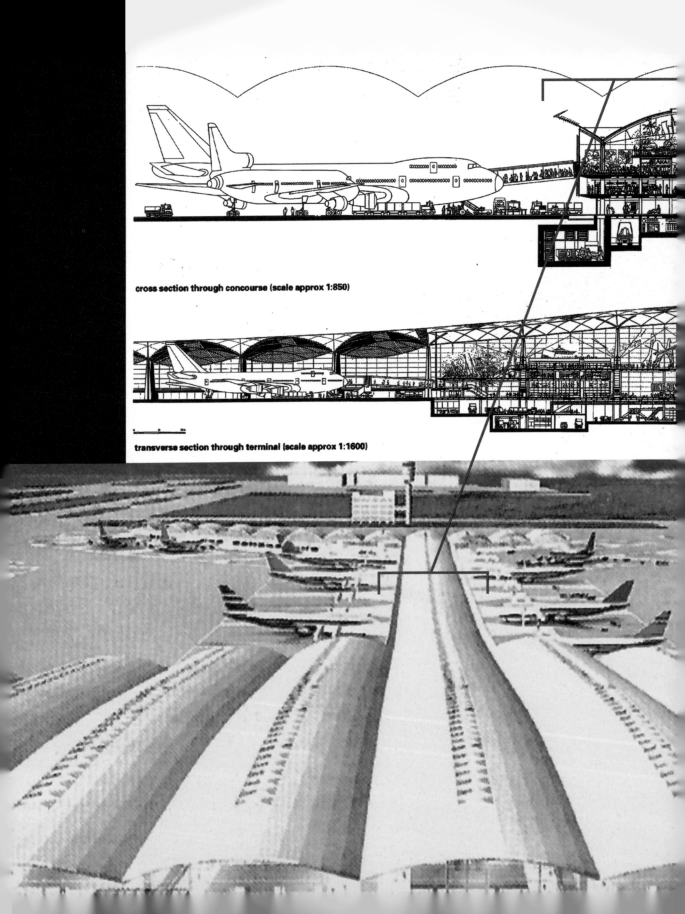

cross section through concourse (scale approx 1:850)

transverse section through terminal (scale approx 1:1600)

HONG KONG
SkyMall
香港機場 購物中心
COMING APRIL 1998

Chek Lap Kok is located off the north coast of Lantau Island, 25 kilometers west of the Hong Kong CBD. The linkage to Hong Kong is made by way of the North Lantau Expressway, Lantau Fixed Crossing, Tsing Ma Bridge, West Kowloon Expressway, Western Harbor Crossing, and Airport Railway. Those infrastructure projects opened in mid-1997. Phase I of the airport cost U.S.$7.2 billion and has the following features: a 3,800-meter-long, 60-meter-wide runway; three parallel taxiways; a 1.2-kilometer (longest in the world) and 490,000-square-meter passenger terminal, on three levels; 288 check-in counters; 38 air bridges for boarding; 150 commercial and retail outlets within the terminal; a 139,000-square-meter cargo terminal; a parking apron for 27 aircraft; 24-hour operation; and a 3,000-car multilevel parking garage.

675 *Pearl River Delta* | INFRASTRUCTURE

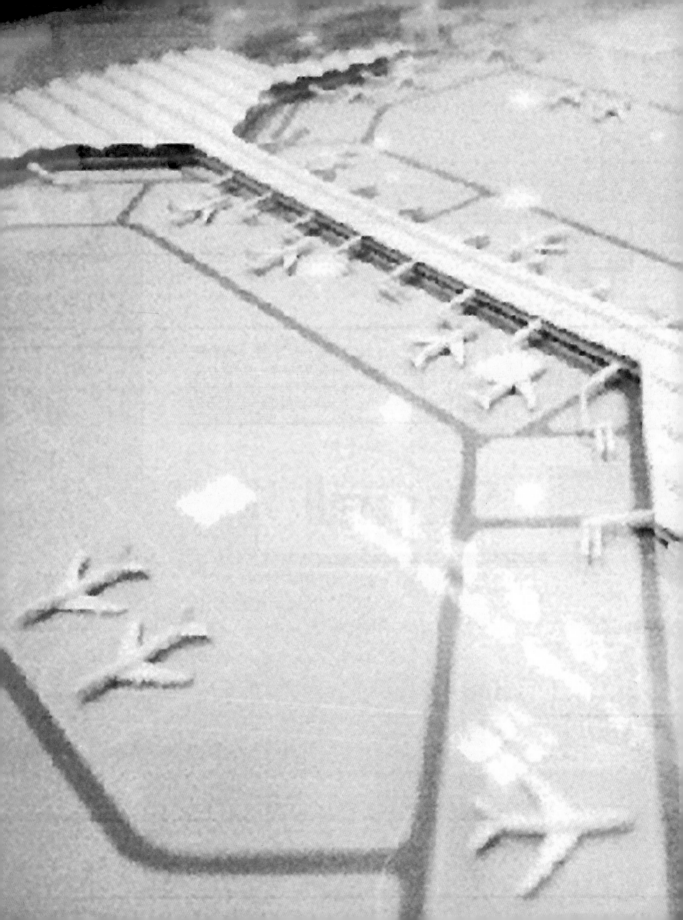

Phase I of Chep Lap Kok Internationl has an annual capacity of 35 million passengers and 3 million tons of cargo. A total of 90 hectares of commercial land is available, 11 of which were leased to Cathy Pacific Airways, for its new headquarters, and to developers of freight-forward centers and hotels. In October 1998, an additional 3,800-meter-long, 60-meter-wide runway, parallel to the first one, was opened. The airport facilities were designed to be expanded in stages: by 2040, Chep Lap Kok International should handle 87 million passengers and 9 million tons of cargo annually.

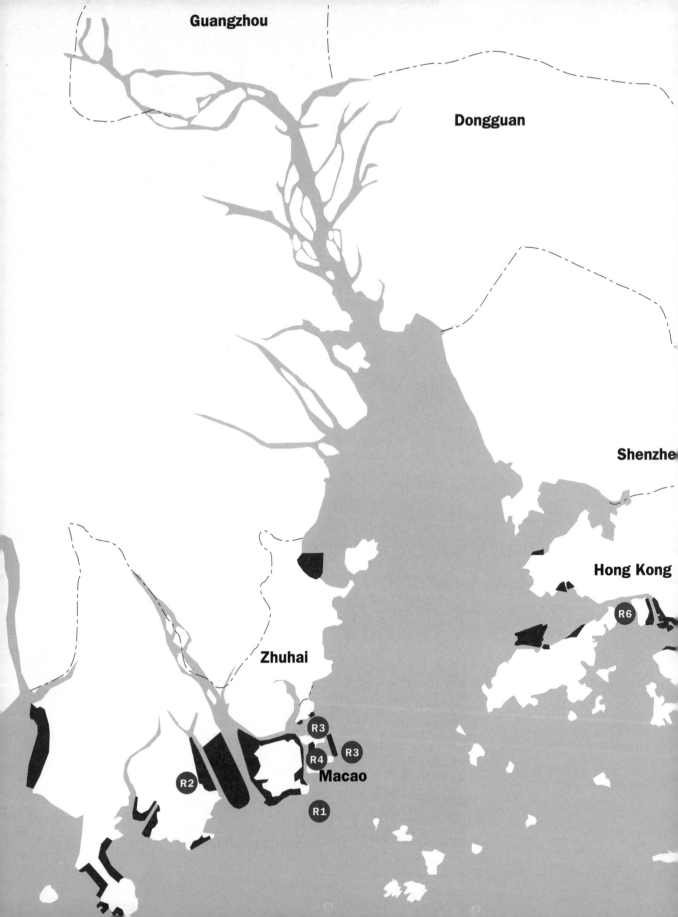

Guangzhou

Dongguan

Shenzhe

Hong Kong

R6

Zhuhai

R3

R3

R4

Macao

R2

R1

RECLAMATION

ZHUHAI HENGQIN ISLAND + HAISHI JIMUA **R1** | 681

ZHUHAI WESTERN DISTRICT **R2** | 683

MACAO NAMVAN LAKES DEVELOPMENT **R3** | 685

MACAO COTAI **R4** | 689

MACAO INTERNATIONAL AIRPORT **R5** | 691

HONG KONG URBAN DEVELOPMENT **R6** | 693

Reclamation has added more than 21,000 hectares of land at the most and least populous areas of the Pearl River Delta for the last five years. In Zhuhai Western District, islands are connected by landfill; they form the Gaolan Port, which is distant from any development. Before the reclamation, the site could only be reached by boat. Zhuhai has also used reclaimed land for landscape that will remain green and unoccupied. The size of Zhuhai's Hengqin Island, which has a population of 3,000, has been doubled for future economic development. Since 1860, reclamation has been reshaping Victoria Harbor, the Central Business District (CBD) of Hong Kong, by the addition of commercial parcels along the waterfront. The Chep Lap Kok airport sits on a 1,250-hectare land mass; 938 hectares of that land was formed by reclamation off Chep Lap Kok Island, which remained undeveloped until 1992.

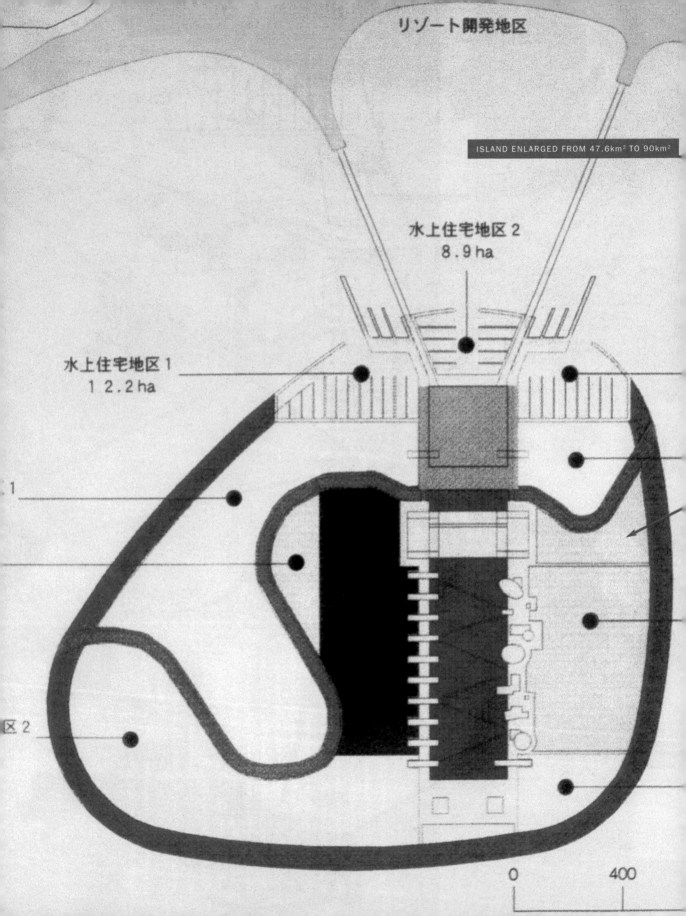

リゾート開発地区

ISLAND ENLARGED FROM 47.6km² TO 90km²

水上住宅地区2
8.9 ha

水上住宅地区1
12.2 ha

区1

区2

0   400

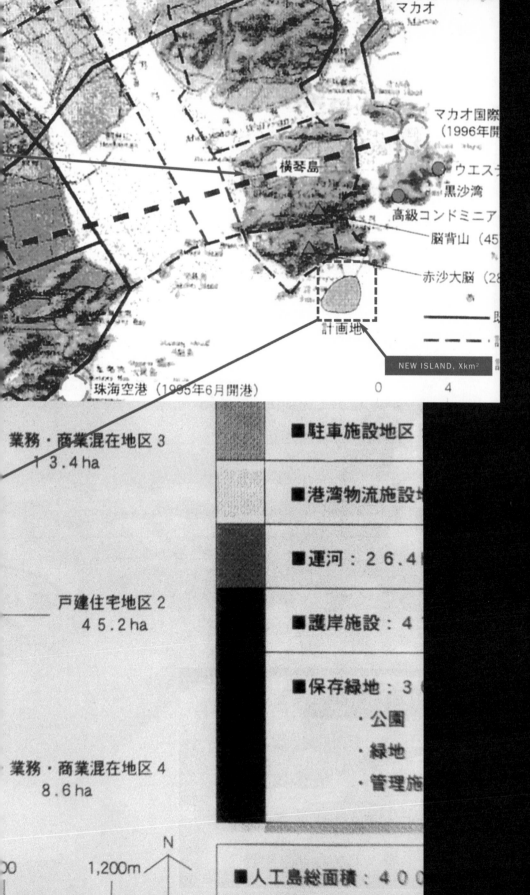

Hengqin Island, west of Macau and 20 kilometers south of the Zhuhai Special Economic Zone (SEZ), will be developed into an Open Economic Zone (OEZ). The original size of the island was 47.6 square kilometers; reclamation enlarged the island to 90 square kilometers. Hengqin had a population of 5,000 people in 1995; it is expected to reach 650,000 by 2010. Development has been concentrated on the periphery of the island; its road network, a total length of 56 kilometers, comprises three major roads. One connects the island with Zhuhai Harbor District, in the north. Since 1999, linkages have been established between the Hengqin OEZ administrative center and Macau Taipa Island. Ultimately, the Guangzhou-Zhuhai Railwa will reach Macau via Hengqin. In 1995, the Zhuhai municipal government invited Arata Isozaki to create a proposal for an artificial island off the southern tip of Hengqin Island. The 400-hectare island, named Haishi Jimua by the architect, was planned to become the Central Organization of Asian Political Communities and is strategically located within 3,000 kilometers of all Asian countries.

マカオ
Macao

マカオ国際
（1996年開

横琴島

ウエスタ

黒沙湾

高級コンドミニア

脳背山（45

赤沙大脳（28

計画地

NEW ISLAND, Xkm²

0   4

珠海空港（1995年6月開港）

業務・商業混在地区 3
+3.4ha

■駐車施設地区

■港湾物流施設地

戸建住宅地区 2
45.2ha

■運河：26.4

■護岸施設：4

業務・商業混在地区 4
8.6ha

■保存緑地：3

・公園

・緑地

・管理施

N

00   1,200m

■人工島総面積：400

NEW EDGE

Islands in the Zhuhai Western District are connected by landfill for port development. The land mass created by reclamation serves as a buffer between the urban development of the SEZ and the industrial development of the Western District.

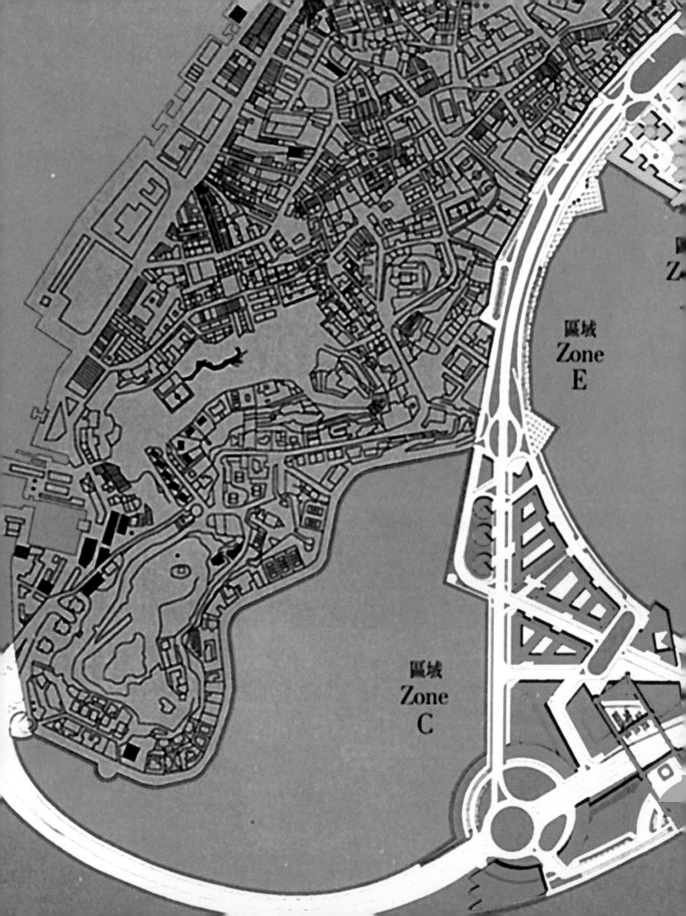

區域
Zone
E

區域
Zone
C

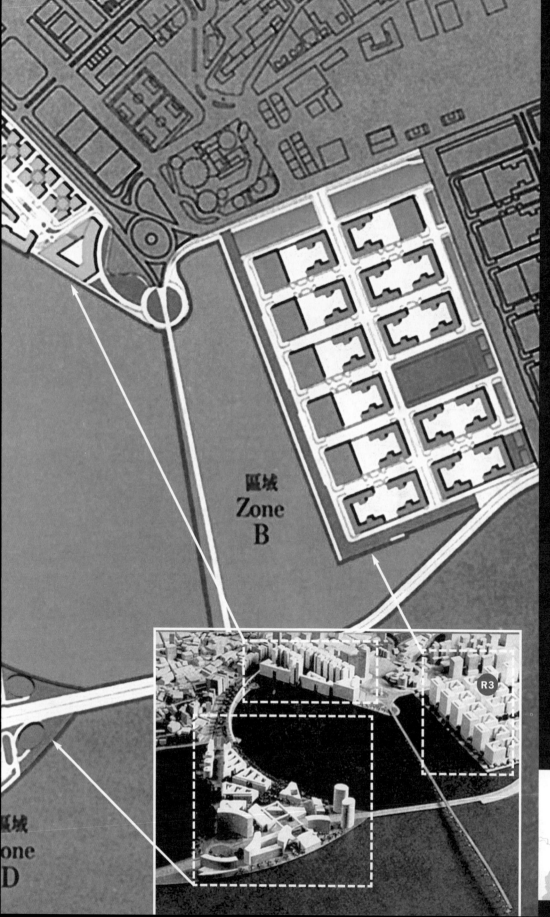

區域
Zone
B

區域
one
D

R3

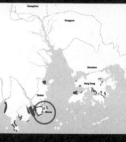

RECLAIMED

R3

COTAI (COloane + TAIpa) is a new urban space, or new city, in Macau and will be located between Coloane and Taipa islands. The site for the new city has a total area of 6.2 square kilometers. 5.3 of which was created by reclamation on the east and west sides of the causeway between the islands. The master plan for COTAI includes 6.25 million square meters of residential development, which will accommodate a population of 150,000; 2.37 million square meters of commercial development; 740,000 square meters of office space; 750,000 square meters of hotel development; 475,000 square meters of warehouse storage; and 200,000 square meters of public and administrative areas.

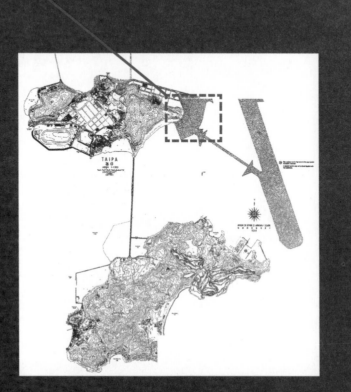

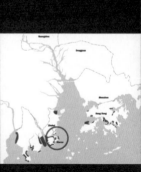

1977 - 1994

LAU FAU SHAN

TIN SHUI WAI

SHUEN WAN

TAI PO

TOLO HARBOUR

YUEN LONG

Plover Reso

TAI PO KAU

EP BAY

Light Rail Transit operational in 1988

TAI MO SHAN
▲957 m

MA LIU SHUI

Sha Tin Race Course completed in 1978

Nam Wan

Castle Peak Tunnel 1957

SHA TIN

Catch Tunnel operational in 1991

LUNG KWU TAN

▲583m
CASTLE PEAK

TUEN MUN

Route 3 under construction

Shing Mun Tunnel operational in 1990

PILLAR POINT

Pearl Island

TAI LAM CHUNG

TSING LUNG TAU

TSUEN WAN

1st MTR Tsuen Wan Line operational in 1982

LION ROCK
▲494 m

1931

Mass Transit way (MTR) operational 1979

▲KOWLOON PEAK

MA WAN CHANNEL

MA WAN

Ma Wan

Tsing Yi

KWAI CHUNG

SHAM SHUI PO

INTERNATIONAL AIRPORT

Airport Tunnel operational in 19

Chek Lap Kok

MONG KOK

Airport under construction

Proposed Airport Railway

Proposed North Lantau Expressway

YAM O

KOWLOON

TSIM SHA TSUI

HUNG HOM

Eastern Harbour Crossing operational 1990

MTR Kwun Tong Line operational in 19

Discovery Bay

TAI HO

Proposed Western Harbour Crossing

VICTORIA HARBOUR

NORTH POINT

MTR also operational

Peng Chau

SAI YING PUN
CENTRAL

CAUSEWAY BAY

HAU KEI WAN

TAI SHUI HANG

552m ▲
VICTORIA PEAK
1877

Cross Harbour Tunnel operational in 1982

CHAI WAN

TUNG CHUNG

MUI WO

POK FU LAM

HONG KONG ISLAND

LANTAU ISLAND

ABERDEEN 1932

1917

▲934 m
LANTAU PEAK

Ap Lei Chau

STANLEY

Cheung Chau

Lamma Island

up to 1887

1888 -1924

Kowloon-Canton Railway operational in 1910

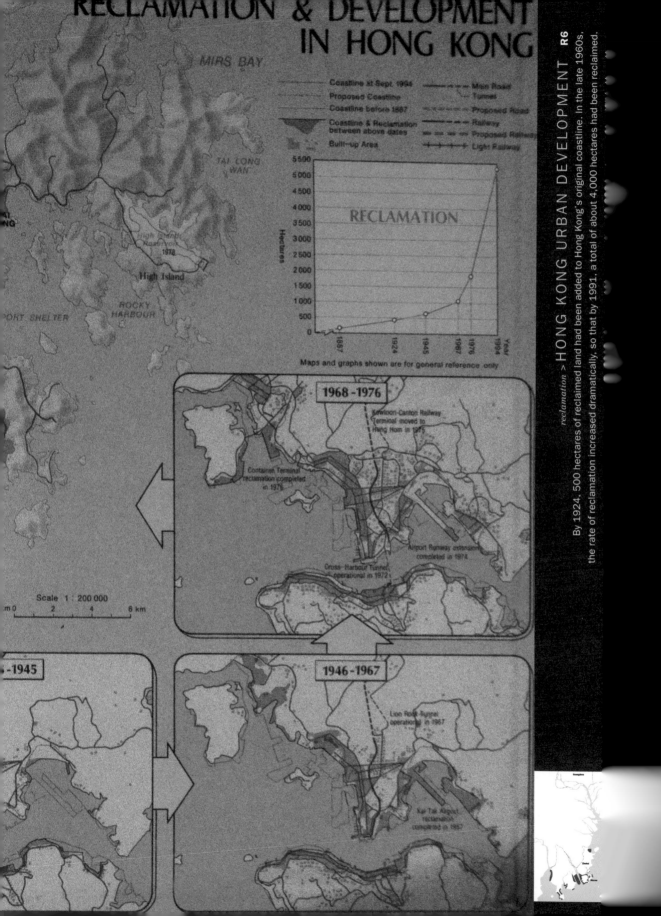

reclamation > HONG KONG URBAN DEVELOPMENT R6

By 1924, 500 hectares of reclaimed land had been added to Hong Kong's original coastline. In the late 1960s, the rate of reclamation increased dramatically, so that by 1991, a total of about 4,000 hectares had been reclaimed.

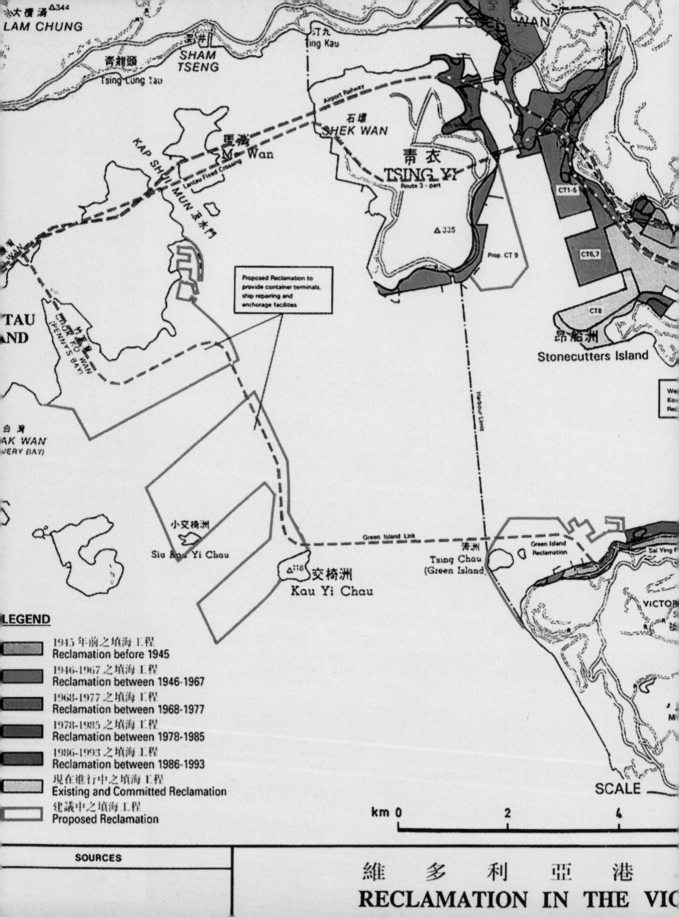

大檻涌 △344
LAM CHUNG

喬龍頭
SHAM
TSENG
Tsing Lung Tau

汀九
Ting Kau

TSEUNG WAN

Airport Railway

石壩
SHEK WAN

KAP SHUI MUN 汲水門

Lantau Fixed Crossing

馬灣
M-Wan

TSING YI 青衣
Route 3 - part

△335

CT1-5

CT6,7

Proposed Reclamation to
provide container terminals,
ship repairing and
anchorage facilities

Prop. CT 9

CT8

昂船洲
Stonecutters Island

TAU
AND

竹篙灣
CHOK KO WAN
(PENNY'S BAY)

Harbour Limit

白灣
AK WAN
VERY BAY)

小交椅洲
Siu Kau Yi Chau

交椅洲
△118 Kau Yi Chau

Green Island Link

青洲
Tsing Chau
(Green Island)

Green Island
Reclamation

Sai Ying P

VICTOR

We
Ko
Re

LEGEND

1945 年前之填海工程
Reclamation before 1945

1946-1967 之填海工程
Reclamation between 1946-1967

1968-1977 之填海工程
Reclamation between 1968-1977

1978-1985 之填海工程
Reclamation between 1978-1985

1986-1993 之填海工程
Reclamation between 1986-1993

現在進行中之填海工程
Existing and Committed Reclamation

建議中之填海工程
Proposed Reclamation

SCALE

km 0   2   4

SOURCES

維 多 利 亞 港
RECLAMATION IN THE VIC

望夫石
MONG FU SHEK

△ 577

筆架山
PAT KA
SHAN
452 △

獅子山
SZ TSZ SHAN
(Lion Rock)

FEI NGO SHAN
(Kowloon Peak)
602
△
飛鵝山

Cheung Sha Wan

KOWLOON

Kowloon Bay

To Kwa Wan

九龍灣
KOWLOON BAY

Kwun Tong

Hung Hom

Airport Railway

△781

T.S.T. East

Hung Hom
Bay

Kowloon Point

Eastern Harbour Crossing

VICTORIA HARBOUR

Quarry Bay

Harbour Limit

鯉魚門
LEI YUE MUN

CR1

WCR1

CR3

CR4

WCR2

Central

Causeway Bay

Aldrich Bay

CR2

Wan Chai

HONG KONG ISLAND

抬架山
531 △ PAK KA SHAN

NSON

Reclamation at Hung Hom Bay has produced 36 hectares of land for residential and commercial development, and for the extension of the Kowloon-Canton Railway freight yard. The development will accommodate 11,500 residences. The relocation of the Kai Tak airport released 670 hectares of land in southeast Kowloon for redevelopment, 200 hectares of which were reclaimed from Kowloon Bay.

海 地 圖

...IA HARBOUR

8 km

Plan 1

The site preparation for Hong Kong Chek Lap Kok International Airport was the biggest reclamation contract ever granted in Hong Kong. The contract, representing 20 percent of the cost of the airport, created 938 hectares of land off Chep Lap Kok Island by the dredging and offsite disposal of 70 million cubic meters of marine deposits, the extraction of 60 million cubic meters of sand from marine sorrow areas, and the excavation of 95 million cubic meters of shot rock from the islands. The site preparation of phase I of Tung Chung New Town, one of the Airport Core Projects, involved 52 hectares of reclamation. Located on northern Lantau Island and adjacent to the Chep Lap Kok airport, Tung Chung is expected to accommodate a population of 20,000, which will largely be composed of the airport support community

NEW LAND

The Central and Wan Chai reclamations on Hong Kong Island, which extend along the waterfront from Sheung Wan to Causeway Bay, cover an area of 108 hectares. The first phase of the Central reclamation created 20 hectares of land for the Hong Kong Airport Railway terminal, the relocation of the ferry terminals, and the extension of the Hong Kong CBD.

NEW LAND

The second phase involved 5.3 hectares of landfill in the Tamar Basin area, for commercial and open-space development. Phase I of the Wan Chai reclamation created an island for the expansion of the Hong Kong Convention and Exhibition Center. On the west side of the island, the Belcher Bay reclamation provided 10 hectares of land for the construction of the Belcher Bay Link, which upgraded the existing road network. On the east side of the island, the Aldrich Bay reclamation and the Siu Sai Wan development produced 30 hectares and 56 hectares respectively, of land for residential, government, institutional, and community use.

GLOSSARY

ARCHITECTURE© Stocks, commodity, profit, status; otherwise only marginally related to the art and science of building. ARCHITECTURE© is designed in the Pearl River Delta under unprecedented pressures of time, speed, and quantity.

AMBIGUITY© Policy of indeterminacy, or half-hearted embrace, to exploit possibilities for political or economic gain. AMBIGUITY© allows tensions and contradictions to coexist in matters of state sovereignty and territory. AMBIGUITY© used by the Chinese Communist Party in one circumstance becomes leverage in another.

ASYMMETRY© All phenomena that restore, maintain, or intensify the inequalities that define the CITY OF EXACERBATED DIFFERENCE©.

BANKRUPTCY© Although in the West, bankruptcy is seen as a business fatality, in China, BANKRUPTCY© offers the chance for rebirth, the freedom to start over. China's Trial Enterprise Bankruptcy Law does not make enterprises bankrupt, assures *Workers' Daily*. It "increases their vitality." The fundamental inconsistency in the BANKRUPT© socialist market system—an economy that embraces both communist-style sustainability (the resuscitation of a failing industrial base) and CHINESE©-style reincarnation (the evolution and perfection of market strategy in a cycle of death and rebirth)—is responsible for multiple smaller BANKRUPTCIES©.

BASTARD METROPOLIS© Wholeness and coherence can only be achieved at the expense of editing, of control. The BASTARD METROPOLIS© does not even aspire to such status; its vitality is guaranteed by the systematic avoidance of perfection.

BLOCK© In the ZONE©, the BLOCK© is an ideal of INFRARED© versatility, an ideological *unit*. Its theoretical as well as physical extent may be stretched or dwarfed to absorb the unpredictability of the market. The BLOCKS© are test grounds where the opportunities and failures of the market are played out, "structured" and phased in a search for illusory control.

BORDER© Boundaries in the Pearl River Delta that are drawn and redrawn, and opened or closed according to changing policies of inclusion or exclusion of the desired or undesired population.

BUBBLE DIAGRAM© Once a derogatory term used to describe the oversimplifications of planners—a city dismantled, robbed of its complexity and layerings—the BUBBLE DIAGRAM© has in the Pearl River Delta become a blueprint, if not a manifesto. BUBBLES© are connected—usually by POTEMKIN CORRIDORS©—but not integrated. The city is not understood as the product of common interests, but rather as a new form of centrifugal coexistence of divergent interests.

BUSINESS VACATION© The way for a few to inhabit the largest possible territory in shifts. In the Pearl River Delta, the reduction of program (STREAMLINING©) coincides with the reduction of city (THINNING©).

CHINESE ARCHITECT© The most important, influential, and powerful architect on earth. The average lifetime construction volume of the CHINESE ARCHITECT© in housing alone is approximately three dozen thirty-story highrise buildings. The CHINESE ARCHITECT© designs the largest volume, in the shortest time, for the lowest fee.

There is one-tenth the number of architects in China than in the United States, designing five times the project volume in one-fifth the time, earning one-tenth the design fee. This implies an efficiency of twenty-five hundred times that of an American architect.

CHINESE SUBURBIA© Urbanization without a doctrine of the city. If in the West *suburban* is a derogatory term for unwelcome spin-offs of the city, in China SUBURBIA© is the essence of urbanization. The newness of the Chinese city strives for the SUBURBAN©.

CITY OF EXACERBATED DIFFERENCE© (COED©) The traditional city strives for a condition of balance, harmony, and a degree of homogeneity. The CITY OF EXACERBATED DIFFERENCE©, on the contrary, is based on the greatest possible difference between its parts—complementary or competitive. In a climate of permanent strategic panic, what counts in the CITY OF EXACERBATED DIFFERENCE© is not the methodical creation of the ideal, but the opportunistic exploitation of flukes, accidents, and imperfections. Although the model of the CITY OF EXACERBATED DIFFERENCE© appears brutal—to depend on the robustness and primitiveness of its parts—the paradox is that it is, in fact, delicate and sensitive. The slightest modification of any detail requires the readjustment of the whole to reassert the equilibrium of complementary extremes.

COOP-ETITION© Newly minted Singaporean word that perfectly describes the constructive component that competition can have in the Asian context. Without COOP-ETITION©, there can be no COED©.

COORDINATION© Retroactive task, by politicians and planners, of creating coherence in urban development in order to regain lost power in an exploding socialist market economy. An attempt, as in the Pearl River Delta, to mediate various parts of an outwardly unified, but inwardly competitive, whole.

CONCESSION© Policy of yielding as tactic. Reformulation of the traditional notion of concession: the forceful insertion of a foreign entity into sovereign Chinese territories or the forced yielding of territory as admittance of defeat. Deftly reinterpreted by the Chinese Communist Party to control the importation of Westernness, it allows most of China to remain untainted. The Special Economic Zones, as land sacrificed for free-market experimentation, are examples of CONCESSIONS©.

CORRUPTION© Eases thousands of square kilometers of construction into existence each year in the Pearl River Delta. Asian business practice has never acknowledged CORRUPTION© as anything but a "gift"; now the Open Door Policy relies on CORRUPTION© to mediate between Chinese Communist Party dogma and MARKET© demands. CORRUPTION© lessens foreign investors' risk, and it cements complicity with the Communist bureaucracy. CORRUPTION© in China is punishable only when an example is needed to sate the global market's hunger for sacrifice (transparent—"honest"—business practice is the Western market's utopian ideal).

CULTURAL DESERT© China's euphemism for the Pearl River Delta. The fortuitous result of NEGLECT©, geographical circumstance and relentless ideological campaigns. Under Mao Zedong, the Cultural Revolution tried to force the victory of the *red* ideals by imposing a moratorium on the cities and on the market. To the INFRARED© ideology, the CULTURAL DESERT© is ground for an equally efficient ideological counter-purge that uses urbanization and the exaltation of the MARKET© to save Utopia. The ZONE© is the planned equivalent of the CULTURAL DESERT©.

CULTURAL REVOLUTION© A leveling of cultural terrain to create an ideal condition of social blankness. Culture : CULTURAL REVOLUTION© :: city : TABULA RASA©.

CURTAIN WAR© A battle between different ARCHITECTURES© to utilize the maximum variety in glass-panel systems on one façade to form a competing whole; includes the use of multiple curtain-wall systems to distinguish separate programs on one façade. The curtain wall in the PRD is no longer associated with simplicity, precision, and tautness, but with a new baroque, assuming a vital role in the PICTURESQUE© order.

DEMOGRAPHICS© The use of dramatic changes in population patterns to justify grotesque planning and architectural doctrines. Under socialism, DEMOGRAPHICS© dictated development; under capitalism, development dictates DEMOGRAPHICS©.

DIALECTICS© A classic method of argument that weighs contradictory facts or ideas with a view to the resolution of their real, or apparent, contradictions. In the Pearl River Delta, the concept has acquired enough fuzzy logic to be used to justify any contradiction— political policy or otherwise.

DICTATORSHIP OF THE EYE© After all other logic has been subordi-nated, the visual provides the dominant system of organization in the contemporary city. Under DICTATORSHIP©, objects coexist and are understood (or not) in terms of their visual relationships.

FACTORY/HOTEL/OFFICE/HOUSING/PARKING© The status of all floor space in the Pearl River Delta is generic. Each programmatic function is provisional, and every occupancy is only temporary. A consequence of MORE IS MORE©, in which the changing market forces buildings to transform rapidly to accommodate multiple uses.

FAUSTIAN© In the same way that Faust entered a joint venture with Mephistopheles, China's communist state entered the global market searching for FAUSTIAN MONEY© (investment, foreign currency, foreign bribes). A FAUSTIAN© contract can exist on any scale. An entire nation of 1.3 billion people made a deal with the devil (or rather Deng made it for them) when the Open Door Policy introduced the socialist market economy into China. Just as the Hell Bank Note in Confucianism finances an ancestor's stay in the hereafter, FAUSTIAN MONEY© in China finances the interval between the present speculative excess and the eventual collective wealth in a socialist market economy.

FENG SHUI© Geomancy originally used to determine optimum site and building orientations, FENG SHUI© now is used to fabricate ideal conditions from scratch, functioning as advertisement and becoming a self-fulfilling prophecy that both predicts and insures the inevitable success of commercial development. FENG SHUI© also is used retroactively to correct bad *qi* (energy) accumulated in modern architecture. In pursuit of financial profitability, FENG SHUI© coalesces ARCHITECTURE© and landscape into the PICTURESQUE©, providing the necessary precursor to SCAPE©.

FLATNESS© The spatial condition of FLATNESS© is a direct result of the PICTURESQUE© (where space is FLATTENED© into vertical surface, to be consumed by the EYE©) and the MARKET© (where mountains are FLATTENED© into horizontal surface, to be consumed by development).

FLOATING© A migrant condition, held by two-thirds of Shenzhen's population, who do not have jobs, legal status, or homes in the SEZs, yet are officially registered in their original provinces of residence. Attracted to the hyperdevelopment of the coastal cities and the SEZs, FLOATERS© form mobile reservoirs of flexible labor, a necessary ingredient for SHENZHEN SPEED©.

GREAT LEAP FORWARD© 1. Extravagant hyperdevelopment marked by periods of stagnation. 2. Optimistic production even in the face of immanent disaster or prolonged suffering. 3. An unofficial campaign to modernize China, overseen by a socialist structure leaping toward a market economy that simultaneously achieves staggering success and catastrophic failure. 4. A modern reinterpretation of Mao Zedong's early campaign, the Great Leap Forward.

GREEN CARD DREAM© Shenzhen's policy of "Buy a House and Get Registered; Fulfill Ones' Green Card Dream" allows the establishment of residency in Shenzhen when purchasing a home. Residency in Shenzhen is a highly desirable achievement, providing home-buy-

ers an immediate elevation in social status. The GREEN CARD DREAM© also provides Shenzhen's FLOATERS© immediate permanent residency. The GREEN CARD DREAM© keeps the buying of housing in Shenzhen at an accelerated pace.

"HAS BECOMING"© Future perfect tense invented in the Pearl River Delta that combines the immediacy of achievement with eternal deferment. Terminal striving: "Zhuhai city, with beautiful scenery and good environment, HAS BECOMING a famous scenic spot for tourism and a garden for investment, it is the result of Zhuhai people's wisdom and courage." Essential to an understanding of the Asian condition: there is now, no now there, only later.

INCORPORATION© Using capitalist tactics as a method of protection from STREAMLINING©.

INFRARED© Driven underground by the forces of global economy, the Chinese Communist Party safeguards its totalitarian ideology by moving into the invisible spectrum of politics. INFRARED© is a covert strategy of compromise and double standard, a peremptory reversal of history that links nineteenth-century idealism with the realities of the twenty-first century.

INFRASTRUCTURE© Infrastructures, which were mutually reinforcing and totalizing, are becoming more and more competitive and local. They no longer pretend to create functioning wholes but now spin off functional entities. Instead of network and organism, the new infrastructure creates enclave and impasse: no longer the *grand récit* but the parasitic swerve. Malfunctioning is also a form of functioning. Each INFRASTRUCTURE©

has both a positive and a negative program: it enables and prevents.

LEARNING© A mode of permanent experimentation that has eliminated the notion of failure, which is now declared a LEARNING© experience. In a subversion of the educational process, China recycles received (often discredited) Western and Soviet ideas and adapts them in order to gain access to the new (see VISIONARY VS. FUTURISTIC©).

LINEAR© The *socialist market economy* defines the present as an era of opportunistic juxtapositions and uses the LINEAR© city as the blueprint for an ideological puzzle of urban forms and programs. The *socialist market economy* exposes, therefore, the LINEAR© city as being akin to the PICTURESQUE©; the irrational is rationalized, planned according to a logic that finds beauty in disorder and virtue in the bizarre.

LINGNAN© "South of the Nanling mountain range" refers to the geographical barrier between ancient Chinese civilization in the north and the CULTURAL DESERT© of southern China. The word LINGNAN© is claimed by both sides; inevitably synonymous with "tasteless and unrefined"—culturally bankrupt—to those in the north, it means "natural, reasonable, practical, and flexible" to those in the Pearl River Delta. LINGNAN© encompasses the pragmatic and the unworthy: LINGNAN© Garden, LINGNAN© Architecture.

MARKET REALISM© Socialist Realism is the Stalinist doctrine that art should depict, in the most realistic way, a final condition of realized utopia rather than dwell on the imperfections of the present or the sacrifices on the road of implementation. It is a brilliant formula for desire simultaneously deferred and consummated. The present interval between market promise and market delivery is explained by MARKET REALISM©, a speculative fervor that does not demand instant gratification in the form of profit, rentability, or a real relationship between supply (overwhelming) and demand (defined by ORACULAR MAGIC©). Socialist Realism : MARKET REALISM© :: toil : speculation.

MERGE© In the Pearl River Delta, DIALECTICS© collapse into MERGE© (the first a method to understand and synthesize opposites, the second a brutal collapsing of opposites to create new conditions: Landscape + city = SCAPE©, business + pleasure = BUSINESS VACATION©, socialism + the MARKET©—the socialist market economy . . .

METABOLISM© The paradox that certain contemporary conditions can best be understood through concepts developed by architectural movements that are now largely irrelevant. Many of the phenomena currently visible in the Pearl River Delta, such as the heightened collective effort triggered by DEMOGRAPHIC© pressures leading to an overall acceleration of the production of urban substance, were anticipated in the speculations of the Metabolists and Team X.

MORE IS MORE© The conclusion of an evolution that began with Mies as "less is more" and passed through Venturi as "less is a bore," now ends in a paroxysm of the quantitative in the PRD as MORE IS MORE©. Five hundred square kilometers of urban substance is built every year, of which 6.4 million square meters is found

in Shenzhen alone. In addition to quantity, redundancy proliferates: five international airports exist, with two more nearing completion; in one building alone, twelve different curtain wall systems are used (see CURTAIN WAR©), while five lighting systems are deployed in a single 15-square-meter room; ten revolving restaurants are constructed within four square blocks; 414 holes of golf are open for play, and 720 more are under construction.

NEGLECT© Policy of the Chinese Communist Party to chronically disadvantage the Guangzhou region of the Pearl River Delta; it is a policy that has suspended development in the region since 1949.

NEGLECT REVERSAL© Method of reversing NEGLECT© for self-advantage by seeking more NEGLECT© or autonomy. Used by the Guangdong province since 1979 to achieve unprecedented economic growth.

ORACULAR MAGIC© Seemingly random, essentially unpredictable way to define aims, goals and deals that depends on an amalgamation of Confucian and communist tradition and practice. Now operative in a new market-based context as the foundation of MARKET REALISM©.

PARADISE© The final Edenic condition, whose ultimate realization remains as elusive as a mirage yet inspires and justifies the neverending effort to achieve it.

PEARL CITY© A fiction, a fairy tale, the PARADISE© of the Pearl River Delta. Lured by the optimism of PEARL CITY©, the region unwittingly generated its double, the CITY OF EXACERBATED DIFFERENCE©.

PEASANT VACATION VILLAGE© Outposts of hotels, flower beds, alligator shows, tomato parks, swimming pools, karaoke bars, golf courses, theme restaurants and romantic paddle boats, VILLAGES© are strategically located in remote areas to lure urban conditions.

PHOTOSHOP© The same power offered by Photoshop, to combine everything into anything—the uncritical accumulation of desire—is exercised literally in the Pearl River Delta as urbanism. In the Pearl River Delta, PHOTOSHOP© is the freedom to manipulate not images but urban substance, regulated only by the rules of FENG SHUI©.

PICTURESQUE© Revenge of the anti-idealistic. A mode of making and perceiving space, invented by Chinese gardeners in the sixteenth century, which insists on the juxtapositions and relationships between objects, rather than their singular presence. "We may look upon pictures as a set of experiments in the different ways in which trees, buildings, water, and etc. may be disposed, grouped, and accompanied in the most beautiful and striking manner, in every style, from the most simple and rural to the grandest and ornamental: many of those objects, that are scarcely marked as they lie over the face of nature, when brought together in the compass of a small space of canvas, are forcibly impressed on the eye, which by that means learns how to separate, to select and combine. . . . " —Uvedale Price, *An Essay on the Picturesque*, 1794

POTEMKIN CORRIDOR© Just as the Russians, under Potemkin, built villages bigger and healthier than the actual ones for inspection by the czar, so during the Great Leap Forward the entire trajectory of Mao's travels through the country was transformed into linear zones of engineered perfection, where all the ambitions of the Revolution were realized as if by magic. Today, the BUBBLES© of the CITY OF EXACERBATED DIFFERENCE© are connected by development corridors that play a similar role as prefigurations of THINNING©.

RECLAMATION© Originally China's strategy of territorial expansion, now the reoccupation of abandoned REAL ESTATE© by an indigeneous culture, (re)emerging to exercise the new Chinese ideology of permanent adaptation. RECLAMATION© is the process that turns the Pearl River Delta's coastal landscape into fresh ground for development. The Pearl River Delta's buildings undergo a similar takeover, turning China's relentless mimicry of the West into a triumph of kitsch.

RETROFIT© To install or fit an improvised device or system in order to repair an existing structure. Used in the Pearl River Delta as a strategy to repair anything—architecture, ideology, politics.

SCALE© Communist planning defines the city in terms of numbers; the Chinese Communist Party has traditionally followed a logic of urbanism that replaces hierarchy with quantity. During Mao's era, ideological commitment was measured by the relative size of each economic absurdity, disaster, or famine. In reverse logic, the socialist market economy measures the success of the Open Door Policy in terms of each victory of the MARKET© over communist ideology. For the Chinese Communist Party, size is a measure of truth.

SCAPE© An (exploded) mountain, a highrise, and a rice field in every direction—nothing between excessive height and the lowness of a continuous agricultural/light-industrial crust, between the skyscraper and the scraped. SCAPE©, neither city nor landscape, is the new posturban condition, the arena for a terminal juxtaposition between architecture and landscape, the apotheosis of the PICTURESQUE©.

SCENERY© The suddenness of construction in the Pearl River Delta turns landscape into a backdrop inhabited by people who unwittingly become spectators. Public space under DICTATORSHIP©.

SHENZHEN SPEED© Unit of abrupt growth. Architectural design in China has accelerated to keep pace with SHENZHEN SPEED©. Designers in the Shenzhen Special Economic Zone have set records: 5 designers x 1 night + 2 computers = 300-unit single family housing development; 1 architect x 3 nights = 7-story walk-up apartment; 1 architect x 7 days = 30-story concrete residential highrise.

SMOOTHING© The replacement of the traditional urban fabric with the SMOOTH© green crust of THIN© urbanism. Ultimately generates the UTOPIA OF GOLF©.

SPECULATOR'S SEARCHLIGHT© The sudden, often inexplicable click with which a developer's attention is switched to a newly hot subject (as surveyed from one of Shenzhen's revolving restaurants . . .). The ever-shortening interval between new discoveries means that the attention span of the developer is rushed—too short to actually realize development. His activity becomes merely

speculative—a self-fulfilling prophecy of nonoccurence.

SPILLOVER© Fantastic growth, when concentrated in a clearly demarcated economic system (the freewheeling capitalism of the island of Hong Kong, the schizophrenic socialist market in the Shenzhen ZONE©), eventually SPILLS© over into ideologically unprotected VIRGIN© territory. In China, this excess (most visible as export processing factories and luxury housing developments) taints a socialist hinterland with the temptations of unadulterated capitalism.

STEALTH© China's cities aspire to quick growth through modernization (see SHENZHEN SPEED©) and the global fame (or is it infamy?) that follows. Cities victimized by NEGLECT© (i.e., not Special Economic Zones) are unable to attract the necessary foreign capital. They therefore devise STEALTH© strategies in order to prosper. STEALTH© tactics simultaneously quicken growth and insure continued invisibility, thus facilitating business CHINESE©-style (see CORRUPTION©).

STITCHING© The creation of synthetic wholes, based on each city's radical identification—and subsequent annexation—of what is missing.

STRATEGY© Policy of systematic, abrupt reversal, by which the Chinese Communist Party operates internally to negotiate with external forces. STRATEGY© has defined a perpetual swaying pattern of social and economic development in the Pearl River Delta.

STREAMLINING© Deregulation or simplification of political bureaucracy to enable the accelerated development of a socialist market economy.

SYSTEMATIC DISADVANTAGE© A condition in which successive forms of NEGLECT©—natural, political, economic, cultural—create an explosive mixture of resentment and recklessness that can be harnessed for sudden spurts of drastic change.

TABULA RASA© The notorious clean slate that was the underlying myth of modernist planning. Discredited in the West, it is the norm—the sine qua non—in the East. In the Pearl River Delta, TABULA RASA© has achieved an autonomous status: no longer an initial scraped condition on which a new condition is projected, it is a project independent of need. FLATNESS© as an affordable platonic luxury. Initially applied to a physical condition, TABULA RASA© now includes other "scrapings," where political or cultural regimes have sponsored the removal of all earlier layers. Major irony: the West now pursues folded authenticity, the East FLATTENED© artificiality.

THEME© In the Pearl River Delta, the (more or less precise) idea of program is replaced by the infinitely more mutable concept of THEME©, a general category intended to stimulate a regime of as-yet unidentified future programs. Urban space, no longer zoned, but THEMED© according to vastly different needs (high-tech park, ethnic town, business center), reaches its pinnacle in the THEME© park, a ubiquitous, all-encompassing typology capable of operating at any scale (golf course, amusement park, city ...).

THINNING© The coating of the largest available territory with the minimum concentration of substance necessary to generate an urban condition.

TRANSITIONAL REVERSAL© The conceptual shift, and mutual adjustment, in the balance of contrasts that now defines the CITY OF EXACERBATED DIFFERENCE© that will inevitably take place when China—space, no freedom—and Hong Kong/Macau—overcrowding, freedom—are reversed. It predicts that after 1997, the shared absence of freedom will make Hong Kong and Macau seem overcrowded slums while the spaciousness of Shenzhen and Zhuhai, by comparison, will acquire a sudden glamour.

UTOPIA OF GOLF© The golf course as the main carrier of urban activity. The first installment of the UTOPIA OF GOLF© takes form in the Shenzhen Special Economic Zone, where three eighteen-hole golf courses and four theme parks radiate from the city center.

VIRGIN© Untouched (pre-inhabited) urban substance; i.e., VIRGIN© city.

VISIONARY VS. FUTURISTIC© Possibly as a result of the hybridization of Confucianism, communism, and capitalism, the Pearl River Delta reveals an overabundance of VISIONARY© projections that paradoxically totally resist the FUTURISTIC©; i.e., they aim for difference more than progress.

ZONE© Imposes limits, but not spatial content. A vague term, ZONE© is preferred by the Chinese Communist Party over "city" because it is conceptually blank. A ZONE© is open to the impurities of ideological manipulation. It purges historical contents from territories where they have been imposed and replaces them with the dynamics of global economy. A ZONE© remains programatically unfulfilled, an urban condition that never achieves focus or intensity. ZONE© is the birthplace of CHINESE SUBURBIA©.

All reasonable efforts to secure permissions for the visual material reproduced herein have been made by the authors of each essay. The publisher and authors apologize to anyone who has not been reached.

KEY

The location of an image on a page is indicated by the following key: t = top row; m = middle row; b = bottom row; t2 = second row from top; t3 = third row from top; etc. . . . l = left column; c = center column; r = right column; l2 = second column from left; l3 = third column from left; etc. . . . o = overlay; u = underlay. The key locates images from top to bottom, left to right. Notations can be used in combination, for example: t2l3 = image is located in the second row from top, third from the left. Illustrations are also keyed according to the figure numbers used in the essay.

FRONTMATTER 6(t), 7(b), 8, 9(tl, tr, t2r, b), 12–13, 16: Bernard Chang. 8(tl, tr, br), 9(t3r): Marcela Cortina. 8(bl), 10–11: Jun Takahasi. 18(u), 20–23: Landsat™.

IDEOLOGY 46(1): *Constructivist Graphics*. 46(2): Film still from Dziga Vertov's *Man with a Movie Camera* (1929). 46(3, 4): Khan-Magomedov, *Alexander Vesnin and Russian Constructivism* (1920). 46(5): Alessandro de Magistris, *La Citta di Transizione, Politiche Urbane e Ricerche Tipologiche nell'URSS degli Anni Venti* (1988). 46(6): V.A. Korol, *Mikroraiony Belorussii* (Minsk, 1963). 48, 50(3): *Taiwan Magazine* (1997). 50(1, 2), 84: Alfred Schinz, *Urbanization of the Earth, Cities in China* (Berlin: Gebruder Borntraeger, 1989). 54(1): Rui Guanting, *The People's Commune is Good* (1958). 54(2): Moisei Ginsburg and Mikhail Barshch, project for a "Green City" (1929). 56(2): John King Fairbank, *China: A New History* (Cambridge: The Belknap Press of Harvard University Press, 1992). 56(3), 60(1, 2): Robert Vexler, *China: History, Culture, People* (New York: Globe Book Company, Inc., 1981). 58: Leonardo Benevolo, *Storia della Citta Orientale* (Rome: Laterza, 1988). 62–5, 92–114, 136(2): Mihai Craciun. 66: Timepix. 78: www.pathfinder.com/time/deng/. 86: Shenzhen Special Economic Zone, May 1995. 115(3): Shenzhen Institute of Planning (1996). 116(2), 118, 128, 132(1), 134, 136(1): *Shenzhen Urban Planning and Design: A Compilation for the First Decade Celebration of*

Shenzhen Special Economic Zone, 122(1): H. Gonzales del Castillo, *Ciudades Jardines y Ciudades Lineales* (Madrid, 1913). 122(2): Tony Garnier, *Cite Industrielle* (1901–1904). 122(3): Ivan Leonidov and OSA Group (1929). 124(4): Nikolai Miliutin, *Sotsgorod* (Moscow, 1930). 124(5): Nikolai Miliutin, *Traktorstoi* (Stalingrad, 1930). 124(6): Le Corbusier and ASCORAL Group (1942). 124(7): Kenneth Frampton, "The Other Le Corbusier: Primitive Form and the Linear City 1929–52," *Le Corbusier Architect of the Century* (London: Arts Council of Great Britain, 1987). 126(8): Alison and Peter Smithson, *Urban Structuring* (London: Studio Vista, 1967). 126(9): G. Candilis, A. Josic, S. Woods, *Toulouse le Mirail* (1962–1970). 126(10): "Utopia and Reality in City Planning," *Bauen + Wohnen* (issue 1, 1960). 138(b): Marcela Cortina.

ARCHITECTURE 164: *Business Weekly of China: Cash*. 166–171, 184(t), 194–203, 212(b), 218–241, 242(b), 244(b), 246, 250–251, 252–253: Nancy Lin. 176(tl): City Development Co. 176(tr): Pau Ju Mountain Villa. 176(bl): Shenzhen Baoan Housing Co. 176(br): Xi Hu Co. and Ping Di Development Co. 177(t): Shenzhen Longgang Real Estate Development Co. 177(b): Shenzhen Xing Mao Industries Co. 182: *Shenzhen Commercial Daily* (17 July 1996). 184(b): *Beijing City's Excellent Residential Design Collection* (Beijing: Beijing Planning and Construction Committee, 1993). 186: *Pictorial Guide to Speedy Architectural Design*, 1993. 187–189: *Jian Shu Xue Bao (An Architectural Resource)* (Jiansu Design Institute). 204, 208(b): *Cash* (20 August 1996). 252: *Shenzhen Commercial Daily* (7 August 1996).

MONEY 266–274(tl, tm, tr), 276(t), 283, 286, 296–308, 326–334: Stephanie Smith. 274(bl, bm, br), 294, 319: Chashan Town of Dongguan Government. 276(b): Dongguan Foreign Economic Relations Commission. 280: Camdor Harbour City. 284: *Chang'an in South China*. 290(b): *A Tourist Guide to Dongguan China*. 309: *South China Morning Post*, January 1996. 316–317: Guangdong Winnerway Real Estate Development Co. 319(t): Yanshan Hotel, Heshan Guangdong China. 320(t): The People's Government of Zhangmutou Town, Dongguan, Guangdong, China. 321: Wu Sha New Technological Park. 322–23: Licheng Development Zone.

LANDSCAPE 340–41, 391(bl): Mihai Craciun. 342–43, 346, 350(tl), 354, 360, 361(t), 365, 367–68, 373(tl), 378–79(u), 380, 381(m, b), 382, 384, 387, 388(br), 391(m, b), 392(tr), 395(tl2, tr, t2l, t2,l2, t2l3, t3l2, t3r, bl3), 400(tr), 403–05: Kate Orff. 357: Zhuhai Tourism Board. 361(b), 366(b), 371, 373(t3l, bl, br): Marcela Cortina. 369(r): Zhuhai Programme Bureau. 372(m, t3), 373(t2l, t3r): *Zhuhai Yearbook 1995*. 388(bl): Shenzhen Urban Planning and Design. 395(bl2): *Asian Golfer*. 395(br): Jincheng Industrial Development Zone. 400(br): © 1998 by the New York Times Co., reprinted by permission. 402(u): T.R. Treagear, *China: A Geographical Survey* (New York, Wiley and Sons, 1980). 412–13: Nancy Lin.

POLITICS 420–21: Immanuel Hsu, *The Rise of Modern China* (New York: Oxford University Press, 1995). 424–425, 426–27: Bettmann/CORBIS. 428–29: *Asian Golfer*. 441, 454: Charts by Yuyang Liu; for sources see p.441 and p.454. 460, 461: The Planning for Urban Agglomeration of Pearl River Delta Economic Region.

INFRASTRUCTURE 470 (t,b), 482(o), 484–85, 488–91, 498–501, 512–13, 516–19, 524, 525(t), 548–49(u), 550–51, 555, 560–63(u), 564–565, 572–573, 576–577, 598–599(u), 612–615, 616–617(u), 630–39, 648–49(u), 648(b), 650–51, 654, 682–83: Bernard Chang. 480–1, 492–3, 496–7: Hopewell Holdings Ltd. 502(t), 507, 509, 542, 588–89, 622, 667: *150 Years of Public Works: Foundation for the Future* (Hong Kong). 522–23, 526(l): Chu Kong Tourism Co., Ltd. 525(b): *Macau Getting There*. 530, 534–35, 601, 602–03, 604–05 (t), 628–29(u): *Shenzhen Urban Planning and Design: A Compilation for the First Decade Celebration of Shenzhen Special Economic Zone*. 541: Qianshan Town. 546–47: *Welcome to China: Guangdong* (vol.4 no.4, 1995). 554: *City Planning and Construction of Zhuhai* (1994). 573, 575–76, 660(l), 690–91(u): *Macaensis Momentum a Fragment of Architecture: A Moment in the History of the Development of Macau*. 582–83, 677, 698–99(u): The Government of Hong Kong Special Administrative Region. 589, 619: *Hong Kong 1996*. 621: *Hong Kong Review* (12 January 1996). 648(t): Zhuhai Airport Group Corporation. 653: *Chinese and Foreign Real Estate Times* (no. 177, November 1995). 684–5: Nam Van Development Co. Ltd.

Authors

Bernard Chang is a native of Hong Kong. The Pearl River Delta research project brought him back home and allowed him to rediscover the region and study the infrastructure projects that have been instrumental to its urban development. He is the cofounder of Index Architecture, a firm with offices in Hong Kong and New York, which conducts architecture and urbanism projects in Hong Kong, Dongguan, Tianjin, Ningbo, and other cities in China. He has worked at Kohn Pedersen Fox and the Office for Metropolitan Architecture, Asia. Chang received a B.Arch. with High Distinction from California College of Arts and Crafts in 1994 and a M.Arch. from Harvard University in 1997. He is a member of the American Institute of Architects.

Mihai Craciun was born in 1959 in Sibiu, Romania. After studying art, he attended the Ion Mincu School of Architecture and Urbanism. In the 1982 Space/Object exhibition, a critique of the subjugation of ideals to ideology, his project, Table, polemically reinforced the split between concept and accepted form. In 1983, as the Romanian dictatorship reached its apogee, proven by complete censorship and vast construction projects, Craciun defected to the U.S. as did many of his peers. In the early 1990's, Craciun and a fellow expatriate formed Westfourth Architecture in New York, whose projects have been transforming post-communist Romania. In 1994, they won a Progressive Architecture Award for the International Film and Television Center in Bucharest; the headquarters of a private bank, also in Bucharest, was completed in 1999. Motivated by his interest in the polemical role of architecture and the lessons from the PRD, he is working on a documentary on Bucharest. He lives in New York.

Nancy Lin was born in Taipei and moved to the United States at the age of 12. Before attending Harvard in 1997, she studied civil engineering and architecture at Princeton University. This training has provided her with strengths in statistical research and numerical analysis, which naturally led her to decipher architecture and the profession in the PRD through numbers, volumes, speeds, and rates. Since finishing the PRD project, she has return to Taiwan where she has been based since 1997. She currently teaches at Tamkang University, writes articles for architecture magazines, and practices architectural design. She is a registered architect of New York State and a member of the American Institute of Architects.

Liu Yuyang, born in Taiwan, is the son of a journalist-turned-politician, making Liu the ideal candidate to study the Pearl River Delta's urban conditions vis-à-vis politics. Liu received a B.A. in urban planning from the University of California at San Diego, and a M.Arch. from Harvard University. Upon completing his research, Liu worked with Skidmore, Owings & Merrill to design a skyscraper in New York City. In 2000, Liu cofounded Index Architecture, which is currently designing a French cosmetic counter in Hong Kong, a 1,200-unit residential complex in Dongguan, and a 400,000-square-meter master plan for the economic and technology zone of the northern Chinese port of Tianjin.

A landscape architect, planner, and artist, **Kate Orff** graduated from the University of Virginia and Harvard University, escaping to California in search of palm trees and pleasantness shortly thereafter. After working for several design firms, she started Gnome, an ongoing project that focuses on the infiltration of the city by suburban culture, and on the subsequent evolution of the landscapes of both realms. Gnome explores the creative potentials of these shifting territories, and is based on the conceptualization and construction of landscapes and installations in collaboration with architects, artists, and politicians. Born in Maryland in 1971, Orff currently resides in Brooklyn, New York.

Before going to the Pearl River Delta, **Stephanie Smith** focused her design studies on urban planning and real-estate development, forming an interest in how architecture can make money. After receiving her M.Arch. from Harvard University in 1997, Smith worked with Jon Jerde in the retail-entertainment industry for three years before starting Architecture NOW (www.architecture-now.com), a Los Angeles-based design strategy consulting firm, which is devoted to helping companies use architecture and design to enhance their business strategies. Smith is a frequent lecturer on market-driven design, design strategy as a new design discipline, and the merge of design and business. Smith is also a design critic and instructor, and has taught a design studio at SCI-Arc (Southern California Institute of Architecture) since September 2000. Smith is from Portland, Oregon.

Editors and Design

Alice Chung is a designer with 2x4 in New York City, where she has worked on a diverse range of projects that includes print, Web, exhibition and signage design. She designed *Great Leap Forward* in her "spare" time.

Chuihua Judy Chung is principal of CODA Group (Content Design Architecture), in New York City. The firm's projects encompass editorial and publication work, and graphic and architectural design. She is currently editing *Owning a House in the City*, a forthcoming study on low-income housing in the United States.

Jeffrey Inaba is researching institutional environments designed by architects Gordon Bunshaft and Kevin Roche. He is a principal of AMO Inc., an architecture-based firm that addresses issues of culture, design, and knowledge.

Rem Koolhaas is an architect, writer, and professor of architecture and urban design at the Harvard University Graduate School of Design. He is the author of *Delirious New York*, a retroactive manifesto for Manhattan, and *S,M,L,XL* with Bruce Mau. He is principal of the Office for Metropolitan Architecture (OMA) in Rotterdam, and of AMO, a think tank.

Sze Tsung Leong is principal of CODA Group (Content Design Architecture), in New York City. With Chuihua Judy Chung, he has designed and edited *The Charged Void: Architecture*, the complete works of Alison and Peter Smithson. Leong is the co-editor and designer of *Slow Space* (Monacelli, 1998).

Qingyun Ma was born in Xian, China. He received a B.Arch. at Qinghua University, in Beijing, and a M.Arch. from the University of Pennsylvania. When the Harvard group visited the Pearl River Delta in 1996, Ma was the associate dean of the school of architecture at Shenzhen University and a practicing architect in Shenzhen. He provided invaluable help and guidance in coordinating the group's research in the delta. Ma is currently a founding principal of MRMADA, an architecture firm with offices in Shanghai and Beijing.